GODS, MEN, AND WINE

GODS, MEN,

THE WINE AND FOOD SOCIETY

WILLIAM YOUNGER

AND WINE

With a Foreword by
JAMES LAVER

and a chapter on Wine in America by
JOHN N. HUTCHISON

in association with WORLD PUBLISHING COMPANY

A Publication of
The Wine and Food Society Limited
in association with
World Publishing Company
2231 West 110th Street, Cleveland, Ohio

© *Elizabeth Younger 1966*

Library of Congress Catalog Number 66–17305
This book was designed and produced by
George Rainbird Limited, 2 Hyde Park Place, London, W. 2
Phototypeset in 'Monophoto' Bembo by
Oliver Burridge Filmsetting Limited, Crawley, Sussex, England
The paper was supplied by
Leykam-Josefsthal, Vienna 1
Printed and bound in Hungary
House Editors: J. E. M. Hoare & Rosemary Joekes
Designers: Ronald Clark & Nan Quelle

For Dennis, who taught me to love good wine.
William

Contents

List of Colour Plates

Acknowledgments

I wish to thank the following for the invaluable information and research facilities which they so kindly gave me.

His Excellency Eliahu Elath, for a long time Israeli Ambassador to the court of St James; M. Paran Esq., Agricultural Attaché to the Embassy of Israel; Dr Epstein, Principal of the Jews College, London; Asaph Goor Esq., Director of the Department of Horticulture, Israel; Y. Yadin Esq., the James A. de Rothschild Expedition at Hazor; Maurice Callender Esq.; A. F. Shore Esq., Department of Egyptian Antiquities, British Museum; Seton Lloyd Esq., C.E.B., F.B.A., lately Director of the British Institute of Archaeology in Ankara; D. E. L. Haynes Esq., Keeper of Greek and Roman Antiquities, British Museum; S. Hood Esq., Miss Virginia Grace, Mrs Elizabeth Lyding Will, Professor Mabel Lang, all of the American School of Classical Studies, Athens; and Mrs Karouzou of the Photographic Department of the National Museum, Athens; Geheimrat Dr F. von Basserman-Jordon; S. F. Hallgarten Esq.; Dr Karl Schultz, Director of the Historisches Museum der Pflaz, Speyer; Dr Erich Gose, Director of the Romische Abteilung des Deutscher Weinmuseums der Stadt Trier; Dr Gredecke, Staatliche Weinbaudomäne, Waldboeckelheim; Graf Matuschka-Greiffenclau, Schloss Vollrads; the firm of Deinhard and Co., Berncastel; Baron Philippe de Rothschild of Mouton Rothschild; M. Margory, Director of Mouton Rothschild, Armailhacq, etc.; Baron Elie de Rothschild of Lafite Rothschild, and M. Portet also of Lafite; M. Barailhé, Secretary of the Conseil Inter-professionnel du Vin de Bordeaux; M. Jean Hugel, M. Jean Hugel fils and M. Georges Hugel of F. Hugel et Fils,

Riquewihr; M. Marcel Wolff, Chambre de Commerce, Colmar; M. Albert Bichot and M. Albert Bichot fils of Bichot et Cie., Beaune; M. Delissey, Conservateur du Musée du Vin de Bourgogne, Beaune; M. Jean Richard, Centre des Études Bourguigones, Dijon; Baron Le Roy de Boisseaumarié, Chateauneuf de Pape; M. Alain and M. Georges Rochard of Hennessys, Cognac; M. Marcel Lugan, Institut National des Appellations d'Origine des Vins et Eaux de Vie; M. and Mme Jean Heidsieck, Rheims; Dr Norman Penser; the firm of Richard and William Teltscher Ltd; Senor Manuel M. Gonzalez Gordon, of Gonzalez Byass; Captain Guy Williams, M.C., and the late Charles Williams Esq., of Williams and Humbert; The Marques de Santurce and the Marques del Merito; The Marquesa Origo; Exmo. Senor E. Costa Lima, and Dr Joao Ribero Mesquita, of the Instituto do Vinho do Porto; The Duke of Richmond and Gordon; Francis Steer Esq., County Archivist, West Sussex County Council; K. W. Dickens Esq., Curator of Deeds, Sussex Archaeological Society; N. E. S. Norris Esq., Hon. Secretary and Curator, Sussex Archaeological Society; Geoffrey Bill Esq., Archives, Christchurch, Oxford; R. W. Hamilton Esq., Keeper of the Department of Antiquities, Ashmolean Museum; Dr T. B. Heaton, Curator of the Common Room, Christchurch, Oxford; Professor Peter Russell of The Queen's College, Oxford, and Professor Peter Fraser of All Souls, Oxford; Dr G. Taylor, Director of the Royal Botanic Gardens; and the Royal Society of Herbalists.

I am especially grateful to Mrs James de Rothschild for her great help; and to Eddie Tatham for all his very valuable introductions.

I am deeply indebted to the many friends who offered generous hospitality and tireless patience in answering my questions and I thank Norah, Ron and John Symington, Claire Bergqvist, Ronnie and Anthony Barton, Betty and François Chasseloup Laubat, Arthur Golding Barrett, Desmond Haselhust, John Baber, and many others, for contributing so much to the pleasure of my work.

WILLIAM YOUNGER

My thanks to Edward Bacon Esq., of the *Illustrated London News* for his great help and kindness, and my deep gratitude and thanks to Ruby Millar and Kathleen Osborne for their splendid work in preparing this manuscript for publication.

ELIZABETH YOUNGER

The publishers and producers wish to express their gratitude to all the museums, art galleries, photographers, agencies and collectors who have courteously assisted them in obtaining the material for the illustrations reproduced in this volume. They would especially like to thank the following:

(The figures refer to the page numbers of the plates)

The Maps on pages 40-41 were drawn by Sheila Waters, and the End-papers by Stewart Black.

Foreword

BY JAMES LAVER

When I was young some forty years ago it was difficult for a young man to be knowledgeable about wine. If he had occasion to call upon the family solicitor he might perhaps be offered a glass of sherry and a dry biscuit. If he dined with a bachelor uncle the older man might set before him two glasses of port and, flattering his immaturity, ask him which he liked better. At home there might be white Bordeaux, 'because the ladies liked it', or, on special occasions, a bottle of champagne. George Saintsbury's *Notes on a Cellar Book* might have come his way and inspired an interest in different wines and vintages. The old-fashioned wine merchant was always, of course, a mine of information, but the young man with modest requirements was probably too shy to take advantage of it. There was astonishingly little in print.

Now all this is changed. Handbooks pour from the press; little celluloid charts of vintages find a place in many pocket books; wine merchants issue 'Lists' which are often miniature treatises, and great national newspapers retain a 'Wine Writer' on their staff. Few however have been willing to undertake the formidable task of writing a history of Wine.

William Younger was a lively and ingenious writer whose *Hammersmith Maggot* is recognized as a classic among Whodunits. *Trample an Empire, The Lobster Guerillas* and *Skin Trap* were only less successful, and it seemed that a distinguished future lay before him in this branch of fiction. His untimely death put an end to these hopes, but he was able to complete a *magnum opus* in a different field: the present volume.

It is, in the first place, an astounding piece of erudition. Most historians of wine have been content to begin with the Greeks and Romans. Not so William Younger. After a lyrical chapter describing a vintage in Portugal with all the vividness and authenticity of an eye-witness, he plunges into his story, clears away the mists of legend and takes us back to neolithic times and beyond. He reminds us that in Egypt, as early as 3000 B.C., Osiris was already hailed as 'lord of wine at the inundation'; and we learn that the wine jars of the later Egyptian dynasties were labelled with the date of the vintage. Cleopatra, in spite of her deplorable habit of putting things in wine, must surely have offered one of these vintage jars to Roman Antony.

It is not the function of a foreword to offer a précis of the work nor to duplicate the chapter headings, but rather to whet the appetite of the reader for the feast which is to come. And a feast it certainly is; stimulating to the palate and satisfying to the stomach. It excites the imagination and warms the heart. It will promote the rational drinking of civilized men. And if any reader should not be among these but, having drunk to excess, should decide to abjure wine for ever, there is something for him too. He is advised to try a 16th-century remedy for alcoholism: 'To provoke hatred of Wine . . . mark diligently where the owle haunteth that so you may get some of her egs, frie them, and give them to the drunken gallant to eate.' The book is full of these *trouvailles*, is indeed a social history as well as a history of wine; and what a sad thing social history would be if the grape had never been trodden under foot.

CHAPTER ONE

Vintage on the Douro

A bunch of grapes is beautiful, static, and innocent. It is merely fruit. But when it is crushed it becomes an animal, for the crushed grapes become wine and wine has an animal life.

Wine suffers a heaving birth. It has a rough, groping childhood. It develops into adolescence. Then, if it does not sicken, it matures; and in this it is almost human since it does not mature according to a fixed rule but according to the law of its particular and individual personality. The act which gives it personality is the act of fermentation. In this metamorphosis it is changed from fruit into animal: sometimes even into an animal of splendour.

It is this strange metamorphosis which makes every vintage dramatic. In many vineyards, however, the drama is not open and visible and has to be imagined, since in those vineyards the birth of wine is hidden away behind the wooden shells of cask or vat. But in order to comprehend what man has done to wine during the six thousand years of wine history, and in order to comprehend the nature of wine itself, one must first comprehend the whole act of vintaging. One must see it and watch it from the gathering of the fruit until the running off of the wine.

It is for this reason that I have chosen to describe the port wine vintage on the River Douro. This is one of the most visible, one of the most 'open', of all vintages. Hence it is also one of the most sensual: it is known at one and the same time by sight and smell and skin. The drama is comprehended not by the mind alone but also by the blood; it is as intimate as an embrace.

There is a second reason for my choice. The vintage of the modern Douro brings one closer than any other to the feeling of antiquity. It thus reflects into the modern world an outline picture of ancient wine-making. That the flavour of antiquity should happen here in this river valley is an accident, since the Douro is the latest of the great European vineyards. It is a geographical accident, for the wild, rough country in which the wine is grown cannot easily be handled by modern machines. The pace of life is unable to move much faster than the speed of an ox-cart and a man with a mattock: and this, to a great extent, is the speed of antiquity.

Monday October 1st, 1956, at the Quinta de la Rosa in the High Douro. Dawn has begun, but only far away over the remote uplands of Trás-os-Montes – 'behind the mountains' – where the Douro runs in its gorge between the north-east of Portugal and Leon in Spain. Here in the valley at La Rosa it is still dark. A sickle of moon, looking as though it were painted by Raphael, is high over the bulk of the opposite hill. Below the Quinta there are two lights reflected in the river and there is the splash of oars from an unseen boat. A bird starts to sing, the light grows, and from behind me, from a terrace above the house of the Quinta, comes a mutter of voices as the *roga* gathers to begin its work.

Day floods into the valley. I can now see the beaked boat moving slowly across the river. The sun is striking onto Valença do Douro, a white village huddled high up above the valley. There at Easter the village stumbles in the thick dust and on the naked rock of the streets in a lantern-lit procession of mourning for the death of Christ. There also at Easter in the tiny village square are guttering, reeking lamps of pig fat. (On the remote north-eastern uplands where the dawn began this morning there are lowering stone idols of pigs which, like the lamps, bear witness to the civilization that existed here before the Romans came.) To the east the Quinta do Noval is perched up on the side of its conical hill. Below it in a bend of the river sits the village of Pinhão, the heart of the country of great port. Pinhão is quite modern: it has two garages, a post office, and a railway station whose walls are decorated with scenes of the vintage in coloured tiles. For the rest it is much like any other fairly prosperous Portuguese village. Its houses cluster along the main street and when it is washing day the women go down to the river and wash their clothes by the water-side.

It is now full dawn and the *roga* has gone up the hill behind La Rosa to bring in the first load of grapes. The *roga* is the team of men and women who do the picking, the carrying and the pressing. At vintage time they come down over the hills into the Douro, each team led by its musician, a man with a drum or an accordeon, while often among them is their own clown or jester. They straggle down the dusty roads singing, shouting, laughing and sometimes dancing, for although they are walking into ten days of gruelling work they view it as a strenuous holiday. They come from upland villages 'beyond the mountains' where the hot earth is pale yellow and the rocky hills are pale mauve and grey. They come down over the hill behind the Quinta where the villages are lost clumps of huts, where there are wolves in a hard winter and where, if you walk past a village at night, your footfalls alert a bedlam of watchdogs.

The hillside of La Rosa is an enormous staircase of terraces. Even the Quinta house itself is a terraced building. First is the *adega*, a barnlike structure filled with the wooden vats or tonels, each one almost the size of a peasant's hut; in these the new wine is stored until the early spring. On the next terrace up are the living quarters of the Quinta, or rather most of them since the dining-room and kitchen are yet one terrace higher. Higher still, and on the fourth terrace, are the house of the *caseiro*, or farm manager, and the long building in which the *roga* will have its meals. Behind the *caseiro*'s house, stretching far up to the fringe of pine trees and cistus bushes at the top of the steep hill, are the terraces of vines. Each terrace is faced with a rough stone wall in which, set sideways, is a ladder of rough stone slabs. The walls vary in height. Sometimes they are only a few feet but where the ground is steepest or where the edges of the hill jut out into the valley some of the walls are massive constructions twenty feet high. Occasionally a wall bursts under the winter rain. It bulges and breaks taking with it the terrace below and the terrace below that. The tumbled masonry looks exactly like the breached walls of a castle, and as castle walls must be rebuilt before the next siege so must these before the next vintage. They are of course all built by hand; and when you look up from the floor of the valley at the walled hillside you cannot help wondering at the patience of human labour.

The women of the *roga* do the picking. They began this morning at dawn and now down the hill come the men on their first *caminhada*, or long walk, of the vintage. Led by their accordeon they file down the stone ladderways and then, still in file, along the white road to the Quinta. Each man carries a *cesto*, a tall basket full of grapes. It is carried on the back, resting against a roll of sacking placed in the nape of the neck, and slung from the forehead on a broad canvas band. Some men steady the top of the basket with their hand but most of them use a stick with an iron hook at its upper end. (A 4th-century mosaic found at Carthage shows a vintager on the Estate of Julius carrying a basket of exactly the same shape and in almost exactly the same way.[1] When the Portuguese *cesto* is full of grapes it weighs 130 lb. and during the vintage of 1927, for example, each man made 160 *caminhadas*.[2] But these men of the *roga* do not seem to feel the weight. They walk fast down the road, swing round the top terrace of the Quinta house, trot down the grey stone steps and with a final blare of music arrive at the *lagares*.

The pressing shed is on the same terrace as the living-rooms of the Quinta; in fact it adjoins the house itself. It is long, cool and dark and, like everything else at this Quinta, it is terraced. Its lower terrace is a 'landing' which runs the length of the shed; its upper terrace – also running the full length – is a stone platform four feet above the level of the 'landing'. On top of this platform are the treading tanks, the *lagares*, huge rectangular tanks made of grey granite. There are seven of them in a row down the length of the platform and in the central *lagar* the heavy metal screw of the hand press sticks up.

It is still only seven in the morning as the grapes come in. The men of the *caminhada* climb to the platform and, with a shout, tip their baskets into the first *lagar*. Then they have ten minutes rest: that is to say they have ten minutes dancing for the vintage seems to give them unlimited energy and whenever they rest they dance, with each other, with the women, or with the children. Now there are no women and it is still too early for the children: so they dance with each other. At the end of ten minutes off they go with their cock-a-doodle music, out again into the sunlight. It will not be the yellow inferno of August reflected and intensified by the rock walls of the valley but, if the vintage is lucky, a mellow golden heat that has lost its summer intolerance. Even so it will be a long, hot walk up the hillside.

When the men have gone the pressing shed is silent and empty. This is always a moment of anti-climax for although the vintage has begun the only sign of it is an untidy heap of white grapes in the corner of a *lagar*. They look cold and lonely, lost

[1] Ros., *SEHR*, Pl. lxxix.

[2] Vintage Records, *Quinta de la Rosa*.

19

in the unfriendly grey space of the tank, mere tumbled fruit that is remote from drama. So I have a tot of *aguardente bagaçeira*, young brandy that smells of butter and is made of flame, and go off and have breakfast. When I return another *caminhada* has come down with more white grapes from the Upper Quinta and by lunchtime the first 'white' *lagar* is filled. The second 'white' *lagar* is sulphured before the grapes go in and by evening that too is filled and waiting for its transformation. These two 'white' *lagares* will make *jeropiga*, a sweet wine, and also an ordinary, unfortified – and very good – white wine for the use of the Quinta. There is white port but it will not be made here at this vintage. Perhaps that is why there seems to be a lull as though the vintage would not move into its excitement until the red grapes came down and the Quinta began the making of its port wine.

Next morning the excitement has begun. Down below the house the Douro is a sullen, jade green moving slowly over ribs of grey rock. With equal slowness a file of women is winding up from the river to the Quinta garden, carrying water in red earthenware pots balanced on their heads. The look of them and the labour of them is timeless. Across the river is a plodding ox-cart with heavy wooden wheels. The axle screeches plaintively in its sockets making 'the music of the Douro' which here becomes part of one's life. There is always 'music' in the Douro: a woman singing, an ox-cart wailing, two men calling to one another from somewhere in the valley. Even when you are in the hush of the pine trees above the Upper Quinta and sit there looking at the small white clouds drifting in the sky over Pinhão, you hear, from far below on the river bank, the voices of women who chatter as they spread out their white squares of linen to dry in the sun. Now this morning the air is a tangle of vintage music. A drum is beating across the river as a neighbour's *roga* crawls up the slope of its vineyards. The accordeon of our own *roga* is strident behind the house and fades into the pressing shed. From round the corner of our hill comes intermittently the music of the *caminhadas* of Val da Figueira. The air is infected with the vintage and overnight the tempo has changed. Now it is eager, restless, active, an irresistible impulsion as though life itself were in ferment.

After dark this evening rockets curve up from the Quinta to welcome the son of the house who has been travelling overland to arrive for the vintage. On the sanded drive outside the *adega*, and under the harsh light from a carbide jet, is the group of welcome. There stands La Rosa's owner, with a quantity of her dogs which range from dachshunds to the big Serra wolfdogs who (up in the hills) wear spiked collars when they hunt the wolves. There are the *caseiro* and the chauffeur with their wives, a number of children who are about to fall off a wall, and the Quinta's maids. The youngest of these, a shy and pretty girl from up in the hills, is balancing on her head a lighted candle in an old-fashioned candlestick. In this aspect, with a flame above her dark hair, she seems to have wandered in from one of the margins of mythology but she is being perfectly natural. Portuguese peasants carry anything, and everything, on their heads.

We go straight to the pressing shed. The two white *lagares* have been run off. They were trodden yesterday but they were reluctant to become wine and it was twenty-six hours before they began to 'move'. The skins were left in with the juice and when fermentation began the juice was allowed to ferment upon the skins. This is rare among white wines for normally the juice is run off the skins and allowed to ferment by itself. One of these white *lagares* was permitted only a very short fermentation – little more than half an hour – since its sugar had to be kept high and the longer a wine ferments the more it loses its sugar. When they were first trodden the white *lagares* looked like rectangular seas of green-brown squelch. When the must was run off and went down the pipes to its tonels in the *adega* it was an opaque, yellow-brown liquid that looked like flood water. At its birth wine is not beautiful. But when it has been educated this pungent mess will have been guided into a bright clarity.

In one of the bigger *lagares* the men of the *roga* are lined up, knee deep in black grapes. Twelve of them stand along each of the longer sides of the *lagar*. They are small, swarthy men, brown-eyed and dark-haired, dressed in shirts and a carnival assortment of white, pink or blue pants. Some of them are still wearing their hats and some have stuck into the grapes in front of them the iron-tipped sticks which they use to balance their *cestos*. The *lagar* has already been washed with water and sterilized with sulphur before the grapes went into it. Now more sulphur, a lumpy powder beaten to dust in a wooden bowl, is sprinkled on the grapes to slow down a too rapid fermentation for once fermentation starts it can become explosive, spitting the must up into the air over the *lagar*, and if it rushes through its work the wine will not be of the finest. A sugar-reading of the grapes has been taken and now there is nothing left to do but change the sugar into alcohol.

Sour grapes make no wine. It is the sweetness in the grapes which becomes alcohol and the amount of alcohol in a naturally fermented wine corresponds to the amount of sugar in the pressed or trodden grape juice. To summarize the process in its least romantic form one can say that yeasts on the gathered grape transform the sugar of the grape juice into alcohol and carbon dioxide gas. The agents of the metamorphosis are the *saccharomyces*, the wild yeasts which produce only a feeble fermentation, and the wine yeasts which have prodigious energy and achieve the full fermentation. One of the reasons for putting sulphur into grapes which are about to ferment is that it may kill off the wild yeasts and leave the wine yeasts in full control of the transformation. These latter will work away until they have changed all the sugar into alcohol and gas, so that, from a grape juice of ordinary sweetness, the sugar will have been fermented right out and the resulting wine will be dry. But the wine yeasts will not go on for ever, and when the wine which they are making contains between 16 per cent and 17 per cent of alcohol the yeasts will die and fermentation will stop. Where the grape juice is exceptionally sweet, in Sauternes for example, the yeasts will start to die at 16 per cent alcohol, but there will still be sugar left in the wine and there it remains, giving Sauternes its outstanding sweetness. The juice of the Douro grapes is not as sweet as that of Sauternes and if it were left to ferment to the full it would end up as a dry wine of about the same strength as claret.

The transformation begins. There is a confusion of shouting and stamping from the men of the *roga* as they start treading – 'cutting' it is called in the Douro. Then the leader shouts out the time and the moving legs come into a steady rhythm. Slowly, very slowly, the two files of men advance towards each other across the *lagar*.

Treading looks easy. Lyrically one might consider it to be merely a stroll among grapes. It is not so. When you get into a *lagar* your first shock is one of coldness. You expect the grapes to hold the warmth of sunshine that has ripened them out on the hill. But they are as cold as the pebbles on a river bed. You expect also that they will crush easily, that they will be merely frail skins of tissue around the pulp. But under the naked foot they are agile, evasive and resistant, trying to avoid their approaching change into alcohol. Only gradually does the juice spurt between the toes. And when you stand with the bare backs of your knees against the granite wall of the *lagar*, cold stone against your legs and cold grapes under your feet, and when you look at the tumbled sea of fruit that you must crush – 10,000 lb. of grapes – the labour seems Herculean and the naked foot too frail.

Some people are squeamish about feet, especially when the feet are in their wine. They have no need to be. In these days the feet are washed before they go into the *lagar* and in any case fermenting grape juice is a sterilizer. As a matter of fact, the Douro is one of the few great *vignobles* in which this sort of treading is still the practice and it is kept so because it helps in the making of this particular wine. With other wines there are other techniques; and when, for example, you are making white wine from black grapes, then treading is too slow, for the juice must be run off the skins before it can take colour from them. Then you must press and not tread.

The cutting of this red *lagar* will go on for hours. In the meantime we go back to the house and Maria Emilia comes down from one of the upper terraces to sing to us. She is a big-boned girl, finely built, with heavy dark eyes and a quick sense of humour. She also has one white eyelash. She leans against the door post looking reluctant but the reluctant look is only shyness and this she forgets when she begins to sing. She sings in the plaintive, strident voice that is the singing voice of all Portuguese women. Unlike many of the girls whom you hear singing in the Portuguese hills, Maria Emilia can read and write; but like those other girls she has never used the printed words of a song for she has learnt them all from memory. The art of memory is alive among these people as it was among the ancient peoples. And, like the ancient songs, Maria Emilia's have come down to her from memory to memory, from her mother and grandmother and from God knows how many more of the disappeared and the disappearing generations.

Back in the pressing shed the men of the *roga* are still cutting the red *lagar*. Until they began the only liquid among the grapes was that which had oozed from them before they were trodden. This was the *lagrima* – the 'tear'. Now the grapes have lost their single identities and have been trodden into a runny pulp of juice and grape skins. This innocent and unexciting pulp has not yet begun to ferment, and not until it does, not until it begins to turn into wine, will it be dignified with the name of must.

There seems now to be another lull in the vintage. It is nearly midnight. The only people in the long shed are ourselves and the men wading through the pulp in the *lagar*. There is no music. It is a hushed and rather lonely scene. Even the *égrappoir*, the machine that is used for separating some of the stalks from the grapes before the grapes go to be trodden, stands forlornly in an empty *lagar*, stalks hanging out of its mouth like the unswallowed ends of a monster's meal.

Next morning it is raining. Fortunately it does not rain for long, so that if the sun comes out the grapes on the vines will soon dry. But as one walks up through the vineyards it is still cool: cool enough perhaps to retard the start of a fermentation. Walking on, and up, round the shoulder of the hill one moves away from the mass of vines and into a narrow valley, silver green with olives. These too belong to La Rosa and their fruit will be harvested later in the year to make olive oil. If the vintage fails there are always the olives but if both fail there is nothing. That small archaic valley is sombre under a grey sky. One remembers how long they take to grow, those trees, and thinks of the Portuguese proverb –

> '*Vinhas,*
> *Minhas;*
> *Olivaes,*
> *Dos meus paes . . .*'[3]

> (Vines,
> My own;
> Olives,
> My parents' . . .)

and one imagines the fury of ancient Greek farmers whose vines had been burned and whose olive trees cut down by the army of another city. But then the sun breaks through the grey sky and covers the Douro once more with gold, and the little valley is no longer a grim picture out of Thucydides but an idyll from Theocritus. Over the river, beyond Pinhão one can see the sun on the tiled roofs and the white walls of the pressing sheds at the Quinta do Bomfim. Under those tiled roofs are more of the spitting, heaving, red rectangles of must which dominate the Douro during the days of vintage; and one can visualize them also in the grey tanks of Quinta after Quinta all the way up the gorge of the river towards Spain.

At La Rosa the red *lagar* which was cut last night has started to 'move'. It literally is moving, as though it were stretching itself and twisting itself to try and escape from the grip of fermentation. It is talking too; hissing and muttering like a strange animal caught in a strange dream. The top of it is a convulsed mat of grape husks, driven to the top by the gas which breaks through in a continual spluttering of bubbles. Balanced on the narrow granite walls round the tank are men with wooden rakes – *macacos* or 'monkeys' – with which they break up the clotted mat. Beside this toiling *lagar* another tank is being filled with grapes from the middle vineyards. They are black grapes; or rather they are a dusty grey blue in colour except that where they have been rubbed by a picker's hand they are a shining brilliant black. Soon they too will be cut.

The pressing shed is heavy with the reek of fermentation, the tingling heady smell of carbon dioxide gas that is everywhere and unforgettable. Only outside among the vines are you free from it for even when you go to bed it will drift from the *lagares* across the house, and when you wake the first thing you know is fermentation. From now on the reek will be persistent as more *lagares* are filled and cut and labour in their ferment.

From now on too the activity in the pressing shed will be multiplex, the various

[3]Rodney Gallop, *Portugal: A Book of Folk-Ways*, Cambridge: 1936, 28.

23

lagares moving at different times through the various stages of the metamorphosis. It will simplify the picture if we isolate certain threads in the general pattern.

When the grapes have been cut the men of the *roga* are given a glass of the fiery *aguardente bagaçeira*; then they are given their *liberdade*, their 'freedom' or respite. They dance in the red juice of the *lagar* and they sing their song of *Liberdade*:

> '*São tão bonitas as carvoeiras*
> *São tão catitas as feiticeiras*
> *O que lindo rancho*
> *Bela mocidade*
> *Vivam as raparigas*
> *Viva a Liberdade*.'[4]

> (So lovely are the coal-women,
> So neat and fine the witches.
> What a handsome crew.
> Youth to me has beauty.
> Hurrah then for the girls, the girls
> And to be free from duty.)

When the grapes have been cut, and not until then, there is music in the vintage shed. On the narrow ledge of the platform, in front of the *lagares*, struts the musician of the *roga* with his accordeon. Down below on the 'landing' everyone is dancing: children from the cottages down by the river, girls dancing with one another, guests dancing with Maria Emilia, with Conceiçao, a young woman who looks as though she were made of ivory, and with the little maid who carried a candle on her head. (Some of these names have an aura of baroque religion. Conceiçao means conception and one year in the *roga* there was a woman called Perpetual Conception.) The dance is a cross between a highland reel and complete exhaustion and it is complicated by '*O Mudo*', 'the dumb one', a small boy who was run over by a train, lost his leg, and became dumb from shock. He hops about with the agility of a goat, using his crutch as a propellant rather than as a second leg. He is a general favourite and is entirely enjoying himself. Under the carbide jets, on a bench along the 'landing', sit old women in black. They look as though they had been carved by a neolithic sculptor and left there until they should be needed.

The dancing takes place against a purgatorial background. Up on the platform, in the middle of the row of *lagares*, the screw-press is being filled. From a *lagar* that has 'moved' and been run off the wet grape skins are being shovelled into the slatted, barrel-like container of the press. Two semi-circular halves of a wooden cover, each two inches thick, are fitted over the top of the pulp. The mere weight of this cover is enough to press down the pulp: not much, but enough to make it 'bleed' between the slats of its container. On the cover are laid three layers of short and heavy wooden beams and down onto them comes the metal girder-beam of the press itself. The press is wound down and its tightening thrust is marked by a staccato, metal clicking. The pawls which hold the ratchet-wheel against the pressure are short, metal bars and they click up and down round the top of the press like the keys of an extraordinary typewriter.

[4]Trans., Author; (there is an earlier verse).

24

The press is wound down by a thick horizontal bar stuck into the rim of the ratchet-wheel and at first there is only one man on this bar. The action is rapid and easy. As the clicking slows down another man comes onto the bar. Three steps forward, three steps back. Again and again. Juice is running between the wooden slats of the container and the grape skins creak and protest as they are driven down. The work is harder now and a third man comes onto the bar. The shadows of the straining, sweating, bare-footed men are thrown enormous on the wall by the harsh white light of the carbide jets and they seem to be labouring out their redemption in a corner of Purgatory. They are as it happens enjoying themselves but though Purgatory is absent, death is not impossible. The press is strained to the point at which it is explosive. If it breaks the wooden slats will fly outwards like spears and if the ratchet fails the metal bar will spin in a bright decapitating circle. This is possible but rare: far rarer than a Portuguese peasant who does not want to dance. Even the old women in black on the bench would dance if they could; but their minds are away among neolithic dreams.

A finished red *lagar* is being run off. The must runs from the bottom of the granite tank, down through filters and into the pipe which will take it to its first home. It is dark purple-red with pink froth and while it is beginning to be wine it is not yet port. If you look down from the 'landing' into the *adega* on the terrace below, you see down there on the sanded floor a solitary man. He is in a crude circle of light from a carbide lamp, and all round him are the enormous shadows of the vats. With a monotonous resolution he is turning the wheel of a hand pump. He appears to have gone mad. He seems to imagine that the Quinta is a ship and that he is pumping the water out of her to save her from shipwreck. He is, however, quite sane and he is pumping brandy.

This is where the new wine becomes port, or anyway fundamental port. The *lagar* has been run off while there was enough sugar left in it to keep it fermenting. As it rushes down into its vat it is given a dose of grape brandy. This brings the alcohol in the must up to a point where fermentation has to stop and where the unfermented sugar remains to give some sweetness to the wine, a technique not used with wines such as (for example and among many others) claret and burgundy whose fermentation is allowed to finish, but which with port is a vital step in the creation of a great wine.

At the end of ten days (the time can, of course, vary), the vintage is over. The commonplace miracle has been brought to happen in the grey *lagares*. Grapes have become wine. The new wine has been born and caged in the wooden hulks of the *adega*. All that remains is the Curtain Call.

The *roga*, all of them, men and women, are gathered on the sandy drive outside the *adega*. In anticipation of the dancing later there is a spurt of impatient music from the accordeon but nobody moves for this is still a formal occasion. Down the long flight of granite steps from the Quinta house walks the owner with her son, followed by a Serra wolf dog. As they reach the drive the leader of the *roga* steps forward and presents the *roga*'s gift of the *ramo*.

The *ramo* is an elaborate bouquet. It is made of corn stalks, branches, ribbons, flowers, bits of coloured paper and grapes. It is sincere but it is not a surprise for it follows a traditional pattern of the Douro. Nor, surely, is it surprising that it should have some resemblance to the *Eiresione*, the harvest branch, of ancient Athens. This was a branch of olive, twined with white or purple wool, pots of wine, figs, acorns, and cakes.[5] And the song sung by those who went in procession with the *Eiresione* applies to La Rosa as it applied to ancient Athens:

> 'Eiresione brings
> All good things,
> Figs and fat cakes to eat,
> Soft oil and honey sweet,
> And brimming wine-cup deep . . .'

[5]Harrison, *Prolegomena*, 78–80.

CHAPTER TWO

The Ancient Middle East and Egypt

In the Shadows

Wine was first discovered by a woman. King Jemsheed, so runs the story, was fond of grapes and was accustomed to store them in jars so that through the year there should always be grapes for him to eat. On one occasion, however, he found that the grapes were no longer sweet – (they had fermented) – and, imagining that the liquid in the jar was poisonous, he labelled the jar accordingly. One of the ladies of his harem noticed the label on the jar. Having been distracted by the pain of 'nervous headaches' and, desiring death in preference to this continual pain, she drank some of the 'poison'. She was overpowered by the wine, fell asleep, and awoke refreshed. With pleasure she returned to the 'poison' and finished the jar. She was forced, however, to communicate her secret to the King, upon which 'a quantity of wine was made; and Jemsheed and all his court drank of the new beverage'.[1]

Jemsheed is Jamshíd, one of the culture-heroes of Persian mythology. This story about him is late and undoubtedly 'poetic', but in its poetic guise it speaks the truth. This is how wine must have been discovered. And the suggestion that it was discovered by a woman cannot be dismissed as a mere poetic invention, since in the Sumerian *Epic of Gilgamish*, one of the oldest poems in the world, there is close connection between a woman and the making of wine.

This, then, in the remote past, is how wine happened. Grapes, either fresh or dried into raisins, would have been kept for eating in a pottery jar, a stone bowl, or a cavity in the rock. The juice would have run and, under the right conditions of temperature, it would have fermented. Often the bubbling juice must have been thrown away as unfit for consumption. But once, somewhere, fermentation finished and wine was made. The first drinker, with his first draught, may have thought it was poison; with his second draught he – or she – began the history of wine.

We can argue with some assurance about the discovery of wine but the type of

[1]Malcolm, Sir John, *The History of Persia*, I, 10, fn. b. For Jamshíd as culture-hero: see Firdausí, *The Sháhnáma of*, trs., A. G. and E. Warner, I, 129 sqq.

27

wine which humanity first drank must remain a matter for speculation. It was either *vin ordinaire*, the fermented juice of fresh grapes, and not very good at that, or it was raisin wine, the fermented juice of dried grapes and, in those early days, a very much better drink. The latter is the more likely simply because it is more likely that grapes would have been dried into raisins before they were stored for the winter, and raisins would therefore have been the first grapes to find themselves in the right conditions for fermentation. If this were so, then the first wine tasted by mankind would have been a sort of Tokay essence, very sweet and only moderately alcoholic.

It is generally assumed that the making of wine began somewhere in the 4th millennium B.C., although it may have begun a little earlier. But we may be able, at least in argument, to push the original date of wine-making back to the distant age of the Magdalenian rock painters, 10,000 years ago or more. In this Upper Palaeolithic Age which marks the emergence of 'modern' man, some of the conditions existed for the deliberate making of wine although they did not exist for the deliberate growing of grapes.

The vine itself goes back much further than the Palaeolithic period. The earliest vine of which we know, the *Vitis sezannensis*, which seems to have been an American type, occurs in the Tertiary period, a million to sixty million years ago. Strictly speaking, this is not relevant to our story. What is relevant, however, is the fact that a prehistoric vine *Vitis silvestris* is more or less resistant to frost and that its grapes will make drinkable wine. (This vine still grows in Hercegovina, Yugoslavia, where it is called 'Iosnica'.) Thus even in the somewhat cold climate of the Magdalenian period this vine may have been able to ripen its grapes; and if it could do so, then the rock-painters may well have drunk wine. More relevant to the historical part of our story is when, in the Quaternary, we find the 'European' vine. The Quaternary runs from about a million years ago and includes the Upper Palaeolithic which ends about 8000 B.C. and the vine which we find – at Montpellier, in Tuscany, and near Rome – is the *Vitis vinifera*, the famous vine of Europe and the Middle East and the vine which is the basis of most historical wine.[2]

The conditions may thus have existed for the making of Palaeolithic 'wild wine' and when we consider the skill of the Magdalenian rock paintings it is hard to believe that men who exploited such an art did not also exploit the accidental discovery of wine – assuming, of course, that the accidental discovery had already been made. But an artistic sense does not necessarily involve material progress. At Early Neolithic Jericho, about 6000 B.C., the inhabitants modelled in plaster, and modelled with skill, human features upon the actual skulls of the dead. Yet this people, which could model so remarkably in plaster, did not possess pottery.[3] From Lerna, a site on the Bay of Argos in the Peloponnese, comes the remarkable 'Lerna Aphrodite', a small terracotta statue which is outstanding, not only for its beauty, but also because it foreshadows the great sculpture of civilized Europe. Yet it is Neolithic and this particular culture of the early 3rd millennium is not outstanding in terms of material progress.[4]

We do not know whether the Magdalenian cave dwellers of southern France, the plastered-skull people of Jericho, or the Neolithic inhabitants of Argos knew the pleasures of wine as well as the satisfactions of art. Nor are we any better off when we look at the earliest attempts at urban civilization. It is at this point in history,

[2] V.V., *A.*, I, 486 sqq.; Zeuner, F. E., *Pleistocene Period*, 183-4. Vitis silvestris ('Losnica'), *The Wine and Spirit Trade Review*, London, April 8th, 1960, ' "Extinct" Vine Discovered'.

[3] Kenyon, K. M., 'The World's Oldest Known Township', *ILN*, May 12th, 1956; cf. the story in Herodotus IV of the Issedones, who gilded and kept the heads of dead men. See also Kenyon, K. M., 'Jericho and its Setting . . .', *Antiquity*, XXX, 1956, for the controversy about the Jericho dating: Zeuner, F. E., 'The Radiocarbon Age of Jericho', *Antiquity*, XXX, 1956; Braidwood, R. J., 'Jericho and its Setting . . .', *Antiquity*, XXXI, 1957, with Miss Kenyon's reply; and later articles in *Antiquity*.

[4] Caskey, J. L., 'Where Hercules slew the Hydra . . .', *ILN*, Jan. 12th, 1957; Caskey, J. L. and Eliot, M., 'A Neolithic Figurine from Lerna, *Hesp*, XXV, 1956.

when a community becomes static, when it settles down to village life and to agriculture, that we might expect to find the first viticulture, the first deliberate growing of grapes. The conditions are there: the evidence is not: and once again we are forced to speculate.

About 8000 B.C. at Anau in Turkestan, on the borders of Russia and north-east Iran, there appear the beginnings of settled agricultural life.[5] The people of Anau lived in houses, cultivated barley and wheat, and had painted pottery. The Siyalk culture in north-central Persia, one of the earliest cultures of Iran, also had grain and pottery.[6] The combination of agriculture and pottery is important since, if these people were accustomed to harvesting and to storing their harvest in pottery vessels, then they might also have stored their grapes for eating, and thus given the grapes the chance of reasonable fermentation. Pottery is not essential to the making of pre-historic wine but the pottery jar is convenient for storage and it is to storage that we must look for the earliest wine.

When we find silos, or grain bins, of pottery in these Early millennia, then the conditions become even more propitious, for these silos would allow the fermenting of grapes in some bulk and the making of wine in some quantity. Tell Hassuna, a few miles south of Mosul in Mesopotamia, is one of the earliest static communities yet discovered in that part of the Middle East, and at Tell Hassuna we find large spherical silos of clay 'coated outside with bitumen and sometimes lined with gypsum plaster'.[7] We find silos at Mersin in Cilician Asia Minor, to the north-west of Syria, just after the end of its Neolithic period and, which is even more suggestive, a jar stopper of about 4000 B.C., one moreover that is not radically dissimilar from a type of stopper used much later in Mycenaean Greece.[8] The stoppered jar of Mersin, may not, of course, have contained a liquid; but on the other hand it may represent one of the earliest attempts to prevent the air from getting at the wine and thus to prevent the wine from turning into vinegar. And while we do not know that the silos were ever used for the storage of grapes or the making of wine, we can note that pottery jars were sometimes used (though much later) for the treading of grapes and the making of wine in the Middle Kingdom of Egypt.

These things only indicate the possibility of the making and storing (and growing) of wine. They do not indicate that wine had either been discovered or become 'deliberate' any more than the existence of a farming community at Olynthus and Neolithic cauldrons at Knossos mean that the 4th millennium peoples of Greece and of Crete had discovered that wine could be a part of their life.

In fact it seems clear that the possibility of wine was seldom realized in the earliest days of Western civilization. So much the old gods tell us. It seems equally clear that there was a fairly sudden change when, instead of beer or of mead, wine became the chosen drink of the gods. So much they also tell us. In detail their testimony is confusing: in general, however, it is accurate, for, since men made the gods, these gods must reflect what happened in the lives of the men who made them.

First, and most famously, the ancient deities drank honey-wine – mead, the nectar of the gods.[9] There is an Orphic story that when Zeus defeated his father Kronos, Zeus first made the older god drunk on mead.[10] When Zeus himself was born, so runs another story, he was nursed and suckled by bees.[11] And in the Homeric Hymn to Hermes there is a curious story about the honey-priestesses of Parnassus, the

Terracotta Figure
4000–3500 B.C.
Baghdad, Iraq Museum

[5]Pumpelly, R., *Explorations in Turkestan*, I, 38, 57; *CAH*, I, 86 sqq.

[6]McCown, D. E., 'The Material Culture of Early Iran', *JNES*, I, 4, 1942.

[7]Lloyd, S., and Safar, F., 'Tell Hassuna', *JNES*, IV, 4, 1945.

[8]Garstang, J., *Prehistoric Mersin*, 45–8, 76; Chadwick, J., and Bennett, E. L., 'The Mycenae Tablets II' (Bibl. Ch. 3), 7 and figs. 36, 37.

[9]Hes., *Theogony*, 642.

[10]Kerenyi, C., *Gods of the Greeks* (Bibl. Ch. 3), 20; Harrison, *Prolegomena*, 422.

[11]Kerenyi, C., *Gods of the Greeks* (Bibl. Ch. 3), 83.

Thriae, the 'swarming sisters', 'three virgins gifted with wings' who practised sooth-saying when they had fed upon honey.[12] Surely their honey was mead? And surely these stories, late though parts of them may be, must contain reflections of a far earlier age?

Such a reflection certainly exists in an old story of Hathor, the great cow-headed goddess of Egypt. Ra, wishing to be revenged upon a rebellious mankind, sent Hathor against men. The goddess slaughtered them without mercy and could only be stopped when Ra poured beer over the earth and Hathor, drinking it, became intoxicated and 'recognized mankind no longer'.[13] It was perhaps only natural that she should have been the Egyptian goddess of intoxication but this seems to have made her merciful for she became also the goddess of love and joy, of music, singing, dancing and of the making of garlands.

If first of all in Greece it may have been mead, and in Egypt beer, in Mesopotamia it may have been date-wine. The *Epic of Gilgamish* presents us with the type of savage man, Enkidu, a 'wild man of the woods' who lived on plants and drank only water. He was given his first experience of civilization by a temple woman, in this case one of the *shamkhāti* and a temple harlot, who showed him human manners and gave him wine to drink – the first fermented drink that he had ever had. 'He drank seven times. His thoughts wandered. He became hilarious. His heart was full of joy and his face shone.'[14] Is it coincidental that Jamshíd's benefactress was a woman and so was Enkidu's teacher?

[12]Hes., *Homeric Hymns*, IV, 'To Hermes', 550 sqq.; and see Harrison, *Prolegomena*, 442.

[13]Erman, 268–9.

[14]Contenau, G., *Médecine en Assyrie . . .*, 194; and Thompson, R. Campbell, *The Epic of Gilgamish*; pref., *CAH*, I, 539.

Enkidu's drink was probably date-wine and the early Sumerian world in which he moved was one that was largely, or completely, without the wine of grapes. But soon we find the rise of the deities of wine – (and in this book where I use the word 'wine' by itself it means the wine of grapes). For a time the connection between Early woman and Early wine persisted in religion for one of the earliest of these deities was Gestin, the Sumerian goddess of the Vine, a specialized form of the primitive earth-goddess of Central Asia. Later, at Ugarit on the coast of Syria, we find the woman Pagat helping her father Danel, a hero-figure or demi-god, to cultivate the vine; and although the clay tablets which record the Ugarit story date only from about 1500 B.C., the story itself is almost certainly a reminiscence of life in an earlier period.[15]

It is not surprising that early deities of wine should have been women since these early deities were naturally associated with the early goddesses of the fertility of the earth. Nor were they confined to Sumeria or Syria, for in Egypt in the 15th and 14th centuries B.C. the snake goddess Renen-ūtet, patroness of plenty, was 'present' at the vintaging of the grapes.[16]

Nevertheless the male principle had begun to assert itself in Egypt as early as 3000 B.C. By the time of the Early Dynasties Osiris had taken the titles of 'lord of wine at the inundation' and 'lord of carousing at the festival *ouag*'.[17] The name of this latter festival, which took place at the time of the inundation, was written with the signs of three wine jars on the table and a fourth jar being offered by an outstretched arm. Although it was a feast of drinking and carousing it was a feast for the dead as well as for the living and it is interesting to compare it to the Spring festival of the Anthesteria in Classical Greece.

The gods were fond of drinking. At the beginning of the 3rd millennium Egyptian gods, resplendent in dark red linen, enjoyed themselves 'living on figs, drinking wine'.[18] Towards the end of the 3rd millennium, in the time of the Third Dynasty of Babylon, the Babylonian gods were quite prepared to drink and equally prepared to get drunk. The *Epic of Creation* puts the matter bluntly: 'the sweet drink put far away their cares. As they drank liquor their bodies became satiated. Much they babbled and their mood was exalted.'[19] Once again the old gods followed the actions, or at least the aspirations, of their human creators.

The First Vignerons

'Noah' is generally accepted as the type of the first *vigneron* and the story of his first vintage has lost nothing in the telling. '. . . Noah began to be an husbandman, and he planted a vineyard: And he drank of the wine, and was drunken; and he was uncovered within his tent.'[20] The description is a summary statement of the beginnings of viticulture, but the statement is too summary. Did Noah deliberately get drunk and was he, like the early gods of Babylonia, happily intemperate? The story as it is told in Genesis does not bear this interpretation. It implies rather that Noah was taken by surprise and was overwhelmed by his first experience of wine. But the story cannot bear this interpretation either. Wine would not have been made from cultivated grapes until some time after it had been made from the fruit of the wild vine, and any cultivator of vines must already have known of the intoxicating

[15]*Ras Shamra*, Vol. XXI, 78, 82, 85 sqq., 93, 99.

[16]Davies, N. de G., *Two Officials of Tuthmosis the Fourth*, Pl. xxx, 31; *Tomb of Nefer-Hotep*, I, Pl. xlviii, 37.

[17]Mercer, S. A. B., *Pyramid Texts*, 1524a; and Vol. IV, Excursus XXI (Driotin, E.); cf. Mercer, S. A. B., *Literary Criticism of the Pyramid Texts*, 1924, 1880b, 716c, 2118b.

[18]Mercer, S. A. B., *Pyramid Texts*, 1511b; and comm. to 1511a.

[19]Langdon, S., *The Babylonian Epic of Creation*, 125.

[20]*Genesis*, IX, 20-1.

properties of his vintage. 'Noah' may thus stand as the figure of the first viticulturalist but he cannot claim to be the first maker of wine. This title, as we have suggested, must surely go to a woman.

This woman occurs in the *Epic of Gilgamish*. There, the hero, after considerable travelling, finds the Tree of Life 'Bearing its fruit . . .(?) . . . ruby, and hung about with (its) tendrils'[21] and meets 'Siduri, the Maker of Wine . . .'. It is possible that this Tree of Life was the vine, and that Siduri used its fruit. She may, it is true, be merely a remote personification of an 'ale-wife', and only a seller of wine, but we may suspect that she both made and sold the new and exciting liquor of grapes.

Siduri may have been 'created' in the 4th millennium, or even in the 5th millennium, B.C. and thus the first historical wine may bear the same dating. At all events the archaic texts of Ur, which are among the earliest agricultural documents in the world, show that the vine was much in favour and that wine (presumably grape-wine) was being drunk. It seems possible, moreover, that by the time of these early texts viticulture was being practised and the era of 'wild wine' had gone past.[22] Certainly by the middle of the 4th millennium B.C. the first Dynasties of Egypt practised viticulture and made wine.[23] It is indeed conceivable that wine was known in the Badarian civilization at the beginning of the pre-Dynastic period of Egypt, but more than that we cannot say and we have to settle for our certainty that it was both known and made in the first Dynasties.[24]

Owing to the approximate nature of these early datings, we cannot be sure whether viticulture began first in Mesopotamia or in Egypt. For that matter we cannot be sure whether it began in either. It has frequently been maintained that the homeland of *Vitis vinifera* was south of the Caucasus and south of the Caspian,[25] but one writer suggests that its homeland may originally have been the Mediterranean and that it travelled by Egypt into the Middle East.[26] It is probable, indeed, that the vine existed all round the Mediterranean as well as in Asia Minor and viticulture could thus have begun in the south of France or in northern or central Italy.[27] It is unlikely that it did. Another view is that it began in Armenia and spread thence into Mesopotamia, Syria and Egypt and this is the view that is usually taken.

But I believe it reasonable to suggest another theory. If we accept the probability that viticulture began in Asia Minor, may we not also accept the probability that it began in Syria rather than Armenia? We go back once again to Siduri. Is it not remarkable that the *Epic*, which seems to have originated with very early Sumerians, should locate Siduri and the 'Tree of Life' in a region which may be identified as Western Syria? There were, admittedly, later editions of the *Epic* so that we cannot be certain of the Sumerian dating of all of it, but the story of Siduri has the stamp of great antiquity. Admittedly also the *Epic* does not make it certain that Siduri actually cultivated the vine but it is not unreasonable to assume that a people who deliberately made wine tried deliberately to cultivate the tree from which wine was made.[28]

Furthermore it seems undoubted that there was trade between Syria and the pre-Dynastic Badarian civilization of Egypt and it is not at all impossible that the knowledge of the cultivated vine travelled to Egypt by this route.[29] However that may be, and wherever viticulture did begin, it is to Egypt, and not to Syria, that we must go for our fullest knowledge of man's early and deliberate growing of wine.

[21] Thompson, R. Campbell, *Epic of Gilgamish*, 43–4; and Addenda.

[22] *Ur Excavations*, II, 6–11.

[23] Mercer, S. A. B., *Pyramid Texts, passim*.

[24] Brunton, G. and Caton-Thompson, G., *The Badarian Civilisation . . .*, 41, 63, trade (?) from Syria.

[25] Hehn, V., *The Wandering of Plants . . .* (Bibl. Ampelography), 73; Laufer, B., 'The Grape Vine', *Sino-Iranica*, XV, 1919.

[26] Mortillet, G. de, 'Les Boissons fermenteés, 265, *Rev. Mens. de l'Ecole d'Anthrop.*, 1897; cf. Aribaud, A., *Le Dieu de Pourpre et d'Or* (Bibl. General), 13.

[27] V.V., *A.*, I, 504.

[28] Thompson, R. Campbell, *The Epic of Gilgamish*; Contenau, G., *Everyday Life in Babylon and Assyria*, 72–3, 204; and see *CAH*, I, 362, 462.

[29] Brunton, G., and Caton-Thompson, G., *The Badarian Civilisation . . .*, 63; Bruijning, F. F., 'Tree of the Herakleopolite Nome', *Anc. Egypt*, Pt IV, 1921.

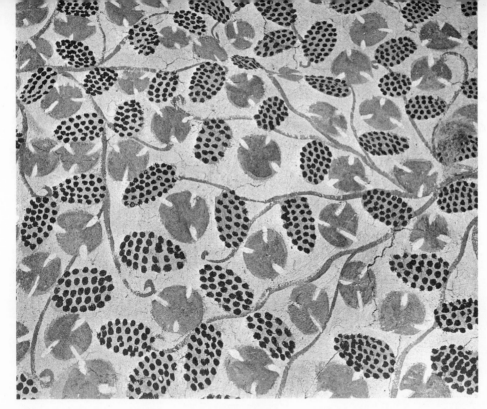

*Vine Motif: ceiling
decoration
Tomb of Sennefer
c 1500 B.C.
Thebes*

EGYPT

'The Wine Store of the Hog'

The Egyptians were a beer-drinking people. From the pre-Dynastic period onwards they quenched their thirst and their cares in beer that was made from emmer wheat and, also perhaps, from barley.[30] In the Pyramid Texts of the Early Dynasties beer is frequently mentioned as a religious offering and it was even thought suitable to be the drink of the dead Pharaoh.[31] So popular did it continue to be that when in somewhat later times the Egyptians gave a party – and they were very fond of parties – they called it arranging a 'house of beer'.[32]

Nevertheless they had wine as well. In the Pyramid Texts of Sakkâreh which date from the 5th, 6th and 7th Dynasties but which reflect a good deal of pre-dynastic life, wine is frequently mentioned, and not only wine but wine from various places.★ For example, one incantation runs: 'To say four times: . . . a lifting up of the offering, four times. Two jars of wine of the North. Wine: Two bowls of the North; two jars of *bš*; two bowls of Buto; two bowls of (wine) *ḥzmw*: two bowls of Pelusium.'[33] The 1st Dynasty tombs at Abydos not only record the existence of vineyards but give us such tantalizing phrases as 'the wine-press of the Eastern nomes and the Western nomes', 'wine of various kinds from the place of the Golden Bull', 'wine from the fortress Khent', and 'the wine-store of the Hog', this latter being one of the earliest recorded wine 'cellars' in history.[34] From the tomb of King Zoser of the 3rd Dynasty comes the resounding description 'Vineyard of the red house of the king's house in the town of Sen(?)pu in the Western nomes' and also the title of that

★For wines of ancient Egypt and of the ancient Middle East, together with the location of their vineyards, see Appendix A.

[30]Lucas, 19, 22–3; Erman, 192–3 and 193, fn. 1.

[31]Mercer, S. A. B., *Pyramid Texts, passim*. For types of beer, 61a, 61b, 89b, 91b; III, 113 sq., 119; and Murray, Margaret A., *Saqqara Mastabas*, Pt I, 34.

[32]Erman, 256.

[33]Mercer, S. A. B., *Pyramid Texts*, 92b.

[34]Petrie, W. M. F., *History of Egypt*, 19 sq., 21 sq.

famous Egyptian vineyard 'Praised be Horus who is in the front of Heaven'.[35] The wine in the long, yellow-brown wine jars of this 3rd Dynasty was made five thousand years ago and it is interesting to note that, even at this early date, the wine was 'labelled' with seals stamped on the conical caps of mud which covered the mouths of the jars.

We do not know what type of wine went into these jars. It has been suggested that, since only dark grapes are depicted in the Old Kingdom of Egypt, the wine would generally have been red. It could also, of course, have been a rosé. But it is quite likely that both red and white wine was made at this time and it might be that the *bš* wine of the Pyramid Texts was in fact a white wine. By the 5th Dynasty, which is not very much later, both red and white wines were usual, the red (or dark red) representing the right eye, and the white the left eye, of Horus. The white – was this the wine known as *Green Horus-Eye?* – was thought to be the better of the two.[36]

Most of the wines of the first seven Dynasties came from the Nile Delta in Lower Egypt. From here came the 'wine of the North' of the Pyramid Texts, as did the wines of Buto and Pelusium and the wine of *ḥzmw*. This latter name, which is perhaps that of a vine-growing district, may well have meant the area near Lake Mareotis in the north-western Nile Delta and from this area may also have come that wine of ancient Egypt called *Ḥm* or 'wine of the fishermen-village'. From the Western Delta too, or so it would seem, came wine from Zoser's 'Vineyard of the red house of the king's house in . . . Sen(?)pu . . .' while from the Eastern Delta, near Tanis, came the wine 'of Imet'. There may have been vineyards in the Faiyum by the 3rd Dynasty but it seems likely that the vineyards of the Delta were the earliest and that 'the wine-press of the Eastern nomes and the Western nomes' dealt with grapes that were grown near Mareotis and Tanis.[37]

Some two thousand six hundred years after the end of the 7th Dynasty two writers of the Roman Empire recorded that the wine of Mareotis was white, fragrant, and thin, but of good quality and that the wine of Sebennytus, in the Central Nile Delta, ranked quite highly for its excellence.[38] But we cannot use these statements as any real guide to an appraisal of the earliest Egyptian wines. During the early Dynasties the techniques of wine-making and wine maturing may have been rather different from those that were employed in Egypt under the Roman Empire. The vines, also, may have been different since we know that, by the 1st century A.D., Greek vines had been introduced into some of the vineyards of the Delta.[39] I think we would be right in assuming that the Delta wines which the Romans knew were finer than those which celebrated the lordship of Osiris at the Inundation and finer than those which went into the tombs of the earliest kings. How much finer we cannot guess. All we know is that the Early men greatly esteemed the Early wines.

'*Wine of the Basin*'

There were two kinds of Early Egyptian vineyard. Either it was a creation of beauty or else a work of agriculture. To put it another way, one was a formal garden and the other an orchard-garden. Both produced wine and it is impossible to decide

[35] *Bêt Khallâf*, 3, 10, 11, 19 sqq., Pl. xxxi.

[36] Grapes: *Ancient Egypt*, Pt I, 1914, 38. Colours of wine: Mercer, S. A. B., *Pyramid Texts*, 1082a; Murray, M. A., *Saqqara Mastabas*, Pt I, 40; Erman, 196. *Bš*: Mercer, *Pyramid Texts*, 92b, 92d; cf. *Meir*, III, 29-30; *Green Horus-Eye*: Lutz, *VB*, 7, 8; and cf. Frazer, Sir J. G., *Golden Bough* (Bibl. Ch. 3), Vol. VII, 263 for Osiris often represented as green on monuments; by analogy, Green Horus Eye might have meant a wine drunk in the Spring.

[37] *Bš*: see fn. 36 above; Buto, *Ḥzmw*, Lower Egypt (Wine of the North). Pelusium: Mercer, S. A. B., *Pyramid Texts*, 92b, 93b, 93d, 94; and Buto: *Meir*, III, 29-30. Pelusium: *Meir*, V, 29; *Ḥm* (same as the later Hemy [?]. Breasted, *ARE*, IV, 734), Lutz, *VB*, II, 13. 'Imet: Lutz, *VB*, II, 14; Praised be Horus . . ., *Bêt Khallâf*, 21 sq., Breasted, *ARE*, I, 201; Sen (?) pu: *Bêt Khallâf*, 22; vineyards in the Faiyum – Methen: Breasted, *ARE*, I, 173; Erman, 196; another wine of ancient Egypt was Esneh. See fn. 207 below.

[38] Ath-E, I, 33d; Plin., XIV, 74.

[39] Plin., XIV, 74.

34

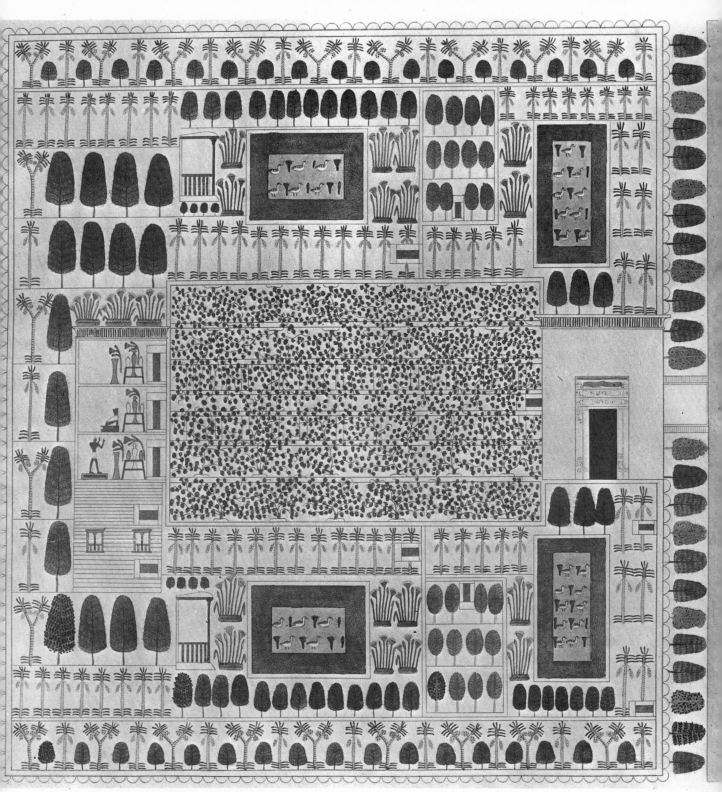

Garden Vineyard: painting from Theban Tomb

which came first. By the end of the 3rd Dynasty (about 2600 B.C.) both types appear to have existed, since at that time Methen, an administrator in Northern Egypt, had a garden-vineyard outside his house and another one, but this time a vineyard 'by itself', in another place.[40]

The full development of the garden, or leisure, vineyard had been attained by the time of the 18th Dynasty. The tomb of Nebamūn, who was an official of Tuthmosis IV, shows us the formal garden with its T-shaped lake or tank, bordered by trees. Vines are trained up between the columns of a pergola.[41] Another of the Theban tomb paintings shows us the garden of the harem of King Ay, who followed Tutenkhamon and who reigned in or about 1350 B.C. In this garden are pomegranates, figs, sycamores and vines, the latter being trained on a horizontal trellis between the decorative pillars of a pergola or summer-house.[42] The same tomb, which is that of Nefer-Hotep who was 'superintendent of the oxen and heifers of Amūn', that is to say an official of the temple administration of the god Amūn, has preserved for us the picture of a garden before a temple. There are avenues of trees, beds of papyrus, a T-shaped lake with lotus, and in each of the beds an apparently unsupported vine.[43] Ramses III, of the 20th Dynasty, recounting at considerable length his various benefactions, gives us yet another picture of these gardens. Addressing the great god Amon-Re, he says:

'I made for thee wine-gardens in the Southern Oasis, and Northern Oasis likewise without number; others in the South with numerous lists; they were multiplied in the Northland by the hundred-thousand. I manned them with gardeners from the captives of the countries; having lakes (of my digging), supplied with lotus flowers, and with shedeh (*sdh*) and wine like drawing water, in order to present them before thee in "Victorious Thebes" I planted thy city, Thebes, with trees, vegetations, isi-plants, and menhet flowers for thy nostrils.'[44]

These benefactions of Ramses III are recorded in the great Papyrus Harris, an enormous document one hundred and thirty-three feet long. It gives detailed information about the property of the temples of Egypt and from this we can discover that they owned 513 vineyards.

We must, however, make certain observations about this statement. In the first place not all, and perhaps not even the majority, of these vineyards were made by Ramses III. Some existed before his time. In the second place not all of them were actually transferred to the temple by Ramses III. In a number of cases he must merely have confirmed the temple in its possession of a vineyard which already belonged to it. Therefore we cannot say for certain that the reign of Ramses III marked any sudden, or any great, increase in viticulture.

And in the third place the 513 vineyards appear in the Papyrus as 'vineyards and tree gardens' or 'gardens and groves'. They may thus have been garden-vineyards or orchard-vineyards. At all events, not all of them were devoted to the sole purpose of growing wine and the total figure of 513 does not greatly help us to make a satisfactory estimate of the size of Egyptian wine-growing. Even if we double or treble this figure to take into account the royal and private vineyards which existed as well as those of the temples, and if we then reckon that there were at this time 1,000 or

[40]Breasted, *ARE*, I, 173, and 173, fn. a; cf. Erman, 196.

[41]Davies, N. de G., *Tombs of Two Officials of Tuthmosis the Fourth*, Pl. xxx

[42]Davies, N. de G., *Tomb of Nefer-Hotep*, I, 26 and Pl. xiv; II, Pl. i.

[43]I, Pl. xlii.

[44]Breasted, *ARE*, IV, 213 – (Papyrus Harris). *Shedeh*: Breasted, *ARE*, IV, *passim*; *Tell El-Amarna*, I, 161, 166; Gardiner, A. H., *Anc. Egyptian Onomastica*, II, 235.

1,500 vineyards in Egypt, our figures will still mean little. Apart from the fact that they are guesswork, since we do not know the proportion of temple to other vineyards, we have no means of calculating how much of them was actually vineyard and how much was garden or orchard.[45]

The vineyards of leisure were the prized possession of the upper classes of Egypt and it must have been delightful to sit in them looking at the colours of the lotus and of the black grapes among the foliage, while the 'bearers of cool drinks'[46] performed their proper office. The colours would have pleased almost as much as the wine for the Egyptians loved colour. They painted many of their statues, much of their temples, and a great deal of their houses. The richer houses, built of mud-brick with wooden columns and rafters, were brilliant with colour. Door frames of yellow, red pillars, and ceilings of bright blue were only the basis of one colour scheme and to this were added door tops in yellow, red and green, and passageways barred horizontally with red and blue. Round the top of the walls might run a frieze of lotus leaves in blue and white. The lotus design, which often became a combination of lotus flowers and bunches of grapes, was a popular motif with the Egyptians and it occurs in many of their tombs. The vine pattern, with its green leaves and black fruit, was also popular and in a temple at Tell El-Amarna in the reign of Akhenaten there was a design of green vine leaves, blue grapes and red lines of trellis-work, all on a yellow background. Also, so it would seem, the rafters which held up the ceiling were decorated with bunches of grapes in faience.[47]

The vines of the leisure-gardens had a triple purpose: they gave decoration, they gave shade, and they gave grapes. Some of these grapes would have been kept for eating; the rest would have been made into wine. The grapes of the orchard-vineyard, though some may have been picked for the table, were mostly destined for the wine-press. These orchard-vineyards existed from the early Dynasties though it seems that they did not become really common until Hellenistic times.[48] But we do not know a great deal about them in the 3rd and 2nd millennia so that one cannot be precise on this point. I believe myself that they were commoner in the older period than some people have suggested. At least, however, even if we do not know much about the number or location or productivity of the older vineyards, we do know a considerable amount about the way in which they were worked.

From the 2nd until at least the 12th Dynasty vines were grown as cordons and the old hieroglyphic sign for a vineyard is a picture of a vine branch stretched between two crotched sticks. The height of the vine branch from the ground varies very little and is usually that of the height of a man when he is kneeling. The 4th millennium vine, its branch heavy with grapes and trained horizontally between two sticks, shows us the earliest recorded form of viticulture. In Egypt, with its emphasis on formal gardens, it was probably not long before the horizontal vine branch was exploited more decoratively and trained either along the horizontal trellis of a pergola, or from ground to ground in the shape of an arch. By about 1500 B.C. the arch of vines had become a common structure and in this case, as in that of the pergola, it may have been that the vines were no longer single-stemmed, but many stemmed, cordons. The arch seems also to have been common in the orchard vineyards and the height of it was generally the same as that of the horizontal branch in the early Dynasties. From the earliest times the vintage was made by kneeling

[45]Breasted, *ARE*, IV, 151 sqq.; Erman, 300.

[46]Erman, 188.

[47]Erman, 167 sqq., 413; *Tell El-Amarna*, Pt I, 5 sqq., 37 sqq., 116, 117; Pt II, 24, 25; Mackay, E., 'Theban Borders of Lotus and Grapes', *Anc. Egypt*, Pt II, 1921.

[48]For an interesting lease, dated 170 B.C., see Turner, E. G., 'A Ptolemaic Vineyard Lease', *Bull. John Rylands Library*, XXI, 1948.

The Vintage: detail from painting from the Tomb of Nakht, c 1372–1350 B.C., *Thebes, Valley of Nobles*

men.[49] On this point the tomb pictures are remarkably consistent and we do not have to assume that the artists who painted them were merely following a stylized convention. It is possible, of course, that the arch in the garden-vineyard may sometimes have been grown higher so that it would serve as a shady alleyway in which the owner could walk. If this were done, then it seems to have been the exception rather than the rule. It is possible, too, that vines were grown without any support but this also seems to have been exceptional.

It is, as we have seen, difficult to separate Egyptian viticulture into precise departments and to be sure where the 'garden' ends and the 'orchard' begins. Frequently they were the same thing; and to illustrate the possibility of confusion here once more is Ramses III in the Papyrus Harris:

'I made for it Kanekeme, inundated like the Two Lands, in the great olive-lands; bear-

[49]Petrie, W. M. F., *Royal Tombs of the First Dynasty*, Pt II, sealings of the 2nd Dynasty; and see Pt I, 44; *Bêt Khallâf*, 22; Murray, M. A., *Saqqara Mastabas*, 34; Davies, N. de G., *Mastaba of Ptahhetep . . .*, Pt I, Pl. xxi; *Meir*, v, Pl. xx; Davies, N. de G., *Five Theban Tombs*, 33, Pl. xxxi.

ing vines; surrounded by a wall around them . . . planted with great trees in all their many paths, wherein was oil more than the sand of the shore; in order to bring them to thy kâ, to "Victorious Thebes"; wine like drawing water without measure, to present them before thee as a daily offering. I built for thee thy temple in the midst of its ground. . . .'[50]

[50]Breasted, *ARE*, IV, 216

Kanekeme, in the Delta, had in fact been a religious vineyard in the reign of Ramses II in about 1250 B.C. and at one time in their history the vineyards of Kanekeme produced 'sweet wine of Kenkēme, surpassing honey'.[51] Ramses III 'made' many vineyards: 'wine-gardens' in the oasis of Dakhel and in the oasis of Khârgeh while at Heliopolis he 'made' '. . . great gardens . . . bearing shedeh and wine. . . .' These 'great gardens' were made for a temple and during his reign there were also 'gardens with wine' which belonged to a temple and were at Tanis in the Delta.[52] Whether

[51]Gardiner, *JEA*, V, 185–6, 1918, quoting Pap. Anastasi III.

[52]Dakhel: *Tell El-Amarna*, III, Vol. I, 166; Breasted, *ARE*, IV, 213, 734; Khârgeh: Breasted, *ARE*, IV, 213, 734; and 6th century B.C., IV, 992; Lutz, *VB*, 13, 14; Heliopolis: Breasted, *ARE*, IV, 262; Tanis: Breasted, *ARE*, IV, 217.

Wine Areas of the Ancient World

these were leisure-vineyards or orchard-vineyards remains uncertain; and equally uncertain in some cases must be the fact that Ramses himself 'made' them.

At Tell El-Amarna in the time of Akhenaten there is wine listed as 'Wine of the Basin of . . .'. This type of description leaves us with yet another uncertainty for we do not always know whether 'Basin' means the canal system from which a vineyard was irrigated or the artificial tank which graced a formal garden.[53] Tomb paintings show us the gardeners or vine-dressers at their work of irrigation. About 1500 B.C. we see them watering the roots of the vines from small jars carried on a yoke.[54] A little later, about the beginning of the 14th century B.C., the *shādūf* method was introduced, by which the water is raised from a canal in a jar or bucket at the end of a long lever[55], and this method has lasted in Egypt until the present day. The former practice may have continued in the leisure vineyards, the water being taken from the ornamental tank, while the latter would have been more suitable to the orchard-vineyards, but in either case the water supply may have been known as a 'Basin'. This confusion in terms – a very natural one – may even have been carried over into the titles of the men who grew the wine. At Tell El-Amarna 'the Master of the Vineyard' is a usual title, and one which in later Ramesside times changes into 'Master of the Vine-dressers'. But equally at Tell El-Amarna occur the titles 'Master of the Basin' and 'Chief of the Basin'[56] and he, in his turn, could have been the head of a vineyard. But what sort of vineyard it was, leisure or orchard, is concealed behind the word 'Basin'.

'Ernūtet Goddess of Plenty'

The harvesting of the grapes was a time of bustle and noise and from the faces of some of the pickers, as they have come down to us in the vivid paintings of the tombs, one can see that they were as vocal and ribald as many a modern vintager.

First of all the grapes were piled into yellow baskets. Then they were taken to the wine-press and trodden. The treading scenes of the 6th Dynasty differ only in detail from those of the 18th and one may well believe that the same techniques, in almost exactly the same form, go back into the earliest days of dynastic Egypt. The simplest picture of the scene is from the Tomb of Pepiankh, a nomarch of the 6th Dynasty, and in it we see three men treading in a shallow tank, the right hand of one man gripping the shoulder of the man next to him. The picture is dated about four thousand seven hundred years ago, about the time of the first settlement at Troy and the first period of Minoan civilization, and there is little in it that is different from the treading of the grapes in modern Portugal.

This is the simplest, but not the most usual, picture of Egyptian vintaging. Even earlier than Pepiankh a refinement had been introduced which consisted of a pole, supported on two crotched sticks, and running high and horizontal across the treading tank. The pole is gripped by the men who are treading and this type of structure, elaborated and modified, runs down for one thousand five hundred years into the New Kingdom of Egypt. Later pictures show us the horizontal pole set even higher and sometimes forming part of a light roof which was supported on columns over the tank and which shaded the men while they trod. From this high pole or rafter, ropes were hung and to these the men could cling and get purchase

[53] *Tell El-Amarna*, III, Vol. I, 167.

[54] British Museum, copy of a wall-painting from the *Tomb of Kha-'emwēse at Thebes* (No. 261), by Mrs N. de G. Davies.

[55] Davies, N. de G., *Tomb of Nefer-Ḥotep*, I, 36, Pls. xlvii, xlviii.

[56] *Tell El-Amarna*, III, Vol. I, 168.

The Vintage: copy of painting
Tomb of the Sculptor Apuy
c 1250 B.C.
London, British Museum

while they trod the grapes. It has been suggested that the ropes were there so that the men could prevent themselves from sinking too deep into the pulp in the tank, but this cannot have been their reason. Anyone who has trodden grapes will know that, at the beginning of the treading, some sort of purchase is almost a necessity and is certainly a relief. This Egyptian method of obtaining purchase by means of ropes or straps is particularly interesting because it seems to have been unique in the ancient world.

The more elaborate of these treading tanks show all the Egyptian delight in decoration. The tank – in these cases possibly a permanent structure made of stone or wood – is mounted on a platform to give it height enough for the must to flow out of a spout into a smaller tank built at the side of the platform. From the corners of the treading tank papyrus-shaped columns support a light roof, or else they support a beam from which hang ropes and sprays of shading foliage. Sometimes the panels of the structure are decorated with the vine shoots and papyrus. Near the wine-press may be a small shrine at which a thank-offering is made to 'the Snake Renen-ūtet, Patroness of Harvests'; or else, on the spout from which the trodden juice runs into its receiving tank, is set a figure of 'Ernūtet Goddess of Plenty'.[57]

It is more than likely that the earliest wine-presses of Egypt, the 1st Dynasty 'wine-press of the East in the nomes of the North', and the 'wine-press of the West in the nomes of the North'[58] were simple forms of these treading tanks. For the smaller vintages of early Egypt, however, it is possible that they used large pottery jars in which the grapes were trodden by foot. Jars are certainly used for this purpose in the Middle Kingdom, about 2000 B.C., and the wooden model which shows us Egyptian servants at work in this way is most probably the reflection of an archaic usage.

Another Egyptian method, and one which we know to have been archaic, was the use of the sack-press. This consisted of a sack or bag, made of cloth or light, yellow matting. It was filled with grapes or with trodden grape-skins and then twisted tight until as much as possible of the juice had been squeezed out. The action is like that of wringing out a wet cloth but the power needed to twist the sack was, naturally, very much greater. This extra power was obtained by putting poles

[57] 5th Dynasty: Davies, N. de G., *Mastaba of Ptahhetep*, Pt I, Pl. xxi. 6th Dynasty: *Meir*, v, Pl. xx. 12th Dynasty: Newberry, P. E., *Beni-Hasan*, Pt I, Pl. xii. New Kingdom: British Museum, copy of a wall-painting from the *Tomb of Kha-'emwēse at Thebes* (No. 261), by Mrs N. de G. Davies; N. de G. Davies, *Tomb of Nakht*, 69, 70, Pl. xxii; *Tombs of Two Officials of Tuthmosis the Fourth*, 31; *Tomb of Nefer-Ḥotep*, I, 37, Pl. xlviii; *Two Ramesside Tombs*, Pl. xxxiii.

[58] Petrie, W. M. F. (and Griffith, F. Ll.), *Royal Tombs of the First Dynasty*, Pt I, 44.

through the loops at each end of the sack and twisting the poles in opposite directions. As the sack tightened the pressure became so strong that it threatened to stop the poles or even to untwist them. At this moment one of the vintagers would stretch himself like an acrobat between the upper ends of the poles, his hands gripping one, his feet on the other, and thus keep them apart. A less agile method was to use a fixed frame to hold the sack and it is this method that we find as early as the 1st Dynasty.[59] And here again one might remark that, like the straps of the treading tank, the sack-press seems to have been an Egyptian invention for it does not appear in any other of the ancient civilizations of the Middle East or the Mediterranean.

Once the grapes had been trodden, or squeezed, the juice was left to ferment. It is not always easy to say how this was done, for the artists of the Tomb paintings may have telescoped into a single picture the work of weeks, or even months. In the Tomb of Nebamūn, a Captain of Police in the reign of Tuthmosis IV in the latter part of the 15th century B.C., some of the storage amphoras are shown with the fermenting wine overflowing the necks of the jars and this may have been either the first or the second fermentation. It is more likely to have been the first. On the whole we may assume that the wine was run straight off the treading tank and left to ferment in open jars. The jars were then stoppered and only a small hole left to release the gas from the second fermentation. When the second fermentation was over the small hole was stoppered in its turn and then the jar was left to await the thirst of its Master.[60]

The Seal of the 'Red house'

Egyptian wine jars were stoppered with mud. These stoppers, in the New Kingdom at least, were either shaped like a fez which fitted over the neck of the amphora, or were cones which fitted into the neck. That part of the stopper which actually covered the mouth of the jar was usually built up of mud on some sort of pad, the pad being made of palm-wood fibres or a piece of pottery and a wad of papyrus.[61]

[59] 1st Dynasty: Petrie, W. M. F., *Soc. Life in Anc. Egypt*, 136. 5th Dynasty: Davies, N. de G., *Mastaba of Ptahhetep . . .*, Pt I, Pl. xxi. 6th Dynasty: *Meir*, v, 29, Pl. xx, and Erman, 197 sq. 12th Dynasty: Newberry, P. E., *Beni-Hasan*, Pt II, Pls vi, xvi. New Kingdom: Davies, N. de G., *Tomb of Nakht*, Pl. xxii; *Two Ramesside Tombs*, Pl. xxx.

[60] Davies, N. de G., *Tombs of Two Officials of Tuthmosis the Fourth*, Pl. xxx; Carter, Howard, *Tomb of Tut-ankh-Amen*, III, 148

[61] *Tell El-Amarna*, Pt I, 161; Quibell, J. E., *The Ramesseum*, 8.

Pressing the Wine: copy of painting from Theban Tomb

In many cases, the stopper was 'sealed' with an inscription which labelled the contents of the jar and it is from these seals that we learn a good deal of what we know about the wines of ancient Egypt. Sometimes the seal could be as bright as the label on a modern wine bottle. In the time of Akhenaten, for example, some of the stoppers were painted in one colour while the hieroglyphs of the 'seal' were picked out in another. Some were painted in patterns of red and blue while on others the hieroglyphs were white or yellow on a blue ground.[62]

Generally speaking, the seals indicate possession and this possessive element seems to have become even more important in the New Kingdom. In the 3rd Dynasty the royal seals state the name of the king while the private seals state the name and the titles of the owner of the wine. In each case they are a declaration of ownership. But sometimes they indicate both possession and location for some of the seals of King Kha-sekhemui refer to vineyards of the 'Red house' and 'the Palace of Lower Egypt', and from an inscription we know the name, though we cannot be certain of the location, of King Zoser's vineyard 'Praised be Horus who is in the Front of Heaven'.[63]

The possessive element is seen again in the jar sealings from Akhenaten's city at Tell El-Amarna. Here we have 'Wine of the House of Aten', 'Very good wine of the House of Aten', 'Very good new wine (šdḥ?) of the House of Aten', 'Good wine of the House of Akhenaten, the living'. These do not indicate the particular vineyards from which the wine came though we may assume that in many cases the vineyard formed part of the estate of the House of Aten or the House of Akhenaten. They show that the wine belonged to the temple or to the king and was for the use of either of them – temple wine, it would seem, was often used by the royal family. Then there are also bureaucratic seals which record 'Wine of the Treasury', 'Wine of the Chancellor' and 'Wine for offerings (?) of the Storehouse of Tribute'. More romantic in style, but to us equally unrevealing, is the hieratic inscription from the 13th century: 'Year 50. Wine of the Sanctuary Millions of years of the king of Upper and Lower Egypt, Usermarê-Setepenrê' (Ramses II) 'in the Temple of Amon . . . By the hand of the Superintendent of Vine-dressers, Paḥeripedet'.[64]

The question of responsibility was almost as important as that of ownership and even in the earliest Dynasty there seems to have been a 'Royal Sealer of the Wine (?)'.[65] A 3rd Dynasty jar bears the seal of the official who was in charge of the vineyard of King Zoser and these official sealings of royal wine jars appear to have been quite common at this period. We find them again in the time of Akhenaten where the ordinary type of formula is: 'Year . . . Wine of the House of Aten. West river. Chief of the Vineyard . . .' and where a complete inscription runs: 'Year 7. Wine Good Good of the House of Aten. The inspector Tu'. Another inscription is that at Tell El-Amarna which runs: 'Year 9. Wine of the House of Aten. Brought by the inspector Ab?'.[66]

Where to us the seals are unhelpful (as are also some of the tomb paintings), is in their naming of vineyards. Sometimes indeed they are informative but only too often they use general terms which make it difficult for us to locate the vineyards with any precision. In a tomb painting of the 6th Dynasty we have 'Wine of Pelusium' (in the Eastern Delta) but we also have simply 'Red Wine'. In a 12th Dynasty painting we get 'Wine of Eastern Buto', 'Wine of Mareotis', and 'Wine of

[62] *Tell El-Amarna*, Vol. i, III, 145.

[63] Petrie, W. M. F., *History of Egypt*, 28; *Bêt Khallâf*, 3, 11, 19, 21 sq.

[64] *Tell El-Amarna*, Pt I, 161–2; Vol. I, III, 148–9; Davies, N. de G., *Two Ramesside Tombs*, 39–41.

[65] Petrie, W. M. F., *History of Egypt*, 19 sq.; Petrie, W. M. F. (and Griffith, F. Ll.), *Royal Tombs of the First Dynasty*, I, 44.

[66] *Bêt Khallâf*, 19, 21; *Tell El-Amarna* (Petrie and Griffith), 32–3.

Wine Jar Seals: c 1360 B.C., Tell-el-Amarna, City of Akhenaton. 1st Row: (a) Wine of the House of Aten; (b) Wine of the offering of the Storehouse of the Tribute; (c) Wine of the Western River of 'Aten Gleams'. 2nd Row: (d, e, f) Wine of Lower Egypt.

Syene' (all in the Western Delta) but we also get just 'Wine of (the Delta)' and *'irp bš'* – white(?) wine.[67] In the 18th Dynasty, in the time of Akhenaten, we not only come up against the purely possessive appellations such as 'Wine of the Mansion of the Aten' but also such general descriptions as 'Wine of the Southern Pool', 'Wine of the Eastern Side', 'Wine of the Western Side', and 'Wine of the Western River'. These latter three must have been from the eastern and western vineyards of the Nile Delta, as was 'Wine of Lower Egypt'. Other stamps, seeming to translate as 'Wazyt' may mean 'Wazyt-Buto', the snake-goddess of the Delta. Another type of inscription – this from the reign of Ramses II – is 'Year 53. (Superfine) Wine (of the . . .Th day) of the vineyard of the district(?) which faces(?) the water of Neti(?) . . .'[68]

In many cases we can suggest limited areas for the origin of these wines but the limits will not always be exact. To the general picture, however, this does not matter. We know that most of the wine of Egypt came from the Nile Delta while other vineyard areas were in the oases of Bahriyeh, Khârgeh, and Dakhel. There were also vineyards at, or near, Abydos, Memphis, and Thebes.[69] Altogether there were many vineyards and there was quite a lot of wine in Egypt and some of the wine was no doubt quite good. Perhaps it was very good. But even so, and at least until Hellenistic times, foreign wine was not unwelcome in the Land of the Pharaohs.

In the 15th century B.C. the Vizier Rekhmara received, on behalf of his master, offerings brought by foreigners to the Pharaoh Thutmose III. Among these foreigners are men from the 'Great Green' – the Mediterranean – who appear to be Cretans and who carry the graceful, conical vases which are familiar to us from Minoan frescoes.[70] The wine in the vases (if it were wine for it might equally well have been olive oil), was in this instance a present from one King to another but it is not impossible that from time to time a small amount of Cretan wine was imported into Egypt. At a much later date, in the 6th century B.C., a considerable quantity of wine was imported from the Greek islands of the Eastern Aegean and as Herodotus says in the 5th century B.C. 'Throughout the year, not only from all parts of Greece but from Phoenicia as well, wine is imported into Egypt in earthenware jars. . . .'[71]

It was Phoenicia, Palestine and Syria whence came much, and probably most, of the wine that was brought into Egypt. From early times Egypt regarded Palestine as a land much richer in wine than she was herself. In the Tale of Sinuhe, which

[67] *Meir*, v, 29; III, 29–30; cf. *Pyramid Texts*.

[68] *Tell El-Amarna*, I, 162–3, 167; Vol. I, III, 148, 150; 165–7; Petrie, W. M. F., *Six Temples at Thebes*, Pl. iii, No. 23; Carter, Howard, *Tomb of Tut-ankh-Amen*, II, 32; Davies, N. de G., *Two Ramesside Tombs*, 39–41.

[69] Bahriyeh: Breasted, *ARE*, IV, 213; *Tell El-Amarna*, III, Vol. I, 166. Khârgeh: Breasted, *ARE*, IV, 213, 734, 992; *Tell El-Amarna*, I, 166; III, Vol. I, 166; Lutz, *VB*, 13, 14. Dakhel: Breasted, *ARE*, IV, 213, 734; *Tell El-Amarna*, III, Vol. I, 166; and for *Dsds* as Dakhel: Lutz, *VB*, 10, 10, fn. 1. Abydos: Breasted, *ARE*, IV, 1021. Memphis: *Bêt Khallâf*, 21 sq., Breasted, *ARE*, IV, 313; *Tell El-Amarna*, I, 162; III, Vol. I, 149, 166; Frank, Johnson, II, 315. Thebes: Ath-E, I, 33f; Frank, Johnson, II, 347, fn. 21. Thebaïd (Coptic and Diospolan): Ath-E, I, 33f; Lutz, *VB*, 13; Lucas, 38. See also Elephantine in fn. 207 below.

[70] Virey, *Rekhmara*, 33, Pl. v; cf. Hall, H. R., 'Keftiu', *Essays in Aegean Archaeology Presented to Sir Arthur Evans*.

[71] Herodotus, II, 135; III, 6; Glotz, *AGW*, 75, 119; Ros, *SEHH*, 1252.

dates from about 2200 B.C., the Egyptian Sinuhe finds that in the land of Upper Retenu (Palestine) 'More plentiful than water was its wine'. Not only was the 'sheik' Emuienshi able to give Sinuhe land with vines but wine was drunk on every day.[72] This state of affairs may, to some extent, have existed even earlier since the Egyptian army which invaded Northern Sinai in about 2750 B.C., was able to cut down the figs and the vines of the 'sand-dwellers'.[73] Thutmose III received honeyed wine as tribute from the chiefs of 'Rotenou' and when Megiddo, south-west of the Sea of Galilee, surrendered to him, wine from its territory was also offered in tribute.[74] A clear comment upon the richness of Syria, and also upon the behaviour of the Egyptian army, comes to us from the Annals of the campaigns of Thutmose III. The army took Arvad, a city on the coast of Syria and, say the Annals:

'Behold, his majesty overthrew the city of Arvad with its grain, cutting down all its pleasant trees. Behold, there were found (the products) of all Zahi' (Phoenicia and Western Syria). 'Their gardens were filled with their fruit, their wines were found remaining in their presses as water flows, their grain on the terraces (upon -); it was more plentiful than the sand of the shore. The army were overwhelmed with their portions.'

At the end of the list of tribute gathered on this campaign the Annals remark:

'Behold, the army of his majesty was drunk and anointed with oil every day as at a feast in Egypt.'[75]

'Wazyt, Lady of Profusion: Good (Wine)'

How good was Egyptian wine? We find that it could be labelled as *nfr*, good, or *nfr-nfr*, very good. But what did these designations mean?

It is hard to know. If the seals and inscriptions were put on the jars at the time of the vintage they may indicate only that the wine was grown in a better or in a worse vineyard. If they were put on some months later they may refer to the quality of the wine as it began to mature. If we knew this latter to be the case we should know that the Egyptians took a real interest in the maturing of wine. But we do not know.

We might have expected that, after a few months in the jars, the wine would indeed have been tasted to see if it were in good condition. I would hesitate to say that this is more than a possibility although the cellar masters cannot always have been sure about the keeping qualities of their wines. To begin with, fermentation in the hot Egyptian climate may often have been too rapid and would have produced a difficult wine which could easily turn sick. The wine-makers may have cooled their fermenting vessels with water (an early version of a system used nowadays in North Africa), but we have no evidence to show that they did so.

Then again there is the question of the jar in which the wine was stored. If the fabric of the jar was porous, or too porous, it might have to be coated. Admittedly one can make a jar less porous by smoothing or polishing its surface when it is not quite dry and no doubt this was often done. Glazing would, of course, make it

[72] Breasted, *ARE*, I, 496.

[73] Breasted, *ARE*, I, 313.

[74] Virey, *Rekhmara*, 37; Breasted, *ARE*, II, 434.

[75] Breasted, *ARE*, II, 461, 462. For Syrian jars in Egypt see: Carter, Howard, *Tomb of Tut-ankh-Amen*, III, 148.

47

impermeable but glazing was not a successful technique in Egypt until a late date. It is possible, therefore, that jars may have been coated and the most likely coatings would have been oil or resin. Pottery was sometimes – in the 18th Dynasty for example – given a coating of resin varnish but coatings of this type seem to have been infrequent in wine jars until the Greco-Roman period. It is true that some of the wine jars in the tomb of Tut-ankh-Amen show a black coat on their inner surface but this is not necessarily resin.[76] Thus, although most Egyptian wine probably did not taste of resin, we cannot discount the possibility that some of it had taken the flavour of the inner coat which made the jar impermeable.

Nor do we know whether the wine was clarified by being racked from jar to jar. We may doubt that it was. But we do know that it was sometimes strained before it was drunk. In the banquet scene of Rekhmara a funnel shaped like a V, and probably made of cloth, hangs down into a large bowl. It may be a funnel for mixing but it is much more likely to be one for straining. And in the tomb of Tut-ankh-Amen there is a calcite wine-strainer to show that the Egyptians were at least aware of the possibility, if not the desirability, of straining their wine.[77]

An obvious method of straining wine is by siphoning it and the Egyptians were well acquainted with the siphon. A Theban tomb picture shows one made out of 'two reeds jointed at a right angle'. This particular siphon is inserted into a decorated jar which stands under a shelter by a quayside and the liquid in the jar is being sold to thirsty sailors. Since it has a siphon, the jar can be covered and its contents kept free from dust and flies. Here, I think, its only purpose is to avoid the dirt outside, and not the dregs inside, the wine – if indeed it is wine in the jar and not some other drink. Another type of siphon from the New Kingdom is much more interesting. It consists of three curved tubes which lead from three jars of wine into a single

[76]Lucas, 12, 26-9, 178, 422-4, 523; Carter, Howard, *Tomb of Tut-ankh-Amen*, III, 148.

[77]Virey, *Rekhmara*, Pl. xli; Carter, Howard, *Tomb of Tut-ankh-Amen*, I, 116.

Treading Grapes: Wooden Models
Egyptian, 2000 B.C.
London, British Museum

Faience Drinking Cups
Egyptian, c 1900 B.C.
London, British Museum

bowl in which the three wines are being mixed together for a feast.[78] That the Egyptians liked to mix their wines in this way does not mean that they strained them by the same method but it does mean that they could do so if they wished. There is not a great deal to indicate that they did so wish.

If the triple siphon tells us that at one period the Egyptians liked to mix their wines, we may wonder whether they liked to ring the changes of taste in other ways. It is very common in the ancient world to find that wines have been 'improved', or at any rate altered, by the addition of honey, spices or perfume. The honied wine received as tribute by Thutmose III from the chiefs of 'Rotenou' does not mean that the Egyptians themselves regarded such a wine as commendable and we have little reason to think that they followed the same practice. But we may suspect that on occasion they altered their wines. At a feast in the 14th century B.C. Nebamūn (this time a 'Superintendent of Sculptors' and not the other Nebamun who was a Captain of Police), is offered wine by his 'wife', Henetnofret. With her right hand Henetnofret offers the wine in a bowl; in her left hand she holds a small vase and from a finger of that hand dangles a small jug; it seems therefore quite possible that she has added, or may be called upon to add, 'some spicy cordial' to the wine of her lord and (possibly) husband.[79]

One of the notable things about the wine jars of the later Dynasties is that a number of them were dated with the year of the vintage. This has given rise to the belief that the Egyptians were aware of the benefits to be obtained from maturing their wines, and the inference is that with their finer wines they had more or less the same view of 'vintage years' as we ourselves have today. This may have been so but I think we can accept this inference only with considerable reservations.

As we would have expected from this civilized people they drew a distinction between qualities of their wines – good and very good – and we also find, at Tell El-Amarna for instance, that some jars were labelled only with the simple inscription *'irp* – 'wine' – which doubtless meant that the jars contained *vin ordinaire*[80] and were

[78]Davies, N. de G., *Two Ramesside Tombs*, 57-8, Pl. xxx; Erman, 199.

[79]Davies, N. de G., *Tomb of Two Sculptors at Thebes*, 53, Pl. v.

[80]*Tell El-Amarna*, I, 167.

49

thus less good. But this sort of evidence, while it shows that they appreciated the quality of wine, does not show that they appreciated the quality of age in wine.

It is in fact clear that the primary purpose of the seals and inscriptions was one of accountancy. The amount of wine that was produced had to be checked by those to whom it was due. The name of the estate on which the wine was grown: the name of the vineyard-master who was responsible for growing it or of the inspector who was responsible for delivering it: these helped the 'Superintendent of the Provision House' or the 'Scribe of the Sideboard' to keep the accounts of their cellars. The seals would also, of course, have enabled the proper official to keep a check on the honesty of the vineyard-master and the efficiency of the estate. Another type of 'label' is that which indicates the use of the wine – 'Very good wine for offerings (?)' – and here again the purpose of the 'label' is purely bureaucratic.[81] These seals and inscriptions on Egyptian wine jars were designed by accountants and not by epicures.

In some illustration of this theme it may be interesting to cite once again the Papyrus Harris. During the reign of Ramses III the annual income in *shedeh* and wine of the great god Amon of Thebes was 819 'various jars'; that of the great god Re of Heliopolis was 77 'various jars'; that of the great god Ptah of Memphis was 13. (If we want to put these figures into modern terms, we may, I think, reasonably assume that the 'jar' held, at its lowest, about 10 litres and at its highest about 45 litres. The income of Amon would, therefore, have been, in round numbers, between 8,200 and 37,000 litres.) In the case of Amon, some sort of accountancy would obviously have been necessary; in the case of Ptah the need is not so obvious. But then one has to remember that these figures most probably do not represent the real total so that the real annual income of wine may have been larger, and possibly very much larger.[82]

The seals – from the Early Dynasties onwards – which we have already noticed when we were dealing with the location of vineyards all fit naturally into a system of accountancy. They indicate the owner of the vineyard or the ownership of the wine, or both – the royal vineyards of the 'Red House' and the 'Wine of the House of Aten'. They allocate responsibility for the production and delivery of the wine – 'By the hand of the Superintendent of Vine-dressers, Paḥeripedet', 'The Inspector Tu', 'the Inspector Ab (?)'. And where it is necessary they define the distribution of the wine or the department in charge of its distribution – 'Wine of the Treasury', 'Wine for offerings (?) of the Storehouse of Tribute'.

In the eyes of the Egyptian accountant the year-date on the seals must have been the least vital piece of information. To the cellar master, however, it would have been of more value, especially if he were in charge of a big storeroom such as that of the Pharaoh or of the Temple of Amon. The date on the jar would have enabled him to select that wine which was next on his list for consumption and there can be little doubt that his selection was made on the basis of the age of the wine. But I suggest that the Egyptian view of this age was exactly the reverse of our own. We use the date on a bottle to tell us when a good wine ought to be drunk. The Egyptians used the date on a jar to tell them when a young wine must be drunk. They were not concerned with maturity but with soundness. When an Egyptian cellar-master saw that he still had some jars of, let us say, three-year-old wine, he would have

[81]Erman, 186; *Tell El-Amarna*, I, 162.

[82]Breasted, *ARE*, IV, 169, 170; my minimum and maximum estimates of jar-capacity are only 'guesses', but cf. Grace, Virginia R., 'The Canaanite Jar', *The Aegean and the Near East – Studies Presented to Hetty Goldman*, 84-6 (Bibl. Ch. 3).

noted that wine as being the next on the list for drinking – and for drinking before it went bad.

This is my own interpretation of the jar-datings and I must point out that, while (so far as I know) there is no evidence to prove me wrong, there is little evidence to prove me right. The most telling factor in my support is that, as one studies the attitude which the men of the more ancient civilizations held towards the age of wine, the less their attitude appears to be like our own. The Egyptians may have been exceptional. They may have adopted a 'modern' attitude. But I see no reason to believe that they did.

We know, however, that they kept some of their wine and that they kept it for a number of years. In the Ramesside Tomb of Apy, for example, the inscriptions on the fragments of wine jars record Year 49, Year 50, and Year 53. In the Annexe to the Tomb of Tut-ankh-Amen, thirty-six wine jars were found and each of them bore 'a docket, written in hieratic, which gives the date, place and vintage of the wine . . . far the larger quantity of wine came from the Aten Domain and dates from the IIIrd to the XXIst years, thus showing that the Aten estates were maintained for at least twenty-one years . . .'.[83] But whether these old, or comparatively old, wines were put into the Tombs because they were matured, and thus considered to be particularly fine and particularly suitable to the dignity of the dead man, is a question which has no certain answer. I believe myself that it was only in unusual circumstances that wine in Egypt was kept for longer than three or four years.

'Wreaths of Lotus Flowers for the Limbs . . .'[84]

At the feasts of the upper classes wine was the crowning glory. It was not, however, the inevitable accompaniment since they had other drinks: beer, date wine, palm wine and, at a very late date, pomegranate 'wine' which was, perhaps, imported from Palestine.[85] They also had the 'shedeh' drink which has been variously translated as new wine, or must, or 'a beverage akin to wine' or even '[Shed]h of eating, good, good'. Sometimes it may have been grape juice, or must, boiled down and thus different to the mrs of the 20th Dynasty which has been translated merely as 'must'.[86] If it were '[Shed]h of eating, good, good' then it would probably have been juice or must boiled down into a syrup or paste. It could thus have been served at Egyptian banquets either as a sweetmeat or as a sweet(?) drink.

Gay, colourful and noisy these banquets often were, and uninhibited by the statuesque solemnity which we tend to associate with so much of ancient Egyptian life. The dresses of the women, which in the older dynasties were red or yellow or white and which in the Middle Kingdom were sometimes green, were by the time of the Middle Kingdom and in the New Kingdom usually white, as were the clothes of the men; and this whiteness of the linen made a fine background for the colours of the flowers and of the decorated wine jars. Serving girls, as well as guests, wore collars of flowers though in the case of the serving girls a flower collar was all that they wore, apart from a narrow and unconcealing belt around the hips. Garlands of flowers or sprays of foliage were hung round the wine jars and over their mouths were placed lotus flowers to protect the wine from the flies and the heat. Sometimes the jars were also decorated with embroidered work or with

[83]Davies, N. de G., *Two Ramesside Tombs*, 39-41; Carter, Howard, *Tomb of Tut-ankh-Amen*, III, 147-8.

[84]Erman, 255.

[85]Lucas, 23.

[86]Erman, 257; Breasted, *ARE*, IV, passim, esp. in Papyrus Harris; *Tell El-Amarna*, I, 161, 166; Gardiner, A. H., *Anc. Egyptian Onomastica*, II, 235*. Pomegranate wine; Lutz, *VB*, 17-18; but Lucas, 23, 33.

painted designs. Lotus flowers were given to the guests to hold or to smell but the lotus was not the only flower of pleasure for on occasion the garlands could be made of cornflowers.[87]

Flowers, too, graced the 'presentation bowls' which appear occasionally at these feasts. These bowls are about the size of small soup tureens and are decorated with a fencework of flowers which stands just inside and all round the rim. The design of the flowered fencework varies. Sometimes it is of alternating lotus flowers and lotus buds, the flower leaning its head sideways to rest upon the bud; or else it is of lotus flowers, all open, in a circle round the rim. At other times the fencework is made of other kinds of flowers, standing one by one around the circle, or arranged in a pattern of a group of three flowers together, then a single one, then a group of three, then a single one again. It has been suggested that on special occasions of formality or celebration these vases were used as bowls to drink from, although it is hard to see how anyone could drink from them without disturbing the meticulous arrangement of the flowers. Perhaps a siphon was used, or a small cup dipped into the bowl, or perhaps the circle of flowers was not complete? I find such theories unconvincing. I do not believe that these bowls were used as drinking bowls at all. In the Tomb of Rekhmara, for example, they are borne by five of the men who are bringing tribute or presents to the Vizier of Egypt. Here they must be formal offerings, symbols to be shown, not cups to be drunk. At the banquet of Amenhotpe-si-se, as at that of Nebamūn, this same type of bowl, which is presented to the host and which stands on a table before him, must also be a formal offering of good will to the great man of the occasion. May we not take as an analogy an incident engraved on a seal of the 3rd Dynasty of Ur, some thousand years before Rekhmara was Vizier of Egypt? This seal is dedicated to Nusku, the god of the new moon, and shows the King Dungi 'pouring a libation into a tall jar from which protrude two lotus buds'. Dungi is pouring his libation in the presence of the god Nusku. However unusual this design may be in the art of ancient Sumeria, its meaning is clear. It is an offering to a god. May not the flowered bowls of the Egyptians also have been offerings, symbols of a hoped-for happiness on the occasion of an act of friendship or at the beginning of a joyous feast?[88]

[87]Davies, N. de G., *Tomb of Nakht*, Pl. xv; *Tombs of Two Officials of Tuthmosis the Fourth*, 28, Pl. xxiii; 6, Pl. vi; Virey, *Rekhmara*, Pl. xli; Mackay, E., 'Theban Borders of Lotus and Grapes', *Anc. Egypt*, Pt II, 1921.

[88]Davies, N. de G., *Tombs of Two Officials of Tuthmosis the Fourth*, Nebamūn, Pl. xxiii; Amenhotpe-si-se, 6, Pl. iv; Virey, *Rekhmara*, Pl. v; *CAH*, I, 438.

Feast: detail from painting Tomb of Nebamūn, Thebes
c 1400 B.C.
New York, Metropolitan Museum of Art

Banquet Scene: detail from painting
Tomb of Nebamūn,
Thebes
c 1400 B.C.
New York, Metropolitan
Museum of Art

Here is one of the joyous feasts of Egypt in the 15th century B.C. It is the banquet of Nakht as it was painted in his tomb to help or to console him throughout eternity. On the left are the guests, each of the women with 'a pinch of fragrant ointment' on the top of her head. On the right sit Nakht and his wife, Tawi. In the centre are the musicians. A blind harper plays a six-stringed harp. Dancing girls play the harp and the double flute, and the girl who plays the lute is naked except for a collar and a belt of beads. There is a big jar on a stand, its mouth covered by lotus and there are decorations of hanging vine sprays. Beneath the chairs of Nakht and Tawi is Tawi's pet cat 'of a rich orange colour on the back, turning through yellow to white on the under parts and barred from head to tail with wavy black stripes'. It is having its own feast of a fish.[89]

The Egyptians were fond of pets. Nebamūn, the sculptor (or his 'wife' Henetno-fret), has a cat, a small, long-tailed, yellow-bodied cat, which, at a feast given by Nebamūn, sits alertly beneath a chair of a woman guest, its red tongue lolling out. In another tomb is User with his pet dog, a white animal lightly marked in red and, oddly familiar to modern ears, bearing the name of 'His favourite, Trust'.[90] In some other matters, however, the taste of the Egyptians was remote from our own. They wore wigs, short wigs as well as long, elaborate wigs, and at banquets there was placed on the head of each of the women guests a small cone of ointment which melted and ran down over the hair or the wig. At feasts, too, it was not at all un-known for men to have an absorbent oil-ball placed on their heads, from which the oil would slowly trickly down over their hair. Perfumes were commonly used at these carousings and in the general atmosphere the bouquet of a fine wine would certainly have been overwhelmed.[91]

We do not have to assume that the wine was fine or that anyone was interested in its bouquet. They were interested in drinking; and of course in talking and eating

[89] Davies, N. de G., *Tomb of Nakht*, 59, Pls. x, xv.

[90] Davies, N. de G., *Tomb of Two Sculptors at Thebes*, Pls. v, vii; *Five Theban Tombs*, 26, Pl. xxviii.

[91] Erman, 231; and the various feast-paintings referred to, above; Virey, *Rekhmara*, Pl. xli.

53

House and Garden of Apuy
Tomb of the Sculptor Apuy
c 1250 B.C.
New York, Metropolitan
Museum of Art

as well. They chattered while a dancing girl played on the double pipes and her companions squatting round her clapped their hands to the rhythm of the music. From the provisions piled up at the beginning of these feasts we can be sure that the guests did not go hungry. They would have eaten their favourite foods: roast goose (particularly a favourite), beef, the finer sorts of fish, cakes, and fruit. Their general diet was based on these things too – bread, birds, fish, beef, and fruit – although the poor had to rely mainly on dried fish and on whatever bread they could afford. For the wealthier people the diet was more complex than it sounds since they had many kinds of meat, ate several varieties of birds, and took some care in the choosing of their fish. Priests, however, or at least in later times, were forbidden to eat fish but they had a daily ration of beef and goose-meat and wine.[93]

One of the most enjoyable pleasures of the feast was drinking. 'Give me 18 cups of wine, behold I should love drunkenness.' This frank enthusiasm comes from a lady of the 17th Dynasty,[94] and we have good reason to believe that she was not exceptional. They drank their wine from shallow, metal cups like flattened bowls. These could, so it seems, sometimes be held by a spike inserted vertically into the base of the cup and it is interesting to note that a pottery cup of this type – a 'ceremonial dish with grip handle' – occurs in Asia Minor at Mersin as 'a unique example' in an Early Chalcolithic level which is dated about 4000 B.C. In Egypt, however, at the period with which we are now dealing these shallow cups were usually held on the flat of the hand.[95] That they were filled with a beguiling frequency is demonstrated by a painting of the 18th Dynasty. Here one of the guests, a woman, is being sick and so suddenly that a servant girl, running with a vase, is not in time to help

[92]Davies, N. de G., *Tombs of Two Officials of Tuthmosis the Fourth*, 27, Pl. xxiii.

[93]Erman, 188 sqq., 239; for fish in later times, see: Erman, 239; Herodotus, II, 37.

[94]Petrie, W. M. F., *Soc. Life in Anc. Egypt*, 102.

[95]Virey, *Rekhmara*, Pl. xli; Davies, N. de G., *Tombs of Two Officials of Tuthmosis the Fourth*, 6; cf. Herodotus, II, 37; Garstang, J., *Prehistoric Mersin*, Pl. xi(a).

54

her. It might be charitable, although probably inaccurate, to assume that she had merely over-eaten. At another feast in the same Dynasty a vase was placed beneath the chair of each guest – a precaution, it has been suggested, against the effects of over-drinking.[96] Or were they for bones and scraps of food? We may believe that they were not.

Yet these were only the accidents of pleasure, and the Egyptians took great pleasure in their feasts on 'the joyful day'. They had, as well as their varied views about immortality, an awareness at times that the joy of life was fleeting and that 'you can't take it with you'. 'Celebrate the joyful day . . .' went one of the songs that was sung at their feasting. And it continued:

> 'For no one can take away his goods with him,
>   Yea, no one returns again, who has gone hence.'[97]

In their bodies they cannot come back. But they return to us most living in the paintings which they placed in their tombs.

MESOPOTAMIA

'. . . the female slaves of E-Rarzida'

The Mesopotamian cities which drew their life from the two great rivers Tigris and Euphrates, the cities of Lagash, Larsa, Erech, Kish, Nippur, Eridu and Ur, rose and fell in power like the weights of some intricate game. In prehistoric times the Sumerian people, so it would appear, had come down from Iran. They had moved, perhaps, through Elam on the south-western border of Persia and had come by Susa into southern Mesopotamia – The Land of Sumer, and into northern Mesopotamia – The Land of Akkad, both of which Lands became known as Babylonia. Dynasties rose and fell: first the Dynasties of Kish and Erech: then the 1st Dynasty of Ur: to be followed by the 3rd and 4th Dynasties of Kish, the Dynasty of Agade (Akkad) and the 3rd Dynasty of Ur: later still to be followed by the Dynasties of Babylon and Assyria. And among all these Dynasties founded by greater or lesser men, it seems at first sight incongruous to find that the Fourth of Kish was founded 'by a female wine merchant'.

She was Azag-Bau. She is legendary, a queen who ruled 'after the Flood'; but she is probably also historical and ruled about 3089 B.C. There is no reason why the tale of her trade should be untrue for in the Age of Hammurabi, a thousand years later, 'convent' priestesses often engaged in business.[98] As the founder of a Dynasty Azag-Bau is no doubt a romantic figure; as a wine-merchant rather less so for the wine in which she traded may not have been wine of the grape but wine of the date.

There was a story in the Greek world that Dionysos fled from Mesopotamia because the Mesopotamians drank beer.[99] The story may be poetical or satirical but it contains a fraction of the truth about Dionysos and more than a fraction of the truth about the drinking habits of Babylonia, for there beer was a national drink. The beer was made from barley and it was brewed from the early days of the Sumerian civilization in Mesopotamia.[100] In later Dynasties there were various

[96]Davies, N. de G., *Tomb of Nefer-Hotep*, I, 27, Pl. xviii; II, Pl. i; *Tomb of Two Sculptors*, Pl. v.

[97]Erman, 255.

[98]*CAH*, I, 370–1, 538, 669.

[99]*Hist. Tech.*, I, 282.

[100]*Ur Excavations*, II, 7, 9, 17.

kinds of beer, 'fine dark beer', 'ordinary dark beer', 'dark, or brown, beer and pale beer'; and there was also small beer, the 'one-third' beer which the Mayor of Nippur ordered his servant to give to that semi-humorous character of Babylonian fiction, Gimil-Ninurta, the Poor Man of Nippur.

> 'Give him, the citizen of Nippur, a bone and a sinew,
> give him a drink of 'one-third' (beer) from your can,
> send him away and show him out of the gate!'[101]

Barley was not only important to the brewing of beer. It was also one of the basic foods of Mesopotamia and we find it again and again in the lists of rations which are to be paid out to workers or officials. In the Third Dynasty of Ur the standard ration seems to have been barley, oil, and dates. This at any rate was the ration 'for the female slaves of E-Rarzida'.[102] The standard could vary, though not radically: sometimes the temple employees got beans as well: sometimes they would not get oil: sometimes they would get date wine and not dates. Fish could also be part of the ration and it was eaten by all classes, either as food for slaves or as 'fish carried to the Palace for the King'. A tablet from Lagash (Tello), dated about 2900 B.C. or a little earlier, gives a list of fishermen's offerings and it includes both dried and salted fish.[103] The rather monotonous diet of the poor would have been barley bread dipped in oil, or barley paste mixed with oil, fish, onions and dates. They might have eaten figs but would only seldom have eaten grapes. Now and again they might have been able to eat cheese but it would no doubt have been the ordinary curdled ga-har and not the 'green' cheese which was made from cheese, butter and herbs.[104]

From various sources we can gain an idea of the diet of those who were better off or in the higher official positions. A tablet of the 3rd Dynasty of Ur, about 2400 B.C., which gives an inventory of temple stores, includes fats (butter and two qualities of oil), honey, cheese, dates, white grapes, pomegranates, and figs. Spices were available at this time and there is a receipt of 'two kinds of spices to sweeten oil, received from the Tablet Office by the oil-carrier'. This 'sweetened' oil, however, would probably have been for religious annointing and not for secular consumption. Another tablet consists of a report on the palace flocks of sheep and goats. There are records of cattle and although sometimes they are of 'fat cattle' at other times they have a more melancholy ring and note 'old asses to feed dogs' and 'old oxen to feed the dogs'.[105]

If barley beer was a usual drink, so too was date wine. The date-palm was always a tree of vital importance in the civilization of Sumeria and one remembers that when the wild man Enkidu was made drunk in the ancient *Epic* the wine given to him by the temple harlot of Erech was most probably date wine.[106] *Sikaru* was one of the names by which it was called and Xenophon later recorded, as some modern travellers have found, that it was apt to cause headache.[107] The ancient Mesopotamians were, of course, well aware of its qualities. They named it *sikaru* – 'strong drink' – and we find the distinction drawn in a tablet of about 2900 B.C.: 'one (measure) of wine, 2 of strong/for the king . . .'.[108]

In this particular case the word 'wine' is likely to have meant the wine of grapes,

[101] *Ur Excavations*, III, 200, 202; *Tello, Inventaire des tablettes de*, Vol. II, Pt II, 16, 20; beer occurs in many of the documents; Gurney, O. R., 'The Sultantepe Tablets', *Anat. Studs.*, VI, 145 sqq., 1956.

[102] *Ur Excavations*, III, 239, 240; and see: 198.

[103] Lau, R. J., *Old Babylonian Temple Records*, 10–17; *Ur Excavations*, III, 239, 250; Pinches, T. G., *Amherst Tablets*, Pt I, Tablet 1; see also: *Tello, Inventaire des tablettes de*, Vol. II, Pt II, 38.

[104] Genouillac, *TSA*, xlvii–xlix; Contenau, G., *Contrib. à l'Histoire Economique d'Umma*, xxxvii; *Tello, Inventaire des tablettes de*, Vol. II, Pt I, 36 sqq.; *Ur Excavations*, III, 196, 241.

[105] Hussey, M. I., *Sumerian Tablets in the Harvard Semitic Museum*, Pt II, 3–6 (inventory); 10 (flocks); cf. *Tello, Inventaire des tablettes de*, 36. *Ur Excavations*, III, 246 (flocks); 248 (dog-food).

[106] Contenau, G., *Médecine en Assyrie*, 194; for a possible very early mention of date-wine, see *Ur Excavations*, II, 9.

[107] Xen, *An*, ii, 3, 15–16.

[108] Pinches, T. G., *Amherst Tablets*, Pt I, Tablet II.

but where the word occurs alone on the tablets without any context to indicate that it is grape wine we may have to suspect that it is wine made from dates. In some of the tablets of Ur III, in those, for example, which give the rations of officials, it is made clear that date wine is meant; but in other tablets of the same period the entries may bear either meaning – '. . . wine for the royal smiths', 'expenditure of wine and meal for the *satukku* offering and wine for the royal scribe'.[109] To some extent rank must have played its part and the higher the official the more likely it would have been that his wine was grape wine. The royal scribe may have got grape wine, the royal smiths date wine. But in the absence of other evidence even rank is not decisive since date wine was popular and the prestige value of grape wine was probably not as high in Babylonia as it was in Egypt. In Babylonia the grape vine was both literally and metaphorically overshadowed by the date palm.

We also have to remember that when the term 'wine-shop' occurs in the documents it does not necessarily mean a shop that sold grape wine. Much later, in Greco-Roman times, it may have borne this meaning but during the first four thousand years of Sumerian and Babylonian history it usually meant a shop or a tavern which sold the various qualities of beer and of date wine: sometimes 'common date wine', sometimes 'drink of the first quality'.[110]

[109]Lau, R. J., *Old Babylonian Temple Records*, 10, 11, 12–13; Hussey, M. I., *Sumerian Tablets in the Harvard Semitic Museum*, Pt II, 2, 14.

[110]Lau, R. J., *Old Babylonian Temple Records*, 15 – (mentioned in temple expenses); Tello, *Inventaire des tablettes de*, Vol. I, 21.

Watering the Roots of Vines: copy of painting from the Tomb of Kha-emwēse Thebes, Tomb 261, 12th century B.C., London, British Museum

57

The Babylonian wine-shop appears to have had a doubtful reputation. The Code of Hammurabi, of about 2090 B.C., states that 'If a priestess or holy sister who has not remained in the Convent shall open a wine-shop, or enter a wine-shop for drink, that woman shall be burned'.[111] On the other hand, of course, this enactment may only have been designed to protect the trading position of the temple, or 'convent', priestesses who had remained in the convent. The penalty seems excessive but it is in line with the exaggerated cruelty of certain other punishments. One, also recorded from the 1st Dynasty of Babylon, says that the offending party shall have his head asphalted with hot asphalt.[112] Perhaps the asphalt was not very hot? A repellent example comes from the Middle Assyrian Laws, in the last half of the 2nd millennium: 'If a woman has crushed a man's testicle in an affray, one of her fingers shall be cut off; and if, although a physician has bound it up, the second testicle is affected with it and becomes inflamed, or if she has crushed the second testicle in the affray, both her (nipples?) shall be torn out.'[113] The state of the tablet on which this savagery is recorded leaves us in some doubt as to whether it was actually 'nipples' but it is almost certain to have been so since, for one reason, a similar punishment has been recorded in the Code of Hammurabi. Moreover the text of 'An Incantation against the Female Demon Lilitum' goes:

'Lilitum who struts in the desert
Has committed evil spell, sorcery . . .
May her sorcery rage fiercely against her own self,
May her breast be cut off by inches.'

It is, to our eyes, something of an anti-climax that the desired result for the man who is being released from the Demon should be this:

'May he be cleansed like a vessel of lard!
May he be clean like a vessel of butter!'[114]

The stated law of Babylonia seems ferocious but in reality the legal cruelties may never, or seldom, have been inflicted. About the reality of the Demons, however, there was no question. They were imminent, everywhere, and malignant. Although each man had a guardian spirit who protected him, evil demons lay in wait and if the guardian were absent they would attack a man and inflict upon him those woes which have always fascinated the human imagination. In addition to the evil spirits, wizards were abundant and one rather pathetic 'Prayer to a Goddess' complains: '. . . I am surrounded with the power of evil . . . Sorcery, witchcraft, poisoning. . . .'[115]

All in all it was a pretty gloomy outlook. The after-life was dim and depressing and this life was a battleground for contending spirits. It is small wonder that the temple was a focal point of daily life, for there prayers could be offered for protection against the dangers of being alive. One might have thought that the temples would reflect this atmosphere of pious pessimism and be doleful structures but they were, on the contrary, gay with colour. One of the very earliest, which dates from before the Dynastic period of the Sumerians in Mesopotamia, is the 'Painted Temple' at Tell 'Uqair, south of Baghdad. The inside walls of this temple were washed in

[111] (Section 110.) Edwards, C., *The World's Earliest Laws*, 28.

[112] Lutz, H. F., *Legal and Economic Documents from Ashjâly*, x, 13 fn., quoting Thureau-Dangin.

[113] Driver, G. R., and Miles, J. C., *The Assyrian Laws*, Tablet A, and 31.

[114] Lutz, H. F., *Selected Sumerian and Babylonian Texts*, 56 sqq.

[115] Lutz, H. F., *Selected Sumerian and Babylonian Texts*, 24

colour or were decorated with painted designs and figures on a white background. A red dado about a yard high ran round the room and above it there was often a band of formal, geometric decoration. Some of the decoration consisted of 'vertical and horizontal bands of geometric ornament which had lines of plum-colour separating black and white diamonds, producing a brilliant effect'. Among the colours used in this temple were deep plum-red, orange, yellow, and white and black. On the white of the higher part of the walls were figures of human beings or animals, one of the latter being a 'leopard' with a white body and black spots.[116]

These early people may have had a happier and brighter religion than that of later Sumeria and Babylon. It is quite likely that they did. But whether they did or not, the sense of colour persisted in the temple building of Mesopotamia. A Neo-Babylonian, or partly Neo-Babylonian, *ziggurat* or temple tower at Ur, which was about 70 feet high, was built in three storeys, the lowest being coloured black, the next storey red, while on top of the whole tower was a small shrine 'surfaced with enamel bricks of a beautiful deep blue'.[117] The seven storeys of the *ziggurat* at Khorsabad 'were successively painted white, black, red, white, reddish orange, silver and finally gold'.[117]

The innumerable rituals of religion, and the temple liturgies with their music of drum or flute, formed around man a protective apparatus of some complexity. When this apparatus failed there was always the simpler consolation of drink. There were many drinks to choose from and, although we cannot be sure of the characters of all of them, many were variants of beer or date wine. Date wine could be amended by the addition of (perhaps) cassia, or with sesame and in the latter case it was (again perhaps) the drink called *kurunnu*. On the other hand *kurunnu* might possibly have been a sort of beer.[118] At the beginning of the 3rd millennium there were two drinks known as *kas-kal* and *kas-gig*. *Kas-kal* was made from one-third date wine and two-thirds beer and it must have had an interesting effect. *Kas-gig* – known as the 'black drink' – was made from approximately equal parts of date wine, paste, and 'old liquor'.[119] The Mesopotamians may also, although infrequently, have drunk wine made from the actual palm tree itself and this may be the meaning of the old Sumerian word *áš-an*.[120] Other drinks of the 3rd millennium were '*dida*-drink' which was possibly herbal, *kaš-šeg*, perhaps fresh or unfermented drink, and *kaš-gin*, perhaps 'kept' or fermented drink. '*Ulušin*-drink', a special type of beverage, has been translated by one commentator as 'schnapps' but this cannot be so.[121] Among the tablets from the 3rd Dynasty of Ur we find the record of '. . . best sweet drink . . . sweet drink . . . sweet *usa* drink . . . best *du* drink . . .'.[122] Finally from the temple expenses on the tablets of Tello we get '1 *qa* of beverage from the plant *SA*'.[123] It would be interesting to know exactly how these drinks were made.

'*The Plantation of the Vine of the bank (of Bau-hengala)*'

Nevertheless there was also *kas-geštin* – grape wine – in the Land of Babylonia. (Here again I should repeat that when in this book I use the word 'wine' by itself it means grape wine.) It is not likely that there was a great deal of *kas-geštin* and what there was would have been the pleasure only of the royal families, the temples, the higher officials and the wealthier merchants. In the 7th century B.C. Sennacherib

[116] Seton Lloyd and Fuad Safar, 'Tell Uqair', *JNES*, II, No. 2, 1943.

[117] Contenau, 277–8.

[118] Dubberstein, 28–9; Lutz, *VB*, 41. For the possible meaning of beer, Thompson, *Botany*, 328; Lambert, W. G., and Gurney, O. R., 'The Sultantepe Tablets, III', *Anat. Studs.*, IV, 87 and notes, 1954; and cf. Plin., XIII, 44.

[119] Genouillac, *TSA*, LI, and tablets, *passim*.

[120] Genouillac, *TSA*, LI, tablet 3, II; cf. Xen, *An*, II, 3, 16; cf. Plin., XIII, 27, 40–1.

[121] Pinches, T. G., *Amherst Tablets*, Pt I, Nos. 63, 68, 102, 103, 115.

[122] Nies, J. B., *Ur Dynasty Tablets*, Nos. 39, 83; see also Contenau, G., *Contribution à l'Histoire Economique d'Umma*, xxxv–xxxvi, and tablets 1, 56.

[123] Lau, R. J., *Old Babylonian Temple Records*, II.

commemorated his creation of a 'great park' by a Bull Inscription in which he says: 'By command of the god, within the orchards, the vine, every fruit-bearing tree, and herbs throve luxuriously. The cypress and mulberry, all kinds of trees, grew large . . . the cane-brakes developed rapidly; the birds of heaven . . . built their nests. . . . At the dedication of the palace I drenched the foreheads of the people of my land with wine, with mead I sprinkled their hearts'.[124] The distinction between the outer use of wine and the apparent inner use of mead makes it probable that the mass of the people who celebrated Sennacherib's feast of landscape gardening did not get drunk on grape wine.

It seems that the growing of grapes for wine was known in Mesopotamia in the earliest days of the Sumerian civilization.[125] About the very early times we know little more than that, but from the beginning of the 3rd millennium the records become more plentiful. About 2900 B.C. at Lagash, in Sumer or Southern Babylonia, vines were grown, most probably in irrigated 'gardens', and wine was 'kept in ground floor cellars'. To supplement the home-grown vintages of Lagash, however, wine was imported from 'the mountains of the East', from Hulbunu and Izallu which must be in Elam on the south-western border of Persia.[126]

Other 3rd millennium tablets from Lagash mention vineyards; one, for example, gives the valuation of a vineyard at Tigabba; others record 'the vine-plantation of Karsum' and 'the plantation of the vine of the bank (of Bau-hengala)', these two latter being temple vineyards.[127] But while it is obvious that the entry on a temple

[124] Footnote deleted.

[125] *Ur Excavations*, II, 11.

[126] Genouillac, *TSA*, xlvi, xlvii, xlix, li, and fn. 3.

[127] *Tello, Inventaire des tablettes de*, Vol. II, Pt I, 58; Pinches, T. G., *Amherst Tablets*, Pt I, No. 54; see also No. 7.

Prisoners and spoil from Lachish
Stone Relief
Babylonian, c 2900 B.C.
London, British Museum

pay list of 'grain to men for taking care of a vineyard'[128] is not in any way unusual, one still has the impression that vineyards were less important in Babylonia than they were in Egypt.

Many of the vineyards, perhaps even most of them, belonged to the city temples which also owned vegetable and fruit gardens as well as rich farmlands. These vineyards, which were tended by men who, in the 3rd Dynasty of Ur, were called 'the gardeners of the vine'[129] were wine-gardens in both the Egyptian senses of the word, though the leisure-vineyards seem to have been less formal, and were probably less frequent, than they were in Egypt. The usual type of wine-garden in Mesopotamia was the orchard-vineyard of the type of the 'vine orchard' which is described in the farm accounts of the 3rd Dynasty of Ur. In one instance we have '6 acres of vines below *nurmu*-trees among which are 91 full grown palm trees . . . $1\frac{1}{2}$ acre of vineyard below *nurmu*-trees, among which are 36 full grown . . . palm trees'; in another we have 'acres of vineyard under the *gis-ma* fig trees'. Yet another entry of the same time has 'barley from the "vineyard" field' and although this proves nothing, it indicates the probability that a 'vineyard' was normally an integral part of a farm unit which produced grain, fruit, and vegetables.[130] The mixing together of fruit trees makes it difficult, as in Egypt, to estimate the actual size of Mesopotamian viticulture. For example, an Assyrian 'Domesday Book' of the 7th century B.C. which deals with the district round Harran (Carrhae) in northwest Mesopotamia, lists vineyards, or plantations, which contain between 2,000 and 29,000 trees.[131] Harran was, it seems a well-known wine-growing area from which came, perhaps, the wines called Bilak and Habur.[132]

The production of fruit was not the only function of these other trees in the plantations for, unlike the Egyptian vineyards, they also gave support to the vines which were trained up them or from branch to branch across the vineyard. The documents of the 3rd Dynasty of Ur are not explicit on this point but with some confidence we may assume that in the 25th century B.C. vines were tree-trained in this way. Nor is it unreasonable to assume that this method goes back into the remotest age of Mesopotamian civilization since the only vines known to the earliest *vignerons* would have been wild vines climbing in the woods from tree to tree. A picture of this type of vineyard – the 'high-vineyard' – is in a 7th-century B.C. bas-relief of Ashurbanipal. Here, in a formalized orchard, or plantation, clusters of grapes are shown hanging from long vine branches strung from tree to tree, and the vine branches themselves sprout from a vine stem which is twisted round the trunk of a tree. We see the same type of scene a little earlier, in the 9th century B.C., in a stela of Aššur-Nasir-pal II which shows us vines at Kalhu (or Calah, the modern Nimrud) planted between fruit trees in irrigated land and growing upwards into the trees.[133]

It might be argued that, since these two Assyrian scenes are representations of pleasure parks, the vine-branches were allowed to grow long among the foliage of the trees only in order to produce a pattern that was pleasing to the royal eye. But I think we can accept the scenes as being basically representative of the typical Mesopotamian vineyard and although – again in the Assyrian period – we see vines trained in the shape of a fan[134] we can take it that in Mesopotamia the high and tree-trained vine was both the oldest and the most popular form.

[128]Lau, R. J., *Old Babylonian Temple Records*, 17.

[129]Hussey, M. I., *Sumerian Tablets in the Harvard Semitic Museum*, Pt II, No. 2.

[130]*Ur Excavations*, III, Nos. 1109, 1364, 1368, 1371.

[131]Johns, C. H. W., *Assyrian Domesday*, 21, 31.

[132]*CAH*, I, 452; Johns, C. H. W., *Assyrian Domesday*, 7, 20-1.

[133]Hall, H. R., *Babylonian and Assyrian Sculpture in the British Museum*, Pl. xli, 2; Wiseman, D. J., 'A new Stela of Aššur-Nasir-pal II', *Iraq*, XIV, Pt I, 1952.

[134]Lutz, *VB*, 70, fig. 13.

'Ur-Ninezen the musician . . . pours out wine for the King'[135]

Ur-Ninezen lived during the 3rd Dynasty of Ur and the wine which he poured for the king must often have been white wine. White grapes are specifically mentioned in a list of produce which dates from the dynasty of Agade at the beginning of the 3rd millennium[136], while half-way through this same millennium white grapes are mentioned quite frequently, and white wine occasionally, in the documents of Ur.[137]

Before we consider the quality of the wine that went into the jars and the 'sheep-skin bottles' of Babylonia,[138] we might pause to note a 'drink' which may seem to us now little more than a curiosity, but which in ancient times had some sort of importance. It not only occurs here in Mesopotamia but also in Homeric Greece. In Babylonia this 'drink' was 'wine, mixed with *Eša*' and it was a compound of wine and some sort of flour.[139] It may have been considered as a specially palatable, or even luxurious, blend of food and drink, as a sort of tipsy-cake in fact, or it may have had a religious purpose: possibly both. And one might not be wrong in assuming that the double purpose, as well as the original recipe, was prehistoric.

We do not know a great deal about the wine-making of the early Mesopotamians and it is difficult therefore to judge the nature of their early wines. Fermentation would often, as in Egypt, have been affected by the heat of the climate and the wine resulting from it would have been unstable. If the wine were not sealed from the air it would quickly have gone sour and here again we meet the question of the impermeable container. Some of their pottery was no doubt impermeable enough, but equally some of it, and in addition the wine skins, may have needed treatment and where this treatment involved a coating of resin, then the wine would have taken the flavour of resin. The men of those times would not necessarily have minded such a taste any more than they minded wines which had been aromati-sized with herbs or spices. Some wines indeed may have needed an aromatic to make them pleasurable at all.

Nor do we know how much they racked and clarified their wine. Strainers were known in Sumeria in quite early times while in the 1st millennium in Babylonia 'clear grape wine' fetched a relatively high price, costing more than eight shekels a jar as against ordinary date wine which cost less than one shekel a jar.[140] In any case,

[135] *Ur Excavations*, III, No. 853.

[136] *Tello, Inventaire des tablettes de*, Vol. II, Pt II, No. 4658.

[137] *Ur Excavations*, III, Nos. 282, 1021; Hussey, M. I., *Sumerian Tablets in the Harvard Semitic Museum*, Pt II, No. 5; *Tello, Inventaire des tablettes de*, Vol. II, Pt I, Nos. 892, 1006; see also Genouil-lac, H. de, *Tablettes de Dréhem*, No. 5530.

[138] *Tello, Inventaire des tablettes de*, Vol. II, Pt II, No. 4685.

[139] *Ur Excavations*, III, Nos. 67, 149, 944.

[140] Contenau, 78; Dubberstein, 29.

the argument about ancient wine being racked or unracked, being clarified or left on its lees, has to be put into historical perspective. It is not the practice now to leave wine for long unracked, yet a century ago in Cyprus wine was purposely left upon its lees in order to help it to become clear.[141] There is evidence that a similar custom, though not necessarily for the same purpose, existed in Palestine, or in Palestinian tradition, about the 6th century B.C. and I think we may assume that this custom was not unusual in Near and Middle Eastern antiquity. We may surmise that, as in more modern Cyprus, the lack of racking was not so much due to carelessness as to a belief that wine improved if left upon its lees. In this surmise we may be correct. But at the same time we must not discount the possibility that much of the ancient wine was unracked and unclarified simply because many of the ancient peoples were somewhat rough in their taste.

This would not have been at all surprising for life itself was rough. Comfort was sporadic, personal liberty precarious, and pain inevitable. Even the after-life was sometimes viewed with gloom. In Babylonia, for example, the dead went down into a seven-walled city. They arrived at the heart of it naked and there, locked in forever

Faience Wine Strainer
Egyptian, c 1900 B.C.
London, British Museum

> 'Dusk is their nourishment
> And their food is mud.'

Wine would have lulled many a man in this life to forget the precariousness of the Here and the doubtful promise of the Hereafter, and whether his wine was clarified or not may have seemed to him largely irrelevant.

His view of the roughness and the precariousness of life can also be seen in his attitude to human sacrifice. In the 12th Dynasty of Egypt, which is contemporary with the 1st Dynasty of Babylon, Hapzefi, Prince of Siut, was buried at the Third Cataract and into the grave with him went 'the bodies of Nubian slaves who were killed in order to accompany him to the next world'. It is possible that this superstition exacted its toll elsewhere in the Egyptian Middle Kingdom. But much more striking, and very much earlier, are the large-scale human sacrifices which took place in the death-pits of the 'Royal Tombs' of Ur.

These tombs are pre-Dynastic and date from somewhere in the 5th millennium B.C. 'The number of people sacrificed in a single tomb might vary from a mere half-dozen to between seventy and eighty.' The ritual of their immolation is brilliantly re-created and described in Sir Leonard Woolley's *Ur Excavations*:

'When the principal body had been laid in the tomb with the attendants about it . . . and when the offerings had been set on the floor or on the shelves which might line the chamber walls, the doorway was blocked with brick and stone and plastered smoothly over, and the first part of the ceremony was complete.

'The next act is best illustrated by the graves . . . where the "death-pit" lies outside the chamber and there is therefore a clearer distinction between the two parts of the ceremony. . . . In these graves, that of "the King" and of Shub-ad . . . we must imagine the burial in the chamber to be complete and the door sealed; there remains the open

[141]Redding, 294, 296.

63

pit with its mat-lined walls and mat-covered floor, empty and unfurnished. Now down
the sloping passage comes a procession of people, the members of the court, soldiers,
men-servants, and women, the latter in all their finery of brightly coloured garments
and head-dresses of lapis lazuli and silver and gold, and with them musicians bearing
harps or lyres, cymbals, and sistra; they take up their positions in the farther part of the
pit and then there are driven or backed down the slope the chariots drawn by oxen or
by asses, the drivers in the cars, the grooms holding the heads of the draught animals,
and these too are marshalled in the pit. Each man and woman brought a little cup of
clay or stone or metal, the only equipment required for the rite that was to follow.
Some kind of service there must have been at the bottom of the shaft, at least it is evident
that the musicians played up to the last, and then each drank from the cup; either they
brought the potion with them or they found it prepared for them on the spot – in
PG/1237 there was in the middle of the pit a great copper pot into which they could
have dipped – and they composed themselves for death. Then someone came down
and killed the animals and perhaps arranged the drugged bodies, and when that was
done earth was flung from above on to them, and the filling-in of the grave-shaft was
begun.'

This type of sacrifice must seem to us an abomination; and if the victims were killed
in order to continue their service to the 'King' or 'Queen' or 'Prince' in the after-
world, then it must seem to us the most selfish of all superstitions. But the human
victims of the ancient world may often have seen their sacrifice in a very different
light. Life was hard and, to many of them, cruel. There was much death in their
life for not only was death a commonplace but they lived much nearer to the dead
than we do. The passage from life to death may have seemed to most of them to be
less momentous than we might ourselves imagine.

The grave-victims, moreover, may have died with pleasure. As Sir Leonard
Woolley has pointed out, they may have considered their sacrifice as 'a privilege

rather than a doom'. They were accompanying the Great Dead into the after-life and in that after-life they would continue to receive the benefits which in this life had accrued to them from their status as members of the 'royal' court. When they drank the drink and lay down to die, they may have felt that they were not abandoning life but increasing it.[142]

The Wines of the 'Gate of God'

The conditions of life in this world may thus have taught many a man to take whatever drink he could get and to take it gladly. He may have been inclined, or obliged, to view the quality of his wine with resignation or even with indifference.

This is not to say that there were no gradations in taste. Clearly and obviously there were. We have already seen that in the early history of Mesopotamia a distinction was drawn between the qualities of drink. In later times at least there was also some distinction of age for in the contract tablets of the firm of Murashû Sons of Nippur, which date from the 5th century B.C. we find an entry for the delivery of '200 good jars full of old wine', part of this consignment being 'first class 3-year-old wine'.[143] We cannot be certain that this was grape wine though it seems probable that it was. But here again, in Babylonia as in Egypt, we may suspect that wine was seldom kept longer than three years and that most of it was drunk when it was only one year old.

Babylonia grew its own local wines but it also imported wines from outside, from Elam, Armenia, and Syria. In the first half of the 1st millennium B.C. she imported wine from 'the land of Asallu'. This was presumably the same as the wine from 'Izallu', which was known in Sumeria in the 3rd millennium B.C., and it came therefore from Elam on the south-west border of Persia. From Elam also came the wine called Bit-Kubati while from the district of Lake Van in Armenia came a favourite wine of Sargon II. In the period of the 7th to 5th centuries B.C. wine from 'Ebir Nari, in the Harran area of Syria, was imported. Other wines which were known in Babylonia during this period (but whose places of origin I find it difficult to locate) were Amabanu, Tuḫimmu, and Zimzini, and – an import – wine from 'the land of Shushu'.[144] We may reckon that still more wines were imported, mainly perhaps from Syria but possibly also from the Iranian region, and particularly after 538 B.C. when Cyrus, King of Persia, conquered Babylon. The Hellenistic period doubtless saw a further increase in the traffic of wine from Persia for there was certainly no lack of it in that country. Strabo tells us that, in the 1st century B.C., many parts of the Iranian region abounded in wine. In Aria the wine was said to keep for three generations in unpitched vessels – which is unlikely. Bactria produced wine as did Hyrcania on the southern shore of the Caspian where each vine, so Strabo says, made eight gallons of wine. In Margiana he reports that some of the grape clusters were about three feet long.[145] And somewhere about this period there was also wine in Fergana and Sogdiana.[146]

How much wine was actually imported into Babylonia, and how much was locally grown, are both questions which admit of uncertainty. A wine cellar recently excavated in a royal fort at Assyrian Calah (Nimrud), south of Nineveh, 'contained four rows of huge terracotta jars with a narrow gangway between them' and the

[142] *CAH*, I, 305, 321, 531; *Ur Excavations*, II. Text 33 sqq. Babylonian quotation according to *Larousse Encyclopedia of Mythology*, 64, 1959.

[143] *Murashû Sons of Nippur, Business Docs. of*, x, No. 12. See also Dubberstein, 29.

[144] Asallu: Dubberstein, 28, fn. 37; Contenau, 91; Izallu (Isallan): Johns, C. H. W., *Assyrian Domesday*, 21; Lutz, *VB*, 43; Genouillac, *TSA*, LI, fn. 3. Bit-kubati: Johns, *Assyrian Domesday*, 21. Van: *Hist. Tech.*, I, 282. 'Ebir Nari: Dubberstein, 28, fn. 37. Amabanu: Johns, *Assyrian Domesday*, 21. Tuhimmu: Johns, *Assyrian Domesday*, 21. Zimzini: Johns, *Assyrian Domesday*, 21. Shushu: Dubberstein, 28, fn. 37.

[145] Strab., 11, 10, 1; 11, 1, 14; 11, 10, 1–2.

[146] Laufer, B., 'The Grape Vine', *Sino-Iranica*, XV, 221, 1919.

amount of wine that could have been stored (with a relative degree of coolness) would have been considerable. The cellar 'was at one time set aside for the provisioning of the king's male Kassite choir, specially selected singers from the Persian hills. Their ration was 'about a quart a day'.[147] The ration seems reasonable and it argues that wine was plentiful; but was it always grape wine? How many cellars of this kind were there in Mesopotamia? And how often were they filled with wine from grapes and not with wine from dates?

We would know more about the vineyards and the vintaging of the Mesopotamians if they had recorded their lives in paint. But they were sculptors and engravers rather than painters and we miss in Mesopotamia those scenes of daily life which make vivid the tombs of Egypt. Unless it were a carving made to celebrate the great deeds of a King, the Mesopotamian was comparatively uninterested in pictorial autobiography. The details of his life, its business dealings, and sometimes its joys and sorrows, he wrote down on tablets of clay; the colour in his life he kept for display and not for reminiscence.

He liked his art to be formal, dramatic and symbolic. These qualities, together with a rich impressiveness, suited his taste and decorated his religion. A cow of copper inlaid with silver was given to Ur, the moon-god city. Lion heads of copper were ornamented with inlaid eyes. Samsu-iluna of Babylon, son of Hammurabi, gave to the temple of the sun 'figures of lions . . . fearsome copper creatures, life size, doubtless arranged in an avenue, in pairs facing each other, to protect the approach'. At Babylon, 'the gate of God', a 'processional road was flanked by high protecting walls which guarded the approach to the gate of Ishtar, between long avenues of lions on the walls picked out in low relief with brilliant enamelling; lions to left and right, a hundred and twenty snarling monsters to frighten away all evil from the city'; while near it was the Palace of Nebuchadnezzar, its main courtyard magnificent with enamelled tiles.[148] And as well as working with metal and enamel, the artists were also lovers of ivory, covering the wall of a great palace room with uncarved ivory or else carving its panels into scenes of vivid, but formal, action.[149] Formalism was engrained in the Babylonian mind.

Perhaps Dionysos (as he was later to become) 'fled from Mesopotamia', not because of beer, but because he was stifled in the Land between the Two Rivers. The hot land, netted by innumerable irrigation canals and guarded by great mud-brick walls of the cities and temples, had achieved a fertile work of civilization. The

[147] Mallowan, M. E. L., 'Nimrud and "Fort Shalmaneser"', *ILN*, Nov. 23rd, 1957.

[148] *CAH*, I, 545, 585, 554, 506–7.

[149] *ILN*, Nov. 23rd, 1957; and later *ILN*, Supplement, Mallowan, M. E. L., 'Nimrud and "Fort Shalmaneser"'.

Ashur-bani-pal feasting with his Queen after the Defeat of Teuman
Stone Relief
Nineveh, 660 B.C.
London, British Museum

palm trees clustered outside the cities continued to give their abundance but the copper palm trees dedicated in the temple of Larsa, were losing their magic, as were the carved bulls of Babylon. The towering *ziggurats*, often visible to each other across the land, watched over a civilization whose life had become static. It was time to go.

PALESTINE AND SYRIA

'Wine of Charu'

Who is wealthy? . . . Rabbi Tarfon said: 'He who possesses a hundred vineyards, a hundred fields and a hundred slaves working in them.' Rabbi Akiba said: 'He who has a wife comely in deeds.' Rabbi Jose said: 'He who has a privy near his table.'[150]

Rabbi Jose was a practical man. He knew that a man who did not have to go out to a privy in the fields, because he had one in his own house, was a man of some wealth. And, with respect, this Talmudic quotation is a summary in miniature of much of the life of ancient Palestine. There is the emphasis on agriculture and particularly on vineyards; there is the recognition of the value of 'righteousness' or 'good' deeds; and there is a demonstration of the small size of material wealth when a man with his own privy could be considered 'wealthy'.

This picture of Palestine does not apply in quite the same terms to Syria and the Lebanon with their old and important sea coast cities – Tyre, Sidon, Beirut, Byblos and Ugarit (Ras Shamra). But one form of wealth that was common to the small farmers of Israelite Palestine as it was to the traders of the Phoenician cities was wine.

We may briefly recapitulate what we have already learnt from Egyptian records about the wines of Syria and Palestine. In about 2750 B.C. the 'Sand-dwellers' of Northern Sinai grew vines. The Tale of Sinuhe, dating about 2200 B.C., remarks upon the abundance of wine in Upper Retenu, or Palestine. The Annals of Thutmose III, in the middle of the 2nd millennium, record with pleasure the wine of Zahi, or Western Syria.[151] On the clay tablets of Ugarit which are also from the middle of the 2nd millennium, appears the figure of the 'wine-goddess' Pagat who helps her father, the hero, demi-god Danel, to cultivate the vine.[152]

Pagat's work must have been rewarding, as must that of her less mythological sisters in Palestine, for when Moses sent out his spies to search the land of Canaan, they cut down in Hebron 'a branch with one cluster of grapes, and they bare it between two upon a staff'.[153] No wonder then that, in later times, at Jerusalem 'A golden vine stood at the entrance to the temple trained over posts, and whosoever presented a leaf or a berry or a cluster would bring it and hang it thereon'.[154] The devout who added to this vine could scarcely have been poor, since the leaves and berries and clusters were made of gold. The offerings may have had a mixed piety; on the one hand, gratitude to the tree which made up so much of their livelihood; and on the other, a recognition of the Tree of Knowledge, for the Talmud, in *Sanhedrin*, relates the view of some that:

'The Holy One, blessed be He, said unto Noah: "Noah, should'st thou not have taken

[150] *Talmud-B*, Shabbath, 112; cf. *FAC*, II, Eubulus, 53.

[151] Breasted, *ARE*, I, 313, 496; II, 461, 462.

[152] *Ras Shamra*, Vol. XXI, 85 sqq.

[153] *Numbers*, XIII, 23.

[154] *Talmud-B*, Hullin, 506.

a warning from Adam, whose transgression was caused by wine?" This agrees with the view that the (forbidden) tree from which Adam ate was a vine. For it has been taught: Rabbi Meir said: That (forbidden) tree from which Adam ate was a vine, for nothing else but wine brings woe to man.'[155]

The wild inaccuracy of Rabbi Meir's statement about woe seems to herald the more eccentric utterances of yet unborn prohibitionists.

Apart from the tablets of Ugarit we have other local records which tell us something about Syrian viticulture in the 2nd millennium B.C. The tablets of Alalakh, in the Plain of Antioch, inform us that, in the 18th century B.C., Arammu sells a part of his vineyard to Wari-muša. Others of these tablets, in this case dating from the 15th century B.C., list the tenants or the owners of vineyards and from one of them it is interesting to note that there are eighty-one vineyard-holders in a single village.[156] Ugarit gives us a picture, although only a basic one, of the work of these Syrian *vignerons* at about this latter date for we are told that there are those who prune the vines, those who tie them up, and those who take the stones away from the vineyard.[157]

Ugarit is of great interest for other reasons, for many of the documents deal with trade and principally with the trade in wine. We may note as a significant incidental that wine is distinguished into *yn ṭb*, or good wine, and *yn d l ṭb*, or wine which was not good.[158] The fact that this distinction existed is important to any assessment of ancient wines and to any assessment of ancient taste. But the main importance of the Ugarit documents, so far as we are concerned, is in their demonstration that there was a commerce in wine. Ugarit lies on the coast of Syria opposite the eastern tip of Cyprus and was 'since the 4th millennium an important stage on the route between East and West'.[159] From very early times, therefore, it may have been concerned with any wine-trade that there was between Syria and Egypt as well as with any that there was between Syria and Cyprus, Anatolia or Crete.

It is possible then that Syrian, as well as other wine, was traded from this part of the coast in the 4th and 3rd millennia. Of this we cannot be certain. But when we come to the 2nd millennium we have definite knowledge. 'Wine of Charu', an Egyptian name for Palestine and Syria, was sent to Egypt in the 19th and 20th Dynasties, that is to say, from the middle of the 14th century onwards.[160] During the 12th century, towards the end of the 20th Dynasty, there is an Egyptian record of 'Wine of Khor', which means wine from Palestine and Syria, and another – 'Wine of Amor' – which may mean wine from a district between Laodiceia (the modern Latakia), Tripolis, and Homs. Since this period at least, Syrian wines achieved a considerable reputation. 'Wine of Lebanon', and in particular its fragrant bouquet, is mentioned by Hosea when he is recalling Israel to righteousness: 'O Israel, return unto the Lord thy God; for thou hast fallen by thine iniquity;' and he adds of those who will return that they shall, 'grow as the vine: the scent thereof shall be as the wine of Lebanon'. The Prophet may well have been referring to the wine of Byblus, the modern Gebal, in the Lebanon since Bybline was widely esteemed for its fragrance. We may strongly suspect that the vine on which it was grown was some type of muscat and if we could prove this suspicion to be true it would give us a further insight into the nature of ancient wine drinking.

[155] *Talmud-B*, Sanhedrin, 478.

[156] Wiseman, D. J., *Alalakh Tablets*, Nos. 62, 207-11.

[157] Virolleaud, C., 'La Naissance des Dieux Gracieux et Beaux . . .', *Syria*, XIV, 133, 1933.

[158] Virolleaud, C., 'Les nouveaux textes alphabétiques de Ras Shamra', *Syria*, XXX, 191-2, 1953.

[159] *Ras Shamra*, Vol. XXXI, 9-10.

[160] Erman, 516.

The Syrian wine trade continued to be important and we even find in the 1st century A.D. that some wine of Laodiceia was exported down the Red Sea, on the voyage to Abyssinia, the Somali coast, East Africa, Southern Arabia, and India. Nor was it only from the sea coast of Syria that good wine was exported, for in the 7th, and probably also in the 6th, centuries B.C. the wine which Ezekiel calls 'Wine of Helbon', and which is elsewhere called Chalybonian or Chalymonian and probably also Ḥilbunim, was exported from Aleppo and later from Damascus. It was sent into Babylonia and was considered good enough to be drunk by the Persian Kings.[161]

A curiosity of early Syrian wine is the drink called *msk* which occurs in the Ugarit legend of Danel and Paġat. During the course of this legend Paġat's brother Aqhat is murdered by an enigmatic character named Yṭpan. Paġat, however, is induced to accept a cup of wine from Yṭpan and this is not merely *yn*, ordinary wine, but *msk*, a more stimulating drink and one which seems to have brought on a sort of prophetic intoxication.[162] It is extremely likely that *msk* was a doped drink and one, therefore, which can take its place in the intriguing, but incomplete, pattern of the doped drinks of antiquity. To this pattern belongs the drugged or poisoned potion which was given to the victims in the death-pits of Ur. And then, some five or six hundred years after the appearance of the Paġat legend at Ugarit, the Odyssey tells us that both Helen of Troy and the enchantress Circe were skilled in the mixing of drugged drinks and, furthermore, that Helen got her knowledge from Egypt. We know little about these various potions. Helen's was obviously a narcotic; the effect of Circe's may have been similar to the effect produced by Indian hemp. If we knew more about the *msk* of Ugarit, which seems to have been in the Circean class, we should be able to probe deeper into this special department of ancient intoxication.[163]

The 'Romantic' Vineyard

The Book of Judges records the use of a vineyard for a purpose which, though not strictly in line with modern practice, would certainly enliven modern viticulture: '. . . they commanded the children of Benjamin, saying, Go and lie in wait in the vineyards; And see, and, behold, if the daughters of Shiloh come out to dance in dances, then come ye out of the vineyards, and catch you every man his wife of the daughters of Shiloh, and go to the land of Benjamin'.[164] The Song of Solomon takes the more poetic view: 'A bundle of myrrh is my wellbeloved unto me; he shall lie all night betwixt my breasts. My beloved is unto me as a cluster of camphire in the vineyards of En-gedi. Behold, thou art there, my love; behold, thou art there; thou hast doves' eyes.'[165]

For the first time in history the vineyard becomes a romantic symbol. The vine had long been used as one aspect of fertility-religion but the vineyard had never, it seems, been made into a symbol of poetic mysticism. The Jews of Palestine gave it this poetic meaning. So too with wine. Libations of wine were common in religious ritual throughout all early history and the wine-offering is no innovation of the Jews. But they gave the emphasis which, in the Christian religion, made wine the supreme symbol of unity between human and divine. The idea of partaking of the

[161] Khor: Gardiner, A. H., *Anc. Egyptian Onomastica*, I, 180* sqq.; II, 235*. Amor: Gardiner, A. H., *Anc. Egyptian Onomastica*, I, 187*; II, 236*. Lebanon: Hosea, XIV, 1, 7. Bybline: See Ch. III, fn. 64. Laodicean: Strab., 16, 2, 9; *Periplus*, 24; Ros., *SEHH*, 1253. Chalybonian; Johns, C. H. W., *Assyrian Domesday*, 21; Ath-E, I, 28d. Chalymonian: Strab., 15, 3, 22. Helbon: Ezekiel, XXVII, 18. See also Tripoline: Plin., XIV, 74. Ḥilbunim: Thompson, *Botany*, 329.

[162] *Ras Shamra*, Vol. XXI, 100; and see 115.

[163] *Ur Excavations*, II, Text, 33 sqq.; Odyssey, IV, X.

[164] XXI, 20-1.

[165] I, 13-15.

Feasting and pastoral Scenes: from the Standard of Ur
Lapis lazuli, Limestone and Shell Inlay, c 2759 B.C., *London, British Museum*

god, of 'eating the god', of being 'intoxicated with the god' is not uncommon in the pagan world and indeed it is at the root of much primitive religion, but the rigorous mysticism of the Jews prepared the way for a somewhat different concept of communion.

The Syrians were a middle point on the great highway between East, West, and South-west, between Babylonia, the Aegean, and Egypt. They were cosmopolitan. The Jews were not. The Jews were a small people in a small land. They were free from the ponderous complexity of the great River Civilizations whose life depended so much upon organization, upon the control of the irrigation system for the benefit of the whole community. The Egyptian and the Babylonian farmer was caged in his network of canals. Not so the Jew. He was not confined in a fixed and physical apparatus of social agriculture. His livelihood depended upon his energy and his ability. It is small wonder that, in a life shaped to the size of the individual, he should concentrate all his thoughts upon personal values: upon his family, his faith, and his own vineyard.

The Israelites might hanker after strange gods and they often did so. But there came to be only 'one' temple in Israel, the great Temple of Jerusalem, and this was physically remote from the daily life of most of the Jews. Unlike the Mesopotamian, the Jew did not live under the shadow of a *ziggurat*; unlike the Egyptian, he was not watched by the great temples of the Nile. His Temple was distant and thus it tended to become a spiritual rather than a physical object. Its presence, for most of the Jews, was abstract and spiritual. It was a presence which depended upon the effort of the individual mind; and it is this combination of individualism and spirituality which seems to me to be the hallmark of the earlier Jews.

The basic quality of a wine is made by the *terroir* of the vineyard in which it grows. The *terroir* is the geological shape – the soil – of a vineyard: but it is not unfair to

70

extend the word to mean the whole 'shape' of a vineyard – its soil, its situation, and its climate. It is this *terroir* which makes a *vignoble* unique and which determines that its wine shall be basically different (in greater or in lesser degree) from the wine of any other *vignoble*. The *terroir* will also, though only to a certain extent, dominate the individuality of vines, for the same vines grown in different *vignobles* will produce different wines.

Is it too fanciful to believe that this happens also to a people? Might one not suggest that it was the '*terroir*' of Palestine which helped the Jews to develop their distinctive genius? Pliny, it is true, remarked tersely that the Jews were 'a race remarkable for their contempt for the divine powers'[166] but his 'divine powers' were not theirs and his statement is interesting merely for its prejudice. It is doubtful, indeed, if many of the Romans could have understood the Jews, even if they had tried, for in their religion the Romans were not Puritans and the Jews were the Puritans of the ancient world. They acquired all the energy and idealism and fanaticism of a Puritan faith. They were poets so long as the poetry was mystical and religious so long as the religion was intolerant. Their idealism developed the high concept of individual and responsible righteousness. But, as has happened so often with the Puritan impulse, the high endeavour could not be maintained. The intensity faltered and the impulse became lost in a labyrinth of ritualistic observance.

Having said all these things about this remarkable people, it is an anti-climax to have to add that they seem to have made no original contribution to the growing of wine. One would have thought quite differently. One would have thought that these hard-working small farmers, devoted to their vines, would have sought new, and perhaps better, ways of growing them. This does not appear to have happened. Admittedly most of our information comes from the *Mishnah* and the *Talmud* which cover between them a period from the 2nd century B.C. to the 6th century A.D. During this period Hellenism was a powerful influence in the Near East so that any new technique which we discover in Palestine in these centuries might be attributed to Hellenistic influence rather than to Jewish invention. But in fact we find no new techniques at all.

The Israelites continued the ancient custom of the 'orchard-vineyard'. They trained their vines onto the branches of fruit trees, and in addition to growing fruit trees in their vineyards, they were prepared to grow crops of vegetables or grain between the vines. (In time this latter practice may have become less common.) As well as training their vines onto trees, or from tree to tree, they grew them on trellises. And they also had ground-trained vines whose grapes grew almost at foot level. This latter practice sounds as though it might have been a real development and in a sense a forerunner of the modern 'low' vineyard. I do not think that it was. It is more likely that these low vines were only vines whose branches were allowed to sprawl along the ground – a common method in some parts of the ancient world – and that the reeds used as props in the vineyards of Palestine were put beneath the branches to keep the fruit just above the earth. Then again when we learn from the *Mishnah* that a vineyard could be planted 'in irregular fashion' or else with the vines in rows, we still cannot say that the vines-in-rows constituted anything like a 'modern' vineyard. They may have been individually staked with reeds which would have given them something of a modern appearance but the reeds may

[166]Plin., XIII, 46–7.

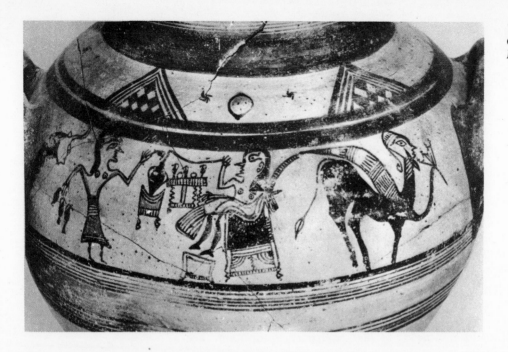

The Hubbard Amphora
Cyprus, 900 B.C.
Nicosia, Cyprus Museum

equally well have served the purpose of giving the vines support until they could reach up onto a high 'un-modern' trellis.[167]

The grapes were trodden or pressed in 'wine-presses' of stone or wood or earthenware, or, as at Gibeon, in 'wine-presses' cut into the bedrock. The word 'wine-press' has of course a double connotation. Here, as in the earliest times, it usually means a receptacle or tank in which the grapes were trodden. But there were also in the Talmudic period presses in the more technical sense of the term. The references to them in both the *Mishnah* and the *Talmud* are unclear, so that we cannot be certain what types of press were actually in use. One seems to have been only a pile of beams placed on the grape skins to press out the remaining juice, but it is probable that a real beam press of the lever type was also used, rough in construction no doubt, but quite efficient in its action.[168]

The wine-growers of Palestine seem to have gone to some trouble to try and get their wine clear. Filters are often mentioned – they were sometimes merely a basket of rushes[169] – but how far the Jews really went in the clarifying of their wine is another matter. Isaiah proclaims: 'And in this mountain shall the Lord of Hosts make unto all people a feast of fat things, a feast of wines on the lees, of fat things full of marrow, of wines on the lees well refined.'[170] This delight in 'fat things' reflects the attitude of the 7th or 6th century B.C.; but may not a desire for 'fat wines', for wines 'bodied' by being left upon their lees, have persisted into the time of *Mishnah*? It is quite possible, and racking may not have been at all usual. Yet a statement in the *Talmud* makes one hesitate to be dogmatic on this point. In the Tractate 'Abodah Zarah' it says that 'A man was drawing wine through (a siphon consisting of) a large and small tube', and a further explanation is given that wine was being drawn from a full to an empty cask.[171] (For cask we should read jar.) This need not, of course, mean that the wine was being deliberately racked, since

[167] *Mishnah*, Kilaim, 4, 5; 4, 7; 4, 8; 4, 9; 5, 1; 6, 1-9. Peah, 7, 8. *Talmud-B*, Peʿah, 40. Kilʾayim, 99, 119-24. Baba Bathra, 274. Baba Meziʾa, 592.

[168] *Mishnah*, Tohoroth, 10, 8, and fn. 1. Shabbath, 1, 9; Pritchard, J. B., 'Wine Making in Biblical Gibeon', *ILN*, Sept. 10th, 1960.

[169] *Mishnah*, Shabbath, 20, 1. Kelim, 28, 9. *Talmud-B*, 'Abodah Zarah, 285.

[170] XXV, 6.

[171] *Talmud-B*, 'Abodah Zarah, 348.

it might have been drawn off into another vessel for the purpose of sale or transport. Still, we cannot discount the possibility of racking for which the siphon is the obvious instrument. All we can say is that if it had been commonly used we should expect to find it more frequently mentioned.

In Palestine, as in Egypt, the siphon had a practical function. In Mesopotamia and Syria, on the other hand, it had a peculiar and rather puzzling religious connotation. The motif of seated persons sucking 'drink' through tubes out of a jar set between them is quite frequent in pre-dynastic Ur and in the 4th millennium in Mesopotamia, if not before, these seated figures are those of gods. The same theme is common on West Asian cylinder-seals and one version of it is claimed to represent a goddess drinking through a reed from a jar. An unusually graphic portrayal of this latter scene comes from the Hubbard Amphora which was found in Eastern Cyprus and which dates from somewhere about 900 B.C. A throned woman drinks through a jointed tube from a jar placed on a stand before her. On the other side of this jar is another woman holding three smaller jars and filling, or refilling, that from which the goddess (?) is drinking. The theme of two drinkers appears on Syro-Hittite cylinders towards the end of the 2nd millennium and it has been supposed that these represent either two gods drinking from the same jar or a god and a worshipper in a 'communion scene'. It has also been suggested, at least in the case of the Hubbard Amphora, that the woman drinking through a siphon is a deceased human being who is being worshipped, or perhaps served, with wine.

But here, before we go on to the argument about the meaning of these siphons, we ought to note another instance of the use of the drinking tube. In the 'royal' tomb of 'Queen' Shud-ad of pre-Dynastic Ur there was found 'the silver mouthpiece' of[31] a long drinking-tube of silver decorated with rings of lapis-lazuli and gold and having this silver mouthpiece which was bent at right angles so as to fit more easily into the pot. . . .[172]

Now, with the exception of Shud-ad and the possible worshippers these Asian siphon-drinkers are either deceased humans, or deified humans, or deities who have never been human, and they are all doing their drinking in another world. Even Shub-ad is on her way into another world in which (if she were not already thought of as being divine) she might confidently expect to be deified. Is the drinking-tube, therefore, a prerogative of the other world and is it, in particular, a prerogative of the gods?

It is reasonable to assume that the use of the siphon in the world of the dead and the deified is simply a reflection of its use in the world of the living. Men in this world would have drunk their wine through a reed or tube in order to get their wine clear. Since gods were the reflections of men, they too would have preferred the clearest wine and would have used the siphon of their earthly worshippers. The argument is attractive; and if it is true it will indicate either that wine was seldom racked or that it was only racked 'at table'.

We may consider, then, that Shub-ad used her drinking-tube in this earthly life as well as taking it with her into the Hereafter. And we may argue with conviction that the drinking-siphon was a well-known instrument. Why then does it not appear more frequently in the records? It was the cup, and not the tube, that was the normal instrument of drinking. And why, when the siphon does appear in the

[172] *Ur Excavations*, II, Plates 193, 194, 200; II, Text, 81; *CAH*, I, 376; Ward, W. H., *The Seal Cylinders of Western Asia*, 243-5, figs. 734, 738; Ward, W. H., *Cylinders and other Oriental Seals in the Library of J. Pierpont Morgan*, 81-2, fig. 173 in Pl. xxiv; Dikaios, P., 'An Iron Age Painted Amphora in the Cyprus Museum', *BSA*, xxxvii, 56 sqq., 1936-7; and cf. Barnett, R. D., 'The Treasure of Ziwiye', *Iraq*, III sqq., xviii, 1956.

Asian records, does it appear insistently in a religious context? Because it is becoming a symbol. It has lost its value in the world of men, for men now seldom use it, but in the older world of the 'gods' it retains its older value. The wine of the gods must be the purest wine of all and the gods still use the ancient instrument for the purest drinking. And may it not have attracted an even more symbolic meaning? May it not have come to signify that the lips of the god cannot touch the earthly wine of his worshipper and that he must 'drink' it at one remove through a tube? May not the tube have symbolized both the gap between the god and the earth, and the link of communion between the god and his earthly worshipper?

'. . . Wine of the juice of my pomegranate'

'Give strong drink unto him that is ready to perish,' says the Book of Proverbs, 'and wine unto those that be of heavy hearts.'[173] Many a time the Jews of Palestine, heavy-hearted with the tribulations of rebellion, civil war, and conquest – and in their sufferings they were not at all unique among ancient peoples – must have alleviated their misery with a cup or two of wine. They seem, on the whole, to have been a moderately temperate people. It is true that 'Raba said: It is the duty of a man to mellow himself [with wine] on Purim until he cannot tell the difference between "cursed be Haman" and "blessed be Mordecai".'[174] This, of course, is ritual intoxication but on the other hand the Old Testament is enthusiastic in its denunciation of ordinary drunkenness. We need not take these things too seriously. An occasional feast is a rare release and social criticism cannot always be taken at its face value. The Jews were not prone to incessant intoxication any more than they were plunged into a fit of continual and sober sadness.

They liked their wine and they made many kinds of it. Mostly it was red. They made also a black wine which in the *Talmud* is contrasted with the red of red wine.[175] It is clear that white wine, and 'mustard-coloured' wine, were not uncommon although they were not always of good quality for the word 'Gurdeli' was used as a nickname for an inferior white wine.[176] They made two general kinds of sweet wine. One was made from 'sweet' grapes, although the word which describes it can

[173] XXXI, 6.

[174] *Talmud-B*, Megillah, 38.

[175] *Talmud-B*, Baba Bathra, 405; Niddah, 453.

[176] *Talmud-B*, Yoma, 78; Baba Bathra, 405, and see 405, fn. 8; Shabbath, 294, in a graphic but curious context, and 294, fn. 7.

Libation to the Gods
Stone Relief
Assyrian, 7th century B.C.
London, British Museum

also be held to mean must or new wine and thus it may sometimes have been grape juice which had been kept from fermenting or else boiled down into something approaching syrup. The other was a raisin wine made from dried grapes; *Simmūqīm* or *Yen zimmukin*. At certain times it seems also to have gone under the name of *Hīlīṣṭon*, presumably from the Greek ἡλαστήριον which means a place for drying fruit.[177] It was, of course, sweet and tended to be low in alcohol.

Of the wines which were received as Temple offerings those which were considered to be of the first quality were Hattulim and Keruthin. Hattulim may have come from Kefr Hatla, north of Gilgal, while Keruthin, or Keruhim, may have come from Coreae in the Jordan valley. Second-class wines offered in the Temple were those from Beth Luban, north-west of Jerusalem, from Beth Rimmah, also north-west of Jerusalem, and Kefar Signah which seems to have been grown at Sukneh near Jaffa. Other wine-growing areas were Ammon, north-east of the Dead Sea, Carmel, Gibeon, the Plain of Sharon which produced a light-red wine said to be 'exceptionally weak', Petra in Jordan, and Pelugto (perhaps the same as Perugitha) near Tiberias in Galilee. Of the wines of Syria and the Lebanon, Berytian from Beirut, Tripolitican from Tripolis, and Tyrian from Tyre were classed by Romans in the 1st century A.D. as being of second quality. This, however, is quite a distinction since it means second quality compared to all the wines of the Roman Empire.[178]

New wine for old bottles?

'Corn shall make the young men cheerful, and new wine the maids,' says Zechariah, thus giving the young men the raw end of this particular deal.[179] In the *Talmud* we find the terse proposition '. . . wine is unattractive until it is forty days old'.[180] We would agree with this view, since new wine is not alluring. Some of the Jews, though doubtless a small and rash minority, seem not to have agreed, for the *Mishnah* delivers the following advice upon higher education: 'He that learns from the young, to what is he like? To one that eats unripe grapes and drinks wine from his wine-press. And he that learns from the aged, what is he like? To one that eats ripe grapes and drinks old wine.'[181] Only the inexperienced or the very thirsty could have found much pleasure in drinking the *tirosh*, or new wine, as it was becoming ready to leave the press.

For the most part Palestinians drank *yayin*, ordinary fermented wine which would usually have been less than a year old.[182] They appreciated old wine but not in modern terms for *yayin yashan*, a term for one-year-old wine, also means 'old wine', and *Yayin meyushshan*, a term for three-year-old wine, means 'very old wine'. In certain cases they may have aged their wines for four or five years but it is probable that three years was considered to be the more usual upper limit of maturity.[183] When we come across the man named Ḳarna who was 'a judge of the Exile' and find that he 'was (regularly occupied in) smelling tests at a wine store . . .' in order to advise the owner of the store which wine would keep for some time and which would not, then it does seem that we have found an early expert in the knowledge of the ageing of wine.[184] But it is to be feared that when Karna said a short time he meant a very short time indeed and that even the better wines which he smelt were

[177] *Talmud-B*, Menahoth, 525–6; Baba Bathra, 405, 405 fn. 9; Lutz, *VB*, 26, 27.

[178] Hattulim, Keruthin, Keruhim, Beth Luban, Beth Rimmah, Kefar Signah: *Mishnah*, Menahoth, 8, 6; *Talmud-B*, Menahoth, 524, and fn. 6. Ammon: *Talmud-B*, Sanhedrin, 723. Carmel: *Talmud-B*, Niddah, 137. Gibeon: Pritchard, J. B., *Hebrew Inscriptions and Stamps from Gibeon, passim*; Pritchard, J. B., 'Wine Making in Biblical Gibeon', *ILN*, Sept. 10th, 1960. Sharon: *Mishnah*, Niddah, 2, 7; *Talmud-B*, Shabbath, 364. Petra: Plin., XIV, 75. Pelugto, Perugitha: *Talmud-B*, Shabbath, 750, and fn. 3. Berytian: Plin., XIV, 74. Tripolitican: Plin., XIV, 74. Tyrian: Plin., XIV, 74; but for Pliny's Tyros (Theophrastus has Tylos) as Bahrein, see Tylos, fn. 207 below.

[179] IX, 17.

[180] *Talmud-B*, Sanhedrin, 476.

[181] *Mishnah*, Aboth, 4, 20.

[182] Tirosh, *Talmud-B*, Sanhedrin, 476. Yayin, *Talmud-B*, 'Erubin, 454.

[183] Yayin yashan: *Mishnah*, Aboth, 4, 20; *Talmud-B*, Yoma, 78. Yayin meyushshan: *Jewish Encyclopedia* (Bibl. Dictionaries). See also *Talmud-B*, 'Abodah Zarah, 148, 319; Krauss, S., *Talmudische Archäologie*, II, 243; and *Talmud-B*, Pesahim, 200.

[184] *Talmud-B*, Kethuboth, 675, and 674, fn. 5.

not destined to a long life. And how much one wonders was his sense of smell disturbed when the wine was stored, as it may often have been stored, in pitched containers?[185]

It is difficult to decide when Palestine first adopted the custom of diluting wine with water. At all events, the Jews of the Talmud period were quite accustomed to drinking *mazug*, wine mixed with water, and it seems that the most usual dilution was three parts of water to one part of wine.[186] Whether Hellenistic influence, or home economy, or the delights of sobriety induced them to dilution cannot certainly be known. The one case where economy was the obvious motive was in their making of *tamad*, a 'wine' made from grape skins steeped in water and an old Palestinian version of the modern *piquette*.[187]

They had various other drinks and concoctions. One of these was 'boiled wine' or *yayin mebushal*, grape juice or must boiled down to a required consistency and it is possible that the Karina of the *Talmud* was not only a wine which came 'from Asia Minor', or alternatively from Essa, east of the Sea of Galilee, but a Palestinian equivalent of the Greek *karynon* or 'sweet wine boiled down'. Sometimes, it would seem, the *yayin mebushal* was treated as a sort of jam or syrup into which bread was dipped.[188] For cold weather there was wine mixed with hot water which, as the Talmud of Jerusalem disparagingly remarks, was in use among the 'pagans' at Tyre. It was, however, also drunk by the Jews.[189] In this connection one might remark that pagan contact could make wine into a forbidden thing – *yen nesek* or wine which, to the Jewish mind, had been defiled because it might have been dedicated by a pagan as libation wine to a heathen idol or a heathen god.[190]

In a country which grew many kinds of fruit, and among them mulberries, pomegranates, dates, and apples, it is only natural that the Palestinian farmers would have tried to make wine out of other fruit than grapes. *Shekar* was a word of somewhat general application, apparently covering beer and mead as well as date wine. The last meaning, coupled with that of 'strong drink' was probably its most usual meaning as it was of the *šikaru* of ancient Babylonia. A more precise name for date wine in Palestine was *yen temarim*. 'Strong drink' was a wide term and one that could be disapproving as well as descriptive.[191] *Deuteronomy*, laying down the law of the Temple offerings, is merely descriptive: 'And thou shalt bestow that money for whatsoever thy soul lusteth after, for oxen, or for sheep, or for wine, or for strong drink, or for whatsoever thy soul desireth: and thou shalt eat there before the Lord thy God, and thou shalt rejoice, thou, and thine household.'[192] *Proverbs*, however, is disapproving: 'Wine is a mocker, strong drink is raging: and whosoever is deceived thereby is not wise.'[193]

'If a man vowed to abstain from wine, he is permitted the wine of apples . . .' says the *Mishnah* and it seems that cider, or *yayin tapuhim*, was not at all uncommon.[194] But how much was it esteemed? One might embark upon the perilous argument that the apples (and the apple wine) of antiquity were bitter, and carried the stigma of their bitterness into mythology, because, when they appear in mythology, they are almost always a fruit of contention and woe. The Golden 'Apples' of the Hesperides do not really count since they may not have been apples at all but clouds or the 'flocks of heaven'. But look at the other appearances. There are the three golden apples which Melanion, or Hippomenes, got from Aphrodite to

[185] Krauss, S., *Talmudische Archäologie*, II, 236.

[186] *Talmud-B*, Niddah, 123 and fn. 8; Menahoth, 526, fn. 6; 'Erubin, 378; 'Abodah Zarah, 291, and fn. 3.

[187] *Mishnah*, Maaseroth, 5, 6; Maaser Sheni, I, 3; Hullin, I, 7; *Talmud-B*, Pesahim, 200 and fn. 12.

[188] *Mishnah*, Terumoth, 2, 6,, Menahoth, 8, 6; *Talmud-B*, Menahoth, 525 sq.; 'Abodah Zarah, 148 sq.; 'Erubin, 201, and fn. 3; 'Abodah Zarah, 151.

[189] *Talmud de Jérusalem*, XI, 232 ('Aboda Zara).

[190] *Talmud-B*, 'Abodah Zarah, 153, fn. 6, 282 sqq., 318 sqq.; Pesahim, 139, fn. 10.

[191] Shekar, Yen temarim: *Jewish Encyclopedia* (Bibl. Dictionaries). Beer, date-wine: *Talmud-B*, 'Erubin, 202, fn. 2. Sikaru: Pinches, T. G., *Amherst Tablets*, Pt I, No. 11 and fn. to line 1.

[192] XIV, 26.

[193] XX, 1.

[194] *Mishnah*, Terumoth, II, 2, 3; Nedarim, 6, 9.

divert Atalanta in the foot-race in which she herself was the prize. The lovers, however, came to a disturbing end for they were turned into lions.[195] Unhappier still was the outcome of the Judgment of Paris who gave the golden apple 'For the fairest' to Aphrodite and thus, by the intervention of divine jealousy, brought about the Sack of Troy. Most fatal of all was the fruit of the Tree of Knowledge which Eve ate, and gave to Adam to eat, and which, at all events in later tradition, was an apple. Nevertheless some degree of bitterness or 'sharpness', whether in apples or elsewhere, was not at all unwelcome to the taste of the ancient world and bitter 'wines' had a place, and quite an important place, in the ancient life. These 'wines' pass under a variety of names, which is sometimes confusing, and they range in type from vinegar to 'absinthe'. They fall into two main classes, sour wine and bitter wine.

Sour wine can sometimes mean ordinary wine of an inferior quality. Usually, however, it means *verjuice*, or vinegar. It was used in preparing food and it went into the Jewish *Ḥaroseth* which was 'a pap made of fruits and spices with wine or vinegar, used for sweetening the bitter herb on Passover night'.[196] As *verjuice*, the juice of unripe, or only partly ripe, grapes, it went under the general names of *Omphacium* or *Omphacites* but another name for it in Palestine was *semadar*. *Semadar* means 'tender grape', as in the verse of the Song of Solomon: 'The fig tree putteth forth her green figs, and the vines with the tender grape give a good smell.'[197] Wine from these young, unripe grapes was found in the north Galilean citadel of Hazor in the 8th century B.C. In the 1st century A.D. both Pliny and Dioscorides give *omphacium* or *omphácites* as being made from particular vines, Dioscorides naming the Thasian or Aminaean for this purpose and Pliny the Psithian or Aminaean. At this time it was not only the juice of unripe grapes but also the pulp that was used, the latter being dried and sold in small cakes. It was made in the Aegean – Dioscorides mentions Lesbos – and also in Egypt, for in the same 1st century, some was exported from Diospolis parva in the Thebàid.[198]

But Sour Wine also had the meaning of grape juice which has fermented and become sour and turned into vinegar. This too had its various names, *oxos* in Greek and *acetum* in Latin. It was made in the Aegean, at Cos for example, while in the 1st century A.D. the best *acetum* was made in Egypt.[199] The commonest use of sour wine was in the cooking and seasoning of food but it could also, when mixed with water, be a refreshing drink in times of great heat.

Bitter Wine can signify either the juice of unripe grapes or wine which has gone sour. But it seems more than likely that it can also mean Wormwood Wine, a form of 'absinthe', though not of course the same as the modern absinthe. In this guise 'bitter wine' is *absinthiatum* or, as it was called in Palestine, *pesintiton*. The making of it was not confined to Palestine for it appears in many other countries of antiquity. Indeed, in this particular form, 'absinthe' may well be one of the oldest compounded drinks in the world.[200]

The ancients not only compounded wines to make them bitter but also to make them sweet and to make them aromatic. The only sweeteners which they could add were fruit syrups, in particular in the Middle East date-syrup or 'date-honey', and the honey from bees and it must have been one of these which sweetened the honied wine that went as tribute from Palestine to Thothmes III of Egypt. It was still being

[195] Ovid, *Met.*, X, 560 sqq.

[196] *Talmud-B*, Pesahim, 190, fn. 8.

[197] II, 13.

[198] Plin., XII, 60, 130; XIV, 98; Dioscorides, *Herbal*, V, 6, 12; *Song of Solomon*, II, 13; Catalogue of the Hazor Exhibition at the British Museum, 22; Lucas, 38. (See also Ch. 3, p. 132.)

[199] Frank, Johnson, II, 315, 347, fn. 21; Pritchett, W. K., 'The Attic Stelai, Part II', *Hesp.*, XXV, 187-8, 1956; *Mishnah*, Nedarim, 6, 9; *Talmud-B*, 'Abodah Zarah, 147; Mart., XIII, 122; Plin., XIV, 102-3.

[200] *Talmud-B*, 'Abodah Zarah, 151.

made in Palestine in the time of the *Mishnah*, some fifteen hundred years later, and we know that at the time pepper was sometimes mixed in as well.[201] This mixture of wine, honey and pepper was known as *anomalin* and perhaps also as *tila*. *Tila*, however, might only mean wine mixed with pepper though another view has it as a strong wine with a remarkably pungent taste or as an acrid wine 'which makes the wine-skin burst'. It should, presumably, not be confused with *ṭilia* which was 'an inferior kind of wine' or with 'white *ṭilia*' which was the 'worst of all wines'.[202]

Spiced or aromatic wine could be used for a doleful purpose, as when it was sprinkled before the bier of a dead person, but it had also its more pleasurable connotation. *Alontith*, made of 'old wine, clear water, and balsam', was 'used (as a cooling drink) in the bath-house'.[203] And, more romantically, there is the 'wine' of the Song of Solomon: 'Come, my beloved, let us go forth into the field. . . . Let us get up early to the vineyards; let us see if the vine flourish, whether the tender grape appear, and the pomegranates bud forth; there will I give thee my loves . . . I would lead thee, and bring thee into my mother's house . . . I would cause thee to drink of spiced wine of the juice of my pomegranate.'[204]

Yet spiced and aromatic wine – *yayin ha-reḳaḥ* – was not always a mild and gentle joy. As 'mixed wine' it could produce the result so graphically described in *Proverbs*: 'Who hath woe? who hath sorrow? who hath contentions? who hath babbling? who hath wounds without cause? who hath redness of eyes? They that tarry long at the wine; they that go to seek mixed wine.'[205]

A happier view of wine, although not necessarily of 'mixed wine', is given to us in the *Talmud* story about Rabbi Ishmael, a man who was notable for his stoutness: 'Rabbi Ishmael son of Rabbi Jose visited the home of Rabbi Simeon. . . . They offered him a goblet, which he accepted at the first invitation and drank at one draught. Said they to him: "Do you not agree that he who drinks his goblet in one draught is greedy?" Said he to them: "This was not said when your goblet is small, your wine sweet, and my stomach broad." '[206] Such common sense deserved another goblet.

Virey, *Rekhmara*, 37; *Mishnah*, Shabbath, 20, 2; Terumoth, II, 1; Menahoth, 8, 6.

Anomalin: *Talmud-B*, 'Abodah Zarah, 148, 151 and fn. 1. Tila: *Talmud-B*, 'Abodah Zarah, 151 and fn. 1. Tilia: *Talmud-B*, Gittin, 333.

Talmud-B, Sanhedrin, 321; 'Abodah Zarah, 148.

VII, 11–12; VIII, 2.

XXXIII, 29–30.

Talmud-B, Pesahim, 456.

NOTE: References for wines listed in Appendix A, but not discussed in the text of this chapter: 'Andjet: Gardiner, A. H., *Anc. Egyptian Onomastica*, II, 176* sq., 236*. Antyllan: Ath-E, I, 33f. Aranabanim: Thompson, *Botany*, 329. Arsinoitic: Strab., 17, 1, 35; Lutz, *VB*, 6. Bitâtim: Thompson, *Botany*, 329. Carmanian: Strab., 15, 2, 14. Coptic: Ath-E, I, 33f. *Dsds*: see fn. 69; and Lutz, *VB*, 10, 10, fn. 1. Elephantine: Breasted, *ARE*, II, 798; Lutz, *VB*, 14; see also Theophrastus, *Enq. into Plants* (Bibl. Ch. 3), I, 3, 5, and Varro, 1, 7, 6, though the context in Varro may qualify his statement. Esneh: Petrie, W. M. F., *Soc. Life in Anc. Egypt*, 136. Geštin Dug-Ga: Thompson, *Botany*, 328. Geštin-Kalag-Ga: Thompson, *Botany*, 328. Hardai: Gardiner, A. H., *Anc. Egyptian Onomastica*, II, 236. Lower Egypt, Wine of: Mercer, S. A. B., *Pyramid Texts*, 92b; Virey, *Rekhmara*, 48; Tell El-Amarna, I, 162, 167; III, Vol. I, 148. Myrrh wine: New Testament, Mark, xv, 23; cf. Plin., XII, 35; XIV, 92-3, 107. Nham, T: Lutz, *VB*, 14. Simmini: Thompson, *Botany*, 329. Smoked wine: *Mishnah*, Menahoth, 8, 6; *Talmud-B*, Menahoth, 525 sq.; and see discussion on smoked wines in Ch. 4, p.   sq. Strip-Wine: Ath-E, I, 33e. Sûham: Thompson, *Botany*, 329. Taeniotic: Ath-E, I, 33e. Tbui: Lutz, *VB*, 14. Tharu: Quibell, J. E., *The Ramesseum*, 8, 16. Thel: *Tell El-Amarna*, I, 166; *JEA*, Gardiner, v, 242-3, 1918. 'Three-leaf' wine: Lutz, *VB*, 27. Tylos: Theophrastus, *Enq. into Plants* (Bibl. Ch. 3), IV, 7, 7; cf. Plin., XII, 40 with Tyros - is he repeating Theophrastus? Ua-wine: Murray, M. A., *Saqqara Mastabas*, Pt I, 35.

CHAPTER THREE

Greece and the Aegean

The Winged Jars of Poliochni

The Aegean first gave a European meaning to the drinking of wine and it is to the Aegean that we must look also for the first development of European viticulture.

To find the Aegean beginnings is not easy. In the earlier Cycladic, Minoan, and Helladic civilizations the signs are few and their interpretation is guesswork. In the later Minoan, and in the Mycenaean, civilizations they are more frequent but they are still secretive; they speak to us of the wines of these brilliant peoples but their message is incomplete. Reading them is like reading a face in the fragments of a broken mirror.

The attempt to read that face is important for some of its features mature into the beauty of Classical Greece. Constantly the mirrors flash back and forth across Greek history, each supplementing and illuminating the message of the other. The clear people of Aristophanes light up the shadowy subjects of Agamemnon; an Attic vase-painting is a comment upon the dim vintagers of Nestor's Pylos. And throughout, reflecting others yet himself remaining mysterious, moves the changing figure of Dionysos, the greatest of the gods of wine.

It was not, it would seem, until the 16th century B.C., in the time of the golden death-masks of Mycenae, that wine entered the life of mainland Greece. In the Early and Middle Helladic periods, before this Shaft Grave Dynasty at Mycenae ushered in the Late Helladic, the peoples of Hellas would have had to confine their drinking to beer – if they made beer – and to honey-wine or mead. Zeus of the bees, and the honey-priestesses of Parnassus, demonstrate this side of life in an early and wineless Greece.[1]

We may accept this picture as being substantially accurate, but at the same time we must ask if it is completely true. If wine was known in Western Asia Minor before the 16th century B.C., and if at the same time the civilization of the Aegean

Note: except where otherwise stated the references to the *Iliad* and the *Odyssey* are from the Lang, Leaf and Myers translation of the *Iliad* and from the Butcher and Lang translation of the *Odyssey*.

[1] See Ch. 2, pp. 29-30.

was vigorous, then we may say that wine could have travelled, either as an article of trade or as a gift between princes, from Asia Minor through the Aegean and into mainland Greece. The conditions existed for this to happen and we may suppose that, occasionally at least, it did happen.

Beycesultan lies on the Upper Meander river in south-western Asia Minor. There, among broken votive pottery behind the horned altar of an Early Bronze Age shrine, were found the remains of barley, lentils, and also grape pips.[2] The dating of this shrine is about 2400 B.C., in the time of the Second City of Troy. At the same period Poliochni, on the Island of Lemnos in the North Aegean, was a flourishing city, larger even than the Second City of Troy. The houses of Poliochni were many-roomed, the streets and squares were in part paved, and there was a system of drainage. Poliochni must have been one of the major settlements in the Aegean and its urban sophistication is matched by the sophistication of its pottery. It had beautiful drinking beakers each shaped like the end of a trumpet with two semi-circular handles running from the base to a point below the rim. It had jars of distinction, round jars with short necks, and with handles rising like wings from the curve of the jar towards the neck.[3] Sometimes, perhaps, these beakers and jars held wine. If they did, then sometimes, also, this wine may have been traded into Lemnos from the vineyards of Asia Minor. The grapes of Beycesultan cannot have been unique and the city of Poliochni cannot have been isolated.

Seaborne traffic in the Aegean must have begun in the earliest Bronze Age, a thousand years or so before this city of Poliochni; by then, commerce, or at least communication, in the Aegean must have been quite considerable.

None of this is evidence that, in the 3rd millennium, wine actually did travel among the islands of the Aegean or on to the mainland of Early Helladic Greece. Later, however, and somewhere between 2000 and 1600 B.C., we have reason to suggest that wine was known on the mainland, for, at Middle Helladic Orchomenos in Boeotia we have 'grape seed discovered in connection with a *pithos*'.[4] Whether the grapes were locally grown, or imported as raisins, we cannot tell. In any case they denote no more than the possibility of wine. An earlier, and more interesting, though less satisfactory, piece of 'evidence' is a cooler from Tiryns which is now in the Museum at Nauplion. This cooler is a large jar with a sort of guttering in the shape of a truncated cone constructed all the way round its upper interior. Through the hole of the truncated cone was poured the liquid to be cooled while in the guttering itself was put the cooling material. It has been given an Early Helladic dating, that is to say, between 2600 and 2000 B.C., and if we can suppose that it was a wine cooler then we can say that some of the mainland drank wine in the 3rd millennium and drank it, moreover, in the hot days with some degree of comfort.

Minoan Crete: 'bulls, wine, women and snakes'[5]

When we stand before the remains of Minoan Crete it seems that the Minoans are no further from us than the tips of our own fingers. They lived three and a half thousand years ago; but they are so near that we can almost touch them, they are nearer than any of the archaic peoples, they are suddenly and surprisingly 'modern'. This 'modernity' beats in their art as it does not beat in the art of the other ancient

[2] Lloyd, Seton, and Mellaart, James, 'Beycesultan Excavations, Fourth Preliminary Report 1957', *Anat. Studs*, VIII, 1958. I am indebted to Mr Seton Lloyd for giving me this information prior to the publication of the Report.

[3] Brea, L. B., 'A Gold Treasure . . .', *ILN*, Aug. 3rd, 1957; see also 'Greater than Troy . . .', *ILN*, Apr. 18th, 1959.

[4] Vickery, 33.

[5] Guthrie, W. K. C., 'Early Greek Religion in the light of the decipherment of Linear B', *Inst. of Class. Studies*, 1959, Bull. No. 6, 41, quoting Kerenyi.

civilizations. The Minoans delight in movement; they love rhythm; they are excited by the changing beauties of the human body. Their figures move with the real movement of personality, utterly different from the stiff poses of Egypt and the statuesque declamations of Mesopotamia.

Look, for example, at the individual faces and the natural bodies of the men who sweep by in a singing procession on the Harvester Vase of Haghia Triada. The naturalism is both 'modern' and European. Look, too, at the Cretan seal which shows two tumblers practising handstands in a field of lilies. The rhythm of the limbs is observed and portrayed from life.

Modern also is their observation of movement in natural things. When the Middle Minoan vase-painters paint an octopus, they make it a pattern of beauty; but it is still an octopus and it moves with an octopod life. This acute sense of movement is echoed in a fresco from the Second City of Phylakopi in the Island of Melos where again it is a marine motif though here of pale-blue flying fish. These fish live as the painter saw them live; they are fish, not formalities.

The Minoans anticipated modern naturalism; and, curiously enough, they anticipated rococo as well. What else but rococo is the wonderful wine *crater*, or mixing bowl, which comes from the early Palace of Phaistos? Its huge painted bowl stood on a painted stem; from hooks on the rim of the bowl hung chains of white rings; and from the shoulder of the bowl and from the stem jutted out the white trumpets of lilies.[6] It was in the Palace of Phaistos about 2000 B.C., and it would not have been out of place in the 18th century of Christian Europe.

Artistically the Minoans were the first to give a European idiom to Early experience. We might have expected that they would have given the same idiom to all of their experience (including wine) and that they would thus have been the first real makers of the European attitude. Somehow this did not happen; somewhere there was a gap; and the Minoan influence, great though it may have been, was not the dominant factor in the growth of European consciousness.

One instance of this occurs in architecture. The great Burnt Palace at Beycesultan in south-west Anatolia, which dates from about 1900 B.C., is an agglutinative building whose rooms seem to have been added to it like the cells of an undisciplined honeycomb. In style it is akin to the Cretan palaces of Phaistos and Mallia, and, evading the question as to whether Anatolia influenced Crete or vice versa, we may call this the 'Minoan style'. But there existed also at Beycesultan another style of architecture and, evading another question as to whether or not it was invented by 'Greek people', this we may call a 'Greek' style. The basis of this 'Greek' style was the megaron house which consisted of a porch, and of a rectangular hall with a round, raised hearth at the end, or in the centre, of the hall. Three of the megaron houses have been excavated from this 'residential district of an earlier Bronze Age city.... Undoubtedly the Megaron with its porch or porches constituted a standard domestic unit, and these columned facades, lining streets and market places in irregular grouping, create a picture which can be mentally constructed'. The antiquity of the style is demonstrated by the 'miniature megaron' also excavated at Beycesultan and dated to approximately 3250 B.C.[7] It was this 'Greek' megaron, and not the honeycomb Minoan, that was to endure into the architecture of classical Greece.

Cupbearer: from the Freize of the Bearers of Tribute 6th century B.C. *Persepolis*

[6]Zervos, C., *L'art de la Crète . . .*, Pls. 552–5; Kenna, V. E. G., *Cretan Seals*, Pls. 9, 204, and Pl. 23. Phylakopi: Nat. Museum, Athens, No. 5844; Levi, D., 'Pottery from the Earliest Phaistos Palace', *ILN*, Supp. Nov. 24th, 1956.

[7]Lloyd, Seton, and Mellaart, James, 'Beycesultan Excavations, Second Preliminary Report, 1955; Fourth Preliminary Report, 1957', *Anat. Studs*, VI, 1956; VIII, 1958. (The hearth could also be oval); Pernier, L., *Il Palazzo Minoico di Festos*, II, fig. 285. Mallia, Gournia: Hutchinson, R. W., 'Prehistoric Town Planning in Crete', *Town Planning Review*, XXI, 1950.

*Black Steatite Rhyton
(detail) from the Palace of
Hagia Triada
Late Minoan, c 1550–
1500 B.C.
Crete, Heraklion Museum*

In other ways, too, Minoan influence proved ultimately unacceptable. Cretan religion was, in part at least, a cult of 'bulls, wine, women and snakes' and this cult, or perhaps one should say the Mycenaean version of this cult, lasted among the Pelasgian people of Greece long after the Minoan and Mycenaean civilizations had been destroyed. In various disguises or transformations it even lasted through Olympian Greece. But the intellect of Olympian Greece was against it. The importance of the female principle in religion became, though only gradually, less and less. Demeter, the Earth Mother of Crete, faded before Zeus the Sky Father.[8] The importance of the snake as a symbol faded also, though again only gradually. So did that of the bull, and the 'bull-game', the Minoan bull 'fight', was never really popular in Europe after Minoan and Mycenaean times. In fact the only places where it ever achieved a comparable status, though not in a religious sense, was in Christian Spain and Portugal.

Wine had a sacred and symbolic value in the libations of the Greeks as it did in the sacrifices of the Romans. It may, in part, have drawn this value from the rituals of Crete. But while it is not too difficult to imagine its rôle in Minoan religion, it is much harder to estimate its importance in Minoan life.

One of the really striking things is the rarity of the vine motif in Minoan art. One would have thought that, if wine were important to the Minoan civilization, the vine would often have been portrayed in frescoes or on vases and on seals. Yet it is not. And we might argue, therefore, that wine was not important to the Minoans. But, apart from its other defects, this argument is disproved by the Mycenaean parallel. There we have indeed, as Sir Arthur Evans has recorded, 'the Goddess on the well-known signet-ring from Mycenae' who 'was certainly seated beneath a vine, if we may judge from its grape-like bunches'. If this does represent a vine the scene is unusual, since the vine is also rare in Mycenaean art; and yet all the same we know from the Linear B tablets that wine played a prominent part in Mycenaean life.[9]

We can argue very little from the Minoan vessels. The *crater* from the Palace of Phaistos may well have been a mixing-bowl for wine; if so, it merely tells us that wine was drunk in Crete at the beginning of the 2nd millennium B.C. It does not tell us how often it was drunk and it does not tell us that the wine was grown in Cretan vineyards. The giant *pithoi* in the magazines of the Palace of Knossos are just as unhelpful for, although some of them must have held wine, we cannot estimate how many of them did so. Most of them, in fact, would have held oil and grain and vegetables, and we might perhaps cite here the example of a prosperous Late Minoan farmhouse to show, or at least to suggest, the preponderance of food-growing over wine-growing towards the end of the Minoan civilization. This farmhouse, which was at Gortynia, near Phaistos in southern Crete, had storerooms 'crowded with huge jars or *pithoi*' and it appears certain that they held peas, broad beans and oil.[10] No trace of wine.

There may have been many reasons why the farm at Gortynia did not grow wine and it is in itself no proof that other farms were equally wineless. Nor is it fair to make any comparison between the life of a Minoan farm – even of a prosperous one – and the life of the Palace of Knossos. Minoan Palaces may have had vineyards where Minoan farms may not.

[8]Pandora, and Pandora into Aphrodite, see Harrison, *Prolegomena*, 283 sqq.

[9]Evans, *Palace of Minos*, IV, 627–8; Furumark, A., *The Mycenaean Pottery*.

[10]Levi, D., 'Country Life in Minoan Crete', *ILN*, Jan. 2nd, 1960.

In his *Palace of Minos*, Sir Arthur Evans wrote: 'It is probable that . . . beer brewed from barley malt was drunk in Minoan Crete from a very early epoch, though its use may have been supplemented in Late Minoan times by wine from the juice of the grape'. While it is difficult to argue with any certainty about the antiquity or the prevalence of beer, it does seem likely that grapes were grown in Middle Minoan times – by 1700 B.C. at the latest – and almost certain that they were grown and that wine was made from them in the Late Minoan period, from 1600–1400 B.C. At the Palace of Phaistos the bottom of a storage jar was found to be full of grape-pips.[11] These may have come from raisins which had been kept for eating but whether they did so or not is largely irrelevant to our purpose for, as we have already seen, the combined presence of grape-pips and jars in the ancient world always infers the possibility of wine. But when we come to Mycenaean times we are in no doubt at all, for the decipherment of the Linear B tablets has told us that wine was well known at Knossos. We need not assume that it was imported, for two of the Knossos tablets suggest the local existence of orchards or vineyards, and this suggestion of Cretan vineyards is confirmed by the discovery of a Mycenaean wine-press at Palaikastro.[12] The press is no temporary or random structure. On the contrary, it is built into a house and the pressing-bed slopes to a *pithos* which is 'built into the fine, hard plaster of the bed to its lip. Into this *pithos* the juice would flow off the slightly sloping bed'.

Now let us return for a moment to the Minoan farm at Gortynia. In one of the largest storerooms of this farm there were 'two large square stone basins set into the floor. These have small central hollows where sediment would collect, and were apparently used for settling the oil . . . a similar basin was found in the storeroom nearby'. It may be that one of these basins was in fact used for making and settling wine since there is a striking resemblance between the Gortynia basins and the fermenting tanks – one thousand two hundred years later – of the Hellenistic winery at Mirmeki in the Crimean area of Southern Russia. At Mirmeki the fermenting tanks were let into the ground and in the south-eastern angle of each of them there was a round, cup-shaped cavity to collect the sediment in the wine.[13] The argument that what was done at Mirmeki was earlier done at Gortynia is of course extremely fallible and the resemblance between the two sets of tanks may only mean that a Hellenistic technique for the making of wine had earlier been a Minoan technique for the making of oil. Still, the resemblance is interesting.

There is, however, another argument and one which also has to do with an oil-making technique. The Gortynia basins seem to have been designed to cope with a comparatively large-scale production of oil. The more normal method for small-scale production was to put the oil together with water into large earthenware jars or settling vats. As the oil floated on the water, the water was drawn off from the jar through a spout near its foot, and after the water came the oil. This method was undoubtedly in common use in Crete and the Cyclades in Middle Minoan times, as we may legitimately infer from the *pithoi* of this type which had been discovered at Knossos and Thera. (To show how widespread this method became we can cite a basically similar vessel of red terracotta which dates from the 4th century B.C. and was discovered at Olynthus in north-eastern Greece, and also the fact that the same method has still been used in Crete in modern times.[14] Now this type of spouted

[11] Evans, *Palace of Minos*, IV, 627–8; Phaistos; Levi, D., *ILN*, Sept. 29th, 1956.

[12] General: *Mycen. Docs.*, 129; cf. Glotz, *Aegean Civilisation*, 163. Knossos: 'The Knossos Tablets', Bennett, E. L., Chadwick, J., Ventris, M. (2nd edn . . . etc.). *Inst. of Class. Studies, Bull.* Supp. No. 7, 1959; *Mycen. Docs.*, 270, 273. Palaikastro: Dawkins, R. M., 'Excavations at Palaikastro, II', *BSA*, IX, 295.

[13] *Mirmeki*, 140 sqq., and fig. 66; cf. Evans, *Palace of Minos*, IV, 631.

[14] Zervos, C., *L'Art des Cyclades*, fig. 344; *Olynthus, Excavations at*, Pt XII; Robinson, D. M., 'Domestic and Public Architecture', 138 and fig. 5.

*The Harvester Cup (detail)
from the Palace of Hagia
Triada
Late Minoan, c 1550–
1500 B.C.
Crete, Heraklion Museum*

pithos could equally well be used for fermenting wine and for drawing off the juice from under the blanket of skins floating at the top of the jar. So far as I am aware there is no proof that such *pithoi* were ever used for this purpose but I see no reason why they should not have been. The Mycenaean wine-press at Palaikastro need not be considered as a standard type of installation. Those who farmed on a small scale, who grew only a few vines and made only a little wine, would have found it much more convenient to ferment their wine in movable *pithoi* without going to the trouble of having a fixed installation. For this purpose the spouted jar would have been ideal. The scarcity of discovered wine-making installations in ancient Crete is no proof that there was a corresponding scarcity of wine.

Such then is the Cretan evidence and it adds up to very little. We may know more if the Minoan Linear A script is deciphered for, whereas the Linear B records of Crete so far deal only with Knossos, Linear A occurs over the rest of the island as well. Meanwhile our picture of Minoan wine is curiously and tantalizingly incomplete.

We get the impression that the Middle Minoans were seldom able to turn to a cup of wine. But I cannot believe that this impression is anywhere near the truth. Even if they did not grow wine themselves, they must have known about it from their overseas contacts, not only from their contact with Egypt in about 2000 B.C., but from other wine-bearing countries as well. And once they had known it, they must have esteemed it; it is inconceivable that a civilization as sophisticated and sensuous as that of the Minoans would have failed to appreciate the new pleasure of

wine. Once discovered, then appreciated, then desired, the ships of the Minoan traders would have done the rest and the harbours of Crete would often have seen the wine-jars of the Eastern Mediterranean.

This is one possibility. The other is that the Middle Minoans, having discovered wine, discovered how to grow it, planted their own vineyards and grew their own wine. It is more than likely that there were vineyards in Crete about 1500 B.C., in the Late Minoan period, and I find it hard to believe that they did not exist at least five hundred years earlier. They may not have been large; and, except for the vineyards which served the Palaces, the viticulture of the Minoans may always have been on a small and 'household' basis. Nevertheless it may have been, and it probably was, perfectly adequate to supply the needs of those of the Cretans who could afford to drink wine.

I suggest then, that one way or the other there must have been wine in earlier Crete, and wine, moreover, in reasonable quantity. We can imagine how it would have appealed to the artistic sensibility of the Minoans, and to their sensual and emotional character; and we can imagine also how it would have fitted into their religion with its ecstatic and orgiastic dances. Did not Daedalus make a dancing-place in Crete for 'Ariadne of the lovely tresses': and did not Ariadne, the daughter of King Minos, become the wife of Dionysos?[15] True that Dionysos was not yet the Great god of wine but the wine of Crete may still have played some part in the beauty of his antique youthfulness.

Wine for Mycenaean Heroes

In the 12th century B.C., the last century of the Mycenaean Age, Agamemnon, '. . . wide-ruling Agamemnon . . . king of men . . .'[16] had his Palace at Mycenae. Menelaus, the husband of Helen of Troy, ruled over Sparta. In the south-west, at 'sandy Pylos' lay the Palace of Nestor, the old man, 'the shepherd of the host'.[17] These Hero-Kings dominated the Peloponnese and ruled over a civilization whose contacts with Minoan Crete were manifold and intimate.

The Mycenaean civilization was more artistic than one could have assumed from the scattered glimpses which Homer gives of it in the *Iliad* and the *Odyssey*. The Hero-Kings and their predecessors on the thrones of the Peloponnese lived among many things of fine imagination and developed skill. From the Shaft Graves of Mycenae come the thin, gold cups which brightened their banquets or the rites of their religion.[18] From the beehive tombs of Pylos come wonderful ornamented daggers. One of them is hilted with pure gold, and inlaid in gold and silver and niello with the figures of leopards stalking among rocks and woods. Another is 'decorated with nautiluses, alternately in silver and gold, swimming among sea creatures in gold, silver and niello'.[19] These daggers are comparable in richness and design to other daggers of the Mycenaean Age, inlaid with gold, silver, electrum and niello, and showing scenes of men hunting lions and of cheetah chasing wild duck in a papyrus marsh.[20]

Artistic skill not only decorated daggers but also painted the walls of palaces. It did so at Pylos, as it did at Mycenae, and at Tiryns on the Bay of Argos below Mycenae. Frescoes from the later palace at Tiryns, in the 13th century B.C., show a procession of women bearing gifts, a boar hunt, and a bull fight. The boar hunt, watched by women in a chariot, is painted in colours of white, yellow-brown, brick-red and pale blue. In the bull fight, or bull-game – a scene of great vitality – the bull's body is white dappled with brick-red, while the body of the acrobatic bull-fighter is also white, and both of them are painted against a background of pale blue-grey.[21] The reference to the bull-game of Crete is obvious. The octopus motif of Minoan Crete is present too, for at Pylos in one of the tombs there was found not only 'a great jar with octopus and sea-scape decoration' but also an offering table whose circular top was painted with an octopus in red.[22]

In the beehive tomb of a Mycenaean prince at Pylos lay a carnelian gem-seal. On the seal is cut the figure of a naked-breasted woman wearing a flounced skirt.[23] She offers lilies at an altar which bears olive branches between, or behind, the horns of consecration. Without much doubt the cult in which she is taking part is Minoan as well as Mycenaean but how much the religion of Mycenaean Greece was made

[15] *CAH*, I, 175; *Iliad*, XVIII.

[16] *Iliad*, I.

[17] *Iliad*, II, X.

[18] Nat. Museum, Athens, Nos. 220, 392, 393.

[19] Marinatos, S., '. . . an unplundered tomb at Nestor's Pylos . . .', *ILN*, Apr. 6th, 1957.

[20] Nat. Museum, Athens, Nos. 394, 765.

[21] Nat. Museum, Athens, Nos. 5878–5882 (including a fresco of spearmen from the older Palace), and No. 1595. Pylos: see Blegen, C. W., 'The Palace of Nestor Excavations of 1955', *AJA*, 60, 1956.

[22] See fn. 19.

[23] *ILN*, Apr. 27th, 1957.

by the Minoans and how much by the Mycenaeans themselves is difficult to tell. Perhaps the histories of Artemis and Pan will serve to illustrate two forces that worked in the making of the Mycenaean religion.

Primitive Greek Artemis was a Goddess of Fertility. She was of Minoan origin and her cult included ecstatic and orgiastic dances. Pan was a local god of Arcadia in the Central Peloponnese and he was no doubt an Arcadian 'invention'. They each have a different birthplace but they both move in a world of primitive, emotional religion, a world which, in Mycenaean times, included such Minoan characteristics as the sacred doves, the sacred bull and worship of the Great Mother, the Goddess of the Double-Axe.[24]

Then observe the different fates of the two divinities. Artemis is transformed under the pressure of the Olympian religion and from being a mother-deity she becomes a virgin goddess. Pan eludes the Olympian embrace. It is true that Athens welcomed him after the Battle of Marathon and, near the Acropolis, 'the worship of Pan was established in the ancient dancing-ground of the Agraulids'.[25] He remains nevertheless a primitive god, an old deity who lives below the intellect of classical Greece and who continues to reflect the attitude of an earlier world.

This brief disquisition is not meant to be a sortie into comparative religion. It is an example – there are many more – of how the threads run through from one period into another. We can thus argue, or at least imagine, backwards from a later period to an earlier one, from the time of Hesiod and Homer to the time of Nestor and Agamemnon. We cannot, of course, do so with certainty for sometimes the threads are transformed in their growth – as was Artemis. But viticulture – like Pan and the religion of the people – is on the whole a conservative thing and our argument backwards from a known fact will tend to produce a reasonable guess. And therefore also, since the relations between Greece and Crete were so intimate in the time of the Later Minoans, it will be reasonable to apply to Minoan Crete the experience of Mycenaean Greece.

Fortunately the Mycenaeans were a literate people. Fortunately also they were literate in a minute and bureaucratic way. The Linear B tablets which record the details of their administration record also the presence of wine. From excavations we could have assumed that wine was a part of Mycenaean life; among the modern vines of Rutsi near Pylos, for instance, lies the tomb of the Nautilus Dagger and there a complete wine-jar was set by the door of the tomb.[26] But what we could have assumed from archaeology is now confirmed by Linear B.

Mycenaean wine occurs both in a religious and a civil context.★ A Linear B tablet from Pylos four times mentions wine and seems to record 204, or perhaps 216, litres of wine as a contribution to the worship of Poseidon – Poseidon, of course, in Mycenaean, not in Olympian, dress. There are a number of other mentions of wine on Pylos tablets of about 1200 B.C. and four of the clay sealings recently found in the wine magazine of Nestor's Palace are inscribed with the ideogram for 'wine'. There is also an ideogram at Pylos which appears to mean either must or some particular kind of wine, while on one of the inscribed seals there is a possible reading of *melition*. This may have been mead; but it may also have been a version of the

★For wines of the ancient Greek world, from Minoan and Mycenaean times onwards, and for the location of their vineyards, see Appendix B.

[24]Nilsson, N. M. P., *The Minoan-Mycenaean Religion and its Survival in Greek Religion*, 503-4, 509, 513; *CAH*, II, 464.

[25]Harrison, *Prolegomena*, 289.

[26]See fn. 19.

melitites, or honied wine, of the later Greeks. At Mycenae a tablet, which is possibly a ration list, records twenty-four litres of wine.[27] At Tiryns the evidence is less explicit. On a gold ring the Great Goddess is shown being given a first offering of wine, or probably of wine, and in the ruins of Tiryns the excavators found quantities of grape-pips 'of unusual size'. From Sparta we have two clay jar-sealings of Mycenaean date and impressions on the lower face of each are almost certainly those of vine leaves.[28] The decipherment of Linear B has not only confirmed the existence of wine in Mycenaean Greece but has also enabled us to get some idea of the quantities of wine that were produced in Peloponnesian vineyards. Individual figures on a Pylos ritual tablet build up to the total of 204, or possibly 216 litres of wine as a contribution to Poseidon. This ritual tablet, taken by itself, does not point to any large scale production since the amount of wine which it records is only about that of a single *barrique* in modern Bordeaux. Another tablet from Pylos, however, shows a little over twice as much: '. . . due from Dunios: 2220 (litres) of barley, 526 of *eating* olives, 468 of wine, fifteen rams . . .'[29] This is doing better, but it is still not evidence of large-scale viticulture.

These figures, or at least the Poseidon figures, cannot be telling us the whole story. Human beings do not grow wine simply and entirely for the service of their gods, and a community which produced half a litre of wine a day for Poseidon – did the dove-goddess at Pylos,[30] one wonders, get a similar ration ? – would certainly have produced wine for its own consumption or, at any rate, for the consumption of its wealthier or more powerful members. In fact we do have some evidence to show that the production of wine at Pylos was not inconsiderable.

This evidence is the wine-cellar of Nestor's Palace. The cellar, only recently excavated, not only indicates the extent of production but also gives us a valuable picture of the wine-organisation of a Mycenaean king. The cellar – it is really a magazine – is about forty feet long; down one wall was set a row of large jars; a double row ran down the middle of the cellar; and there may have been a fourth row of jars down the other long wall. There were at least thirty-five jars in the magazine when the Palace was destroyed by fire, 'and there may have been a good many more'. The capacity of the best preserved of the jars is somewhere about 200 litres so that the cellar could have held at least 6,000 litres of wine. This may mean that 6,000 litres were made for the Palace at every vintage, but, if some of the wine in the cellar was being matured for two or three, or more, years, then the annual intake of the cellar (and perhaps also the total size of the vintage) would of course have been less than 6,000 litres.

That it was wine which went into the jars we know from the seals which have been discovered at the Palace and from them too we can argue something about the delivery of the wine. It was, it seems, brought to the Palace in skin bags, was there checked in by an official, and was then emptied into the *pithoi* of the magazine.[31] It must have been a busy time after the vintage, as the labourers arrived with their bulging wine skins and the cellar was filled up for another year of Mycenaean drinking.

We can make some general and, I think, reasonable assumptions about the wine that was drunk by Nestor at Pylos, by Agamemnon and Clytemnestra at Mycenae, and by Menelaus and Helen at Sparta – assuming that Helen was a real person and

[27] Pylos: *Mycen. Docs.*, Tablet 171, pp. 172–4, 219–20, 223. Nestor's Palace and melition: Lang, Mabel, 'The Palace of Nestor Excavations of 1958', AJA, 63, 1959, 133–4. Melites: refs in fn. 142. Mycenae: Chadwick, J., 'The Mycenae Tablets, II'; ed. Bennett, E. L., *Trans. American Philosophical Society*, New Series, XLVIII, Pt I, 1958.

[28] Tiryns: Nilsson, N. M. P., *The Minoan-Mycenaean Religion and its Survival . . .*, 288; Schliemann, H., *Tiryns*, 83. Sparta: Dawkins, R. M., 'Excavations at Sparta', BSA, XVI, 1909–10.

[29] *Mycen. Docs.*, 220, 281 sqq.

[30] *Mycen. Docs.*, 287.

[31] Blegen, C. W., and Lang, Mabel, 'The Palace of Nestor Excavations of 1958', AJA, 63, 1959, and Pt II of this report, by Mabel Lang, on the Tablets. I am more than grateful to Miss Lang for giving me the estimated capacity of the cellar. Miss Lang emphasizes that the estimate is of necessity vague since no intact jar has been preserved.

not the goddess of an ancient tree-cult.[32] Their wine would usually have been a *vin ordinaire*, or perhaps one should say a carafe-wine, and it would have been drunk in the year after the vintage. It may have been racked by means of a siphon, from one pithos to another but this, I think, is unlikely. Nevertheless, it would have been moderately clear. In the first place, the newly fermented wine would have been run off the grape husks into the wine skins destined for the Palace. In the second place, any sediment left in the wine would have sunk to the bottom of the store-room pithos and the wine ladled from the pithos for drinking would have been more or less clear until the level sank towards the bottom of the jar. In other cases, however, and particularly with small, domestic vintaging the grapes may have been trodden, the must fermented, and the wine kept on its lees in one and the same pithos and the wine, when it came to be drunk, may have been far from translucent. Perhaps strainers were used. Two of them, semi-spherical dipper-scoops whose bases were pierced, have been found in the House of Sphinxes at Mycenae but it is very doubtful if these were used for wine.[33] It is possible, of course, that the wine was strained through a cloth before it came to table but of this we cannot be certain. Furthermore, we must remember that the drinking in Mycenaean Greece, as in Minoan Crete, was done from vessels of wood or pottery or metal, none of which gives the best opportunity for judging the clearness of a wine.

We can suggest that the Mycenaeans had three types of drink: one-year-old wine, mead, and honied wine, but we cannot be sure that they had both the latter. I think it likely that they did and I think it likely also that they had raisin-wine, as did the other ancient peoples by all of whom its extra body and sweetness would have been much appreciated. To these four types of Mycenaean drink we can, perhaps, add a fifth - matured wine, wine kept in the cellar for longer than the one year after its vintaging.

There is no reason why the Mycenaeans should not have matured their wine. Provided that the wine, when it was made, was potentially stable, and provided that the jars were properly sealed, the wine should have kept quite well for a period of years. That the jars could in fact be properly sealed we know from Mycenaean Sparta and this, at Sparta, is how it was done: 'In the mouth of the jar was placed a potsherd, roughly shaped into a circular form . . . . The disc prevented the soft clay from falling into the jar. On the lower faces of the sealings are the impressions of leaves, almost certainly of the vine. These leaves were evidently laid above the round sherd, to prevent any clay falling into the jar at its edges . . . . Over these leaves was put the mass of clay which served as a stopper. This was kept in place by cords . . .'[34] A variant technique can be seen in the stoppered spouts of oil jars in the House of the Oil Merchant at Mycenae. Here a clay stopper, shaped somewhat like a cork, was first put into the spout of the jar. It was then fastened with a string and sealed in with a clay cap which covered the whole spout. Homer called this type of clay cap Κρήδεμνον which meant a woman's head-dress, and the word was so used because the clay hung over and round the spout like a veil or kerchief hung over and round the head of a woman.[35] Interestingly enough, Homer uses it to describe the fastening of a lidded jar of old wine in the cellar of Nestor at Pylos and Homer is thus describing a technique which actually existed in the Mycenaean world. But this does not allow us to say that, when he speaks of Nestor's old wine, he is also

[32]Nilsson, N. M. P., *The Minoan-Mycenaean Religion and its Survival . . .*, 528, 531, though see also 532; cf. Page, Denys L., *History and the Homeric Iliad*, 257-8, 287, fn. 90.

[33]Wace, A. J. B., 'Light on the Earliest Greek Culture . . .' *ILN*, May 28th, 1955. For conical strainers, dating M.M.III or L.M.I, in the Aegean, see Vickery, 26-7; but these may have been used for making cheese.

[34]Dawkins, R. M., 'Excavations at Sparta', *BSA*, XVI, 1909-10.

[35]Chadwick, J., 'The Mycenae Tablets, II', ed. Bennett, E. L., *Trans. American Philosophical Soc.*, New Series, XLVIII, Pt I, 1958; *Odyssey*, III, 392.

describing the fact of Mycenaean maturing, for his description of the clay cap may be taken from his own, later, Homeric Age; and so, of course, may his description of old wine.

Like the Egyptians, the Mycenaeans labelled their jars and at Sparta, for instance, one of the seals was stamped nine times in all by a Mycenaean gem. Four of the Pylos sealings carry the ideogram for 'wine'. None of these, however, implies any system of recording vintage years for the purpose of maturing the wine. They are, like the Egyptian 'labels', records of responsibility and accountancy. So much wine came from so-and-so and it has been checked in. This wine was made by so-and-so and he is responsible for its goodness. The same practice seems to have existed – not unnaturally – with oil as well as with wine. On the oil jars at Mycenae there are signet stamps, one showing 'a cow or an ox scratching its ear with its hind leg', while another more romantically shows 'three girls dancing',[36] and these stamps appear to have recorded either the producer of the oil or the merchant's trade-mark under which the oil was sold.

In the Mycenaean Age traders from the Aegean had ventured into the central Mediterranean. They touched south-eastern Italy at the harbour of Tarentum. As early as the 16th century B.C. Greek sailors had voyaged to the Lipari Islands off the north coast of Sicily. In Sicily itself Acragas was in contact with the Mycenaeans while the harbour of Syracuse attracted a flourishing trade. There, near the site of modern Syracuse, were the Siculan settlements of Thapsos, Cozzo Pantano, Milocca, and Plemmirio; and there the native Siculi received the pottery, the glass

[36]Spara: fn. 34. Pylos: fn. 31. Mycenae: fn. 35.

*Odysseus putting out
Cyclop's Eye
Proto-Attic Amphora from
Eleusis
7th century* B.C.
Eleusis, Museum

beads and the gold rings of Mycenaean civilization as well as instruction in the art of building beehive tombs.[37]

Oil may have been one of the articles of commerce carried in Aegean ships. Wine may have been another. But the extent of a trade in wine is much more doubtful than that of a trade in oil. It depended, of course, upon the amount of wine produced in Greek and Aegean vineyards and upon the amount which the Mycenaeans were willing to release for export. We have as yet no reason to assume that Greek production was over-abundant and therefore we cannot say that the trade in wine was anything except a small-scale luxury commerce. Greek ships were no doubt accustomed to carry wine as a ration for the crews and the first vinous experience of many a western native would have been when he shared a cup of wine with a Mycenaean sailor. Once the native got the taste he would have demanded more and the wine first offered in courtesy would later have been offered for sale. In the *Odyssey* Homer illustrates the rougher side of this type of intercourse when he tells the story of the milk-drinking Cyclops being doped by the strange and potent drink of wine which Odysseus gave him.

'Then I stood by the Cyclops and spake to him, holding in my hands an ivy bowl of the dark wine: "Cyclops, take and drink wine after thy feast of man's meat, that thou mayest know what manner of drink this was that our ship held. And lo, I was bringing it thee as a drink offering, if haply thou mayest take pity and send me on my way home' . . . again I handed him the dark wine. Thrice I bear and gave it him, and thrice in his folly he drank it to the lees.'[38]

The Cyclops, a simple creature at the best of times, not unnaturally became intoxicated.

This is the archetypal story of the coming of wine to an unskilled native people. Homer has adapted it to the purpose of his plot but basically it is no different from the obvious original which Pindar reflects in his lines:

> Then when the wild men knew
> The scent of honeyed wine that tames men's
> > souls,
> Straight from the board they thrust the white
> > milk-bowls
> With hurrying hands, and of their own will flew
> To the horns of silver wrought
> And drank and were distraught.[39]

Sometimes the experience was unnerving. Icarios, the mythological shape of an undoubtedly real person, introduced the vine into Attica and first made Attic wine. The villagers of Icaria to whom he gave this new gift rapidly became drunk and their neighbours, believing that the intoxicated men had been poisoned, killed Icarios.[40] Such are the rewards of careless benefaction. But, while the intoxication of the Cyclops may have been a Mycenaean phenomenon, the fate of Icarios would

[37] *CAH*, I, 104; II, 459, 463, 590; Dunbabin, 28, 29, 309-10; Phillips, E. D., 'The Isla of Aeolus', *Antiquity*, 120, 1956; Peet, T. E., *The Stone and Bronze Ages in Italy and Sicily*, 432 sqq.

[38] Bk IX. But note that, near the land of the Cyclops, there were vines which 'know no decay'.

[39] Frag. 44, quoted in Harrison, *Prolegomena*, 385.

[40] Kerényi, C., *The Gods of the Greeks*, 236; Harrison, *Prolegomena*, 148.

certainly not have been a Mycenaean disaster; or not, at all events, in the 14th and
13th centuries B.C. The later Mycenaeans knew far too much about wine.

It was an Age of power and magnificence. Kings who delighted in gold and
bronze lived in the massive citadels which dominated Mycenaean Greece. Tiryns
'of the great walls'[41] guarded the Bay of Argos. Mycenae with its huge walls
watched the route that went north through the hills towards Corinth and central
Greece where, in Boeotia, lay the Mycenaean cities of Thebes and Orchomenus
and the great, four-gated citadel of Goulas. Gold cups, gold-inlaid daggers, and
bronze mirrors with ivory handles were among the treasures of Mycenaean rank.
The magnificence of its more powerful kings is exemplified in the beehive tomb
of Mycenae – the 'Treasury of Atreus' – for this sepulchre of a 14th-century king
was decorated with bronze and gold and ivory.[42] Jewellery was an intimate part
of their lives as it was also of their deaths. In the tomb among the vines of Rutsi
near Pylos lay a young Mycenaean princess wearing a necklace of polychrome
beads and two of the men in this same tomb wore 'huge necklaces of amber'.[43]

The humbler folk, the merchants and craftsmen, and some of the farmers and
vine-dressers, who lived in the neighbourhood of the Palaces, like those who lived
in residential areas on the hills around Mycenae and those in the plain around
Tiryns, may have admired the metallic splendour of their rulers but most of them
had to be content with simpler ware. They would have drunk their wine, and this
goes for many of the wealthy too, out of pottery; sometimes from stemmed goblets
which in shape are not unlike the modern champagne glass, and sometimes from
shallow, stemless cups. It is curious to think that they would often have done so in
houses that may have resembled the black-and-white houses of English Tudor

[41] *Iliad*, II.

[42] *CAH*, II, 457–8.

[43] Fn. 19.

93

architecture; or such, at any rate, would have been the case at Mycenae for the House of Sphinxes there had upper walls made of mud-brick strengthened by horizontal and perpendicular beams of wood[44] and if the wood were neither painted nor plastered over, the effect would indeed have been 'Tudor'. It is hard to imagine the Heroes looking down from their citadel upon an 'English' village in the brilliant light of Argolis.

It must have been even harder for those Heroes to imagine that the power and magnificence of their civilization would be obliterated. Somewhere about the beginning of the 12th century the City of Troy had fallen and the Heroes returned home to their various fates of triumph or misfortune. And then, towards the close of that same 12th century, there came the end. The Dorian Invasions moved south through Greece, bringing with them a Dark Age. In that darkness Mycenae was burnt and the Mycenaean civilization was shattered and forgotten.

The Homeric Mirror

In the 11th, 10th, and 9th centuries B.C. – the dark centuries at the beginning of the Iron Age – the rather coarse artistry of Geometric vase-painting seems to show that the old beauty had been lost. But how much of the older Minoan and Mycenaean world had really been forgotten? How much had lingered on in Attica and the eastern Aegean where the peoples had not been overwhelmed by the Dorian Invasion?

An answer lies in Homer but the answer is unsatisfactory. In the first place Homer lived, most probably, in the 8th century B.C. In the second place the *Iliad* which we now have, and for that matter the *Odyssey* also, are derived from 'standard' editions which were made in Athens in the 6th century B.C. 'Homer's' *Iliad* and *Odyssey* may thus have reflected a certain amount of the life of the 8th, or even the 9th, centuries, while 'our' Athenian versions may have incorporated something of the experience of the 6th or 7th centuries. Some of the threads in the Homeric poems may therefore run back to Mycenaean times; others may have been incorporated during the 9th and 8th centuries; yet others, though perhaps fewer, may have been added to the pattern in the 7th and 6th.

A vexed question in the Homeric Argument is that of the personality of Homer. Was 'he' a multiple person, a group or craft-college of bards, or was he an individual poet? The latter seems the more likely, even though nothing is known about the man himself. But fortunately for our argument the personality of Homer does not greatly matter. Our concern is with four factors, all of them widely accepted: the existence of a 'standard' Athenian version in the 6th century; the existence of a Homeric 'personality' in the 8th century; the great probability that some of the poems which went into the Homeric *Iliad* were sung, in one form or another, throughout the Dark Ages of the Dorian Conquest; and the near-certainty that a few of the passages in 'our' *Iliad* go back into the Mycenaean Age itself.[45]

One thing is quite clear: the Homeric mirror does not reflect anything like the full reality of the Mycenaean world. We could never have gathered from Homer that the Mycenaeans were a literate people; his poems give us scanty information about Mycenaean art; they tell us even less about Mycenaean religion. About

[44] Wace, A. J. B., 'Domestic Life in Ancient Mycenae . . .', *ILN*, Feb. 2nd, 1957.

[45] See Bibliography to this Chapter for works on the Homeric Argument; also *CAH*, II, 502 sqq.; *OCD*, 'Homer'.

Mycenaean wine, however, they may prove to be a fairly accurate mirror. Viticulture in the ancient world was, as I have already remarked, a conservative profession and I see little reason to think that viticultural methods changed in any radical degree – if they changed at all – between the time of Agamemnon and the time of Homer. And there is this point too, that in the ancient world a viticultural practice is always older than its first literary record. When Homer sings of wine, he is singing of an ancient thing.

Telemachus, seeking for news of his father, came to Sparta, 'to the hollow land of Lacedaemon'. He drove to the house of Menelaus where the neighbours and kinsmen of Menelaus were feasting in the Great Hall: '. . . among them a divine minstrel was singing to the lyre, and as he began the song two tumblers in the company whirled through the midst of them'.[46] We can accept this is a true picture of one side of Mycenaean feasting, for the presence of musicians or dancers or acrobats was almost *de rigueur* at the wealthier feasts of the older world; and in this context we may perhaps recall the seal from Knossos which showed two tumblers practising in a field of lilies. We find the acrobats again in classical Greece. Xenophon describes in his *Symposium* an imaginary feast which is supposed to have taken place at a house in the Piraeus on the occasion of the Panathenaic Festival of 422 B.C. The guests were entertained by a troupe owned, or at least managed, by a Syracusan impresario. The troupe consisted of a flute-girl, a dancing girl who was also a juggler and acrobat, and a boy who both danced and played the harp. Part of the dancing girl's performance was to juggle with twelve hoops while she was dancing, and to somersault into and out of 'a large hoop studded with a bristling row of upright swords'.[47] Professionally she was a descendant of the tumblers of Menelaus.

But here we must remark upon a difference, and a striking difference, between the Heroes of Homer and those who actually lived in the Mycenaean Palaces. This is in the matter of diet. The Homeric nobles, as described by Homer, lived almost entirely on bread and meat, varied, if one can call it variety, by such delicacies as 'the great pudding, stuffed with fat and blood' which Antinous gave to Odysseus. Their sacrifices to the gods, too, were usually of barley-meal and meat.[48] It seems

[46] *Odyssey*, IV; (and Loeb edn.).

[47] Xen., *Symposium*, II, 1–11.

[48] *Odyssey*, XVIII; *Iliad*, II, IX, etc.

*The Trojan Horse (detail)
from Relief Amphora
Mykonos,
late 7th century* B.C.
Mykonos, Museum

that this insistence on meat, and especially on roasted meat, came down into Greece with the Dorians for the Mycenaean diet was much more diverse and much more vegetarian. The Minoans and Mycenaeans did, it is true, eat the meat of sheep and pigs but they also ate fish, which the Homeric Heroes did not, and we know that, at Mycenae at least, oysters and mussels were eaten too. The basis of the Minoan, as of the Mycenaean, diet was grain, either in the form of wheat, or barley, or flour. These are common entries on the Linear B tablets and the rations are often accompanied by an issue of figs or olives. Among the vegetables in general use were peas, chick peas, broad beans and lentils while the tablets also list 'coriander . . . the most frequent . . . and . . . celery, cumin, cyperus, fennel, mint, pennyroyal, safflower and sesame'.[49]

Oil is a frequent mention on the Linear B tablets and the written record is exemplified by the oil store-rooms behind the throne room in the Palace of Nestor. Some of it would have been used for food: some perhaps for anointing the body, as was done in Homeric Sparta: and some for anointing the statues or vestments of the gods and for making fragrant their sanctuaries. The Pylos tablets even allow us to catch a faint breath of this fragrance for they tell us: 'Sage-scented for anointing – oil' and 'rose-scented for anointing – oil.'[50]

Now this matter of diet must make us pause and consider. When Homer is dealing with the eating habits of his Heroes, he is, it would seem, describing Dorians and only Dorians. He is not describing Mycenaeans. But when he is dealing with their drinking habits, is he then describing only Dorians? Or can we assume that his wine references go back to an earlier, and Mycenaean, context?

I think that on the whole we can. And I think that one case in point is the extraordinary 'drink' that was 'drunk' by Nestor during the Siege of Troy. Hekamede, the 'fair-tressed', Hekamede whom the old man Nestor won from the sack of Tenedos, mixed it for him.

'First she drew before them a fair table, polished well, with feet of cyanus, and thereon a vessel of bronze, with onion, for relish to the drink, and pale honey, and the grain of sacred barley, and beside it a right goodly cup, that the old man brought from home, embossed with studs of gold, and four handles there were to it, and round each two golden doves were feeding, and to the cup were two feet below. . . . In this cup the woman, like unto the goddesses, mixed a mess for them, with Pramnian wine, and therein grated cheese of goats' milk, with a grater of bronze, and scattered white barley thereover, and bade them drink. . . .'[51]

This 'drink' is more accurately described in the *Odyssey* as food. There Circe, the enchantress, mixed up for the followers of Odysseus 'a mess of cheese and barley-meal and yellow honey with Pramnian wine' (but she also 'mixed harmful drugs with the food to make them utterly forget their own country').[52]

One might imagine that this alcoholic porridge was a relic bequeathed to Homer by semi-barbarous Dorians, but I have little doubt that he is going back behind the Dorians and is describing a drink of much greater antiquity. An early Mycenaean context for Hekamede's stirabout might possibly be indicated by the fact that Nestor's cup, as described by Homer, is not unlike a smaller, and two-handled,

Carriers of Offerings from the Tomb of Nakht c 1360 B.C. Thebes, Valley of Nobles

[49] *Mycen. Docs.*, 59, 129, 130, 131, 215; Vickery, 32 sqq.; and for other fruits, 54; Bennett, E. L., Chadwick, J., Ventris, M., and Householder, F. W., 'The Knossos Tablets', *Inst. Class. Studs., Bull.* Supp. No. 7, 48, 49, 50, 65, 76, 1959; Chadwick, J., 'The Mycenae Tablets, II', ed. Bennett, E. L., *Trans. American Philosophical Soc.*, New Series, XLVIII, 107 sqq., 1958.

[50] *Mycen. Docs.*, 129, 130; Blegen, C. W., 'The Palace of Nestor Excavations of 1955', *AJA*, 60, 1956; Bennett, E. L., 'The Olive Oil Tablets of Pylos', *Sem. de Filol. Clasica, Univ. de Salamanca*, 54, 57, 1958. Homeric Sparta: *Odyssey*, IV.

[51] *Iliad*, XI.

[52] *Odyssey*, X.

golden cup with doves on the handles, which comes from the fourth Shaft Grave at Mycenae.[53] If Homer was describing a Mycenaean cup, he may also have been describing a Mycenaean drink. But this argument is remarkably frail and we have to seek support from elsewhere. We find it in the 3rd millennium in Sumeria where *kas-gig*, or the 'black drink', was made from more or less equal parts of date-wine, paste, and old liquor. We find it also during the 3rd Dynasty of Ur, when wine was 'mixed with Esa', the latter being a kind of flour.[54] The continuing popularity of this type of mixture is witnessed by the fact that it was known among the classical Greeks who called it ὀινοῦττα – Aristophanes mentions it – and who made it from barley mixed with wine, water, and oil. As a cake or porridge, it was eaten by the rowers in the Greek ships. In other parts of the Greek world a somewhat similar, though more liquid, mixture was treated as a drink. Hegesander, for example, reports that the people of the 'Therad' islands drank 'wine with pulse instead of barley-meal sprinkled on it . . .'[55] From its antiquity, therefore, this 'drink' could easily have existed in Mycenaean times; from its continuing popularity it is likely that it did so. And here one might observe that the diet of classical Greece was basically like that of the Mycenaeans. The ὀινοῦττα, or some variant of it, may thus have appealed to the Mycenaean, as it did to the classical, Greeks. Let us, at least tentatively, give a Mycenaean dating to Nestor's drink and to Circe's potion.

Pramnian wine occurs in both these stirabouts and it is tempting to believe that Pramnian was a raisin wine and one which, from its nature, would stand long keeping. Old, sweet wine might thus have been a Mycenaean pleasure. But here, when we are trying to decide on a Mycenaean liking for sweet wine, we get no help from Homer. To describe wine he uses a word which has been translated as sweet; and he uses it so frequently that it is almost a stock description; but it does not mean that the wine was sweet so much as that it was sound. His constant use of the word is surely illuminating for he is writing about the high-born ones of the Mycenaean world and they were the ones who get the best of whatever was going. Naturally also they got the best of the wine: but if the best is described as being sound, what was the worst like? On the other hand there does seem to be a real mention of sweet wine in the *Iliad* where Hector's mother says to him 'tarry till I bring thee honey-sweet wine, that thou mayest pour libation to Zeus and all the immortals first, and then shalt thou thyself also be refreshed if thou wilt drink' and 'great Hector of the glancing helm answered her: "Bring me no honey-hearted wine, my lady mother, lest thou cripple me of my courage and I be forgetful of my might".'[56] Admittedly this may not have been a 'Pramnian' raisin wine. It could have been a Trojan version of the *melition* which (possibly) appears in the cellar of Nestor at Pylos and it may thus have been either mead or wine mixed with honey.

Even so we cannot discount the probability that the Mycenaeans did make raisin wine. Hesiod, in his *Works and Days*, describes the drying of grapes to make such a liquor. In September, he says, cut off all the grape-clusters, dry them for ten days and nights, cover them for five, 'and on the sixth day draw off into vessels the gifts of joyful Dionysos'.[57] Hesiod, it is true, may be a little later than Homer but it is obvious that he was not the inventor of raisin-wine. Homer himself, in his description of the garden and vineyard of Alcinous, refers to grapes drying in the heat and seems to imply a grape-drying floor which, in other circumstances, would no

[53] Nat. Museum, Athens, No. 412.

[54] Genouillac, *TSA*, li, and tablets, *passim* (Bibl. Ch. 2); *Ur Excavations*, III, Nos. 67, 149 (Bibl. Ch. 2).

[55] Aristophanes, *Plutus*, 1121; Ath-E, X, 432d.

[56] *Iliad*, VI

[57] Hes., 609–17.

Feast:detail
from wall painting
Tomb of Neb–Amun,
c 1400 B.C.
Thebes

doubt have served also as a threshing floor and a dancing ground.[58] Homer's picture most probably represents the typical orchard-vineyard of Mycenaean times and we can plausibly imagine the Mycenaeans drying their grapes on the threshing floors of Pylos and Argolis, as the Minoans may have done on the threshing floors or dancing-grounds of Crete.

In earlier, as in later, times the drinking of raisin-wine may have been an occasional, rather than a usual, occurrence, the wine being treated as an *aperitif* or as a luxury. We know nothing about its use in Mycenaean or Minoan times, but we know that in later centuries it had a wide and lasting popularity. Psithian, which was both the name of a vine and of the raisin-wine made from it, was known in Classical Greece and Imperial Rome and it seems to have been a muscatel wine.

> 'When I'd gathered a thirst,
> After giving me first
> For a sample, and neat,
> Some Psithian Sweet . . . .'

says Eubulus while Anaxandrides, another poet of the Middle Comedy, has merely left us the haunting remark '. . . half a gallon of Psithian mixed'. In Roman times Crete made the best raisin-wine of all and it was this wine which Dioscorides equated with Pramnian and *protropon*. A raisin-must called *scybelites* was made in Galatia or Pamphylia in Asia Minor while Tmolitan, a sweet wine made in Lydia in Asia Minor and considered by Virgil to be excellent, was sometimes used for blending with dry wines and may have been made from dried, or partly dried, grapes.[59]

In the course of his Epic, the *Iliad*, Homer several times mentions vineyards and from the context in which some of these passages occur we can properly assume that he is recording actual vineyard areas of the Mycenaean world. From Boeotia he cites 'Arne rich in vineyards', from north-western Euboea 'Histiaia rich in vines'. From Argolis in the Peloponnese he gives us 'Epidauros full of vines', and from, most probably, Messinia in the Peloponnese 'Pedasos land of vines . . . on the uttermost border of sandy Pylos'. From north-western Greece we have the vineyards of Ithaca, the kingdom of Odysseus, which may be either the modern Ithaca or Leucas a little to the north. And from Asia Minor comes 'Phrygia, the land of vines' whose wine had perhaps been drunk by Priam and his sons in the doomed city of Troy.

Of the number of reasons why we can say that some of these vineyards were Mycenaean, one in particular is instructive. Homer speaks of 'Arne rich in vineyards'. But by the time when 'Homer' lived, in the 8th century B.C., the vineyards of Arne had ceased to exist. They had completely disappeared in the Dorian Invasion. They must, therefore, have been Mycenaean. And since the vines of Histiaia and Epidauros are recorded in the same context they must surely be Mycenaean as well.

At last then we can supplement the evidence which we have from excavations and from Linear B, and we can add these vineyards to those which have been (almost certainly) given to us by the jar-seals of Sparta and (certainly) by the

[58] *Odyssey*, VII; see Ure, A. D., 'Threshing Floor or Vineyard', *The Classical Quarterly*, New Series, V, 1955.

[59] Psithian: *FAC*, II, Eubulus, 138; Anaxandrides, 71; Ath-E, I, 28f; Virgil, II, 93; Plin., XIV, 80, 81. Cretan: Plin., XIV, 81; Ath-E, X, 440e-f; Dioscorides, *Herbal*, V, 9; and *CIL*, IV, Supp. I and II, No. 5526. Scybelites: Plin., XIV, 80. Tmolitan: Virgil, II, 98; Plin., XIV, 74; Strab., 14, 1, 15; Ovid, *Met.*, VI, 15; XI, 86.

Linear B tablets of Pylos. These latter confirm also the probability of the Homeric 'Pedasos land of vines'. Ithaca is a different matter. We cannot be sure of the existence of the vineyards of Odysseus and, even if they did exist, we cannot be sure of their location for the location of Homeric Ithaca is, to say the least of it, unproven. It has been suggested that the Ithaca of Odysseus is the modern Leucas, off the north-west coast of Greece; if so, then we may imagine that the wine of Odysseus was of quite good quality, since, in the 3rd century B.C., Leucadian wine was held in some esteem. At any rate it would probably have been better than the Mycenaean wine of Epidauros, for the Meilissian wine of Epidauros was considered in the 4th century B.C. to be only just drinkable. We might add that, if the Mycenaean wine of Histiaia was the same as that which in the 3rd century B.C. was called Oretic (which may well have been the case), then it was in the same class of quality as the wine of Leucas. Homer's Phrygian vineyards may have been Mycenaean.[60]

The wine which Homer has made most famous is the wine that came from Maronea in Thrace for it was Maronean which Odysséus carried with him in a goat-skin and gave to the Cyclops. It was a fragrant, dark wine, so dark that it was almost black; and it was so strong that when Maron, the legendary priest who had originally given it to Odysseus, drank this 'red wine honey sweet' he would dilute its strength with twenty measures of water.

More interesting still than the quality of this (Mycenaean?) wine of the *Odyssey* is the story which Homer tells in the *Iliad* of 'many ships from Lemnos' bearing wine to sell to the Greeks before the walls of Troy. This was clearly a trading venture of some magnitude and a vague idea of its size may be gained from the fact that, accompanying the wine-fleet, went a thousand measures of wine as a personal gift from the son of Jason to Agamemnon and Menelaus. It is very likely that the wine in the 'ships from Lemnos' was in fact Maronean, or Ismaran which was probably the same thing, and that it was exported through Lemnos to the Troad. This seems to be made clear by a later passage of the *Iliad* in which Nestor says to Agamemnon: 'Thy huts are full of wine that the ships of the Achaians bring thee by day from Thrace across the wide sea'. Maronea is in Thrace and Maronean is the one Thracian wine which Homer singles out for praise. The men of Lemnos then (if the ships were really Lemnian and not Thracian ships journeying via Lemnos) were wine-traders and not wine-growers. Or is this unjust to them? Aristophanes has the purple Lemnian grape which ripened early and this purple grape may have been in Lemnos long before he wrote his plays. Perhaps it was both Lemnian and Maronean for which the besieging Greeks in the Troad bartered bronze and 'gleaming iron', hides, and cattle, and captives.[61] If this incident in the Troad can bear a Mycenaean dating, then it would suggest that Mycenaean merchants were prepared to trade in larger quantities of wine than has hitherto seemed likely. But, if they did, I rather suspect that any quantity trade in wine was confined to the circle of the Aegean. There may perhaps have been an eastern extension of trade though whether it exported wine is another question. It may even have imported wine. Hesiod, speaking of the month of June when 'goats are plumpest and wine sweetest; women are most wanton, but men are feeblest . . .' says that the ideal picnic under a shady rock should consist of cheese, meat of a young kid or from a 'heifer fed in the woods, that has never calved' and Bibline wine. From the Boeotian

[60] *Iliad*, II, III, IX; *Odyssey*, II. Arne: see also Strab., I, 3, 18. For Leucadian wine see also: Plin., XIV, 76; Ath-E, I, 29a, 33b. Meilissian: *FAC*, II, Eubulus, 131. Oretic: Plin., XIV, 76. For Mycenaean (?) dating of Homeric vineyards, also for Maduwattas, see Page, D. L., *History and the Homeric Iliad*, 98, 120–34, 152.

[61] *Odyssey*, IX; *Iliad*, VII, IX. (Later refs: Plin., XIV, 53-4); Ath-E, I, 26b, 30f; Coins, B. M., Pl. 21, 6-7, 37; and cf. *FAC*, I, Cratinus, 147. Lemnian: Aristophanes, *The Peace*, 1159 sqq. Homer's 'gleaming iron' does not invalidate a pre-'Iron Age' dating for the incident – see the iron-bladed sword at 3rd millennium Dorak.

context of Hesiod one might have expected this to be the name of a local Greek wine. But at a later date 'Bibline' was introduced into Sicily where it was a sweet wine known as Pollian and the name Bibline may, therefore, be the name of a vine or perhaps even of a style of wine. Alternatively the wine, or the vine, of which Hesiod is speaking and which later became Pollian in Sicily, may have come from Byblus in the Lebanon. It seems a long way for it to have travelled in the time of Hesiod but Homer speaks of women brought to Troy from Sidon and if women were brought from the eastern coast of the Mediterranean, either in Mycenaean or in 'Homeric' times, there is no reason why wine, or vines, should not have been brought as well.[62]

There are other passages in Homer which give us grounds for speculation. It is noticeable that when he describes a vineyard the grapes which he portrays are black. They are black on the great shield which the lame god Hephaistos wrought for Achilles and in the vineyard of Alcinous they are 'growing black to vintaging'.[63] We might suspect, therefore, that much of the Mycenaean wine was red as, of course, was the 'red wine honey sweet' of Maronea.

And then there is the difficult question of the age of Mycenaean wine. In Homeric Ithaca, in the treasure-chamber of Odysseus 'there stood casks of sweet wine and old, full of the unmixed drink divine, all orderly ranged by the wall, ready if ever Odysseus should come home . . . .' When Telemachus was about to set off in secret to gather news of his father he said to Eurycleia, the woman who guarded this cellar, 'come draw off for me sweet wine in jars, the choicest next to that thou keepest mindful ever of that ill-fated one, Odysseus, of the seed of Zeus . . . . So fill twelve jars, and close each with his lid . . . .'.

Let us leave the question of age for a moment and make some calculation of the amount of wine which Telemachus did take with him, he and 'the long-haired youths of the company' in the swift, black ship whose white sail, hauled up with twisted ropes of oxhide, was filled at the command of grey-eyed Athene by 'a fresh West Wind, singing over the wine-dark sea'. If we set twelve litres as the capacity of each jar, and this is about the most frequent capacity of the Mycenaean stirrup-jars which have been excavated, then Telemachus took with him on his voyage 144 litres of wine. He had a crew of twenty oarsmen and his journey should have lasted at least a couple of weeks so that the wine ration can scarcely have been much more than half a litre a day for each man. But how much of the wine was for drinking? The provisions of the ship seem to have consisted only of barley-meal and wine, and these may have been mixed together in the mixing bowls to produce a form of that tipsy porridge which Nestor had eaten on the shores of Troy. If, on the other hand, the wine was only for drinking, then they may have taken skin-bags full of water, or reckoned on landing each night by a stream, in order to be able to drink their wine diluted. Perhaps also Telemachus hoped that they would be entertained with wine at Pylos. And indeed, as far as he himself was concerned, the hope was nobly fulfilled, for when he got to Pylos: 'Then Nestor of Gerenia, lord of chariots, led them, even his sons and the husbands of his daughters' (and Telemachus also) 'to his own fair house. But when they had reached this prince's famous halls, they sat down all orderly on seats and high chairs; and when they were come, the old man mixed well for them a bowl of sweet wine, which now in

[62]Bibline: Hes, 589; *FAC*, I, Philyllius, 24; II, Antiphanes, 114; Theocritus, *Idyll* XIV. Pollian: Ath-E, I, 31a-b; Dunbabin, 93-4. Bybline (Lebanon): Ath-E, I, 29b-c. Women of Sidon: *Iliad*, VI; for Mycenaean jars from, probably, Syria, see Grace, Virginia, 'The Canaanite Jar', *The Aegean and the Near East – Studies presented to Hetty Goldman*, 88.

[63]*Iliad*, XVIII; *Odyssey*, VII.

the eleventh year from the vintaging the housewife opened, and unloosed the string that fastened the lid'.

Here we are back to the age of wine. Homer's three statements, two from 'Ithaca' and one from Pylos in the Peloponnese, bear the interpretation that the men of Homeric times were prepared to mature some of their wine and to mature it for quite a long time. This practice must surely have existed in the 8th century B.C. when Homer 'wrote'. Can we push it back into a Mycenaean context?

Not with any assurance. The cellar which Homer describes in Odyssean Ithaca is not quite the same type as the Mycenaean cellar which has been excavated in Nestor's Pylos. The difference, however, is not radical. Moreover, the lidded jars of Homeric Ithaca and of Homeric Pylos were not uncommon in Mycenaean times. Then again Nestor's 'housewife opened, and unloosed the string that fastened the lid' of Nestor's eleven-year-old wine and we know from the excavations at Sparta that the stoppers of Mycenaean jars were held in place by cords. Homer's descriptions would thus fit well into a Mycenaean context. But since they would fit equally well into Homer's own century we cannot say that his descriptions are really drawn from an inherited memory of Mycenaean practice; and therefore we cannot say that his descriptions of old wine are Mycenaean either.

There is a further difficulty. The age of Nestor's wine is stated in years and a statement of this sort is exceptional in the Homeric Epic. Why, then, is it here in the *Odyssey*? Surely it is a poetic device? The wanderings of Odysseus were supposed to have taken ten years from the Fall of Troy and it was in the tenth year of those wanderings that Telemachus went to Pylos. Nestor's vintage would have been the last vintage before the Fall of Troy. Surely the explicit statement of the age of the wine is a device to remind the poet's audience of the lapse of time between the last year of the Trojan War and the imminent return of Odysseus? And since the *Odyssey* is a romance, not a history, and the time of the wanderings is poetic, not historical, the age of the wine is poetic, not actual. All the figure means is that Homer's audience would have found nothing grotesque or unbelievable in the thought that wine could be kept for eleven years. That they did keep it as long as that, we do not know. And there we are left: with an answer which is a question.[64]

About the nature of Mycenaean vineyards, however, I believe that we can obtain from Homer a somewhat more satisfactory answer. He describes three vineyards: that of Alcinous, that wrought by Hephaistos on the Shield of Achilles, and that tilled by the old man Laertes, the father of Odysseus. ('Hesiod' gives us another description in his *Shield of Heracles* but this is partly an imitation of Homer's Shield of Achilles, probably not the work of Hesiod himself, and possibly as late as the end of the 7th century.) Homer may, of course, only be describing the vineyards of his own experience in the 8th century but I do not think that this is likely and I see no good reason for supposing that his vineyards differ substantially from those of Mycenaean Greece.

Homeric vineyards were hedged or fenced, and they were orchard-vineyards, in which grew not only vines but other fruit trees as well: pears, apples, figs and olives. When Odysseus was a boy Laertes gave him in a garden thirteen pear trees, ten apple trees, forty fig trees and fifty rows of vines 'whereof each one ripened at diverse times'. This latter statement, if it is not poetic licence, seems to mean that

[64] *Odyssey*, I, II, III; Blegen, C. W., 'The Palace of Nestor Excavations of 1955', *AJA*, 60, 1956; Blegen, C. W., and Lang, Mabel, 'The Palace of Nestor Excavations of 1958', *AJA*, 63, 1959; Dawkins, R. M., 'Excavations at Sparta', *BSA*, XVI, 1909-10; Mycenaean jar-capacity, Appendix D.

there were several varieties of Homeric vine and not that the rows were all planted with the same variety and were harvested at different periods. This seems also to have been the meaning of the curious remark of Homer in his eulogy of the Garden of Alcinous: 'In the foremost row are unripe grapes that cast the blossom and others there be that are growing black to vintaging'. It cannot literally have been true. What else can it be but a poetic way of describing the several varieties of vine?

It seems clear that the vines were grown in more or less orderly rows and that they were given some form of support. On the Shield of Achilles 'the vines hung throughout on silver poles'. Whether that means that they were tied to stakes, or trained up stakes onto trellises or trees, or grown on some form of pergola, we do not know. Homer might be thought to imply a trellis but even if we accept this view we cannot take the trellis as being the only method used in Homeric or Mycenaean times.[65] It is quite possible that the vines were tied to stakes and trained as cordons; and I suggest also that in many vineyards the vines were unstaked and stood by themselves, their branches trailing along the ground and their fruit raised above the earth by short and summer propping.

About the vintage scenes of Homer there clings a haze of sunlight as though they were the idealised harvest-homes of a romantic poet. The grapes which the men gather are carried away in plaited baskets by girls and children. Some of the grapes are being dried. The rest have been taken to the wine-press where they are being trodden. While this is going on there is a dance by those whose 'feet falling together kept time with the music and song'. The truth in this picture is evident and timeless and it is made pungent by the song. This was the Linos song, a sweet but mournful vintage lament for the end of the summer and for the death of the god who had brought the grapes into being.[66] It goes back without question into remote antiquity. It may have sounded among the mountains of Minoan Crete and it must have been known to the early vintagers of Boeotia and the Peloponnese. Did they take it, together with the Homeric poems, eastwards across the Aegean when they fled from the darkness of the Dorian Invasion? And did they also find it there, ageless and enduring, sung among the Islands and along the coast of Asia Minor?

'. . . *sweetly-smiling Sappho*'

After the Fall of Troy the Ionian Migration gathered impetus. Landless or adventurous men from the mainland of Greece moved eastwards to the Islands and the coast of western Anatolia. The Dorian Invasion of Greece can only have hastened this process and many of those who sailed across the Aegean fled from the wreckage of the Mycenaean Empire. They carried with them some of the traditions of the broken civilization and perhaps some memory of the beauty that had been in Crete. However much these traditions and memories may have become muted among their children, something must have remained and it was surely this which helped the cities of the Islands and of Anatolia to produce in the 8th and 7th centuries B.C. a Greek civilization that was far in advance of the mainland of Greece.

The record of the eastern Aegean is a proud one. Homer, most probably, came from Ionia – from Chios or Smyrna. Hesiod came from Cyme in Aeolis, not far to the north of Smyrna. So too, from Aeolis and Ionia came the poets of wine and love:

[65] *Odyssey*, VII, XXIV; *Iliad*, XVIII; Hes, *Shield of Heracles*, 285 sqq.; Hehn, V., *The Wanderings of Plants and Animals* . . . (Bibl. Ampelography), 75, and note 28; for possible Linear-B vineyards (or orchards) see *Mycen. Docs.*, Nos. 153, 155, 164.

[66] *Odyssey*, VII; *Iliad*, XVIII; see Frazer, Sir James G., *The Golden Bough*, VII, 216, 257-8, 263-4; Herodotus, II, comments on the 'Linus' song in Egypt, and gives it as being sung also in Cyprus and Phoenicia.

*Marines on a ship: from
Proto–Attic plaque
Sunium, 700 B.C.
Athens, National Museum*

Alcaeus of Mytilene in Lesbos and Sappho of Lesbos, both towards the end of the
7th century: and, in the first part of the 6th century, Anacreon of Teos whose death
at a ripe old age was supposed to have been caused by a grape-pip in the throat.
Homer continues and completes the Epic tradition. His is the deep-sounding chant
of great deeds. But in the others there is a new voice at work, sensual with the
beauty of the Minoan knowledge, Greek – unmistakably later Greek – with the
note of the hard, curious mind moving in the sensitive artist, and lyrical with the
feeling which it has for the curious and individual beauty of man. In this it is fully
European for it sings of man as an ordinary person who is at the same time extraordinary, as a fallible and fleeting marvel, an irreplaceable child with an unpredictable intellect. It was not, perhaps, unfitting that when the new Greece stirred, the
personal voice should have come most sweetly through a woman to whom after
all a child and a man are so often the same person.

'Violet-haired, holy, sweetly-smiling Sappho!' – this is Alcaeus describing her.
The tradition is more explicit: she was very dark, it says, small, and not at all good
looking; she was compared to 'a nightingale with clumsy wings enfolding a tiny
body'. She may not have shone in beauty among the girls who surrounded her, 'rose-
bud Gongyla' who came from Colophon in Asia Minor, and little Timas who came
from Phocaea in Asia Minor and who died very young. But she was still the nightingale and, in her own words, she was the '. . . angel of the Spring The Nightingale'.[67]

There is the breath of springtime about her in Aeolis. 'Weave garlands, maiden,
from the strands of dill . . . .', she writes. Also:

> 'Many a coronet
> Of rose and violet,
> Crocus and dill upon your
> > brow you set'

and to Dica she says: 'let your dainty fingers twine a wreath of anise-sprays and
bind your lovely locks'.[68] Alcaeus in a drinking song commands:

[67] Higham, T. F., and Bowra, C. M.,
*Oxford Book of Greek Verse in
Translation*, Nos. 136 (trs. Anon.),
155 (trs. Ben Jonson); Brown,
Ivor, *Dark Ladies*, 107-8, 124.

[68] Higham, Bowra, *Oxford Book of
Greek Verse in Trans.*, Nos. 144
and 147 (trs. Bowra, C. M.);
Anacreon, *Lyra Graeca*, I, Sappho,
117.

103

> 'Now bind the woven necklaces
> Of dill about your throat . . . .'

while Anacreon of Teos has some favour for '. . . little garlands of celery'. The custom of using garlands, and in particular at drinking parties, runs right down through Greek times and among the flowers which they used were roses, violets, red and white lilies, larkspur, thyme, hyacinth and crocus.[69]

At last we can see ordinary Europeans at their wine – ordinary people, not Heroes – and at last we can see them clearly. They may not have been as dramatic as the Heroes before the walls of Troy or in the Palaces of Pylos and Ithaca, but they are usually loveable and always very human. Like Alcaeus:

> 'Drink! Why wait for lamps? The day
> Has not another inch to fall.
> Fetch the biggest beakers – they
> Hang on pegs along the wall.'[70]

Naturally enough the wine-party was not an invention of the later Greeks. It was invented millennia before their time. But we may believe that in this 7th century B.C. it played a greater part in Greek life than ever before since it was at this time that vineyards were spreading widely through the Islands and over the mainland of Greece. Even Hesiod's father who settled at Ascra on the slopes of Mount Helicon in Boeotia, a spot which was 'bad in winter, unpleasant in summer, and good never', grew a little wine as well as some corn and vegetables.[71] In the same 7th century wines are signalled from Arcadia and Sparta in the Peloponnese: Carystian from Arcadia and 'Five Hills' from Sparta.[72] From the time of Solon onwards, that is to say from the beginning of the 6th century, vineyards spread in Attica, their spread being helped no doubt by growing deforestation as trees were cut down for the building of houses or ships or for burning into charcoal. Some indication of the extent of the Attic vineyards in the time of Solon can be gathered from the property qualifications of the four property-classes of Athens. The Thetes, in the lowest class, had, roughly speaking, less than seven acres of vineyard; the next class up, the Zeugites, owned between seven and ten acres of vines; the larger landowners, those of the knight's class, had twelve to fifteen acres of vineyard and the greatest landowners twenty to twenty-five acres. These qualifications could have been expressed in terms of grain or oil, as well as of wine, so that they do not necessarily show the actual amount of land that was under vines[73]; but in any case, in the days of Aristophanes, his 'Athmonian, skilled in vines . . .'[74] who came from north-east of Athens, would have been typical of a numerous class of Attic viticulturalists.

The pattern of life in Attica was to some extent conditioned by the proximity of Athens since market gardens were needed to provide the city with vegetables and fruit for eating and with flowers for making garlands. But the conditioning was only a matter of degree and on the whole the life of the Attic peasant or smallholder, with his vineyards and olives and hives of bees, was little different from that of other rural workers in the Aegean. An example from the 2nd century B.C. is the life of Pidasa, a small city of Caria in south-west Asia Minor.

[69] Alcaeus: Higham, Bowra, *Oxford Book of Greek Verse in Trans.*, No. 135, II (trs. Bowra, C. M.). Anacreon: *Lyra Graeca*, II, Anacreon, 56; *FAC*, I, Cratinus, 98; and see Theophrastus, *Enq. into Plants*, I, XII, 4.

[70] Higham, Bowra, *Oxford Book of Greek Verse in Trans.*, No. 135, III (trs. Bowra, C. M.).

[71] Glotz, *AGW*, 41, 64.

[72] Carystian: Ath-E, I, 31d; and Strab., 10, 1, 6. 'Five Hills': Ath-E, I, 31c.

[73] Glotz, *AGW*, 129, 246; *CAH*, V, 4, 13.

[74] *The Peace*, 190.

Two-handled Clay Cup
Mycenaean, 1300–1200
B.C.
London, British Museum

'The land belonged partly to the city and to the temples, but most of it was owned by the citizens. The main income was derived from the olive groves; next came cattle and bee-keeping, the last a speciality of Caria. . . . Corn was probably produced mostly on the mountain slopes. . . . The yield of these corn fields was probably small. . . . In addition to land in the territory of the city the citizens of Pidasa owned vineyards in the territory of the city of Euromus. The estates were large: some of them produced more than 1,000 *metretai*' (about 39,000 litres)★. 'The wine was probably of excellent quality. . . .'[75]

The Aegean smallholder would not, of course, have had vineyards which produced as much wine, nor would his wine always have been of excellent quality.

Another picture of Aegean life, and one which covers the 3rd and 2nd centuries B.C., is taken from the Island of Delos in the Cyclades and shows us the pattern of work on the estates which were owned and leased by the Temple of Apollo. (Delos was supposed to have been the birthplace of Apollo.) The estates were on Delos itself, on the nearby Island of Rheneia, and on the Island of Mykonos, and in general the picture which is given to us by the Temple accounts is one of mixed farming. Vines, figs, olives, and apples were grown; there was some grain; and cattle and sheep, probably also goats, seem to have been kept by nearly all the

★For measures of the ancient Greek world, see Appendix D.

[75]*CAH*, v, 4, 14–15; Ros, *SEHH*, 670–1.

estates. The size of the vineyards is interesting. 'In 250 B.C. nine of the ten Rheneian estates contained a total of 16,772 vines, and if the numbers listed elsewhere for other estates are added, the total is greater than twenty thousand.' In the 2nd century the single estate of Dorion-Chersonesos on Mykonos had 2,750 vines. What again is interesting, and even more illuminating, is that, in this 2nd century B.C., when the price of wine in the Aegean had fallen sharply, many of the Temple estates still kept their vineyards. Yet their wine does not seem to have been highly esteemed, for Delos imported some wine – Coan and Cnidian – although these wines, it is true, were for use in the religious ceremonies.[76] The wine made on the Temple estates of Delos must have continued to satisfy some part at least of the local market or else the size of the vineyards would have been drastically curtailed. After 220 B.C., for example, they do not seem to have been of any great value and yet the local vineyards continued to exist. Surely this points to the maintenance of local production at a very low rate of profit to the farmer since, if the price of his wine had been high enough to give him a good profit, he would have faced severe competition from imported wine which was very much better than his own. And what happened at Delos must have happened in many another area of the Greek world.

If low profit margins were a hardship to the small farmer, war was a disaster, for his olive trees were cut down and his vineyards were destroyed. With an angry humour in *The Acharnians* Aristophanes tilts against this hazard of Greek life. There we have the ruined vineyard with its trampled vines and the burning of the vine props which, in happier days, would have supported the welcome harvest.[77] Thucydides puts it in a sober recital of fact: 'Next summer the Peloponnesians . . . and their allies invaded Attica . . . . The invading forces destroyed everything that had started to grow up again in the districts which they had laid waste previously, and they went on to destroy such property as had been left untouched in earlier invasions. Thus, this was the worst invasion of all except the second. The enemy prolonged their stay in Attica and overran most of the country . . . .' On certain occasions an understandable self-interest guided the decisions of those who were threatened. This happened at Acanthus in Macedonia (and Acanthian, it might be noted, was considered to be a good wine) when Acanthus was faced with an army led by Brasidas 'just before the time of the vintage. The people of Acanthus . . . voted by ballot, and the majority, partly because they were swayed by Brasidas's oratory, partly because they were frightened about their fruit, decided to revolt from Athens'.[78] Less able to exercise any choice in the matter were the inhabitants of Decelea which, being only about fourteen miles from Athens, was taken over by the invading Spartans; perhaps the Deceleans were resigned to their fate for their wine was notorious for its sourness. It was, in fact, joked about as 'home-made vinegar'.[79] But, whatever the quality of his wine, many a harassed Greek, weary of the waste and destruction, must have thought longingly of the vision of peace conjured up by Aristophanes:

> 'The bleating lambs, the ivy-leaf, the vat,
> Full-bosomed matrons hurrying to the farm,
> The tipsy maid, the drained and emptied flask,
> And many another blessing.'[80]

[76] Kent, J. H., 'The Temple Estates of Delos, Rheneia, and Mykonos', *Hesp.*, XVII, 243 sqq., 1948; see also Frank, Larsen, IV, 392 sqq. In Pliny's time the wine of Mykonos was considered third class – Plin., XIV, 75. For Delos in general, see Ros, *SEHH*, 787 sqq., 1488.

[77] *Acharnians*, 232, 985-6; see also *The Peace, passim*.

[78] *The Peloponnesian War*, III, ii; IV, vi; 175-6, 278, 280.

[79] *FAC*, II, Alexis, 285; Thucydides, *The Peloponnesian War*, VII, ii, 442.

[80] *The Peace*, 535 sqq.

The Golden Mean?

Everything in moderation, nothing too much. This was one of the keynotes of the classical Greek civilization. But the idea that the Golden Mean was universally observed among the Greeks is just as untenable as some of the other ideas which, from time to time, have been held about them – their courage and their kindness, for example. They were a remarkably brave people but their courage was sometimes tempered by the application of the maxim 'Discretion is the better part of valour'. In one battle Alcaeus of Mytilene threw away his shield and ran; so, in another, did Archilochus of Paros. Both poets, however, were brave men and both joked afterwards about these mishaps, so that their admissions of temporary prudence may only have been made in mockery of the more boring soldiers who boasted about their valour.[81] But other instances of discretion in battle were not unknown.

Kindness was not an invariable manifestation of the Greek character. During the Peloponnesian War the Athenians, by a cunning manoeuvre, captured six ambassadors, and then 'without giving them a trial or allowing them to say what they wished to say in their defence, put them all to death and threw their bodies into a pit'. Thucydides goes on to say: 'They regarded this action as legitimate retaliation for the way in which Spartans had been behaving, since they also had killed and thrown into pits all Athenian and allied traders whom they had caught sailing in merchant ships round the Peloponnese'. The Attic orator Isaeus, in his speech *On the Estate of Ciron*, says to those who are trying the case, 'Both in your public and in your private capacity, gentlemen, you consider that torture is the surest test of truth. When slaves and freemen are both available, and it is necessary to clear up a disputed point, you do not rely on the evidence of the freeman, but rather put the slaves to torture, and seek thus to discover the real facts.'

On the other hand, slave owners would not always allow their slaves to be put to the torture and, even if they did, 'extreme cruelty was forbidden, and any injury done to the slaves, temporarily or permanent, had to be paid for'. In the cause *Against Neaera*, for example, Demosthenes has this statement: 'I proposed that he should deliver up for the torture the women-servants, Thratta and Coccalinê . . .'; and the offer is made to pay for any injuries which the women sustained under torture. Stephanus, however, at whom the challenge was directed, refused it and Thratta and Coccalinê went unharmed.[82]

Temperance in drinking, though much admired in theory, was not always observed in practice. Aristophanes jokes, possibly with some injustice, about the vinous enthusiasm of Athenian women: 'They love their wine unwatered, as of old.' (We need not assume that the women of older Athens did in fact drink their wine unwatered.) In *The Knights* Aristophanes commits an almost Falstaffian speech in praise of wine:

> 'Nicias: Pure wine indeed! Is this a tippling matter?
> How can one get, when drunk, a happy thought?
> Demosthenes: Aye, say you so, you water-fountain-twaddler?
> And dare you rail at wine's inventiveness?
> I tell you nothing has such go as wine.
> Why, look you now; 'tis when men drink they thrive,

[81] *Lyra Graeca*, I, Alcaeus, 121; Murray, Gilbert, *The Literature of Ancient Greece*, 87-8.

[82] Thucydides, *The Peloponnesian War*, II, 7; Wright, F. A., *Greek Social Life*, 164, quoting Isaeus; Murray, Gilbert, *The Literature of Anc. Greece*, 328; Demosthenes, *Private Orations*, LIX, 120, 124-5.

Grow wealthy, speed their business, win their suits,
Make themselves happy, benefit their friends.'

and adds in the same scene:

'Quaff-quaff the loving cup of Pramnian Fortune.'[83]

Many a Greek was just as devoted to wine though his devotion was not always due
to its inventive properties. In the 6th century B.C. Xenophanes (?) of Colophon in
Ionia, remarked that some of the inhabitants of Colophon were so 'dissolute in
carousing' that they never saw the sun either rise or set. In the 4th century B.C. Plato
makes the Lacedaemonian Megillus say that 'among our Tarentine colonists I have
seen the whole city drunk at a Dionysiac festival . . .'. Even the company at Plato's
Symposium was raw with the memory of hangover. When the guests were about to
begin drinking 'Pausanias said, And now, my friends, how can we drink with least
injury to ourselves? I can assure you that I feel severely the effect of yesterday's
potations, and must have time to recover; and I suspect that most of you are in the
same predicament, for you were of the party yesterday. . . . I entirely agree, said
Aristophanes, that we should, by all means, avoid hard drinking, for I was myself
one of those who were deeply dipped yesterday. . . .' It was then agreed that 'drinking is to be voluntary'. Nevertheless, the party was interrupted by intoxication, for
'suddenly there was a great knocking at the door of the house, as of revellers, and
the sound of a flute-girl was heard'. Alcibiades was shouting drunk in the court
outside 'and at length, supported by the flute-girl and some of his attendants, he
found his way to them. "Hail, friends," he said, appearing at the door crowned
with a massive garland of ivy and violets, his head flowing with ribands'. The same
party was interrupted once again by a crowd of revellers: 'great confusion ensued,
and everyone was compelled to drink large quantities of wine'. Towards daybreak
only three of the guests were still awake, one of them being Socrates, and they 'were
drinking out of a large goblet which they passed round, and Socrates was discours-
ing to them'. The other two dropped off to sleep in their turn and Socrates, unaffected by the wine which he had drunk, left them and went off about his day's
business.[84]

These are no isolated instances. Aristophanes in *The Frogs* describes a scene at the
Spring festival of Anthesteria:

'When the revel-tipsy throng, all crapulous and gay,
To our precinct reeled along on the holy Pitcher day.'

Athenaeus quotes Menander as writing: 'Byzantium makes all the traders tipsy.
The whole night through we were drinking for your sake, and, methinks, it was
very strong wine too. At any rate I got up with four heads on me.' In Plutarch's
Dinner of the Seven Wise Men Anacharsis defends his heavy drinking at an earlier
party by saying: 'And why not? . . . Prizes were offered for the man who drank the
most, and I was the first to get drunk. . . .' To round off this chronicle of intemperance one might cite a cylix, or drinking cup, of the potter Brygos, from between

[83] Aristophanes, *Ecclesiazusae*, 227;
Knights, 87 sqq.

[84] Xenophanes (?): Ath-E, XII, 526a;
Plato, *Dialogues of* (trs. Jowett,
B.), *Laws*, 637b; *Symposium*,
212c-e, 223b-d, 176a.

Marines on a Ship (detail)
*from Attic Cup of Brygos
the potter*
530–480 B.C.
*Würzburg, University
Museum*

530 and 480 B.C. This, from the period of the archaic red-figured style, shows a young Athenian 'After the Banquet'. He is leaning on a staff, his head is being held by a girl, and he is relieving himself by vomiting 'of the wine he has imbibed too freely'.[85]

Basically, however, the Greeks were a temperate people and they distrusted Mothon, the goblin-spirit of drunkenness and bestiality. For the most part they drank their wine diluted with water and they regarded as somewhat barbaric the peoples who drank it unmixed. The Scythians and Thracians, says Plato, 'both men and women, drink unmixed wine, which they pour on their garments, and this they think a happy and glorious institution'. Herodotus records the view that Cleomenes went mad because he spent a certain amount of time with the Scythians 'acquired the habit of taking wine without water – and went off his head in consequence'. How puzzling to the Greek mind must have been the custom which Herodotus relates about the Persians: 'If an important decision is to be made, they discuss the question when they are drunk, and the following day the master of the house where the discussion was held submits their decision for reconsideration

[85] Aristophanes, *The Frogs*, 211 sqq.; Ath-E, x, 435d sqq.; x, 442c–e; Plutarch. Moralia, *Dinner of the Seven Wise Men*, 156A. For drinking in Boeotia, see Glotz, *AGW*, 333. The Brygos *kylix*: Buschor, E., *Greek Vase Painting* (trs. Richards, G. C.), Pl. lxix.

109

*Two Revellers: from Red-
figured Cup
c 490 B.C.
Paris, Louvre*

when they are sober. If they still approve it, it is adopted; if not, it is abandoned. Conversely, any decision they make when they are sober, is reconsidered afterwards when they are drunk.'[86]

Mnesitheus seems to have summed up the Greek view about diluting wine: 'Mix it half and half, and you get madness; unmixed, bodily collapse.' By madness he only means 'fighting drunk', but it is a striking comment on the drinking powers of the Greeks for we ourselves would not consider the mixture of half and half as readily conducive to intoxication. In quantity, no doubt, it would have produced

[86]Mothon: Aristophanes, *The Knights*, 635. Scythians and Thracians: *Dialogues of Plato* (trs. Jowett, B.), *Laws*, 637e; Herodotus, VI, 389. Persians: Herodotus, I, 69. For Scythians, see also Anacreon, in Higham, Bowra, *Oxford Book of Greek Verse in Trans.*, No. 176 (trs. Higham, T. F.).

'madness' but it must have taken quite a time to do so. Anacreon called for one of wine to two of water but the more usual mixture seems to have been two of wine with five of water, and even then was considered by Eupolis, a poet of the Old Comedy, as being a mixture for those who took their drinking seriously. Naturally the amount of dilution varied according to the type of party and the lateness of the hour, but the mixing bowl never lost its importance in festive drinking.[87] The counsel of perfection as Eubulus put it, was this: 'Three bowls only do I mix for the temperate – one to health, which they empty first, the second to love and pleasure, the third to sleep. When this is drunk up wise guests go home.'[88] His sage advice was frequently forgotten.

Greece was always a poor country and the Greeks were always conditioned to a sense of frugality. Their sparseness of living was undoubtedly one of the reasons why they mixed their wine with water. As happens in some parts of modern Greece, many a farm and many a village of ancient Greece would have made only enough wine to last, if drunk neat, for nine or ten months of the ensuing year. Sadly Hesiod warns: 'Take your fill when the cask is first opened and when it is nearly spent, but midways be sparing: it is poor saving when you come to the lees.'[89] Hence, to make the wine last out the full year, it had to be mixed with water. And, of course, dilution was a financial economy as well.

But economy was not the only, and perhaps not even the major, reason. The Greek was temperate by nature. He may have committed, and he often did commit, excesses of all kinds but it was instinctive in him to regard excess as a distortion of human dignity. The dignity of life and the value of the individual lay in the exercise of consciousness and any diminishment of this exercise diminished the individual himself. Gluttony, sottishness, and stupefaction were 'madness' – they dulled and distorted the active, appreciating mind. Dilution delayed, if it did not ultimately avoid, the onset of the madness.

I do not say for a moment that the Greeks regarded wine as a demon. Quite the contrary. They loved their wine as they loved the other delights of life. The presence of those delights was always welcome; but their absence was not thought to be a disaster.

Luxury, moreover, was considered to be an extravagance worthier of ridicule than admiration. After the Eastern conquests of Alexander the Great money-wealth increased in the Greek homeland but it was never comparable with the wealth of Rome and the richer Greeks in Hellas seldom displayed that lust for luxury which characterized so many of the richer and less intelligent Romans. The Greek character could never quite accept lavish ideas of comfort and its general attitude seems to be expressed in a passage of Thucydides which speaks of a time prior to the Peloponnesian War. The Athenians, he says, 'were the first . . . to adopt a way of living that was more relaxed and more luxurious. In fact the elder men of the rich families who had these luxurious tastes only recently gave up wearing linen undergarments and tying their hair behind their heads in a knot fastened with a clasp of golden grasshoppers'; and he adds: 'It was the Spartans who first began to dress simply and in accordance with our modern taste, with the rich leading a life that was as much as possible like the life of the ordinary people.'[90] One can hardly count the golden grasshoppers of the Athenians as evidence of an outrageous luxury. And even if it

[87] Mnesitheus: Ath-E, II, 36a-b; (but was it Mnesitheus? - see fn. a). Anacreon: Higham, Bowra, Oxford Book of Greek Verse in Trans., No. 176 (trs. Higham, T. F.). Variant mixtures: Ath-E, X, 426; see also Aristophanes, The Acharnians, 354; Eupolis, FAC, I, Eupolis, 8.

[88] Ath-E, II, 36b-c; cf. Panyasis of Halicarnassus, in Murray, Gilbert, Lit. of Anc. Greece, 70.

[89] Hes., Works and Days, 368-9.

[90] The Peloponnesian War, I, i, 16.

were considered to be so by the Athenians themselves it was not, or at least not until Hellenistic times, carried through into the other departments of their life. Fifth-century houses were by no means grandiose. Their furniture was simple – to our minds scanty – and the frugal bareness of their rooms showed an emphasis on use rather than display. Even the Gorgon mask that watched over this domestic simplicity was not merely decorative since it served the practical purpose of warding off the Evil Eye.[91]

Hellenic food was neither complicated nor excessive. In fact the Persians said that the Greeks left the table still hungry because they never had anything worth mentioning after the first course.[92] Even when some sense of gastronomy made itself evident in Greece, its limited range can be seen from the fact that, although among professional chefs there were those who specialized in pastry, other artists in cookery 'enjoyed a pan-Hellenic reputation for black puddings, stews, lentil soup, fish and, above all, congers'. The Greeks set no store by the finer manifestations of eating. Indeed they found the whole subject a matter for mockery and satire.

Excess in eating was also a matter for mirthful comment, yet the many stories of gluttony, however, exaggerated and unjust they may be, do show that frugality was not an invariable habit. The Boeotians, in particular, were always being accused of over-eating which no doubt they did if and when they could afford it.[93]

> 'A. I'm a Boeotian and I act as such,
>   Speaking but little –
>
> B. Good!
>
> A. And eating much.'

But if this was true of Boeotia it was certainly not typical of the rest of the Greek world. Breakfast in Sappho's Lesbos was bread dipped in wine (though on special occasions this could be accompanied by roasted chestnuts) and this would have been a usual breakfast in Hellas. There were, of course, variations and Aristophanes, accurate within the bounds of his derision, describes the countryman's breakfast as being seasoned with garlic and vinegar. Nevertheless, whatever the variations, it would have meant little more than its literal meaning of breaking the fast since the main meals of the Greek day were a midday lunch and an evening supper. The simple country lunch is pictured by Aristophanes as being a small goatskin of wine, two onions, three olives and a loaf, and his picture must have been as commonplace to most of the Greeks, whether they were country men or dwellers in a city.[94]

Fundamentally, Greek eating (except for 'Homeric' times), was based on the 'Mediterranean triad' of grain, oil, and wine. Cheese was also, as it still is, a commonplace, and ground corn, wine, and cheese were specifically mentioned by Thucydides as forms of food 'useful in a siege'. One might also note that at this particular siege – the Athenians were besieging the Spartans on an island – 'Divers . . . swam in under water from the harbour, dragging behind them by a cord skins containing poppy-seed mixed with honey and pounded linseed'. The basic Hellenic diet was filled out with vegetables, and with fruits such as figs and olives and 'grapes-in-wine',[95] and a good picture of its early simplicity is that given in a play called *The*

[91] For the shape of a lower middle-class house in Athens, see Lysias, *On the murder of Eratosthenes*, 9–10. Other refs for Athenian life: *CAH*, v, 462; Harrison, *Prolegomena*, 191.

[92] Herodotus, I, 69.

[93] Glotz, *AGW*, 223; Murray, Gilbert, *The Literature of Anc. Greece*, 73; Ath-E, x, 417b-f. Boeotian gluttony: *FAC*, II, Mnesimachus, 2; also Eubulus, 34, and Demonicus, 1.

Beggars which has been attributed to the Old Comedy poet Chionides. In this he declares that 'when the Athenians prepare breakfast for the Dioscuri in the Town-Hall, they set upon the tables cheese and heavy-cake with ripe olives and leeks' and this 'breakfast' was supposed to be a reminder of the ancient way of life.[96]

The cake was important not only to 'the ancient way of life' but to the classical way of life as well. There may be overtones of sophisticated, urban derision in the greeting 'O welcome, dear Boeotian muffin-eater' as indeed there may be in the description 'bun-eating Thessaly'.[97] But the bun or muffin was as necessary to Attica as it was to the more provincial Hellenes. Cheese cakes, honey-buns, and honied cheese cakes were popular and 'cheesecakes of every sort and every name' were served up for dessert at a feast. The flat-cakes of Samos were supposed to be so good that we come across the title of 'Samos whose name is flat-cake-maker'. A poet of the Middle Comedy asks what is the civilized life and replies: 'Cheesecakes, sweet wine, eggs, cakes of sesame, perfumes, and crowns, and female flute-players.' Here perhaps one might add that sometimes at a drinking party a prize was given to the man who managed to keep awake all night: the prize was a cake.[98]

Meat was not despised by the Greeks. On the contrary, they were well prepared to eat it on occasion and these occasions, among the poorer people at least, were usually those of holiday or rejoicing. Pork was a favoured meat but they also liked thrushes, finches, and hares, and, though not necessarily in the meat class, 'the stuffed paunch of an ass was accounted a delicacy at Athens'.[99] Hog's puddings, haggises and sweetened sausages were very popular and many of these dishes must have been remarkably pungent since among the seasonings in use were salt, raisins, cheese, boiled must, thyme, cummin, honey, vinegar, 'green-tops for sour-sauce', olives, capers, eggs, salt-fish and fig leaves.[100]

The 'Mediterranean triad' remained basic. In the life of most of the Greeks, however, it was expanded into a Mediterranean quintet for to the grain and oil and wine there were added not only vegetables but also fish. They ate a lot of fish, dried or salted as well as fresh, and among the favoured foods of Attica were the eels from Lake Copäis. These were often served 'lapped in beet' or, as Eubulus has it:

'A bride unwedded shall come,
    Skin fair, body beetroot-veiled –
    Eel's the name she bears –'

or alternatively: 'Asp-bodied eels Boeotian, Goddesses beetroot-enrobed.' The most usual method of c king fish was most probably by frying in oil in the casseroles which were such a common feature of the classical Greek kitchen. There is a glimpse in the *Acharnians* of this type of meal, with the 'small fish . . . lying all in order for the frying' over a charcoal brazier while some of the people present are dipping the fish into pickle.[101]

A more festive glimpse of Greek family eating is given by Eubulus or Ephippus – Athenaeus is not certain which but they were both poets of the 4th-century Middle Comedy – who describes the family celebration of the Amphidromia which was held five days after the birth of a child. Then the custom was 'to toast a slice of Gallipoli cheese, to boil a cabbage glistening in oil, to broil some fat lamb chops, to

[94] Brown, Ivor, *Dark Ladies*, 127; Zimmern, A. E., *The Greek Commonwealth*, 48; Aristophanes, *Ecclesiazusae*, 289 sqq., and fn. a, 302 aqq.

[95] Zimmern, A. E., *Greek Commonwealth*, 47; *CAH*, v, 21; Thucydides, *Peloponnesian War*, IV, 245. Grapes-in-wine: *FAC*, I, Pherecrates, 148; II, Eubulus, 49.

[96] *FAC*, I, Chionides, 5.

[97] Aristophanes, *Acharnians*, 872; Ath-E, III, 112f; cf. *Acharnians*, 245–6.

[98] [99] Ath-E, xiv, 644c; Aristophanes, *Ecclesiazusae*, 224; *Knights*, 276–7, and fn. a; *FAC*, I, Nicophon, 5; II, Antiphanes, 140.

[100] Aristophanes, *The Peace*, 1140 sqq.; *The Wasps*, 194–5, fn. a; Glotz, *AGW*, 259; *FAC*, I, Crates, 17; Pherecrates, 108; II, Antiphanes, 140. Seasonings: *FAC*, II, Antiphanes, 142.

[101] Aristophanes, *Acharnians*, 670 sqq., 967; *The Peace*, 1005 sqq., and fn. b, c; *Lysistrata*, 36; Talcott, Lucy, 'Attic Black-Glazed Stamped Ware . . .', *Hesp.*, IV, 1935; and for food in much detail see, of course, Ath-E, *passim*. Eels: *FAC*, I, Pherecrates, 108; II, Eubulus, 35, 37.

pluck the feathers from ring-doves, thrushes, and finches withal, at the same time to devour cuttle-fish and sprats, to pound with care many wriggling polyps, and drink many a cup not too diluted'.[102] It must have made a welcome change from the frugality of daily life.

The Cost of Drinking

But what, in fact, was the economic measure of Greek frugality? Or, to put it into the context of wine, how much wine could they afford to buy and how often could they afford to buy it?

We have a number of figures; some are from literature, some from graffiti on wine jars excavated in Athens; others are from the building accounts of the Athenian Erechtheum, and yet others from the Temple records of Delos. From the information which these give us we can form some idea of the cost of living. But the idea is only approximate since there are gaps in the information. We can, for example, estimate the cost of living of a family in Delos in 250 B.C. and against this we can set the known wages of skilled labour in the island. But we cannot assess the actual income of the whole family because we do not know how much, if anything, was brought in from work done by the wife or the children. And then again the standard of living may have been a little higher than the actual income would indicate since the family may have had vegetables and herbs, and perhaps a little home-grown wine, from its own plot of ground. These unknown factors hold true, of course, for the rest of the Greek world for even in the great city of Athens many a family owned a few olive and fruit trees, a few beehives, or a vegetable garden with its borders of parsley and rue. The standard of living of the country farmer is even harder to assess since it depended upon the amount and the quality of the land which he owned and upon the efficiency with which he worked it.

Even where we do have the figures of wages and prices we still cannot translate them with any exactitude into terms of modern money. We can calculate the amount of barley or wheat or wine which the Greek drachma would have bought at certain periods; but we cannot calculate the actual value of the drachma to the man who owned it since that value depended, among other things, on what he wanted to buy and what he was prepared to do without. Any comparison between ancient and modern values has to be treated with the greatest caution, and any assessment we make must therefore be made in ancient times. So far as wine is concerned we may be able to get some idea of its real cost by comparing the amount of its price with the amount of a daily wage.

In the later 5th century B.C. the daily wage of a dicast, or 'juryman', at Athens was 3 obols a day. (There were six obols to a drachma.*) In 409-8 B.C. a sawyer working on the building of the Erechtheum got a drachma a day, as did some of the other skilled workmen employed on the job, and a drachma a day seems to have been a standard wage at this time for this type of labour. Now it has been calculated that, in the late 5th century, an unmarried townsman could have lived on 2 obols a day while a married couple in a town would have needed 3 obols a day. Thus, a dicast was paid a living wage and not much more, and the same thing is probably true

*For money of the ancient Greek world, see Appendix D.   [102] Ath-E, II, 65c-d.

of the workmen on the Erechtheum, for their higher wages had to meet the higher prices which resulted from the Peloponnesian War.

In the 5th century at Athens, then, low incomes ranged from 3 to 6 obols a day and during this same century ordinary wine at Athens cost between 2 and 10 obols the *chous*, the *chous* being about 3¼ litres. Mendean wine cost 12 obols the *chous* and so did wine from Chios. Chian wine was one of the most esteemed wines of the Greek world and it appears that its price could go much higher, up to 50 obols or more the *chous* which, if one can believe Plutarch's story, was considered by Socrates to be an extravagant price. In the 4th century B.C. Attic wine could fetch the price of 72 obols the jar at Athens which, if the capacity of the jar in this case really was that of a *metretes*, would have meant a price of 6 obols a *chous*. Demosthenes seems to have considered this an exorbitant price for Attic wine.

At Delos in the 3rd century B.C. the wage of an unskilled labourer was usually 2 obols a day and that of a skilled labourer 4 obols a day, both exclusive of any allowance for clothing. These seem to have been the minimum wages for those in regular employment. If we can assume that these men worked for 300 days in the year then the annual wage of the unskilled labourer would have been 100 drachmas and that of the skilled workman would have been 200 drachmas, again exclusive of clothing. The cost of living in Delos in 250 B.C. has been estimated in approximate figures as being 115 drachmas a year for a single man and 321 drachmas a year for a family of four. The disparity between the money wages and the cost of living seems to indicate a real degree of hardship for the family of four but as we have already seen, it is quite possible that the family's total income was augmented by the labour of its other members. Even so, there cannot have been much room for extravagance. In 296 B.C. one type of wine at Delos cost 5½ obols the *chous*, and local wine may sometimes have been very much cheaper. But even with lowered prices there may still have been many a Greek who had to make do with the poor man's drink of *deuterias*, a 'wine' that was pressed out of wine lees or made from grapeskins soaked in water.[103]

The price of labour tells its own part of the Greek economic story. So, possibly, does the price of the human body. From Herodotus we learn that Greek prisoners of war were normally ransomed for 200 drachmas a head; from the Attic Stelai that the price of certain slaves was about 174 drachmas each. This latter figure was probably on the low side for Demosthenes in the next, the 4th, century, says the minimum price of a slave was 300 drachmas. (The lower price of the slaves whose sale is recorded on the Attic Stelai may be due either to the fact that they were unskilled or that they were being sold off as the confiscated property of Alcibiades and those others who had been accused of mutilating the Herms and profaning the Eleusinian Mysteries.) A marked contrast to all of these prices is that of 3,000 drachmas for a courtesan. The courtesan was Neaera and the story, which is related by Demosthenes, is a minor example of the use of capital as against income.

The Deposition in the case against Neaera relates:

'Hipparchus of Athmonon deposes that Xenocleides and he hired in Corinth Neaera, the present defendant, as a courtesan who prostituted herself for money, and that Neaera used to drink at Corinth in the company of himself and Xenocleides the poet.'

[103] Athenian wages, etc.: Aristophanes, *Knights*, 51; Stevens, G. P., Paton, J. M., and others, *The Erechtheum*, 331, 381, 419, 422; *CAH*, v, 21-2. Delian wages, etc.: Frank, Larsen, IV, 347 sqq., 410 sqq. Wine prices, Athens: Lang, Mabel, 'Numerical Notation on Greek Vases', *Hesp.*, XXV, 13 sqq., 1956; Plutarch, *Moralia*, De tranquill. An., 47F. Demosthenes, *Private orations*, XLII, Ad Phaen., 20; and see also Talcott, Lucy, 'Attic Black-Glazed Stamped Ware . . .', *Hesp.*, IV, 1935. Wine prices, Delos, etc.: Frank, Larsen, IV, 392; Kent, J. H., 'The Temple Estates of Delos, Rheneia and Mykonos', *Hesp.*, XVII, 311 sqq., 1948; Deuterias, Plin., XIV, 86. For wages at Delos in 170 B.C., see Frank, I., 188, who gives the labour wage at about 1 drachma a day.

*Woman wearing dark-red
and black garments
Lekythos from Gala
460–450 B.C.
London, British Museum*

*Dionysos with Dancers
and Youths
Attic Amphora
Amasis the Painter
c 540 B.C.
Basle, Museum of
Antiquities*

Two other of Neaera's lovers, however, preferred the system of capital investment. They paid thirty minae (3,000 drachmas) 'as the price of Neaera's person and purchased the girl outright . . . to be their slave'.[104] Perhaps it was worth it but the price was high.

There may not have been much comfort in the frugal life but at least there was a good deal of colour. It is true that during the 5th century clothes were becoming plainer and simpler and instead of being brightly coloured as they had been in the past, were now either white, or else some dark colour which would conceal the dust and the wear of daily life. But there was still colour about. There were the red Laconian shoes of the men. There were the crimson robes worn at the ceremonies in placation of those who inhabited the underworld. And there were the yellow dresses of the curious and ancient ritual of the Attic Artemis Brauronia, 'the goddess in whose honour all Athenian maidens danced the bear-dance before marriage . . .'[105]

[104]Herodotus, V, VI, 339, 388; Pritchett, W. K., 'The Attic Stelai', Pt II, *Hesp.*, XXV, 1956; Demosthenes, *Private Orations*, XXVII, Against Aphobus, I, 9; LIX, Against Neaera, 28, 29; see Ath-E, XIII, *passim*, for courtesans.

[105]*CAH*, V, 21; Aristophanes, *Thesmophoriazusae*, 142; *Lysistrata*, 645, and Ecclesiazusae, 332; Harrison, *Prolegomena*, 248-9.

Though colour lingered principally in the garments of ritual and tended to disappear from the clothes of everyday life, this does not mean that the Greek world became visually drab. The intense blue of the Aegean was ridden by warships with purple beaks and by ships with eyes painted on each side of their bow. To the homes of the poorer citizens the cheaper types of pottery would have lent what colour they could – red or rose, buff or fawn; but into those which were more prosperous would have come the coloured and figured art of the vase painters. The 6th century provided them with the heavily decorated Corinthian and Chalcidian ware, coloured in black and purple and mauve and red, and decorated with figures of bulls, panthers, griffons and geese. In the same century Athens produced black-figured pottery, and a little later the red-figured pottery, decorated with the people of mythology or Homeric legend, and with scenes of Dionysos and Maenads and Satyrs. By the 5th century some of the houses of Athens had painted walls and in the Hellenistic period rooms and the walls of colonnades' were often decorated with brightly coloured frescoes.

And then, against the pale Aegean sky, there were the temples. They were not altogether as some of us now are accustomed to think of them. They were not simply and sheerly dazzling white, or chaste grey, or pale fawn. Many of them, and much of them, glowed with a colour which can scarcely, at least to our eyes, have enhanced their real beauty. The Acropolis at Athens, for example, must have been an amazing sight, its temples rich with paint and gilding and inlaid glass.[106]

The Greeks enjoyed colour but even more than colour they enjoyed a festival; and this, too, gave a sensual excitement to fill out the sparse comfort of the daily life. Those festivals which concern us here are mainly Dionysiac. But before we look at the enigmatic figure of Dionysos and the equivocal nature of his rites, we might take as representative of one Greek attitude towards festival the more or less idyllic scene described by a character in Plutarch: 'Gorgus then told us that his offering of the sacrifice had taken three days, and on the last day there was a dance and merry-making, lasting the whole night long, down by the shore. The moon was shining bright upon the sea. . . .'[107]

Dionysos

'On, on! Run, dance, delirious, possessed!
Dionysos comes to his own;
Bring from the Phrygian hills to the broad streets of Hellas
The god, child of a god,
Spirit of revel and rapture, Dionysos!'[108]

This verse comes from the opening chorus of Euripides' *Bacchae*, a difficult play about a difficult god, and it summarizes one aspect of the strange wild Dionysos who was lord of delirious dancing and the revel-rout, the god of intoxication who irrupted into civilized Greece with a beauty that was partly bestial. The intellect of Greece regarded him with suspicion and alarm. Dionysos was not so difficult, perhaps, when he was the daemon of the dancing-floor with its rattle of drums and the shrill music of flutes; but when the dance changed into a rout and the women

[106] Ships: Aristophanes, *Knights*, 551 sqq.: *Acharnians*, 95. Pottery: see Bibl. Ch. 3. Houses: *OCD*, 'Houses'. Temples: see *CAH*, v, 455.

[107] Moralia, *Dinner of the Seven Wise Men*, 160E-F.

[108] *The Bacchae*, trs. Vellacott, P., 184.

streamed out, ecstatic and beyond reason, to run wild on the mountains, then his power became a danger which the Greek mind was not prepared to accept.

In the satyr-play *The Cyclops* the chorus of phallic satyrs laments the absence of Dionysos:

> 'No Bacchus here! Not here the dance,
> or the women whirling the *thyrsos*,
> or the timbrels shaken,
> where the springs rill up!
> Not here the gleam of wine,
> and no more at Nysa with nymphs,
> crying *Iacchos! Iacchos!*
> *Where is Aphrodite?* . . .
> she that I used to fly after
> along with the bare-footed Bacchae!
> Dear lord Bacchus, where do you run,
> tossing your auburn hair!'

This was the intoxication which alarmed the Greek intellect.

But as god of the vine, of wine, and of the intoxication of wine, he was readily acceptable and this became a usual disguise. It is all the more interesting to note that in his early days he was not the god of wine, nor was he specifically the god of the vine; and it would even appear that wineless libations were made to the god whom we have come to accept as the greatest wine god of all.[109]

In his early personality he is a nature god, a god of growing things and of plants and animals, and he is worshipped as a tree god and as a bull. The ivy is his sacred plant, the pine tree has a particular affiliation, and the thyrsus, the wand carried by the maenads in his ecstatic rites, is wreathed with ivy and sometimes tipped with pine cones. His early connection with animals is remembered in the fawnskins worn by those who celebrate him with their dancing.[110] It is only later that the vine becomes important in his worship and even then it is some time before it becomes predominant. When, in the *Bacchae*, his followers run on the mountains, there is wine indeed, but there are also the other gifts of the god: 'the earth flows with milk, flows with wine, flows with nectar of bees'. His composite god-head is shown even more clearly in a lovely and dramatic painting on a cylix, for here he is primitive nature-god, tree-god, and also wine-god. As wine-god he holds the thyrsus and the vine branch while a bearded, horse-tailed Satyr pipes to him on a double flute. Round him as tree-god maenads in flowing robes dance in a circle while one of them, also, plays on the double flute. And the Dionysos in the centre of this whirling dance of thyrsus-carrying women is not only tree-god; he is a plank or pillar 'draped with a splendid ritual garment. It is a primitive herm decorated with great bunches of grapes, but also with ivy sprigs and honeycombs and a necklace of dried figs . . .'[111] The centre of the dance is the god of fertile nature. Clearly in these passages and in this painting we have Dionysos in both the Early and the Middle stages of his history. As Early Dionysos he is the decorated herm worshipped by dancing women; as Middle Dionysos he is the god in particular of the vine.

[109]Euripides, *The Cyclops*, trs. Arrowsmith, W., ed. Grene and Lattimore, 63–75; Harrison, *Prolegomena*, 508–9.

[110]Harrison, *Prolegomena*, 426–8; Euripides, *Bacchae* (Vellacott), 182, 184–5.

[111]Harrison, *Prolegomena*, 426–9.

[112]Nilsson, N. M. P., *The Minoan-Mycenaean Religion and its Survival . . .*, 572, 575–6, 577, but 579; Harrison, *Prolegomena*, 478 sqq.; Kerényi, C., *The Gods of the Greeks*, 220 sqq.; Hes., *Homeric Hymns*, XXVI.

That there was an Early Dionysos seems to me beyond doubt, for the religion of Minoan Crete had a strongly Dionysiac flavour. The story that Dionysos was the son of Demeter, or alternatively of Persephone (Kore), both of whom are corn-goddesses, is a late one but it may reflect a conception which existed in Minoan Crete. If he were in Crete he would probably have been subordinate to the Great Mother and he would probably have been worshipped in a cult with a specifically feminine emphasis. His marked association with women is later seen in the *Homeric Hymn* 'To Dionysos' which dates from somewhere about the 6th century B.C. or perhaps a little earlier. Here the boy-god 'ivy-crowned Dionysos . . . splendid son of Zeus and glorious Semele' is brought up by nymphs 'in the dells of Nysa' and when they had brought him up 'then began he to wander continually through the woody coombes, thickly wreathed with ivy and laurel. And the Nymphs followed in his train with him for their leader; and the boundless forest was filled with their outcry. And so hail to you Dionysos, god of abundant clusters!' We meet these worshipping women again in the 5th century maenads of Euripides and it is difficult not to see in them a late recurrence of Minoan religion.[112]

Since the cults of the Mycenaean Greeks seem to have been much the same as those of the Minoans, it is possible also that there was a Mycenaean Dionysos. There again he would have been subordinate to the Great Mother, and he would have been a young god of the fertility of nature. Whether he was present, in one form or another, in Mycenaean Greece, we do not know. But we have seen that one of the Pylos Linear B tablets was a record of contributions to Poseidon. Now Dionysos is only another aspect of Poseidon, or Poseidon of Dionysos, since in his earlier days, and before he became specifically a sea-god, Poseidon was a god of earth-fertility and was probably also the husband of the earth-goddess. Another point is that the bull occurs in both the cults of Poseidon and Dionysos and although this does not necessarily imply a Minoan origin for either of the two gods one cannot help remembering the importance of the bull game in Minoan life and of the Minotaur in Minoan tradition.[113]

If Dionysos had been in Mycenaean Greece, he would have been one of the company of older and wilder divinities who were later accepted into the Olympic religion. Artemis was one of them, not the classical virgin, but a goddess who roamed the mountains and hunted and danced with her nymphs and was concerned with the fertility of animals and of man himself. Athene too, grey-eyed Athene, the goddess of Athens, was one of the older company but she, although at times interested in fertility, seems always to have been a virgin and never to have had the more primitive wildness of Artemis or Dionysos.[114] Athene changed little at her entry into Olympic Greece; Artemis was largely transformed; Dionysos resisted, and resisted with some success, the more sobering aspects of the Olympic trans-mutation. He remained a god of the common people of Greece, a real god of power and excitement, close to emotion and close to nature. In this sense he continued far on into Christian Europe, for the squalid and subterranean black magic of Christen-dom was often no more than a faint remembrance of the 'Old Religion'. Faint, and distorted, it may have been, but it was none the less an attempt to reach the old emotion and the old closeness to nature.

When discussing the existence of Early Dionysos one cannot help remarking that

[113]*CAH*, II, 464, Guthrie, W. K. C., 'Early Greek Religion in the light of the decipherment of Linear B', *Inst. of Class. Studs.*, University of London, *Bull.* No. 6, 1959; *Mycen. Docs.*, Tablet 171; Harrison, *Prolegomena*, 146, 433, 545, fn. 2; but see Page, D. L., *History and the Homeric Iliad*, 210, fn. 59, and 210-11.

[114]Nilsson, N. M. P., *The Minoan-Mycenaean Religion and its Survival . . .*, 503.

he plays an insignificant part in the Homeric Epic, and that even when he does appear, this may be due to interpolation.[115] He may not, therefore, have been a Mycenaean god at all; or, at any event, not in his 'ecstatic' guise. Alternatively, he may have been submerged beneath the flood of the Dorian Invasion and his existence forgotten as completely as was the existence of Mycenaean writing. But whatever the Homeric omission does mean, it must at least mean this: Dionysos was not a god who was recognized among the upper classes of the Homeric world. He may have lived beyond the borders of 'Homeric Greece' or down among the ordinary and 'un-Heroic' Greeks of the villages and the countryside. He may have moved in the shadows behind the Epic. To the Epic itself he is a stranger.

By the time of Hesiod, in the 7th century at the latest, he steps out into the gaze of the Greek world. But he is still something of a stranger. His figure is still a little shadowy. The Greeks are not sure of him. In the *Theogony* Hesiod has him with golden hair. In later legend he is a dark-haired god, as he is in the *Homeric Hymn* 'To Dionysos' which tells the famous story of the god being taken prisoner by pirates. In the Cyclops of Euripides his hair is auburn. Perhaps these differences are not those of uncertainty but merely reflect him in his different aspects. The Greeks, after all, recognized both a Green and a Black Demeter and they 'sacrificed to the Green Demeter in spring with mirth and gladness'. Perhaps, then, Black Dionysos is the winter god of the tilled earth and Golden Dionysos is the god of the summer harvest.[116]

And then there is his birthplace. Where had he come from, this confident stranger of whose origin the Greeks themselves were so uncertain? Had he fled westwards in disgust from the beer drinkers of Mesopotamia? Had he emerged from his hiding place among the long-memoried peasants and farmers of Greece? Or did he come from Aeolis, the homeland of Hesiod, in Western Asia Minor?

He may well have come in the earliest times from Mesopotamia. An old divinity of the Sumerians was Gestin, goddess of the vine, who in this form was only one aspect of the Great Earth-Goddess. Another aspect of the Earth-Goddess was Innini, the virgin deity whose mystically begotten son was Tammuz. Another version was that Ishtar, who could be either a goddess of war or love, had in her youth loved Tammuz, god of the harvest, and thus caused his death. The cult of the death and resurrection of Bêl is in all probability only another variant of the cult of Tammuz. Tammuz was the god of vegetation and in his earliest form he had probably been a tree-god. The resemblance to Dionysos is clear. Yet another god who closely resembles Tammuz is Tarku, god of Amurru, who is shown on a rock sculpture of Ivriz with clusters of grapes at his waist. He too is a god of fertility, and not only of grapes, for he also holds the ears of grain of a harvest god.[117]

There were thus plenty of Middle Eastern exemplars from whom an Early Dionysos of the Aegean could have been drawn. Considering the age-old route westwards from Syria to Cyprus and Crete it would not be surprising to learn that a god of fertility and harvest had travelled that way towards his future and most famous home. There is indeed a story, apparently a Cretan story, that Europa was the daughter, or the sister, of the king of Phoenicia and that she was ravished by Zeus in the shape of a bull which then carried her over the sea to Crete. It is noteworthy that she is often shown as carrying vine branches heavy with grapes. The

[115]For example, *Iliad*, VI; the view is expressed in Murray, Gilbert, *Lit. of Anc. Greece*, 67-8.

[116]Hes., *Theogony*, 947; *Homeric Hymns*, VII; Euripides, *Cyclops*, trs. Arrowsmith, W., ed. Grene and Lattimore, 75. Demeter: Frazer, Sir James G., *The Golden Bough*, Vol. VII, 263.

[117]*CAH*, I, 396; Langdon, S. (trs. etc.), *The Babylonian Epic of Creation* (Bibl. Ch. 2), 45 etc. Tarku: Contenau, G., 'Les Tablettes de Kerkouk' (Bibl. Ch. 2), 89 sqq., and Pl. vii.

story is somewhat poeticized but its Dionysiac flavour, with the bull and the grapes, is suggestive and it may reflect a Minoan tradition of the travelling westwards of a 'Dionysos-divinity'. There is also the insistent legend that the wife of Dionysos was Ariadne, the daughter of Minos of Crete and that Dionysos married her on the Island of Naxos in the Cyclades. (Fittingly, no doubt, the poet Archilochus of Paros compared Naxian wine to nectar.) Can this legend, in its turn, be the remnant of an old tradition and did the Cretan civilization also – or first – meet Dionysos in the islands of the Aegean? And, if so, was he an Aegean god or had he come to the islands from Anatolia?[118]

It was generally said that the birthplace of Dionysus was 'Nysa' although Euripides gives it as Thebes in Boeotia. 'Nysa' is usually translated as meaning Thrace, and the view which commands wide acceptance is that, towards the end of the Mycenaean Age, Dionysos went with the emigrants from Thrace who were colonising Phrygia in Asia Minor. There, during the dark centuries which followed the Dorian Invasion, he acquired, or met with, his Lydian name of Bacchus. Then, later, he returned to the mainland of Greece.[119]

When he did return he was Middle Dionysos, still a god of nature and fertility, but now with growing emphasis upon wine and the vine. This is clear from the *Homeric Hymn* which tells how he was kidnapped by pirates and how, when he manifested his power, not only did a dark ivy-plant twine 'about the mast, blossoming with flowers, and with rich berries growing on it; and all the thole-pins were covered with garlands' but also 'a vine spread out both ways along the top of the sail with many clusters hanging down from it' and 'sweet, fragrant wine ran streaming throughout all the black ship'. Here he is still the 'old' god of the sacred ivy but he is also the 'newer' god of the grape and the wine-cup, and it is in this latter guise that Alcaeus of Mytilene sees him in the 6th century B.C.

> 'Bacchus, son of Sémelê
> And of Zeus, discovered wine
> Giving it to man to be
> Care's oblivious anodyne.'

Of the 'older' elements which persisted in the cult of Middle Dionysos, the most remarkable is the presence of the intoxicated maenads, the raging women. These ecstatic women were not intoxicated by wine; they were god-intoxicated, 'possessed' by the god, raging with the superhuman 'rage' of joy or love or anger. They were delivered over entirely to the rapture and emotion of the moment. Under the compulsion of the god they left their homes in the city and streamed out to the woods and mountains where they ran and danced in company, and while they were 'running with the rage' they tore an animal to pieces and ate it in a raw communion. It was irresistible mass madness. Euripides' Dionysos says of Boeotian Thebes: '... The whole female population ... every woman there was in the town, I drove raving from their homes.' The same thing happened at Boeotian Orchomenos though here not all the women swarmed out to run and dance in the mountains. Three remained in the city and scorned the maenad madness. Dionysos appeared to these three sisters and warned them that they must go and dance. They

[118] Europa: Kerényi, C., *Gods of the Greeks*, 96. Ariadne: Nilsson, N. M. P., *Minoan-Mycenaean Religion and its Survival* . . ., 523–5; Hes., *Theogony*, 947. Naxian (and the vine Naxia): Ath-E, I, 30f; II, 52d.

[119] *Iliad*, VI; Kerényi, C., *The Gods of the Greeks*, 227; Euripides, *Bacchae* (Vellacott), 181; Nilsson, N. M. P., *Minoan-Mycenaean Religion and its Survival* . . ., 567–76; *Greek Piety*, 21; *Griechische Feste von religiöser Bedeutung*, 271; Farnell, L. R., *Cults of the Greek States*, V, 88; Harrison, *Prolegomena*, 378.

refused. 'The god turned himself into a bull, then into a lion, and finally into a leopard. Ivy and vines grew over the weaving-chair, serpents nested in the baskets of wool.' As a sacrifice to the god the terrified women tore a child to pieces and then 'wreathed with ivy, bindweed and laurel, they roamed over the mountains . . .'.[120]

The historical maenads were not intoxicated by wine and they did not indulge in unbridled orgies of sex. They were, in legend, accompanied by revelling satyrs, wild men who were sexually excitable but there is little evidence that sexual intercourse (or for that matter the tearing apart of an animal or the sacrifice of a child) played anything but a symbolical part in the Dionysiac orgies of later Greece. These things were only reflections of very primitive rituals which must have existed much earlier than the Age of the Mycenaeans. There is, of course, no doubt that there were maenads in Greece in Classical and in later times and there is no doubt that they did hold Dionysiac 'orgies'. Aeschylus, in the 5th century, testifies to their existence and so does Pausanias in the 2nd century of the Christian era. Pausanias is interesting, 'The former passage,' he says, 'in which Homer speaks of the beautiful dancing-floors of Panopeus, I could not understand until I was taught by the women whom the Athenians call Thyiads. The Thyiads are Attic women, who with the Delphian women go to Parnassus every other year and celebrate orgies in honour of Dionysos. It is the custom for these Thyiads to hold dances at places, including Panopeus, along the road from Athens. The epithet Homer applies to Panopeus is thought to refer to the dance of the Thyiads.' This sounds as decorous as the protracted outing of a Women's Club, but it was not without its hazards. Plutarch, a little earlier than Pausanias, relates that the Thyiades on Parnassus were once trapped by a fierce gale and a snowstorm and that those who climbed to rescue them had 'their capes . . . frozen so stiff and wooden that when they were opened out, they broke and split apart'.[121]

In later times, both Classical and 'Christian', the maenads appear to have been chaste and worthy women, quite untouched by drunkenness or sexual licence. There is every reason to think that, in general, this was so. But in the 7th and 6th centuries B.C. this may not always have been the case and there may have been sporadic instances of over-indulgence in wine or excited indulgence in sex. It would scarcely have been surprising if there had been, since the earlier orgies gave opportunity for an explosive release of emotion and an uninhibited delight in sensual energy. Some of the women, too, may have used them as an excuse to escape from the boredom and restraint of everyday life. Not all the maenads were driven by the madness. In the words of the anonymous poet:

> 'Many the Bacchi that brandish the rod:
> Few that be filled with the fire of the God.'[122]

As the 'raging god' Middle Dionysos was not acceptable to the higher thought of Greece. Accordingly an effort was made to tame him. The man – and some people think that he really was a man and not a myth – who tamed him most was Orpheus, 'the sweet singer', for Orpheus translated a cult of possession into one of purification. Dionysos remained the central divinity of the Orphic religion but he was now

[120]Hes., *Homeric Hymns*, VII. Alcaeus: Higham, Bowra, *Oxford Book of Greek Verse in Trans.*, No. 135, III, trs. Bowra, C. M.; Euripides, *Bacchae* (Vellacott), 182; Kerényi, C., *Gods of the Greeks*, Greeks, 228–9; Harrison, *Prolegomena*, 388 sqq.

[121]Aeschylus, *Eumenides*, 22–6; Pausanias, X, 4, 3. Panopeus in Homer: *Iliad*, XVII, 307; *Odyssey*, XI, 581; Plutarch, *Moralia*, De prim. frig., 953D. There is an interesting discussion in Harrison, *Prolegomena*, 388 sqq. For a maenad in a frenzy, see Buschor, E., *Greek Vase Painting*, trs. Richards, G. C., Pl. lxx, red-figured archaic period.

[122]Higham, Bowra, *Oxford Book of Greek Verse in Trans.*, No. 692, trs. Richard Garnett.

Apollo and Muses
Boeotian Cup
450–425 B.C.
Dresden

a mystic, rather than an ecstatic figure. He is Dionysos-Zagreus, for Zagreus is the mystery shape which he took in the mystery religion of Orpheus. The omophagy – 'the red and bleeding feast' – of the animal torn to pieces in the Dionysiac running was given a mystic explanation in which Zagreus himself was the sacrifice who was torn and eaten. It was the ancestors of Man who killed and ate Zagreus and it is because of this ancestry that Man has a sinful nature. To purify himself from sin and thus to obtain a happy life in the after-world a man must be initiated into the mysteries of Dionysos and through those mysteries become pure.

This was no creed of raving maenads and revelling satyrs. It was the opposite. It was a religion which condemned the body as inherently evil, which emphasised the sinful part of man's nature and which called upon the initiate to abstain from killing animals and from eating meat. The early animosity between the Dionysos of the raging maenads and the Dionysos-Zagreus of the Orphic mysteries is dramatically pictured in the death of Orpheus for the sweet singer with his lyre was torn to pieces by Thracian maenads.

But the head of Orpheus, still singing, was found by the Muses and buried in Lesbos. This was the triumph. The gentler, more spiritual song of Orpheus prevailed over the wild music of the maenad rout. There is something of Apollo about Orpheus. They were both musicians. In Lesbos the head of Orpheus gave oracles; so did the Oracle of Apollo at Delphi. Nor is it mere coincidence that at Delphi the Oracle spoke through the mouth of the Pythia, a woman possessed and 'intoxicated' by the god, and that the religious year at Delphi was shared by Apollo and by Dionysos. Here again, with Apollo as with Orpheus, Dionysos is being tamed.[123]

Tamed though he almost was by the Olympic religion, and transmuted by the

[123]Harrison, *Prolegomena, passim.*

123

Oenochoë
Mycenaean, 15th century
B.C.
Marseilles, Musée des
Antiquités

Orphics in their mystic speculation, he continued nevertheless to play an important part in the life of the ordinary Greek. His mark is stamped firmly on many of the festivals of the Attic year: the Haloa in December to January, the Lenaea in January to February, the Anthesteria in February to March, and the Eleusinian Mysteries in September to October. He was connected also with the Rustic Dionysia in December to January and the City Dionysia in March to April. Despite the Orphic emphasis in some of these festivals the older god is not entirely banished: or rather the two older gods, for when we meet him here he is Early as well as Middle Dionysos. He is not only the god of wine and of revel (though no longer raging) but he is also the earlier god of the harvest and fertility and of growing things.

The remote ancestry of the Haloa is quite clear. It was the harvest festival of the threshing floor. In Attica 'they were wont to carry first-fruits from Athens to Eleusis and to sport upon the threshing-floors. . . .' It is one of the oldest festivals of a settled, agricultural community. It has lain for so many millennia so close to the heart of religious emotion and of human happiness that it is difficult now to see one of the threshing floors of the Mediterranean and not to feel the throb and the pulse of the past. These, in their simple form, are the dancing-grounds of Ariadne and of Panopeus, and the hard, round threshing-floors of modern Greece bring one close to the world which knew Ariadne and her husband Dionysos.

In Attica the Haloa was a festival of Demeter, Persephone (Kore, the maiden daughter) and Dionysos. There was a procession of Poseidon, who, as we have already seen, had some affinities to Early Dionysos. The rites were largely performed by women and on the tables at the culminating banquet there were 'cakes shaped like the symbols of sex'.[124] But to the primitive meaning of the Haloa, Attica added the meaning of Dionysos as a god of wine, since the Athenian feast was made 'on the occasion of the cutting of the vines and the tasting of the wine made from them'. Thus, instead of being held in the late summer, it was held at mid-winter which was the time of one of the festivals of Dionysos. The shift of meaning from grain to wine is made even clearer by a late story that the Haloa was celebrated in memory of Icarios who first received Dionysos into Attica and first made Attic wine.

The feast of Lenaea, which was held in January to February, is somewhat obscure but there is no doubt about its Dionysiac flavour since it takes its name from the word *lenos*, meaning a tub or vat. It was probably much less important than the Anthesteria which followed it in the early spring.

The Anthesteria, the festival of flowers, is as primitive in its origin as the festival of the threshing floor. The Anthesteria is a festival of fertility and of the spirits of the dead; it is also a festival of blessing the new wine and then drinking it. In its origin it was probably older even than Early Dionysos and in its origin it was by no means a revel. It was a feast of the spirits of the dead and in earlier times the opening of the jars was not the opening of wine jars but the opening of jars which had been the graves of the dead. At Anthesteria these guests from the grave were placated so that no bad influence should fall upon the fertility of the coming year.

With the arrival of Dionysos the Anthesteria cheered up enormously and, as we can see from Aristophanes, 'the Pitcher-feast' became a festival of wine and drinking. For some time at least it kept some association with the dead but more and more it became devoted to the 'revel-tipsy throng'.[125] The festival lasted for three days, the drinking was considerable, and everybody enjoyed themselves. The first day, the Pithoigia, was the opening of the jars – wine jars and not grave jars – and the broaching of the new wine. This done, the revel began. The next day was the *choes*, the jugs, when the new wine was blessed before Dionysos. Everyone carried in their own jug of wine and drank from it and even the children were given little jugs. The jugs, or *choes*, were wreathed with flowers or garlands of ivy;

[124] For all these festivals, see Harrison, *Prolegomena, passim*; and for possible Mycenaean, or Minoan, origin of the Mysteries, Nilsson, N. M. P., *Minoan-Mycenaean Religion and its Survival . . .*, 443, 576-7.

[125] Aristophanes, *Acharnians*, 1068; *Frogs*, 215 sqq.; Harrison, *Prolegomena*, IX, 32 sqq.; van Hoorn, G., *Choes and Anthesteria*, 10, 15, etc., and interesting collection of Plates.

so were the Attic children. Branches were carried, or hung from walls and tables, while dancers were crowned with white or purple blossoms. There was a ceremony of the wedding of Dionysos. The third day was the *chytroi*, the pots, and on this day pots of food were offered to the dead. The drinking, however, went on and sombre thoughts were dissipated by Dionysos. Of the wine-feast itself the climax was a drinking contest, the prize for the winner being an *askos* filled with wine or a cake. The three days of ceremony and merry-making were the pagan Easter of the Mediterranean.

The most famous of the festivals with which Dionysos is connected are the Eleusinian Mysteries. They took place in September to October and they were an ancient harvest festival. But, so far as we can tell, the ancient rite had been considerably developed by Orphic influence and it seems that Dionysos – Iaccos at Eleusis – was a combination of the Early Dionysos of growing things and the sacred child of Orphic speculation. No doubt the Orphics elaborated and evolved what they found at Eleusis but the 'Mysteries' which they found there were in their origin Mycenaean, and probably Minoan as well, and Dionysos may have played his Early part in them long before Orpheus sang his gentle and sin-conscious song.

Early Dionysos had been a god of growing things. Middle Dionysos was a god of wild and fertile Nature, of the vine and wine and of the raging maenads. Then came the third, the Late Dionysos, the god of wine and only of wine. In this guise he is no longer religious, his power is diminished, and his beauty has become a toy. In early Classical Greece he is often shown as a grown man, bearded and mature. The later 5th century Parthenon Dionysos of Phidias shows him as a young man, yet still fully masculine and with power. But by the 4th century he is losing his dignity. The mimic scene of Ariadne and Dionysos in the *Symposium* of Xenophon is rococo and faintly erotic and quite unworthy of the Great God. At Pella, the capital city of Alexander the Great, a floor mosaic shows him as a naked and voluptuous youth riding on the back of a panther.[126] He is becoming degraded into a minor deity of petty sensual indulgence. The god who drove the revel rout at Thebes has become the perfunctory toast of dissolute topers. It is a sad end for one of the gods.

But he has, though very indirectly, a happier culmination. Simple and joyful country festivals are bound to include drinking, singing, and dancing. These are all Dionysiac and from these simple revels developed the drama of the Greeks. The Dionysia were festivals of Dionysos at which dramatic performances were given. Those at the Rustic Dionysia may not perhaps have been very elevated. They may, for the most part, have been mummer-shows, interrupted by the Attic game of trying to balance on greased and inflated wine-skins, but here, with all its ribaldry and dressing up and exaggerated mimicry, is the germ of drama. And if Dionysos moved men to drama through the Dionysia of the countryside and the city, he moved them also towards song, for the Dithyramb which became a serious poetic form began as the Song of Dionysos. In early times it was a choral song to the god and although it may always have been serious it may not always have been quite so stately as it later became. It is pleasant to know, for example, that the early poet Archilochus of Paros claimed 'he knew how to lead the Dithyramb in honour of King Dionysos when his wits were thunderstruck by wine'.[127]

[126]For a discussion of the Eleusinian Mysteries, see Harrison, *Prolegomena*, 539 sqq. Pella: Petsas, P., 'Alexander the Great's Capital...', *ILN*, Aug. 2nd, 1958.

[127]Rustic Dionysia: see in particular, Aristophanes, *Acharnians*, 242 sqq.; also *Plutus*, 1129; and *CAH*, v, 115, 116, 138. For leaping on wine-skins: *FAC*, II, Eubulus, 8.

'. . . vineyard-lovingest of all'

This is Aristophanes praising 'Peace, the Goddess best and greatest, vineyard-lovingest of all'.[128] Many a hard-working Greek must have echoed the playwright's comment for in the 5th century B.C. vineyards were important to the economy of Greece and their destruction in warfare was a heavy loss. So important had they become that the agricultural emphasis was shifting from the growing of grain to the growing of olive oil and wine and this emphasis continued into the Hellenistic period. By the 4th century at the latest there was a change also from 'subsistence' to 'industrial' farming: the produce was no longer consumed entirely, or almost entirely, by the farmer and his household but was more and more sent out to fetch its price in the market.

It was in Greece, and in Classical Greece, that viticulture first became a widespread and expert profession. The foundations of European viticulture are not Greek; if one can trace them back to any single starting place that place, as I have already suggested, may well have been Syria. But the growing of wine on a really large and commercial scale, and the adoption of a more or less scientific attitude towards viticulture, must be considered as primarily an achievement of the Greeks. They wrote works on agriculture, including viticulture, of which the first was Hesiod's *Works and Days*, to be followed much later by Xenophon's *Oeconomicus* which gives some picture of life on his estate at Scillus near Olympia. The scientific research of Aristotle includes the occasional mention of the vine as, for example, when he speaks of 'kapnias', the 'smoky vine' so called from the colour of its grapes.[129] But it was left for his friend and pupil Theophrastus of Eresus to attempt, in his *Enquiry into Plants*, a scientific system of botany and it is to Theophrastus that we owe the first real approach to ampelography, the study of the vine.

Lest it be thought, however, that the scientific attitude was all-pervasive, one might remember that Pausanias – and this was as late as the 2nd century A.D. – was amazed by the wind-ritual at Methana in Troezen. 'A wind called Lips, which rushes down from the Saronic gulf, dries up the tender shoots of the vine. When the squall is upon them two men take a cock, which must have all its feathers white, tear it in two, and run round the vines in opposite directions, each of them carrying one half of the cock. When they come back to the place they start from they bury the cock there.'

Nevertheless, the scientific, or at least the articulate, approach gradually became more general. That there were many writers on agriculture can be seen from the list of names cited in the 1st century A.D. by the romanised Spaniard Columella.[130] But what is surprising is that so little of their work has come down to us, so little indeed that we cannot form any detailed idea of Greek viticulture.

On the form of the vineyard the statements of Theophrastus are ambiguous. He makes it clear that pruning was known to be important but he is unclear as to the ultimate shape to which the vines were cut. (Pruning, of course, was no innovation for Hesiod speaks of it.) Theophrastus does indicate, however, that vines were commonly grown in rows and he states the view that 'low ground is most suitable for the olive, fig and vine'.[131] We might thus imagine that the typical vineyard of the ancient Greeks was much like the modern vineyards between Patras and Pyrgos

[128] *The Peace*, 308.

[129] *Generation of Animals*, 770b, 20; see also Theophrastus, *Enq. into Plants*, II, iii, 2. For kapnias: Ath-E, I, 31e; IV, 131f; Plin., XXIII, 39, 40.

[130] Pausanias: Harrison, *Prolegomena*, 67; Colum., I, i, 7 sqq.

[131] Theophrastus, *Enq. into Plants*, I, ix, 1; II, v, 7; vii, 2; IV, iv, 8; Hes., *Works and Days*, 564 sqq.; also Aristophanes, *Acharnians*, 986; *The Peace*, 1147; Xen., *Oec.*, XIX, and Hehn, V., *Wandering of Plants and Animals* (Bibl. Ampelography), 75, for a generalized view.

and Olympia in the Western Peloponnese, where the vines are pruned to a height of about 4½ feet and stretch out across the flat ground in long, luxuriant rows. The ancient vineyards could not always, of course, have been on low ground. Some of them would have been on terraces on hillsides; others would have been small and windswept enclosures like those which one now sees high up in the mountains of Locris on the Gulf of Corinth. The commonest form of modern Greek vineyard, in Crete as in Attica and Boeotia, is that comprised of 'bush vines', unstaked, cut down to about 3 feet, and planted in rows; and I am inclined to think that this was also the commonest form of vineyard in Classical Greece. I must stress, however, that this is only my opinion.

We know more about Greek vintaging than we do about Greek vineyards but

The Vintage: Satyrs
preparing the grapes
Attic black-figured Amphora
Amasis the Painter
c 550 B.C.
Würzburg, University
Museum

we still do not know enough for a complete picture. There is no reason to suppose that the vintage changed much from Homeric to Classical times. Indeed, one would not expect it to have done so. The fruit would still have been collected and carried to the vat in those plaited baskets described by Homer on the Shield of Achilles. For very small vintages the vat may have been a pithos in which the grapes were mashed or trodden. More frequently it would have been some form of treading tank in which the grapes were trodden by foot and from which the must ran off into a *pithos* that was, it would seem, often sunk into the ground. A gay and interesting picture of this type of vintage is given on an Attic black-figure amphora painted by the Amasis painter about 550 B.C. Satyrs are picking grapes from an overhead vine and putting them into a large bowl-shaped container which seems to be made of basketwork and which stands on a flat, shallow tray raised on legs about a foot above the ground. To the music of the double flute a satyr is treading out the grapes in the container. The juice runs through the meshes of the basketwork and onto the shallow tray: thence it is led off by a spout into a *pithos* which appears to be sunk in the ground. In the use of the basket container, this amphora may illustrate a special technique, but it is likely, to say the least of it, that the shallow tray on legs was a common form of treading tank in ancient Hellas.[132] And as a matter of fact this type of structure is still used today in parts of Central Greece.

A development of later Greek times was the more efficient use of the wine-press. In his pastoral novel *Daphnis and Chloe* Longus writes: 'Now one of the peasants needed a rope to haul up the stone that was used for crushing the grapes after they had been trodden down . . .'. Longus is a very late author, probably of the 3rd century A.D., but in this instance he may be committing a deliberate archaism. It is extremely likely that heavy stones were used to crush grapes in very early times as in fact they were used in 6th-century Greece to weight the beam of the press. The beam-press itself was not invented by the later Greeks, since one (for olives) has been found in the Cyclades and dates from Late Helladic, the age of the Mycenaeans. It became commoner after the Geometric Age, but its use still required considerable exertion as can be seen from an illustration on a Greek vase. This shows the beam being pulled down by a man who clings to it like a monkey while at the same time a huge stone is being roped to the beam. More efficient, and more sparing of the labours of these village Hercules, was the invention of the screw-press which happened most probably in Greece and somewhere about the 2nd century B.C. The knowledge of this mechanism spread all over the Hellenistic world and many a slab of stone once stained with sweat or grape juice must thenceforward have rested idly in the sunshine.[133]

One example may suffice to show the spread of viticulture as well as the spread of efficient (or fairly efficient) methods of vintaging. This example is the 'winery' which has recently been excavated at Mirmeki in that part of the Russian Crimea which in ancient times was known as the Cimmerian Bosporus and the Bosporan kingdom. This winery lay on the northern rim of the Hellenistic world. It may have been built in the 3rd century B.C. and was probably still functing in the 1st century B.C. It consists of three treading tanks and two cisterns to receive the juice, all of them being surfaced by a form of cement. There is also a flat, circular pressing bed made of limestone which measures about a yard and a half across and has two

[132] *Iliad*, XVIII; Buschor, E., *Griechische Vasen*, 122, Pl. 139. Cf. the Mycenaean wine-press at Palaikastro, Crete: Dawkins, R. M., 'Excavations at Palaikastro, II', *BSA*, 9, 295; for the modern equivalent, see Grace, Virginia, 'Wine Jars', *The Classical Journal*, 42, 445, 1946-7.

[133] *Daphnis and Chloe*, II, 13; *Hist. Tech.*, 113 sqq.; Ros., *SEHH*, 364.

concentric grooves running round its circumference. Into the inner groove would have fitted the bottom edge of the container which held the grape-skins while into the outer would have run the juice from the pressed grapes. The capacity of the cisterns (if they were only filled once at each vintage) do not in themselves indicate any large-scale viticulture, even if they do indicate some degree of efficiency. But then we must remember that five other wineries have so far been discovered in the Bosporan area.[134]

With fragments from authors and scenes from vase paintings we can build up a reasonably coherent picture of the life of a Greek *vigneron*. In January he shivers in the 'wretched days, all of them fit to skin an ox' and it is in these harsh days that he is urged by Hesiod to 'pass by the smithy and its crowded lounge . . . when the cold keeps men from fieldwork, – for then an industrious man can greatly prosper his house'. In these days too he must often have yearned for the mulled wine of which the poet Strattis speaks. Then, towards the end of February before the swallow comes, he must prune the vines and laboriously dig round them until May. In June 'the chirping grasshopper sits in a tree and pours down his shrill song continually from under his wings in the season of wearisome heat'. In high summer, if the *vigneron* has gathered in his own small grain harvest or helped with that of his neighbour, there is the winnowing 'on a smooth threshing-floor in an airy place', when, in the words of Phrynicus, he would have said: 'I'll whistle a winnowing-tune for you and me.' Later he must strip the vines of some of their leaves so that the fruit shall ripen. Next, September and the vintage: the piling of grapes into plaited baskets: the drying of grapes for raisin wine: the treading of the fresh grapes and the juice running from the platform into the waiting *pithos*. To accompany the treading there would have been 'a vintage flute-melody', a later variant, perhaps, of the 'sweet Linos-song' which sounded in the pages of the *Iliad*. And there would also have been the hard work of the press, the sweating at the heavy beam as it came slowly down upon the grapes. Then, finally, the desired moment, the 'vineyard-lovingest' moment of all, the Dionysiac celebration, the thanksgiving.[135] No wonder that Dionysos lived on in the hearts of the Greeks.

Salt in the Wine

'Wine is sweet when sea-water is poured into it,' says Athenaeus, and it is remarkable to find that the Greeks not only tolerated, but even admired, this peculiar mixture. In fact, they made quite a lot of '*oinos thalassikos*', or sea-water wine. Coan was considered to be a first-class wine yet one style of it, a white wine, was strongly flavoured with sea-water. So, though less esteemed, were several others: Clazomenian, Ephesian and (probably) Erythraean, all from Ionia in Asia Minor; Halicarnassian and Myndian, both from Caria in Asia Minor; Rhodian from the Island of Rhodes; and Phorinean which possibly came from Attica.[136] The origin of this apparently strange custom of salting is ascribed by Pliny to an act of dishonesty on the part of a slave who used sea-water to fill up a *pithos* of wine to its proper measure. The incident may have occurred but it was certainly not the origin of '*oinos thalassikos*'.

When they were preparing for the vintage the early wine growers of the coast

[134] *Mirmeki*, 140 sqq.; a preliminary report with photographs, appeared in *ILN*, Jan. 5th, 1957.

[135] Hes., *Works and Days*, *passim*; *FAC*, I, Strattis, 57; Xen., *Oec.*, XIX; *FAC*, I, Phrynicus, 14; also for 'vintage flute-melody'; *Iliad*, XVIII; for mulled wine see also *FAC*, II, Mnesimachus, 4. 'Sport upon the threshing floors': Harrison, *Prolegomena*, 146.

[136] Sea-water wine: Ath-E, I, 26b; Dioscorides, *Herbal*, V, 27. Coan: Varro, II, Intro., 3; cf. Cato, CV, CXII; Plin., XIV, 78-9. Clazomenian: Plin., XIV, 73-4. Ephesian: Plin., XIV, 75; Ath-E, I, 31d; and Strab., 14, 1, 15. Erythraean: Theophr., O., 48, 52; cf. Strab., 13, 1, 64. Halicarnassian: Ath-E, I, 32e. Myndian: Ath-E, I, 32e. Rhodian: Plin., XIV, 79; Ath-E, I, 31e, 32e. Phorinean: Plin., XIV, 79.

Circe giving a Potion to Odysseus
Boeotian Cup
450–420 B.C.
London, British Museum

and the islands would most probably have washed their *pithoi* in sea-water. This is a reasonable, and respectable, technique and it has a long history. At the time of the Renaissance in Christian Europe, it was recommended that 'when casks which have held wine are empty, wash them quickly with salted water' while today, in some of the *vignobles* of Western Europe, new wooden casks are washed with sea-water or with solutions of sea-salt so that the new wood shall not give any unpleasant taste to the wine.[137] Modern casks are always washed afterwards with fresh water, but if this had not been done with the ancient *pithoi* some of the sea-salt may have remained in the fabric of the pottery. If the effect had been pleasing to ancient taste, then sea-water would have been introduced into the wine itself.

The effect was pleasing and the practice continued. That it did continue is a revealing comment on the taste of the ancient world. But it is also a comment on the quality of ancient wine for the use of this technique has a double interpretation. In the first place, it was used to give 'bite' or piquancy or, as Pliny says in a passage of his *Natural History*, to 'enliven the smoothness of their wines'. In the second place, it was undoubtedly used to amend or disguise a deficient wine as well as to preserve its life and prevent it from going sour – a method which was still used at the end of the Middle Ages in Europe.[138] When dealing with ancient Greece it is difficult to separate these two motives and to decide which was the more important. We may be inclined to feel that taste provided the major, or at least the initial, motive.

To some extent this view is supported by the fact that the Greeks liked to put perfume into their wine. 'A strange, thirsty wine is this precious perfumed stuff,' says Poseidippus, who does not seem to be sure whether he liked it or not, and who, for that matter, may even have been referring to wine whose extra bouquet may have been given to it by the addition of sea water. Dexicrates, on the other hand, seems to be quite sure:

> 'And if I tipple, I drink my wine with snow
> And a dash o' the finest scent Egyptians know.'

[137] Plin., XIV, 78; Petrus de Crescentiis, *Liber ruralium commodorum* (Bibl. Ch. 5), Bk IV, cap. xxxiii; Nègre, E., Françot, P., *Manuel Pratique de Vinification . . .*, 75–6 (Bibl. Gen.).

[138] Plin., XIV, 120; cf. Henderson, 244; Petrus de Crescentiis (fn. 137, above), Bk IV, cap. xxxviii.

The testimony of these two men is not conclusive; by perfume Poseidippus might conceivably have meant 'bouquet' and the Egyptian scent of Dexicrates could have been used to perfume the room and not the wine. But a treatise of Theophrastus clears up at least some of the doubt: 'Perfume . . . and other fragrant things . . . give a pleasant taste to wine', he writes, adding that it gives a relish or bouquet to the liquor and 'this effect indeed it has on wine which is sweet and specially needs the addition of perfume, because it has no "relish" of its own'. Elsewhere he explains in slightly more general terms: 'The object of the mixture . . . is a desire to produce, as it were, a pleasanter taste: this for instance is the object of flavouring wine with perfumes or of putting spices into it.'[139]

Honey was also used to give a 'pleasanter taste' to wine. Here, again, is the comment of Theophrastus: 'the wine which is served in the town-hall of Thasos, which appears to be of wonderfully delightful quality, is thus flavoured. For they put into the jar a lump of dough which has been kneaded up with honey, so that the wine gets its fragrance from itself, but its sweet taste from the honied dough.'[140]

Honey in wine was probably popular throughout all the centuries of ancient Greece, not merely because it made harsh wine better and bad wine drinkable but also because sweet wine seems always to have been appreciated. Some people, it is true, have given a different, or a wider, interpretation to the honey technique and have supposed that honey was added to the must before fermentation in order to increase the alcohol content of the wine. This may have happened, but I do not know of any evidence to show that in ancient Greece it ever did happen. I suspect that the Greeks were largely unaware of the connection between the degree of sugar and the amount of alcohol.

Honey was used to soften or sweeten wine and it was used in other drinks as well. Two of these 'honey-hearted' drinks were Oxymel and Melitites. Oxymel was made from honey, vinegar, salt and rain water, heated ten times to boiling point, then kept till old. Melitites, or 'honey-wine', was made of must or wine, honey and salt, the whole mixture being just brought to the boil. Here again, in both these drinks, we meet the emphasis upon the piquant taste, an emphasis which could sometimes go as far as a liking for actual sourness. The Sour Wine of the Island of Cos was well known; so was the Omphacium or Omphacites of the Aegean – and particularly of Lesbos – which was the juice of unripe or only partly ripe grapes.[141] The 'Sour Wine' of Cos may have been a euphemism for vinegar but it need not always have reached the vinegar stage. And although it may have been used, like Omphacites, for seasoning food or medicinally, one may also consider that both of them were found to be refreshing drinks in the great heat of summer.

The taste for piquancy which was manifest among the ancient Greeks finds a modern expression in the resinated wine of their descendants. A great deal of ancient Greek wine was *retsina* also, either because resin had been mixed into the wine when it was made or because the wine had been in contact with the pitched coating of the inside of its amphora. There was very little glazing on the inside of the old Greek amphoras so that if they were not rendered impermeable by polishing they would have been coated with oil or smeared with pitch. The latter was the most frequent method. But the pitch coating was not universal. Few Coan amphoras show a pitch lining and it is rare to find it in Rhodian jars. And here one

[139] Poseidippus: Ath-E, I, 31f–32b. Dexicrates: *FAC*, II; Theophr., O., 9–11. For spiced wine, see also *FAC*, I, Eupolis, 122 B.C.

[140] Theophr., O., 51.

[141] *Iliad*, VI. Oxymel: Plin., XIV, 114; Dioscorides, *Herbal*, V, 22. Melitites: Plin., XIV, 85; Dioscorides, *Herbal*, V, 15; Ath-E, I, 29a. Coan: Frank, Johnson, II, 315. Omphacium: Plin., XII, 60; Dioscorides, *Herbal*, V, 6, 12; Ompacium could also be the dried pulp of unripe, or partly ripe, grapes, which, sometimes, had been sun-dried before pressing. See also fn. 197–9 in Ch. 2, and fn. 27 in this chapter.

might remark that there is so far no trace of a pitch coating in the wine jars which have been excavated at the Mycenaean Palace of Nestor.

But retsina was not only produced, as one might say, casually, by its transport and storage in pitched jars but also deliberately, since it was not at all uncommon for resin to be mixed into the body of the wine. Chian wine, for example, was considered to be in the first class of Greek wines, yet the Chian wine which was imported into Athens about 430 B.C. was resinated, and heavily resinated at that. At Mirmeki in the Crimea the process is apparent for, beside the tank which held the grape juice, there is a mortar for grinding resin.[142] These resinated wines of Chios and the Crimea were certainly not exceptional. It was fortunate indeed for the wine-makers of the ancient Greek world that the taste of the resin which they used to preserve the life of their wines coincided with the taste for piquancy which animated the palates of their customers.

The Scarlet Ships

Herodotus tells us that 'all ships in the old days had their topsides painted scarlet' and we remember that, when Odysseus went to Troy, 'with him followed twelve ships with vermilion prow'.

In the 8th century B.C. the scarlet ships of the Greeks were plying into the Central and Western Mediterranean. Cumae, near Naples, was founded about 750 B.C., Syracuse in Sicily in 733, Sybaris in Southern Italy in 720; and, at about the time of the founding of Syracuse, Greek imports were going into Hyères on the French Riviera.[143]

Among the Greeks who had been adventuring to the South of France in the 8th century were men from Phocaea, an Ionian city in Asia Minor. These Phocaeans played an important part in opening up the Western Mediterranean and about 600 B.C. they founded a colony at Massilia, the modern Marseilles. To begin with their ships, like those of the other Greeks, may have carried wine to the new colonies whose vineyards had not yet had time to mature. But later on the arrival of the scarlet ships would have been welcomed more by the vineyard-less native tribesmen than by the vineyard-minded colonists for although the natives may for some time have resisted the sophistication of Greek culture, they had no inhibitions about the pleasures of Greek wine.

The Celts – an intemperate lot in any case – were eager admirers of this new pleasure. Their admirations occasionally took a strange turn. Poseidonius relates that at 'dinner parties' some of them '. . . would collect silver or gold, or a number of jars of wine from the audience . . . and having exacted a pledge that their award would be carried out, they would decree that the collection be distributed as presents to their dearest relatives; they then stretched themselves on their backs over their shields and someone standing near would cut their throats with a sword'.

This uneconomical practice was, at least in its recording, as late as the 2nd or 1st centuries B.C. Much earlier than that, trade had been moving north from Marseilles, going up towards central France by the Rhône and the Saône, and north-eastwards through Franche Comté to the Upper Rhine. The number of Ionian 6th-century wine amphoras which have been found in the valley of the Upper Saône and in the

[142]For the information about amphoras I am much indebted to Miss Virginia Grace of the American School of Classical Studies in Athens. Chian: Grace, Virginia, 'Stamped Amphora Handles, found in 1931-2'. Appendix A, 'Selected Seals . . .', *Hesp.*, III, 296, 1934. Mirmeki: see fn. 134. The Palace of Nestor information has most courteously been given to me by Miss Mabel Lang.

[143]Herodotus, III; *Iliad*, II, and *Odyssey*, IX; Dunbabin, *passim*; and for possible earlier foundations, 34, 35; Blakeway, A., 'Prolegomena to the Study of Greek Commerce with Italy, Sicily and France in the Eighth and Seventh Centuries B.C.', *BSA*, 33, 1935; Clark, J. G. D., *Prehistoric Europe, The Economic Basis*, 273 (Bibl. Ch. 2).

Jura testifies to the activity of Greek commerce and to the barbarian liking for Greek wine. Some of these jars, of course, might have held olive oil but they would not have been in the majority. Most of them would have travelled with Ionian wine, good wine at heart perhaps, but almost certainly doctored with resin, and shipped only seven months after its making.[144]

The barbarians would have got their resinated wine about mid-summer for the earlier Greeks were much averse to sailing in the winter. One sympathises. A Mediterranean storm is not a tranquil experience. Ancient writers thought so too and with a reluctant fascination they point out the hazards and perils of the sea trader's life. Hesiod, who admits that he knows little about sea-faring, goes to the extreme of prudence. Mid-summer, he says, 'is the right time for men to go sailing ... At that time the winds are steady, and the sea is harmless. Then trust in the winds without care, and haul your swift ship down to the sea and put all the freight on board; but make all haste you can to return home again and do not wait till the time of the new wine and autumn rain and oncoming storms with the fierce gales of Notus who accompanies the heavy autumn rain of Zeus and stirs up the sea and makes the deep dangerous'. Spring, he allows, is also a time to go sailing; yet sombrely he adds, '... my heart does not like it. Such a sailing is snatched, and you will hardly avoid mischief'.[145] The Greek merchant, however, was less cautious (or more avaricious), and he extended his time of sailing from spring to autumn so that the wine for the thirsty men of Gaul would have left Ionia when the young leaves were showing a bright pale green on the trees.

As the years went on and the Greek settlements and cities became secure they too would have played their part in this western commerce. This applies particularly to the cities of Southern Italy and Sicily. Whether they planted their vineyards with imported Greek vines, or whether they 'educated' the local wild vines, we do not really know but it is more than probable that their wine was first grown on imported Aegean vines. The somewhat unsatisfactory story of Pollis, King of Syracuse, may be a reflection of the truth. He is supposed to have imported a celebrated vine from Greece (or possibly from Italy which itself may have imported the vine from Greece), and to have made from it a wine which was called Pollian in Sicily but Bibline in Greece. One has to doubt whether Pollis existed at all but one need not doubt that the story of the importation is basically true.[146]

With the planting and development of their own vineyards the wine-growers of Southern Italy and Sicily entered into competition with the wine traders from the Aegean. The extensive vineyards of Sybaris, on the Gulf of Tarentum, ministered to the thirst of their own city which, although blotted out in 510 B.C. by the neighbouring city of Croton, left its name alive as an adjective for luxury. But before Sybaris was obliterated it also exported wine 'which the growers led down to the coast by a system of underground channels'. In south-western Sicily, Acragas, the modern Agrigento, which had been founded in 582 B.C., quickly developed its vineyards and exported wine, as well as oil, to Carthage.[147] And these two examples of commercial wine-growing are by no means unique among the cities of the Central Mediterranean.

Of the nature of these wines we know something, though we do not know anything like enough. Theocritus seems on the face of it to be helpful. He describes

[144] Dunbabin, Blakeway, as in fn. 143. Poseidonius: Ath-E, IV, 154a-c.

[145] Hes., *Works and Days*, 646 sqq.

[146] Dunbabin, 93-4. Also Bibline: Hes., *Works and Days*, 589; Ath-E, I, 31a-b; Theocritus, *Idyll*, XIV. Pollian: Ath-E, I, 31a-b.

[147] Glotz, *AGW*, 122; cf. 246. Also Sybaris: Strab., 6, 1, 14.

Bybline as 'fragrant', as 'four years stored' and as 'sparkling as run from the vat'. The indication of age is interesting but the other references have little descriptive value; and moreover we do not know whether he is referring to wine made in Sicily, in Greece, or at Byblus in the Lebanon. The bouquet of Bybline seems to have been its distinctive characteristic for Archestratus of Gela, who was a contemporary of Aristotle, comments on the 'fragrance it retains for a very long time'. (He adds that in his opinion the wine is inferior to Lesbian.) But Archestratus is talking about the Bybline from the coast of Palestine. The final answer, therefore, would seem to be this: Pollian and Bybline were much the same style of wine, they were sweet, and they were made from the same grape which was, possibly, a type of Muscat.[148]

The early wine trade was not seriously handicapped by its limited sailing season for the wine-filled amphoras did not take too long to reach their destination. In the 5th century it took between nine and eleven days to travel from the Piraeus to Syracuse and between seven and nine days from the Piraeus to Egypt, sailing via Rhodes. Later, in Hellenistic times, the voyages were quicker since the ships then crossed the open sea and also sailed during the night.[149] The ships themselves remained small (they were usually somewhere about fifty tons in the time of the Roman Empire) but this does not mean that the wine trade itself was small, for the considerable number of amphoras which can be carried in a modern Greek caique gives some idea of the number which could have been carried in the ancient vessels.

The loaded amphoras were, of course, risk-cargo as was everything else throughout much of the ancient world since, in addition to the hazards of storms, uncharted rocks, and inadequate navigation, there was often the menace of piracy. In the early days too, there was always the risk that the potential customer, like the Cyclops, would be initially hostile. This double crop of dangers and strange places must have produced seafarers' tales as innumerable and as plausibly improbable as those of many later mariners: tales charged with demons, wrecks, savage barbarians, sea monsters and welcoming girls. The *Odyssey* is the finest of all mariner's tales; yet it is only different in quality from the minor Odysseys with which unpoetic seamen would have enlivened hot September evenings on the quaysides of Ionia or in the taverns of Corinth. The monster Scylla, twelve-footed and six-headed, who lived in a cave opposite Charybdis and lived on fish and sailors, and the whirlpool Charybdis which sucked ships to their doom, would have been adjustable material for these hardy *raconteurs* and their equally hardy listeners.

The story of Sappho's brother would have been a welcome addition to the stock of Aegean gossip. He was Charaxus and he was in the wine trade with Egypt. He would have sailed from Lesbos to Egypt down one of the oldest trade routes in the Mediterranean, down among the Ionian islands of Chios and Samos and Icaria, along the Carian coast to Rhodes, and thence by Cyprus or across the 'Great Green' of the sea to Naucratis in the Western Delta where the Greeks had a station for the sale of their wine and oil. Charaxus was not only interested in the commerce of Naucratis, for at Naucratis lived the courtesan Rhodopis (or Doricha), a Thracian girl who was reputed to have been a fellow slave of the fable writer Aesop. She had been taken to Egypt for professional purposes and Charaxus, much to the fury of Sappho, fell in love with her. Generously, and as it happened expensively, he bought her freedom.

[148] See fn. 62, 146, 147. Archestratus: Ath-E, I, 29b-c; see also Ath-E, I, 31a; and p. 68 in Ch. 2.

[149] Glotz, *AGW*, 294-5, 368.

Rhodopis stayed in Egypt and built up a fortune. But, said Herodotus, in a disparaging mood: 'There is no sense in pretending she was excessively rich, for the tenth part of her property can be seen today by anyone who cares to go and look at it: for wishing to be remembered in Greece by some sort of temple-offering such as nobody had ever thought of before, she spent a tenth of her money on as many iron roasting-spits as it would buy, and sent them to Delphi. They still lie in a heap behind the altar which the Chians dedicated, opposite the actual shrine.' Innocently or illogically, he adds: 'For some reason or other Naucratis must be a good place for beautiful prostitutes . . . .' It is perhaps only an odd coincidence that the iron roasting-spits of Rhodopis lay in a heap behind an altar dedicated by the Chians and that in Chios itself there has been excavated a faience amulet of a cat which is probably Egyptian and, even more probably, a present brought back by a Chian wine merchant from Naucratis.[150] Did Rhodopis, or one of her beautiful colleagues, give it to him to take back to the Aegean?

As well as going southwards to Egypt the wine trade of the Aegean went north into the Black Sea. The size of this trade may perhaps be indicated by the shipment of 10,000 *keramia* of wine sent from Rhodes in about 220 B.C. to supply the city of Sinope which was then under siege. We cannot be sure of the capacity of the *keramion* so that we cannot reckon the size of the shipment but the total can scarcely have been less than 100,000 litres and it may have been very much more. Sinope, which is on the north coast of modern Turkey, was, it is true, a flourishing city and occupied an important position in the trade network of the Black Sea. And, of course, the city was under siege. Yet even so the shipment was probably not exceptional for much wine was sent across the Black Sea to the Chersonesus Taurica and the Bosporan kingdom in the Crimean area of Southern Russia. This commerce with the Crimea was as old at least as the 6th century and it continued into Hellenistic times. The wine was not only consumed in the cities of the Crimea and the Sea of Azov but was traded into the interior where it was drunk intemperately by the wild Scythian nobility of the South Russian steppes. Olbia, near the mouths of the Bug and the Dnieper in south-western Russia, had been founded from Miletus about 645 B.C. and through this Ionian colony Greek wine and oil could be traded towards Central Europe.[151] Another colony of Miletus, and one that was founded also in the latter half of the 7th century, was Istrus near the mouth of the Danube and in the 3rd century the better and the more popular of Greek wines, Thasian and Rhodian, travelled through Istrus up the Danube as far as Turnu-Severin in modern Rumania.

But as time went on, as viticulture spread, and as the colonies developed their own vineyards, the wine trade from the Aegean encountered stiff opposition. In the 3rd century B.C., under the Ptolemies new vineyards were planted in Egypt and the import of Greek wine was hampered by protective tariffs. In Hellenistic times the Bosporan cities, as we have seen from Mirmeki, themselves became wine producers. The cities of Sicily and Southern Italy had already become producers of some importance and their share of the Italian market must have been considerable. When Italy herself became a wine-grower the outlet for Greek wines diminished still further and the fall in prices towards the end of the 3rd century shows that wine was becoming a surfeit in the Aegean.

[150]Herodotus, II; Glotz, *AGW*, 119; Boardman, J., 'Four Thousand Years of Chios . . .', *ILN*, Dec. 31st, 1955.

[151]Ros., *SEHH*, 93-123, 394, 1252-3, 1331, etc.; and see Pârvan, V., *Dacia*, 81-93.

Nevertheless, the better Greek wines remained in favour. The most distinguished of them, and they are the top ranking wines of the ancient Greek world, were Chian, Coan, Thasian and Lesbian, followed, though at a little distance, by Cnidian and Rhodian. There were, at any rate in the 1st century B.C. three styles of Chian, dry, medium and sweet, of which Ariusian, which came from a particular district on the island of Chios, was considered to be the best of the Chian, as well as being the best of all Greek, wines. Chian wine had, in fact, held this title much earlier, in the 5th century. So far as we can tell Chian wines were generally white and generally rather light in body though some of them could be mild and rich. Chian was much favoured in Athens and a pleasant picture of Athenian life is conjured up by the find of six Chian-stamped wine amphoras which most probably belonged to a better-class tavern near the Agora in the years just before the beginning of the Peloponnesian War. One must remember, however, that some of the Chian wine was resinated.

Next after Chian came Thasian, these two standing by themselves in the topmost grade of Greek wines. Thasian was noted for its fragrance which Hermippus compared to 'the smell of apples'. It was probably a little heavier in body than Chian, though it is difficult to be sure on this point; nor can we be sure how much of it, like that served in the Town Hall of Thasos, was sweetened with honey. In colour it seems usually to have been red or even black:

> 'Some more femininity
> Past its virginity
> Fetched out some fine
> Black Thasian wine,
> And flouting decorum
> Filled each a decanter
> And swallowed instanter
> An over-full jorum . . . .'

Coan and Lesbian were also rated as first-class wines though not quite as fine as Chian and Thasian. Coan was, at least sometimes, white and strongly flavoured with sea-water and it seems that in general it was not a *retsina*. Lesbian, although it had a flavour of the sea, was not, it would appear, actually mixed with sea-water. Some of it was a fairly light wine and some was probably on the sweet side, for Eubulus writes of 'old Lesbian nectar-fraught'. It may also have been the sweet style which occasioned the forthright comment of Alexis – 'there is no better drink than Lesbian' – and perhaps these two poets were thinking of the sweet wine *protropon* which was a speciality of Lesbos.

Protropon, wine made from juice which had 'bled' from the grapes before pressing, was also made at Cnidos, in south-western Asia Minor. Cnidian wine was imported into Athens from the 3rd to the 1st centuries B.C. but we cannot be sure that this was necessarily *protropon*. Rhodian wine, which was flavoured with salt or sea-water though not, perhaps, with resin, was esteemed by gods and men: or such, at any rate, was the compliment which Virgil paid to it. That men esteemed it highly can be seen from the number of Rhodian stamps on amphoras or on amphora handles which occur in the Aegean and the Eastern Mediterranean. Rhodian seems indeed to have been pre-eminently the trade-wine of the Greek world. It was imported into Athens (as were many other wines) but though in Attica it may only just have held its own with its rivals, in the Eastern Mediterranean it must have had a clear lead. Many more Rhodian than Cnidian amphora stamps have been found at Tarsus while at Antioch there is a clear predominance of Rhodian over both Cnidian and Thasian. It is not likely that the preference for Rhodian was due entirely to its quality. Some of the modern Rhodian wine is fruity and full -bodied but it lacks distinction; one might class it as the 'ordinary Chianti' of the Aegean; and there is no especial reason to think that ancient Rhodian was markedly different or very much better. Its popularity among men may have been due to the fact that it was cheap.[152]

The Speaking Amphoras

In the ancient world of the Eastern Mediterranean there were no wooden vessels for wine. For local work, wineskins could be used and in Babylonia, or so Herodotus tells us, wine travelled in casks made of palm-wood. But wood was never used in the Eastern Mediterranean where pottery was the normal container. These pottery jars, and in particular the twin-handled pottery jars called amphoras, carried all sorts of things, among them dried, salted, or pickled meat and fish and, of course, olive oil. They also carried wine and the wine-amphoras travelled in their thousands over the seas of the Greek, and later of the Roman, worlds.

The Greek amphora may have developed under the double influence of the oval, short-necked jars of Canaan and the longer-necked wine jars of Egypt, but it achieved a personality, and usually a beauty, which, so it seems to me, is distinctively Greek. And it achieved this in many variations (although the variations are on a common theme), for the Greek amphoras vary in shape, they vary in colour, and they vary in size. This latter variable makes it difficult (unless the jars themselves are actually there for measurement) to calculate with accuracy the size of a shipment or the price of a litre of wine. In the 5th to 4th centuries for example, Mendean amphoras appear to have varied in capacity between 26 and $32\frac{1}{2}$ litres while other amphoras of this same period could hold as much as 39 litres.* Chian amphoras of the 5th to 4th centuries usually held a minimum of about 22 litres. In the 2nd to 1st centuries Cnidian amphoras varied from 27 to 34 litres. The commonest size seems to have been somewhere about 26 litres and, where other evidence is lacking, this is the size which I have used in calculation. Such calculations must, naturally, be treated with reserve and so must any estimate of price based on this 'common' capacity of the amphora.

Being made by hand, one would expect the amphoras of a single city-state to vary, however slightly, in their size. Being made in the individualistic world of the Aegean, one would expect the sizes to differ from city to city. But what one might not expect is the variation in shape. One would have thought that, as time went on, the jars of the Aegean would have conformed to a single pattern. But they did not.

*For the capacities of the amphora, with equivalents in British and American gallons, and for a note on the 'standardization' of the amphora, see Appendix D.

[152] Ariusian: Strab., 14, 1, 35; Plin., XIV, 73; Ath-E, I, 32f. Chian: Aristophanes, *Ecclesiazusae*, 1139; Ath-E, I, 29e; Talcott, Lucy, 'Attic Black-Glazed Stamped Ware . . .', *Hesp.*, IV, 1935; Grace, Virginia, 'Stamped Amphora Handles found in 1931-1932', *Hesp.*, III, Appendix A, 1934; Virgil, II, 98. Other refs: Varro, II, Intro., 3; Strab., 14, 1, 15; Plin., XIV, 25, 73, 96, 97; Hor., *Sat.*, II, 8, 15; Ath-E, I, 26b, 28e, 29e, 32f-33a. Cnidian: Grace, V., 'Stamped Amphora Handles . . .', *Hesp.*, III, 200, 1934; 'Stamped Amphora Handles', Goldman, Hetty (Ed.), *Excavations at Gözlü Kule, Tarsus*, I, 135. Other refs: Strab., 14, 1, 15; Plin., XIV, 75; Ath-E, I, 32e-f; cf. *CIL*, IV, Supps. I and II, 5535. Coan: Varro, II, Intro., 3; cf. Cato, cv, cxii; Strab., 14, 1, 15; Plin., XIV, 78-9; Ath-E, I, 32e; Hor., *Sat.*, II, 4, 29; *CIL*, IV, Supps. I and II, 5536, 5537, 5538; Frank, Johnson, II, 315. Lesbian: Virgil, II, 89-90; Strab., 14, 1, 15; Plin., XIV, 73-4; Ath-E, I, 28f; IV, 129d; *FAC*, II, Eubulus, 124, 125; Alexis, 274; Propertius, I, xiv; Hor., *Carm.*, I, xvii; Galen (Bibl. Ch. 4), II, 734. Protropon: Ath-E, I, 30b; II, 45e. Rhodian: Virgil, II, 101; Polybius (Bibl. Ch. 4), 4, 56; Plin., XIV, 79; Ath-E, I, 31e, 32e; Grace, V., as above, *Tarsus*. Thasian: Aristophanes, *Ecclesiazusae*, 1119-21; *Plutus*, 1021; *FAC*, I, Aristophanes, 350 (quotation); Theophr., O., 51; Xen., *Symp.*, IV, 41; Ath-E, I, 28d, 29c and e, 32a; IV, 192d; VIII, 364d; Virgil, II, 91; Plin., XIV, 73; Dioscorides, *Herbal*, v, 6; Grace, V., both refs above.

Red-figured Kylix from
Vulci
510–500 B.C.
London, British Museum

They kept their distinctive shapes. Conservatism may have been the main reason why they did so: conservatism in the workshops and among the merchants of the city-state. But there may have been a more deliberate reason. A distinctive shape may have served as a trade-mark and have guaranteed to a customer overseas that the wine he was buying came, or was supposed to come, from one particular city. Such a method of recognition would, of course, have lent itself to fraud.

Whatever the reason, the variety remained. There are the graceful, rose-brick-coloured Chian amphoras with their long handles and their long necks. There are olive-grey Lesbian amphoras with narrow base points and slightly swan-necked handles. Cnidian amphoras, some of them the colour of pale rose brick, others with a greyer tinge, are long-necked and long-handled and some of them have an evolved form of base, a spike and circle stub which looks as if it had been designed to fit into a socket. Among the most beautiful of the amphoras are the Coan, mainly fawn with a tinge of green, though sometimes rust coloured and occasionally a mauve-grey. Their handles curve up from the shoulder of the amphora to a point, then curve down again to meet the neck, and they remind one faintly of the wing-handles on the jars of Early Bronze Age Poliochni. Corinthian (or related) amphoras of the 3rd and early 2nd centuries, brown-pink in colour, diverge from the oval form and are almost spherical. Remarkably divergent, also, though in a different way, are the long, thin Thasian amphoras which are elongated almost into pottery tubes.[153]

An empty amphora is neither heavy nor unwieldy. But when it is full it is a different matter for the 'common' amphora holds 80 lb. weight of wine and then

[153]Herodotus, I. Amphora capacities: see Appendix D; Grace, Virginia, 'The Canaanite Jar', Weinberg, S. S. (Ed.); *The Aegean and the Near East – Studies Presented to Hetty Goldman*. I should like here, and again, to record my deep gratitude to Miss Virginia Grace for her help, and for her patience in showing me the magnificent collection of amphoras of the American School of Classical Studies at Athens.

it becomes a ponderous object. It is most easily carried by three men, one to each of the neck-handles and one gripping the stub point of the base. More economical in labour is to sling it from a pole carried by two men, a method which was in use among the ancient Egyptians. More economical still is for one man to roll it. This could have been done with Greek amphoras, whose fabric is quite sturdy, since many of them have the handles so put on that they do not project beyond the bulge-line of the shoulder, and the handles would not break when the jar was rolled.

It was when the amphora reached its customer that it became really unwieldy. Once it was opened it had to be leant against something or stuck into something. Usually, perhaps, it would have been leant against the wall of the house. At other times a hole to receive its tapering base would have been made in the ground or in the floor. The most attractive method was to set it upright in a stand or tripod and this method was practised both by the ancient Egyptians and by the Mycenaeans. In the Old, as in the New, Kingdoms of Egypt it was not unusual to have stands into which the jars were set and by the time of the New Kingdom legged stands were frequent. The Mycenaeans had tripod stands for their jars and, as one might expect, those of the nobility were fashioned with art as well as craft. One of these, Late Mycenaean and now in the National Museum at Athens, was found at Tiryns. It is a bronze tripod about one foot four inches high and is decorated with birds and flowers hanging from its upper ring. It would have added beauty to any Mycenaean palace.

But even supposing that the Classical Greek amphora were set upright in a ring-stand or tripod, there still remained the act of emptying. These big wine-jars are not ideal for pouring. You can empty them by siphoning but there is little to show that the siphon was widely used among the Greeks. Normally, and for domestic use, the wine would have been poured off into smaller amphoras or into wine jugs and mixing bowls. But, except for the wholesale trade, why retain the big amphora at all? A much better system was in use in Palestine. There they had tubular jars, small to medium-small, and looking like neckless bottles. These jars stood in pottery ring-stands and were in every way convenient for domestic use, easy to cellar, easy to handle, and easy to empty. It is remarkable that they were not more widely copied. But then inconvenience was an integral part of so much of the ancient world.[154]

At all events the big amphora remained the standard transport and storage vessel of the ancient Mediterranean. It was stoppered and sealed with plaster and in many cases the sealings appear to have been tied down by cords. On the body of the amphora was sometimes incised or written the price of the wine, while sometimes on the handle of the amphora was stamped its guarantee. These handle stamps, at any rate in the Greek world, seem to have been workshop and not vintage guarantees, enabling a check to be made on the work of the potter, or else certifying the capacity of the jar. Since they give the geographical location of the workshop the stamps are of the greatest importance in building up a picture of the ancient wine trade. Where complete, or largely complete, amphoras exist they can indicate by their shape or fabric from what island or city they came; but where only the handles exist then the stamps can give the same information.[155] All archaeological discovery is in a sense a detective investigation, the building of a composite and

[154] Davies, Mrs. N. de Garis, copy of a wall-painting from the *Tomb of Kha-'emwēse at Thebes* (No. 261), British Museum; *Abydos, The Cemetries of*, Naville, E., Peet, T. E., and others (Bibl. Ch. 2), Pt I, Ch. IV, by H. R. Hall, Pl.xvi, No. 7, *Tomb of Kha-'emwēse*, as above; *Tell El-Amarna*, Pt I, 137; Davies, N. de Garis, *The Tombs of Two Officials of Tuthmosis the Fourth* (Bibl. Ch. 2), Pl. xxx; Grace, V., 'The Canaanite Jar', see above fn. 153, Pl. x, 1-4, and 101; and for 'tubular' Punic (?) jars, fig. 6. Hazor. Cf. the multiple 'ring-stand' goblet holder: Ghirshman, R., 'Temples and a Palace of the Elamites: New Finds at Tchoga-Zanbil', *ILN*, June 13th, 1959.

[155] Two of the scholars who are devoting themselves to this research are, for Greek jars, Miss Virginia Grace of the American School of Classical Studies at Athens and, for Roman jars, Mrs Elizabeth Lyding Will of Pennsylvania, U.S.A. For Miss Grace's publications, see Bibliography to this chapter; for Mrs Lyding Will, see Bibliography to Ch. 4. For amphora handles found at Pella, see Petsas, P., 'Alexander the Great's Capital discovered . . .', *ILN*, Aug. 2nd, 1958.

coherent picture from scattered and sometimes uncertain clues. Such is the picture which is gradually being built up from the finds of amphoras and of stamped amphora handles, and although the building of such a picture may seem to lack drama, it is far from lacking in interest. As it becomes increasingly detailed and increasingly complete, it will tell us more about the trade of the Ancient World; and it will tell us more about the daily life of the people of that world, of their preferences and their taste and their pleasures. These fragments of stamped pottery are, so to speak, the fingerprints of ancient drinkers.

'. . . *after the feast, drinking*'

> 'Rise up above thy troubles, and with me
> Drink in a cloud of blossoms.'

This was the advice of Heracles in Euripides' *Alcestis* and the carefree state which he advocated was, naturally, one of the pleasures of the Greek symposium. Another of its pleasures, and one which particularly appealed to the Greek mind, was the opportunity for almost unlimited talking.

In the earlier days the Greek need for getting together and talking – and drinking – was often satisfied by the arrangement of a 'common feast', a banquet whose cost was met by the contributions of those who attended. Hesiod, among the social advice which he gives and which in parts is more basic and much funnier than that given by Polonius in *Hamlet*, comments on this subject with what was perhaps a necessary frugality: 'Do not be boorish at a common feast where there are many guests; the pleasure is greatest and the expense is least.' At other times the Greeks resorted to taverns which, of course, varied in the quality of their wines. They varied, too, in the honesty of their owners and we hear the inevitable complaint of the watering-down of the wine that was sold. Nicostratus, of the Middle Comedy, voices this grievance:

> 'The keeper of the tavern nigh,
> Be it wine or vinegar or a light you buy,
> Is sure to water it ere he sends it, damn him.'

The high end of the quality scale of tavern drinking is represented by the Chian wine that was offered in a better-class tavern on the fringe of the Athenian Agora. The lower end may be represented by the wine sold in the 'tavern of Aphrodite' at Corinth – assuming this to have been Corinthian wine – for, as Alexis said: 'home-made Corinthian (is) torture'. Since both he and the tavern were flourishing in the 4th century his verdict may also have been that of the tavern's customers and they may have been offered imported wine instead. But perhaps they did not mind what they drank, for the tavern had other attractions. Facing on to its courtyard, there was, it seems, a small stage for the provision of some sort of theatrical entertainment, while for the further consolation of the customers there were narrow cubicles into which the assorted worshippers of Aphrodite could retire.[156] The women of Corinth were famous.

The hetaerae of Classical Greece have become famous and in doing so they have lost their reality. The famous hetaerae were as outstanding in their own way as the accomplished mistresses of later times, but they were very much in the minority. The great mass of the hetaerae were prostitutes, some common, some moderately common, and some whose capabilities were enlivened by a humour which, if not always intellectual, was at least appreciated. Many of them must have exhibited the strict commercial sense of the courtesan Clepsydra who was 'so called because she timed her favours by the clepsydra or water-clock'. (Other courtesans were nick-named Crow, Lamp, and Tipsy.) Even the flute girls were frequently talented in more than music.

> 'Of the gay danseuse of ripened charms
> I've told you; hear me, pray,
> Of the budding flute-girl who saps the strength
> of the sailorman for pay.'

And at the symposia flute-girls were often called upon to exercise all their talents.

The symposia of the Greeks have also tended to lose their reality. They were not always gatherings for metaphysical argument. Some of them, probably many of them, were as conversationally brilliant as any dinner which has happened since. But the wine cup was always there. The symposium, the drinking party, is also the *potos*, the drinking bout. Much noise was made, much wine was drunk, and much enjoyment was had. There was a strong sensual element in the Greek nature and they were not always inclined to repress it.[157]

[156] Euripides, *Alcestis*, trs. Gilbert Murray, 45; Hes., *Works and Days*, 722-3; *FAC*, II, Nicostratus, 22. Chian: Talcott, Lucy, 'Attic Black-Glazed Stamped Ware...', *Hesp.*, IV, 1935; *FAC*, II, Alexis, 290; Morgan, C. H., 'Investigations at Corinth, 1953 – A Tavern of Aphrodite', *Hesp.*, XXII, 1953.

[157] Clepsydra: *FAC*, II, Eubulus, 54. Flute-girls: *FAC*, I, Metagenes, 4. Other nicknames: Ath-E, XIII, 583d-e.

'Joy to those who sit and drink in groups of twenty,
  When the soul warms with compulsion soft and sweet . . .'

sang Bacchylides in a 5th-century drinking song written for the son of the King of
Macedon. But was the joy really increased by the habit of lying down at a symposium? This curious posture seems to have come into fashion somewhere about the
beginning of the Classical period. Before that time people had drunk sitting. The
Egyptians sat or squatted, the Homeric Heroes sat, and the sitting position was
habitual among the Greeks until about the 5th century. At the symposia of Classical
times, however, the drinkers lay on couches, or *clinai*, with a cushion or bolster
under the left arm. It is not really the most suitable position for drinking. However,
the Greeks thought so, as later did the Romans, and the couch was even more
essential to a symposium than was the flute-girl or harpist.

'After the sacrifice, a feast . . . after the feast, drinking.' Thus Epicharmus in the
5th century, summarizing the two parts of an evening, the dinner itself and the
drinking which followed it. At a meal which included wine a libation was made
and some of the wine was poured onto the floor as an offering to the good spirit
of the house – 'to have a gulp for the Good Spirit', as Theopompus says. But drinking was not an important part of the actual dinner. When the meal was finished and
the tables were cleared away, then – or at least this was the Athenian custom – three
libations were poured, one to the Gods, one to the departed Heroes, and one to
Zeus. A paean, or hymn, was sung, sometimes to Apollo, and it was usual for a
flute-girl to play an accompaniment to the libations. Garlands were handed round,
as on occasions were perfumes – 'We've Thasian wine and garlands and perfume. . . .'
Then the drinking party began. Or, as Plato has the procedure: 'Socrates took his
place on the couch, and supped with the rest; and then libations were offered, and
after a hymn had been sung to the god, and there had been the usual ceremonies,
they were about to commence drinking. . . .'[158]

The wine was drunk diluted and it was mixed with water in a large urn-shaped
crater or mixing-bowl. In his Polonius-aspect Hesiod warns 'never put the ladle
upon the mixing-bowl at a wine party, for malignant ill-luck is attached to that',
recording a superstition which may have as much, or as little, reason behind it as
the modern custom of passing the port from right to left. The 'ladle', in which the
wine was transferred from the *crater* to the cups, was usually a wine-jug or *oinochoë*,
often shaped like a modern ewer but sometimes, or at least sometimes in Attica in
the 8th century B.C., shaped like a modern tankard. Hesiod's ladle, however, would
have been a scoop on the end of a rod. One of these is shown on a 5th-century Attic
cylix and it is very similar to the modern Spanish *venencia* which is used to lift
samples of sherry out of the butts at Jerez de la Frontera.

The most usual drinking cup was the *cylix*, a shallow two-handled bowl on a
short stem whose beauty of shape was enhanced by the wonderful art of the vase-
painters. Naturally enough these pictures were frequently Dionysiac. Snake-bodied
nymphs are seen rejoicing at the vintage. Satyrs accompany Dionysos or pursue
women. Maenads carry the thyrsus, and 'rage' or dance or play the double flute.
Dionysos is there with his mother Sémêle, or he is listening to a satyr's flute, or
holding out his characteristic wine-cup, the *cantharos*.

[158] Bacchylides: Higham, Bowra,
*Oxford Book of Greek Verse in
Trans.*, No. 311, trs. Bowra, C. M.
Epicharmus: Ath-E, II, 36c; *FAC*,
I, Theopompus, 76. 'Thasian
wine', etc.: *FAC*, II, Antiphanes,
242; Plato, *Symposium*, 175e-176a.
Libations: *FAC*, I, Pherecrates,
131, and fn. a; II, Eriphus, 4. In
general: *CAH*, V, 123; Xen.,
Symp., II; Plutarch, *Moralia, Din-
ner of the Seven Wise Men*, 150D.

Cup
Geometric Period
Athens, Cerimachos
Museum

Attic Red-figured Kylix
Found at Capua
490–480 B.C.
London, British Museum

The *cantharos* was a deeper drinking cup than the *cylix*, a vase-like bowl mounted, usually, on a slender stem, and having twin handles which curved up above the rim of the bowl. Its frequent use at a party would have produced that state of elation described by Bacchylides:

> 'Dionysos mingles in the wine new powers,
>   Sending high adventure to the thoughts of men;
>   This man thinks he sacks a city's crown of towers,
>   That man dreams himself a monarch then.'

Often the *cantharos* was, like the *cylix*, a work of beauty and some of the black Boeotian ones are very graceful indeed. But they could also adopt the comic note and a 6th-century Athenian *cantharos* has, for example, a mule's head on the front of the bowl and long ears rising up almost to the height of the handles. The drinking cups and drinking horns called *rhytons* could also follow much the same fashion; one from Aegina is shaped like a large knucklebone; others are modelled to form the heads of boars or mules; while yet another is double-faced with the heads of a satyr and a nymph.[159]

We know that the wine which was drunk at the symposia was sometimes strained before drinking – 'Chian and Thasian ready strained', says Epilycus – but we do not know that this was the invariable practice. Nor for that matter can we always be sure how it was done. A cloth is the obvious method but Epigenes mentions 'a silver strainer' and it is likely that the strainer pierced with holes was quite a common

[159]Hes., *Works and Days*, 744–5. Type of Hesiod's ladle: Brit. Mus., E. 65, Attic cylix. Bacchylides: ref. in fn. 158. Dionysiac cylix pictures are illustrated in Harrison, *Prolegomena*, figs. 58, 121, 123, 128, 130. For descriptions of drinking cups I have relied largely on the collections of the Ashmolean Museum, Oxford, and the British Museum. Brit. Mus. refs are: E786, E799, E801, E804.

instrument. We know, too, that in the hot weather those who were able to do so were accustomed to cool their wine. Snow was used and when that was either unobtainable or too expensive, the wine was chilled by being lowered down a well.

> 'Nobody would take mulled claret;
>   everybody chose, you know,
>   Wine that had been "welled", or mingled
>   not with water but with snow,'

says one character of the Comedy, while another remarks:

> 'If I'm no fool,
> Dad's put us down the well, like wine, to cool.'[160]

Theoretically the symposium was under the control of a symposiarch. He could elect himself, although he was usually chosen by a throw of the knuckle bones. He decided upon the proportion of water that was to be mixed with the wine and in this and other ways he could moderate, or accelerate, the inebriation of his fellow drinkers. But there were other amusements besides drinking. Poets, among them Xenophanes and Pindar, wrote *scolia*, or short songs, to be sung after the dinner and when the symposium was about to begin. An Attic *scolion* goes:

> 'The man who betrays not his friend hath great honour methinks both of men and of Gods.'

Another, less elevated, sighs:

> 'O would I might become a pretty ivory lyre, and pretty lads might take me with them to Dionysos' choral dance.'

A less artistic, but very popular, form of *scolion* was that invented or adapted by the guest himself. As the sprig of laurel or myrtle, or whatever else was being used as the mark of the singer, was passed to the guest, he had to sing a *scolion* which would answer or complete or criticize the one which had been sung just before.

Another type of amusement, and one that was very popular in the 5th and 4th centuries in Sicily and in Greece was the game of *cottabus*. In conception the game was extremely simple; in its proper execution it demanded skill. Basically it consisted in shooting at a target the last drops of wine in the wine-cup and the throw had to be made while the player was lying on his couch. The most commended, and possibly one of the more difficult, ways of doing this was to flick the wine from a shallow-bowled *cylix*, one of whose handles was gripped in the player's right hand. 'You must bend your wrist right back, To throw the *cottabus* nicely,' says a courtesan to Heracles. The least attractive method was for the player to shoot the wine out of his mouth. The mess in the room depended upon the expertise of the players.

The targets varied. Sometimes they were cups floating in a bowl of water and

[160] Straining: *FAC*, I, Diocles, 7; Epilycus, 6; II, Epigenes, 5. 'Racked-off wines': *FAC*, II, Nicostratus, 11. Cooling, quotations: *FAC*, I, Strattis, 57; Lysippus, I. Other refs: *FAC*, I, Euthycles, I; II, Alexis, 141; Dexicrates, I.

they had to be sunk by the wine shot into them. A more complicated version was the 'dropping *cottabus*'. Here the wine had to be shot into the pan of a scale so that the pan should descend and bump on the head of Manes, or 'Little-Old-Man', a small, bronze statuette placed beneath the pan of the scale.

> 'He's only to touch the pannikin
> And down it goes and strikes upon the mannikin
> And makes a clatter.'

Sometimes the target was human.[161]

Where money and opportunity offered, the better wines were chosen for drinking at symposia, as indeed they may have been in ordinary life as well. But many a Greek had to rely on the wine of his local vineyards. Sometimes it was good, sometimes not: or, to use Alcaeus' phrase, 'drawing it sometimes honey-sweet, and sometimes as bitter as burdocks'. Only too often the wine must have been inferior, like the *amphias* of Nicostratus, or like Samian which seems to have been nothing like as good as it is today. Then again we must remember that in an opened amphora whose contents were not all drunk at once, the wine would have tended to go 'off' as more and more air got to the wine. The surface of the wine could, of course, have been sealed with a layer of olive oil; but that this technique was by no means invariable, or successful, can be seen from the pessimistic comment of the poet Antiphanes:

> 'Life's like draught wine – turns sour when running low.'

Dryness in wine was not always a desirable quality. The Athenians 'liked not the hard, stiff poets any more than they liked Pramnian wines, which contract the eyebrows as well as the bowels'. This particular Pramnian was grown on the Island of Icaria, in the Sporades, but either tastes differed or the island grew other wine as well for Icarian seems to have been esteemed by some people. In Athens, however, or so the quotation goes on, 'they want wine with delicate bouquet and nectar-distilling ripeness'.

On occasions, it would seem, this result was obtained by blending. Heracleotan, which most probably came from Bithynia in Asia Minor, was a strong and fragrant wine; Erythraean, from Ionia, on the other hand, was a mild wine with no bouquet; and it appears that these two were sometimes blended, for, says Theophrastus 'the effect is that they simultaneously destroy one another's inferior qualities'. 'There are,' he adds, 'many other such blends mentioned by and known to experts'. The same technique may often have been used to 'improve' a harsh or inferior wine.

A degree of sweetness in their drinks was obtained in other ways than by blending. Grapes were allowed to dry on the vine or were spread out in the sun to dry and the result was a rich, sweet wine. One of these raisin wines was made in Cilicia. Another of the sweet drinks was *gleucos* – sweet, new wine or must – and a variety of this may have been the 'ὑπόχυτυς or 'doctored wine' which, at least in Rhodes, was said to resemble must. A further method was to make *hepsema* by boiling down 'wine' until it became sweet.[162]

[161] Scolia, etc.: Bowra, C. M., *Early Greek Elegists*, 121 (Xenophanes). Pindar: Higham, Bowra, *Oxford Book of Greek Verse in Trans.*, Nos. 293, 294, trs. Bowra, Higham; *Lyra Graeca*, III, 569, 573; Aristophanes, *Wasps*, 1222, and fn. a; *Lysistrata*, 1237, and fn. b. Cottabus: Aristophanes, *Peace*, 1244, and fn. c; *Frogs*, 965, and fn. a; *FAC*, I, Cratinus, 116; Hermippus, 47; Plato, 47; II, Eubulus, 16; Antiphanes, 55. Cottabus in general: Ath-E, I, 28b; XI, 479c–e, 487d, 782e; XV, 665d, sqq.

[162] *Lyra Graeca*, I, Alcaeus, 168; *FAC*, II, Nicostratus, 18. Samian: Strab., 14, 1, 15; Ros., *SEHH*, 221. Draught-wine: *FAC*, II, Antiphanes, 240a. Pramnian: Ath-E, I, 30b–c. Icarian: Ath-E, I, 30b; *FAC*, II, Amphis, 40; Strab., 10, 5, 13; 14, 1, 19. Oeneatic, which may be an Icarian wine: Plin., XIV, 76; Ath-E, I, 30b–d. Heracleotan: Theophr., *O.*, 52; Xen., *An.*, VI, 5, 1. Erythraean: Theophr., *O.*, 48, 52; cf. Strab. 13, 1, 64. Cilician: Plin., XIV, 81; Ath-E, I, 33b. Gleucos: cf. *Bible*, *Acts*, 2, 13; *FAC*, I, Phrynicus, 65; Ath-E, I, 31d–e. Hepsema: *FAC*, I, Plato, 149.

There were special wines for medicinal purposes. Cilicia, as well as making raisin-wine, made a laxative wine called *abates*. From Asia Minor also, though this time from Amblada in Pisidia, came a wine that was particularly well suited for use in medicinal diets. In the 4th century B.C., and perhaps earlier, the *vignerons* of Mende in Macedonia 'sprinkled the grapes on the vines with an aperient, so that the wine becomes a laxative'. The effect, unless this was merely the result of over-drinking, is described by Hermippus:

> 'Of good Mendaean the holy race
> Of Gods wet each his bed.'

But Mendaean was also well-considered for ordinary drinking and it was sometimes classed among such favourite wines as Chian, Lesbian, Thasian, Bibline, and, most probably, Magnesian.[163]

Magnesian, which probably came from Magnesia in Ionia, is given high praise by Hermippus who writes of it as 'Magnesian with its gift of grace'. The area from which it came (if it was Ionia), and which includes Ephesus and Mt. Mesogis, was a famous wine-producing district from which not only came the various styles of Ephesian but also the Mesogitan. Among the Ephesian wines were a Pramnian, a wine called Phygelites, and a wine that was, in the 1st century A.D. if not before, seasoned with salt-water and boiled must. Mesogitan, grown inland from Ephesus, was an excellent wine of which the best variety came from Aroma, near Nysa.

A high proportion of the finer wines of the Greek world came from the islands of the eastern Aegean or from the mainland of Asia Minor. From Pontus, in north Asia Minor, came Naspercenian – a good wine; from Calpe in Bithynia, on the

[163] Abates: Ath-E, I, 33b; Ambladian: Strab., 12, 7, 2, dating 1st century B.C. Mendaean: Ath-E, I, 29d-f; IV, 129d; *FAC*, I, Hermippus, 82; also *FAC*, I, Philyllius, 24; II, Eubulus, 126; Ros., *SEHH*, 353; Coins, Brit. Mus., Pls. 10, 11–16, p. 20.

Attic Red-figured Kylix
Found at Capua
490–480 B.C.
London, British Museum

shores of the Black Sea not far from the Bosporus, came a wine that was sweet and sound. Lampsacus, in Hellespontine Phrygia, was a fine district for wine in the 5th century B.C. and the city of Lampsacus was given to Themistocles by the Persian king so that Themistocles could be assured of his supply of wine. And here, perhaps, one may look back for a moment and recall the phrase in the *Iliad* about 'Phrygia, the land of vines'.

This Hellespontine Phrygia was part of Mysia, and Mysian wines were classed quite highly. So, too, were those of Lydia, further south, and Strabo in fact recorded the opinion that the Catacecaumenitan of Lydia was inferior in quality 'to none of the notable wines'. Maeonian, also from Lydia, occurs in Roman times as late as the Edict of Diocletian of 301 A.D. although there it figures as 'Maeonian wine, boiled down one-third'. Among the wines of Ionia, south-west of Lydia, was Metropolitan, while from Lycia, in south-western Asia Minor, came Telmesican. Pamphylia, on the south coast, had fine vineyards and its Selgean wine was noted. The island of Cyprus produced a good wine and from Melitene in Cappadocia came the Monarite wine which, as Strabo says 'rivals the Greek wines'.[164]

Nearer the heart of Greece grew other favoured wines. In the 3rd century B.C. Ambraciotan, from the north-west coast of Greece, was held in some esteem, while Issan, from the island of Issa in the Adriatic, was said by Agatharchides in the 2nd century B.C. to be the best of all. Corcyraean, from Corfu, was thought to be 'a very pleasant wine, when old'. From the wines of the western Aegean we might single out Euboean, Peparethian, and Sciathian. Euboean was described as a 'sweet dark wine' in the 2nd century A.D. and it may have been this also when it was recorded by the poet Alexis in the 4th century B.C. Peparethian, from the island of Peparethus off northern Euboea, had a somewhat contradictory reputation. Hermippus disliked it and, contrasting it with another wine, wrote:

> '. . . Ambrosia 'tis and nectar too;
>   That, when I dine in state,
> That is the liquor for those I love,
>   Peparethian for those I hate.'

But on the other hand Apollodorus, two centuries after Hermippus, declared that it was a good wine but 'less well thought of on account of its not being fit to drink before it was six years old'. Hermippus may have drunk it too young; and in any case Peparethian coins of the same century as Hermippus are a witness to the importance of the Peparethian wine-trade. About the wine of Sciathos, an island of the Northern Sporades, we do not know a great deal but in the 4th century B.C. it seems to have attracted some moderately favourable notice:

> 'Wine gushes out for passers-by to quaff,
> Black wine of Sciathos mixed half-and-half.'[165]

The comment which Apollodorus made about the age of Peparethian shows that the Greeks could, and perhaps did, keep some of their wines to mature; it shows also that they were generally reluctant to do so. Pliny, in the 1st century A.D. made the

[164] Magnesian: *FAC*, I, Hermippus, 82; and I, Philyllius, 24. Phygelites: Dioscorides, *Herbal*, V, 10. Mesogitan: Strab., 14, 1, 15; 14, 1, 47. Aromian: Strab., 14, 1, 47. Naspercenian: Plin., XIV, 76, quoting Apollodorus. Calpian: Xen., *An.*, VI, 4, 6. Lampsacan: Thucydides, *Peloponnesian War*, I, 10; Strab., 13, 1, 12; 13, 1, 19; *Iliad*, III. Mysian: Pindar, *Isthmian*, VIII; Theophrastus, *Enq. into Plants*, IV, 5, 4; Plin., XIV, 75. Catacecaumenitan: Strab., 13, 4, 11; Plin., XIV, 75. Maeonian: Strab., 13, 4, 11; 12, 3, 20; 13, 3, 2, 4, 5; *Edict. Dioc.*, II, I, 13. Metropolitan: Strab., 14, 1, 15. Telmesican: Plin., XIV, 74. Selgean: Strab., 12, 7, 3. Cyprian: Strab., 14, 6, 5; Plin., XIV, 74, 79. Melitene and Monarite: Strab., 12, I, I.

[165] Ambraciotan: Plin., XIV, 76, quoting Apollodorus. Issan: Ath-E, I, 28d, quoting Agatharchides. Corcyraean: Ath-E, I, 33b. Euboean: Wright, F. A., *Greek Social Life*, 237 sq.; *FAC*, II, Alexis, 299. Peparethian: *FAC*, I, Hermippus, 82; Plin., XIV, 76, quoting Apollodorus; Ath-E, I, 29a; Coins, Brit. Mus., Pls 4, 18–20, pp. 7–8. Sciathian: *FAC*, I, Strattis, 61.

sweeping statement that Greek wines took between five and seven years to become properly mature, but his is most probably the Roman, and not the Greek, view. What, in fact, did happen?

'Raise in their honour a clearly sounding strain, and, while thou praisest the wine that is old, thou shalt also praise the flowers of songs that are new.' Thus Pindar. Archestratus dwells upon the theme with enthusiasm: 'after that, when ye have taken full measure from the bowl dedicated to Zeus the Saviour, ye must drink an old wine . . . grown in Lesbos . . .'; and he adds 'the Thasian, to be sure, is also a generous wine to the taste, providing it be old with the fair seasons of many years'. Theocritus, with the poetic brevity of a parched man, merely remarks: 'And the cap from the wine-jar we tore that was sealed four years ago.'

It is clear that the Greeks set some store by wine that was 'old', for *saprias*, or old, mellow wine – '*saprias oinos*' – is occasionally mentioned by the writers of the Old Comedy and when it is mentioned it is included among the wines of high quality. In the Middle Comedy, however, there appears to be some confusion as to who really did like old wine. Eubulus writes:

> 'Strange how the praises of old wine are sung
> By ladies gay, while men prefer it young!'

But he may be referring to sex and not to wine. Alexis, on the other hand, applies the liking generally:

> 'Man's nature's not a bit the same as wine's:
> He loses flavour as his life declines;
> We drink the oldest wine that comes our way;
> Old men get nasty, old wines make us gay.'

The partial inaccuracy of Alexis' comment on the age of man does not mean that his comment about the age of wine is equally inaccurate. And it does, I think, give us the answer to the whole question. Alexis assumes that wine gains in flavour as it grows very old. But it does not do so when it grows very old in modern terms. Thus we may believe that Alexis never drank wine that was very old in our terms and we may also believe that what was true for Alexis was true for the great majority of the ancient Greeks. Their references to old wine are not infrequent but they are not frequent enough to show that they considered the long maturing of wine to be a matter of first importance. Athenaeus, it is true, records that a 'small' wine which was poured out for the courtesan Gnathaena was supposed to be sixteen years old. If it was, it must have been exceptional. I believe that the 'four years' of Theocritus represent the usual, upper, age-limit for ancient Greek wines before the Roman era, and that most of the wine that was drunk in Greece was drunk within the year of its vintaging.[166]

While the Greek at his wine may not greatly have cared for age, he certainly appreciated bouquet. Sometimes, of course, this bouquet may have been 'improved' by the art or craft of man: even so he liked his wine to have fragrance. Perhaps it is fitting to take, as just one example, Hermippus eulogizing *saprias*:

[166]Plin., XIV, 76, 79; Pindar, *Olympian*, IX, 48. Archestratus: Ath-E, I, 29b-c; Theocritus, *Idyll* VII; cf. *Idyll* XIV, for four-year-old Bybline. Saprias: *FAC*, I, Hermippus, 82; Philyllius, 24. Middle Comedy: *FAC*, II, Eubulus, 125; Alexis, 278. Gnathaena: Ath-E, XIII, 584b.

'Yet there's another, by that same token,
  Saprian or Old Amber,
Of which no sooner the seal be broken
  That lo! we're sniffing posies –
The breath divine of that splendid wine
  Fills all the raftered chamber
With violet scent and bluebell scent
  And the scent of sweetest roses . . .'[167]

And here, finally, is Xenophanes of Colophon[168] twenty-five centuries ago in another raftered chamber:

'Now, at last, the floor is swept, and clean are the hands of all the guests, and their cups as well; one slave puts plaited wreaths on their heads, another offers sweet-smelling perfume in a saucer; the mixing bowl stands full of good cheer; and other wine is ready, which promises never to give out – mellow wine in jars, redolent of its bouquet; and in the midst the frankincense sends forth its sacred fragrance; and there is water, cool and fresh and pure. The yellow loaves lie ready at hand, and a lordly table groans with the weight of cheese and luscious honey; an altar in the middle is banked all round with flowers, and singing and dancing and bounty pervade the house. But men of good cheer should first of all praise the God with pious stories and pure words; they should pour libations and pray for power to do the right (for that is the duty closer to hand); 'tis no sin to drink as much as you can hold and still get home without an attendant, unless you be very old.'

[167] *FAC*, I, Hermippus, 82.

[168] Ath-E, XI, 462c-f.

NOTE: References for wines listed in Appendix C, but not discussed in the text of this chapter: Apameian: Plin., XIV, 75. Colophonian: Frank, Broughton, IV, 690-11. Cretan: *Mycen. Docs.*, 128, 129, 308; Plin., XIV, 81; Ath-E, X, 440e-f; Dioscorides, *Herbal*, v, 9; *CIL*, IV, Supp. I and II, 5526; Frank, Johnson, II, 352. Cyzican: Ros., *SEHH*, 589. Eurean: Coins, Brit. Mus., Pl. 22, p. 39. Hippodamantian: Plin., XIV, 75. Melian: Theophrastus, *Enq. into Plants*, VIII, 2, 8. Methymnian: Virgil, II, 90; Propertius, IV, 8. Miletan: Theophrastus, *Enq. into Plants*, IV, 14, 9. Mystian: Plin., XIV, 75. Naxian (Sicily): Coins, Brit. Mus., Pls 7, 27, p. 13. Phlian: *FAC*, II, Antiphanes, 236. Protagian: Plin., XIV 76.

CHAPTER FOUR

Rome

Before the Foundation

In Imperial Rome the centurion's staff of office was the sapling of a vine and the Legions made the 'Latin vine-rod' famous throughout Europe. It was fitting that they should have done so, for, whereas the Greeks had given wine a European meaning, the Romans gave it a European dominion.[1]

It is possible that there had been wine in Italy for many years before the traditional date of the foundation of Rome in 753 B.C. The *terremare* – the lake, or rather the swamp, dwellings of Northern Italy – and particularly those of Emilia and Lake Garda have revealed that towards the end of the Bronze Age the inhabitants of these moated dwellings knew of the *Vitis vinifera*, the European grape vine. The vine seeds discovered in these swamp settlements may only mean that grapes, either fresh or as raisins, were eaten for food and, in fact, it has been suggested that the accumulation of seeds in some of the deposits are merely due to human defaecation. On the other hand, these swamp dwellers were an agricultural people and although there is no evidence that they cultivated the vine there is no reason to deny them the exercise of a rudimentary skill in the making of wine from wild grapes. If we needed any evidence of the 'wine'-making propensities of Bronze Age peoples, even though it comes from a very different area, we may point to the 'cranberry wine deposited in a birch-bark pail in the bronze age oak-coffin buried in the Danish Guldhøj'.[2]

The *terremare* wines of Italy are problematical. So, too, is the suggestion that viticulture was first introduced into Northern Italy by the Etruscans. But this latter theory has much to recommend it. The Etruscans, who came into Italy about 800 B.C. and who were probably Lydians from Asia Minor, came from a country which was later famous for its wine. They would certainly have known about viticulture in the 9th century and since they were a people who were fond of luxury and pleasure and the lighter amusements (they claimed to have invented dice), they

[1] Plin., XIV, 19; Mart., X, 26.

[2] Peet, T. E., *The Stone and Bronze Ages in Italy and Sicily* (Bibl. Ch. 2), 320 sqq., esp. 362; Munro, R., *The Lake Dwellings of Europe* (Bibl. Ch. 2), 194, 218, and see 498; V.V., *A.*, I, 496–7; Mortillet, G. de, 'Les Boissons fermentées' (Bibl. Ch. 2), 261 sqq.; Vogt, E., 'Swiss Pile Dwellings', *Antiquity*, XXXI, 68 sqq., 1957, for swamp, versus, lake dwelling discussion. Cranberry wine: Clark, J. G. D., *Prehistoric Europe: The Economic Basis*, 128.

would certainly not have been content to lead a life without wine. They were a curious and interesting people: great artists, lovers of music and of the dance: yet, at Cerveteri, for example, twenty miles north-west of Rome, their living city was flanked on either side by an extensive city of the tombs of the dead.[3] Perhaps they saw death merely as a continuation of life and thought that in the after world they would be able to drink the same wine which they were the first, or probably the first, to grow in the vineyards of Tuscany.

The beginnings of Italian viticulture may have been in Tuscany but it was the influence of the Greek cities of Southern Italy and Sicily which came to dominate Italian viticulture. With the foundation of these cities towards the end of the 8th century B.C. there came into the Italian world all the skill and experience of the wine-growers of Greece. Vineyards flourished around the southern cities: so much so that Herodotus called the southerly part of Italy Oenotria, 'the land of vine-poles', and Sophocles named it the beloved land of Bacchus.[4]

The early Latin inhabitants of the village that was later to become the City of Rome were shepherds and farmers who lived in round huts constructed from wattle and daub. In those early days of the City there may have been little, or no, Roman wine. Pliny argues a scarcity of wine in early Rome from the story that Romulus 'used milk and not wine for libations' but this may have been due to a religious prohibition on the use of wine in certain libations. Pliny goes on to say that Roman women were forbidden to drink wine and cites as an instance of this masculine rule that 'the wife of Egnatius Maetennus was clubbed to death by her husband for drinking wine from the vat, and that Romulus acquitted him on the charge of murder'. The incident, if it happened, may have been due more to plain bad temper than to an over-balanced sense of thrift in the use of wine. Nevertheless it seems clear that, although it was not grown in any quantity, there actually was Latin wine quite soon after the foundation of the city.

It was not, however, until the middle of the 2nd century B.C. – Pliny gives the year 154 B.C. – that wine-growing in Central Italy became really important. In his dating Pliny may have been right for it was about 160 B.C. that Cato wrote his *De Agri Cultura* which deals, among other things, with the growing of the vine in Latium and Campania,[5] the two districts which were to produce the most famous wines of the Roman Empire.

Some idea of the importance of the vine in Italy in the 2nd and 1st centuries B.C. can be gained from the extent of the Italian wine trade at this time. In the island of Delos, which was one of the great markets for Aegean trade, there were Italian merchants in the 2nd century, and towards 100 B.C. they were settling there with their wives and children. For the greater part they sold Italian oil but they sold some Italian wine as well. In the Central Mediterranean there was a certain amount of trade and it has been suggested that one of the motives behind the Roman destruction of Carthage was fear of competition from North African vineyards. This motive may have existed but it is doubtful if it played any important part in the attitude of Rome towards her political rival. In any case, Italian wine was already being imported into North Africa before the Third Punic War.

At about the same date there was a valuable export trade in wine from Italy to Gaul. Diodorus Siculus, writing about the middle of the 1st century B.C., shows us

[3]Lydian (?) origin: Herodotus, I, 94. Cerveteri: Bradford, J., *Ancient Landscapes* . . ., III sqq. General: Whatmough, J., *The Foundations of Roman Italy*, 220 sqq.

[4]Hehn, V. (quoting Herodotus), *The Wandering of Plants and Animals* . . . (Bibl. Ampelography), 75. General: Frank, Scramuzza, III, 269 sqq.; Sophocles, *Antigone*, 1116 sq.

[5]Plin., XIV, 87 sqq.; XVIII, 24.

*Etruscan Couple
from Sarcophagus at
Cerveteri
Rome, Mus. di Villa Giulia*

the receiving end of this northern and western trade. The Gauls, he tells us, were only able to make beer and a kind of mead but they were

> '... exceedingly addicted to the use of wine and fill themselves with the wine which is brought into their country by merchants, drinking it unmixed and since they partake of this drink without moderation by reason of their craving for it, when they are drunken they fall into a stupor or a state of madness. Consequently many of the Italian traders, induced by the love of money which characterizes them, believe that the love of wine of these Gauls is their own godsend. For these transport the wine on the navigable rivers by means of boats and through the level plain on wagons, and receive for it an incredible price; for in exchange for a jar of wine they receive a slave. ...'

It was doubtless this characteristic love of money which, in the earlier days of the trade with Gaul (about 118 B.C.), led to the enactment upon which Cicero makes comment: 'We ourselves, indeed, the most just of men, who forbid the races beyond the Alps to plant the olive or the vine, so that our own olive groves and vineyards may be the more valuable, are said to act with prudence in doing so but not with justice. ...'[6] There has been some argument about the exact meaning of this prohibition but at least it testifies to the importance which the Italians attached to their own viticulture.

On the whole, however, Rome was remarkably unprotectionist about the growing of wine and as the Italian wine trade prospered so, inevitably, was Rome's example followed by the other countries of the Western Mediterranean. North Africa, except for its raisin-wine or *passum*, had never been noted for its wine, some

[6]Hatzfeld, J., 'Les Italiens résidant à Délos', *Bull. de Correspondance Hellénique*, XXXVI, 1912; Ros., *SEHR*, 22, and fns. 15, 16, 17; Diodorus Siculus, V, 27, 2-3; Cicero, *De Re Publica*, III, 16; Frank, I, 172-3. On the question of Carthage, as well as Ros., *SEHR* above, see Frank, Tenney, *An Economic History of Rome*, 115, and fn. 15.

of which was inclined to be rough. North African output was not large and it was no competitor with the vineyards of Italy. Quite different was the case of Spain. Some Iberian vineyards may have existed before the beginning of the Roman domination in the 2nd century but by the time of the Early Empire the vineyards were already extensive, particularly so round Tarragona and in Andalusia. Strabo indeed remarks upon the large quantities of wine exported from the vineyards of Southern Spain. There were even vines at this date on an island in the Tagus near ancient Moron which is now the Portuguese Almerim.[7] But whereas Portuguese, or rather Lusitanian, wine was never very important in the Roman world, that of Spain was destined to play a great part and already in the time of Augustus Spain was on the way to becoming the chief competitor of the Italian wine growers.

It was not for a long time that the south of France – the Province of Gallia Narbonensis which lay between the Alps, the Cevennes, and the Pyrenees – presented any threat to the Italian wine trade. The first French vineyards had most probably been made at Marseilles as early as the 6th century and either by Greeks or under Greek influence, but it was only slowly that the vine spread outwards from this focal point. In the 1st century B.C. Diodorus remarked of Gaul that Gaul produced neither wine nor oil since the temperateness of the climate was vitiated by excessive cold, while Strabo took a slightly more cautious view and said that north of the Cevennes '. . . the vine . . . does not easily bring its fruit to maturity'. The early wine of the Province was grown in the south and most of it was either drunk in the Province itself or sent north to the wineless tribes of Central and Eastern Gaul where it may have been traded in serious competition with the better but more expensive wines of Italy.[8]

The Wines of Italy

In the time of Augustus at the end of the 1st century B.C. and until at least the rule of Vespasian in the later part of the 1st century A.D., the district of Campania, that fertile district which included Capua, Naples, Mount Vesuvius and Sorrento, was a thriving and prosperous land of vineyards. Campania could in truth have been called 'the beloved land of Bacchus' since the vines produced abundantly in the volcanic soil of the Bay of Naples a number of the best wines of the Roman Empire. The country villas of Pompeii, which we shall later consider in some detail, offer an eloquent testimony to the style of life of the Campanian farmer and to the important rôle which wine played in the pattern of his life.

Campania, however, was not unique in the excellence of its wines for Latium, which extended northwards from Campania to the Alban Hills and Rome, claimed at least an equal degree of distinction for the vintages which it produced. The Falernian of Campania had been at one time the outstanding wine of Roman life. But, as we shall see, its pre-eminence was not always justified and the fame which it gave to the vineyards of Campania has overshadowed that which should rightly have belonged to those other vineyards of Campania and Latium which grew the Caecuban, Calenian, Setine, and Statanian wines, all of which were considered to be first-class, as, it would seem, were also the Alban and the Massic.

These top-ranking wines, and also the question of the maturing of wine, will be

[7]N. Africa: Plin., XIV, 81, 120; XV, 8; Frank, Haywood, IV, 22 sqq.; Frank, Tenney, 'The Inscriptions of the Imperial Domains of Africa', *Am. Jrnl. of Philology*, XLVII, Pts 1 and 2, 1926. Spain: Plin., XIV, 71; Strab., 3, 2, 6; 3, 3, 1; 3, 4, 16; Frank, van Nostrand, III, 132 sqq.

[8]Diodorus Siculus, V, 26, 2–3; Strab., 4, 1, 2; Frank, Grenier, III, 583–4.

*Wall Painting from the
Tomb of Leopards,
Tarquinia
Etruscan, c 500 B.C.*

discussed later in this chapter. For the moment one may merely record some of the
lesser wines which were grown in this part of Italy and for this purpose it is convenient to consider Latium and Campania as a single district.★ The lesser wines
varied greatly in quality. Arician, from south of the Alban Lake, was a somewhat
rough wine made from vines which were trained high upon trees. Its quality can be
gauged from the fact that it was one of the cheapest of wines and the price at which
it sold was so low that the vines were only pruned every other year, a yearly pruning
being found to be too expensive. It was not necessarily the height of the vines which
made this poor quality for Capuan was an excellent wine – or so Polybius thought –
and this was also made from tree-trained vines. For this reason the Capuan was
sometimes called 'anadendrite' from *anadendras*, or a vine which grew up trees. Also
from near Capua came Cauline which, in Pliny's time, was a new name though one
which then was beginning to excite attention. Pliny notes two other names, both
of wines from Campania, which had also 'lately excited consideration', Trebellican
and Trifoline. Trebellican, which grew four miles from Naples, seems to have been
a mild and 'tasty' wine; Trifoline, somewhat earthy in taste, was so called because
it matured in three years. A light wine which was ready for drinking after five years
was the Ulban which was grown near Cumae and which may occasionally have
passed under the name of Cumanum. Gauran, on the other hand, which grew
between Cumae and Naples in the district of the modern Monte Barbaro, was a
rich and vigorous wine, of a fairly oily texture, and 'both rare and excellent'.

★For wines of the Roman World and the locations of their vineyards see Appendix C.

Pompeian wines, which grew, of course, in the vineyards of Pompeii and Mount Vesuvius and which may sometimes have been labelled as Vesuvinum, were made, or at least some of them were made, from the Murgentina (renamed the Pompeiana) vine which had been imported from Sicily. They appear to have been rough, strong wines which, as one commentator wryly remarks, could induce 'a headache which lasts till noon on the following day'. It is interesting to note that some of the local wines of Pompeii were 'labelled' with the names of the estates which were responsible for them: such, for example, were the Geminianum, Marianum and Tironianum: but while this labelling may have served to indicate some degree of quality it is not, I think, comparable to the *château*-labelling of modern times. In fact it is quite possible that it was only an indication of ownership for the purposes of accountancy.[9]

Of the lesser wines grown further north in Latium one of the better ones seems to have been Formian. Horace, at any rate, thought well of it. Another was Labican, from vineyards near the modern town of Frascati, 'sweet and oily to the taste' and 'may be drunk at the earliest after ten years'. Privernatian at one time attained a fairly high ranking, as did Veliternan though the latter, again 'sweet to the taste', 'has the peculiar quality of seeming to be mixed'. Tiburtine, from near modern Tivoli, was a thin wine although, curiously enough, it took at least ten years to mature. Signine, a very dry wine, acquired some renown for its power of constricting relaxed bowels. The worst of these wines seems to have been Vatican which was grown in the neighbourhood of the modern Vatican City. Martial hated it and, always caustic about the wines which he disliked, called it 'venom'.[10]

There were few good wines in Central Italy, either in Umbria to the north of Rome, in the country of the Sabines to the north-east of Rome, or in the territory of the Aequi and the Marsi to the east of the City. The best of them appears to have been Nomentan which was harsh when new, and probably very dark and full of dregs, but which nevertheless improved greatly with age. It is from Martial that we hear of its quality when it had matured and since he possessed a small farm at Nomentum he ought to have known. Aequan, and thus perhaps also Carseolan,

[9]Arician: Plin., XIV, 12; XVII, 213. Capuan: Polyb, XXXIV, 11, 1; Ath-E, I, 31d (quoting Polybius); *CIL*, IV, 2833 may refer. Cauline: Plin., XIV, 69; cf. Strab., 5, 4, 3. Trebellican: Plin., XIV, 69; Ath-E, I, 27c. Trifoline: Plin., XIV, 70; Mart., XIII, cxiv; Ath-E, I, 26e; *CIL*, IV, Supp. I and II, 5518, 5570. Ulban: Ath-E, I, 26f. Cumanum (?): *CIL*, IV, Supp. I and II, 5553. Gauran: Ath-E, I, 26f; Auson., *Mosella*, 157; *CIL*, IV, Supps I and II, 5511. Pompeian: Plin., XIV, 70; *CIL*, IV, Supps I and II, 5559; and Frank, V, 258. Vesuvian (?): *CIL*, VIII, 22640, 31; see also *CIL*, IV, 2557-9. Murgentina and Pompeiana: Cato, VI, 4; Varro, I, XXV; Colum., III, 2, 27; Plin., XIV, 35. Geminianum, Marianum, Tironianum: *CIL*, IV, Supp. I and II, 5578, 5579, 5581-2; and Day, J., 'Agriculture in the Life of Pompeii', *Yale Class. Studies*, 205, fn. (See also last part of fn. 10.)

[10]Formian: Ath-E, I, 26e; Hor., *Carm.*, I, 20; *CIL*, IV, Supp. I and II, 5577. Labican: Ath-E, I, 26f. Privernatian: Strab., 5, 3, 10; Plin., XIV, 65; Ath-E, I, 26e; possibly *CIL*, XV, 4587. Veliternan: Plin., XIV, 65; Ath-E, I, 27a. Tiburtine: Ath-E, I, 26e; Hor., *Carm.*, I, 18; *Edict. Dioc.*, II, I, 2. Signine: Strab., 5, 3, 10; Plin., XIV, 65; XXIII, 36; Mart., XIII, cxvi; Ath-E, I, 27b. Vatican: Mart., VI, xcii; also I, xvii; x,xlv. For those wines of Latium and Campania listed in Appendix C but not discussed in the text, or in this part of the text, references are – Ardeatan: Colum., III, 9, 2. Latiniensian: Strab., 5, 2, 1; Plin., XIV, 67. Leucogaean (?): *CIL*, IV, Supps I and II, 5590. Liternine: Hor., *Epist.*, I, 15. Petrinensian: Hor., *Epist.*, I, 5, 5; and possibly *CIL*, XV, 4625. Praenestine: Ath-E, I, 26f.

both of which came from the ancient territory of the Aequi, had a tendency to be thin and rather dry. Marsic, from the territory of the Marsi, was a dry wine and inclined to be turbid. Sabine was also a thin wine, sometimes, if not usually, white, and its only real distinction seems to have been that some of it was grown by the poet Horace on his Sabine farm. In an Ode of invitation to his friend Maecenas he says 'Come – drink with me – cheap Sabine, to be sure, and out of common tankards, yet wine that I with my own hand put up. . . .' Even without Horace's company to ennoble it, cheap Sabine was doubtless better than the wine made at Sulmo, the Paelignian town in the Abruzzi which was the birthplace of Ovid. (It was Paelignian wine-growers who made the turbid Marsic despised by Martial.)[11]

The wines of the South were better than those of Central Italy but, though they were regarded as acceptable, they were not greeted in Rome with great enthusiasm. Venafran from Samnium was a light wine. Beneventine, also from Samnium, was better; the nickname of 'smoky' which was occasionally given to it did not mean that it tasted of smoke but that it was made from the *Kapneos*, or smoky, vine which was probably imported into the South of Italy from Greece. This same vine, whose name comes from the colour of its grapes, grew also on the hills at Thurii where it made, or helped to make, the mild, soft and fairly sweet Thurine wine. The same combination of mildness, softness, and moderate sweetness seems to have been characteristic of many other wines of the Gulf of Taranto and of Calabria, wines such as Tarentine, Lagaritan, and Tempsan. There were, however, also dry wines, among them Buxentine from Lucania and Barine which probably came from the district of modern Bari in Apulia.[12]

Sicilian wines had a long history which went back into the early days of the Greek cities and their history continued, though with various fluctuations, under the Romans. The emphasis in Sicilian agriculture tended to shift towards the growing of grain but even in the 1st century of the Empire when Sicily was rich in corn, she both grew and exported wines of a high quality. Virgil mentions the Sicilian wine which Acestes had given to Aeneas and his companions; and indeed it seems that Sicilian wines only began to be drunk in Rome a few years before Virgil was writing his *Aeneid*. According to Pliny it was Julius Caesar who first brought Mamertine to the favourable notice of the Romans, this being a good, and possibly a very good, wine grown near Messina. And here it is worth remarking that, of the Mamertine growths, the one called Potitian, after the name of the original grower, was held in particular esteem, for this is one early attempt – there were others in Italy – of the '*château*-labelling' of a good growth. Tauromenitan, from Taormina, ranked next after Mamertine, under which name indeed it was often sold. Three other wines which found favour were the Iotaline (or possibly Italiot), a 'sweet, light, and vigorous' wine, some of which grew near Syracuse, Catanaean from Catania, and Mesopotamian from near Gela in Southern Sicily.[13]

A less favourable view was taken of the wines of Etruria, north of Rome. Wine may have been grown here under the Etruscans; it was certainly grown here later, and in some quantity; yet none of it attained any degree of fame. This must appear curious to us when we think that it is Tuscany which now makes the good wines called Chianti and is one of the best wine-producing regions of Italy. It was not so in Roman times. Then the only Tuscan wine that was singled out for praise was

[11]Nomentan: Colum., III, 2, 14; Plin., XIV, 23; Ath-E, I, 27b; Mart., I, cv; X, xlviii; XIII, cxix. Aequan: Ath-E, I, 27b. Carseolan: Colum., III, 9, 2. Marsic: Plin., XVII, 171; Mart., XIII, cxxi; XIV, cxvi; Ath-E, I, 26f. Sabine: Strab., 5, 3, 1; Mart., X, xlix; Ath-E, I, 27b; Galen., II, 753; Hor., *Carm.*, I, 9, 20. Sulmonian: Ovid, *Amores*, 2, 16, 1-10; Plin., XVII, 250. Paelignian: Ovid, *Amores*, 2, 16, 1-10; Mart., I, xxvi; XIII, cxxi. For Spoletine, from Umbria – 'sweet to the taste and of a golden colour', see Ath-E, I, 27b; Mart., XIII, cxx; XIV, cxvi.

[12]Venafran: Ath-E, I, 27c. Beneventine: Ath-E, I, 31e; *CIL*, xv, 4544. Thurine: Strab., 6, 1, 14; Plin., XIV, 39, 69; and Ath-E, I, 27c. Tarentine: Plin., XIV, 69; Mart., XIII, cxxv; Ath-E, I, 27c. Lagaritan: Strab., 6, 1, 14; Plin., XIV, 39, 69; Virgil, II, 93 – Lagean, referring to Lagaritan (?); see also Dunbabin, 35. Tempsan: Plin., XIV, 69; and Ath-E, I, 27c. Buxentine: Ath-E, I, 27a. Barine: Plin., XIV, 69; Ath-E, I, 27b (note that the text may be corrupt. Ath-E, gives Barine but Athénée de Naucratis, *Les Deipnosophistes*, trs. Desrousseaux, A. M., gives Babia. I think, on wine probability, that Barine must have been meant). Other wines of Southern Italy – Consentin: Plin., XIV, 69. Rhegine: Ath-E, I, 26e; *CIL*, xv, 4590 (?); Frank, v., 136. Servitian: Plin., XIV, 69.

[13]Ros., *SEHR*, 67, and fn. 28; Frank, Scramuzza, III, 269 sqq., 350f; Virgil, *Aeneid*, I, 195-6. Sicilian vines imported into Italy – Murgentina: Cato, vi, 4; Colum., III, 2, 27; Plin., XIV, 35. Eugenia: Colum., III, 2, 16; Plin., XIV, 25. Mamertine: Strab., 6, 2, 3; Plin., XIV, 66, 97; Mart., XIII, cxvii; Ath-E, I, 27d; Dioscorides, *Herbal*, v, 10. Potitian: Plin., XIV, 66. Tauromenitan: Plin., XIV, 25, 66; *CIL*, IV, 2618; IV, Supp. I and II, 5563-8. Iotaline or Italiot: Ath-E, I, 27d, but compare the reading in Athénée de Naucratis, *Les Deipnosophistes*, trs. Desrousseaux, A. M. Catanaean: Strab., 6, 2, 3; Frank, Scramuzza, III, 350-1. Mesopotamian: *CIL*, IV, 2602-3 (?); VIII, 22640, 8; Kleberg, 108, fn. 16. Other wines – Adranu-

Lunensan (which properly, perhaps, should be called a Ligurian wine), and which came from vineyards near La Spezia and Carrara in the general area which now produces the rather special wine of Cinque Terre. The repute of the ancient Lunensan, attested by Pliny, may find some confirmation in the fact that it was also imported into Pompeii. Of the other Tuscan wines, however, there is little to say, except to mention their names: Caeretan, Graviscan, Statoniensian, and Veientan, the latter from the old Etruscan city of Veii just north of Rome and described as a red and turbid wine, inferior and full of dregs.

I do not know why the Tuscan wines did not achieve popularity. Many of them were made from the Apian, or 'bee-vine', which was a variety of Muscat and was possibly the same as the Greek Psithian and the medieval Muscatel. The Apian was renowned for its 'precious flavour' but, although the wines made from it began sweet, they were said to acquire roughness with age. Perhaps Tuscan wines were too harsh for Roman taste; perhaps they were just indifferently made. Harshness was, at all events, a characteristic of the wine of Genoa which was rated as the best of the 'Ligurian' wines and one might note in passing that Ligurian wines were generally treated with resin, although in this they were by no means exceptional. Corsican wine was summed up briefly and bitterly by Martial in the phrase 'we drink the black poison of a Corsican jar'.[14] Martial also thought poorly, although not quite so poorly, of Tuscan wines in general.

On the other hand the wines of Venetia, and those of Cisalpine Gaul – Emilia and the Po Valley – attracted considerable attention and one of them was classed among the top-ranking wines of the Roman Empire. This was Rhaetic. It was grown on the Rhaetic vine whose name must have come from Rhaetia, the name of the Roman Alpine province which included the Tyrol. (There was a Rhaetic vine in the Maritime Alps but this produced a low grade wine while fine Rhaetic only came from the north and north-east of Italy.) It was Virgil who raised Rhaetic to the highest peak of its renown, and it was also, or coincidentally, the favourite wine of Augustus. 'What poem,' wrote Virgil, 'can do justice to Rhaetic?' Having been born near Mantua, and educated at Cremona and Milan, the poet would have had plenty of opportunity to drink the good Rhaetic wine, some of which was grown around Verona and some, most probably, around Aquileia in the north-eastern part of Venetia. His praised was thus based upon experience and it was not prejudiced by native patriotism since he does in fact admit that Rhaetic 'cannot compete with Falernian'.

The Romans grew wines right down the Po Valley to the Adriatic coast. There were vineyards, for example, at Modena, Faenza, Cesena and also at Ravenna where wines were grown on the Spionian vine which produced a good quantity of must. Ancona too, further south in Picenum, produced a quantity of wine at the beginning of the Empire. But none of these wines of Cisalpine Gaul or of Picenum commanded the respect which was given to the wines of Venetia. Apart from the fact that the grapes grown in the marshes of Padua had a flavour of willow, which cannot have been much of a recommendation to any wine that was made from them, the rest of the wines of this region seem to have been of fair quality, and they were on the whole probably dry and white. The best known of them, excepting Rhaetic, was Pucine, grown near the river Timavaus on the Gulf of Trieste, a mild, dry wine

menitan: Dioscorides, *Herbal*, v, 10. Aluntium ('a kind of must'): Plin., xiv, 80.

[14]Lunensan: Strab., 5, 2, 5; Plin., xiv, 68; *CIL*, iv, 2599–2601; Kleberg, 108, fn. 16. Caeretan: Mart., xiii, cxxiv; cf. Colum., iii, 9, 6. Graviscan: Strab., 5, 2, 8; Plin., xiv, 67–8. Statoniensian: Plin., xiv, 68. Veientan: Mart., i, ciii; ii, liii; iii, xlix; *CIL*, xv, 4595. Apian: Colum., iii, 2, 17, 18; Plin., xiv, 24, 81; *CIL*, xv, 4536; V.V., *A.*, ii, 55–6. Genuan: Strab., 4, 6, 2; Plin., xiv, 68, 124. Corsican: Mart., ix, ii. Tuscan wine in general: Mart., i, xxvi. Other wines – Maecenatian (but for doubtful location see Appendix C): Plin., xiv, 67. Psithian: Virgil, ii, 93; Plin., xiv, 80, 81; *FAC*, ii, Anaxandrides, 71; Eubulus, 138.

with a 'sweet scent' which may sometimes have passed under the names of Praetutian and, possibly, of Adrian.[15]

These finer wines, however, do not indicate the real commercial importance of
the vineyards of Venetia for Aquileia not only became the centre of a vineyard
district but grew also to become a great and prosperous city which, among other
things, exported her own wine to the Danubian lands beyond the Alps. Through
Aquileia the Italian wine trade moved out eastwards to dominate Pannonia and
most of the Danubian provinces. The western extension of the Italian wine trade
was motivated principally from Campania and partly from Tuscany, and the wine
went out to Gaul and, sometimes at least, to Spain. The range of the Italian commerce in wine is further shown by the fact that, in the 1st century A.D., 'wine of
Italy', which most probably meant wine from Campania or Southern Italy or
Sicily, was exported, though not in great quantity, down the Red Sea to East Africa
and India.[16] As far as wine was concerned this latter commerce was exotic and un-
important. Far more important to the Italian wine trade in general was the presence
of the Legions in the Provinces of the Empire for the Legions attracted supplies of
wine and in the north-west and north-east most of this wine would have come
from Italy herself. The centurion's vine-rod may have been a symbol of the authority
under which trade could prosper but to the Italian merchants the legionary's wine-
cup was the beckoning emblem of personal good fortune.

The Wines of the West

The main threat to the prosperity of Italian viticulture did not come from those
vineyards which were planted in Dalmatia, and even in the Danube provinces, but
from those which grew up in Spain and Gaul. Of these two western regions Spain
was the major producer. In the Early Empire wine was sent from Italy into Spain
but no attempt seems to have been made to prevent the Spaniards growing their
own wine and we find, on the contrary, that there was even a 'Procurator for improving the Falernian vines in Baetica'. By the beginning of the 1st century A.D.,
Baetica, the modern Andalusia, exported a considerable quantity of wine, as did
Turdetania, the south-western part of Baetica, and most of this wine would have
been traded outwards by the merchants of Gades, the modern Cadiz. Baetica was
not, of course, the only Spanish wine-growing area, for Carpetan wine was grown
at Valdepeñas in La Mancha. But Baetica's main rival, for quality as well as for
quantity, was the eastern seaboard of Spain.

From the north-eastern coast, between modern Barcelona and Gerona, came
Laeetanian, a quantity wine which, in all probability, was exported to Rome as a
cheap wine to be sold in the taverns of the great city. It must be this wine to which
Martial refers when he says contemptuously to a Roman soak: 'Get from the
taverner dregs of Laeetanian. . . .' A further use of the cheap Laeetanian may well
have been to 'stretch' the more expensive and better known Italian vintages and
thus to increase the profit of the fraudulent taverner. Other wines from eastern
Spain, however, could not only hold their own under their own names but could
even be compared in quality to the top-graded wines of Italy herself. The three
Spanish wines which held this high rank were Lauronensian, which probably came

[15] Virgil, II, 95-6. Rhaetic: Suet.,
Augustus, 77; Strab., 4, 6, 8; Plin.,
XIV, 41, 67; Mart., XIV, c; Frank,
V, 109, 146. Veroniensan (Ver-
ona): Strab., 4, 6, 8; Plin., XIV, 67.
Mutine (Modena): Plin., XIV, 39.
Feventine (Faenza): Colum., III,
3, 2. Caesenian (Cesena): Plin.,
XIV, 67. Ravenna, and Spionian:
Colum., III, 2, 27; 21, 10; Plin.,
XIV, 34. Anconitan (Ancona):
Strab., 5, 4, 2; Ath-E, I, 26f. Also
Picenian: Plin., XIV, 37, 39, 67;
Edict. Dioc., II, 1, 1a. Patavian
(Padua): Plin., XIV, 110. Pucine:
Plin., III, 127; XIV, 60; XVII, 31.
Praetutian: Plin., XIV, 60, 67, 75;
Ath-E, I, 33a; Dioscorides, *Herbal*,
V, 10. Adrian: Plin., XIV, 67; see
also XIV, 124-5; and Dioscorides,
Herbal, V, 10.

[16] Aquileia, etc.: Ros., *SEHR*, 70-2;
Frank, V, 113; and see Chilver,
G. E. F., *Cisalpine Gaul*, 138,
140-2. Western trade: Ros.,
SEHR, 70; Frank, V, 258-9;
Frank, van Nostrand, III, 186.
Eastern trade: *Periplus of the Ery-
thraean Sea*, passim.

*Bronze Figures
Etruscan, c 500 B.C.
London, British Museum*

from the modern province of Valencia, Tarraconensian from the region of modern Tarragona, and Baliarican from the Balearic Islands.[17]

Some idea, though only a partial one, of the attraction of the Italian market for Spanish wines can be gathered from the fact that by the middle of the 2nd century A.D. twenty million amphoras of Spanish wine had been shipped into the territory of the City of Rome. This estimate is possibly conservative and it takes no account, of course, of the amphoras shipped into other parts of Italy. At the least, however, we can say that, about A.D. 150, the province of Spain was one of the major suppliers of wine to the populace of Rome.

Spain did not only export wine, olive oil, minerals, fish, sauce and dancing girls; she also exported her brains. Lucan and Seneca were born at Cordoba; the poet Martial was born at Bilbilis; Columella was a Spaniard of Cadiz. Indeed Spain seems, in a way, to have become the most Romanized province of all; certainly she has remained so. It is tempting to compare the announcements of gladiatorial shows at Pompeii during the summer months with the posters advertising the modern bullfights in summer Spain and to find in these modern posters a lingering continuity of Roman life.[18] But the comparison is superficial in every respect and particularly so because the Spanish bullfight is not the lineal descendant of the gladiatorial combat. Even so, one still feels that it is in Spain that one comes closest to the living feel of the Roman world. The huge pottery jars of Tarancon and Ocaña in Central Spain are reminiscent of the *dolia* in which the Romans fermented their must. And then on the south-east coast between Alicante and Murcia and Almeria, pale yellow-green jars are carried about the streets on the heads or the hips of girls, or in slots in wheel-barrows shaped like triangular ladders, and these jars, though smaller in size, are the same in shape as the amphoras of the ancient Mediterranean. These resemblances, if such they be, sound rather petty but in Spain they seem to

[17]Dalmatia: see Ros., *SEHR*, 628, fn. 12. Spain, general: Frank, van Nostrand, III, 132 sqq. – the Falernian vines on p. 149 referring to *CIL*, II, 2029. Gades: Frank, Tenney, *An Economic History of Rome*, 312. Baetica: Strab., 3, 2, 6; Colum., XII, 21, 4; Pauly-Wissowa-Kroll, *Real-Encyclopädie . . .*, Hispania. Turdetania: Strab., 3, 2, 6. Carpetan: Pauly-Wissowa-Kroll, *Real-Ency.*, Hispania. Laeetanian: Plin., XIV, 71; Mart., I, xxvi. Laletanian: Mart., I, xxvi, VII, liii. Lauronensian: Plin., XIV, 71; *CIL*, IV, Supp. I and II, 5558; XV, 4577–9 (?); Kleberg, 108, fn. 16. Tarraconensian: Plin., XIV, 71; Mart., XIII, cxviii. Baliarican: Plin., XIV, 71. Among the vines, apart from 'Falernian', grown in Spain, was the Coccolobis or Basilic (?), otherwhere called Baliscan; see Plin., XIV, 30; Colum., III, 2, 19–20 and textual readings in fn. 5; III, 7, 1; 21, 10. Possible 'stretching' of Italian wines, see Frank, V, 273, fn. 14.

[18]See Frank, V, 220, discussing Monte Testaccio. Gladiatorial shows at Pompeii, dating and frequency: Tanzer, 81–2.

take a different aspect, and at least one may believe that Spain has kept in its fingers the ancient feeling for the uses of pottery.

In France the development of viticulture was less rapid and less widespread than it was in Spain. It is not likely that there were many French – or rather Gallic – vineyards before the Roman domination of Narbonensian Gaul in 121 B.C. and of the vineyards which may have existed most would have been in the neighbourhood of Marseilles. If we can argue anything from the statement of Cicero which we have already quoted, then the slow development of the Narbonensian vineyards may have been due to the Roman prohibition of Gallic viticulture. But in the 1st century B.C. when the Province became heavily Romanized – almost in fact Italianized – the prohibition must have become either ineffective or abrogated, and by A.D. 79 vineyards had spread up the valley of the Rhône as far as Vienne, westwards to Béziers near Narbonne, and westwards also to the neighbourhood of Bordeaux.

The wine of Marseilles, or in this instance perhaps merely wine which was exported from Marseilles, was given a bad reputation by Martial who speaks of 'Massilia's vile smoke-rooms' in which the wine was rashly and improperly matured. But the poet's mockery of Massilian finds little confirmation in other writers who appear to distinguish two kinds of Massilian, the one, locally called 'juicy', being 'uncommon, rich, and full-bodied', and the other, or apparently the other, being a light, dry, white wine. We may suggest that the wine to which Martial referred was not necessarily Massilian since, at about the same date, Narbonensian wines – a general term for the wines of the Province – were maltreated by dealers who had 'set up a regular factory for the purpose and colour them by means of smoke, and . . . also by employing noxious herbs and drugs . . .' This is Pliny's view but I think we may suggest that the 'maltreatment' was not always a malpractice and that some of the products of the factory were spiced and aromatic wines deliberately and honestly made to satisfy the taste of the Roman market.

Loading Wine Casks on a Ship
A.D. *113*
Rome, Trajan's Column

From Vienne in the Rhône Valley came a curious wine with a natural flavour of pitch. This *vinum picatum* had its flavour of pitch given to it by a particular grape, the Allobrogian, which took its name from the tribe of the Allobroges of whose territory Vienne was the capital. The wine achieved a certain notoriety and some of it was even sent to Martial by Romulus, a friend of his at Vienne. That the wine was really popular may be doubted since Pliny, here being poker-faced, remarks that the people of Vienne only sold it at a high price in their own city, 'out of patriotism'. Wine growers are patriotic men, but this is carrying patriotism too far.

In the more westerly part of the province, Baeterrensan was made at Béziers. This wine, some of which was white, seems in the 1st century A.D. to have been drunk only inside Gaul, although towards the middle of the 2nd century A.D. some Baeterrensan, and 'five years old' at that, was exported to Rome. More westerly still, but of no importance to the mind of Rome in the 1st century A.D., was the wine which was (probably) grown in the vineyards of Bordeaux. We have outspoken evidence that wine was grown at Bordeaux in the Later Empire but that there was Bordeaux wine in the 1st century of the Empire must remain, even though probable, yet still uncertain.[19]

This moderately exhaustive survey of the *vignobles* of Italy and the Roman West has been necessary to show how viticultural Europe was gradually assuming a more or less modern pattern. At one moment, however, it seemed that this growing pattern would be abruptly checked. Towards the end of the 1st century A.D. the Emperor Domitian issued an Edict which was intended to limit the growing of vines. The Edict prohibited any extension of the vineyards of Italy and ordered the provincial vineyards to be reduced by half. It has been suggested that one of the motives was to protect Italian wine growers by reducing competition from the provinces. Another motive, however, may have been to use the Edict merely as a threat which, by officially discouraging viticulture, would thereby encourage the growing of corn. This seems to have been the real purpose since the order for the suppression of the provincial vineyards was never fully carried out and Suetonius goes so far as to say that Domitian 'took no steps to implement this Edict'. At all events, Asia Minor managed to keep her vineyards and it appears that there was little, if any, reduction in the vineyard area of Narbonensian Gaul and Southern Spain. The order may have been enforced in Africa, which in any case was scarcely a competitor in the wine trade, and it may have applied to Central and Northern Gaul, though it is doubtful if these two latter districts had any vineyards worth mentioning. Nearly two hundred years later the Edict was rescinded by Probus and although Probus set his legions to work planting vineyards in Gaul and Pannonia, this does not necessarily mean that they were re-planting vineyards which Domitian had destroyed.[20]

Even though the Edict of Domitian may have been generally ineffective in Gaul, the progress of Gallic vineyards was still slow. It is quite possible, as we have already seen, that there were vineyards at Bordeaux in the 1st century A.D. but we have no satisfactory news of them until the 4th century when Ausonius owned vineyards in the Gironde and praised 'our famous wines'. However much his praise may have been genuine, and not due to local pride, the wines of Bordeaux were never famous under the Roman Empire. Nor were the wines of Burgundy. There were vineyards

[19]Cicero, *De Re Publica*, III, 16; Frank, I, 172-4; but see Ros., *SEHR*, 548, fn. 17. Massilian: Strab., 4, 1, 5; Plin., XIV, 68; Ath-E, I, 27c; Mart., III, lxxxii; x, xxxvi; XIII, cxxiii; XIV, cxviii; Galen, II, 753. Viennan (Vienne) and *vinum picatum*: Plin., XIV, 18, 26, 57; Mart., XIII, cvii. Allobrogian: Plin., XIV, 18, 26-7. Helviolan: Cato, VI, 4; Plin., XIV, 29, 46; Colum., III, 2, 23, 25; *CIL*, xv, 4574 (?). Narbonensian: Strab., 4, 1, 2; Plin., XIV, 68, 83, 84. Baeterrensan: Plin., XIV, 68; *CIL*, xv, 4542-3; Frank, Grenier, III, 582. Biturigiaca: Plin., XIV, 27; Auson., *Epist.*, v, 21; *Mosella*, 160. Biturica: Colum., III, 2, 19-20; 7, 1; 21, 10. For Gallic wine exported to Ireland: Ros., *SEHR*, 574, fn. 12.

[20]Suet., *Domitian*, 7; Ros., *SEHR*, 202-3, and fn. 12; Frank, van Nostrand, III, 177-8; Frank, Grenier, III, 582; West, L. C., *Roman Gaul: The Objects of Trade*, 35.

in the Côte d'Or by the 3rd century at the latest, and possibly, even probably, they had been planted in the 2nd century; but by A.D. 312 the *Incerti Gratiarum Actio Constantino Augusto* gives us a sad picture of their state of decay. Ditches had become blocked, the low-lying lands were swamps and the vines themselves – 'of unknown age' – were a tangled mass of huge roots.

A brighter picture is afforded by the vineyards of the Moselle Valley. These may have been planted about the same time as those of Burgundy, or possibly a little later, but in the 4th century they were prospering. In his *Mosella* Ausonius describes 'the hill-sides green with vines' and, apart from Ausonius, there is a great deal of evidence to show that viticulture was important in the life of the Moselle under the Late Empire. The presence of the Legions near the German frontier must have provided a local and thirsty demand which, since the Rhine vineyards scarcely existed, the Moselle was in an excellent position to meet. The most famous example of the wine trade in this part of the Empire is the Weinschiff of Neumagen, a ship with a dolphin beak and an animal figure-head, freighted with four huge barrels of wine which it is carrying along the Moselle river. We cannot, of course, say that the wine in these barrels was actually Moselle since Trier was a clearing house for imports into the Germanic province and wine from Gaul or Italy may have travelled down the Moselle in the beaked wine ships. But from the numerous and graphic monuments of this area there is no doubt at all that the vineyards of the Moselle were as flourishing as any in the Empire.[21]

Roman Britain

Somewhere about 300 B.C. a Massilian sea captain called Pytheas sailed along the shores of Britain. Fortunately he made an account of his voyage and this has come down to us through the writings of Diodorus Siculus. It is not surprising to find that the climate of Britain was described as being 'extremely cold'; nor is it unexpected to hear that the inhabitants were versed in the making of beer and mead.

[21] Bordeaux: Auson., *Epist.*, v. Burgundy: ed. and trs. Galletier, E., *Panégyriques Latins*, II, viii (5), 94-5; and V.V., *A.*, I, 513, for praise of Burgundian wine in the 3rd century. Moselle: Auson., *Mosella*, 21, 25, 152 sqq., Loeschcke, S., *Denkmäler vom Weinbau aus der Zeit der Römerherrschaft an Mosel, Saar und Ruwer, passim.*

The men of Cornwall, however, found a special mention for they were said to be 'especially hospitable to strangers and have adopted a civilized manner of life because of their intercourse with merchants of other peoples'. This, of course, accounts for the fragments of wine amphoras found at Chûn Castle in Cornwall. In addition to these, amphoras have been found at a number of pre-Roman sites in south-eastern England, most of which were probably for wine and not for oil, and at this same time the British were buying wine from the merchants of Gaul. But it was still a luxury import and the British as a whole drank little wine until the coming of the Roman Legions.

The picture of a post-Conquest Britain urbanized and civilized by the Romans tends to conceal the fact that the Romanization was less complete than in most of the other provinces of the Empire. The towns and cities carry the stamp of the conquerors but they do not show the full and undiluted culture of the Mediterranean. A number of the Romano-British houses were decorated in more or less Mediterranean fashion, boasting painted wall plaster and mosaic floors worked into geometrical patterns or representing mythological scenes. Villas of the 3rd and 4th centuries, though not entirely comparable to those of Italy (and for climatic reasons one would scarcely expect them to be so), again give some evidence of a more or less Romanized civilization. Red Samian ware, which Gaul had copied from Arezzo, frequently served the inhabitants as dishes. Martial even felt able to declare that 'Britain is said to hum my verses' and, if he were not merely referring to the legionaries, his claim might show the British avidity for Roman culture. But from none of this Romanization can we argue that the Mediterranean gift of wine became an integral part of British life.

It is very difficult to estimate the extent of the wine trade into Britain. It may have been quite large. But, from what we know of it, it was not large enough to support the theory that Britain was a 'wine-drinking country'. Nor can we accept without question the other theory that it was in Roman times that Britain began its preference for the wines of Bordeaux. In the first place we cannot really tell how much wine was available for export from the Gironde; and in the second place a quantity of the amphora stamps point to a Spanish, and not a French, origin for the wines that were brought into Britain. At Corbridge, for example, most of the amphoras identified by stamps came from the South of Spain and in particular from that stretch of the Guadalquivir which lies between Seville and Cordoba. These amphoras, it is true, may have carried olive oil, or fish sauce, but it is equally likely that they held wine and we must therefore consider as plausible, if not probable, the theory that Britain began her real drinking history on wine from Andalusia and not on wine from Bordeaux. We might also suggest, though lack of evidence makes it no more than a suggestion, that wine could have been shipped into Britain from the Moselle. There was some contact between the east coast of England and the Rhine estuary and as late as A.D. 360 corn was exported from Britain to the valley of the Rhine. It is not inconceivable that this corn could, in part, have been traded for the wine of the Moselle.[22] But on the other hand the production of the Moselle vineyards may have been taken up entirely by the Legions along the frontier and by the population of the valley and its nearby cities, and there may have been little to spare to meet the needs of a far-off British market.

[22]Diodorus Siculus, V, 21, 1; 22, 4; Rivet, A. L. F., *Town and Country in Roman Britain*, 37, 45, 72 sqq., 101. Chûn amphoras: Hencken, H. O'N., *The Archaeology of Cornwall and Scilly*, 127; and cf. 186; Frank, Collingwood, III, 109; Mart., XI, iii; Haverfield, F., *The Romanization of Roman Britain*, 19, 44, 76-7; Callender, M. H., 'Corbridge Amphora Stamps', *Arch. Aeliana*, 4th Series, XXVII, 1949; (I am also indebted to Mr Callender for his views on Spanish amphoras, given to me in conversation); Collingwood, R. G., and Myres, J. N. L., *Roman Britain and the English Settlements*, 71, 226-7, 245; see West, L. C., *Roman Britain: The Objects of Trade*, 88-9, for queried identifications of Italian or Bordeaux wines in Britain. Trade with the Rhine: Haverfield, F., *op. cit.*, 76-7; *CMH*, I, 377, chapter by Haverfield, F. J. For trade between Britain and Aquitaine, see the comment of Richmond, I. A., 'A Roman Monumental Candelabrum . . . from York', *Antiquaries Journal*, XXVI, 1946.

The permission given by Probus to replant, or to extend, vineyards in the provinces has sometimes been interpreted as giving that permission also to Britain. If the decree did refer to the island of Britain, which is, to say the least of it, debatable since it may just as well refer to some district of Gaul, then it is still no real evidence that vines for wine were actually grown in Britain. A frequent argument is that in any case the climate would have been against the making of British wine. It is true that in Caesar's *Gallic War* the climate was said to be 'more temperate than in Gaul, the cold seasons more moderate'; but Tacitus dismally records that the 'sky is obscured by continual rain and cloud'. The weather argument, however, is one which we can scarcely allow, and for this reason: it appears that, in the first four centuries of the Empire, the climate of Central and Western Europe was much the same as it is today and, since wine is produced in a few modern English vineyards, there is no reason why it should not have been produced in Roman Britain.

There is this point too: both Strabo and Diodorus Siculus suggested that Central and Northern Gaul were too cold for the proper production of wine, yet we know that vines were later grown in the Côte d'Or and it seems that they were introduced into the valley of the Seine; thus the views of these two authors were ultimately irrelevant to the spread of Gallic viticulture. Is it not possible then that the comments of earlier authors on the climate of Britain may have been equally irrelevant to the establishment of British viticulture?

We do in fact know that there was some viticulture in Roman Britain for 'a quantity of vine-stems have actually been found near a villa in Hertfordshire, on a sheltered south-western slope'. But whether the vines grew grapes for eating or grapes for wine we do not know. All we can say is that if vineyards for wine existed in Roman Britain, they were of minor importance and that even when the supply of wine from Spain stopped, as it appears to have stopped, at the end of the 2nd century, it is unlikely that this gave any real impetus to the growing of British wine.[23]

Ship, Donkey, and Tavern

All over the Roman world there were merchants who dealt in wine. They were not only in the greater cities such as Gades, which sent wine to Rome, or Lyons, which sent wine to Northern Gaul, but also in the smaller cities such as Vienne where, for example, we discover a *negotiator vinarius Viennae*. And there must have been many a humbler wine-merchant in the smaller towns and harbours along the coasts of the Mediterranean.

These men were not, however, equivalent to modern wine merchants, nor was their trade organized with anything like a modern complexity. The ancient commerce was highly individualistic and it was operated by merchants who acted either singly or in a small family partnership. Each 'firm' had its own ship which it could freight with wine or with anything else that happened to turn up. Then, if the firm grew prosperous, it might have two or three ships. Naturally there was room in this system for the big operator – in a sense Trimalchio of the *Satyricon* was one of them – but since there appears to have been no dominating network of middlemen the enterprise of the individual merchant always remained the active factor. Even Trimalchio's trading was a personal venture. Here he is, describing it himself:

[23]Caesar, *The Gallic War*, v, 12; Tacitus, *Agricola*, xii. Climate: Brooks, C. E. P., *Climate through the Ages* (Bibl. General), 340, 343; see also Miller, A. Austin, *Climatology* (Bibl. General), 282-7, 403; Strab., 4, 1, 2; Diodorus Siculus, v, 26, 2-3; West, L. C., *Roman Gaul: The Objects of Trade*, 37. Hertfordshire vine-stems: Collingwood, R. G., and Myres, J. N. L., *Roman Britain and the English Settlements*, 221. Stoppage of supply from Spain, see Callender, M. H., *op. cit.* in fn. 22 above, p. 78.

'I built five ships, got a cargo of wine – which was worth its weight in gold at the time – and sent them to Rome. You may think it was a put-up job; every one was wrecked, truth and no fairy-tales. Neptune gulped down thirty million in one day. Do you think I lost heart? Lord! no, I no more tasted my loss than if nothing had happened. I built some more, bigger, better and more expensive, so that no one could say I was not a brave man. You know, a huge ship has a certain security about her. I got another cargo of wine, bacon, beans, perfumes, and slaves. Fortunata did a noble thing at that time; she sold all her jewellery and all her clothes, and put a hundred gold pieces into my hand. They were the leaven of my fortune. What God wishes soon happens. I made a clear ten million on one voyage. I at once bought up all the estates which had belonged to my patron. I built a house, and bought slaves and cattle; whatever I touched grew like a honey-comb. When I came to have more than the whole revenues of my own country, I threw up the game: I retired from active work and began to finance freed-men.'

The Satyricon shows Trimalchio at the peak of his wealth but although it pillories the vulgar exaggeration of this *nouveau riche* tradesman, behind the mockery one can see the type of hundreds upon hundreds of the wine merchants of the Roman world: young, energetic, adventurous men, determined to make their fortunes, and not overburdened with scruples.

The personal element can be seen at work in other ways. Quite often, for example, an estate wine would have been sold direct, or transported direct, to its consumer. In two of the wine-growing villas of Pompeii a wine shop is connected with the house, and this small-scale selling, though not necessarily through an actual 'shop', must have been extremely common in those vineyard areas that were adjacent to towns of any size. Then, in addition to the direct selling from an estate to its customer, there was the sale of wine by travelling merchants. In Gaul, as Diodorus tells us, they carried the wine on boats and wagons and many of the burial monuments of Burgundy and the Moselle show the long casks of wine, hooped at either end, being carried on the merchants' carts. In Italy, and also no doubt in other Mediterranean countries, wine was carried on carts in a huge skin vessel from which the amphoras of the customers were filled. These carts, too, laden with skins or amphoras, added to the noise and confusion of street life in Rome for the itinerant *vinarii* hawked their wine from house to house for the convenience of the over-crowded inhabitants. Yet another method of transport is depicted for us by Varro when he comments upon the traders 'who pack oil or wine and grain or other products from the region of Brundisium or Apulia to the sea in donkey panniers'.[24]

The last stage in the traffic of wine was often the tavern, which played an important, though not always a respectable, part in Roman life. There were two general classes of tavern: the *caupona* and the *hospitium* which were inns or hotels; and the *popina*, the *thermopolium*, and the *taberna*, which were bars or restaurants. The inns provided travellers with lodging and, in some cases at least, with a basic menu of wine, bread and meat which could be eaten in a restaurant attached to the hotel. This at any rate is the plan of the *hospitium Sittii* at Pompeii and one may believe that, with minor differences, it was not untypical of South Italian inns.

A hundred and eighteen bars or restaurant-bars have been identified at Pompeii

[24]Britain: Rivet, A. L. F., *Town and Country in Roman Britain*, 101. Vienne: West, L. C., *Roman Gaul: The Objects of Trade*, 38, commenting on *CIL*, XII, 1896; Petronius, *Satyricon*, 76; Frank, Tenney, *An Economic History of Rome*, 257; Day, J., 'Agriculture in the Life of Pompeii', *Yale Class. Studs.*, 176-7; Diodorus Siculus, V, 26, 2-3; Loeschcke, S., *Denkmäler vom Weinbau . . .*, 21, 22; Reinach, S., *Rép. de Peintures Grecques et Romaines*, 248, 1; Varro, II, vi, 5; Carcopino, J., *Daily Life in Ancient Rome*, 181. For the distributive system of the wine trade: Frank, V, 270 sqq.

and we observe that nearly every block of houses has its own bar in much the same way that cafés are located in the modern Continental cities. One of the distinctive types of these bars is that of the *thermopolium*, which occurs at Pompeii and also at Herculaneum. The *thermopolium*, like the *popina*, sold wine but its particular feature is the hot drink and food counter. These counters, which face on to the street, are blocks of masonry sheeted with marble in a crazy paving pattern and into them are set a number of pottery jars. In some cases the jars held food, or perhaps we should say snacks, such as olives and dried vegetables and, probably, pickled appetizers. The counters are often fitted with a small furnace which may have served to heat up some particular foodstuff but which may also, and more frequently, have been used to provide hot water for the *caldum*, a hot drink made of wine and boiling water which seems to have maintained a certain popularity in Roman times. Sometimes, however, the *thermopolium* consisted of two rooms, one room with a food counter in front and opening on to the street, and a smaller room behind which may have served as a sort of restaurant. In such a case the *thermopolium* merges into the *popina*, though the distinction between them, if we can draw a distinction, may have been that the *popina* sold 'restaurant food' whereas the *thermopolium* only sold 'snacks'. A curious confirmation of the type of food sold in the *popinae* and the *thermopolia* is provided by an enactment of Nero which restricted 'the food sold in wine-shops to green vegetables, dried beans, and the like – whereas before all kinds of tasty snacks had been displayed'.

The *taberna* was essentially a bar but it could also be a shop which sold food as well as wine, and it could offer other attractions, such as the services of a prostitute or the amenities of a gambling den. The latter was the more popular, for the Romans were passionately addicted to gambling: so much so that, except for the period of the Saturnalia, it was forbidden by law and gamblers caught in the act were fined four times the amount of the stakes. It is obvious that the reputation of the tavern-keepers was not always of the best, but if theirs was bad, that of the *caupones*, or inn-keepers, was worse since, apart from being accused of fraudulent and immoral dealings, the female *caupones* occasionally achieved a reputation for sorcery. Even without the imputation of these doubtful practices people still regarded the whole profession with irritation or contempt. Horace, on his journey south from Rome to Apulia, notes the 'stingy tavern-keepers' of Appii Forum. He seems indeed to have had a bad journey for the boatman in the Pomptine Marshes was 'soaked in sour wine', and at Trivicum Horace stayed up till midnight awaiting a faithless girl. A comment on the injustice of tavern life comes from a less distinguished Italian, a veteran gladiator who recorded his feelings in a *graffito* at Pompeii: 'Curses on you, landlord, you sell water and drink unmixed wine yourself.'[25]

Naturally the taverns of the Empire varied greatly and were alike only in their primary purpose. In its simplest form the tavern can be pictured from the wine-shop at one of the villas outside Pompeii. This is merely a rustic 'pub' with a seat along the wall which faced the road. It had a kettle for making hot drinks and the wine was grown on the owner's vines. Nevertheless it must have been pleasant there on a warm, spring day, sitting drinking the wine of a Pompeian vineyard and watching the traffic pass along the road.

A more sophisticated picture of a country tavern comes from the *Copa Surisca*,

Roman 'Legena'
1st century B.C.
Pessione, Turin, Wine Museum

[25]Kleberg, *passim*; Tanzer, Helen H., *The Common People of Pompeii*, 41, 48; Suet., *Nero*, 16; Carcopino, J., *Daily Life in Ancient Rome*, 250, 252–3; Hor., *Sat.*, I, v.

which has been attributed to Virgil. Here we have a trellised arbour shaded with reeds and near to a running stream. Outside the arbour cicadas are monotonously shrilling in the heat and a tired little donkey is padding by. Inside there are garlands of violets, and roses, small cheeses that have been dried in rush baskets, a thin wine from a pitched vessel, and a Syrian girl dancing to the castanets.

In Rome, where pillars 'girt with chained flagons' denoted the presence of a tavern, things were less idyllic, for the wine-shops opened onto shouting streets which, until Domitian cleared them, were rendered almost impassable by protruding stalls of barbers and butchers and by 'the grimy cook-shop monopolizing the whole of the way'. Equally unrestful was the 'sodden tavern' of Bordeaux in which as Sidonius Apollinaris described it, the drunken customers sang raucously, their appetites sharpened by the smell from the reeking kitchen and by the sight of red, thyme-flavoured sausages hanging in succulent rows.[26]

Most of the wine that was drunk in the taverns of the vineyard areas of the Roman Empire would, of course, have been local wine. In the bigger cities, and especially in the maritime cities, imported wines may have been offered but it is not reasonable to assume that the customers always had the money, or for that matter the desire, to drink them. They would have been used to their own wines. Pompeii, a town susceptible to Greek influence, may have been rather different and some of the Greek wines which came into Pompeii – Coan and Cnidian among them – may have been sought by those who frequented the taverns. But even if the customers did not appreciate, or could not afford, imported wines they still had a choice among the qualities of their local wines. A girl named Hedone, a *vinaria* of Pompeii says to her clients: 'You can drink here for one *as*; if you pay double you can have better wine, but if you pay four, you can have Falernian.'[27] A similar range of choice must have existed in other wine-growing areas and in particular it must have existed in the great city of Rome whose wine-shops could draw upon the wines brought in from Italy and from the provinces over the seas.

Smoky and smelling of food many of the taverns may have been but not all of them were gloomy drinking booths. Those which had any pretensions above the lowest rustic level had floors made bright with mosaics or walls enlivened by paintings and it is from some of these paintings that we can get an actual picture of the

[26]Carrington, R. C., 'Studies in the Campanian "Villae Rusticae"', *Jrnl of Roman Studies*, XXI, 122, 1931. *Copa Surisca*: Waddell, Helen, *Medieval Latin Lyrics* (Bibl. Ch. 5), 13-15. Rome: Mart., VII, lxi; *Sidonius, The Letters of*, trs. Dalton, O. M., VIII, xi.

[27]Greek wines in Pompeii, see Kleberg, 108, and fn. 16. Hedone: Tanzer, Helen H., *The Common People of Pompeii*, 51.

drinkers of the time. We see four of them, for example, sitting at a small, round table. They are eating from a bowl and drinking from cups shaped like modern tumblers. Two of the drinkers are still wearing the cowls which protected their heads from the weather, and above the four of them is a rack from which hang various articles of food. In other scenes we see them sitting on a rough bench and drinking from the same type of mug; or else we see them playing dice at a small oblong table.[28] It is not at all difficult to imagine these people as they were when they were living and our imagination is helped by the fact that the taverns in which they are shown are not radically unlike a good many of the *trattorias* of modern Italy.

Relish for the Slaves

Wine was essential to the diet of all classes and not least to that of the poor. In the better and more productive wine districts reasonably good wine would have been plentiful and cheap. In less favoured districts, or in bad years the wine which was drunk by the lowest classes would often have been inferior and much of it we should consider to have been almost undrinkable. The Roman poor may have grumbled at what they drank but still they drank it. They were well accustomed to the inconveniences of sparse living.

'People of old,' says Ovid, 'are reported to have subsisted on pure milk and such herbs as the earth bore of its free will. White cheese is mixed with pounded herbs, that the ancient goddess may know the ancient foods.' The statement is not entirely true for the basic food of the poor, in early as in later times, was bread, porridge, or cake. The porridge was often eaten with salt and vegetables though there were other ways of making it more attractive, and Cato, in the 2nd century B.C., gives a recipe for 'Punic porridge' in which soaked wheat is mixed with fresh cheese, honey, and an egg. Bread, which in Italy was usually of a rather heavy texture, was sometimes sprinkled with poppy-seed to increase its appeal and this was done also to cakes. (In earlier times roasted poppy-seed used to be served with honey at the second course of a dinner.) One of the most popular kinds of Italian bread was that made in the neighbourhood of Ancona. It was kneaded with raisin juice and had to be soaked in milk or honey-water before it was eaten. In Cato's day cakes were made of grain and cheese and honey but there were many kinds of cakes, as there were of bread and pastry. A sidelight on the popularity (or the cheapness?) of cakes comes from those records which show that, on festive or ceremonial occasions, generous citizens would provide the local populace with a meal of pastry and 'mead'. This 'mead' would not, I think, have been a liquor made from honey; it would have been *oinomeli* or *mulsum*, which were both the same thing and which were made from wine and honey mixed together.[29]

Vegetables were part of the staple diet of the poor: chick peas, turnips, onions, and beans: and Martial comments with an enforced good sense 'if pale beans bubble for you in a red earthenware pot you can often decline the dinners of sumptuous hosts'. Salads were eaten as well and here is a recipe given by Columella about the middle of the 1st century A.D.: 'Put into a mortar, savoury, mint, rue, coriander, parsley, chives or, if you have no chives, a green onion, leaves of lettuce and of colewort,

[28] Paintings, etc.: Kleberg, 116, 117, and see 115; Reinach, S., *Rép. de Peintures Grecques et Romaines*, 254.

[29] Ovid, *Fasti*, IV, 369-72. Punic porridge: Cato, lxxxv. Poppy-seed: Cato, lxxix, lxxxiv; Plin., XIX, 168. Bread and cakes: Cato (recipes), lxxv-lxxxiv; Plin. (kinds of), XVIII, 69, 105-6; cf. Longus, *Daphnis and Chloe*, III, 5. Feasts: Dill, S., *Roman Society from Nero to Marcus Aurelius*, 230. Oinomeli: Dioscorides, *Herbal*, V, 16. Mulsum, refs in fn. 60; for 'mead' as *mulsum*, see Varro, III, 16, 2-3; Colum., XII, 41.

green thyme or cat-mint. Also green fleabane and fresh and salted cheese: pound them all together and mix a little peppered vinegar with them. When you have put this mixture in a bowl, pour oil over it'. There were several variants of the mixture, one of them containing walnuts. There was garlic as well and Pliny notes, as many English travellers have done, that 'Garlic . . . gives an offensive smell to the breath. . . ."

Cheese, olive oil, and of course wine, filled out the lower class diet of bread, or porridge, and vegetables. So did fruit, and especially dried fruit. Dried apples and pears and figs were an important part of the food of country people in the winter, the figs being sometimes crushed into a paste which, in Africa and Spain, was then pressed into shapes of flowers or stars. Fish, too, was sometimes a supper food for the people, but meat only seldom, though, if they had the money, they could buy sausages from 'the pieman, who bawls as he carries round in his warm pans smoking sausages'.

The most illuminating picture of the diet of the very poor lies in the terse instructions which Cato gave for the maintenance of farm labourers. Cato was a hard and thrifty man and we can take it that these rations represented little more than the minimum needed to keep a worker in reasonable health. Each slave on the farm got about a bushel of wheat a month and Cato noted: 'The chain-gang should have a ration of 4 lb. of bread through the winter increasing to 5 when they begin to work the vines, and dropping back to 4 when the figs ripen.' The ration of wine was nearly three-quarters of a litre a day to each man and although this sounds not unreasonable we must remember that some of it was *lora*, an 'after-wine' made from grape skins soaked in water. In addition to this each slave got a pint of oil a month, a certain amount of salt, and probably vegetables and some fruit. As a consolation for this meagre existence Cato recommended a relish for the slaves: 'Store all the windfall olives you can, and later the mature olives which will yield very little oil. Issue them sparingly and make them last as long as possible. When they are used up, issue fish-pickle and vinegar. . . .'[30] Cato was never one for luxury.

The Size of the Vineyards

'Vineyards are commonly tended by slaves in fetters,' remarks Columella. Elsewhere he speaks of 'men of enormous wealth who, possessing entire countries of which they cannot even make the rounds, either leave them to be trampled by cattle and wasted and ravaged by wild beasts, or keep them occupied by citizens enslaved for debt and by chain-gangs'. These remarks are admittedly generalized but even so they do not give a generally accurate picture of Italian agriculture or viticulture, for vast estates operated by gangs of slaves were by no means the rule.

In the 3rd century B.C., in Latium, the average farm plot was between five and ten acres and the farmer did not have to go far from the town to reach his daily work. In the 2nd century B.C., however, large farms owned by absentee landlords did become a feature of Roman agriculture but even so the small farmer continued, and for a long time continued, to be a vital element in the life of the countryside. It was not until the 4th century A.D. that the small and independent farmers lost their status and became tenants bound to the soil. They became, in fact, serfs.

[30]Mart., XIII, vii; Colum., XII, 59, 1–4; Plin., XIX, III. Dried fruit: Colum., XII, 14, 1–15, 5. Fish: Varro, III, 17, 7. Itinerant sausage-sellers: Mart., I, xli. Rations: Cato, lvi, lviii; *Lora*, Cato, lvii; Varro, I, 54, 3; Colum., XII, 40, 1; Plin., XIV, 86 and for deuterias.

During the Republic and the Empire there must have been innumerable 'cottage vineyards' whose few vines provided the wine for the farmer's own household. But larger, 'professional', vineyards existed from quite early times. In the middle of the 2nd century B.C. Cato lists the equipment of a vineyard and among this equipment we find: '. . . 2 oxen, 2 draft donkeys, 1 for the mill; 3 complete presses, vats for holding five vintages. . . 20 jars for holding grape pulp. . . 2 funnels, 3 wicker strainers . . . 2 carts . . . 3 baskets for wine-lees . . . 5 rush hooks . . . 3 pruning hooks . . . 4 manure-hampers, 1 manure-basket, 40 grape-knives . . .' and many other things, all enumerated in such minute detail that we can mentally re-create the atmosphere of the farmstead. But for our present purpose one of the important things to note is that the size of the vineyard is 66 acres – or 25 hectares. This is indeed a reasonable size. A later instance is when Pliny speaks of a vineyard near Rome which had 37 acres of vines;[31] and it is clear that vineyards of this type must have played an important part in the wine production of Italy.

The country villas of Pompeii and Stabiae give us a valuable picture of Roman country life in the time of Augustus. To some extent Campania may have been subject to special conditions: extreme fertility of soil, comparative proximity to Rome, easy access to busy harbours: and thus the Campanian pattern of life may not have been typical of the rest of Italy. But there were other wine-growing areas in which almost the same conditions existed and it is not unreasonable to believe that the Campanian pattern may have been repeated in other parts of the country.

The notable thing about these Campanian villas is that so many of them belonged either to citizens of Pompeii or Stabiae, or to local men who lived on their farms and not in one of the cities. It is notable, also, that these villas are not mere country houses to which a wealthy Pompeian or Stabian could escape for relaxation from the heat and bustle of the city. Some of them do indeed have the luxury of wall paintings but even these villas are working farms whose fields and vineyards were intended to be run at a profit. In some cases they would undoubtedly have been used as summer residences by those of their owners who lived in the cities, but they were still considered as economic propositions rather than luxurious playthings.

There were, however, two villas owned by absentee landlords and operated on slave labour. In one of them, the villa of Agrippa Posthumus, in addition to the living quarters, there was an *ergastulum*, a prison house for the slaves, complete with a set of iron stocks. Lest this should be thought an eccentricity one might record the advice proffered by Columella: 'for those who are in chains there should be an underground prison, as wholesome as possible, receiving light through a number of narrow windows built so high from the ground that they cannot be reached with the hand'. This is the less attractive side of Pompeian farming.

In the main these villa estates were devoted to the growing of wine and oil, though some of them had threshing floors and one, near Stabiae, had a large factory for the making of cheese. In size the estates varied, some comprising only a few acres while others must have been much larger. The cellar capacity of one villa, for example, is calculated to have been about 84,000 litres and if this were designed to hold only the produce of a single vintage, then it would argue a very sizeable vineyard. Cato, however, recommended that a fairly large vineyard should have 'vats for holding five vintages' and if this were the case at Pompeii, then the yearly

[31]Colum., I, 3, 12; 7, 1; 9, 4-7; Cato, xi; Plin., XIV, 48; Frank, I, 163; V, 147 sqq., 168 sqq.; and Frank, Tenney, *Aspects of Social Behaviour in Ancient Rome*, 66 sqq.

Transport of Cask on Cart
Gallo-Roman Relief
Langre, Museum

produce of this Campanian villa may only have been about 16,800 litres. Possible support for this view might be drawn from an inscription which appears to record a five-year-old Tironianum, for this was a wine grown on one of the properties near Pompeii and it may have spent those five years in the cellar of the farm where it was first made.[32]

So much then for the Pompeian pattern which demonstrates that there was still a healthy localism in one of the richest areas of Italy. The prosperity of Pompeii depended largely upon wine and it depended, therefore, upon the skill and vigour of the local men who worked in the vineyards. There is no question about their vigour. But what of their skill?

The Growing of the Vines

Inspired by the value of education and the general desirability of profit, the Romans compiled manuals of instruction for those who wished to become farmers or who, so they hoped, wished to become better farmers. These manuals deal, among other things, with the growing of vines and the making of wine and they provide us with a picture of Roman viticulture which is far more complete than the picture we have of the vineyard practice of any other ancient people.

The Roman knowledge of wine-growing was based upon the knowledge of the Greeks. But how much the Romans elaborated upon that knowledge is a question which we cannot satisfactorily answer, because we do not know enough about the details of Greek viticulture. It is probable that the Romans did elaborate upon the Greek knowledge and that what has come down to us in the manuals is, so to speak, Greek architecture with Roman carving. But the Romans may also have taken some of their knowledge from another source, for Varro hails as the greatest of agricultural writers the Carthaginian Mago who died about the beginning of the 3rd century B.C., and through Mago the experience of Syria and the Lebanon may have passed into the experience of Rome.

The first of the Roman books which we have is the *De Agri Cultura* of Cato – Marcus Porcius Cato, the Censor, famous for his adherence to the old Roman virtues and also for his bitter opposition to Carthage. His book was written about

[32]The Campanian villas: Ros., *SEHR*, 550, fn. 25; 551, fn. 26; 564, fn. 23; Frank, Tenney, *Aspects of Social Behaviour in Ancient Rome*, 86; Carrington, R. C., 'Studies in the Campanian "Villae Rusticae"', *Jrnl of Roman Studs.*, XXI, 1931; Day, J., 'Agriculture in the Life of Pompeii', *Yale Classical Studs.*, 1932. Slaveprison: Colum., I, 6, 3; and Ros., *SEHR*, Pl. x. Cellar capacity: Day, J., *op. cit.*, 180; Frank, v, 172; Frank, Tenney, *An Economic History of Rome*, 265–6; Cato, xi, l. Tironianum: *CIL*, IV, Supp. I and II, 5581–2.

160 B.C. and deals mainly with Latium and Campania. Over a century after Cato, in 37 B.C., came Varro's longer and more coherent *Rerum rusticarum* which borrowed from Cato and which in its turn influenced later writers such as Pliny, Columella, and Palladius. The best of these Roman treatises is the *De Re Rustica*, written by Columella about A.D. 60. He was brought up, or at least partly brought up, with his uncle who was a skilled farmer and wine-grower in the south of Spain, but most of his life was spent in Italy. He owned farms in Latium at Ardea, Albanum, and Carseoli, and another farm which was perhaps at Caere in Etruria. He had some influence upon Pliny and more upon Palladius who wrote in the 4th century A.D. and whose work may have been available to literate *vignerons* in the Christian Dark Ages. Pliny himself is encyclopaedic rather than expert but the undiscriminating zeal with which he collected facts and fancies makes his *Natural History* a valuable warehouse of information and belief. Pliny also has the merit of being the most comprehensive of the ancient writers on ampelography.

For us these books have great historical value. But what was their practical value to the Roman farmer? How much were they read and how much was their advice handed on to the overseers of vineyards and the managers of estates?

We cannot possibly tell. All we can say is that, if instructions had been copied from these manuals, they could at least have been read by many of the farming populace. Varro remarks quite casually that the man in charge of a herd of animals should keep in written form a list of the symptoms of animal diseases, while elsewhere on the subject of animal health he says that 'there are many rules . . . I see to it that my head herdsman is reading some of them repeatedly'. In a light-hearted, but even more telling, context we may note the high degree of literacy evinced by the 15,000 *graffiti* which were scribbled on the walls of Pompeii by the lower classes of the city and its neighbourhood. These *graffiti* show that the Campanians were avid writers, even if most of what they wrote was scarcely literature. One individual, for example, who must have been waiting for an appointment, occupied his time by walking between two points, and he recorded his findings – '640 paces for ten turns back and forth'. Another *graffito* sends good wishes to a girl – 'Farewell, Victoria, and everywhere you wish may you sneeze agreeably'.[33] Varro's literate herdsman would not have found himself out of place in the company of these spontaneous chroniclers.

But the fact that a number of *vignerons* could read does not necessarily mean that they read viticultural manuals. The reading of books, however, does not in itself make a *vigneron*, for most of his knowledge is gained from inherited tradition and from his own experience. And new knowledge – new methods of cultivation, new types of vines to cultivate – would have reached the Roman *vigneron* as easily by word of mouth as they would have done by means of the written word. The works of the Roman writers must have had some influence and it can only have been a good one; but that it was limited can be seen from the frequent examples of men to whom wine-growing was a mere financial mechanism and not a profitable art.

An interest in the different varieties of vine is in evidence as early as Cato. He gives a brief ampelography and mentions six vines by name. The brevity of his list does not mean that these were the only vines known to him or cultivated in Italy but we can probably take it that these six were the vines most widely grown at that time in Latium and Campania. In particular Cato mentions the Aminean which

[33]Varro, I, 1, 10. For other writers see: Varro, I, 1, 8 sqq.; Colum., I, 1, 7 sqq. Pompeian graffiti: Tanzer, Helen H., *The Common People of Pompeii*, 6, 88, 93. Varro's herdsmen: II, 1, 23; 5, 18.

was the top-graded vine of the Roman world. We can possibly identify it with the
vine with golden-yellow grapes which, in Christian Europe, became known as the
Greco bianco. It made white wine of good body and good keeping qualities; or, as
another writer said, it provided 'wines of more or less true taste and to surpass all
other varieties in flavour'. Cato also mentions the double Eugeneum and this may
have been the same as the later Eugenian which was imported from Taormina in
Sicily but which was grown successfully only on the Alban Hills.

Roman writers put the Eugenian into the second class of vines and in this class
also, as well as the Apian or Muscat vine, they put the Nomentan or Nomentana
which both Columella and Pliny rank immediately after the Aminean. Italian vines
– the Rhaetic of the Alps is an obvious example – were often given the name of the
tribe, or of the place, in whose territory they grew and identification of these vines

in modern terms is thus made difficult. Fortunately with the Nomentan, which took its name from the old Sabine town of Nomentum, we have descriptions which indicate that it was the relative, if not the ancestor, of the *teinturier mâle* with its rosy foliage and the red-black juice of its grapes. Another Roman vine which we may identify, though with more hesitation, is the Trebulan which made good wine only when it was grown in a district south of Caserta in Campania, and this may have been the same as the medieval and modern *trebbiano* of Italy. If the identification is acceptable then the Trebulan is the same also as the *ugni blanc*, a vine which seems to have originated in Asia Minor or the Aegean and whose grapes are green touched with gold, though sometimes flushed with a rosy tint and sometimes even turning to copper.[34] To some extent, then, we can get the 'feel' of the ancient Roman vineyards by visualizing the types of vine which filled them and the types of grape which gave them colour.

With considerably more clarity we can visualize the shape of the vineyards in which they grew. Varro, in 37 B.C., gives us the general picture and this, as amplified by Pliny, remains generally true for all the centuries of the Empire. In Spain, Africa, Egypt, Syria and 'the whole of Asia', the most usual method was to plant 'low vineyards'. In these vineyards the vine was unstaked and supported itself, its branches were allowed to sprawl out over the ground, and the ripening grapes were either left to lie on the earth or were raised off the surface of the earth by means of short

[34]Cato, vi, 4 (Varro, I, 25, repeats Cato). Aminean: Cato, vi, 4; Colum., III, 2, 7-13, and fn. a; Plin., XIV, 21-2, 25; Virgil, II, 97; *CIL*, XV, 4510 (probably), 4532-3, 4534 (?), 4535 (?); *Edict. Dioc.*, II, 1, 4; V.V., *A.*, Dict. Eugeneum: Cato, v, 4. Eugenian: see Eugenia in fn. 13. Apian: see fn. 14. Nomentana: Colum., III, 2, 14, 15; Plin., XIV, 23; V.V., *A.*, III, 363-7; for Nomentan wine see fn. 11. Rhaetic: see fn. 15. Trebulan: Plin., XIV, 69-70; V.V., *A.*, II, 256, and Dict., 'Trebulanus'. Roman ampelography in Columella and Pliny: Colum., III, 2, 7 sqq.: 7, 1-2; 9, 1 sqq.; XII, 45, 1, Plin., XIV, 21 sqq.

Silver Cup from Pompeii
Naples, Museum

175

props. 'Modern vineyards' in which the vines were fastened to a vertical stake and trained out along horizontal cross-bars, were not uncommon in Italy although the most usual Italian practice was to train them in the form of a *compluvium*, a rectangular trellis raised above the ground and which, when covered with vines, formed a sort of arbour. The name comes, in fact, from the roofs of Roman houses which sloped inwards to a quadrangular opening which let in the light and collected the rainwater. The *compluvium* vineyard is a 'high vineyard' but the highest of all and one which seems to have been particularly favoured in the north of Italy, was the *arbustum* in which the vines were trained up other trees or led from one tree to another in long festoons.[35]

The popularity of the low vineyard was due to the fact that it was simple and economical. Apart from cultivating the ground, all you had to do was to prune the vinestocks and then let the branches grow. You had to waste no time in cutting props, making trellises or tying the vines to their supports. Even when the fruit-bearing branches were propped, this was for the most part done on forked sticks which needed very little labour and could be used year after year with no extra cost. There was, however, one great disadvantage in that type of low vineyard where the grapes lay on the ground for, as Varro says, 'the foxes often share the harvest with man in such vineyards, and if the land breeds mice the yield is cut short unless you fill the whole vineyard with traps, as they do in the island Pandateria'.[36]

Much more laborious than the setting of mousetraps was the construction of the *compluvium* on which the vine was spread out along the cross rods of the horizontal trellis; and this was particularly laborious when the rods of the trellis were made of reeds which had to be tied together in bundles to give them strength. We might wonder why the Romans went to the trouble of training vines by this method but they believed that the *compluvium* vineyard produced more wine than a vineyard arranged in straight rows. In the hotter districts of Italy this may well have been the case for the overhanging branches would have shaded the grapes from the full heat of the sun and thus have prevented them from becoming shrivelled and burnt before the vintage.[37]

Less complicated than the *compluvium*, and to modern eyes more antique, was the *arbustum* in which the vines were 'wedded' to trees. Strictly speaking, an *arbustum* might be taken to mean a vineyard specially planted with the trees up which the vines were trained. But the *arbustum* vineyard, the 'high vineyard' *par excellence*, need not have been based on a deliberate plantation and vines would have been grown up trees, and looped from tree to tree, wherever trees happened to offer themselves. Again, the *arbustum* vineyard could vary in its trellising, either using trellises to take the vines up onto the boughs, or to spread them out among the boughs, or to lead them along and beyond the boughs from tree to tree.

Elms and poplars, twined and hung with vines, were a usual sight to the Roman poets. Virgil in his *Georgics* has:

> 'Ash stakes for the forked uprights,
>   Upon whose strength your vines can mount
>   and be trained to clamber
>   Up the high-storied elm trees. . . .'

Dionysios by Exekias the Potter
535 B.C.
Munich, Staatl.
Antikensammlung.

[35]Varro, I, 8, 1–7; Plin., XVII, 164–6, 184–6; and XIV, 13–14; Colum., IV, 1, 5.

[36]Varro, I, 8, 5; see also Plin., XIV, 32.

[37]Colum., IV, 17, 1, 4–5, 8; 24, 3; 26, 3; Plin., XVII, 166.

Horace seems to have a liking for poplars but Martial and Catullus prefer elms. Other trees were also used for the purpose: the ash, the fig, sometimes the olive, and in Northern Italy, in addition to these, maples, limes, oaks, and the guelder rose. In Venezia, 'because of the dampness of the soil', the willow was found to be most suitable. Pliny, referring to Italy, and to Cisalpine Gaul – the Po Valley – describes the scenes which gave pleasure (and wine) to the Roman poets: 'Our Italian method of pruning drapes the tree with tresses of vines festooned along the branches and clothes the tresses themselves with bunches of grapes, but the Gallic method spreads out into growths passing from tree to tree. . . .'

In another context Pliny relates that vines climbed so high up the poplars in Campania 'that a hired vintager expressly stipulates in his contract for the cost of a funeral and a grave!' There may be an element of truth in this tale but it is more likely to be one of those good stories which Pliny loved to collect, for in a more sober-sided discussion of the *arbustum* he says that the maximum height of an elm is usually kept at twenty feet. A vintager, and even a tipsy vintager, who fell from this height should not normally have needed a funeral.

The principal reason for the high vineyard was again the reason of economy. Crops could be sown between the trees so that on a high level the *arbustum* produced wine and on a low level it grew corn or vegetables. But by the 1st century A.D. the reason was also given that 'high-class wines can only be produced from vines on trees, and . . . even so the choicer wines are made from grapes at the top of trees, while those lowest down give a large quantity: so beneficial is the effect of height'. This is not at all in accord with the modern view which holds that finer wines come only from lower vines, and indeed the *arbustum* method was condemned as early as the 1st century B.C. by the two Sasernas, father and son, who wrote between the time of Cato and Varro and who were reputed to be experts on farming. Even Scrofa, who wrote about the same time, would only concede that the practice was allowable in Italy. But the Sasernas' view was rejected, Scrofa's prevailed, and the *arbustum* remained an essential part of ancient Italian viticulture. Three vines to a tree were considered to be the reasonable minimum though some *vignerons* grew as many as ten, and one viticulturalist at Novara, near Milan, trained his tree-hung vines into so many branches that, in addition to the poor soil of his vineyard, the method of training gave his wine an extra harshness.[38]

We need not think that the Romans were particularly archaic in their practice since all of their methods are still in use in various places today. 'Low vineyards' exist in the islands of Crete and Rhodes as they do in some parts of the Peloponnese. They are to be found in some areas of Old and New Castile in Spain and also in the south at Jerez de la Frontera, where the grapes are raised off the ground on props. Since sherry is one of the outstanding wines of the world it shows that the low vineyard does not necessarily produce poor wine. The *compluvium* system can still be seen in Italy – around Frascati for example. The high trellis is a common sight in the Minho province of Northern Portugal while the *arbustum*, in this case with vines festooned from tree to tree, is by no means unusual in the vineyards of modern Venezia.

For the most part, however, modern vineyards consist of vines planted in rows. They grow to a height of between three and five feet – occasionally a little higher –

Greek Wine Party: detail from Corinthian Crater 600 B.C. London, British Museum

[38] Virgil, II, 359–61; Horace, *Epode*, II; Mart., IV, xiii; Catullus, LXII, 48 sqq.; Cato, i, 7; xxxii, 1–2; xlvii, xlix, 2; Varro, I, 8, 4–5; Colum., III, 3, 2; Plin., XIV, 10–12; XVII, 199–213.

Black and White Glass Jug from Pompeii Naples, Museum

and their branches are kept short and trained horizontally along wires. Most of the great vineyards of Western Europe grow their fine wines in this way.

The Romans were not ignorant of this method. Cato accepted without comment the practice of growing vines in rows and although these may not have been trained in quite the modern pattern, the basis of the pattern was certainly there. Pliny stated that vines trained in a straight row and on single crossbars made better wine, and Columella suggested that five feet was the right height for a vine though he qualified this statement by setting the topmost height of the trellis at seven feet.

The *juga*, or horizontal crossbars, together with the vertical stakes to which they were tied, formed the *canterius* or 'horse' on which a vine was sometimes trained. The framework could be made of sticks or reeds or ropes, ropes being a speciality of Southern Italy and also used to some extent in Spain. It seems possible, or so it might appear from a relief found on the Moselle, that vines could sometimes be trained in cordons along a line of props without necessarily having the *juga* to make up the *canterius*. A different, and very interesting, Moselle relief shows a vine fastened to a prop in a figure of eight[39] and although this design was clearly pleasing to the sculptor there is no reason to think that it was merely an artistic invention. It might have been, of course, that the vine was merely tied in this way while its branches were being grown long enough to climb up into a tree; but the *arbustum* method would have been very improbable in such a northerly vineyard. And one might also remark that vines in the modern Moselle are often tied to their stakes in a slightly variant form of this Roman figure of eight.

All in all, then, we can say that the Romans showed themselves capable of skilled and orderly viticulture. They were well versed in the various ways of planting, grafting, and pruning vines and it is probable though not certain, that the Roman

[39]Cato, xxxiii, 3; Varro, I, 7, 1-4; 8, 1-4; Colum., III, 13, 1-5; 15, 1; IV, 12, 1-2; 19, 1-3; 30, 5; Plin., XVII, 78, 165-6; for the use of reeds in Egyptian viticulture in A.D. 280 see *Oxyrhynchus Papyri* (Bibl. Ch. 2), 1631. Moselle reliefs: Loeschcke, S., *Denkmäler vom Weinbau . . .*, 8 (cf. 6, Abb. 4); and Espérandieu, E., *Rec. Gén. des Bas-Reliefs de la Gaule Romaine*, V, 4199, 4212.

knowledge of viticulture was much more expert and comprehensive than that of any other ancient people. But the knowledge was not always used. And here, in sorrow and in anger, is Columella quoting Graecinus on the shortcomings of the Early Empire:

'Why, then, is viticulture in disrepute?' asks Columella. 'Not, indeed, through its own fault, but because of human failings, says Graecinus; in the first place because no one takes pains in searching after cuttings, and for that reason most people plant vineyards of the worst sort; and then they do not nourish their vines, once planted, in such a way as to let them gain strength . . . and if they do happen to grow, they are careless in the matter of cultivation. Even at the very start they think that it makes no difference what kind of ground they plant; or rather they pick out the very worst section of their lands, as though such grounds alone were particularly fit for this plant because incapable of producing anything else. . . . Most people, in fact, strive for the richest possible yield at the earliest moment; they make no provision for the time to come, but, as if living merely from day to day, they put such demands upon their vines and load them so heavily with young shoots as to show no regard for succeeding generations . . . they complain that their vineyards do not yield them a return – vineyards which they themselves have ruined through greed, or ignorance, or neglect.'[40]

Sulphur and the Moon

Wine-farming, even in Italy, was not always easy. Pliny the Younger writes to Mamilianus: 'I am in the midst of my vintage . . . it has proved an extremely bad one this season'; to Romanus he writes: 'You tell me also your vintage has proved extremely moderate. That complaint, notwithstanding that we are separated and in such distant countries, is common to us both.' Apart from hailstorms, and rain at the wrong time, some vineyards had difficulty in ripening their grapes, and here Columella is insistent on stripping leaves from the vines so that the grapes should be properly exposed to the sun. There were other hazards, too, and farmers who were anxious for the safety of their vines were advised to make bonfires so that the smoke should protect the vineyards, an expedient still practised by modern growers against the disastrous frosts of early summer.[41] And then there were, of course, the diseases which made war upon the summer vines.

The modern wine grower owes a deep, though unromantic, debt to sulphur. The vines themselves are protected by being sprayed with sulphur; wine barrels are sterilized by having sulphur burnt inside them; sulphur is used to control fermentation and it is used to preserve the health of a wine once it is made. Sulphur is thus invaluable and since, in the making of good wines, it is used in only the minimum necessary doses, it should impart no disagreeable flavour to the wine and cause no offence at all to the drinker. The use of sulphur is a technique which can certainly encourage, and should never impair, the proper quality of a good wine.

In the ancient world sulphur, as such, was hardly ever used in viticulture. It was known to the ancients and it had been known to them for many hundreds of years, but to them its use was medical or magical. After Odysseus had returned to Ithaca, after he and Telemachus had slain the suitors of Penelope and the maidservants who

[40]Colum., III, 3, 4-7.

[41]Pliny the Younger, *Letters*, IX, 16, 28; see also Mart., IX, xcviii; Colum., IV, 27, 3; Plin., XVIII, 278, 285, 293.

179

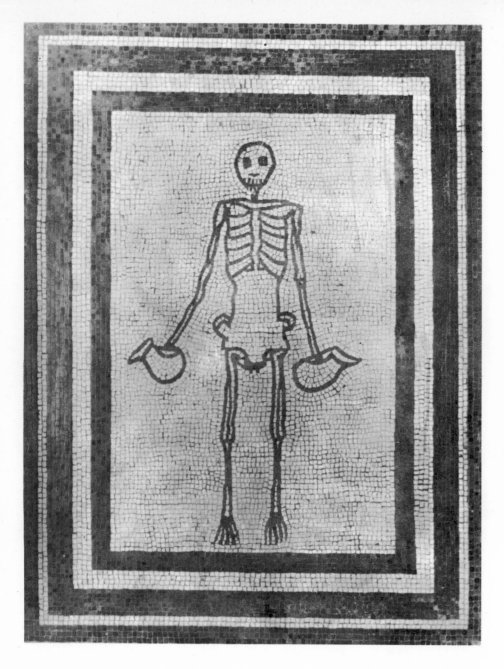

had slept with them, Odysseus called to Eurycleia: 'Bring sulphur, old nurse, that cleanses all pollution and bring me fire, that I may purify the house with sulphur. . . .' According to Strabo the Telchines, who 'were the typical magicians of antiquity' were reputed to 'besprinkle animals and plants with the water of Styx and sulphur mixed with it, with a view to destroy them'. In the Peloponnesian War sulphur and pitch together were employed by the Greeks to burn besieged cities and at the siege of Delium the mixture was used in an ingenious 'flame-maker' to burn down that part of the wall 'that had been principally constructed of vines and other wood'.

Some such military use may account for the jarful of sulphur which was found in the ruins of Beth-Pelet, south of Gaza on the borders of Egypt and Palestine, and which probably dates from somewhere about 1000 B.C.

The Romans, too, knew about sulphur. It was exported from Sicily and from, or through, Puteoli and sulphur 'matches' were sold in Rome. But in Roman times the main uses of the chemical, apart from any uses which it had in warfare, were again either magical or medical and it is often difficult to decide where magic ended and medicine began. Ovid in his *Fasti* seems to record a double use since, at the April festival of the Parilia which was celebrated in protection of the farmers' flocks and herds, he says: 'Make blue smoke with pure sulphur, and let the sheep, touched with the smoking sulphur, bleat.' This looks like an attempt at both magical and 'medical' fumigation. Tibullus likewise seems to have used it in a double aspect, for in a poem to his erstwhile and still desired mistress he says that it was he 'whose vows snatched thee from peril when thou layest exhausted in sickness' gloomy hold. It was I who scattered all about thee the cleansing sulphur, the beldame first chaunting her magic spell. I appeased the cruel Dreams that had thrice to be honoured with offerings of holy meal, that they might work no harm'. More strictly medical were the well-known sulphur baths of Baiae, of which Horace wrote. Propertius, on the other hand, in a splendid and disastrous drinking scene, pays a presumed tribute to its magical power. His mistress Cynthia being false to him, he has decided on other entertainment and summons to a party Phyllis – 'sober she pleases me little; when she drinks all is charm' – and Teia – 'fair is she, but when the wine is on her, one lover will be all too few'. It was a summer night and there was Lesbian wine; Phyllis played the castanets, Propertius played dice, and both the girls sang to him. Suddenly however, 'Cynthia hurled back the folding portals, Cynthia with hair disordered, yet lovely in her fury. . . . Her eyes flashed fire: she raged with all a woman's fury. The sight was fearful as a city's sack'. She scratched Phyllis's face, tore the girls' dresses, and then, as Propertius wryly remembers, 'hastened back to me victorious, and bruised my face with cruel hands, and marked my neck with her teeth. . . .' When Propertius had made peace, Cynthia who, for all her impetuosity, seems to have been a trifle bureaucratic 'purified with fire each place that the foreign girls had touched, and cleansed the threshold with pure water . . . and thrice touched my head with burning sulphur'. Magic or 'fumigation'? At all events, the story ends without dismay to the poet and without surprise to us: 'I bowed to her will and we made up our quarrel on the couch we knew so well.'[42]

Sulphur thus played its part on the varied occasions of Roman life but those occasions seldom included the growing or making of wine. Indeed, I know of only three instances where sulphur is mentioned in the context of viticulture. Cato recommends that a plaster for mending cracks in wine jars should be made from resin, wax, sulphur and pulverized gypsum. But there is nothing in this recipe from which we can infer that the sulphur was added because of its sterilizing quality. Another of Cato's recipes, however, does seem, in its own way, to anticipate modern practice for he uses sulphur in a mixture which, when smeared on the trunk and the branches, kept caterpillars away from the vines. Pliny adds that 'Some growers are content with submitting vines for three days on end to smoke from this concoction boiled to the windward of them' and this again might be thought to

[42] *Odyssey*, XXII; Harrison, *Prolegomena*, 171-2; Thucydides, *The Peloponnesian War* (Bibl. Ch. 3), II, 143; IV, 287-8; Petrie, Sir Flinders, *Beth-Pelet*, I (Bibl. Ch. 2), 18; Ros., *SEHR*, 67, 208; Frank, V, 135; Mart., XII, lvii; Carcopino, J., *Daily Life in Ancient Rome*, 56; Ovid, *Fasti*, IV, 739-40; but see also *Fasti*, I, 271-2; Tibullus, I, 5; Propertius, Elegies, IV, 8.

anticipate the modern sulphuring of vineyards. If so, the anticipation is unconscious. The Roman writers are so detailed in their instructions that, had they been fully conscious of all these qualities of sulphur, they would certainly have said so and frequently have commended them. This they do not do. Their use of gypsum in the making of wine would have been some substitute for the modern use of sulphur but they still made no adequate use of sulphur for protecting their vines and sterilizing their vessels.

Here, however, one must point out that a lack of sulphur, or even of gypsum, in wine would not have meant that the wine was inevitably inferior. Red wines with a proportionately high content of tannin need less sulphur than the richer and more alcoholic of the white wines, and, generally speaking, *vin ordinaire* needs it least of all. Untreated Roman wines, therefore, were not necessarily unsound or unstable.

The Romans did at least know that cleanliness and fumigation were important in wine-making. Vats and vessels were washed out before the vintage with water, either with sea water or with fresh water. Then they were scoured, carefully dried, and finally fumigated, sometimes with myrrh, or else with myrtle, bay or rosemary. Before the vintage, too, when all is being made ready, 'the wine cellar', says Columella, 'must be cleansed of all filth and fumigated with pleasant odours, that it may not smell at all mouldy or sour. Next sacrifices must be offered in the greatest piety and purity to Liber and Liberia and to the vessels of the wine-press. . . .' Liberia was an Italian goddess associated with Ceres, and in some way with the growing of corn; Liber is the Italian god of wine though he is only a pale shadow of the great Aegean Dionysos.[43] One wonders if these preparations included a 'magical' fumigation by sulphur; if so, the sacrifice would have been more efficacious.

Whether because of tradition or because of genuine belief, religion (or magic) played its not inconsiderable part in the life of the Roman farmer. 'Above all, worship the gods,' says Virgil and continues his counsel:

> 'Let all your labouring men worship the Corn-goddess:
> For her let the honeycomb be steeped in milk and mild wine. . . .'

'Offer to Jupiter Dapalis,' says Cato, 'a cup of wine of any size you wish, observing the day as a holiday for the oxen, the teamsters, and those who make the offering. . . . The feast to Jupiter consists of roasted meat and an urn of wine. Present it to Jupiter religiously, in the fitting form. After the offering is made plant millet, panic grass, garlic, and lentils.' A vow to ensure the health of the farm cattle was performed by making an offering to Mars Silvanus 'in the forest during the daytime'; the offering consisted of grain, bacon, meat, and wine, and, says Cato severely, 'a woman may not take part in this offering or see how it is performed'.

Reliance upon magical protection, or at any rate the taking of magical precaution, is exemplified by the Spring Festivals of Vinalia, Floralia and Robigalia. The Vinalia, or rather the First Vinalia, for there was a Second Vinalia towards the end of August, was held on April 23rd. It was a festival at which the new wines were tasted and at Rome some of the new wine was offered to Jupiter. The Floralia, a movable feast, seems usually to have been celebrated, according to Pliny, about April 23rd, though Ovid puts it a little later and has it extending from April into May. It was a

[43]Cato, xxxix, 1–2; xcv, 1–2; Plin., XVII, 264; Plin., XIV, 134; Colum., XII, 18, 3–4; 21, 3; 25, 4; 28, 1–3.

six-day festival whose purpose was to invoke the good will and the protection of the goddess Flora at the time of the blossoming of plants and trees, including, of course, vines; but it was, or it became, a Spring Carnival. Ovid comments with remarkable common sense upon the games which were held at the Festival: 'I was about to ask why these games are marked by greater wantonness and broader jests; but it occurred to me that the divinity is not straitlaced, and that the gifts she brings lend themselves to delights. The brows of wassailers are wreathed with stitched garlands, and the polished table is buried under a shower of roses. Maudlin the guest dances, his hair bound with linden bark, and all unwitting plies the tipsy art. Maudlin the lover sings at the hard threshold of his lady fair: soft garlands crown his perfumed locks.' There were, adds Ovid, nocturnal revels.

On April 25th there was the Robigalia, the Mildew Festival. It was celebrated in honour of Robigus or Robigo (we are not certain of the sex of the divinity), the god or goddess Mildew who must be placated in order to protect the crops. To achieve this desirable result a dog and a sheep were sacrificed to the divinity. Another somewhat unpleasant rite, and one which took place in the spring at about the same time as the Robigalia, was the 'Doggy Sacrifice', the dog-victim being sacrificed in order to appease the inimical influence of the Dog-star whose rising at the beginning of August heralded the hottest part of the summer.

We may view the protective magic of these festivals as the sad elaboration of archaic thought. We may regard the people who took part in their ceremonies as being just about as foolish as the *haruspices* who predicted the future from the entrails of animals; and we might treat them all with the same scorn which Ennius directed at 'shameless gut-gazers'. The state of mind which accepted these activities, and which was prone to believe in portents, might even have believed the remarkably silly story related by Pliny: 'A portent that will eclipse all those ever heard of occurred in our own day in the territory of the Marrucini, at the fall of the Emperor Nero: an olive grove . . . bodily crossed the public highway, and the crops growing on the other side passed over in the opposite direction to take the place of the olive grove.' Equally silly, we may think, is the advice recorded by Varro 'that a vineyard suffers less damage from storms if, at . . . the beginning of autumn, a picture of a bunch of grapes is placed among the vines as a votive offering'. Pliny adds to the record two other precautions taken by some farmers of the Roman world: to prevent vines being blighted three crabs should be burnt alive among the vines; to aid the proper storing of corn a toad should be hung up at the entrance to the granary. A more decorative device was current in the time of Virgil in Campania where the inhabitants were accustomed to hang small images of the Wine-god from the branches of pine trees.[44]

In addition to the magic of ritual the magic of the moon influenced the course of Roman agriculture. 'Manure must not be touched except when the moon is waning, but manuring should chiefly be done at new moon or at half moon. . . . Put eggs under the hen at the new moon. Make ditches at full moon, in the night-time.' These are some of the instructions to be observed by the prudent farmer. Grafting ought to be done while the moon is waxing while trellis-rods for vines 'cut between the old moon and the new are immune from all kinds of insects'. It was said to be a general view that vines ought to be planted at the waxing or the

[44] Virgil, I, 338, 343-4; Cato, cxxxii, 1-2; lxxxiii, and cf. cxli, 2-4. Vinalia: Plin., XVIII, 284-9; Ovid, *Fasti*, IV, 863-900. Floralia: Plin., XVIII, 286; Ovid, *Fasti*, V, 183-378 and IV, 947. Robigalia: Plin., XVIII, 284-5; Ovid, *Fasti*, IV, 901-42 and Appendix, 420 sqq. – commentary by Sir James Frazer. Ennius: *Remains of Old Latin*, I, 341. Pliny's portents: Plin., XVII, 241 sqq. Varro: in Plin., XVIII, 294. Other precautions: Plin., XVIII, 293-4, 303; Virgil, II, 385-9.

full moon while another view suggested that they should be pruned at the full moon and by night.[45] This can scarcely have simplified the pruners' task.

It is scarcely needful to point out that a religious ritual which appears ludicrous to those who do not practise it, appears valuable, and even essential, to those who do. Naturally the quality of belief varies from the mere performance of a traditional rite to the genuine attempt at a divine invocation, and most of the rituals of the Roman countryside hovered, no doubt, between the two extremes. It would, at any rate, be arrogant to assume that the Romans were much less sincere than we are ourselves. When, for example, Horace was nearly killed by a falling tree, he vowed to Liber 'a savoury feast and a pure white goat'. The yearly repetition of this feast may have been for Horace only a pleasant occasion for an amusing dinner; but, among less sophisticated Romans such a 'savoury feast' may have been a genuine tribute of gratitude and one as genuine in its own way as the *ex votos* which are found in the churches of the modern Mediterranean. And then again the custom recorded by Pliny of placing a Mulvian quince by the statues of the gods which stood in the bedrooms may appear to have been only a matter of interior decoration. But how merely decorative were those statues of the gods? – more merely decorative than the small, religious images which stand on some of the bedside tables of

[45] Plin., XVII, 57 (an apparent discrepancy here with Pliny's later advice on manuring), 108, 215; XVIII, 321-2. For the picking of grapes and the moon, see Colum., XII, 16, 1; 19, 3; 44, 2. A collection of references, and a discussion of them, has been made by E. Tavenner, 'The Roman Farmer and the Moon', *Trans. Am. Philological Assn.*, XLIX, 1918.

Dionysios
from Mosaic Pavement
Roman Villa at
Halicarnassus
London, British Museum

the modern world? And those who nowadays wear lucky charms, who refuse to walk under ladders, or who count the magpies which fly in front of them across the road, may also take comfort from the fact that they have predecessors in antiquity: the Emperor Tiberius, for example, was frightened by thunder and 'whenever the sky wore an ugly look he would put on a laurel wreath which, he supposed, would make him lightning-proof'.[46]

The Making of the Wine

The fact that viticulture spread into Northern Italy, as well as up through France and into the Moselle Valley, meant that the Romans gained experience of growing wine in climatic conditions which were more difficult than those of Southern Italy or the Aegean or the Levant; and this gives us further reason for believing that the Roman experience was wider and more expert than that of any other ancient people. By bitter experience *vignerons* of the colder climates would have learnt the difficulty of keeping wine made from must that was deficient in sugar; and therefore the proper ripening of the grapes would have been to them a point of major importance.

The drying of grapes to increase their sugar was not, of course, an invention of the Romans, and the *vinum passum*, or raisin wine, which was made in one district of the Rhône Valley is in no sense a development of Roman knowledge. This particular technique is very ancient and, in any case, the Romans took one of its variations from Mago the Carthaginian. But insofar as ordinary wines were concerned, that is to say ordinary as opposed to 'dessert' wines, a deliberate attention to the

[46]Hor., *Carm.*, III, 8; Plin., XV, 38;
Suet., *Tiberius*, 69.

longer ripening and later harvesting of the grapes was quite probably a Roman 'invention'. At the very least we can believe that it was a specifically Roman emphasis. Virgil, remembering perhaps the scenes of his youth in the north of Italy, is certainly emphatic:

> 'Be the first to dig the land, the first to wheel off the prunings
> For the bonfire, the first to bring your vine-poles under cover;
> But the last to gather the vintage.'[47]

Another development which seems to have been made by Roman viticulture was the increased use of the wine-press for it appears that the Romans used the wine-press to a far greater extent than was ever the case with the Greeks. This does not mean that treading was generally discarded and the scene sketched by Tibullus – 'the grapes in the brimming trough when the quick feet tread the gleaming must' – would still have been a commonplace feature of autumn in many of the vineyards in the Roman world. A charming mosaic from Vienne, for example, not only shows a wine-press in action, but also three naked, or nearly naked, men treading grapes in a tank which is surrounded by pillars.[48]

I believe it possible, however, that in the more intensively cultivated vineyard areas of Italy, pressing without previous treading may have been the favoured technique. The installations in the wine-growing villas of Pompeii may perhaps support this view; and it is, it seems to me, a view which is implicit in the manuals of the Roman writers. If this technique was favoured in the bigger vineyards of Italy, then it may have been adopted in some of the bigger vineyards of the provinces. I think that in fact it was, but I must quickly add that my views in this matter are only tentative and that it would be dangerous to be dogmatic. All one can say with certainty is that, under the Roman influence, there was some increase in the mechanization of wine-making.

Undoubtedly primitive methods persisted: or rather we may assume that they persisted. Piranesi gives a drawing of an ancient vintage scene in which a heavy rock is being put on the top of a lot of grapes piled in a rough wicker basket. This particular scene is imaginative and it may even have been a deliberate archaism. Even so, we know that stones were still employed in pressing grapes in the 1st century A.D. for Pliny tells us so, although in his experience they were used as extra weights in conjunction with a screw-press.[49] But it is not unreasonable to assume that in the poorer and remoter districts of the Roman world heavy stones were still occasionally used, without a mechanical press, to help the peasant to crush his moderate vintage.

A type of press which may be very ancient is the wedge-press. This consists of a structure rather like a small guillotine. Horizontal beams are slotted into the uprights and between the horizontal beams wedges are hammered in to press the bottom beam down upon the fruit. It is true that the representations of this wedge-press, one from Herculaneum and one from the house of the Vetii at Pompeii, show it being used in the making of especially fine olive oil but it could equally well have been used for crushing grapes, and in fact a crude wine-press of this type can be seen and studied in the *Musée du Vin* at Beaune.[50]

[47]Passum: Colum., XII, 39, 1, 3; cf. the *vinum dulce*, or sweet wine, in Colum., XII, 27; Plin., XIV, 81, 83; Dioscorides, *Herbal*, V, 9; CIL, IV, Supp. I and II, 5594. Raisin, or 'sweet' wine of the Rhône Valley: Plin., XIV, 83-4; Virgil, II, 410; for the date of vintaging in the 'old days' see Plin., XVIII, 315, and cf. XVIII, 319.

[48]Tibullus, I, v; Reinach, S., *Rép. de Peintures Grecques et Romaines*, 223, 10, 11.

[49]Piranesi, G. B., *Vasi, candelabri . . .*, II, Pl. 563; Plin., XVIII, 317.

[50]Reinach, S., *Rép. de Peintures Grecques et Romaines*, 86, 4; 91, 3; and Ros., *SEHR*, Pl. XV.

Cato gives minute instructions for the building of a pressing room and from these instructions we can tell the degree of 'mechanization' which obtained in the better Italian vineyards at the middle of the 2nd century B.C. The press used was the beam-press and Cato recommends that the beam should be twenty-five feet long. He also goes into detail on the making of the leather ropes which were used on the windlass. Their quality was indeed important for the heavy beam was dragged down on the grapes by a windlass worked with levers and the ropes must have taken a very considerable strain. The working of the press was no light labour as we can see from a picture in the house of the Vetii which shows Cupids sweating away at the long levers which turn the drum of a windlass. Somewhat, though not a great deal, easier was the screw-press, which seems to have been invented in Greece in the 2nd or the 1st century B.C. and which was in use in Roman vineyards in the time of Pliny.[51] This was an advance but there the advance stopped; and both these types of press, the beam and the screw, were to remain the models for European practice for eighteen centuries.

The *égrappoir*, the contrivance which separates the grapes from their stalks and which, in its mechanical form, is used in a great number of modern vineyards, does not appear to have been much favoured by Roman wine-makers. Cato seems to imply the existence of a hand-*égrappoir* made of cords, as well as a sieve made (presumably) of wickerwork, but it is not clear that either of these was used before the grapes went into the press or the vat. If the grapes were in fact taken off their stalks at all, the stripping may have been done simply by the hands of the vintagers; and in some cases at least this would have been part of the process of picking out the best berries and rejecting those that were rotten or unripe.

Fermentation, in the Mediterranean world, was carried out in large pottery jars called *dolia*. (One might mention that at Valdepeñas in Central Spain, huge pottery jars are still used both for fermenting and for storing the wine.) North and west of the Alps it was probably more common for the must to be fermented in stone or wooden tanks or else in wooden barrels. There was no sulphur to control the fermentation and in the hotter parts of the Roman world it would often have been turbulent and explosive. In Italy as in Spain, indeed, the vessels were often burst by the fermentation and it may have been to give them greater strength and to prevent them bursting that the *dolia* were sometimes buried in the ground. (On the other hand the bursting may have been due to secondary fermentation after the jars had been sealed.) But there may have been another reason for burying the jars, since the Romans may have thought that the comparative coolness of the sunken *dolium* would help to moderate the turbulence of fermentation. We may even imagine that Cato is deliberately advocating this technique when he says: 'If you wish to keep grape juice through the whole year, put the grape juice in an amphora, seal the stopper with pitch, and sink in the pond. Take it out after thirty days; it will remain sweet the whole year.' But whether they did use the cooling principle to control fermentation, and if so, how much and how deliberately they used it, are questions which we cannot answer with any degree of reasonable precision. We are equally uncertain as to whether they increased the sugar in their must by adding honey before fermentation. We might have expected to find this technique employed with the thinner musts of more northerly vineyards where, in bad years, extra sugar

[51]Cato, xii; xviii, 1–9; xix, 1–2; cxxv, 3–5; Plin., XVIII, 317–18; Ros., *SEHR*, Pl. xiv; *Hist. Tech.*, II, 116–17.

Wine Cup: 'Kantares'
Southern Italian,
250–150 B.C.
Pessione, Turin, Wine
Museum

would have been invaluable, but lack of evidence defeats our expectation.[52] What
they could have done, and what they probably often did do, was to put *decoctum*
or *defrutum* – must reduced by boiling – into a thin juice to help it begin its labour
of fermenting.

Once the wine was made, the care of it continued. It is probable that, in earlier
times at least, some farmers were content to leave their new wine upon its lees, but
others racked it off and, according to Cato, the best time to perform this racking
was thirty days after the vintage, provided that the fermentation had then stopped.
Midwinter was also thought to be a good time for this operation while sometimes
the wine was not racked off until the spring. But whatever time they did choose,
they were certainly concerned with the clarity of their wine, either by racking, or
by fining it with such things as pigeons' eggs. One cannot say that these refinements
were universally practised, or that they were necessarily in the repertoire of peasants
who merely made wine for their own household; but that the technique of racking
was widespread in the ancient world can be seen from the *Oxyrhynchus Papyri* in
which an Egyptian vineyard contract of A.D. 280 specifically mentions the straining
of wine from one jar to another.[53] We cannot say whether the technique of clarifying wine was a Roman technique or whether the Romans inherited it from the
Greeks but we can, I think, suspect that the emphasis upon it was yet another
development of Roman viticulture.

[52] Cato, xxv, cxx; Varro, I, 13, 6;
Plin., xiv, 83; but see 134 – 'Weak
vintages should be kept in jars
sunk in the ground . . .', etc.

[53] Cato, xxvi; Colum., iii, 21, 10;
xii, 23, 1–4; Plin., xviii, 232; Hor.,
Sat., ii, 4, 55–7; *Oxyrhynchus
Papyri* (Bibl. Ch. 2), 1631, 19.

Sharp Wine or Muddled Wine?

After all these labours what were the wines like?

Those which Cato suggests should be given to farm labourers certainly do not conjure up any picture of rustic beatitude. 'Gather the inferior grapes for the sharp wine for the hands to drink,' he advises. Later he tells us how to make 'wine for the hands to drink through the winter': this brew, which was not a wine at all, was made from must, vinegar, boiled must and fresh water, to which, when it was thoroughly mixed, old sea-water was added. Cato remarks with satisfaction: 'this wine will last you until the summer solstice; whatever is left over after the solstice will be a very sharp and excellent vinegar'. Other consolations for the hard-worked labourer were *lora*, or 'after-wine', made from grape skins soaked in water, and lees-wine, or *faecatum*, made out of lees.

On a somewhat higher plane was *circumsicium*, or *circumcidaneum*, wine made from grapes cut from the 'cake' of the first pressing and then pressed again. Alternatively it could be made from the whole of the cake which was chopped and then re-pressed. A combination of some of these methods made what Columella called 'the best after-wine': the basis was the grape skins from the day's pressing which were then soaked in water; to this were added the boiled down scum of the must and the dregs from the vat. After a day's soaking it was trodden and pressed and the liquid that flowed from it was put into jars and fermented. (It is not unlike the modern *piquette* of France although this, by law, has to have 5 per cent of alcohol.)[54] Some of these Roman 'little wines' may have been refreshing in hot weather but they can scarcely have been satisfying after a hard day's work. Still, the Romans were used to diluting their wine so that these feeble drinks may not have been quite as disappointing to them as they would be to us.

But even their ordinary wines were not always satisfactory. One reason for this was inadequate cultivation of the soil of the vineyards, a fault which seems to have been committed rather more in the provinces than in Italy. Another reason was the unwillingness of vineyard owners to pay for good labour. Columella's reproof of this false economy illustrates its prevalence. 'Admitting that vineyards demand a very generous outlay,' he writes, 'still seven *jugera*' (about 4½ acres or 1¾ hectares) 'require the labour of not more than one vinedresser, upon whom people in general set a low value, thinking that even some malefactor may be acquired from the auction-block; but I, disagreeing with the opinion of the majority, consider a high-priced vinedresser of first importance.' Pliny comments, though in rather a confused passage, on some of the real or apparent shortcomings of 1st-century *vignerons*: 'Before now I have seen vintagers at work even on the first of January owing to shortage of vats, and must being stored in tanks, or last year's wine being poured out of the casks to make room for new wine of doubtful quality. This is not so often due to an over-abundant crop as to slackness, or else to avarice lying in wait for a rise in prices. The public-spirited method of an honest head of a household is to use the output of each year as it comes; and this is also quite equally the most profitable plan.' More telling than this is his comment on the Falernian district. The best Falernian was the Faustian, simply because the estate of Faustus, from which it came, was well and carefully cultivated: and Pliny drives the lesson home by adding

[54]Cato, xxiii, 2; lvii; civ, 1–2. Faecatum: Cato, cliii; Plin., XIV, 86. *Circumsicium*: Varro, I, 54, 3. *Circumcidaneum*: Cato, xxiii, 4. 'Best after-wine': Colum., XII, 40.

189

Old Woman drinking
Roman copy of Hellenistic
original
Rome, Capitoline Museum

immediately afterwards: 'The reputation of this district also is passing out of vogue through the fault of paying more attention to quantity than to quality' – this of the most famous wine of the Roman world![55]

Another indication of the quality of Roman wine comes from the measures which the *vignerons* were forced to take, or which they felt themselves forced to take, in order to keep their wine in a drinkable condition. One of Columella's paragraphs has the depressing introduction: 'On any estate where the wine often turns acid . . .' while elsewhere he says that certain farmers had to consider the amount of preservative which they must use 'owing to the excessive weakness of the wine, which scarcely kept sound for thirty days'. Then also, speaking of a particular type of preservative, he remarks: 'This, though it does not make the flavour of the wine last for ever, yet at any rate generally preserves it until another vintage.' Virgil

[55]Colum., III, 3, 8, 13; Plin., XIV, 62; XVIII, 319–20. Faustian: Plin., XIV, 62–3; *CIL*, XV, 4553.

writes: 'Sweet honey you'll get – not sweet so much as pure, and fit to soften your wine's harsh flavour': but here the poet is probably writing about wine when it is being drunk and not when it is being made. Cato gives advice on how 'to make sharp wine mild and sweet' but his method is more complicated than Virgil's. Cato used small bricks of flour which were soaked in a mixture of wine and *sapa*, or boiled must. These bricks were dissolved in a jar full of wine which was sealed after sixty days and as a result 'the wine will be mild and sweet, of good colour and of good odour'.[56]

Columella states firmly: 'we regard as the best wine any kind which can keep without any preservative, nor should anything at all be mixed with it by which its natural savour would be obscured; for that wine is most excellent which has given pleasure by its own natural quality'; then he launches himself into a detailed discussion of preservatives. One of these was boiled-down must mixed into the wine. This is no more unreasonable than Cato saying that a small amount of concentrated must should be added to any blended wine. But Columella's boiled-down must is no simple concoction. First of all 'the odours boiled with the must which are generally speaking suitable for wine are iris, fenugreek and sweet-rush'. After this herbalized must had been boiled down, the preservatives could be added which, in this case, were liquid pitch and turpentine resin. When these had been stirred into the must spices were added: 'the leaf of spikenard, the Illyrian sword-lily, the Gallic spikenard, the *costus*, the date, the angular rush and the sweet-rush . . . also . . . myrrh, a pound of sweet reed, half-a-pound of cinnamon . . . balsam . . . saffron, and a pound of vine-leafed *cripa*'. A kind of crude pitch was mixed with these pounded spices. Finally, after giving instructions as to the amount of this preservative which should be used in the wine, he adds: 'Care must be taken that the flavour of the preservative is not noticeable, for that drives away the purchaser.' It is hard to believe that the mixture always remained undetected.

It is clear that the use of herbs, or plants, in preservatives was not at all uncommon. They are even used, though here only iris, fenugreek, and sweet-rush, in a recipe which includes graded quantities of gypsum, the whole mixture being diluted with must. One feels that the gypsum by itself should have been enough, but the purpose of the herbs seems pointed by Columella's words – 'if you put in good perfumes (herbs), you will prevent any bad odour or flavour; for there is nothing which attracts to itself the odour of something else more quickly than wine'.[57]

Wine lees were sometimes employed in helping a wine to live until it was 'old', but the more usual 'aid' to an indifferent wine was boiled-down must. This went by various names – *decoctum*, *defrutum*, *hepsema*, *sapa* and *siraeum*, and it was boiled down into varying consistencies. The different names do not, however, indicate with any exactitude the different degrees of consistency. Pliny, for example, has *defrutum* as must boiled down to one-half, but Columella as down to one-third, this latter being the consistency which, to Pliny, goes under the names of *hepsema*, *sapa*, and *siraeum*.

As common as the use of must, and probably even commoner, was the use of pitch. The pitch-coating of wine-skins or wine-jars, was not, of course, intended to be a preservative, but only to seal the skin or the jar. Nevertheless the coating by itself would have been sufficient to give the wine a resinous taste. This, admittedly,

[56]Colum., XII, 20, 7–8; 26, 1; Virgil, IV, 101–2; Cato, cix. *Sapa*: Plin., XIV, 80.

[57]Cato, xxiv; Colum., XII, 19–20, 28; Plin., XIV, 121.

need not have happened to wine that was stored in wooden casks since wood is not as porous as pottery, but we still cannot say that the barrelled wines of Gaul were always free from pitch. Indeed it is evident that some of the inhabitants of the Rhône valley were accustomed to, and even liked, their *vinum picatum*, their wine with its natural taste of pitch. But this flavour in *vinum picatum* was not usually natural; in many cases it came from the coating of the jar; in many others it came from the resin which had been deliberately mixed with the wine, and here we come across resin in its preservative aspect, its purpose being, as Pliny says, to give the wine a 'durable hardness'. It was also used to 'improve' a wine by taking away any bad smell which it might have, and to do this Cato advises heating a clean roof tile, coating it with pitch, and leaving it for two days in the bottom of the wine jar. Yet another motive was to 'enliven' the wine, to make it more piquant, and in order to achieve this both wine and must were seasoned with resin.[58] We cannot escape from the fact that a good deal of Roman wine was very near to what we should now call *retsina*.

And here again, in the Roman as in the Greek world, we meet the double motive of preservation and piquancy. 'In Greece,' says Pliny, 'they enliven the smoothness of their wines with potter's earth or marble dust or salt or sea-water, while in some parts of Italy they use resinous pitch for this purpose and it is the general practice both there and in the neighbouring provinces to season must with resin. . . .' Cato recommended marble dust and Columella gave his approval to 'flower' of marble or plaster. Salt was frequently used and in fact Columella goes so far as to say that 'every sort of vintage in every district ought to be salted . . . for this prevents there being any mouldy taste in the wine'.[59]

From all this we might argue that a great number of Roman wines were basically inferior and hopelessly 'fiddled'. It is doubtful how far we can stretch this argument; certainly not as far as a generalization. But we can say that the ordinary Roman, and more particularly the ordinary Roman provincial, would often have drunk wine that had been given an artificial preservative and would also have been well acquainted with various sorts of *confusum* – mixed or blended wine. We have no cause to think that he grumbled a great deal at these mixtures, or not, at any rate, until the 'fiddling' became outrageous. (Blending, in any case, is not necessarily fraudulent and it may even improve a wine.) And indeed we know for a fact that certain sorts of mixed, as opposed to blended, wines made a welcome addition to the daily diet of pure wine or wine-and-water.

One of the favourite mixtures was *mulsum*, a compound of wine and honey, or sometimes of must and honey and salt – in which case it could be called *melitites*. It was drunk, or rather it was often drunk, with the first course, the *promulsis*, of the Roman dinner and since the *promulsis* consisted of *hors d'oeuvre*, the *mulsum* was thus in a sense an apéritif drink. As a matter of fact it is not at all a bad one. Made with dry wine, and according to the proportions of wine and honey given by Columella, *mulsum* comes out as a drink which, though too sweet for the dry taste of the modern English and Americans, is little sweeter than some of the apéritifs drunk now on the Continent of Europe. But *mulsum* could also be drunk at other times, with the dessert course of dinner, for example, or at public banquets, so that in Roman life it performed the triple function of apéritif, luxury wine, and 'liqueur'.[60]

[58] Colum., XII, 28, 4. *Decoctum*: *Edict. Dioc.*, II, 1, 15. *Defrutum*: Colum, XII, 20, 2–3; 21, 1; Plin., XIV, 80; *Edict. Dioc.*, II, 1, 16. *Hepsema, Sapa, Siraeum*: Plin., XIV, 80. *Vinum picatum*: refs in fn. 19. The use of pitch: Cato, ii, 3; xxiii, l, cx; cf. cxiii, 1–2; Plin., XIV, 18, 120–1; Colum., XII, 18, 5–7; 22, 1–3; 23, 2–3.

[59] Plin., XIV, 120; Cato, xxiii, 1–4; Colum., XII, 20, 8; 21, 2–6; 23, 2–3; 25, 1.

[60] *Confusum*: CIL, IV, Supps I and II, 5584. *Mulsum*: Cato, lxxx; Colum., XII, 41, 1; Plin., XIV, 85; XXII, 113–14; Mart., IX, xciv; Galen, II, 751, 776; CIL, IV, Supps I and II, 5526, 5592. *Melitites*: Plin., XIV, 85; Ath-E, I, 29a. *Mulsum* as a luxury: cf. Varro, III, 16, 2–3.

The Roman taste for compounded wines appears also in two variants of *mulsum*. *Rosatum*, rose wine, was made from roses and wine to which honey was added before drinking, and *violatium* followed the same method but used violets instead of roses. Spiced or aromatic wine – *conditum* – had a certain popularity and, as Pliny relates with disapproval, some people put 'scent' into their drinks. 'I also find,' he says later, 'that aromatic wine is constantly made from almost exactly the same ingredients as perfumes. . . .' By 'perfumes' here he not only means myrrh, but herbs and spices as well. One type of 'aromatic' wine was *piperatum*, or peppered wine, made from wine, honey and pepper, while another, and one which had medicinal uses, was *absinthites*, or wine and wormwood.

But lest it should be thought that the Romans would accept without question any sort of compounded wine, or that they were totally indifferent to the abuses of adulteration, we may cite two indignant passages from Pliny: 'We know that for the sake of colouring the wine colours are added as a sort of pigment and that this gives the wine more body. So many poisons are employed to force wine to suit our taste – and we are surprised that it is not wholesome!' And then in a sweeping condemnation: 'Today indeed not even our nobility ever enjoys wines that are genuine. So low has our commercial honesty sunk that only the names of the vintages are sold, the wines being adulterated as soon as they are poured into the vats. Accordingly, strange indeed as the remark may seem, the more common a wine is today, the freer it is from impurities.'[61] One cannot, I think, accept these passages as being the whole and literal truth but at the same time it is unlikely that they are the mere fantasies of Pliny's imagination. And this being so, we are forced to the conclusion that the taste of many a Roman was as indifferent as the taste of many a Roman wine.

The Roman Epicure

The use of preservatives, the abuse of adulteration, and the existence of aromatics, all bear upon this question of the quality of the Roman palate. When the flavour of a preservative was noticeable, as assuredly it must often have been, did the Romans accept this as being merely inevitable? Had they become so habituated to an alien flavour in their wine that they no longer found it a cause for comment? Could they appreciate the fineness of a fine wine?

We cannot argue, or at least we cannot argue much, from the existence of aromatic drinks since the good taste of modern wine-lovers is not invalidated by the existence of vermouths and these, after all, are aromatic wines. But if we find that the taste of the Roman upper classes leaned heavily towards the use of aromatics in food, or found its greatest pleasure in foods that were strong and rich, and if we find that the epicures took the same view, then we can argue that the Roman palate was not conditioned to the sensitive enjoyment of a beautiful wine.

One of the most famous of Roman gastronomes was Apicius. With disapproval Seneca relates his story. 'After he (Apicius) had squandered a hundred million sesterces upon his kitchen, after he had drunk up at every one of his revels the equivalent of the many largesses of the emperors and the huge revenue of the Capitol, then for the first time, when overwhelmed with debt and actually forced to do so, he began to examine his accounts. He calculated that he would have ten

Still-life with Thrushes Eggs
detail from Fresco,
House of Julia Felix
1st century A.D., *Pompeii*
Naples, Museo Nazionale

[61] *Rosatum*: Apicius, 47; *Edict. Dioc.*, II, I, 19. *Violatium*: Apicius, 47. *Conditum*: Plin., XIII, 129; XIV, 108; *Edict. Dioc.*, II, I, 17; cf. Apicius, 43. *Piperatum*: Plin., XIV, 108. *Absinthites*: Colum., XII, 35, I; Plin., XIV, 109; XXVII, 45 sqq.; Galen, II, 723, 726, 736; Apicius, 45; *Edict. Dioc.*, II, I, 18. Scents in wine: Plin., XIII, 25; XIV, 107 sqq. Adulterated wines: Plin., XIV, 130; XXIII, 33-4. For various 'wines', see Dioscorides, *Herbal*, Bk V, *passim*.

million sesterces left, and considering that he would be living in extreme starvation if he lived on ten million sesterces, he ended his life by poison.' His fame rests also upon the more useful fact that he wrote a cookery book. He was not, of course, the only Roman to have done so.

The book as we now know it was edited towards the end of the 4th or the beginning of the 5th century A.D., whereas Apicius wrote in the 1st century A.D., and thus our *De Re Coquinaria* is a collection of recipes from a number of sources. That some of these sources may have been Greek does not affect our argument since the book was designed for the use of the Latin world; and furthermore, since it does include some recipes from Apicius, it gives us a picture of Roman eating spread out over three or four centuries. It is thus more valuable to our argument than if it had been solely the work of Apicius himself.

One of the things which we notice from this cook-book is the incessant use of pepper. In earlier days, before pepper had been discovered, myrtle berries had served instead and their use was continued, though in a minor way, for a long time afterwards. Their memory lived on in 'myrtle sausage', they were used in a pickle for wild boar, and myrtle wine could be one of the ingredients in a sauce for birds. By the 1st century of the Empire, however, pepper had become essential to the cuisine of Rome and it was used in such various ways as dressing truffles, cooking rissoles of porpoise, and making 'quick digestives'.

The sauces which we have from Apicius – as we will now call the book which has come down to us under his name – use many other ingredients besides pepper and myrtle berries. They rely greatly upon herbs and also upon wine, oil, honey and vinegar. In addition to all these, the recipes use pine-kernels, certain fruits, and various types of wine – *passum*, or raisin wine, *defrutum*, or boiled-down must, and *mulsum*, or wine and honey mixed. Three examples from Apicius will give some idea of the type of sauce that was favoured by the Latin palate:

'Another sauce for boiled crane or duck.
Pepper, lovage, cumin, dried coriander, mint, origan, pine-kernels, Jericho dates, *liquamen*, oil, honey, mustard, and wine.'

'Sauce for meat slices.
Chop hard-boiled eggs and add pepper, cumin, parsley, boiled leek, myrtle-berries, a fair amount of honey, vinegar, *liquamen*, and oil.'

'(Sauce) for soft-boiled eggs.
(Pound) pepper, lovage, soaked pine-kernels. Add honey and vinegar, blend with *liquamen*.'

A less elaborate relish was advocated in his *Epigrams* by the poet Martial who suggested that soft-boiled eggs should be accompanied by fish-sauce.[62]

The sauce for the poet's eggs was, in this case, *garum*, which was a luxury of Roman life and a necessity in the well-appointed kitchen. Basically *garum* was a liquid sauce made from the salted entrails of fish but the finest was that which was made at Cartagena in Spain from the entrails of Spanish mackerel; and the finest variety could be very expensive. The lesser varieties of *garum* (or *liquamen*) were *allec*, which was second-grade *liquamen*, and *muria*, which was made from the entrails of the tunney.[63] The importance of this type of salty sauce can be recognized from the constant appearance of *liquamen* in the recipes of Apicius.

Among the delicacies of the Roman table were oysters, and the celebrity which they have attained in the minds of later ages is justified by the praise which was given to them by the Roman poets. Virgil pays tribute to the oyster beds of Abydos, and Martial to the oysters which were fattened near Baiae in the Lucrine Lake. (Some of these latter had been brought to the Lake from Brindisi in Apulia.) Even Ausonius of Bordeaux writes proudly of 'oysters rivalling those of Baiae, which the surge of the ebbing sea fattens in the lush marshes of Médoc. . . .' These are epitaphs which confer nobility. But can we say that the methods of their eating implied gastronomy? Martial has Lucrine oysters eaten with a relish of *garum*. Apicius recommends this dressing: 'Pepper, lovage, yolk of egg, vinegar, *liquamen*, oil, and wine; if you wish add also honey.'[64] Are these the sauces of a sensitive gastronome? I leave you to express your own opinion.

Fattened also for the table were snails and dormice. Varro goes into minute detail on the keeping of snails and on the right type of 'snail-island'; thriftily he insists: 'They have to be shut in . . . with water, so that you need not get a runaway-catcher.' Dormice, at least when they were being fattened, led a more confined existence. They were put into jars which had ledges for holding their food – acorns or walnuts or chestnuts – and, as Varro remarks, 'when a cover is placed over the jars they grow fat in the dark'. It is no surprise to find that a recipe for cooking them included pepper and *liquamen*.[65]

[62] Apicius: Seneca, *Moral Essays, Ad Helv.*, x, 8-9. Matius: Colum., XII, 46, 1. For the compilation, etc., of 'Apicius', see Apicius, 9-15. Myrtle: Plin., xv, 118; Apicius, VI, v, 1. Pepper: Apicius, *passim*; with truffles: VII, xvi, 3-6; with rissoles of porpoise: IV, ii, 18. 'Quick digestives': Colum., XII, 59, 4-5. Sauces: Apicius, *passim*; and those quoted: VI, ii, 4; VII, vi, 12; VII, xix, 3; (from this footnote alone it will be obvious how much I owe to the edition of 'Apicius' prepared by Miss Barbara Flower and Miss Elisabeth Rosenbaum). Martial's eggs: Mart., XIII, xl.

[63] Mart., XIII, cii, ciii; Apicius, 21-3; for *allec*, cf. Hor., *Sat.*, II, 4, 73.

[64] Virgil, I, 207; Mart., III, xlv, lx; XII, xlviii; XIII, lxxxii. Oysters from Brindisi: Plin., IX, 168-9; cf. Hor., *Sat.*, II, 4, 33; Auson., *Epist.*, xv, 1-3; Apicius, IX, vi. Oysters: see also Juvenal, *Satires*, IV, 140-3.

[65] Snails: Varro, III, 14. Dormice: Varro, III, 15; cf. Mart., III, lviii, 36. Recipe for cooking dormice: Apicius, VIII, ix.

Fish were an object of the epicure's attention and also of his exaggeration. Many sorts of fish were eaten, cuttle fish, sea-urchins, and eels among them, and 'lampreys' too, the best of these being the 'floating lampreys' which came from Sicily and were so called because of the fatness which made them float. Shad was considered by Ausonius to be 'food for the vulgar' while pike was no better, being found 'fried in cook-shops rank with the fumes of his greasy flavour'. Perch, on the other hand, he thought to be 'the dainty of our tables' and one which 'can vie on equal terms with the rosy mullet'. His view seems to have been somewhat personal for the majority of Roman epicures gave the mullet a unique place in their occasionally misdirected esteem. They thought much of the turbot also but it was the mullet which sent them into the highest transports of fishy fervour. Significantly enough, the fervour increased in proportion to the size of the mullet. Size, not quality, was the criterion. Martial, with a wry humour which is not entirely devoid of envy, contrasts the inexpensive crab (or prawn) which he himself ate off a dish of ordinary red pottery with the food served up to Candidus: 'Mullets of huge size cover your yellow gold-inlaid dishes.' And thus he addresses another 'epicure': 'You sold a slave yesterday for twelve hundred sesterces, Calliodorus, that you might dine well once. You have not dined well: a four-pound mullet which you bought was the ornament and chief dish of your dinner. A man may cry, "This is not a fish, not a fish, you profligate: 'tis a man; a man, Calliodorus, whom you eat." '[66] Beside this disproportionate folly Trimalchio's dinner is a minor buffoonery.

Birds found their place on the Roman table. The fieldfare was extremely popular, and not merely among pretenders to good taste. In the late Republic there were aviaries which reared them for the market and sold them to be served at public banquets or on the occasion of a triumph, and at the same period they seem to have been almost obligatory at the numerous club dinners. They were not only eaten at Rome, for Horace had them at Beneventum (lean ones it is true) where the kitchen was nearly burnt down while they were being cooked. They were also given as presents at the family festival of the Caristia, on February 22nd, at which family quarrels – if they existed – were settled – if possible. Perhaps, since Martial rated the fieldfare as the greatest delicacy among birds, the excellence of the food helped the not always easy process of adjusting a family difference.

' "But a big fish on a big dish outstretched! That's what I'd like to see!" cries a gullet worthy of the greedy Harpies'; and in the same *Satire* Horace attacks the fashionable compulsion to serve a peacock at a rich dinner. It is the rarity of the bird, he complains, it is the extravagance of its cost and the panoply of its feathers, and not the quality of its eating, which makes it the delight of the pretentious host. Unusual the peacock may have been; but in this it was not alone for Apicius gives us a 'sauce for boiled ostrich'. He also instructs us how to cook flamingo and adds 'the same recipe can . . . be used for parrot'.[67]

Much the same thing happened with vegetables as with fish, for here again size became the coveted distinction. Indignantly, Pliny relates that kale was so fattened 'that there is not room for it on a poor man's table' and adds, as another example of gastronomic folly, that the cultivated asparagus at Ravenna 'produces heads weighing three to a pound'. Pliny is condemning size, not lack of quality and Martial is much nearer to the epicurean truth when he says: 'The succulent stalk that has

[66]Fish, and methods of cooking: Apicius, IX and X. 'Lampreys': Varro, II, 6, 2; Colum., VIII, 17, 8; and see Plin., IX, 76, 81; cf. Mart., XIII, lxxx; Hor., *Sat.*, II, 8, 42-4. Perch, pike, shad: Auson., *Mosella*, 115-27; Hor., *Sat.*, II, 2, 30-8. Turbot: Mart., III, xlv; X, xxx; xiii, lxxxi; Hor., *Sat.*, I, 2, 116. Mullet: Mart., II, xliii; X, xxxi; Hor., *Sat.*, II, 2, 33-4.

[67]Varro, III, 2, 15-16; Hor., *Sat.*, I, 5, 71-6; Mart., III, lxxvii; IX, liv, lv; XIII, xcii. Peacock: Hor., *Sat.*, II, 2, 23 sqq. Ostrich, flamingo, parrot: Apicius, VI, i, I; VI, vi, I. For flamingoes' tongues, see Mart., XIII, lxxi.

Roman Dishes: 'Lucasta Assa', Roast Lobster, with Pepper Sauce; 'Patina Mullorum', Soused Mullet in Honeyed Wine with Pepper

grown in watery Ravenna will not be more palatable than wild asparagus.' It is a pity that his words are not heeded today.

Martial, as a matter of fact, seems to have been rather fond of vegetables which is hardly surprising since they formed a large part of the diet of the poor and Martial was an impoverished poet. Apart from the commoner vegetables, however, he set great store by mushrooms, a preference in which he was by no means alone, and he also considered the truffle to be a welcome and worthy object. This was the saner side of Roman gastronomy as was their recognition that the hams of Gaul were among the best which could be procured, and in Varro's day Comacine and Cavarine hams (which probably came from Narbonensian Gaul) were every year imported into Rome.

Some of us might not consider that the good taste of the Romans is shown at its best in their liking for the stuffed womb of a sow; but then we should not necessarily rate the good taste of the modern Scots by any predeliction which they might have for haggis. Many of us, on the other hand, would find nothing to criticize in the recipe of Apicius which goes 'Meat roasted plain in the oven, sprinkled with plenty of salt. Serve with honey', for this is only an ancient variant of British roast lamb and red-currant jelly. We might, perhaps, disagree with Martial's view that the hare was the finest of the four-footed animals and the Romans themselves disagreed with him too for they thought that the finest meat was that of the boar. These boars came from Umbria, Lucania, Tuscany and the Laurentine Marshes, and they could be either wild or else reared and fattened in *vivaria*. One of these *vivaria* belonged to Quintus Hortensius at Laurentum, just south of Ostia, and it provided manifold pleasure; the greedy, or the hungry, could feed their imagination with the sight of

197

succulent meat 'on the hoof'; the romantics could find their enjoyment in the scene which Varro has described: 'In it was a high spot where was spread the table at which we were dining, to which he (Quintus Hortensius) bade Orpheus be called. When he appeared with his robe and harp, and was bidden to sing, he blew a horn; whereupon there poured around us . . . a crowd of stags, boars, and other animals. . . .'

The boar produced a rich and festal food – 'a bilious Rome is still belching my boar' was Martial's comment on a Laurentian monster which he had sent as a present to Garricus. The boar at Trimalchio's dinner was in every sense an exaggeration though one which may not have been too far from the occasional truth. On its tusks hung two baskets full of dates; 'round it lay sucking-pigs made of simnel cake'; and when the boar was carved, out of its body flew a number of thrushes. But let us return from the fictional Trimalchio to the real Martial and an occasion on which he had a boar in his own house – 'a booty abhorrent to my hearth', he says, lamenting the cost of cooking it:

'Let my household gods joyously grow fat with the steaming reek. . . . But ah! the cook will consume a huge heap of pepper, and add Falernian mixed with his treasured fish-sauce. Go back to your owner: my fire is too small for you, O boar that would bankrupt me! 'tis less ruinous to starve.'[68]

Pepper and fish-sauce again.

One must be wary in using the records of Roman extravagance. They chronicle exaggerations but they do so in a moral and satirical spirit, and throughout these Roman writers there runs a consistent vein of disapproval. They condemn the wealthy glutton and mock the pretentious gourmet. Horace's *Satire* (II.4) on the finer points of gastronomy as expounded by a conceited lecturer is a charming slaughter of the finicking epicure. 'Give good heed to serve eggs of an oblong shape, for they have a better flavour and are whiter than the round,' says Horace's lecturer, who advises his audience also how to deal with a difficult emergency: 'If a friend suddenly drops in upon you of an evening, and you fear that a tough fowl may answer ill to his taste, you will be wise to plunge it alive into diluted Falernian: this will make it tender.' The mockery and disapproval of the poets and moralists do show that exaggerations existed, and frequently existed, among the wealthier classes, but the fact that they criticize and condemn shows too that the exaggerations were only an exotic growth on the normal life of the civilized Roman.

Behind the mockery we can see two things. First, that the wealthier Romans were fond of what they considered to be good food, they were accustomed to it, and they went to great pains to get it. Their taste for pungency and richness does not, however, make them into a race of gluttons. And second, that they were basically accustomed to think of their food in terms of moderation. There was always a sense of frugality in the Roman character and the wealth and the luxury of Rome never entirely destroyed it.

The richer and the duller of the Romans may have led lives of idle self-indulgence. Many of them did. It would be inaccurate to call them typical and mere kindness to call them civilized. But the ordinary and the civilized Roman, whether by choice or necessity, led an active and, on the whole, an abstemious life. In the country, as in

[68]Kale and asparagus: Plin., xix, 54; Mart., xiii, xxi. Mushrooms, truffles: Mart., iii, xlv; xiii, xlviii, i. Gallic hams: Varro: ii, 4, 10-11. Sow's womb: Mart., vii, xx; Hor., *Epist.*, i, 15. Roast meat and honey: Apicius, vii, v, i. Hare: Mart., xiii, xcii. Boar: Virgil, *Aeneid*, x, 707-13; Varro, iii, 13; Ovid, *Fasti*, ii, 231; Hor., *Sat.*, ii, 3, 234; 4, 40-2 (how much in mockery?); 8, 6; Mart., iii, lxxvii; vii, xxvii; ix, xlviii; xii, xlviii; (Boar and myrtle-berries: Plin., xv, 118); Petronius, *Satyricon*, 40.

the town, labourers were up by daybreak. Nor was it only the lower classes who kept these early hours. Cicero, in a letter to Publius Lentulus says: 'I write this on the fifteenth of January, before dawn'; and a letter to his brother Quintus, written in the late October or early November of 54 B.C., gives us an intimate picture of the great Roman at work: 'I am writing this before day-break, by the light of a little wooden torch-stand, which has always been a great delight to me, because they told me that you had seen to its construction when you were in Samos.'

The Roman breakfast, the *jentaculum*, was little more than the barest satisfaction of hunger. A piece of bread, with perhaps a few olives or raisins, seems to have been usual, though boys might eat a pastry. Bread and cheese were sometimes eaten and occasionally, it would seem, a piece of meat. But in general it was a meal of no importance, eaten in haste, and quite without ceremony. Almost as unceremonious, although a little more important, was the *prandium*, or lunch, which was taken about noon. For working people this might consist mainly of the 'insipid beet' but the more fortunate might have meat or eggs, or something left over from the dinner of the night before. Usually the *prandium* was a cold meal and usually it was enlivened with wine.

The important meal of the day was dinner, the *cena*, which began about two o'clock or half-past two in the afternoon. It was a leisurely, pleasant, and undoubtedly talkative, meal and it was divided into three parts: first of all the *promulsis* or *gustus* which consisted of *hors d'oeuvre* and was usually accompanied by *mulsum*; after this the *fercula*, the main part of the dinner, which was composed of several dishes; and finally, the *mensa secunda*, the dessert course of pastry and fruit, which was also sometimes accompanied by *mulsum*.

The quality of the *cena* depended, naturally, upon the taste and the wealth of the host. For most of the Roman people it was not an elaborate affair and there are many literary examples of the simple dinner. These not only explain what sort of a meal it was but bear witness to the ungluttonous side of Roman life. And in the context of eating it will be reasonable also to cite other examples of frugality, even if they do not refer strictly to the Roman dinner.

We can take an historical example from the eating habits of Augustus Caesar. 'He was frugal,' says Suetonius, 'and, as a rule, preferred food of the common people, especially the coarser sort of bread, whitebait, fresh hand-pressed cheese, and green figs of the second crop; and would not wait for dinner, if he felt hungry, but ate anywhere.' Nor was Augustus the only abstemious emperor for Trajan offered to his guests dinners which were both moderate and civilized.

Literature abounds with examples of simplicity and although these are often imaginative they are clearly reflections of the truth. Horace makes the farmer Ofellus say: 'I was not the man to eat on a working day, without good reason, anything more than greens and the shank of a smoked ham, and if after long absence a friend came to see me, or if in rainy weather, when I could not work, a neighbour paid me a visit . . . we fared well . . . with a pullet and a kid; by and by raisins and nuts and split figs set off our dessert.' Pliny the Younger, reproaching Septicius Clarus with not keeping an engagement to dine with him, writes that he had prepared a dinner of lettuce, snails, eggs, olives, beets, and shallots 'and a hundred other dainties. . . . But the oysters, chitterlings, sea-urchins and Spanish dancers of a certain – I know not who, were, it seems, more to your taste'. Lettuce, fish sauce, snails, and eggs, were among the most usual offerings at the *promulsis* although they were not the only ones. Martial, at a modest dinner, offers his guest lettuces and leeks and tunney fish in sliced eggs, and one of his fuller, but still modest, dinners for himself and six guests runs as follows: '. . . squat lettuce and clipped leek, and flatulent mint is not wanting nor the salacious herb (garden rocket); sliced eggs shall garnish lizard-fish served with rue, and there shall be a paunch dripping from the tunney's brine'. This was his *promulsis*. The *fercula* consisted of a kid, meat-balls, beans and young sprouts, a chicken, 'and a ham that has already survived three dinners'. For the dessert they had apples and Nomentan wine.[69]

The Finest Wines

So far there is little to indicate that the upper-class Romans were a class of exquisite epicures. They did, it is true, exercise discrimination in their choice of food and the best foods of the known world were imported into Rome. But discrimination in Roman gastronomy was expressed in antique, not in modern, terms. Undoubtedly there were a few gourmets in our modern sense of the word but in general the taste of the Romans was conditioned by two factors: on the one side a rustic – almost an archaic – simplicity: on the other side a desire for pungency and richness. Neither of these factors impels towards the cultivation of a fine taste, and neither is the mark of a modern epicure. Shall we find, then, that their discrimination approached more nearly to the modern pattern when they were dealing with the finer wines of the Roman world? They were certainly as eager to import the better wines as they were to import the better foods. None of these better wines, however, came from France.

[69]Early rising: Plin., XVIII, 236; Mart., XII, lvii; Cicero, *Letters to his Friends*, I, 2; *Ad Quintum Fratrem*, III, 7; and cf. II, 3. Breakfast: Mart., VIII, lxvii; XIII, xxxi; XIV, ccxxiii. Lunch or dinner: Suet., *Claudius*, 34; *Augustus*, 76; Mart., IV, viii; VII, li; XI, lii; XIII, xiii; Pliny the Younger, *Letters*, III, I; III, 5; and for Trajan: VI, 31. And see Hor., *Sat.*, II, 2, 116–22; Pliny the Younger, *Letters*, I, 15; Mart., III, l; v, lxxviii; x, xlviii; XII, xix; XIII, liii; cf. Juvenal, *Satires*, XI.

Mostly they came from Greece and Spain while some may even have come from Egypt.

If wines were in fact imported into Rome from Egypt they would have been the Mareotic, Taeniotic, Antyllan, and Sebennytic, all of which were grown in the Nile Delta. Mareotic was a light and fragrant wine and its vine, the 'white Mareotic', finds a place in Virgil's *Georgics*. Taeniotic, which was also called 'Strip Wine' from the shape of the *vignoble*, was a pale wine with an aromatic taste and it was considered at one time to be even better than Mareotic. Antyllan, at least in the 2nd century A.D., was considered by some to be the best wine of Egypt, while Sebennytic, in the 1st century A.D., was given a ranking immediately after the top-grade wines of the Aegean. This latter wine was made from three different kinds of grape, one of them being the Thasian, the others, as Pliny has it, being the 'soot grape and the pine-tree grape'.

These Egyptian wines were given their ranking purely, it would seem, because of their genuine quality. (Or should one suspect the 'aromatic' taste of Taeniotic? Was it due to the addition of herbs?) Greek wines, on the other hand, though much more admired than those of Egypt, were not always admired because of their genuine goodness. A case in point is the wine of Cos.

Coan was one of the top-graded wines of the Roman world. Its popularity among the Romans is evident and the reason for its popularity is instructive. Cato's *De Agri Cultura* is not a long book but three times he gives instructions on the making of 'Greek wine': either it is 'directions for making Greek wine', or 'recipe for Greek wine', or – more explicitly – 'recipe for Coan wine'; and at the end of his 'recipe for Greek wine' he observes 'This wine will not be inferior to the Coan'. (He is referring, it seems, to the 'Coan' made in Italy.) Now in each of the recipes the essential points are these: the must is to be comparatively sweet whilst salt, sea-water, or brine is to be mixed with the must; either this or else the grapes are to be soaked in sea-water before they are trodden.

Cato's recipes are nothing more than attempts to counterfeit the sea-water wines of the Greeks and Cato chose Coan as his exemplar because one style of Coan was strongly flavoured with sea-water.

It may be argued that Cato is only expressing a personal preference for sea-water wine and that his taste was not shared by the rest of his fellow Romans. As an argument it is not convincing. Coan wine – 'Coum' – was imported into Italy long after Cato's time and we have no good grounds for believing that later Coan was free from sea-water. Furthermore, of the other two Greek wines which the Romans especially favoured, one – the Lesbian – though not actually mixed with the sea, nevertheless carried a flavour of sea-water. Finally, Columella, two hundred years after Cato, instructs us how 'to make wine like Greek wine' and salt is a vital ingredient.

Pliny made the downright statement that 'wines imported from oversea held the field for a long time and right down to our grandfathers' day' and he implied that these wines were mainly Greek. The reasoning on which he based a part of this statement seems to be somewhat confused but if we interpret his phrase 'held the field' as a referring only to wines which were ranked as wines of high quality, then we may not be far from the truth. Virgil knew of a number of Greek wines and mentions Lesbian, Thasian, Tmolian, Rhodian, and 'the royal Chian' but he may have learnt about them from a visit to Greece, and in any case he does not necessarily mean that all these wines were imported into Italy. Varro, however, writing at about the same date, gives the unequivocal statement that 'the vintage we store comes in ships from the islands of Cos and Chios'. On special occasions Horace drank Chian or Lesbian wine and he also mentions a 'Chian, unmixed with brine'. To celebrate the *Ambarvalia* Tibullus commands: 'Now from the old bin bring me out the smoked Falernians and loose the bands of the Chian jar. Let drinking be the order of the day.'

Writing in the middle of the 1st century A.D. Columella remarks 'we lay up our stores of wine from the Cyclades islands and from the districts of Baetica and Gaul'. His phrase about the Cyclades is admittedly a generalization but even so it is inaccurate for it omits the better known wines from other islands. We ourselves would sum up the position rather differently. We would say that in the Late Republic and Early Empire the Greek wines which were favoured at Rome came almost exclusively from the Aegean islands, and not from the islands of the Cyclades, but from those of Asia Minor. It is possible that other wines were also imported – Thasian, Tmolian, Rhodian, and perhaps the wine of Clazomenae 'now,' as Pliny significantly says, 'that they have begun to flavour it more sparingly with sea-water' – but to Roman palates the top-ranking Greek wines were Chian, Lesbian, and Coan. These three can properly claim a place among the greatest wines of the Roman world.[70] Even so, one must still point out that, however sparing the Clazo-menaeans may have been with their sea-water, 'Greek wine' under the Early Empire was still considered to be a 'salty' wine.

We can make a list, and a reasonably accurate list, of those wines which were ranked by the Romans as the finest wines of the world. There were seventeen, or, if we include one 'probable', eighteen of them. Three of them were Greek – Chian, Coan and Lesbian. One of them was Sicilian – the Mamertine from Messina. Four of them were Spanish – Baliarican from the Balearic Islands, Lauronensian from the modern province of Valencia, Tarraconensian from Tarragona and (this is the 'probable'), Baetican from Andalusia. The remaining ten places are taken by Italian wines: Alban, Caecuban, Calenian, Falernian, Fundanian, Massic, Setine, Statanian, Surrentine, and Rhaetic. Some of these Italian wines varied from time to time in their quality but on the whole they were preferred above all others, even above Chian and Lesbian which ran them close, and sometimes very close indeed.

Falernian was the Great First Growth of the Roman Empire and it is, I suppose, the most famous wine in ancient history. Almost unanimously the Latin writers give it pride of place and even Virgil puts it in front of his beloved Rhaetic of Verona. It is hard to go against the great weight of opinion voiced by the poets and to suggest that Falernian was not always worthy of its proud title. But this does seem to have been the case for, as we have already seen, Pliny relates that the Falernian district was losing its reputation because more attention was paid to quantity than to quality. Pliny is by no means free from inaccuracy yet one can see no reason why he should have been inaccurate in this case and particularly when he is writing about such a famous wine. We must accept the fact that, somewhere about the middle of the 1st century A.D., the vast popularity of Falernian had led

[70]Mareotic: Virgil, II, 91; Ath-E, I, 33d; Strab., 17, 1, 14. Taeniotic: Ath-E, I, 33e. Antyllan: Ath-E, I, 33f. Sebennytic: Plin., XIV, 74. Sea-water wine: Cato, XXIV, CV, CXII. Greek wines known in Italy: Virgil, II, 89-102; Varro, II, Intro. 3; Hor., *Carm.*, III, 19, and *Epod.*, 9; Hor., *Sat.*, II, 8, 15; Tibullus, II, 1, 27-8; Plin., XIV, 73-4, 95-7; Colum., I, Preface, 20; XII, 37 – giving recipe for 'wine like Greek wine'. Coum (Coan) and Pompeii: *CIL*, IV, Supps I and II, 5536-8.

some of its growers to become careless and avaricious; and thus, for a time at least, some of the Falernian vintages suffered in quality from the growers' desire to reap an inflated profit from an almost insatiable market.

Falernian was grown on the borders of Latium and Campania. The *vignoble* was sometimes divied into three *climats*, Caucinian being the highest and on the tops of the hills, Faustian being the middle and half way up the hills, and Falernian being the lowest and at the bottom of the hills. (In my text, unless specifically qualified, Falernian means wine from any part of the Falernian district and not merely from the lowest *climat* of the *vignoble*.) There were two colours of Falernian, white and red, though we should qualify this by saying that the 'white' was sometimes yellowish-brown and the red was the darkest red. There were also two styles of the wine, one dry and one sweet, although a third style – a light wine – makes an occasional appearance. The body and potency of the heavier kind can be gauged from Horace's descriptions: 'stout Falernian' he calls it, and elsewhere asks: 'What slave will swiftly temper the bowls of fiery Falernian with water from the passing stream?' 'It is the only wine that takes light when a flame is applied to it,' writes Pliny referring to Faustian to which (and this to some extent redeems his statement of the lost reputation of the Falernian district) he gives the highest ranking of all the wines of his own day. The charm and attraction which Falernian had for the Romans can perhaps be imagined from one of Martial's Epigrams:

'Breath of balm from phials of yesterday . . . perfume of apples ripening in their winter chest, of the field lavish with the leafage of spring; of Augusta's silken robes from Palatine presses, of amber warmed by a maiden's hand; of a jar of dark Falernian shattered, but far off. . . .'

One might add that Martial is using this Epigram to conjure up the fragrance of remembered kisses.[71]

Two more of the top-ranking wines came from the borders of Latium and Campania and from Campania itself. These were Calenian, from the district of modern Calvi, a lighter wine than Falernian, and Surrentine, from Sorrento in Campania. That the latter should have been in the top class seems peculiar for it was a thin, hard wine which was very rough when young and needed at least twenty-five years to mature. Tiberius called it 'generous vinegar' while Gaius Caligula, a little more kindly, described it as 'best quality flat wine'. Perhaps they drank it too young. At all events, lesser men did not share the Imperial point of view and they considered Surrentine as being fit to rival Falernian.[72]

Out of the ten top-ranking Italian wines, six came from Latium: Alban, Caecuban, Fundanian, Massic, Setine, and Statanian. Alban could be either dry or sweet, although the sweet variety seems to have been the most usual. Caecuban was grown on marshy ground in the Bay of Amyclase (north of Gaeta). It was a full, strong wine but after A.D. 79 it was no longer produced. Fundanian came from near modern Fondi and was grown on trellises or on vines which were trained up small trees; this again was a strong, full-bodied wine which for that reason was 'not often drunk at symposia'. Even so, it managed to make the top class, as did Massic from Monte Massico, and Setine and Statanian, both of which were lighter than Falernian.

[71] Mamertine: Plin., XIV, 66, 97, and fn. 13. Spanish wines: Plin., XIV, 71, and fn. 17. Rhaetic: Virgil, II, 95, and see fn. 15. Caucinian: Plin., XIV, 63; Ath-E, I, 27c. Faustian: Plin., XIV, 62–3; CIL, XV, 4553. Falernian (lowest *climat*): Plin., XIV, 63. Falernian (all *climats*): Virgil, II, 96; Strab., 5, 3, 6; 5, 4, 3; Plin., XIV, 62–3; XXIII, 33, 36; Ath-E, I, 26c, 33a; Mart., II, xl; VI, xxvii; VIII, lvi; XI, viii, 1; Hor., *Carm.*, I, 27; II, 3, 11; Catullus, 27; Galen, II, 753; Dioscorides, *Herbal*, v, 10; *Edict. Dioc.*, II, 1, 7; CIL, IV, 1679, 2566 (?); IV, Supps I and II, 6896 (?); XV, 4511 (?), 4532, 4554 (?), 4559, 4560; cf. 4556 and 4557.

[72] Calenian: Strab., 5, 4, 3; Plin., XIV, 65; Ath-E, I, 27a; Hor., *Carm.*, I, 20. Surrentine: Strab., 5, 4, 3; Colum., III, 8, 5; Plin., XIV, 64; XXIII, 33, 35, 36; Ath-E, I, 26d; Mart., XIII, cx; Dioscorides, *Herbal*, v, 10; *Edict. Dioc.*, II, 1, 6; CIL, IV, 2555; IV, Supps I and II, 5514 (?), 5521–2, 5525, 5560–2.

Setine was certainly 'drunk at symposia' and Martial, when ill and condemned to drink warm water, bewailed the lack both of Setine and of symposia:[73]

'Full Setine bumpers strained through lordly snow,
When shall I see you and no leech say no?'

The Connoisseurs

In the range of their choice the Romans were not at all modern. Either they did not know, or else they did not choose, wines from those areas which have come to be recognized as the great vineyards of the world – France and Germany, for example. This may not have been the Romans' fault since French and German wines may not then have been as outstanding as much later they became. But within the limitations of their choice, how genuine was the connoisseurship of the Romans? How much could they really appreciate a fine, matured wine?

Pliny the Younger tells the story of how he once dined with a man who had the best wine served to himself and his particular friends, the second grade of wine to the other guests, and the third grade to the freedmen. While censoring this conduct, Pliny remarked that, when he himself entertained, all his guests drank the same wine and that 'my freedmen don't drink the same wine I do – but I drink what they do'. Pliny's style is not without pomposity but his sentiments are at least sincere. Nor was he alone in his experience of such stratified entertainment for the same type of discourtesy is related and condemned by Martial and Juvenal. Bad manners, it might be said, have nothing to do with connoisseurship; superficially, perhaps not; but in practice they do, for a genuine appreciation of fine things implies an equal appreciation of good manners and, in modern times at least, it is rare to meet a discourteous connoisseur. Roman manners were not always good – quite often they were abominable – and those who practised the discourtesies of which the writers complain are convicted either of an ill-judged display of thrift or an ill-mannered display of behaviour. In any case, they can scarcely have been connoisseurs in any civilized sense of the word.

Then there was the matter of mixing. Martial upbraids Tucca for mixing old Falernian with Vatican wine (or must): 'it is a crime to murder Falernian, to apply to Campanian wine deadly poison'. We can agree. But Martial and Horace recount without criticism, and indeed with approval, the mixing of fine wine and honey in order to make the apéritif *mulsum*: 'Massic wine with Attic combs', writes Martial as an example of the perfect blend; elsewhere he commands 'You, Attic honey, thicken the nectarous Falernian. It is meet that such a drink be mixed by a Ganymede'; and Horace describes the ingredients of a luxurious *mulsum* – 'honey . . . from Hymettus . . . the wine from Falernum'. (The 'poor man's *mulsum*' was the raisin wine of Crete.) Now logically there is nothing against using the best wine to make an apéritif; it may perhaps make the best apéritif, especially when, as in Rome, the apéritif was a sweet and not a sharp, drink; but we ourselves might hesitate to use the finest burgundy for such a purpose.

Nor would we dilute the finest claret, or any other excellent wine. There is, it is true, a story current in Bordeaux that some years past an Anglo-Saxon visitor

[73] Alban: Strab., 5, 3, 6; Colum., III, 2, 16; 8, 5; Mart., XIII, cix; Hor., *Carm.*, IV, 11; Hor., *Sat.*, II, 8, 16; Juvenal, *Satires*, XIII, 214; Plin., XIV, 25, 64; XXIII, 33, 35, 36; Ath-E, I, 26d, 33a; Dioscorides, *Herbal*, V, 10; *CIL*, XV, 4531. Caecuban: Strab., 5, 3, 5, 6; Colum., III, 8, 5; Hor., *Carm.*, I, 20; Hor., *Sat.*, II, 8, 15; Mart., II, xl; III, xxvi; XII, lx; Plin., XIV, 61; XVII, 31; XXIII, 35; Ath-E, I, 27a; Dioscorides, *Herbal*, V, 10; *CIL*, XV, 4545. Fundanian: Strab., 5, 3, 6; Mart., XIII, cxiii; Plin., XIV, 65; Ath-E, I, 27a; *CIL*, XV, 4566-9. Massic: Colum., III, 8, 5; Mart., I, xxvi; III, xxvi, xlix; Hor., *Carm.*, I, 1; II, 7; Hor., *Sat.*, II, 4, 51. Setine: Strab., 5, 3, 6, 10; Mart., IV, lxix; VI, lxxxvi; VIII, li; XIII, cxii; Plin., XIV, 61; XXIII, 36; *Edict. Dioc.*, II, 1, 5; quotation from *Martial's Epigrams*, VI, lxxxvi, trs. Francis, A. L., Tatum, H. F. Statanian: Strab., 5, 3, 6; 5, 4, 3; Plin., XIV, 65; XXIII, 36; Ath-E, I, 26c.

ordered a bottle of the finest vintage and diluted it with soda water. This story, or myth, is sometimes held in after-dinner reminiscence to indicate the precarious basis of civilization, though comfort is taken from the fact that the incident was exceptional. With the Romans, however, dilution was the general custom, and one part of water to three parts of wine seems to have been considered quite a strong mixture. Dilution with water did not, of course, improve the quality of the wine but this must have been largely irrelevant to the Romans. They diluted in order to mitigate the strength of wine and even a Great Growth like Falernian was watered down to make it less intoxicating. One cannot say that the habit of dilution was universal for there were Romans who drank their wine unwatered.[74] These neat imbibers were treated with sarcasm rather than approval but even so one may suspect that neat wine was a commoner drink at Rome than it had ever been in Greece.

The Romans were careful in the matter of straining, or as we should say decanting, their wines. From this it does not necessarily follow that their wines were any fuller of dregs than ours are today since most of the fine red wines of the modern world need decanting, or careful pouring, before they are drunk. Still, in passing, we may note such phrases as 'thick dregs of red Veientan' (which was in any case an inferior wine), 'Paelignian wine-growers send you turbid Marsic', and 'to pass the turbid Caecuban through the bag'. This bag, or *saccus*, was made of linen and was in common use among the more careful drinkers of Rome. So was the *colum* which was like a little colander with small holes. There even grew up at Rome a theory about the relative merits of the *saccus* and the *colum*. A precious epicure (again mocked and immortalized by Horace) believed that Massic wine 'when strained through linen, is spoiled, losing its full flavour'. Others held that the metal strainer was superior to the *saccus* and it is this view which seems to have prevailed. There were one or two other notions. Pliny states that anise 'placed with bitter almonds on the strainers . . . improves wine'. Perhaps, although I do not think so, he was referring to the strainers made of rushes or of broom which were used in the wine vats; perhaps he meant these, too, when he said that myrtle oil, when 'poured over the wine-strainers before they are used . . . retains the lees and only allows the pure liquor to pass through, and unites with the wine after it has been strained, greatly improving it'.

Pliny has, from time to time, some odd ideas about wine and although we must take it that these methods of 'improvement' were actually in use, we do not have to assume that they were in common use. Nor need we take as widely representative of Roman opinion his very peculiar notion that wines are 'robbed of their virility by being passed through strainers'. One is tempted to read his sentence as meaning that wine lost its strength when it was passed through a strainer full of snow, and was thereby diluted as it was cooled. But if he did mean this, he has failed to make his meaning clear, and in another passage on wine he states flatly: 'Nay, what is more, to enable us to take more, we reduce its strength by means of a linen strainer. . . .'[75] Pliny was no connoisseur.

Cooling was a frequent practice among those of the Romans who could afford it, and both the *saccus* and the *colum* could be used for this purpose. They were filled with snow or ice and then the wine strained through them; and even the finest

[74]Pliny the Younger, *Letters*, II, 6; Mart., VI, xi; IX, ii; Juvenal, *Satires*, V, 24-37. Mixing and *mulsum*: Mart., I, xviii; IV, xiii; X, lxvi; XIII, cviii; Hor., *Sat.*, II, 2, 15; 4, 24. 'Poor man's *mulsum*': Mart., XIII, cvi; and for *Vinum Creticum*, see also Plin., XIV, 81; Dioscorides, *Herbal*, V, 9; *CIL*, IV, 5526. Dilution: Virgil, I, 9; cf. Tibullus, II, 1, 46; Mart., I, xi; I, cvi (for a special reason); VI, lxxxix; Hor., *Carm.*, III, 11; Carcopino, J., *Daily Life in Ancient Rome*, 268.

[75]Mart., I, ciii; (and for Veientan, see fn. 14); II, xl; VIII, xlv; XII, lx; XIII, cxxi; XIV, ciii, civ; and 'wine without lees': X, xlviii; Hor., *Sat.*, II, 4, 53-4; Colum., II, 2, 20; Plin., XIV, 138; XV, 124; XIX, 53; XX, 185-6. Vat-strainers: Virgil, II, 242; Colum., XII, 19, 4. Willow baskets: Cato, xxxi, xxxiii.

wines – Falernian, Caecuban, and Setine – were subject to this treatment. Let us take one of the more idyllic examples of refrigeration:

> 'So, on flower-spangled sward reclining, where in the runnels sparkling here and there the pebble is tumbled by the rippling wave, with all your frets banished far, may you with measures of dark wine break through the ice while your brow blushes with rose-stitched chaplets.'

Or this, in a somewhat elegiac mood:

> 'Pour in, Callistus, two double-measures of Falernian; do thou, Alcimus, dissolve upon them the summer's snow; let my dripping locks be rich with over-bounteous balm, and my temples droop beneath the knitted roses. Yon tombs, so nigh, bid us enjoy life, forasmuch as they teach us that the very gods can die.'[76]

The poet is not here contemplating the death of the rather self-conscious divinities of the Roman heaven. He is looking towards the Mausoleum of Augustus and meditating upon the death of the man whom the Senate had decreed should be set among the gods of the State. And, of course, he is meditating – under the best conditions – upon the perennial theme of 'Gather ye rosebuds while ye may'.

The Age of Wines

One of the most remarkable things about Roman wine is the consistent emphasis upon age. Again and again the Latin writers speak of wines which have years of age, not a few years only but many years, and they speak about these wines so naturally, almost so casually, that there is no doubt whatever of the fact that matured wine was an integral part of civilized Roman life. And from the evidence which we have about the age of wines in the ancient world we cannot but believe that the Romans were the first people to mature wine on anything approaching a modern scale.

'Almost every wine has the property of acquiring excellence with age,' wrote Columella in about A.D. 60. In the same sentence, and immediately before these words, he wrote of wines which could age for fifteen years without deterioration. But age was not always meant in this sense. Cato said that a large vineyard ought to have enough vats to hold five vintages and thus implied that a five-year-old wine was nothing unusual; but the implication seems to be qualified, or at least qualified to some extent, by Varro who wrote: 'I imagine he fixed the number . . . so high in order that the farmer might not be forced to sell his wine every year; for old wine brings a better price than new, and the same wine a better price at one time than at another', and by saying later 'If you wish to drink old wine (and wine is not old enough until a year has been added to its age), it should be brought out when it is a year old. But if it is of the variety of grapes that sours quickly, it must be used up or sold before the next vintage. There are brands of wine, the Falernian for instance, which are the more valuable when brought out the more years you have kept them in store'. And coming round the circle again to Columella we have this: 'Moreover, when vines of different kinds ripen at the same time, the taste of the better kind is spoiled by the worse, and the flavour of many, when blended into

[76]Plin., XIX, 55; Mart., V, lxiv; VI, lxxxvi; IX, ii, xxii, xc; XII, xvii; Pliny the Younger, *Letters*, I, 15.

one, becomes intolerant of age. And so necessity' (incompetence or ignorance) 'forces the farmer to market his wine when it is new, though it would bring a better price if the selling could be put off for a year, or at least until summer'.

We may be sure that most of the wine in the Roman world was *vin ordinaire* and that it was drunk in the year after its vintaging. The small farmer would not have had the capital, nor probably the space, to store his wine for longer than a year; and in any case if it were not potentially a high-grade wine, there would have been no point in his doing so. In this he would have been no different from many of his modern colleagues.

Nevertheless it is clear that, even as early as Cato, some wine was matured for a number of years, and from Cato onwards there was never any doubt in the Roman mind that the better wine was a wine with age. Horace says 'I had a jar full of Alban over nine years old . . .'; and again 'jar of mellow wine as yet untouched has long been waiting for thee' (Maecenas) 'at my house. . . .' We read of 'old Falernian' and 'ancient Massic' and there are innumerable other instances of the Roman pre-occupation with the age of wine. In this they seem to be like ourselves but there is, none the less, a difference; when we talk of vintages we talk of the date of the

Silenus
Rome, Capitoline Museum

vintage year; when the Romans speak of years, it is seldom of vintage years and almost always of the number of years that a wine has lived. The reason, of course, is climatic. To us the date of a year signifies the climatic conditions under which that wine was grown; to the Romans this significance was not so important, for most of the wines which they drank came from Mediterranean regions where the climate was less variable than in those northern and western areas from which we draw so many of our wines.

The question of age interested them with other wines besides those of Italy. Pliny made the flat statement: 'all the overseas wines are thought to take seven years to reach the middle stage of maturity'. He certainly meant this to apply to the wines of the Aegean and the Levant, probably also to those of Egypt, and possibly to the better wines of Spain and France. We know that some French wine was allowed to age, for, towards the middle of the 2nd century A.D. a five-year-old Baeterrensan, from Béziers, was exported to Rome. But there is also a possibility that Bordeaux had begun to mature her wines a century before this. Columella states with every appearance of knowledge that wine made from the 'Bituricus' vine would keep perfectly for fifteen years and even for a few years longer than that. If this vine were the same as the Biturica, the wine of Bordeaux would have been able to age for fifteen years at least. Unfortunately the argument – any argument – about the early vineyards of Bordeaux is peppered with 'probabilities' and we are left with the tantalizing but unproven thought that in the time of Nero a Roman might have drunk Bordeaux vintages as old as many, and older than some, of those which we drink now. But if so, he certainly did not drink them in Rome, for the wines of the Gironde found no favour in the capital city of the Empire.

Pliny also relates that a sea voyage makes a difference to wine: 'the effect of the motion on vintages that can stand it is merely to double their previous maturity'. This seems to be an early example of a far later practice for in the 19th century Madeira, and some sherry, was shipped to the East Indies and back in order to attain age and extra quality. Basically the two techniques are the same; but Pliny can only be referring to wines shipped straight from their home port to their destination, for it is improbable in the extreme that the Romans shipped their wines out and back again simply in order to give them maturity.

On the whole it appears that Italian wines were matured for longer than those which were grown outside Italy. There were, however, exceptions. Trifoline, from Campania, was supposed to mature in three years. Ulban, a light wine from Campania, was ready after five years, while Nomentan (Martial's wine) was 'drinkable after the fifth year'. But then we go into the higher ages. The thin Tiburtine, which was grown near modern Tivoli, needed ten years to mature but it was better when it had even more age. Sabine (Horace's wine), which was medium to light bodied, was 'ready to drink after from seven to fifteen years'. Falernian could be drunk after ten years but it was better with fifteen to twenty. Alban required fifteen years. The controversial Surrentine, as we have already seen, required twenty-five while Caecuban 'a generous wine, but overpowering and strong . . . matures only after many years'. These figures of maturing-age are impressive and, while we may doubt that they were always observed in practice, we can take it as certain that wines of 'many years' were a commonplace of the wealthier side of Roman life.[77]

[77]Cato, xi, i; Varro, I, 22, 4, 65; Plin., XIV, 79, 118; Colum., III, 2, 19-20, 26; 21, 6-7, 10; Hor., *Carm.*, I, I; III, 29; IV, 11; Mart., I, xviii; VI, xxvii; Ath-E, I, 26c-27d; for other references to the wines mentioned, see fns 9–19. For an example of old wine, and very old wine, as a commonplace of life, see Galen, II, 725, 738, 778.

Cask, Bottle, and Jar

In the field of maturing the Romans appear to have anticipated a good deal of modern practice. But, since the Romans lacked some of the modern techniques, we may well ask how far the age and the quality of their wines bears any relevance to the age and quality of a modern vintage.

First, let us look at some of the modern maturing. The fine red wines of Bordeaux and Burgundy spend the first two or three years of their lives in casks (in the mid-19th century Clos-Vougeot spent, on the average, the first six years in cask). The wine is then bottled and in the bottle it spends the remainder of its life which, in the case of the great clarets, may be as long as eighty or ninety years. Now basically the theory is this: the speed of maturation depends upon the amount of air that gets at the wine. The more air it gets the quicker it will mature – though not necessarily with distinction – and if it gets too much it will become vinegar.

The wood of the cask allows a moderate degree of air to get at the wine. But if the wine stayed too long in the cask it would age too rapidly. After a few years in cask, therefore, it is put into bottle. Here its 'breathing' is diminished and its maturing is slowed down. It still has a little air: it will have been aerated by its various rackings before it went into bottle; a small amount of air will have been left in the bottle before it is corked; and the cork, being porous, may allow a minute quantity of air to get at the wine. This last factor is the least important for on occasions the cork will allow no air to pass at all.

This is the basic theory and no doubt there is much truth in it. But it has to be modified. The importance of air in the maturing of wine is not quite as great as has sometimes been supposed, and there are many other factors which go to the maturing of a fine wine. But what we can affirm is that (whatever the reasons), the period in cask makes a wine 'cleaner' and more stable before it goes into the bottle and thus (with some exceptions) prepares it best for the long, slow time of its future maturing.

In general, then, wines which are to mature for longer than a few years need three things: the cask, the bottle, and the cork, the latter being an essential part of the trio because it has so far been the only substance that would properly seal a bottle. It is this trio that has made possible the maturing of nearly all the fine wines of the modern world.

Among the civilizations of antiquity that of Rome was the first to use the cask to any important extent: or, virtually, to any extent at all. It came to the Romans from the Alpine tribes and Strabo records that in the North of Italy some of the wooden wine-jars were as large as houses. Casks and barrels were not only used in the Alpine districts but also in France and on the Roman Moselle. And here in the cask, we have the first of the three instruments of modern maturing.

The other two members of the triad were not lacking either. Glass had been known long before the Romans; as early, in fact, as the 5th Dynasty of Egypt in the 3rd millennium B.C., while the making of glass increased greatly under the 18th Dynasty. But even so, glass was not exactly a commonplace object in the more ancient world and it was not until the 1st century B.C., when glass-blowing was invented, that its manufacture entered a phase of real and rapid expansion. By the 2nd century A.D. the glass industry was established at Trier and Cologne and in its

turn it reached Belgium and Britain. Nor was the industry slow to make cylindrical vessels of glass. From the 1st century A.D. glass bottles and jugs were made, some of the earlier ones being Syrian and some of the later – such as those imported into Britain – being made in Northern Gaul. These Gallic vessels are more purely cylindrical than the modern bottle; their necks rise straight out of the top of the cylinder and do not taper gradually from the shoulders; and, unlike the modern bottle, they are fitted with handles. Much nearer to the modern shape is a beautiful vessel which is now in the Museum at Speyer and which dates from the early 4th century A.D. It would have held about as much as a magnum and, although there are two handles at the base of the neck, they scarcely project over the shoulders so that the bottle could easily have been binned in a horizontal position.

The third instrument is the cork. This too was known before the time of the Roman Late Republic for the Greeks occasionally used corks as stoppers. A wine jug found in the Agora at Athens, and probably dating from the 5th century B.C., was plugged with a cork but in this case the cork was pierced with a small hole through which, no doubt, went a knotted cord to act as a 'cork-screw'. There was thus no question of the wine maturing in this particular jug which was, after all, no more than the pottery equivalent of the modern decanter.

This is, so far as I know, the earliest European instance of the use of a cork as a wine stopper, and one might have expected that the classical Greeks would have adopted such a convenient substance for closing their wine jugs and jars. But it seems that the cork was of little importance in the drinking life of the Greeks and its increased use must be counted as a development of the Romans. Horace proclaims: 'this festal day, each time the year revolves, shall draw a well-pitched cork forth from a jar'. That Horace's cork was not a fashionable toy can be seen from the fact that, a century before Horace, Cato used a cork to stopper a jar and also from a 1st century B.C. amphora which is now in the *Musée du Vin* at Beaune. This amphora, which was dragged up from a wrecked ship, was carrying wine from Pompeii to the Mediterranean coast of France, and in its neck, still firmly embedded, is a sizeable grey-black cork.

On the other hand there is no evidence to show that the use of the cork stopper was habitual among the Romans. Trimalchio's 'glass jars', whose tied-on labels bore the dubious information that the wine was 'Falernian of Opimius's vintage, 100 years in bottle',* were 'carefully fastened with gypsum'. The wine in the bottle at Speyer seems to have been sealed only with a film of oil. Amphoras appear to have been most commonly sealed with pitch or plaster, or both. Finally there is the silence of the Latin writers on the subject; if corks had been frequently used, they would have been frequently mentioned; but mention of them is rare. And there is no evidence at all to show that the cask and the corked bottle were ever used in Roman times to bring about the modern sequence of maturation. The instruments were there but the knowledge of their combination had yet to be discovered.[78]

In the Mediterranean world there was no question of any such combination for the wine-growers of the Mediterranean only used vessels of pottery. It can be argued, however, that the amphora is nothing else than a huge earthenware bottle and that wine in a sealed and impermeable amphora would have matured as well as in a bottle of glass.

The argument is not unattractive but it calls for some further observations. In the first place the wine in an amphora would not have spent its early years in a cask and it would therefore have been less 'clean' and stable than wine which had begun to age in wood. One should not, however, exaggerate the importance of wood and while amphora-wine may have been inferior to cask-and-bottle wine, it need not have been disastrously inferior. (That there was no cask-and-bottle wine does not, of course, affect the argument.)

In the second place there is the question of air. When the Romans were maturing wine, they did not always fill their jars right up to the brim, so that a space for air was left between the top of the wine and the bottom of the sealing. This was certainly a practice recommended by Cato. 'Pour the wine into the jars from the vat immediately, let them stand covered for fifteen days before sealing, leaving space for air, and then seal.' And Cato goes on: 'Forty days later pour off into amphorae, and add one sextarius of boiled must to the amphorae. Do not fill the amphorae higher than the bottom of the handles, and place them in the sun where there is no grass. Cover the amphorae so that water cannot enter, and let them stand in the sun not more than four years. . . .'

It is interesting to note that this appears to be an ancient version of the technique by which the modern *Vin santo* of Tuscany is made. The modern method is to use must from dried grapes which have been pressed, to ferment the must in tightly sealed vessels which are only filled to a little more than half their capacity, and to subject the vessels to the varying temperature of the climate so that the fermentation proceeds sporadically and over a period of from three to six years. If fully fermented the *Vin santo* is dry; if only partially fermented it is sweet, the degree of

*The Opimian vintage was in 121 B.C.

[78] Air and wine: see Pasteur, L., *Études sur le Vin* (Bibl. General), 112 sqq.; Ribéreau-Gayon, J., *Traité d'Oenologie* (Bibl. General), 202 sqq. Roman casks: Strab., 5, 1, 12; Plin., XIV, 132. In France and on the Moselle: see Loeschcke, S., *Denkmäler vom Weinbau . . ., passim.* Glass: Lucas, A., *Anc. Egyptian Materials . . .* (Bibl. Ch. 2), 529; *Hist. Tech.,* II, Ch. 9. Bottles and jugs: Ashmolean Museum, Oxford, 36–7, 1948; 1943–54, etc.; Historisches Museum der Pfalz, Speyer. Corks: Greek – I am grateful to Miss Lucy Talcott, of the American School of Classical Studies, for bringing this jug to my notice in Athens. It is No. P. 20786 and is published in Thompson, Homer A., 'Excavations in the Athenian Agora', *Hesp.,* XX, 50–1, 1951, and Pl. 25a. Corks, stoppers, etc., Roman: Hor., *Carm.,* III, 8, 10; Petronius, *Satyricon,* 34; Cato, cxx; cf. xxvi. Opimian, other references: Plin., XIV, 55–6; cf. Mart., II, xl; X, xlix.

sweetness depending, of course, on the length of fermentation. It was perhaps this ancient *Vin santo* technique which Pliny had in mind when he wrote: 'the best way of treating the finest wines of Campania seems to be to set them out in casks' (jars) 'in the open air, exposed to the sun, moon, rain and wind'.

And then in the third place there is this observation. The sealed amphora can be considered as a huge earthenware bottle; but it can also be considered as a small earthenware tank. Now in some modern vineyards wines are stored in sealed tanks which slows down their ageing and preserves their youthful freshness. The same thing must have happened to some of the wines in the sealed amphoras of Rome; and thus, for example, a Falernian of ten years old would not have been equivalent to a modern cask-and-bottle wine of ten years' age – the Falernian would have 'drunk' much younger than the modern wine. So, therefore, when we look at the age of Roman wines, we have to consider whether they were matured by the *Vin santo* or by the tank method and if they were matured by the latter, then we must scale down their calendar age into terms of their actual 'drinking' age.

As we have already seen, the 4th-century glass bottle from Speyer could well have been binned in a horizontal position and if it had been so binned it would have anticipated one of the techniques of modern cellaring. The Romans were not ignorant of 'flat' binning for, in a shop at Herculaneum, storage amphoras lay horizontally on wooden shelves. But it is doubtful if this system was ever used for glass bottles and the nearest approach to it seems to have come with vessels of pottery and not of glass. 'Bottle-shaped' pottery cylinders were made during the Empire and until the 4th century A.D. In colour they range from pale rose to brick red. They have squat necks with two small handles under the rim of the neck, projecting stub bases about three inches long, and their cylindrical bodies are ribbed horizontally all the way round. These would have been admirably suited for the bottling and binning of wine and they are all the more convenient insofar as they just hold enough for a small party to drink at one sitting. Moreover they are less fragile than Roman glass and they are more naturally fitted to a flat position than most of the glass vessels. But there is no evidence to show that the pottery cylinders, any more than the glass bottles, were deliberately made for horizontal binning or that they were ever thus stored on anything approaching a large scale.

While on this subject of Roman pottery, one might note that Roman amphoras of the late 2nd to the early 1st century B.C. tend to be very much heavier in shape than those of the Greeks and their bellies sag in a way that reminds one irresistibly of a paunch. This sag becomes even more pronounced in the 1st century A.D. One of the curiosities, almost one of the eccentricities, of Roman pottery is the 'sword-amphora', a type of thin, elongated jar about three-and-a-half feet long with scarcely any shoulders and with a body tapering evenly into a long, tapering base stub. The long neck, with its twin handles, looks like the hilt of a sword and the length and the taper of the body looks like a heavy, circular blade. Despite its adventurous name there is nothing attractive about the 'sword-amphora'. It is dull in shape and inconvenient in function.[79]

But we have not yet finished the tale of Roman maturing for there is still another complication. This is the existence of 'smoked wine'. Smoked wine does not mean Beneventine wine which was made, or partly made, from the 'smoke-grape', a

[79] *Vin santo*: for information on the modern technique I am much indebted to the Marchesa Iris Origo. Ancient technique: Cato, cxiii; Plin., XIV, 136. For the effect of the painted casks of Clos-Vougeot (in the 19th century) see Pasteur, L., *Études sur le Vin* (Bibl. General), 116. Herculaneum: see Grace, V., 'Wine Jars', *The Classical Journal*, 42, 1947. Roman amphoras: those described belong to the splendid collection of amphoras in the Stoa of Attalos, Agora, Athens; and see 'Ribbed cylinders': Agora, Nos. P. 9877, 9885, 10611, 14905, 15087.

*Wine Shop at Herculaneum
Bottle and Shelf as
discovered*

variety of grape which was probably the same as the Greek *kapneo* or 'smoky' vine.
It refers to wine which was artificially matured by the action of heat and smoke.
'Storerooms for wine,' says Columella, 'will be situated to advantage over . . . places
from which smoke is usually rising, for wines age more rapidly when they are
brought to an early maturity by a certain kind of smoke.' This action of heat is not
necessarily a bad thing, provided that it is suitably controlled, for at one stage of its
life modern Madeira is subjected to heat for about six months and Madeira, as well
as being a fine wine, lives and continues to improve for a remarkably long time. It is
clear, however, that in Roman times the process was subject to abuse. 'There should
be another loft,' warns Columella, 'to which they' (the wines) 'may be removed, to
keep them from becoming tainted . . . by too much smoking.' That they did
become tainted is shown by Pliny's casual comment that 'the smoke . . . also adds
flavour to wines' and by Martial's bitter complaint about Marseilles: 'Whatever
Massilia's vile smokerooms store, whatever jar acquires its age from the fire, comes
from you, Munna; to your wretched friends you consign over the sea, over long
roads, deadly poison, and not at an easy price, but at one which would satisfy a
crock of Falernian or Setine. . . .' No doubt it was for this reason that Pliny observed:
'Wine matured by age and not by smoke is the most wholesome.' Nevertheless,
smoked wines were acceptable and even the finest wines were not immune to this
treatment. Smoked Massic, for example, was a luxury, and to celebrate an anniversary Horace picks a smoked wine from his storeroom: Tibullus, also in festival
mood, cries: 'Now from the old bin bring . . . out the smoked Falernians. . . .'[80]

We cannot come to any definite conclusion about the 'drinking age' of any
Roman wine unless we know by what method it was matured; and, unfortunately,
it is only too seldom that we have this knowledge. We may, however, suggest three

[80]Beneventine: see fn. 12; and Plin.,
XIV, 39. *Kapnias*: see Ch. 3, fn.
129; Colum., I, 6, 20; Plin., XIV,
16; XXXIII, 39; Mart., I, xxvi; III,
lxxxii; X, xxxvi; XIII, cxxiii; XIV,
cxviii; Hor., *Carm.*, III, 8; Tibullus, II, I.

213

propositions: first, that the old wines of the Romans often drank somewhat younger than the number of their years might lead us to suppose; second, that the more aged wines of the Mediterranean were not quite as good as they would have been if they had been matured by the cask-and-bottle method; and third, that the wines of the 'cask-areas' – which must in large part include Bordeaux, Burgundy and the Moselle – were not able to live for anything like as long as the longer-lived of the wines of the Mediterranean.

But if our picture of Roman maturing has perforce to remain rather general, and therefore rather confused, we may console ourselves with the thought that the Roman taste in wine was itself confused. There is no doubt that pure wine was appreciated; but there is equally no doubt that confused wines were enjoyed. From its earliest years the Roman palate had been accustomed to this confusion, to the taste of resin, to the flavour of herbs, and to the presence even of perfume. It was not only a matter of the 'perfumes' which were put into the wine as preservatives but of perfumes, such as myrrh, which were put into the wine to give it an extra and special fragrance. This habit, we may think, was not of great importance for banquets were themselves sometimes scented with perfume and who, in a scented room, can appreciate the bouquet or the flavour of a wine? 'Fill to the brim with care-dispelling Massic the polished goblets! Pour out perfumes from generous phials! Who will make haste to weave garlands of pliant parsley or of myrtle? . . . 'Tis sweet to make mad holiday when a friend has been regained.' So Horace. His sentiment about friendship is impeccable but his Massic, if it had any grace to show, can scarcely have shown it. It may be fair to assume that the banquets of the Romans did not smell as pungently as the feasts of ancient Egypt but there must have been many occasions when their fragrance was, to say the least of it, perceptible. And again it is only fair to add that perfumes were not inevitable and their use was often a matter for mockery.

But even supposing that perfumes had not been there to mask the delicate qualities of the wines, would these qualities not still have been perverted by preservatives? Columella does, indeed, say that salt need not give any extra taste to a strong wine and he also gives us a way of preserving 'the whole vintage with . . . pitch in such a way that it is impossible to tell from the taste that it has been preserved with pitch'. Obviously he knew what he was talking about, for he was a skilled and intelligent man and something of a purist in the growing of wine. But it is hard to believe – I find it impossible to believe – that he was representative of the majority of Roman wine-growers. Some men made pure wine, or wine which at least appeared to be pure, and I think it probable that the growers of the better wines tried to achieve this result. But for the rest we must take the view that the *vignerons* frequently failed to disguise the taste of their preservatives and frequently, in fact, used that taste to disguise the imperfections in their wine.

It seems to me that the position is summed up by Martial. Addressing Baeticus, who ate and drank those things which had the coarsest and strongest taste, he says: 'You drink resined wine, avoid Falernian.' The implications in the Epigram which contains this line are that Falernian was unresinated, that Baeticus could have afforded to drink it, and that it was, therefore, an expensive wine. The implication is also that the resined wine which Baeticus did drink was not only a coarser, but a cheaper, wine. Thus we get the theorem: 'pure' wine for the rich, *retsina* for the poor. About the *retsina* of the poor there is no doubt; and one remains a little sceptical about the real purity of the wines of the rich.[81]

Intemperance

The excesses of the Few appeal greatly to the imagination of the Many. And many there have been whose imagination was so powerful that it could only picture the wealthier Romans as gross shapes moving in a haze of excess. They have been visualized as bestial gluttons who reeled with unsteady lechery through monstrous orgies. The villas and the palaces echoed, we might think, with the songs of drunkards and the willing screams of wantons. The picture is that of the Golden Age of Vice but the picture is, to put it mildly, over-painted.

No one would seriously suggest that the Romans were a nation of sobersides. On the contrary, they could boast of many a notable drinker. There was the Milanese Novellius Torquatus who won a name for his ability to drink some ten litres at a draught. Pliny tells of 'some men taking a dose of hemlock before they begin in order that fear of death may compel them to drink'. It is possible that Pliny is trying to be satirical but, if so, the satire is veiled. Martial has a galaxy of topers. There was Acerra who always drank till daylight. There was the woman Myrtale – 'flushed and with swollen veins' – who was 'wont to reek with much wine'. And there was the mean figure of Aper who, when he was poor, fulminated against drinking at the baths but, inheriting some money, 'doesn't know how to go home from the warm baths sober'. Then again here is Juvenal fulminating against the luxury of his times:

'Filthy lucre first brought in amongst us foreign ways; wealth enervated and corrupted the ages with foul indulgences. What decency does Venus observe when she is drunken? When she knows not one member from another, eats giant oysters at midnight, pours foaming unguents into her unmixed Falernian, and drinks out of perfume-bowls, while the roof spins dizzily round, the table dances, and every light shows double!'

Alcoholic enthusiasm was not confined to the wealthier classes. On the fifteenth of March the New Year festival of Anna Perenna was celebrated. This, as Ovid says, was a 'jovial feast'. It was held just outside Rome near the Tiber and to it 'the common folk come, and scattered here and there over the green grass they drink . . .' Some of them pitched tents, some made huts of boughs, while others made shelters of cloths stretched on reeds. They sang and danced and drank 'and they pray for as many years as they take cups, and they count the cups they drink'. The young men, being accompanied by their sweethearts, had extra opportunity of merry-making. 'On the way home they reel, a spectacle for vulgar eyes . . . I met the procession lately; I thought it notable; a drunk old woman lugged a drunk old man.' A different holiday vignette is sketched for us by Seneca and records at Baiae, near Naples, 'persons wandering drunk along the beach, the riotous revelling of sailing parties. . . .'

One has to be a stern critic to condemn these outbreaks of popular insobriety,

[81]Plin., XIV, 92-3, 107; Colum., XII, 20, 6-7; 21, 5-6; 23, 2-3; 28, 4; Hor., *Carm*., II, 7; Mart., III, lxxvii; V, lxiv; XIV, cx; but see VI, lv.

and to condemn them as a distinctively Roman vice shows merely an ignorance of history. Our own age is not without its parallels. But the thing which has distorted our view of Roman excess is not this casual intoxication but the deliberate intemperance which led to vomiting. We are too often hypnotized by Seneca's bitter remark: 'they vomit that they may eat, they eat that they may vomit. . . .' It is not a question of doubting Seneca's word, for he is speaking the truth, and not only about gluttony but also about drunkenness. 'What glory is there in carrying much liquor?' he asks. 'When you have won the prize, and the other banqueters sprawling asleep, or vomiting, have declined your challenge to still other toasts. . . .' There is nothing but ugliness also in the conduct of the virago whom Juvenal describes. She comes in late from the baths and 'tosses off a couple of pints before her dinner to create a raging appetite; then she brings it all up again and souses the floor with the washings of her inside. The stream runs over the marble pavement; the gilt basin reeks of Falernian, for she drinks and vomits like a big snake that has tumbled into a vat'.

These criticisms bite deep but they do not bite wide. The fact that people got drunk at the feast of Anna Perenna, and that 'the mob is drunk and vomiting' at the festival of Saturnalia, meant only that these were annual and careless outbursts. They have nothing to do with the prevalence of vomiting among what were supposed to be the more cultured classes. We may doubt, in fact, that vomiting was really prevalent at all. Seneca and Juvenal were attacking particular abuses and while it seems evident that the abuses were not exactly rare, it is improbable that they affected any wide area of Roman life. There is moreover another side to this question of vomiting and one that is exemplified in the conduct of Augustus. By nature he was a temperate drinker and 'in later life his limit was a pint; if he ever exceeded this he would deliberately vomit'. One does not suggest that Seneca's revellers eased themselves for the same healthful purpose but we may assume that 'abstemious vomiting' was not uncommon in Roman manners and that it was a custom of moderation perverted to suit the beastliness of drunkards and gluttons.[82]

Since the Roman people loved their tipsy festivals it is curious that the god of wine played such an undistinguished part in their beliefs. Bacchanalia – the Dionysiac mysteries – were known at Cumae, near Naples, as early as the 5th century B.C. and they attracted a considerable following in the south of Italy. But, in part at least, they became corrupted into a neat blend of lasciviousness and fraud and in 186 B.C. they were suppressed by the Roman Senate. Later they revived, and they continued to be popular, but their motive was mainly religious and had little to do with wine. Bacchus, a Lydian name for Dionysios, played no part in the Roman world as awe-inspiring as Dionysios had played among the Greeks. Even the native Italian god of fertility and wine – Liber Pater – became a dim shadow of the Greek Dionysios. The only contribution of the Romans to the mythology of wine, if in fact it is a contribution and not merely a take-over from Hellenistic art, is the emphasis upon Silenus as an old and rather comic drunkard, soggy with wine, and swaying on an ass.

In this intoxicated posture he might seem to reflect one aspect of the merriest and probably the most drunken of the Roman festivals, the Saturnalia, which took its name from an obscure, and possibly Etruscan, god called Saturnus. It began on

[82]Plin., xiv, 138, 144; Mart., I, xxviii; v, iv; xii, lxx; see also I, xxvi and lxxxvii; Ovid, *Fasti*, III, 523 sqq.; and *Fasti*, Appendix, 405 sqq.; Seneca, *Epist.*, li; Seneca, *Epist.*, xviii, 4; li, 4; lxxiii, 24; *Moral Essays*, *Ad Helv.*, x, 3; Juvenal, *Satires*, vi, 298–305, 425–32; Suet., *Augustus*, 77.

December 17th and was a period of licence, during which gambling became legal, presents were given, slaves were allowed a temporary freedom, and, so it seems, there could be a Lord of Misrule. The cap of liberty was worn and drinking was the order of the day. Pliny the Younger describes how, at the feast of the Saturnalia, 'my villa resounds with the mirth of my domestics' and the happy anticipation of this holiday is summed up in a *graffito* from Pompeii – '*Saturnina Io Saturnalia*'.[83]

The degree of welcome extended by the slaves to this holiday is given point by some repellent advice which Cato offered to the careful farm owner. Counselling him to go over the accounts of the farm with his overseer and to give him instructions as to what must yet be done, Cato adds: 'Sell your oil, if the price is satisfactory, and sell the surplus of your wine and grain. Sell worn-out oxen, blemished cattle, blemished sheep, wool, hides, an old wagon, old tools, an old slave, a sickly slave, and whatever else is superfluous.' This type of merciless economy was not necessarily universal. Yet even Columella, who prided himself on talking 'rather familiarly with the country slaves', and who could remark 'when I perceived that their unending toil was lightened by such friendliness on the part of the master, I would even jest with them at times and allow them also to jest more freely', added as a matter of course: 'it is the established custom of all men of caution to inspect the inmates of the workhouse, to find out whether they are carefully chained, whether the places of confinement are quite safe and properly guarded, whether the overseer has put anyone in fetters or removed his shackles without the master's knowledge'. Columella seems to have been a comparatively humane man; how comparative his humanity was can be seen from a statement of his at the end of the same passage: 'To women too, who are unusually prolific, and who ought to be rewarded for the bearing of a certain number of offspring, I have granted exemption from work and sometimes even freedom after they had reared many children.' To men and women who laboured under such conditions the liberty of Saturnalia must in every sense have been intoxicating.[84]

It would be quite wrong, however, to assume that slaves were always treated as captive animals. Under the Empire at least, a slave could lead a fairly reasonable life; the more capable he was, the more valuable he was to his owner, and therefore the more reasonable were his conditions. Similarly, it would be wrong to imagine that Roman insobriety was divided exclusively between common festivals and private orgies. Like most other peoples the Romans enjoyed a genial drinking party and saw no harm whatever in becoming mellow. One method of attaining this happy end was to number the measures of wine poured into the cup by the letters of one's mistress's name. Other names could also be used in the performance of this courtesy: those of friends, those of patrons, and those even of Caesar himself. The happy effect, not necessarily due to alphabetical drinking, is variously recorded. Cicero writes to Trebatius Testa and confesses that he 'returned home comfortably mellow and at a late hour . . .' Martial – 'I think it was after I had got through ten half-pints' – invited Procillus to dinner the next day: and regretted it. Even Ofellus, Horace's paragon of rustic frugality, says that when a friend came to see him, and when they had dined: 'then we had a game of drinking, with a forfeit to rule the feast. . . .' Doubtless no heel taps. One wonders how often Cato's advice was regarded on these occasions: 'If you wish to drink deep at a banquet and to

[83]Bacchanalia in Italy: Livy, XXXIX, 8 sqq. Bacchus: cf. Ovid, *Fasti*, III, 713, 771-2. Saturnalia: Mart., XV, xlvi; VII, liii; XI, vi; Ovid *Fasti*, 395-6 for speculation about the Lord of Misrule; Pliny the Younger, *Letters*, II, 17; Tanzer, Helen H., *The Common People of Pompeii*, 94.

[84]Cato, ii; Colum., I, 8, 15-19.

enjoy your dinner, eat as much raw cabbage as you wish, seasoned with vinegar, before dinner, and likewise after dinner eat some half a dozen leaves; it will make you feel as if you had not dined, and you can drink as much as you please.'

It was disregarded, perhaps, by Phryx:

> 'The toper Phryx was scant of sight,
> His left eye blind and bleared his right.
> The doctor frankly spoke his mind,
> "Cease drinking, sir, or go stone blind."
> Phryx laughing cried "Farewell my peeper!
> Large glasses, ho! I'll drink the deeper".'[85]

Gilt Dates, and Dancing Girls

The early character of the Romans, simple, practical, and self-reliant, underwent some degree of change when the hard-working farmers became the masters of the world. But the temper of frugality was not destroyed; it persisted throughout the centuries of the Empire. There were many lapses into immorality and dishonesty and ludicrous ostentation. Yet the hard, frugal streak continued to animate the thoughts of philosophers as it did the mockery of satirists, and from economic necessity it dominated the life of the great majority of the people of the Empire.

It was this streak, for example, which underlay the repeated censure of the dancing girls of Andalusia. 'Girls from wanton Gades with endless prurience swing lascivious loins in practised writhings' is the view expressed by Martial and Martial was no prude. Juvenal has almost exactly the same picture: 'You may look perhaps for a troupe of Spanish maidens to win applause by immodest dance and song, sinking down with quivering thighs to the floor. . . . My humble home has no place for follies such as these. The clatter of castanets, words too foul for the strumpet that stands naked in a reeking archway, with all the arts and language of lust, may be left to him who spits wine upon floors of Lacedaemonian marble. . . . .' Yet still the castanets of these Spanish girls clatter unabashed through the pages of the Roman poets.

There may have been in these strictures something of envy – this after all is a not uncommon motive of social criticism – but it seems more likely that the motive was a genuine condemnation, not so much of the erotic, as of the general 'wantonness' – or perhaps we should say the 'unseriousness' – of these performances. The Younger Pliny writes to Genitor: 'I have received your letter, in which you complain of being highly disgusted lately at an entertainment, though exceeding splendid, by a set of buffoons, fools, and wanton prostitutes, who were playing their antic tricks round the tables.' We have no cause to think that Genitor was being insincere. He, like the poets, was attacking that extravagant unseriousness which offended against the deep-seated Roman instinct for a somewhat grave simplicity.

The critics turn, too, upon other extravagances of behaviour. They laugh at the collector of supposedly, but improbably, genuine antiques. They paint the unappetizing picture of the miser Santra who angles for an invitation to a feast, scoops into his napkin the choice bits and the sad leavings of the food and then 'when that

[85]Mart., I, xxvii, lxxi; VIII, li; IX, xciii; XI, xxxvi; the spirited translation of the Epigram on Phryx is from Francis, A. L., and Tatum, H. F., *Martial's Epigrams*, VI, lxxviii; Cicero, *Letters to his Friends*, VII, 22; Hor., *Sat.*, II, 2, 123; Cato, clvi; but cf. Theophrastus, *Enquiry into Plants* (Bibl. Ch. 3), IV, 16, 6.

218

greedy fellow has carried these things home up two hundred stairs, and anxiously shut himself in his locked garret, the next day – he sells the lot'. With unkind precision they describe the cosmeticizing Thais who 'whenever she strips and enters the bath . . . is green with depilatory, or is hidden behind a plaster of chalk and vinegar, or is covered with three or four layers of sticky bean-flour'. When they were castigating folly the Roman poets could write without compassion.

Martial is our daily guide to the richness and poverty of Imperial Rome. In this he was an expert for he came to Rome from Spain when he was about twenty-four years old and could view the Roman scene with the comparative clarity of an adult expatriate. Furthermore his view of the life of Rome was a wide one; it ranged from the Imperial Court to the company of friends such as Seneca, Juvenal and Pliny the Younger and to an intimate knowledge of the life of the poor among whom he himself lived. His poverty sharpened the edge of his satire and gave to his *Epigrams* the hard and living feel of Roman life. The old worn cloak, of which he ironically complains: the splendid toga which was his pride when new and which he laments when threadbare: these are almost as intimate to us as our own clothes. Vividly his experience shows us what life was like for the less prosperous inhabitants of Rome.

Martial lived in a garret 'up three flights of stairs, and high ones' in the Quirinal district. Later he was able to take a house but even so it was one of the few in Rome which did not have water laid on to it from an aqueduct. And in each of these dwellings he could find little peace. 'Do you ask,' he writes, 'why I often resort to my small fields in arid Nomentum, and the unkempt household of my villa? Neither for thought, Sparsus, nor for quiet is there any place in the city for a poor man. Schoolmasters in the morning do not let you live; before day-break, bakers; the hammers of the copper-smiths all day.' Money-changers, gold-beaters, and the clashing of pots and pans increased the din. 'The laughter of the passing throng wakes me, and Rome is at my bed's head,' he ends. 'Whenever, worn out with worry, I wish to sleep, I go to my villa.' He was lucky to have a villa. And though he is rueful about its impoverished smallness, it must have been a blessed escape from the swarming, over-crowded city. It was an escape too from the weary toil of clientship.

In Early Rome clientship was a social bond and the client received the protection of his patron. But in the time of Martial it was little more than a common form of parasitism. The client was a paid hanger-on. His duty was to attend upon his patron and to greet him in the morning. In return he received (sometimes) a free dinner or else the 'hundred worthless farthings' which were a customary payment to a client in Imperial Rome. 'At length spare, O Rome, the weary congratulator, the weary client! How long, at levees, among the escort and the full-dressed throng, shall I earn a hundred worthless farthings in a whole day. . . .' And Martial again: 'I must surmount the track up the hill from the Subura and the dirty pavement with its steps never dry, and I can scarce break through the long droves of mules and the blocks of marble you see hauled by many a cable . . . more annoying still – after a thousand exertions, Paulus, when I am fagged out, your doorkeeper says you are "not at home"! Such is the result of misspent toil, and my poor toga drenched!'

Then, even when the client was invited to dinner – as Juvenal says – 'what a dinner after all! . . . See now that huge lobster being served to my lord, all garnished with asparagus. . . . Before you is placed on a tiny plate a crab hemmed in by half an egg – a fit banquet for the dead'. And much more on the same unappetizing theme.

This form of clientship was ceremonial begging, servile and undignified, and there is something pathetic about the gilded date which poor clients offered as a gift to their patrons on the kalends of January. Martial hated his rôle as a client but at least it gave him some sort of an income, and at least the system was more honest than the practice of legacy hunting which gave scope for a rich display of talented hypocrisy.

Martial did lapse into flattery from time to time but he was no hypocrite. He writes about his clientship with a sense of humour and makes no excuse for his type of life. In his own mind, no doubt, it needed no excuse. He was a good poet; had something to give in return for his dole. And, as a matter of fact, although he was always poor, he did not have such a bad time. Some of his patrons may have been tiresome; but from one of them at least he experienced generosity, and he was rewarded too by the generosity of his friends. When late in life he returned to Spain it was Pliny the Younger who paid for his journey, and there, at Calatayud in Northern Spain, he settled down to a life of frugal ease on a property given to him by a patroness.

From Spain he writes to his friend Juvenal: 'While perchance you are restlessly wandering, Juvenal, in the noisy Subura . . . while, amid the thresholds of great men, your sweaty toga fans you . . . I enjoy a huge unconscionable sleep . . . and I pay myself now in full for all my sleeplessness for thrice ten years. . . . When I get up, a fire, served with a lordly heap of logs from the neighbouring oak-wood, welcomes me, and my bailiff's wife crowns it with many a pot. . . . So I love to live, so I love to die.'[86] He did both well.

The Cost of Keeping Alive

Martial knew a great deal about poverty. Though not himself among the poorest, the surroundings in which he lived would have taught him everything that he needed to know. We do not have the fullness of his knowledge. From other sources, however, we can make some estimate of what, in terms of prices, poverty meant and the part which wine was able to play in the life of the ordinary people.

About 150 B.C. the normal price for an agricultural slave seems to have been in the region of 500 denarii or 2,000 sesterces. At the same period the wage of a free labourer, which naturally kept down near the level of the cost of slave labour, was most probably about 3 sesterces a day, only just above the daily 'wage' of 2 sesterces for a slave. In Central Italy at this time ordinary wine probably cost about 20 sesterces for a 26 litre amphora, or about three-quarters of a sesterce the litre.

But there were other prices. At the middle of the same century, wine in the Po Valley was remarkably cheap and was obviously being sold at glut prices because it could reach no other market. In Lusitanian Spain wine was also cheap at this period and cost only about a sixth of what it cost at Rome. In both of these areas food was cheap when compared to Roman prices and therefore it is possible that the labourer in the remoter districts lived somewhat better than his Roman, or Central Italian, counterpart.

In the next century – in 89 B.C. – the maximum price for 'Greek and Aminean wine' was fixed by the Censors at 400 sesterces the amphora, or about 15 sesterces the litre. (Where the sources do not give the capacity of the amphora, I am assuming it to have been the 'standard' size of 26 litres.) Chian and Falernian wines were, it seems, actually sold at this price so that a jar of one of these two wines would have cost a hundred times as much as the daily wage of a free Roman labourer.

[86]Dancing girls: Mart., v, lxxviii; Juvenal, *Satires*, XI, 162–75; see also Mart., VI, lxxi; cf. Propertius, *Elegies*, IV, 39; and Pliny the Younger, *Letters*, I, 15; Pliny to Genitor, IX, 17. Antiques, Santra, Thais: Mart., VIII, vi; VII, xx; VI, xciii; his cloak and toga: VI, lxxxii; VIII, xxviii; IX, xlix; his garret: I, cviii, cxvii; VI, xxvii; his house: IX, xviii; X, lviii; noise: XII, lvii; his villa: VII, xciii; IX, xviii, xcvii; X, lviii; XII, lvii; clientship: I, cviii; v, xxii; X, lxxiv; XIII, xxvii; and cf. VIII, xxxiii; legacy-hunting: VI, lxiii; XI, lv; retirement in Spain: XII, xviii. Clientship: see also Juvenal, *Satires*, v. For Roman housing, see also Carcopino, J., *Daily Life in Ancient Rome*, 31 sqq., also his comments on the water supply of Rome, 46–7.

221

By the middle of the 1st century A.D. ordinary Italian wine cost 15 sesterces the amphora or just over half a sesterce the litre. It is difficult to tell whether this was the wholesale or the retail price but it is likely that the workman in Rome would have had to pay a little more than half a sesterce for his litre of wine. If, however, he was content, or forced, to drink a cheaper wine, then he could most probably have bought Spanish at rather less.

During the 3rd century A.D. prices began to rise sharply and one result of the inflationary process was the Edict of Diocletian on maximum prices. This gives us a very full picture of the (maximum) price structure in A.D. 301. In the lower wage groups a shepherd got 20 denarii a day, a farm labourer 25 denarii, and a stonemason 50. All of these figures include maintenance. An advocate, however, got 1,000 denarii for pleading a case. In the lower levels of the wine prices we find that ordinary wine cost 8 denarii for half a litre. Twice as expensive, at 16 denarii the half litre, was one-year-old wine of the second quality and this was also the price for one type of boiled-down must. Wormwood wine cost 20 denarii the half litre and spiced wine 24 denarii. This latter, too, was the price of first quality one-year-old wine. The 'named' wines of the Edict – Picene, Tiburtine, Sabine, Aminean, Setine, Surrentine, and Falernian – all had their maximum price fixed at 30 denarii the half litre.

These are, of course, maximum figures and we cannot assume that wine always fetched these prices. But we can at least compare them with the maximum prices which were set for other things. Celtic beer cost 4 denarii the half litre; ordinary oil 12 denarii the half litre; salted fish was 6 denarii for about three-quarters of a pound, fresh cheese 8 denarii for the same amount; green, shelled beans were 4 denarii for about half a litre, cabbages cost 4 denarii for ten, while eggs or oysters were 1 denarius each. A dormouse cost 4 denarii.

These were all, except perhaps for oysters and dormice, in the class of basic food. Moving a little higher up the scale we find that the best quality of honey cost 40 denarii for half a litre although the same amount of Phoenician date honey could be bought for 8 denarii. Three-quarters of a pound of goat's meat, or mutton, cost 8 denarii, of beef sausage 10 denarii and of sardines 16. I cannot resist quoting a few extra details from this long and very interesting list. A wolfskin, untanned, cost 25 denarii. Oil of roses, first quality, cost 70 denarii the pound. Good boots for mule drivers or farm workers cost 120 denarii the pair.

Finally, perhaps, it might not be out of place to mention here the oft-quoted but still instructive inscription of Aesernia which dates from the Empire and which purports to be the comments of a traveller on paying his bill at an inn. Wine appears to have cost him nothing, or at all events its price is not mentioned. Bread cost him one as (a sixteenth of a denarius), meat two asses; he paid two asses for the hay for his animal and to the girl at the inn he gave eight. This traveller was not happy about the price of the hay but he seems to have been happy about the girl.[87]

One cannot argue a great deal from all these figures. To say that the poor lived on, or only just above, subsistence level is not a statement of any novelty. And there are other considerations which we have to take into account. Some of the city poor, for instance, got their baths and circuses and their doles of corn at reduced prices. Along the coastlines, fish, and in the countryside, vegetables, must have

[87]Frank, I, 170, 188-9, 193, 195-7, 200, 284, 384-5. Roman Egypt: Frank, Johnson, II, 176 sqq., 314-15. Roman Syria: Frank, Heichelheim, IV, 184. Roman North Africa: Frank, Haywood, IV, 80-2. Edict of Diocletian: Frank, Graser, V, 322 sqq.; and cf. Coleman-Norton, P. R., *Studies in Roman Economic and Social History* . . . (West, L. C.), 292. See also Frank, Tenney, *An Economic History of Rome*, 338 sq. Colum., III, 3, 10; Mart., XII, lxxvi; Ros., *SEHR*, 190-1, 470. Aesernia: *CIL*, IX, 2689; and Kleberg, 118-19.

eked out many a slender diet. In vineyard areas wine cannot always have cost as much as it did in the cities. And then, when we are looking at the price which the townsman had to pay for wine in a city, we must remember that he drank it diluted so that a litre of wine would have gone further with him than it does with us. That many men of the Roman world were extremely poor is obvious. But we may wonder if they were much worse off than some of their descendants in the modern Mediterranean.

The Sweetness of Life

Dum vixi bi (bi) libenter; bibite vos qui vivitis.

So runs the message left by a Roman legionary who stated that while he lived he drank with a good heart and who recommended his friends to follow his example. This is one view of the enjoyment of life.

Here is another. Beneath a vine trellis loaded with clusters of grapes, and ranged behind a sickle-shaped table, sit eleven Roman people at an open-air feast; and, because it is a feast they are crowned with garlands. This picture, although it comes from a tomb and may thus be a comment upon the shortness of life, must also reflect the sweetness of life and the gaiety of many an autumn holiday. Varro presents us with another charming picture for he relates that some people, when they build a fruit-house, coat the walls and ceiling and floor with marble cement to keep it cooler and 'even spread a dining-table in it to dine there'. This is the charm of the country life but there is a sting in the tale for Varro adds: 'provided always that you do not follow the example set by some, of buying fruit in Rome and carrying it to the country to pile it up in the fruit-gallery for a dinner-party'.

Garlands played an important part in Roman life; how important this was can be seen from Cato's instruction that 'near a town it is well to have a garden planted with all manner of . . . flowers for garlands'. There were, of course, many purposes for which chaplets and garlands were made and by no means all of them were concerned with drinking. They were used on religious occasions, as prizes for sport, and as offerings at tombs. Nor were they only made of flowers. There were the 'chaplets of cinnamon surrounded with embossed gold' which Vespasian dedicated in the temples of the Capitol and of Peace. There was the crown of grass voted by an army to a man who had saved it from a perilous situation. For less heroic occasions there were, in Pliny's day, winter chaplets 'made from dyed flakes of horn' while women who considered themselves smart used chaplets made 'of multi-coloured silk steeped in perfumes'.

In the earlier days of the Republic garlands seemed to have been sparingly used at feasts and banquets and may have been confined to the decoration of the room rather than the adornment of the feasters. Later, however, chaplets became a usual feature of the revels, being worn not so much at the dinner itself as at the drinking bout which followed. In the 1st century A.D. they seem to have been made only of violets or roses. Such at any rate is Pliny's view and as a generalization it is probably true enough. Roses were undoubtedly the most popular, especially those grown at Praeneste outside Rome and in Campania, and in this latter district there grew, though no doubt among other kinds, 'the hundred-petalled rose'.

223

The love of flowers, or the pleasure of flowers, was not confined to the wealthier classes. Pliny gives us a sad insight into the life of the poorer people who crowded the teeming apartment houses of Rome: 'Indeed the lower classes in the city used to give their eyes a daily view of country scenes by means of imitation gardens in their windows, before the time when atrocious burglaries in countless numbers compelled them to bar out all the view with shutters.' Real gardens designed for pleasure belonged only to men of some wealth, but even these were not immune from the depredations of the less well off. A statue of Priapus, a godlet in the shape of a small, grotesque man with outsize genitals, was sometimes put into a Roman garden in order to protect it; but Priapus was himself occasionally stolen from the garden which he was supposed to guard. It was an undignified end for a god who had once been given as his parents the great figures of Dionysos and Aphrodite.[88]

The town garden of pleasure was not an invention of the Romans. The country villa of pleasure was almost entirely their creation. The ancient Egyptian house-with-garden was not comparable with the Roman country villa and the Greeks were not interested in the countryside as a place for pleasure or retreat. It was the Romans who first emphasized the pleasure of living in the country and who laid such stress upon the peace and the beauty of the country house. Many of these houses were not, strictly speaking, country houses but seaside villas, such as the magnificent summer palaces along the coastline of Campania. Others, serving equally as holiday retreats, were along the shores of lakes and among these were the 'several villas' which Pliny the Younger had along the edge of the Larian Lake (Lake Como).

Many of the Roman villas, however, were designed for profit as well as for pleasure, the one part of the villa serving as a farm and the other as the more or less luxurious residence of the owner. The Campanian villas of Pompeii illustrate the theme of profit. That of profit and pleasure combined is illustrated by the huge and splendid villa on the island of Brioni Grande in Istria. This villa, which was devoted in part to the making of oil, had long terraced colonnades, roofed against the sun and looking down on the sea. It owned spacious baths, a fish tank, a harbour, and a garden; and in the curve of the bay three temples, linked by a semi-circular colonnade, formed the background to a fine quay.

The joy which the Romans took in their pleasure-villas is one of the more engaging traits of the Roman character. It is one which brings them close to us because we share their taste for the country house and the country life. Here is Cicero, writing in about 61 B.C.: 'I have built some new reading-rooms in a little colonnade at my Tusculan villa, and I should like to decorate them with pictures: as a matter of fact, if anything of that sort gives me any pleasure at all, it is painting.' And to his brother, in September of 54 B.C., he writes: 'Your landscape gardener won my praise; he has so enveloped everything with ivy, not only the foundation wall of the villa, but also the spaces between the columns of the promenade, that I declare the Greek statues seem to be in business as landscape-gardeners, and to be advertising their ivy.'

Nor is it difficult for us to share the enthusiasm of Pliny the Younger when he writes of his 'Tuscan' villa which lay below the Apennines in Umbria. He describes the view: 'Before you lies a vast extended plain bounded by a range of mountains, whose summits are crowned with lofty and venerable woods. . . .' Lower down there were small and fertile hills and 'at the foot of these hills the eye is presented, wherever it turns, with one unbroken view of numberless vineyards'.

Then, with pride, he turns to the villa itself. 'In front of the portico is a terrace divided into a great number of geometrical figures, and bounded with a box-hedge. The descent from the terrace is a sloping bank, adorned with a double row of box-trees cut in the shape of animals. . . .' He describes the rooms of the villa, how

[88]Dill, S., *Roman Society from Nero to Marcus Aurelius*, 499, and fn. 4; Reinach, S., *Rép. de Peintures Grecques et Romaines*, 257, 1; Cato, viii, 2; Varro, I, 59, 2; Plin., XII, 94; XIX, 59; XXI, 1 sqq.; XXII, 6-8; Mart., III, lviii, 47; VI, xxii; VIII, x; Hor., *Sat.*, I, 8; and Priapus: Strab., 13, 1, 12; Pausanias (Bibl. Ch. 3), IX, 31, 2. Campanian garland industry, see Ros., *SEHR*, Pl. xiv, 4.

some catch the sun, how some remain cool in the hot weather and he dwells lovingly upon one particular room of his private apartments, which, being near a plane-tree, 'enjoys a constant shade and verdure; its sides are covered with marble up to the cornice: on the frieze above a foliage is painted, with birds perched among the branches, which has an effect altogether as agreeable as that of the marble. In this room is placed a little fountain, which, playing through several small pipes into a vase, produces a most pleasing murmur'.

But his delight, or at least his artistic delight, is really in the garden. 'Having passed through . . . manifold winding alleys, the path resumes a straight course, and at the same time divides into several tracks, separated by box-hedges. In one place you have a little meadow; in another the box is interposed in groups, and cut into a thousand different forms; sometimes into letters, expressing the name of the master, or again that of the artificer: whilst here and there little obelisks rise inter-mixed alternately with fruit-trees: when on a sudden, in the midst of this elegant regularity, you are surprised with an imitation of the negligent beauties of rural nature. . . .'

Then, at one spot in the garden, there was 'a semi-circular bench of white marble, shaded with a vine which is trained upon four small pillars of Carystian marble. Water gushing through several little pipes from under this bench . . . falls into a stone cistern underneath, from whence it is received into a fine polished marble basin, so artfully contrived that it is always full without ever overflowing. When I sup here, the tray of whets [hors d'oeuvre] and the larger dishes are placed round the margin, while the smaller ones swim about in the form of little ships and water-fowl. . . .' There must have been many moments here by the marble pool when life had the taste of sweet and scented honey.

Simpler, and nearer – indeed very near – to the heart of the Latin world, is this other picture drawn from the same Pliny: 'In compliance with the advice of the *haruspices*, I intend to repair and enlarge the Temple of Ceres, which stands upon my estate. It is . . . not only very ancient, but small, considering how thronged it is upon a certain anniversary. On the 13th of September, great numbers of people from all the country round assemble there, many affairs are transacted, and many vows paid and offered; but there is no shelter hard by against rain or sun.'[89]

This, like the centurion's vine-rod, is the country reality behind the Roman magnificence.

[89] Ros., *SEHR*, Pls viii, ix, xli; and cf. Pl. lix; Mart., I, cviii; Cicero, *Letters to his Friends*, VII, 23; for his Cuman and Pompeian villas, see VII, 4: Cicero, *Ad Quintum Fratrem*, III, 1; Pliny the Younger, *Letters*, V, 6; IX, 7; IX, 39; for his other villas, see II, 17; and V, 6. On his 'Tuscan villa': Frank, V, 172.

NOTE: References for wines, etc., listed in Appendix C (Wines: Ancient Roman) but not discussed in the text of this chapter are – Aigleucos: Plin., XIV, 83. Crhysatticon: *Edict. Dioc.*, II, 1, 14. Erbulan: Ath-E, I, 27c. Hydromel: Plin., XXII, 110-12; Dioscorides, *Herbal*, V, 17; Celsus, *De Medicina*, I, 497; and cf. Colum., XII, II, 1-2. Mustum tortivum: Colum., XII, 36, 1. Oxymel: Plin., XIV, 114; Galen, II, 726, 728, etc.; Celsus, *De Medicina*, I, 497. Precian: Colum., III, 2, 23; Plin., XIV, 29. Protagion: Plin., XIV, 76. Protropum: Plin., XIV, 75, 85. Semper mustum: Plin., XIV, 83.

CHAPTER FIVE

The Middle Ages

The New Mind

Dramatically it is fitting that Ausonius should have been a man of Bordeaux since it was at Bordeaux, on the line between the Latin and the Gothic worlds, that Ausonius suffered his tragedy. In the vast scale of human pain it was a minor incident. To us, however, it is dramatic because it illuminates a radical movement in the history of the human mind. When we watch Ausonius at Bordeaux, and when we see him caught in bewildered grief like a fly twisted in amber, we are not only witnessing a personal tragedy but are watching also the defeat of the Latin attitude and the approaching triumph of the Gothic vision.

The Gothic line runs through St. André de Cubzac, a small town at the head of the Gironde estuary. To the north, in the time of Ausonius and despite all their romanization, Gaul and Britain remained sensitive to the pressures of either the Celtic or the Germanic consciousness. But to the south of St. André de Cubzac Narbonensian Gaul was deeply permeated by the patterns of the Mediterranean. There, life was cast in a Latin mould and the mind imagined with a Latin predilection. Bordeaux was the space between the two worlds of the spirit.

Ausonius lived, reputedly, at that part of St.-Emilion which is famous among modern wine-lovers as Château Ausone. He may indeed have had a property there but it is possible that his *herediolum* – his 'little inheritance' – of a thousand acres, of which a hundred acres were vineyard,[1] was at Bazas, south-east of Sauternes and that it was near Bazas, as he himself wrote, that 'my own vineyards cast their reflection on the yellowing Garonne'.[2] Ausonius had a pleasant life, cultured, prosperous, and successful. The son of a Bordeaux doctor, he became a Professor of Rhetoric at the University of Bordeaux where he taught for thirty years. Appointed tutor to Gratian, his success followed the life of his pupil. When Gratian became Emperor, Ausonius was made Governor of Gaul and, in A.D. 379, Consul. From his Imperial

[1] Auson., *De Herediolo.*

[2] Auson., *Mosella,* 160.

227

pupil he received honour which he was never weary of recalling. But from another pupil, Paulinus, he received a rebuff which he was never able to understand.

In this lay the tragedy. Paulinus was not only the favourite pupil; he was also the loved friend. Ausonius and Paulinus had much in common. They were both men of Bordeaux, they were both cultured versifiers, they had both been Consuls. Ausonius set a high value on friendship, particularly on this one, and there seemed every reason for it to be prolonged in warm and constant communication. But Paulinus retired into Christianity and communication ceased. Desperately Ausonius tried to prod his friend out of the impregnable silence. The effort seemed to have been successful since it provoked a response, but the success was as bitter as defeat. In fact it was defeat. Paulinus wrote and asserted his love for his old master. He also denied the world which his old master loved. The affectionate rebuff must have seemed as cruel as it was incomprehensible.

It seems that nominally Ausonius was a Christian but it is quite clear that he did not understand Christianity. His was the Mediterranean mind, a mind to which the idea of a living eternity, of a real life for All for Ever, was fundamentally alien. This world was the only world. It was beautiful and desirable and it was not to be denied. It followed as a matter of course that a friendship in this world was of more value than any speculation about an improbable eternity.

But Paulinus, absorbed in the passion of Christianity, relentless in the development of his faith, comprehended the timeless nature of the new Paradise and saw nothing unnatural in disregarding his friends. This life, and the things of this life, were ephemeral. If they stood between the soul and Heaven, then they must be disregarded. And if disregard meant the sacrifice of a friendship in this world, what did that matter? In eternity friendship would be eternal.

'I have a new mind, I confess – a mind not my own,' he wrote to Ausonius.[3] One can imagine how the Professor of Rhetoric, wandering through his vineyards at Bazas, must have resented this Christian God who changed men and gave them new minds and broke up old friendships. And Ausonius was left in no doubt about the new mind of his friend, for Paulinus had also written: 'A short-lived thing is man at best, man with his frail body and passing season, dust and a shadow without Christ. . . .'[4] Then, worse still, he had turned upon life and had spoken of 'the prison of the body'.[5]

To Ausonius this latter view must have seemed a delusion, for he himself could not see life that way. He saw it as a sculptor sees it: immediate, solid, sensual. Or as a poet sees it: present, always present, and in its manifestations beautiful. 'The thrush . . . which has torn the gleaming clusters from the vines'[6]: bird nets which 'in the evening hour float loose like clouds, or in the morn are taut with dew'[7]: Paestrum roses wet with dew in the dawn – (this poem is of the feeling though not necessarily of the authorship of Ausonius)[8]: these things were tangible and inescapable, the bodily things of a bodily world. To love or be loved, to make or to feel beauty, the body was essential. It was the very privilege of life.

The Middle Ages were to reject this simple idea. They were to see the body as a thing of shame, as a trap and a hindrance, and this curious concept was to run riot over the Christian world, distorting art and denying beauty. The note is sounded already by Paulinus: 'Why dost thou bid the deposed Muses return to my affection,

[3] Auson., *Epist.*, XXXI, 142.

[4] Auson., *Epist.*, XXXI, 288-9.

[5] Auson., *Epist.*, XXX, 57-8.

[6] Auson., *Epist.*, XVIII.

[7] Auson., *Epist.*, XVIII.

[8] Auson., Vol. II, Appendix, 277; *De Rosis Nascentibus*, 11-12.

*Vine Training
from 'Livre des Prouffitz
Champetres'
Petrus de Crescentis,
1529 ed.
London, British Museum*

my father? Hearts consecrate to Christ give refusal to the Camenae, are closed to Apollo.'[9] Paulinus was a good man but in his words one can hear, centuries ahead, the cramped yelping of the puritans.

Ausonius did not understand the new faith of his friend. Nor did he suspect – how could he have done? – that this faith would change the whole texture of western civilization. To him the world was still pagan. He could not have guessed that when, in the last years of his life, the Eleusinian mysteries were performed, they were performed – at least officially – for the last time. And to him, also, the world was still Roman. He did not hear, or if he heard he did not comprehend, the ominous thunder along the Roman frontiers. The Huns were in Transylvania. The Visigoths had slain the Eastern Emperor at the Battle of Adrianople. The Roman world was breaking. Fifteen years after Ausonius died Alaric sacked Rome.

Yet even in the century after Ausonius the Roman life persisted. We see the sunset of the Empire in the *Letters* of Sidonius Apollinaris. He, too, was a Gaul, though one from eastern France, from Lyons. He, like other Gallo-Roman nobles, lived in the atmosphere of Roman culture, enjoying the villas and libraries, the sophisticated dinners and literary exercises. But while he and his friends maintained the manners of Rome the Visigoths were the political masters. They were not always bad masters and often the barbarians were treated with curiosity rather than fear. Curiosity is the dominant attitude in the description which Sidonius gives of 'the young prince Sigismer' (who was possibly a Frank) 'on his way to the palace of his father-in-law in the guise of a bridegroom or suitor in all the pomp and bravery of the tribal fashion'. The prince:

[9]Auson., *Epist.*, XXXI, 19–22.

'went afoot amid his bodyguard and footmen, in flame-red mantle, with much glint of ruddy gold, and gleam of snowy silken tunic, his fair hair, red cheeks and white skin according with the three hues of his equipment. But the chiefs and allies who bore him company were dread of aspect . . . their feet were laced in boots of bristly hide reaching to the heels; ankles and legs were exposed. They wore high tight tunics of varied colour hardly descending to their bare knees, the sleeves covering only the upper arm. Green mantles they had with crimson borders; baldrics supported swords hung from their shoulders, and pressed on sides covered with cloaks of skin secured by brooches. No small part of their adornment consisted of their arms; in their hands they grasped barbed spears and missile axes; their left sides were guarded by shields, which flashed with tawny golden bosses and snowy silver borders. . . .'

Nevertheless fear was obtrusive. In another letter Sidonius writes: 'though the Goths have broken their old bounds, though their valour and the impetus of a vague greed have pushed their frontiers to the Rhône and Loire. . . .' And again: 'Our town lives in terror of a sea of tribes which find in it an obstacle to their expansion and surge in arms all round it. We are exposed as a pitiful prey at the mercy of rival peoples, suspected by the Burgundians, almost in contact with the Goths . . .' And again: '. . . a race of uncivilized allies directs the Roman power, yes, and bids fair to bring it crashing to the ground'.[10]

Gothic Wine

Economically as well as politically, the Western Empire was destroying its own achievements. By the 4th century, the century of Ausonius and Paulinus, the senatorial class was rejecting urban civilization. It was withdrawing from the cities to live instead in 'large and beautiful fortified villas in the country' and there its wealthier members were 'surrounded by . . . slaves, a real retinue of armed clients, and thousands of rural serfs and dependents'. A rigid economic policy gave no scope for initiative, whether in trade or agriculture. The small farmer was becoming a bound tenant, in fact a form of serf. Irrigation systems were being left to decay and land was falling out of cultivation.

We have already seen that at the beginning of the 4th century the low-lying lands of the Côte d'Or in Burgundy were swamps and the vines were tangled masses of huge roots. In the next century we come across another aspect of decay in Gaul though this time, curiously enough, it concerns the Church herself: 'Diocese and parish lie waste without ministers. You may see the rotten roofs of churches fallen in, the doors unhinged and blocked by growing brambles. More grievous still, you may see the cattle not only lying in the half-ruined porticoes, but grazing beside altars green with weeds. And this desolation is not found in country parishes alone; even the congregations of urban churches begin to fall away.'[11]

But there were brighter scenes to set beside these sombre ones and now and again the sunlight glows through the pages of Sidonius and lights up the happier stretches of the Gallic countryside. Having stayed for a time with two of his friends, Sidonius describes their estates and comments with pleasure that 'the hills above the houses are under vines and olives'. To another friend he writes: 'I hear that your

[10] *Sidonius, The Letters of,* IV, xx; III, i; III, iv; III, viii.

[11] Ros., *SEHR,* 530-1, and see 522 sqq.; Frank, Tenney, *Aspects of Social Behaviour in Ancient Rome* (Bibl. Ch. 4), 88. Côte d'Or: see Ch. 4, p. 163. The Church: *Sidonius, The Letters of,* VII, vi.

vines have responded to your hard work and our general hopes with a more abundant harvest than a threatening and lean year promised. I expect that you will consequently stay longer at the village of Vialoscum' (probably just to the north-west of Clermont-Ferrand) '. . . of course you have a rich vineyard there, and a large farm besides . . .' And of Auvergne he says: '. . . pastures crown the hill-tops and vineyards clothe the slopes . . . villas rise on the lowlands and castles on the rocks, forests here and clearings there, valleys with springs, headlands washed by rivers. . . .'[12]

This picture of Auvergne is as idyllic in its own way as that which Ausonius gave of the Moselle Valley in the 4th century. Then vines covered the Moselle hillsides, villas graced the banks of the river and, as mute witnesses to civilization, smooth, sawn blocks of marble lay waiting along the course of the Ruwer. Ausonius, of course, adds a classical-romantic filling to his picture:

> 'I can believe that here the rustic Satyrs and the grey-eyed Nymphs meet together on the border of the stream, when the goat-footed Pans are seized with merry ribaldry. . . . Then, wantonly frolicking amid their native waters, the Nymphs duck the Satyrs in the waves, and slip away right through the hands of those unskilful swimmers, as, baffled, they seek to grasp their slippery limbs and, instead of bodies, embrace yielding waves.'[13]

But then there is a breath of chill barbarian wind and suddenly the Satyrs are gone. The wind ripples the surface of the river and gone also is the mirrored reflection of the idyllic scene. A cloud comes over the sun. Its shadow darkens the valley of the Moselle and spreads over the landscape of Auvergne and the storm of the barbarian invasions rises to blow away the brittle peace of the Roman sunset.

When morning comes after the long night of wreckage it is, to be sure, a grey, uncertain morning. Still, there is light again, raw and flickering. One can see that, whatever else of civilization the barbarians may have destroyed, at least the vine-yards of France and Germany had suffered no irreparable disaster. On the Moselle there was no setback – or no permanent setback – for in the latter half of the 6th century Fortunatus takes up the tale which was told by Ausonius two hundred years before. It is also likely, not only that vineyards had existed in the Palatinate in the 3rd century, but that they continued to exist after the fall of the Roman Empire. And then, in the 7th century, vineyards were spreading along the Main in Fran-conia where we find that vines were being planted at Kitzingen and Ochsenfurt by Benedictine nuns.[14]

In fact the barbarian domination was not at all hostile to viticulture. On the contrary, it was beneficial. The vineyard area did not contract. It was maintained and even expanded, and this happened in France as well as in Germany. Gregory of Tours could announce in the 6th century that the Dijon *vignoble* produced a con-siderable amount of quality wine which, not unnaturally, was reckoned by the honest men of Dijon to be superior to that grown at the same period in the vine-yards of Chalon-sur-Saône.[15] Then also the forests of Burgundy were being cleared, new vineyards, fenced and guarded, were being planted and gradually the great names – Gévrey, Vosne, Beaune, and Aloxe – begin to come up into the history of Western wine.[16]

[12] *Sidonius, The Letters of*, II, ix; II, xiv; IV, xxi.

[13] Auson., *Mosella*, 21, 169-85.

[14] Venantius Fortunatus, *Die Mosel-gedichte*, III, 12, 39-40; X, 9, *passim*. An interesting collection of Pala-tinate material is in the Wein-Museum at Speyer. Some of it has been published in Bassermann-Jordan, F. von, *Das Wein-Museum im Historischen Museum der Pfalz zu Speyer am Rhein*. Main: Hall-garten, S. F., *Rhineland Wineland* (Bibl. General), 124.

[15] Salin, E., *La Civilisation Méro-vingienne*, I, 463; Dill, S., *Roman Society in Gaul in the Merovingian Age*, 311.

[16] Dill, S., *Roman Society in Gaul in the Merovingian Age*, 68, 69, 75; Rodier, 6.

In the Ile de France, too, there appears to have been a development of viticulture. We cannot be certain that it was development and not merely a continuation, but development does seem the more probable. At all events, in about A.D. 814 the *Roll of the Abbot Irminon* lists vineyards in the *arrondissements* of Versailles, Rambouillet, Pontoise, Dreux, Sceaux and Fontainebleau. Some of these were very small, being only half or quarter of an acre, but others were of considerable size and could even be as large as a hundred and forty-three acres.[17] The *Roll* shows us, too, the men who worked these Carolingian vineyards. At Villanova, for example, which is now Villeneuve-Saint-Georges in Seine-et-Oise, lived Girelmus, a tenant of the Abbey of St. Germain des Prés, a 'free' man but bound to the soil. With him was his wife Sicleverta and their four children, Gibernus, Girberga, Ildeburs and Hildesindis. The family had four acres of vineyard – which must have kept them busy – and, among other payments, Girelmus had to give two modios* of wine for the right to pasture his livestock.[18]

Further south along one of the tracks of barbarian migration lay the vineyards of Bordeaux and there is little reason to believe that they suffered any worse at the hands of the invaders than did the other vineyards of France. What actually did happen is somewhat obscure for as far as its *vignoble* is concerned Bordeaux passes through the Dark Ages in comparative silence. It is tempting, however, to argue from the fact of the increase of other vineyards and to suggest an analogous increase in the vineyards of the Gironde. Even if this were so, one must still note that, although there seem to have been some vines in the Médoc, they do not appear to have been important. Indeed it seems clear that the development of the Médoc vineyards is a matter of later history.[19]

It is curious to think that the development of gothic vineyards nearly spread as far as the eastern seaboard of North America. In A.D. 1000 Leif Ericson, 'Leif the Lucky', son of Eric the Red, landed near – probably – Boston. There he discovered vines whose grapes were so abundant that on one occasion the crew gathered enough to fill the ship's stern boat. It was considered that wine made from these American wild grapes could be very good and Leif called this new country 'Vinland'. Whether any wine was in fact made in 11th- and 12th-century Massachusetts we do not know. There may well have been several 'Vinland vintages' since the contact with America lasted for a hundred and twenty-one years and in 1112 Pope Paschal II made the Icelander Eric Gnupsson Bishop of Greenland and Vinland '*in partibus infidelium*'. In 1121 the worthy Bishop sailed in search of his flock, or of wine, or – with the civilizing zeal of the Church – in search of both.[20] But no more was ever heard of him. North America receded into shadow and so did the possibility of medieval American wine.

Church Wine

It has often been assumed that a good deal, and even a great deal, of the spread of the northern and western vineyards was due to the spread of the Christian churches. One of the arguments which underlies this assumption goes as follows: where there was a church there was a Mass: if the church had no vineyard to provide wine for

*For medieval measures see Appendix D, below.

[17]Longnon, A., *Polyptyque de l'Abbaye de Saint-Germain des Près (Roll of the Abbot Irminon)*, II, I, 7, 29, 41, 48, 98, 202, 258.

[18]*Ibid*, II, 219. For a picture of life on these estates, see Power, Eileen, *Medieval People*, chapter on Bodo.

[19]Lafforgue, 72.

[20]Fiske, John, *The Discovery of America*, 165-6, 181, 198, 209, 212, 222-3.

the Mass, then a vineyard had to be planted: and thus the impetus for the creation of new vineyards arose from the necessities of the Sacrament.

I do not think this argument is tenable. Many of the early churches would not have had the man-power to plant and cultivate a vineyard. Nor would they have had the incentive to do so, since wine for the altar would more easily have been provided by the offerings of the faithful. Donations for the churches were of common occurrence and out of innumerable examples we may instance three. There was the pious widow, cited by Gregory of Tours in the 6th century, who brought daily to her church – probably the basilica of Sainte-Marie at Lyons – a measure of wine which had been imported from Gaza★ in Palestine.[21] In England in 1076 Robert de Todeni gave the tithes of all his vineyards for the endowment of the Priory of Belvoir.[22] A few years later Robert, Earl of Leicester gave to the Cathedral Church of St. Mary, Evreux, three muids of wine annually from his vineyards at Paci for the celebration of the Mass.[23] Gifts of this kind seemed natural, and indeed inevitable to an age which believed in the awful reality of Hell as much as it believed in the difficult harbour of Heaven. It was only logical, by invoking the special prayers of the Church, to endeavour to ease the translation of a particular soul from the torment of Purgatory to the ecstasy of Paradise; and it was a short step from the gift of wine or tithes to the gift of a vineyard itself. Another element in the transfer of land was the desire of kings or nobles to provide for the economic upkeep of a religious house, but the motivation for all these gifts of land was, of course, a mixed one, guilt, repentance, statecraft, and piety each contributing its quota. The result, however, was the same and the Church took possession of vineyards which had been created by laymen.

The Burgundian donations are clear evidence of the process. About 587 the King of Burgundy gave land near Dijon 'with its vines' to the Abbey of Saint-Bénigne.[24] At the foundation of Bèze by the Duke of Lower Burgundy in the 7th century, vines at Gévrey, Vosne and Beaune were given to the Abbey.[25] The churches received Aloxe in 696, Fixey in 733, Fixin, Santenay, Auxey, and Chassagne in the 9th century, Savigny in the 10th, and Pommard and Meursault in the 11th.[26] And, since there was nothing exceptional about Burgundy, we can visualize the same process at work in the other wine-producing areas of Christendom.

This does not mean that the Church never created its own vineyards and to suggest that it never did so would be ridiculous. The Benedictine nuns who were responsible for planting vines at Kitzingen and Ochsenfurt were by no means unique in their outlook and many a monastic foundation would have laboured to the same purpose. The religious houses had, here and there, the man-power for this type of work and those which were animated by the Benedictine spirit of *laborare est orare* would often have turned their dedicated hands to the making of a monastic vineyard. This they did, to take another example, at Shrewsbury in England where, in the 13th, or possibly even earlier in the 12th, century land was given to the Benedictine Abbey of SS. Peter and Paul for the purpose of planting a vineyard. But at the same time we have no reason for assuming that the Monastic Movement was the great impetus behind the vineyard-makers and we must discard the notion that the Church was supremely responsible for the increase of Western viticulture.

★For medieval wines and their vineyards of origin, see Appendix F, below.

[21] Gazetic, or Gazetine (wine from Gaza): Salin, E., *La Civilisation Mérovingienne*, I, 443, 464, No. 32; see also Sidonius, *Poems*, XVII, 15.

[22] *Monasticon*, III, 284; see also Belvoir in Appendix F.

[23] *Cal. Docs. Fr.*, I, 102.

[24] Rodier, 5.

[25] Rodier, 6.

[26] Rodier, 6.

Another theory holds that it was the Church which brought the tradition of viticulture over from Roman times, safeguarding it during the years of invasion and anarchy, and deploying it once again in the fullness of the Middle Ages. This theory is patently untrue. The Church had little, if anything, to do with the transmission of viticulture from the Ancient into the Christian world. Wine-growing was brought over the Dark Ages by private enterprise, and the traditions of viticulture were continued through the memories of lay *vignerons* rather than through the manuscripts of monastic libraries.

The case of Portugal may illustrate the theme. There, where a militantly Christian civilization drove the Moors back over the Tagus and down into the southern province of the Algarve, one might have expected that the Church would have been mainly responsible for the planting of new vineyards. It is doubtful, indeed, if this was so. For example the *forais*, the charters, of Arganil and Penedono in east-central Portugal, while they demonstrate the existence of vineyards at these places in the last quarter of the 12th century, give us no cause to alter our belief that the vineyards existed for the profit of lay owners.[27] In any event the example of the Church was not necessary to teach viticulture to these newly conquered, or reconquered, lands since viticulture was widely practised under the domination of the Moors.

Witness Muslim Spain. It is true that in Andalusia many of the grapes were for eating or for making into raisins; but nevertheless, although the fermenting of grapes might have to be conducted under the cloak of a tactful silence,[28] wine was still made and it was actually exported from Malaga.[29] Edrîsî's description of Murcia and Andalusia in the middle of the 12th century shows how numerous and how widespread were the *vignobles*. Denia, Alicante, Almeria, and Priego all had their vineyards, while 'Xerès' – our modern Jerez de la Frontera – was surrounded by them. Even the Balearic island of Iviza was planted with vines.[30]

It is fascinating to follow Edrîsî across Southern Spain and from his terse descriptions to build up a picture of the medieval country. One sees it mainly as a green and brown tapestry studded with fortified towns. There are, of course, the vineyards and along the rivers the numerous mills of which Edrîsî makes particular mention. There are many of them, he tells us, on the river Guadalbullón outside Jaén and he notes that when one travels from Seville to Cordoba one passes the 'mills of az-Zarâda' and later those of Nâcih. Then at the centre of the whole tapestry is the great city of Cordoba, a city made up of five separate towns, each one of them walled, and the centre of Cordoba, the centre of the centre, being that wonderful mosque which we see now as a forest of slim pillars and red-and-white arches.[31]

But let us return from the vineyards of Muslim Spain to those of the Christian Church. The Christian vineyards were not solely – and not even principally – intended to provide wine for the Mass. Their main function was not religious but economic. They were donated, or created, in order to contribute to the upkeep of a foundation and the wine which they produced was an important element in the finances of that foundation. It was inevitable that the Church should become a landowner and it was perhaps natural that it should not have been a particularly benevolent one. Its attitude towards agricultural profit was on the whole severely practical and its view of agricultural trade was seldom distorted by sentiment. In the earlier centuries in Germany the monks were in control of the wine trade[32] while in

[27]*Portugaliae Monumenta Historica,* I, 403, 499.

[28]Lévi-Provençal, E., *L'Espagne Musulmane au Xème Siècle*, 168.

[29]*CMH*, III, 433.

[30]Edrîsî, 233, 235, 245, 252, 254, 266.

[31]Edrîsî, 248, 256 sq.

[32]Langenbach, A., *The Wines of Germany*, 23.

234

13th-century France – to cite only two examples – the Bishop of Agen and the Archbishop of Bordeaux sold large quantities of their wines.[33]

Some interesting figures of ecclesiastical wine-growing can be gathered from the early 9th-century *Roll of the Abbot Irminon*. From a property at Villemeux, in the *arrondissement* of Dreux, the Abbey of St. Germain des Près could collect 150 *modii* of wine: from one at Thiais, in the *arrondissement* of Sceaux, it could collect 1,300 *modii*. At the lowest estimate this makes a total of 11,600 gallons and the actual total (which depends upon the uncertain size of the *modius*) may have been very much larger.[34] Not all of this wine would have been available for the market since a proportion of it would have been used for the Mass. The consumption of sacramental wine in a large monastery of modern England is 155 gallons a year, this amount providing for an average of twenty-five to thirty Masses each day. It is possible, of course, that in the 9th century the laity may have had communion in both kinds but even so, and even allowing for any 'dependent' churches which there may have been, the sacramental consumption of the Abbey of Saint-Germain could not greatly have exceeded 2,000 gallons a year. At a low computation this leaves about 9,000 gallons a year for the market – or for the monks.

How much did the monks get? How often was their preoccupation with Eternity interrupted by wine from their own vineyards? The modern imagination has been captivated by the picture of smiling churchmen and laughing monks, well-fed and well-content, gossiping or carousing at the refectory table.

The picture is exaggerated. Still, in varying degrees it had some reality:

'Mother and sister, ease a fuddled man.
Across a sea of wine the table swims . . .'[35]

This was Venantius Fortunatus in the 6th century, a gentle man who loved his food and wine and who became Bishop of Poitiers. Another cleric, Abbot Adam of Angers, located in the 9th century or before, was perhaps only a legend in a drinking song. He was a mighty figure with an inexorable thirst:

'Never did a day or night go by,
But it found him wine-soaked and wavering . . .'[36]

So much did he drink that his skin became dyed with wine and his body immune from corruption. Some three hundred years later that tempestuous Welsh churchman Giraldus Cambrensis acidly noted, when he dined with the monks at Canterbury, that the refectory table carried 'wine, mead, mulberry juice, and other strong drink . . . in such abundance . . . that beer . . . found no place there'.[37] If Giraldus had known of them, he would doubtless have been shocked by the sophisticated habits of an Archbishop of Ravenna . . . 'who was wont to pace through his palace chanting a responsory or an antiphon to the praise of the Glorious Virgin, from one corner of the palace to the other: and in every corner in the summer time, stood a flagon of a truly remarkable wine, cooling in ice-cold water'.[38]

In general, however, ecclesiastical drinking was neither luxurious nor intense. The Rule of St. Benedict, compiled about 529, allowed a pint of wine a day to a

[33] Simon, André L., *The History of the Wine Trade in England*, I, 108.

[34] Longnon, A., *Polyptyque de l'Abbaye de Saint-Germain des Prés*, II, 98 sqq., 202 sqq.; for the modius see Appendix H.

[35] Jack Lindsay, *Medieval Latin Poets*, 35.

[36] Helen Waddell, *Medieval Latin Lyrics*, 138–41.

[37] *Giraldi Cambrensis Opera*, I, xxxii.

[38] Helen Waddell, *The Wandering Scholars*, 179.

sick monk, or more at the discretion of the Prior, and a pint of wine a day is not an extravagant ration. On the other hand the Rule observes rather sadly that, although monks ought not to drink wine, they cannot be convinced of this proposition and therefore '. . . let us at least agree not to drink to satiety, but sparingly'. This argues a certain amount of vinous enthusiasm and the strength of the monks' conviction that wine was a good thing is emphasized by the punishment meted out to those who were late for grace, for their wine was taken from them.[39]

Not all monks were so fortunate as to have wine. Sedulius, the Irish scholar, utterly condemned the bad beer at Liège[40] and what he, for lack of anything better, was forced to drink, monks of all the medieval centuries would frequently have had to swallow. However rich Canterbury may have been, however laden with 'strong drink' its refectory table, the drink of most English monks was beer,[41] as it was of the ordinary people in much of northern and north-western Europe. Even when the monks did drink wine, and even in the wine-producing countries, their wine was – at least sometimes – cloudy and unracked. This complaint, which comes from the *Bible Guiot* in 12th-century France, adds that clear wine went only to certain abbots and cellarers and to those monks who organized the outlying monastic estates.[42] The complaint may have been edged with a genuine indignation against the pampered ranks of the monkish hierarchy but it was also barbed with a personal resentment, for the minstrel who wrote it, 'Guiot de Provins', came to the monastic life as a worldly man with experience of good food and good wine. He liked good company too, as well as good living. The solitary discipline of the Carthusians horrified him and he preferred the more genial life of the Augustine Canons who not only fed well and were well-dressed but also had good wines.[43] But, although Guiot may have been indignant about class-consciousness in the distribution of wine, he should not really have been surprised, for the same principle was common in medieval life. In the previous century, for instance, a class-distinction between the qualities of wine given out as rations was observed at the Court of the Norman Kings.[44] And Guiot should have known as well as anybody that as the Church became more of a worldly organization, so it was bound to reflect the habits of the worldly life.

On occasion it reflected them vividly. Here, from the middle of the 13th century, is the protest of the Renclus de Moiliens:

> 'Clers mangiere, trop me desplais . . .
> Mieus sés sermoner d'un saumon
> Ke des Proverbes Salemon.'[45]

And here the imagination leaps again to the favourite picture of the well-fed monk. But in the same way that not every dinner in ancient Rome was punctuated by visits to the vomitorium, so not every medieval churchman was a gourmand. The majority of priests, monks, and friars were men who lived in poverty and integrity, abstinent from choice or obligation, genuinely trying to help a sinful and suffering world. Whatever one's views about the sin, there is no question about the suffering in those dark and cruel centuries, and one does not grudge the men of religion their occasional cup of clouded wine.

[39] Trs. Cardinal Gasquet, *The Rule of St Benedict*, cap xi, pp. 74-5; cap. xliii, p. 80.

[40] Helen Waddell, *The Wandering Scholars*, 85-6.

[41] *VCH, Hunts*, I, 379. See also *Roll. Swinfield*, II, xlvi-lxvii; *Cart. Mon. Ram.*, II, 206; Neilson, N., *Economic Conditions on the Manors of Ramsey Abbey*, 55.

[42] Langlois, C. V., *La vie en France au Moyen Âge*, II, 74.

[43] *Ibid*, II, 49.

[44] Hall, H., *The Red Book of the Exchequer*, III, fo. 30, 807.

[45] Langlois, C. V., *La vie en France au Moyen Âge*, II, 170.

*Monk with Cask
from 'Livre de Sante'
Aldebrandin de Sienne
14th century
London, British Museum*

The English Vineyards

The vineyards of medieval England have long been accepted as a matter of fact but their full significance has continued to be something of a mystery. The sceptical have doubted their purpose and the romantic have exaggerated their prevalence. On the one hand it has been argued either that they were not vineyards in the proper sense of the term because they were not intended for the production of wine, or that they were little more than token vineyards planted to satisfy a Norman nostalgia for the grapes of France. On the other hand it is theorized that they were a typical feature of monasteries in the more southerly counties of England, and this theory, leaping from an unchecked assumption to an unwarrantable conclusion, asserts that the Church may claim the real honour of having, for a time, turned England into a wine-growing country.

Surmise and uncertainty remain because the subject, so far as I know, has never been fully treated. A few serious writers have dealt with these vineyards but only in the context of themes which did not demand an extensive and numerical analysis.[46] Their work has been of great value since they considered the vineyards with sanity and erudition and put their existence into a proper perspective. Our

[46] See, for example, the useful discussions in: Henderson, 267-73; Simon, André L., *The History of the Wine Trade in England*, I, 1-18; Hyams, Edward, *The Grape Vine in England* (all in Bibl. General); Amherst (Bibl. Ch. 5).

purposes in this chapter, however, demand a numerical investigation and this I have attempted to make. I have worked through the records and have listed a hundred and thirty-nine definite or possible vineyards of medieval England,* a figure which is nearly three times as high as any enumeration yet known to me. Even so, I do not believe that my figure can represent a final count. I think it likely that there were at least a hundred and fifty vineyards and I think it conceivable that there were quite a number more. Nevertheless our list of a hundred and thirty-nine should enable us to form a reasonably detailed picture of the viticulture of England in the Middle Ages.

Bede is our witness for the earlier Anglo-Saxon vineyards. There are vineyards in some places, he says.[47] But we must treat his evidence with caution, as we must also when, in the same chapter of his *History*, he tells us that in Ireland there was no lack of vines. This may have been so, and the plants may have been brought from France by the scholars who travelled to the Irish Schools. Yet when Giraldus Cambrensis visited Ireland – though admittedly some four hundred and fifty years later – he said that there were no vines in Ireland.[48] If they had been there in the time of Bede, it seems curious that the practice of viticulture had died out by the time of Giraldus. The only grounds left to us on which we can build a shaky speculation about the existence of Irish *vin ordinaire* are those of climatic possibility and the liking which medieval Irish scholars had for wine.

They seem to have liked wine as much as they liked cats. 'Three young clerics of the men of Ireland went on their pilgrimage. . . . There was no provision taken to sea save three casks. "I will bring the little cat," says one of them. . . . Not long afterwards they came with Christ's help to a beautiful island. . . . The little cat goes from them. It draws to them a veritable salmon, up to three salmons for every (canonical) hour.'[49] A skilled and worthy cat indeed. Then there was Pangur Bán, the mouse-hunting companion of the scholar who, commenting on the two of them – 'Pangur Bán, my cat, and I' – as they sat together in the scholar's quiet room, observed, not without irony:

'Practice every day has made
Pangur perfect in his trade;
I get wisdom day and night
Turning darkness into light.'[50]

On the other hand there was the sinister story in the Life of Brenainn, son of Finnlug, of the island west of Aran where 'dwelt mice like sea-cats' who ate the buffoon in a ship's party 'save a few of his bones' and 'he was a wonderful martyr'.[51]

The vines of Ireland may not have been as phantasmal as the 'mice like sea-cats', and Bede's English vineyards may have been perfectly real. We remain in doubt. But we can be tolerably sure that vineyards existed in England by the end of the 9th century for the Laws of King Alfred ordain: 'If any one injure another man's vineyard, or his fields, or ought of his lands; let him make "böt" as it may be valued.'[52] Just over half a century later, in 956, we know of a vineyard at Pamborough in Wedmore in Somerset which belonged to Glastonbury Abbey. Six

*They are listed in Appendix F, below. The alphabetical list gives details of the individual vineyard.

[47] Bede, *Ecclesiastical History of England*, Bk I, Ch. 1.

[48] *Giraldi Cambrensis, Opera,* I, xxxix-xl; *Topographia Hibernica,* Distinctio, I, cap. vi.

[49] Stokes, Whitley, *Lives of Saints from The Book of Lismore,* viii-x.

[50] Flower, Robin, *Poems and Translations,* 129-30.

[51] Stokes, Whitley, *op. cit.,* 257

[52] Thorpe, Benjamin, *Ancient Laws and Institutes of England,* Laws of King Alfred, cap. 26.

years after that King Eadgar gave to Abingdon Abbey a vineyard at a place which is probably Watchfield in the Vale of the White Horse in Berkshire. And then we find that sometime in the 11th century a Greek monk called Constantine made a vineyard near the monastery of Malmesbury.

Such scattered references are tantalizing. If there were two, or possibly three, vineyards in England before the date of the Norman Conquest, then there may very well have been others. We should like to know something about them and we should even like to know more about the vineyards which are recorded. What was the size of the vineyard at Pamborough in Wedmore? Where did the Greek monk Constantine get his vine plants and from what stock did they originate?

We know of only two vineyards which were definitely established in England before the Norman Conquest. In 1086, twenty years after the Conquest, we know of thirty-nine and the total *vignoble* area – *Domesday* does not record the size of four of its vineyards – would have been about a hundred and thirty acres.[53] The largest vineyard was at Bisham in Berkshire. It consisted of about twelve acres and belonged to Henry de Ferrers. The next in size was at Belchamp Walter in Essex and belonged to Aubrey de Vere. It was of about eleven acres and one notes that in 1086 it was a new vineyard of which only one acre was bearing. Ranking just below it was Geoffrey de Mandeville's vineyard of about ten acres of Great Waltham in Essex. Altogether eight of the *Domesday* vineyards were of five acres or over but the most frequent size was two acres and the smallest of all was the half-acre owned by Edward of Salisbury at Lacock in Wiltshire.★

Our knowledge of the earlier, Anglo-Saxon, vineyards being so sparse, we cannot say with any certainty that it was the Normans who gave the great impetus to English viticulture. On balance, however, it seems most likely. And it was not a mere temporary enthusiasm, for, in addition to the *Domesday* series, at least another ninety-six vineyards were cultivated in England between the Norman Conquest and the Dissolution of the Monasteries. It is not always easy to identify the exact location of the vineyards but it seems that they occurred in twenty-four of the counties of England, from (possibly) Yorkshire and (certainly) Cambridgeshire to Kent and (most probably) Devon. In numbers Worcestershire leads with seventeen, closely followed by Essex with sixteen. Buckinghamshire has only one.

The pattern of original ownership is enlightening. If we discount Chart Sutton and Leeds in Kent, which we have to do because their status is uncertain, then we are left with twenty-five *Domesday* vineyards which belonged to laymen. Only ten vineyards belonged to the Church. Out of these ten, three were the property of St. Mary of Glastonbury, and two of Ely, while the remaining five belonged, one each, to Shaftesbury, Canterbury, Evesham, Muchelney, and Westminster. Over and above the twenty-five lay vineyards there were two, though curiously enough only two, which belonged to the King, one at Westminster, and one at North Curry in Somerset, the latter being of about seven acres.

In contrast to this royal paucity Aubrey de Vere had four vineyards, one each at Belchamp Walter and Castle Hedingham in Essex, one at Kensington in Middlesex, and one at Lavenham in Suffolk. There were other, and lesser, cases of plural lay ownership: Edward of Salisbury had two, Lacock and Wilcot, both in Wiltshire;

★See also the Statistical Survey in Appendix F, below.

[53]See the Statistical Survey in Appendix F.

Ranulf Peverel had two, at Debden and Stebbing in Essex: Eudo Dapifer also had two, one at Eaton Socon in Bedfordshire and the other at Mundon in Essex.

The preponderance of lay over church vineyards is carried through, though less notably, in the total figures for the whole period. Against the seventy-eight lay and royal vineyards there were fifty-two which belonged to the Church; and although there were in all probability more vineyards than I have been able to trace, thus perhaps altering the proportion of lay to clerical, it is at least clear that the lay interest was marked.

It is as well to point out here that apart from the problems of determining location and original status, there are other difficulties in the listing of the English vineyards. One of these difficulties lies in the words which the records use to describe them. *Vinea*, for example, can mean a vineyard or a single vine. *Vinarium* – York – though possibly used in this case to mean a vineyard, could also be interpreted as a garden containing a few vines. Occasionally the description, as at Kensington, is merely a 'vine-garden'. Equally inadequate is the phrase which occurs in the *Calendar of Inquisitions Post Mortem* and which gives at Portbury in Somerset, 'two gardens with vines . . . in them'. In all these doubtful cases context and probability have to help us towards a decision.

Yet another problem is the extent to which one can use the evidence of place-names. The word 'Wynyard' may seem to imply the existence of a vineyard. It may do so but it may equally mean an enclosed meadow.[54] Thus we find in 1326 that a manor at Erith in Kent included a place called 'la Wynyerd', we have to ask whether it was vineyard or meadow, and here unfortunately, neither context nor probability can help. When on the other hand we come across 'Wine erde' at 12th-century Abingdon probability does indicate a vineyard since Abingdon Abbey owned one in the 14th century. Then again it is tempting to think that the word 'Wineyats', which was applied to certain land in Somerset at the time of the Dissolution, had originally meant 'wine vats'.[55] In this particular case it could have borne such a meaning but when we turn to the 'Wynyates' of Compton Wynyates in Warwickshire the name has a different interpretation for here it almost certainly means a 'pass where the wind drives through'. And finally, when the name 'Vineyard' turns up in the documents of the Dissolution, we cannot, on that evidence alone, be certain whether it means an earlier wine vineyard or a late-medieval 'ornamental' vinery somewhat like those which were occasionally to be found in the England of the 17th century.[56]

A different line of doubt has arisen from the use of the word *vineae* and an ancient argument sought to make out that *vineae* should be read as 'orchards' and not as 'vineyards'.[57] The argument is outmoded, and it is now quite clear that they were vineyards. But at this point we meet a fresh argument for while their existence is admitted their purpose is queried. The vineyards were not intended to make wine, so it is said; they were intended to make verjuice.

Verjuice (in one meaning of the word) is the juice of unripened grapes. It was used in medieval cooking as well as in the making of medieval mustard and the part which it played in the domestic life of the Middle Ages would certainly have led to some of it being made in England. In a bad year the whole of the grape crop would most probably have been turned into verjuice. But verjuice can also be made from other

[54] Ekwall, E., *Concise Oxford Dictionary of English Place-Names* (Bibl. Dictionaries).

[55] *VCH, Somerset*, II, 405.

[56] *Fiennes, Celia, The Journeys of* (Bibl. Ch. 6), 59, 68.

[57] Henderson, 271.

Workers in a Vineyard: from the Echternach Codex, Nürnberg, German Nat. Museum

fruit – apples, for instance – and in normal years this is how most of the English verjuice would have been made. The English grapes would have gone into the wine vat, for there is no doubt at all that the English vineyards were maintained for the making of wine. As late as the end of the 14th century wine was made from the royal vineyard at Windsor and 'some part was spent in the kings house, and some part sold to his profit. . . .' In 1289 the Herefordshire vineyard of Ledbury made seven casks of white wine (Ledbury also made red wine) and about 1400 wine was sent to Lady de Mohun from a vineyard at Minehead in Somerset.

The verjuice theory is part of the general, climatic argument against the making of medieval English wine. The climate, so the argument runs, would not have allowed the grapes to ripen properly: drinkable wine could not have been made; the vineyards, therefore, were either for verjuice or for the visual pleasure of the upper classes.

The premise of the argument is climatic and the premise is false. But let us suppose for a moment that the weather of medieval England was no better than it is today. Wine could still have been made and it could still have been very drinkable. I have drunk a red wine from a modern vineyard in the English West Country and, although the wine was light in body, it was sound and acceptable. It was dry, a little sharp, and had a slight savour of red currants. It would never have been, and it was never meant to be, a 'classic' but its medieval equivalent would certainly have been appreciated by the nobles of feudal England.[58]

If, therefore, we can assume that the medieval English weather was no worse than it is today, then the climatic argument is already answered. But in fact we can assume that the weather was rather better. From about A.D. 400 until the Norman Conquest, and perhaps until the 13th century, it appears to have been warm and dry. After that it is probable that it became colder and wetter, a state of affairs which lasted until the Elizabethan era when it became what it is now.[59] The warm, dry period in the Middle Ages helps to explain the number of medieval English vineyards; and it explains also (if he was speaking literally and not metaphorically) the

[58] Outstanding research work on the growing of wine grapes in modern England has been done by Mr R. Barrington Brock at his Viticultural Research Station, Oxted, Surrey. See his Reports Nos. 1 and 2 (Bibl. Ampelography). Mr Edward Hyams has made a most valuable contribution to English viticulture, both with his own vineyard and with the books which he has written and edited. See his *The Grape Vine in England*, and *Vineyards in England* (Bibl. Ampelography). References for verjuice: see fn. 214.

[59] Brooks, C. E. P., *Climate through the Ages, passim*; see also Miller, A. A., *Climatology*, 282–7, 403 (both in Bibl. General).

comment made by William of Malmesbury in the first half of the 12th century when he said that wine made from the vineyards of the Vale of Gloucester was just as sweet as the wine of France.[60]

The likelihood of a favourable climate in the earlier Middle Ages seems to be borne out by the fact that vineyards were established in Belgium from the 10th to the 14th centuries. The earliest plantings, at Liège, Namur, and Tournai, may have been merely of individual vines but from the 11th century onwards they were definitely of vineyards. Most of them were along the line of the Meuse and many of them were quite large. Vineyards were also cultivated in Limbourg and Brabant. Then in the 14th century there are fairly frequent records of verjuice being made and this again fits into the probability that the medieval climate had begun to worsen. Belgian *vignerons* would have complained about the weather with much the same feeling as their English counterparts.[61]

Before we move on from the arguments about the growing of wine in medieval England we must remark that these arguments often conceal a misconception. When they discuss, or deny, the possibility of English wine, they tend to use the word 'drinkable' and they tend to use it with its connotations of modern quality. But we cannot use it thus in a medieval context, for the Middle Ages had no such standards. Even if English vineyards had produced indifferent wine – which sometimes they must have done – they would still, for a time, have been cultivated. The men of the Middle Ages drank what they could get. Good wine was welcome: inferior wine was tolerated: and almost any wine was preferable to none at all.

It is clear, then, that the English vineyards were neither freaks nor phantoms. However small they may have been in comparison with the vineyards of France, they were still an accepted feature of country life and many an English peasant had at one time or another been accustomed to the craft of a vine-dresser. *Wyn silver*, or *winyard silver*, a rent in commutation of labour in the lord's vineyard, was a frequent payment,[62] though by the end of the Middle Ages its implications were becoming a memory because the English vineyard was itself becoming a rarity.

The real beginnings of this decline must be placed in the 14th century. The causes were manifold: the shortage of labour after the Black Death: the increasing variety and, in many cases, the higher quality of the wines that were imported: and, of course, the gradual worsening of the climate. But the process was slow and its stages uneven. Some of the vineyards died out early. This happened at Severn Stoke in Worcestershire where a vineyard which existed in 1172 had disappeared by 1315. Other vineyards were maintained but I suggest that those which were maintained were devoted more to the making of verjuice than they were to the making of wine. In 1295–6 a vineyard at Holborn which belonged to the Earl of Lincoln sold about fifty gallons of verjuice and in 1372, or thereabouts, the Holborn vineyard of the Prior of Ely made thirty gallons of verjuice. It is possible, too, that in the better years of the 14th and 15th centuries the grapes from English vineyards were destined for eating rather than pressing, as indeed was the case at Windsor in 1420–1.[63]

None of these examples is conclusive and in any case we must remember that wine was still being made in England from the end of the 13th to the end of the 14th century. In 1275 forty gallons, and in 1278 sixteen gallons, of home-grown

[60]William of Malmesbury, *De Gestis Pontificum Anglorum*, Bk IV, cap. 153, 291–2.

[61]Halkin, J., *Étude Historique sur la Culture de la Vigne en Belgique*, 20–6, 74–5, 81–5, 100–4, 115, 117.

[62]Neilson, N., 'Customary Rents', *Oxford Studies in Social and Legal History*, II, 58–9.

[63]Amherst, 25–6; see also Henderson, 270; but cf. Amherst, 24. Eating grapes at Windsor: Amherst, 33; cf. also *VCH, Cambridge*, II, 70 for Ely in 1296.

wine were for sale at Ditchingham, near Earsham in Norfolk, and this wine (which I presume to have been grape-wine) was probably grown in an 'Eresham', or Earsham, vineyard. And then, in about 1400, there was the wine that was sent from Minehead to Lady de Mohun. No doubt there was wine from other English vineyards in the 14th century and it is quite possible that some was still being made in the 15th. But in my reading of the records I find nothing which alters my view that by 1400 the vineyards of England had served their purpose and had either disappeared or were doomed.

It would be interesting to estimate the productive capacity of the English vineyards, particularly in the early days, and at one moment it seems that we are near to the answer, for *Domesday* gives us a set of figures. It tells us that Suain's vineyard at Rayleigh in Essex consisted of about 6 acres and produced 20 muids, or modios, of wine *si bene procedit* – 'if it does well'. At the lowest reckoning of the value of the muid this would amount to 160 gallons and at the highest reckoning 1,260 gallons. But we cannot say that this was the total production of the whole 6 acres since the vineyard was new at the date of *Domesday* and only a part of it was bearing. This was the case also with other of the *Domesday* vineyards. Debden in Essex had about 4 acres but in 1086 only 2 of them were bearing. Stebbing in Essex had about $2\frac{1}{2}$ acres but only a part of them was bearing. Kempton in Middlesex had about 8 acres but in 1086 they too were newly planted. How much of Rayleigh was bearing? We do not know. Suain's 20 modios remain enigmatic.

We can, however, make a guess at the potential capacity of the *Domesday* vineyards since we have some figures from 9th-century France and what happened in the vineyards of 9th-century France can probably be applied to those of 11th-century England. In France the *Roll of the Abbot Irminon* gives the following figures for the vineyards of Villemeux and Thiais: Villemeux – 68 acres of old vineyard, 17 acres of new, total production 150 modii; Thiais – 135 acres of old vineyard, $8\frac{1}{2}$ acres of new, total production 1,300 modii. At the lowest value of the modius the total production of both vineyards was 11,600 gallons and at the highest it was 91,350 gallons. This gives us, at the lowest, a production figure of about 50 gallons to the acre and, at the highest, a figure of about 400 gallons to the acre. If we discount the new acres of vineyard, on the assumption that they were not yet bearing, then we get a minimum production of about 58 gallons per acre and a maximum production of about 457 gallons per acre. At which point let us observe that the capacity of a modern English vineyard should, at the very least, be 600 gallons to the acre.

The *Irminon* figures suggest that the vineyards of Villemeux and Thiais were inefficiently cultivated. Had they been intended for the making of high-quality wine, then we might have expected a low yield, but there is no evidence to show that high quality was a prime consideration of the north-western medieval producers and when we criticize the medieval figures we must do so only on a quantity basis. I think there is no doubt that in this sense the medieval vineyards were comparatively inefficient and not merely in the 9th century but throughout all the centuries of medieval viticulture. I believe that one of the reasons was this: the modern English vineyard, on which I have based my estimate of modern production, has its vines planted a yard apart with a yard between each row of vines but the medieval vineyard most frequently had its vines planted with twice as much distance between them. This type of spacing is shown again and again in medieval pictures and the system, if one can call it a system, is mentioned by Petrus de Crescentiis towards the end of the 13th century.[64] It is probable that the vineyards of England were for the most part planted in the same wide manner and we have therefore no cause to imagine that the production of the English vineyards was any higher than it was in the *vignobles* of France. Judged by our modern standards the medieval north-western *vignerons* were inefficient.

The Vinedressers of Lusignan

Out of all the eras of western history the thousand years of medieval life qualify for the title of the Age of Inefficiency. They were occasionally redeemed by the acts of a skilled vision – in one particular by the creation of the great cathedrals of the 12th and 13th centuries – but on the whole they were grossly and contentedly incompetent. If they had not been so, they would not have been so long and it would not have taken medieval man a thousand years to climb up to humanism from the collapse of the classical mind.

Ignorance and faith were the agents of the long stagnation. The barbarians made ignorance, if not a social accomplishment, at least an aristocratic commonplace and for many centuries the mind of the feudal upper classes lay resting in a locked chamber of unenlightenment. It is the story of the Sleeping Princess. Some kings encouraged education but for the most part learning remained the prerogative of the Church and a profession for the more ambitious members of the lower classes.

The Church dominated learning and the Church was not interested in knowledge. Its purpose lay among the mysteries of sin and salvation. Facts did not guide a man to salvation but faith did. Facts could be disregarded so long as faith was protected, for the only thing that mattered was that Man should be saved. Man was not only sinful but he was also frail, he was easily turned from the pursuit of the Ultimate Glory. That being so, he must be helped, or persuaded, or even forced, towards acceptance of the Ecstatic Will whose workings only the Church had been given authority to interpret.

Within its own compass the attitude is logical. And whatever one may think about the assumptions on which the logic is based there is no denying that the Church led a movement of the spiritual consciousness whose magnitude it is impossible to comprehend. The monastic disciplines were a remarkable creation and the insistent expectancy of God translated human happiness into new dimensions of pain and pleasure.

In view of this general attitude it is hardly surprising that the Middle Ages were for the most part technically uninterested. Despite the mathematical interest displayed by such men as Adelard of Bath and Robert of Chester, and despite the scientific tendency of such thinkers as Roger Bacon, the movement of technical progress was slow and, even when it gathered impetus in the 13th century, its effect upon life was sporadic. Its laggard and uneven growth can be witnessed in medieval viticulture. During the early Middle Ages the area of north-western viticulture increased but the cultivation of the vineyards was certainly no better and probably

[64]The medieval values used in the Suain calculations are: 'arpents' or 'aripennos' equals an acre each; the modios: low value equals 8 gallons, high value equals 63 gallons (see Modius in Appendix H). I am assuming that the gallon is the size of the modern British gallon (see Gallon in Appendix H). For the Rayleigh vineyard, see Appendix F. Modern English production figures: Mr R. Barrington Brock, of the Viticultural Research Station, Oxted, informs me that, from some *cépages*, he gets just over a pint of wine to a vine. Mr Edward Hyams, *The Grape Vine in England*, 96, suggests 1½ pints to a vine; see also his 'A Vineyard in Kent', *ILN*, Nov. 7th, 1959. I have used the figure of 1 pint to a vine. Villemeux and Thiais: Longnon, A., *Polyptyque de l'Abbaye de Saint-Germain des Prés*, II, 98, 202. Illustrations of medieval vineyards: *Calendrier de Charles d'Angoulême*, Mars; *Livre des Propriétés des Choses*, Barthélemy l'Anglais; Miniature – *La Taille de la Vigne*; both in the Bibliothèque Nationale, Paris. Petrus de Crescentiis, Bk IV, cap. vii.

rather worse than it had been in Roman times. This state of affairs must have lasted for seven or eight hundred years for the evidence does not allow us to assume any real technical development until the 13th or 14th centures. Then, when it does occur, its application is unsystematic and it does not seem to be directed by any organized, experimental intelligence.

The Monastic Orders are supposed to have played a leading part in the promotion of 'scientific' agriculture. Doubtless they did; but I find little to support the view that they were also responsible, or rather that they were mainly responsible, for the development of 'scientific' viticulture. I think that in this sphere the rôle of the Orders has often been exaggerated. I believe, too, that unjustified emphasis can be placed upon the idea that the Church, being the keeper of the classical knowledge, is likely to have put that knowledge into practice. The manuscripts in the Abbey libraries may sometimes have been read for their practical advice; if so, their influence is imperceptible. Furthermore, if the ancient knowledge had been applied, it would in many cases have been taken only from the rather unsatisfactory work written by Palladius in the 4th century. For many of the literate *vignerons* of the Middle Ages there can have been little inducement to translate the precepts of the library into the labours of the vineyard. Nor, it would seem, was there any enthusiasm to make the attempt. The desire to propagate this type of knowledge came late and it is not until the 13th and 14th centuries that farming manuals became popular. Walter of Henley's *Husbandry* was one. More informative was the *Liber ruralium commodorum* of Petrus de Crescentiis who quoted frequently from Roman authors and whose book went through many editions at the end of the 15th century.

The spread of knowledge (or at least advice) was slow and it is again not until the later centuries that we have any clear evidence of technical improvement in viticulture. One major advance was the use of sulphur and the credit for this discovery can be ascribed to the medieval alchemists. Sulphur was one of the basic ingredients, or principles, or symbols, of the alchemical art and its importance is reaffirmed at the beginning of the 16th century in the work of Paracelsus. This alchemical emphasis must have led to its being used in the craft of wine. Its application, however,

245

*Picking Grapes ; Pruning the Vine
from 'Livre des Prouffitz Champetres'
Petrus de Crescentiis,
1529 ed.
London, British Museum*

was limited since it does not seem to have been used for the preservation of the vine-plants but only for the preservation of the wine made from them. Even then its use seems to have been confined to Germany where it was regarded with such suspicion that on various occasions the authorities commanded it to be prohibited.[65] Nevertheless an advance had been made and the sulphurous discomfort of German burghers was the price of eventual progress.

It seems that we should also credit the Middle Ages with the development of the 'low-vineyard', that is to say the vineyard whose vines are tied to upright stakes and kept down to a height of about four feet. In this the medieval *vignerons* tended to move away from many of the ideas of the ancient world and closer to most of the ideas of modern wine-growers. But here again it appears that development was late and we must reckon that the ancient 'ground-vineyard' in which the branches of unstaked vines trailed along the ground and were only propped to keep the fruit-clusters off the earth, may have persisted for a long time and, most probably, over a wide area.

Both 'high' and 'ground' vines were grown in England in the early 12th century. William of Malmesbury, when describing the vineyard of Thorney Abbey in Cambridgeshire, says that there were vines trained high on poles or trellises as well as vines which trailed along the ground. The custom of growing high vines existed also in Continental Europe. One of the illustrations in the 11th-century Codex Aureus of Echternach shows a fenced vineyard in which the vines grow on to a crossbar about the height of a man. The depiction of this vineyard may be stylized but without doubt it is only a stylization of what the artist himself had seen. Then, towards the end of the Middle Ages, a miniature in the *Livre des Prouffitz Champestres* of Petrus de Crescentiis shows a 'modern' style of vineyard but backing it is a high trellis. Perhaps a 'high-vine' would have been grown on this trellis for merely

[65]Beckmann, J., *A History of Inventions . . .* (Bibl. General), I, 251–4.

decorative reasons: or perhaps its purpose was to provide grapes for eating. At all events it is certainly not an important part of the vineyard and it is probable that by this time the high vine was seldom used in north-western Europe for the making of wine.[66]

'Ground' vines appear to have been common in the vineyards of France until the end of the Middle Ages. In a 14th-century illustration one sees them being pruned. The pruner wears black ankle-length boots, blue hose, a pink doublet, and has a black hat crammed down on his head. The gnarled vine-stocks look like corkscrews and the thin branches are all cut back, leaving only one shoot to each vine. Another picture, this time of two *vignerons* working in a vineyard, shows the vines as leafless bushes.[67] Their branches straggle from them and, since the time of this picture is March, it is unlikely that they are going to be pruned any further. It seems clear that the vines in these two illustrations were unstaked and probably all that happened in the summer was that the *vignerons* propped the branches to keep the fruit off the ground.

I have said it seems clear because at this point indecision enters. When we turn to a third illustration, one of a scene at the Château de Lusignan, we find the same type of vineyard but here, at Lusignan, the vines have been, or more probably are being, staked.[68] Were the other vineyards going to be staked also? We must admit that it is possible. This being so, we must also admit that the 'ground-vineyard' may have been disappearing from north-western Europe rather more rapidly than one might have supposed. We can be fairly sure that the disappearance is a late phenomenon but it is extremely difficult to decide on the scale and the speed of the disappearance.

There is a certain amount of English evidence but it gives us little help in coming

[65]Beckmann, J., *A History of Inventions . . .* (Bibl. General), I, 251–5.

[66]William of Malmesbury, *De Gestis Pontificum Anglorum*, Bk IV, cap. 186, p. 326. Codex Aureus: Grabar, A., and Nordenfalk, C., *Early Medieval Painting*, 212. *Le Livre des Prouffitz Champestres de Pierre de Crescens*, Bibliothèque de l'Arsenal, No. 5064; cf. James, M. R., *The Canterbury Psalter*, f. 233b.

[67]*Le Livre des Propriétés des Choses de Barthélemy l'Anglais, La taille de la vigne*, Bibliothèque Nationale, Paris; *Calendrier de Charles d'Angoulême* (15th century), *Mars*, Bibliothèque Nationale, Paris.

[68]*Les Très Riches Heures du Duc de Berry, Mars, Les Labours*, Musée Condé, Chantilly.

Vintage in Burgundy: 15th-century French tapestry, Musée Cluny, Paris

March: Tilling
from 'Les Très Riches
Heures du Duc de Berry'
c 1416
Chantilly, Musée Condé

to a decision. A 12th-century plan of the land of the monastery of Christ Church, Canterbury, shows a staked vineyard[69] but the drawing is obviously a scribe's hieroglyph and is intended to indicate the mere presence rather than the actual look of the vineyard. At Abingdon Abbey in 1388–9 the propping of the vines cost 4/6d.[70] Does this mean that the vines were staked or merely that the fruit-clusters were propped? In 1405 at Windsor six hundred 'paxills' were bought for propping vines; fifteen years later at Cambridge there was a purchase of five rails.[71] We do not know the exact function of the paxills of Windsor but we may suspect that the rails of Cambridge were not the cross-bars for a 'low-vineyard'. They are much more likely to have been the bars for a wall-trellis since the dons may well have preferred eating Cambridge grapes to drinking Cambridge wine.

We are thus unable to say that the 'low', staked vineyard was usual in north-

[69]James, M. R., *The Canterbury Psalter*, ff. 284b, 285, 286.

[70]*Acc. obed. Abingdon*, 55, 57; lvii, lx.

[71]TR, III, 545, 548.

September: the Vintage
from 'Les Très Riches
Heures du Duc de Berry'
c 1416
Chantilly, Musée Condé

western Europe towards the end of the Middle Ages. But I do not think there is much doubt that it was coming into vogue at this time and we see it clearly in certain pictures of the 15th century. In the *Livre des Prouffitz Champestres* the vines are trained diagonally along a row of stakes and in a tapestry showing a Burgundian vineyard each vine, laden with heavy bunches of fruit, is tied to its own stake.[72] These vineyards are not yet 'modern' for they do not have the regular neatness of the modern *vignobles* but all the same they are drawing closer to modernity.

On a Roman pillar-drum at Speyer in the Palatinate we see a naked youth reaching upwards over his head to cut the ripe clusters from the overhanging vine-stems.[73] We cannot help contrasting this beautiful design with the pictures of the medieval *vignerons*. The body on the pillar-drum, unself-consciously naked, is natural and sensuous, simply delighting in a fertile and physical world. How

[72] *Le Livre des Prouffitz Champestres de Pierre de Crescens, Les Travaux de la Vigne*, Bibliothèque de l'Arsenal, Paris, No. 5064. Burgundy: Rodier, 35.

[73] Loeschcke, S., *Denkmäler vom Weinbau...*, Abb., 13a, p. 17; also published in Espérandieu, E., *Rec Général des Bas-Reliefs...*, Vol. VIII, 5960; (both in Bibl. Ch. 4).

awkward and graceless in comparison, how near to caricature and grotesque, are the clothed figures of the workers in the vineyards of the Middle Ages. Yet these latter men, lacking in beauty, are vivid with humanity. We can almost smell the sweat of their clothes and feel their rough fingers gripping a pruning knife in the bitter cold of a late winter.

The miniatures which illustrate medieval manuscripts – books of husbandry, Calendars, Psalters and Books of Hours – present these *vignerons* with an unflattering sympathy. *Les Très Riches Heures de Jean de France, Duc de Berry* show us the peasants of Poitou in March, pruning in one of the two walled vineyards outside the Château of Lusignan. One of the vineyards has already been prepared. In the other, three vinedressers are busy cutting the branched vines down to heads of three spurs each. Behind the vineyards looms the Château, a dominant mass of high, round towers and high, angled roofs, rising up from behind defensive walls. In September, we see the men and women of Anjou vintaging outside the Château of Saumur. One of the men is cramming a handful of grapes into his mouth. One of the women is heavily pregnant with a child conceived during the New Year holiday. All of them are picking among knee-high vines. The grapes are collected into baskets and then put into panniers slung on either side of a donkey, or else into two round tubs on a cart. Above the vintagers soar the walls and pinnacled towers of the Château like the spired and turreted dream of a Romantic novelist. And, like the fortress of Lusignan, the castle of Saumur dominates the people who work its land, dwarfing and overlording them, making them seem what in fact they are – the little, parochial people of the Middle Ages. The art of the miniaturist is exactly fitted to their portrayal.

The peasants are also in the big wooden tubs where the wine is being made, men this time, no women, still in miniature and still intensely alive. Grapes brought in from the vineyards are carried in baskets of almost the same shape as the modern *hottes* of Burgundy and the modern *cestos* of northern Portugal. In the *Belles Heures de Jean de France* a man, naked except for a loincloth, is receiving yet another *hotte* of grapes into the tub. The expression on his face is anguished as though the work were too hard for him; and anyone who has begun to tread a vintage will know exactly how he felt. On the other hand the treader in the *Bedford Hours*, dressed this time in a blue hat, green jerkin and white underpants, wears on his face a look of blissful stupefaction. He must have been at the new wine from another vat.[74]

The Grotesque Imagination

The fact that the portraits of these little people should balance always on the verge of the grotesque is perhaps not due to any desire of the artist to caricature but merely to the streak of the bizarre which ran through the medieval imagination. It shows its presence in many ways. Some of the vineyards, for example, suffered from insect invasions and in the absence of chemical control over the insects the vines suffered badly. At the beginning of the 15th century there was a plague of *urebères*, a sort of beetle, in the Côte d'Or. They, with cockchafers, *escrivains*, and other pests, ravaged the Côte for a hundred to a hundred and fifty years. Despite human efforts to exterminate them, the insects lived on and became such a menace that, with the

September: Treading Grapes from 'Les Belles Heures du Duc de Berry'
New York, Metropolitan Museum of Art

[74] *Les Très Riches Heures de Jean de France, Duc de Berry*, Musée Condé de Chantilly; *Queen Mary's Psalter, March*, British Museum, London, Royal M.S., 2 B, vii, f. 73b; *Les Belles Heures de Jean de France, Duc de Berry*, ed. Porcher, Jean, Bibliothèque Nationale; *Bedford Hours*, British Museum, London, Add. M.S., 18850, f. 9.

advice of the Church, supernatural remedies were attempted. In 1460 the spiritual pest-control took a multiplex form: in addition to a general procession, general confession was recommended, together with a general prohibition of swearing.[75] The plague, however, wiped out most of the vines of the Côte de Beaune.

In the middle of the 16th century the medieval imagination was still at work. This time it was the *écrivains* against whom the remedies of the Church were turned. The warning to be addressed to the insects by the priests of the Côte is impressive:

September: Treading Grapes
from the Bedford Hours
c 1420
London, British Museum

'. . . trusting in the divine mercy . . . I summon, and by the power of the holy Cross, armed, with the shield of faith, I command and I conjure a first, a second, and a third time all flies which commonly are called *escrivains*, *urebères* or *uribères*, and all other maggots hurtful to the fruit of the vines, to cease immediately their ravaging, eating, destroying, and annihilating of the branches, buds, and fruits, to cease to have this power henceforward, and to withdraw into the remotest places of the forests so that they can no longer harm the vines of the faithful . . . and if, by the counsel of Satan, they refuse to obey these injunctions and they continue their devastations . . . I curse and hurl sentence of malediction and anathema . . .'

upon them.[76]

It was comfortless enough for the peasant to have to fight against the insects which ravaged his vines but even more discomforting to suspect that the gulf of Hell waited for him beneath the vineyards which he so laboriously cultivated. And what a gulf!

'The horrible cold, the loathsome worms, the stench, hunger and thirst, the darkness, the chains, the unspeakable filth, the endless cries, the sight of the demons, Denis' (the Carthusian) 'calls up all this before us like a nightmare. Still more oppressive is the insistence on psychic suffering: the mourning, the fear, the empty feeling of everlasting separation from God, the inexpressible hatred of God, the envy of the bliss of the elect; the confusion of all sorts of errors and delusions in the brain. And the thought that this is to last for all eternity is by ingenious comparisons wrought up to the fever-point of horror.'

And – how can human beings behave like this? –

'the treatise *De quatuor hominum novissimis*, from which these details are borrowed, was the customary reading during mealtime at the convent of Windesheim.'[77]

The gothic imagination was a very remarkable instrument. At one end of the scale it shaped such fantasies as the Dance of the Dead and the nightmare pictures of Hieronymus Bosch and at the other it elaborated the legend of the Holy Grail. Between these two extremes lies a romance like *The Lay of Yonec* in which the hero, though a devout Christian knight, has nevertheless the power to visit his mistress in the guise of a hawk.

A belief in magic and a delight in marvels were both inherent in the medieval mind. Gerbert, later Archbishop of Ravenna, still later Pope Sylvester II, was

[75]Rodier, 28 sqq.

[76]Rodier, 30, quoting from the Archives of Dijon.

[77]Huizinga, J., *The Waning of the Middle Ages*, 219.

rumoured to have learnt magic at Toledo[78] though what he probably studied were Arab mathematics. John of Salisbury, in his youth in the first half of the 12th century, was – so it was said – apprenticed to a necromancer but 'failed at the profession'.[79] Walter Map tells the story of the merman Nicholas Pipe – an unlikely name for a merman – who lived for long periods on the sea-bed and who, when he descended into the depths, took with him 'pieces of old iron, wrenched away from a cart or from horses' hoofs. . . .'[80] William of Malmesbury records that, in 1100, 'there were many adverse events; but the most dreadful circumstance was that the devil visibly appeared to men in woods and secret places, and spoke to them as they passed by'.[81] And when cruelty was mingled with credulity, then the results were indeed bizarre. 'The people of Arras celebrate the annulment of the sentences for witchcraft, which during the whole year 1461 had infested the town like an

[78]Helen Waddell, *The Wandering Scholars*, 91–2.

[79]John of Salisbury, *Letters*, Vol. I, p. xiii.

[80]Walter Map, *De Nugis Curialium*, 232–3.

[81]*Chronicle of the Kings of England*, 343.

Cultivating the Vine
Stone Relief
Freiburg Minster

epidemic, by joyous festivals and a competition in acting *"folies moralisées"*, of which the prizes were a gold *fleur-de-lys*, a brace of capons, etc.; nobody, it seems, thought any more of the tortured and executed victims.'[82]

Medieval man walked on a thin crust of vulnerable earth. Ice was below, fire above for, if Hell was below him, above him was Heaven, packed shimmering with angels wing-tip to wing-tip. And though the mercy of God might (ultimately) be infinite, that of the Church was much more limited, excluding from its benevolence those believers who believed differently. The perils of heresy – to the heretic – were convincingly illustrated by the Albigensian Crusade, a double crime which destroyed men with one hand and civilization with the other. Without surprise one notes in the records of the Inquisition against the Albigenses that in 1274 there was discovered among the books of Bernard Baragnon, who was accused of heresy, the *Bible Guiot* which begins '*Dou siecle puant et horrible*'.[83] It was this 'stinking and horrible century' which broke the culture of Provence and it was in this century too that no less a person than the Chancellor of the University of Paris could say: 'We are in danger, we who read the writings of the pagan poets.'[84] Jealously the Church guarded the hold of Heaven upon men, refusing to let them be tempted away from the glittering, insistent Paradise of angels. The hearing of the Middle Ages was obsessed by the singing of the angel choirs.

Cow Crumbock

If life on earth was full of distresses for the soul, it was equally full of discomforts for the body. War left its erratic trails of destruction but we can scarcely count them as a special hazard of the times. We kill more people than the Middle Ages, with their technical inefficiency, were ever able to slaughter. Pirates, robbers, and the turbulent retainers of great lords added their quota to the uncertainties of existence. Darkness and cold were commonplace. Where the poor had lighting at all, it was rudimentary, and heating, even in the great houses, was scarcely more advanced than the central hearth of the ancient Greek megaron. Some chimneys existed in England in manor-houses or castles or monasteries but many an upper-class Englishman lit his fire against a screen in the 'hall' where he ate. Charcoal, when used, would have produced little heat since its effect is visually, rather than physically, satisfying.

Perforce our ancestors felt the cold less than we do, but even so they seem to have varied in the degree of their immunity. In the middle of the 15th century fires were allowed in the Hall from the beginning of November until the end of January but at the Court of the Norman Kings they were permitted from the beginning of October until Easter.[85] A draught of wine must often have warmed a chilled courtier, stamping his feet on a fireless evening: and one shivers in sympathy with the Rhenish peasants in those two terrible winters of 1125 and 1126 when men and cattle were frozen to death and birds fell dead out of the sky.[86]

From West German records we can see how hard life must often have been. In the 9th century thirty out of thirty-seven recorded vintages were small or bad. It appears, indeed, to have been a calamitous century for the same annals tell us of earthquakes in six years, one of them 'frightful', of pestilence in two, and, in 873, of a monstrous swarm of 'grasshoppers' which did great damage. The 11th century

[82] Huizinga, J., *The Waning of the Middle Ages*, 26.

[83] Langlois, C. V., *La vie en France au Moyen Âge*, II, 57-8.

[84] Helen Waddell, *The Wandering Scholars*, 15.

[85] *Curtasye, Boke of*, 393-4; Hall, H., *The Red Book of the Exchequer*, III, 813. For 'chimneys' (hearths or chimneys?) in London, see *Munimenta Gildhallae Londoniensis*, Vol. III, 133, and Glossary.

[86] Deichmann und Wolf, *Weinchronik . . .* (Bibl. General).

was not much better: twenty-nine out of thirty-seven recorded years were unsatisfactory. Heat and cold both played their part. In the year 1000 rivers dried up and rotting fish brought sickness: in 1022 men and animals died of heat: in 1056 there was a summer of tremendous heat: the vintages of the years 1067 and 1068 were ruined by heavy frost. A grim ending to the century was its last decade which saw eight years of 'dearth, misery, and want'. Fortunately the next century was, on the whole, better, giving twenty-two plentiful vintages out of forty-eight years recorded, although in 1166 plenty became over-production and in Franconia there was so much wine that it was mixed with lime for building.[87]

It seems that western Germany was not the only area to suffer from occasional over-production since it is more than likely that the same thing happened in the Midi of France. A Letter-Writing Guide of Toulouse from the early 14th century uses this as a reason for not sending money to the student son of the family.[88] The reason, of course, may have been an excuse, for many a medieval student was a happy spendthrift, losing at dice the cash which he had not already spent on his mistress or on wine at the *Pomme-de-Pin* in the rue de la Juiverie in Paris – *'tout aux tavernes et aux filles'* as Villon has part of the story.[89] On the other hand the excuse may equally have concealed a real hardship: low prices for the wine, meagre rations for the vineyard family, near-starvation for the ambitious son. Alongside the dicing students lived those who were genuinely and bitterly poor.

Even when there was enough food for the family, it was not, at least in winter, always enough for health. In most cases meat, and in many cases fish, had to be preserved by pickling or salting, and the vegetables to mitigate this diet were mainly dried peas and beans, onions, leeks, and – possibly – cabbage. And where the basic diet was bread and beer, as it was in many parts of England,[90] a bad harvest foreboded an ominous winter. This scene, from an early Ballad, portrays only the fringes of hardship, but the threat of starvation lurks in the hollows of the wind:

> 'This winter's weather it waxeth cold,
> And frost doth freeze on every hill,
> And Boreas blows his blast so bold,
> That all our cattle may die with chill.
> Bell, my wife, who loves no strife,
> She said unto me quietly,
> "Rise up, and save cow Crumbock's life.
> Man, put thine old cloak about thee." '[91]

No wonder that medieval poets wrote with such yearning of the birdsong which heralded release from winter:

> 'From middle March to April
> When the spray begins to spring
> The little birds of the air desire
> In their own tongue to sing.'[92]

And, at the end of the Middle Ages, Martin Luther in *Frau Musica*:

[87] *Ibid.*

[88] Haskins, C. H., 'The Life of Medieval Students as illustrated by their letters', *Studies in Medieval Culture*, 15, n. 1.

[89] Chatelain, E., 'Notes sur quelques tavernes fréquentées par l'Université de Paris aux XIVᵉ et XVᵉ siècles', *Bull. de la Soc. de l'Histoire de Paris et de l'Île-de-France*, xxv, 106, 1898; Villon, *Ballade de Bonne Doctrine*.

[90] See Rogers, J. E. Thorold, *Six Centuries of Work and Wages* (Bibl. General), 1, 67, 95, 96; also TR, 1, 17; and Amherst, 10 sqq., quoting the accounts of Norwich Priory; see also ref. in fn. 168.

[91] 'The Old Cloak', *Albatross Book of Living Verse*, Ed. Untermeyer, D., London, 33; for a more cheerful picture of winter, see Durrieu, Paul, *Les Très Riches Heures de Jean de France, Duc de Berry, Calendrier*, Pl. ii.

[92] 'Alisoun', *Albatross Book of Living Verse*, 45 (see fn. 91 above); cf. Helen Waddell, *Medieval Latin Lyrics*, 224-7, from the MS. of Benedictbeuern.

*'Die beste Zeit im Jahr ist mein,
Da singen alle Vögelein;'*[93]

Beside the winter pains of actual hunger or inadequate diet, there were other afflictions of medieval life and among them were scurvy and leprosy. Lice – 'flesh-moths', as they were called in the 15th-century *Boke of Nurture*[94] – did nothing to promote good health. Sanitation, where it existed, was as much the ally, as it was the enemy, of disease.

To the peasant the expanses of Nature made the problems of drainage seem unworthy of attention; moreover, the dunghill outside the country door was less lethal than the cesspool in the town-dweller's garden. Urban cesspits leaked into neighbouring wells and in the huddled medieval cities infection became epidemic. Sophisticated drainage is notable only in the larger establishments. The *necessarium* of the great monastery of St. Gall in Switzerland is likely to have had some flushing arrangement, although it was not, perhaps, as ingenious as that shown some three hundred years later on a 12th-century plan of the Priory of Canterbury where the water from the fish-pond flushed out the *necessarium*.[95] At the end of its journey the contaminated water ran into Canterbury town ditch and in this respect the monks were more fortunate than those nobles whose castle moats were the ultimate receptacle. The curious in these matters may study the battlement latrines at Vila da Feira in Central Portugal.

Most fortunate of all were the villages on the upper reaches of rivers, where a swift current provided an obvious sewer. It is doubtful, however, if the villagers realized their hygienic good luck. Twenty years ago, when I was staying in a village of the Western Pyrenees, I was taken for a walk along the local river, and one of the pools was pointed out to me as having the finest drinking water in the whole valley. It was a beautiful pool. It looked like mobile jade. Its water was ice-cold and, at midsummer, greatly refreshing. Yet two hundred yards upstream, through 'chimneys' cut in the house-walls, the village refuse was directed into this poetic torrent. Still, this was in the mountains and in the lower-lying of the medieval towns contaminated water must have been unpleasant, even to the medieval palate. Wine was a welcome alternative.

It may also have been a welcome anaesthetic. There was an abundance of pain in those fierce centuries and part of that pain was the pain of healing, for medical technology was somewhat limited. Among the war rations for Dover Castle were 300 lb. of mutton fat, the only medicine for the wounds and bruises of the thousand men of the garrison.[96] The Leech Books of the *Leechdoms, Wort-cunning and Star-craft of Early England* give us the prescriptions of Anglo-Saxon doctoring and enable us to ponder upon this remedy: 'For swollen eyes, take a live crab, put his eyes out, and put him alive again into water, and put the eyes upon the neck of the man, who hath need; he will soon be well.' 'For a very old headache' we find the recommendation 'take salt and rue, and a bunch of ivy berries, pound all at once, add honey, and therewith smear the temples, and the forehead, and the top of the head'. For tooth trouble: 'Work a tooth salve thus, mingle together oversea rind [cinnamon] and honey and pepper, lay on.'

It is likely that a number of the herbal remedies were more efficacious than these

[93] *Oxford Book of German Verse.*

[94] *Nurture, Boke of,* I, 280.

[95] St Gall: *The Archaeological Journal,* 101, June, 1848. Canterbury: James, M. R., *The Canterbury Psalter,* ff. 284b, 285. General: *Hist. Tech.,* II, chapter on sanitation.

[96] Bateson, Mary, *Medieval England,* 315.

three and one must remember that the beneficial properties (if any) of the herbs could be further increased by the potency of faith or magic. A 'good drink against all temptations of the devil' was made of 'betony, bishopwort, lupins, githrife, attorlothe, wolfscomb, yarrow' and these, having been laid under an altar and having had nine masses sung over them, were scraped into holy water. A magical approach is evident in the view that stones found inside young swallows were not only good for headache but also 'for the fiends temptations, and for night *goblin* visitors, and for typhus, and for the *night* mare, and for knot, and for fascination, and for evil enchantments by song'.[97]

The general fierceness of mind may have seen nothing unusual in the proffered advice: 'In case a man be lunatic; take skin of a mereswine *or porpoise*, work it into a whip, swinge the man therewith, soon he will be well. Amen.'[98] And no doubt the same attitude of mind would have found little cause for comment in a phrase in the Will of Bishop Aelfsige which, forbidding anyone to alter the Will, pronounces: 'If anyone do so, may God destroy him both soul and body, both here and in the future.'[99] The pious hope is, of course, only formal but it still reads oddly in the Will of a Christian Bishop.

Any solace was welcome in that harsh, uncertain world, and wine provided an easy and immediate comfort. The 13th-century song *Or hi parra* baldly states this view:

> '*Bevez quant l'avez en poing:*
> *Ben est droit, car mut est loing . . .*'[100]

Wine, whether good or indifferent, was a luxury in a world starved of luxury and at the same time it enabled man to feel less cramped and caged in what Paulinus had called the 'prison of the body'. This retort to Paulinus comes out of the Middle Ages in the *Patenostre du Vin*:

> '*Et dimitte nobis; Seignor,*
> *El monde n'est joie greignor**
> *Que de vin; debita nostra:*
> *Qui premiers en taverne entra*
> *Preudom**** fu et de sainte vie.*'[101]

A variant on the same theme is Walter Map's famous drinking song:

> '*Mihi est propositum in taberna mori,*
> *Vinum sit oppositum morientis ori,*
> *Ut dicant, cum venerint Angelorum chori,*
> *"Deus sit propitius huic potatori."*'[102]

> I'm resolved that when I die I'll in a tavern do it,
> Place a bowl of liquor where my mouth is neighbour to it,
> So that angel choirs may cry, when I am a sinker,
> 'God have mercy, God have grace upon this honest drinker.'

*'greater'. **'a wise man'.

[97]*LWS*, II, 307, 53, 335, 307.

[98]*Ibid*, II, 335.

[99]Whitelock, D., *Anglo-Saxon Wills*, 17.

[100]Jeanroy, A., et Langfors, A., *Chansons satiriques et bacchiques du XIII siècle*, Song No. xliii, 78.

[101]Jubinal, M. L. A., *Jongleurs et trouvères*, 70.

[102]Percy Society, *Festive Songs*, Intro. Sandys, W., No. 1. I have translated in the spirit of the song.

Wine of rec

Except perhaps in Italy and the Eastern Mediterranean, almost all medieval wine was drunk in the year of its vintaging. Quite a proportion of it, moreover, was drunk before it had even had time to be properly racked. The distinction between 'wine of vintage' – wine that was shipped between October and Christmas and within the three months after its making – and 'wine of rack' (*reek, rek', rec*) – wine that was shipped between Christmas and Easter or in the late Spring – is a commonplace distinction in English records of the 13th and 14th centuries.[103] 'Wine of rack', being clearer, was of course more highly esteemed than 'wine of vintage' and this led also to a social distinction between the two, a type of grading which is exemplified in the Household of Henry I. As his daily ration the Chancellor got 'one sextary' (probably four to six gallons) 'of clear wine, and one sextary of household wine' – '*et j sextarium de vino claro; et j sextarium de vino expensabili*'.[104] The Chamberlain of the Candles, on the other hand, only got half a sextary of household wine. I think one can assume in this case that 'clear wine' meant *rec* and household wine that 'of vintage'. And in case it should be thought that Henry I's Chancellor was a heavy drinker, one might add that the sextary was the allowance served to his 'mess' for dinner or for supper.

The fact that medieval wine was drunk within the year of its birth is not at all remarkable. The same thing happens, and properly happens, to a great deal of modern wine. But at that point resemblance ceases for there is a fundamental difference between the patterns of modern and medieval drinking. We have our *vins de consommation*, our one-year wines, and we have, in considerable quantity, our finer wines which are aged for a number of years. We attach importance to the quality of age. Medieval man did not. He was little interested in age and he made no real effort to improve his wines by ageing them. He remained content with his *vins de consommation* and he did so for one principal reason – lack of interest.

A subsidiary, though only a subsidiary, reason was the lack of quality. If he had been interested in doing so he could have matured some of his wines since some of them would have had sufficient quality to bear maturing. But much of the wine from the north-western vineyards was not good enough to age gracefully and often not sound enough to age at all. Only too frequently it would have been unstable from birth. Then, once in the cask, there was the possibility of ullage which, by exposing the wine to the air, would have turned it towards vinegar. It is true that the danger of ullage was recognized and that in some cases olive oil was used as a covering film[105] but there must have been many more cases where this method was either unknown or ignored. However, there were other techniques for maintaining, or trying to maintain, the soundness of a wine: the addition of burnt salt: plastering, or resinating: mixing it with cloves: or by plunging into it lighted torches tipped with pitch.[106] Yet, despite all this ingenuity, much wine still went bad.

In 1342, for example, Reymund Seguyn, the King's Butler, was commanded 'to distribute certain feeble wine among the poor brethren of York and Notyngham, and to give the putrified wine to other poor who wish to have it . . . as the king has learned that of 50 tuns of wine at York and 5 tuns at Notyngham in the butler's custody, some are putrid and the rest are so feeble that they cannot be kept'.[107] But

[103] Rec: *Close Rolls*, 12, Henry III, mem., 4; 48, Henry III, mem., 6; cf. *Close Rolls*, 15, Edward III, mem., 14; 16, Edward III, mem., 43.

[104] Hall, H., *The Red Book of the Exchequer*, III, 807, 811. For a translation of the text of the Red Book (and Black Book) see Hall, H., *Court Life under the Plantagents*, 242, etc. But note the tenor of J. H. Round's criticism in *Studies on the Red Book of the Exchequer*.

[105] Petrus de Crescentiis, Bk IV, cap. xliii.

[106] *Ibid*, Bk IV, cap. xxxviii.

[107] *Close Rolls*, 16, Edward III, Pt 2, mem., 25.

the disposal of inferior wine was not always undertaken in such a spirit of bene-volence, for, in the reign of Edward III, a white wine of Spain which 'because of its weakness and age . . . may not advantageously be sold in England . . .' was allowed to be shipped out of Great Yarmouth and sent to 'Prucia'.[108] North Germany was not the only market for this wretched stuff. The *Patent Rolls* of Henry IV note in 1401: 'Licence for John Banham and John Walters to ship . . . 30 tuns of old un-drinkable wine . . . in the port of Bristol and take the same to Ireland and make their profit therefrom, and to salt salmon . . . and bring back the salmon . . . to England.'[109]

The malpractices of vintners and taverners produce an equally disagreeable im-pression of what medieval man had often to put in his goblet. In England sound wine was mixed with spoiled or adulterated wines. There was a complaint in 1307 that Gascon vintners and merchants, as well as men from other parts, brought 'mixed, putrid and corrupt wines' into England for sale, while other vintners and merchants in the boroughs and market towns of England mixed unwholesome old wine with new and then sold the mixture.[110] It is likely that part of this complaint was prejudiced since it was made at a time when the Gascons were in a powerful position in the English wine trade, a position which the English merchants coveted and which, within a generation, they gained for themselves.[111]

But, whatever, the prejudice, the type of malpractice alleged was undoubtedly common enough and frequent regulations bear witness to the mixing of wine in taverns. The *Liber Albus* of London forbade taverners to mix corrupt wine with sound or to sell white wine as Rhenish. For these reasons white wine and Rhenish were not to be kept in the same cellar, nor sweet and dry wines in the same tavern. As an additional precaution customers had to be allowed to see their wine being drawn for them.[112] The penalties against those who offended were both practical and symbolic, as witness the case of John Penrose, a taverner of the City of London, who was convicted in 1364 of selling unwholesome wine. He was condemned to lose his right to trade as a vintner, to drink a draught of his own liquor, and to have the rest of it poured over his head.[113]

We need not think that the vintners of England were uniquely reprehensible. Foreign traders were just as crooked. In the Gironde, wine spoiled during fermen-tation was mixed into sound wine. Blending was also practised, white wine being mixed with Red, and Bordeaux wine with that from the 'high country' – the Côtes de Blaye, Périgord, and Cognac[114] – blends which need not necessarily be censured but at Bordeaux were considered to be fraudulent. And whereas the dishonest taverner of London sold white wine as Rhenish, the dishonest merchant of Bordeaux gave false *appellations* to some of the wines which he offered to his customers.[115]

The deceit of merchants in Burgundy was less subtle. They dealt in wine from heavily productive vineyards of Gamay grapes, wine which was of a 'great and horrible bitterness'. It had, however, at one stage in its making, a certain amount of softness and this the merchants prolonged or resurrected at the time of its sale by putting hot water into the barrels. When the doctoring wore off, the wine became 'stinking', at which the buyers were, not unnaturally 'grandement dommagez'.[116] Such wines, and many other medieval vintages, with or without blending, must have produced hangovers like the one warningly described by Eugenius of Toledo:

[108] *Close Rolls*, 48, Edward III (1374), mem., 27.

[109] *Cal. Pat. Rolls*, 2, Henry IV, Pt I, mem., 6 (Jan. 12th, 1401).

[110] *Close Rolls*, 35, Edward I, mem., 13d.

[111] See James, Margery K., 'The Medieval Wine Dealer', *Explora-tions in Entrepreneurial History*, X, No. 2, 1957.

[112] *Munimenta Gildhallae Londoniensis*, Vol. III, 268–71.

[113] *Cal. Let. Bks. Lon.*, Vol. G, 178.

[114] Lafforgue, 78.

[115] *Ibid*, 78.

[116] Archives Nationales, Paris, H', 106, 57.

'Think of the trembling limbs, the void for mind, the hamstrung shambling walk, the eyes half-blind, the deafened ears, the tongue that none can mark, losing its powers to gain a babbling bark. Speak drunkard, are you dead or living now?'[117]

Burgundy provides an interesting illustration of both the good and the bad sides of medieval wine-making. The same Edict which lamented the 'stinking' wine of the merchants also fulminated against the Gamay *cépage*. In vineyards of Dijon, Beaune, and Chalon the Gamay had been planted for quantity and at the expense of quality and the Edict commanded that the '*très mauvais et tre desloyaux plant nommé gamay*' should be rooted out.[118] Now the Gamay makes none of the great modern wines of the Côte d'Or whereas it does make much of the good wine of Beaujolais. It is illuminating, therefore, to find that on the one hand the medieval Edict was concerned with the quality of the wine of the Côte while on the other hand the *vignerons* were quite satisfied to go on with their production of an inferior, but abundant, liquor.

In years of bad weather the must from some of the north-western European vine-yards tends to be low in sugar and sugar is added (by law) to bring up the ultimate alcohol content of the wine. A form of this *chaptalization* would often have been necessary in the Middle Ages. During most of the medieval centuries, however, it would not have been done with cane or beet sugar, as is the practice nowadays, but either with cooked grape-juice or else with honey. Honey was a constant and important factor in medieval life as we can see from its appearance in records so diverse as the Anglo-Saxon Leech Books, the Norman *Domesday*, and the 14th-century cook-book of the *Ménagier* of Paris. But in this latter work, which was written about 1392, we find also the mention of 'powdered sugar' and 'crystallized sugar'[119] and in the next century Margaret Paston was able to write to her husband and say '. . . send me an other sugar loff, for my old is do'.[120] Towards the end of the Middle Ages, therefore, *chaptalization* would have been possible in the modern manner and sugar could have been used instead of honey.

In fact we do not know how much *chaptalization* was practised by the men of the Middle Ages. Petrus de Crescentiis suggested putting honey into the must before it fermented but the purpose of this was to make the wine sweeter[121] and the logical connection between sweetness and strength, between the addition of sugar and the increase of alcohol, never seems to have been fully recognized. If it had been recognized there would not have been so many weak and unstable wines. Even sugaring the must for sweetness does not seem to have been widely practised for this, although its purpose was different, would have achieved the same effect. We can only believe that the medieval *vigneron* seldom put honey into his vat.

It did, however, in one way or another, form part of his technical repertoire, and it is worthwhile looking at that repertoire to note the range and the limit of his skills. First of all he was quite concerned with the cleanness of his vessels. In the medieval Gironde the butts were scrubbed with cold water and scoured. In Tuscany washing the casks with old wine was the method recommended to Francesco Datini. Petrus de Crescentiis favoured washing with salt water, scouring, and then fumigating '*dencens*' which in this instance meant either rosemary or cedarwood, the latter being perhaps the red cedar which was sold in spicers' booths.[122] Then, after

[117]Jack Lindsay, *Medieval Latin Poets*, 39–40.

[118]Archives Nationales, Paris, H', 106, 57.

[119]*LWS*, II, *passim*; Power, *Ménagier*, 284, 293, 295, 296.

[120]*Paston Letters*, ed. Gairdner, James, I, 236 (Letter of July 4th, 1452).

[121]Bk IV, cap. xxi; cf. Sigerist, Arnaldus, 31.

[122]Gironde: Lafforgue, 226. Tuscany: Origo, *Datini*, 293; Petrus de Crescentiis, Bk IV, caps xxxii, xxxiii; and red cedar: Power, *Ménagier*, 260.

Treading Grapes
Cleaning Casks
from 'Livre de Prouffitz
Champetres'
Petrus de Crescentiis,
1529 ed.
London, British Museum

the wine was made, came the clarifying and for this the *vigneron* used all sorts of things: eggs, pine-kernels, peach-stones and pebbles from a river bed. Honey was particularly recommended; it was supposed to maintain the colour of the wine.[123]

From all this it might seem that the *vigneron* was diligent in his efforts to obtain a sound, bright wine and in a sense this was so. But it was a rather desperate sense for most of these recipes were suggested for use with troubled wine and we cannot escape the implication, which is borne out by other evidence, that a lot of medieval wine was extremely difficult to manage. It must also have been unprepossessing to drink, although on occasion, no doubt, and perhaps many an occasion, its patent instability may have been masked by the awkward attractiveness of youth.

Thirsty Men

Like medieval man, medieval wine entered at birth upon a precarious existence. In a good year the natural strength of the wine may have brought it through most of its perils; in a poor year the natural strength of its drinkers may have carried them through the worst of its after-effects. Even so, and weak or strong, wine was still wine and the Middle Ages were thirsty. In her translation from Sedulius Scotus, Miss Helen Waddell has given us one of the incidents of thirst:

> 'I am a writer, I, a musician, Orpheus the second,
>   And the ox that treads out the corn, and your well-wisher I,
> I am your champion armed with the weapons of wisdom and logic,
>   Muse, tell my lord bishop and father his servant is dry.'[124]

[123]Petrus de Crescentiis, Bk IV, cap. xxxix.

[124]Helen Waddell, *Medieval Latin Lyrics*, 133.

There were many cases of vinous drought. The Anglo-Saxon boy who went to school in a monastery 'drinks ale, and, if he cannot get that, water, for he cannot afford wine'. Perhaps, being only a boy, he did not mind drinking water – or, as Langland would have it, drinking 'with the duck'.[125] Others, however, did mind it. Here, from France, is a lament of the hard life of the common people:

> 'Il n'a plus bled pour porter au molin
> On lui oste draps de laine et de lin,
> L'eaue, sans plus, lui demeure pour boire.'[126]

And these poor people, who had no more corn to take to the mill, whose woollen and linen goods were taken from them, and to whom only water was left to drink, were not alone in their misery. In 15th-century Tuscany there is the pious reference to '. . . the men whose bed has been taken from under them, who suffer from the cold or have to give up buying wine . . .' and to this reference is coupled the reasonable exhortation '. . . in the name of God's charity, weep for them . . .'[127]

The injunction to weep may have been heeded by a few devout souls but they would have been in a minority. Men were too accustomed to the enthusiastic savagery of other men to waste much time on weeping. Those who saw the world with alarm or horror, those who were frightened or sickened by a '*siecle puant et horrible*', fled from the world to the monasteries. Those who remained took a robust view of life and got as much fun out of it as they could.

> 'Never yet could I endure
> Soberness and sadness,
> Jests I love and sweeter than
> Honey find I gladness.'[128]

wrote the Archpoet. He was not alone in his dislike of 'soberness'. The pimply, red-faced Summoner who went on pilgrimage to Canterbury loved 'drinking strong wine till all was hazy' while at one moment on the same pilgrimage Chaucer's Miller was 'very drunk and rather pale'.[129] German peasants in the Schwarzwald, having carried wine to the monastery, were 'to be regaled with some of it until "no two men can carry the third to bed"'.[130] Students at the University of Paris celebrated Christmas Eve with 'revelry . . . dicing and drinking and wild Bacchic processions'.[131]

In the more normal course of their University life the Paris students who could afford to would, as Rabelais has it 'cauponisate in the meritory taberns of the Pine-apple, the Castle, the Magdalene, and the Mule'.[132] Affecting other rendez-vous, they could go and drink in *Les Chappelets*, at the corner of the rue Galande and the rue Saint-Julien-le-Pauvre, where a quart of the best wine cost two sous. They could also go to *Le Coq et la Poule (ad Gallum et Gallinam)* which was probably in the rue du Petit-Pont, or to *Le Turbot (ad Turbotum)* which was probably in the same street and where the wine was said to be good. Or else they might choose *Le Chatelet* where, at least in 1357, they could get the wine of Portugal.[133]

The English, afterwards called the German, 'nation' (or sub-organization of the

[125] *LWS*, II, xi; Langland, *Piers the Plowman*; C. Passus, VII, 174, and note.

[126] Huizinga, J., *The Waning of the Middle Ages*, 63, and n. 1.

[127] Origo, *Datini*, 145.

[128] Helen Waddell, *Medieval Latin Lyrics*, 185; see also Miss Waddell's, *The Wandering Scholars*, Ch. 7, for the Archpoet.

[129] Chaucer, *The Canterbury Tales*, trs. Nevill Coghill, Penguin Books, London, 42, 109, 1957 (Prologue and The Miller's Tale).

[130] *CMH*, VII, 745.

[131] Haskins, C. H., 'The University of Paris', *Studies in Medieval Culture*, 69.

[132] *Gargantua and Pantagruel*, Bk II, Ch. VI.

[133] Chatelain, E., 'Notes sur quelques tavernes fréquentées par l'Université de Paris aux XIVᵉ et XVᵉ siècles', *Bull. de la Soc. de l'Histoire de Paris et de l'Île-de-France*, XXV, 87-109, 1898.

Faculty of Arts), at the University of Paris was well known for its alcoholic enthusiasm. Negel Wircker, who was a student, describes the extent of their banquets and the undisciplined manner of their drinking,[134] and in the 13th century, if not before, the English, as a people, had achieved a considerable reputation for drunkenness. However justified this reputation may have been their 'assiduity in drinking' could scarcely have surpassed that of their ancestors. William of Malmesbury disapprovingly records that among the English at the time of the Norman Conquest '. . . drinking in parties was a universal practice, in which occupation they passed entire nights as well as days . . . they were accustomed to eat till they became surfeited, and to drink till they were sick. . . .' 'These latter qualities,' he adds, 'they imparted to their conquerors. . . .'[135] Such regrettable habits were supposed to have been brought to England by the Danes who drank with a fervour which King Edgar felt obliged to constrain. He took severe action, ordering nails to be driven at a certain level into the sides of the drinking cups 'as limits and bounds, which no man . . . should be so hardie as to transgresse'.[136] The writer who tells this story adds that the regulation had no effect.

The Price of Wine

In the centuries after the Norman Conquest wine was sold in most of the towns of England and on the whole it does not seem to have been unduly expensive. In the Household of Henry I the daily allowance to each of the four hornblowers was 3d. while the 'cat-hunters' got as much as 5d.[137] Wine at that time would have cost about 1d. a gallon.* In the next century, in 1230, wine cost about 2d. a gallon at Oxford while in 1258 at London white wine cost 2½d., and red wine 3d., a gallon.[138] Ordinary wages in the 13th century give us some idea of what these prices meant: a day-paid agricultural labourer got about 2d. a day, with extra for harvest: an artisan in London, where wages were higher than in the country, got 4d.–5d. a day. Perhaps a few other prices may fill out the picture: oysters cost ½d. a hundred and a salmon cost 1/– but a dozen lampreys cost 7/–.[139]

Both prices and wages rose slightly in the century of the Black Death. In 1331 wine cost 4d. a gallon. So did Gascon wine in 1342, though this was supposed to be its maximum price while at the same date the maximum price of Rhenish was 6d. a gallon. In 1358, however, Gascony wine had gone up to 6d. a gallon and 6d. a gallon was the price of Spanish wine. In this same year the highest daily wage, outside London, of a carpenter was 4½d. while that of a mason was 6d. It is curious to note that in 1368 a sword only cost 2/–.[140]

A comparison of the prices of wines in London in 1419 shows how much more expensive were the wines of the Mediterranean. Red wine (probably Gascon, or at least French) cost 6d. and Rhenish 8d. – these are all by the gallon – but Provence and Crete cost 1/–, Malvesie (Malmsey) 1/4d. and Vernage went as high as 2/–. As a foil to these prices we might observe that in the same year ale cost about 1d. a gallon.[141]

It is no wonder, then, that while most of the upper classes and many of the more prosperous merchants were accustomed to the drinking of wine, the poorer classes

*For medieval measures see Appendix H, below.

[134]Furnivall, F. J., *Early English Meals and Manners*, p. xli; see also Boyce, G. C., *The English–German Nation in the University of Paris during the Middle Ages*, 160–1.

[135]Chronicle of the Kings of England, 279.

[136]Lambarde, W., *A Perambulation of Kent*, 280–2, 1576.

[137]Hall, H., *The Red Book of the Exchequer*, III, 813.

[138]*Close Rolls*, 15, Henry III, mem., 21d; 42, Henry III, mem., 12.

[139]Wages: Rogers, J. E. Thorold, *Six Centuries of Work and Wages*, 170, 180. Fish-prices: TR, II, 558, 552 sqq.

[140]Wine prices: *Close Rolls*, 5, Edward III, Pt II, mem., 7d; *Cal. Let. Bks. Lon.*, Vol. F, fo. lxvi; *Close Rolls*, 32, Edward III, mem., 2d. Wages: TR, I, 318. Swords: TR, II, 559.

[141]Liber Albus, *Munimenta Gildhallae Londoniensis*, Vol. III, 262, 271.

of England, whether priests or peasants, confined themselves to beer and, to a lesser degree, to cider, perry, or mead. This difference in drinking is reflected as late as the middle of the 15th century by the *Boke of Curtasye* which ruled that it should be ale for men and wine for gentlemen. But there was no hard and fast line between the classes. Wine was available to the monks in some of the more fortunate monasteries and some of the poorer people bought wine to celebrate a special occasion. There must have been many moments of democratic wine for the scene which Chaucer portrays as the mixed company of Canterbury pilgrims refresh themselves at *The Tabard* cannot have been unique in English life:

> 'Our *Host* gave us great welcome; everyone
> Was given a place and supper was begun.
> He served the finest victuals you could think,
> The wine was strong and we were glad to drink.'[142]

The Naming of the Wines

There was never a period in the Middle Ages when wine was completely localized. In the 5th and 6th centuries Sareptan and Gazetic from Palestine were known in France and were most probably imported into that country.[143] Under the Moslem caliphate Spanish wine was exported from Malaga.[144] Rhenish from western Germany was almost certainly shipped to London before the Norman Conquest and quantities of it were imported into England in the 12th, as well as in later, centuries.[145] London in the early 12th century is described as '*constipata negotiatorum*' – crowded with traders, and many of them were German.[146] A poem called the *Bataille des Vins* lists more than fifty of the wines known in France in the 13th century and while many were of local *appellation*, among them were wines of Cyprus, the Moselle, 'Palme', and Spain.[147]

The wine most frequently drunk in medieval England came, not from the Rhineland, but from western France. It was shipped out of Bordeaux, La Rochelle and Nantes, and where the words 'wine' or 'red wine' occur in the earlier records of English imports they usually mean wine from Anjou, Guyenne, and Gascony. The long association of the English crown and nobility with western France encouraged this particular commerce but even without such a link the commerce would still have existed.

When the English merchants went themselves to Bordeaux to ship the wines of Gascony and Guyenne, they often sailed in convoys to the Gironde, hoping thus to be safe from pirates and privateers. One can see the wine fleet assembling in 1384, when ships from Kingston-upon-Hull, Lynn, Great Yarmouth, Scarborough, Newcastle, and Southampton gathered at Sandwich, Plymouth, and Dartmouth to make their voyage to Bordeaux. Once arrived, the English merchants had to buy their wine in accordance with the system of priorities in force at Bordeaux, restrictive regulations typical of the medieval commercial outlook, and designed in this instance to give an advantage to the wine of the citizens. Apart from taxes graduated in its favour, the wine belonging to the men of the city was the first wine that was allowed to be sold. This was mainly Graves, with perhaps some Côtes de Bordeaux.

[142] *Curtasye, Boke of*, 408-12, 841-3; Chaucer, *The Canterbury Tales*, trs. Nevill Coghill, Penguin Books, London, Prologue, 1957.

[143] Gazetic: see fn. 29. Sareptan: Salin, E., *La Civilisation Mérovingienne*, I, 443; Sidonius, *Poems*, XVII, 16.

[144] *CMH*, III, 433.

[145] Thorpe, Benjamin, *Ancient Laws and Institutes of England*, De Institutis Lundonie, cap. ii, 128; and for Rhenish see also Cunningham, W., *The Growth of English Industry and Commerce* (Bibl. General), I, 194; *Close Rolls*, 16, Edward III, mem. 6; *Cal. Let. Bks. Lon.*, Vol. F, fo. lxvi, 1342; Vol. G, fo. lxxxvib, 1360; *Keruynge, Boke of*, 153; *Paston Letters*, Vol. III, p.   .

[146] William of Malmesbury, *De Gestis Pontificum Anglorum*, Bk II, cap. 73, p. 140.

[147] *BdV*, ll. 15-136. Cyprus: see also *BdV*, l. 187. Palme: see also John of Salisbury, *Letters*, No. 33; Origo, *Datini*, 91, 96, 123-6. Spain (and Espaigne): see also *Close Rolls*, 39, Edward III, mem. 4; 48, Edward III, mem. 27; Chaucer, *Canterbury Tales*, Pardoner, C., ll. 565-6; Origo, *Datini*, 91.

Only after a delay of weeks, or even months, from the vintage could an English merchant buy the wines of the 'high country' which meant wines from the Côtes de Blaye (and possibly also the Côtes de Bourg) on the north bank of the Gironde, from further north in Saintonge, from Entre-deux-Mers between the Dordogne and Garonne, and from further east and south-east in Périgord and Armagnac.[148]

To us these restrictions seem merely pointless since the wine of Graves does not need to fear competition. In those days, however, and in a mediocre year, it had to be sold before it went sour or before it had time to show the full range of its defects. It also had to face the competition of the stronger, and therefore better-lasting, wines of the 'high country'. Body, not finesse, was the principal criterion of western medieval drinking.

Medieval connoisseurship was thus a limited faculty, and for the most part it concerned itself only with the relative merits of districts and regions. There was no question of growths or 'crus', no discussion of 'château wines', no distinction drawn between the individual vineyards of a wine-growing area. Medieval taste was able, for example, to compare wine of Graves with that of Saint-Emilion but it was not able to compare Château Haut-Brion with Château Ausone.

There was undoubtedly a more detailed connoisseurship but its range was the range of local gossip. *Vignerons* of a wine-growing area would have discussed in some detail the vintaging of their own neighbourhood. In the Côte d'Or towards the end of the 13th century they would have commented that Jean de Crux at Chassagne-Montrachet worked his vineyard better (or worse) than the Abbey of Maizières did theirs at Volnay.[149] Or else they would have argued the claims of the Clos de Bèze at Gevrey-Chambertin against those of the Clos de Corton at Aloxe. On the Upper Moselle they would have discussed the exploitation by the monks of the vineyards at Eitelsbach and compared their harvests with the monastic vintages of Kasel. And all the way up and down the valley they would have reminisced about the seven wonderful years from 1293 to 1300: how strong the wine was in 1295: how so abundant in 1296 that some of the old wine had to be poured away: and how plentiful again in 1300, that there was a scarcity of casks.[150]

The clergy, nobles, and merchants who lived in *vignoble* areas would have been familiar with much of the wine-gossip of their own district. Some of them may have had the taste to stock their cellars from the better vineyards and to secure for themselves the heaviest and most lasting wines; further than that their discrimination could not have gone for there was no vintage wine in the modern sense of the word and a discussion of vintage years was an exercise of memory which had no practical value. Some of these men, in fact, may have been in the sorry position of the lord of Bischholz who, when receiving rent from his tenants in the form of wine, was obliged to accept their wine even if it were 'so sour that it would corrode a horse's hoof'.[151] Landowners in his position who were unable to sell such bitter wine, or who had not enough capital to buy sounder stuff, faced a year of gloomy flatulence.

Detailed wine-gossip, differentiating (as far as it did differentiate) between *clos* and *clos*, between *climat* and *climat*, remained almost entirely a district matter. On a wider scale wines were known simply as those of the town or village which served as a centre or collecting point for the neighbouring vineyards. In the 13th century, for example, we have from the *Bataille des Vins*:

[148]Lafforgue, 77–9.

[149]Rodier, 240, 259.

[150]Langenbach, A., *The Wines of Germany* (Bibl. General), 22; Deichmann u., Wolf, *Weinchronik* (Bibl. General).

[151]*CMH*, VII, 745.

'. . . vin d'Argentueil,
Vin de Soissons, vin d'Auviler,
Vin d'Espernai le Bacheler,

.   .   .   .

Vin de Verdelai, vin d'Auçuerre,
De Torniere et de Flavigni' . . .[152]

There were also in this same poem other wines designated as those of Montpellier and Narbonne, of 'Quarquassone', of Mossac, of 'Chastel Raoul', or of Le Mans. Where the caprice of the poet involved some description of them, the description was a general one. There was 'le bon vin blanc de Poitiers'; there was the wine of St. Jean d'Angély, near Cognac, whose great strength was noted; and there were the wines of 'Argenteuil' which '*fu clers comme lerme d'ueil*'.[153]

In theory this 'market-town' or 'village' type of designation conveys a reasonable amount of meaning and implies a certain degree of exactitude. In practice, however, this was not always so since, to take one example, a consignment of wine from St. John (St. Jean d'Angély) might easily have included wine from other areas. And in international trade the general tendency was towards the greater inexactitude. Whereas St. Jean had been a collecting point for neighbouring vineyards, as had the other towns of Aunis and Saintonge, the bigger collecting points such as La Rochelle included the consignments of the lesser towns and obscured their identities inside its own. Thus it was usual for the wines of St. Jean, as well as those of Saintes, Taillebourg, and Angoulême, all of which were shipped through La Rochelle, to take a new title from their town of shipment and to be called merely wine of Rochelle. It is sad to have to point out that much of the wine shipped through La Rochelle to England, especially from Saintonge and the Cognac country, would have been hard and acid.[154]

Much the same obscuring of identity happened also on the River Seine, for wine coming down from Auxerre and Paris was shipped out of Rouen and would sometimes have been known as wine of Rouen. Auxerre, however, was often used as the collecting point from which the wines took their name but even so the *appellation* was imprecise since 'Auxerre', or 'Auçuerre', included the wines of Chablis, of Lower Burgundy in general and, on occasion, of Beaune and the Côte d'Or. Inside France there remained some degree of differentiation for 'Chablies' was distinguished from 'Biaune'; but when English drinkers received any wine from Beaune, which was seldom, or from Chablis, which was more frequently, they received it under the general title of Auxerre.[155]

Then we have the designation which is given by a river as such and not by any collecting point along its course. The Rhine is a good example for the wines shipped down the great river did not take the names of collecting points such as Strasbourg, Mainz, Cologne, or Dordrecht but were merely called Rhenish. Rhenish meant west German wine, whether from the vineyards of the Rhinegau, Rhinehessia, the Palatinate, Franconia, Alsace, or the Moselle, although sometimes Moselle wine did travel under its own name.[156]

Two further illustrations of the river theme, each with its own peculiarity, have a Spanish background. Wine from Aragon or Catalonia, shipped out of the River

[152]*BdV*, ll. 28–30, 36–7.

[153]Mossac: probably the same as Muissac', for which see *Liberate Rolls*, 12, Henry III, mem. 5. Poitiers: see also *Giraldi Cambrensis Opera*, I, xxxix–xl. St Jean d'Angély (or St John): see also *Liberate Rolls*, 22, Henry III, mem. 13, etc.; *Close Rolls*, 13, Edward III, mem. 34d.

[154]Rochelle: Barbazan et Méon, IV; Le Credo au Ribaut, 83–4; Ritson, III, 177.

[155]Auxerre (and Auçuerre): *BdV*, 36, 39; Barbazan et Méon, IV; Le Credo au Ribaut, 83–4; *Pipe Roll*, 2, John, rot. 6; *Close Rolls*, 17, Henry III, mem. 9; Dion, *Rev. Hist.*; Helen Waddell, *The Wandering Scholars*, 213. 'Chablies': *BdV*, 39. 'Biaune': *BdV*, 39; Dion, *Rev. Hist.*

[156]Rhenish: see fn. 145. Rhine wine-trade: see for example, Langenbach, A., *The Wines of Germany*, 23, 29. 'Durdraght': *Close Rolls*, 16, Edward III, mem. 6. Moselle ('Moussele'): *BdV*, 17.

Transporting Wine Casks from the Flemish Calender Munich Bay Staatsbibliothek

Ebro was occasionally called 'Torrentyne' 'of Ebrew' but it was more usually known as 'Ryvere' or 'of the river' or sometimes, as in the early 16th century as 'Wyn ryvers'.[157] It seems odd to us that, with so much wine shipped down so many rivers, English vintners should have been content with such an *appellation* but tradition must have given it a meaning which, however general, was thought adequate enough by the medieval drinker.

[157]'Torrentyne': *Nurture, Boke of,* l. 119; Blowbol, 340. 'Ryvere': *Cal. Let. Bks. Lon.,* Vol. F, fo. ccxiv; Vol. G, fos lxxiib-lxxiib, 1357; Vol. H, fo. cclx, 1391; cf. Bacci, 364. 'Wyn ryvers': Blowbol, 328.

266

The other peculiarity is that of Lepe, whose wine, so Chaucer tells us, was mixed with other wine to produce a rapid intoxication in the honest citizens of London. Lepe is most probably ancient Illipula and modern Niebla, a town in the Province of Seville, north-east of Huelva and Moguer. Why Chaucer used its name in the general context of Spanish wine is something of a problem. Niebla and Moguer may have had their medieval vineyards but the bulk of the Spanish wine gathered for transport down the Guadalquivir river-system should more easily have met its shippers at Seville and at the mouth of the river where the sherry town of Sanlúcar de Barrameda now stands. It may have been that sandbanks choked the estuary of the Guadalquivir. But it is more likely that Lepe was merely continuing its long history as a trading centre. Wine and oil, though chiefly oil, were very probably sent this way from Andalusia to Roman Britain and Edrîsî records in about 1154 that Niebla was then an old and beautiful city, surrounded by strong walls, where much trade was carried on.[158] Whatever the answer to the problem, the fame of Lepe is now gone and few modern drinkers know even where it was.

The 'river' titles were still not the most general form of *appellation*. Land areas provided names of very common use and of very considerable vagueness. 'Algarbe', or 'Algrade' was one of them. In all probability it meant wine shipped from the Algarve, in the south of Portugal, but it may also have meant wine shipped down the River Guadiana, or merely wine from Arab Iberia. 'Provence' was another inclusive *appellation*. It could mean a sweet, white wine when imported into England in the 14th century and the odds are that it referred to a wine of Frontignan. Yet the name 'Provence', unless it is qualified, might mean almost any wine from the region of Narbonne, Carcassonne, and Montpellier.[159] These land-area names are wide enough; yet they are not as widely embracing as the political designations which occur so often in the English records – Andegavie, Pictavie, Wasconie, Spain, Portugal, and Romaney.

Andegavie meant the wines of Anjou, and the shipments down the Loire which ended up in English ports as 'wine of Andegavie' may often have included wine of Touraine. Many of the Andegavie wines were white wines, sweet and strong, and they were much favoured by the English. Pictavie – *vinum Pictav'* – meant the wines of Poitou. Wasconie meant those coming from Gascony and included the wines of Saintonge and Guyenne, together with those grown in Périgord and the wine grown, or collected, at Moissac in Tarn et Garonne. (This latter, however, sometimes reached England under its own name and we find in 1228 that thirty tuns of Muissac' were bought for Henry III.) The *appellations* Spain and Portugal were as wide as the frontiers of those countries[160] but Romaney was the widest *appellation* of them all.

It has sometimes been thought that Romaney – or Rompney or Rumney – was so called either because it was made from a particular grape or because it was grown in the Italian Romagna. Alternatively, it has been classed as a white wine of Spain. The possibility that it could have been any one of these three shows clearly the vagueness (to us) of medieval nomenclature. As it happens, it was none of them. It was wine, and some, at least, of it was red wine, grown in the islands and countries of 'Rumania' – the medieval 'East Roman Empire' – and the name covered the vintages of the Adriatic, Dalmatia, Greece, and Anatolia. It is true that in 1482

[158] Lepe: Chaucer, *Canterbury Tales*, Pardoner, C., ll. 563, 570; *Close Rolls*, 8, Henry IV, mem. 29; cf. Bacci, 365. Niebla: Edrisî, 215.

[159] Algarbe: Ritson, III, 176, p. 360; Edrisî, 217. Provençe: *BdV*, 22; *Cal. Let. Bks. Lon.*, Vol. G, fo. cccxiib, 1373; Vol. H, fo. cxxb, 1380. Frontignan: V.V., *A.*, III, 374.

[160] Andegavie (Andegavia): *Close Rolls*, 17, Henry III, mem. 9; *Pipe Roll*, 26, Henry III, rot. 7, mem. 2. Anjou: cf. also *Maison Rustique*, 631. Pictavie (Pictavia): *Pipe Roll*, 3, Henry II, rot. 7, mem. 2; and 26, Henry III. Wasconie (Wasconia): *Cal. Pat. Rolls*, 9, Henry III, mem. 4; *Pipe Roll*, 26, Henry III, rot. 7, mem. 2. Spain: see fn. 147.

'romania' wines were made at Chipiona, near Jerez, and also at Jerez itself, in south-western Spain, but this was probably a Renaissance extension of the term and in medieval times it seems to have applied only to the wines of the Byzantine East.[161]

A number of medieval wines were named from the grapes out of which they were made. Vernage, which was well known in England in the 14th and 15th centuries, took its name from the vernaccia grape. It was a medium-sweet to sweet wine with a fine bouquet and was grown in Italy, mainly, it seems, in Northern Italy. Trebbiano, another sweet wine, and one which grew in Tuscany and the Marches, was called after the medieval trebbiano vine. The 'Trubidiane' which we find in London in 1373 must have been this trebbiano wine, its name corrupted by the irregularities of medieval spelling. Grenache, which came from Crete, and possibly also from Italy, was called after the grenache vine. 'Campelyte' may be another case of this type of naming. It appears in the English records of the 15th century and it has been suggested that it was wine from Campiglia in Tuscany. This may have been so; but its name Campelyte, with its variant writings Campletes and Campolet, is more likely to have come from a white grape called campole.[162]

The most famous of medieval wines is Malmsey. Basically it was a sweet wine and the best of it grew in Crete, or Candia as the island was sometimes called. But inferior Malmsey was also made in Cyprus and the Malmsey 'style' was undoubtedly copied in many other Mediterranean vineyards. It travelled under more names than any other medieval wine. First of all there were the variant writings of its 'style' name, such as Malvoisie, Malevesyñ, and Malvasia. And then there were its geographical titles: Candy, Cret, Cyprus, and Rotimo, the latter being wine that was

[161] Romaney: Ritson, III, 176; *Cal. Let. Bks. Lon.*, Vol. G, fo. clxvb, 1365; Origo, *Datini*, 91; *Nurture, Boke of*, l. 119; TR, III, 512; *Close Rolls*, 2, Henry VII, mem. 10d; cf. Bacci, 333 (Bacci's information, in this general passage, is very confused). 'Romania' wines in Jerez: González Gordon, 70-1.

[162] Vernage, vernaccia: Ritson, III, 176; Chaucer, *Canterbury Tales*, Merchant, E., l. 1807; *Close Rolls*, 34, Edward III, mem. 4; *Nurture, Boke of*, l. 118; Origo, *Datini*, 291-2; V.V., *A.*, Dict. Trebbiano: Origo, *Datini*, 291; V.V., *A.*, II, 255-6, 263. Trubidiane: *Cal. Let. Bks. Lon.*, Vol. G, fo. cccxiib, 1373. Grenache: Froissart, *Hist. et Chron. Memorable*, Vol. IV, Ch. XVIII, 75; Power, *Ménagier*, 226; Petrus de Crescentiis, Bk IV, cap. iv. Campelyte, Campletes, Campolet: *Cal. Pat. Rolls*, Edward IV, Pt II, mem. 10d; *Keruynge, Boke of*, 153, 174; Simon, André L., *History of the Wine Trade in England*, II, 242; Blowbol, 335; Cotgrave.

grown in the Rethymo vineyards of Crete. Malmsey has been immortalized by Shakespeare as the liquid in which the Duke of Clarence was supposed to have been drowned, but it was popular in England for more normal purposes in the 15th century, as indeed it was in the Elizabethan era. Even earlier than the 15th century it was held in favour, for at one time King Edward III had about 500 gallons of Cret wine in the cellars of the Tower of London.[163] Its sweetness might not have appealed to the Duke of Clarence but it certainly endeared itself to the English palate.

The geographic attitude of the medieval mind was almost as unscientific as the attitude which it took towards natural history. The *Mapemonde* of Pierre, of about 1217, states for example that in Asia lies the terrestial paradise which is encircled by a wall of red flame, and it adds that some of the people in Asia have dog's heads.[164] Such an acceptance of the romantic is not conducive to accurate cartography. Nevertheless there did come about some awakening of interest in proper mapping. There is a record of maps in Barcelona at the end of the 14th century.[165] There were the Catalan coast-maps. And in the first half of the 15th century the Jewish cartographer Jaime of Majorca was at the Court of the Portuguese Henry the Navigator.[166] These are the stirrings of exactitude. But for the most part medieval man was content with approximate definition, and this, together with the flexibility of his spelling, leaves us with a number of problems in the identification of medieval wines.

A splendid example of elasticity in naming lies in the use of the phrase 'Greek wine'. Some 'Greek wine' was a style of Malmsey or Cyprus and in this guise it might most reasonably have been called Greek. But in fact its name came, or there seems little doubt that it came, from the greco vine and in this case the wine would usually have been Italian. And to give the customer an extra choice of title the greco wine could also be called 'Latin'.[167] Now to us, with our insistence upon the accurate geography of wines, this medieval elasticity may seem careless and confusing. Viewed from the modern standpoint it is both. But to the medieval drinker it was neither. He was not interested in the precise location of the vineyards which grew his wine. Two things only concerned him: the style of a wine and the general area in which it was grown. Thus the phrase 'Greek wine' gave him everything which he wanted to know. It told him that the wine was made from the greco grape: that it was a sweet, white wine: and that it was the same in style as some of the wines of the Greek islands. The meanings of Greek and greco fit easily into each other. 'Latin' is added, though only occasionally, to indicate that it came from Italy. Armed with this mass of knowledge, medieval man would have been content. To probe deeper into the origin of the wine would have been impossible and, if it had been possible, it would have seemed irrelevant.

Bread, eels, and bacon

There was rather more finesse in medieval eating than there was in medieval drinking but even so we find little emphasis upon the finer points of gastronomy. We find, too, that there was no great difference in taste between the richer people who drank wine and the poorer people who drank beer and, with a few exceptions, the diet of the rich was only a magnified reflection of the diet of the poor. Conditions

[163] Malmsey: Ritson, III, 176; *Cal. Let. Bks. Lon.*, Vol. G, fos lxxib-lxxiib, 1357; *Close Rolls*, 34, Edward III, mem. 4; Froissart, *Hist. et Chron. Memorable*, Vol. IV, Ch. XVIII, 75; *Nurture, Boke of*, l. 120; *Cal. State Papers Venetian*, I, No. 544; Bacci, 331, 333. Candy: *Cal. State Papers Venetian*, I, No. 544; cf. *Blacke Dogg*, A. 4 (A.D. 1638) for 'Amber colour'd' Candy. Cret: *Close Rolls*, 16, Edward III, Pt I, mem. 39; *Cal. Let. Bks. Lon.*, Vol. G, fos iib, lxxiib-lxxiib (1352-3, 1357). Cyprus: *BdV*, 15, 187. Rotimo: Simon, André L., *History of the Wine Trade in England*, II, 218. Duke of Clarence: *King Richard III*, Act I, Sc. iv.

[164] Langlois, C. V., *La Vie en France au Moyen Âge*, III, 122 sq.

[165] Origo, *Datini*, 98.

[166] Elaine Sanceau, *Henry the Navigator*, 52.

[167] Greek: John of Salisbury, *Letters*, No. 33; Ritson, III, 177; *Cal. Let. Bks. Lon.*, Vol. G, fo. cccxiib, 1373; *Close Rolls*, 8, Richard II, mem. 9; Origo, *Datini*, 292; *Nurture, Boke of*, l. 120; Benvenuto Cellini, *Memoirs* (Bibl. Ch. 6), 56; Petrus de Crescentiis, Bk IV, cap. iv. Latin: Simon, André L., *The History of the Wine Trade in England*, I, 282; cf. Bacci, 224. Greco bianco vine: V.V., *A.*, Dict.

differed, of course, between the beer-making countries of the North and the wine-producing countries of the South but it can hardly be said that they differed radically and a general picture of medieval food will be an adequate background for some of the more aromatic details in the taste of medieval drinking.

The basis of the North-Western diet was corn, made into bread, beer, pastry, or porridge; and this staple fare was filled out with such vegetables as were obtainable.[168] For the great majority of people honey was the only sweetener and it served also to enliven dishes which otherwise would have been dull. In the 6th century, for example, we find Venantius Fortunatus at Poitiers eating his vegetables sprinkled with honey, a recipe which, no doubt, had been inherited from Roman times.[169] In the spring and summer eggs were common, as were milk and cheese: there were pork, bacon and beef: there was fresh fruit, apples, cherries, pears and, sometimes, grapes. Then, to cheer up the monotonous diet of winter, there were nuts, either eaten raw or made into preserves with cloves, honey and ginger.[170]

But although winter conditions were often hard, and sometimes very hard indeed, we must not think that the Middle Ages were a thousand years of unlimited wintry distress. In the better parts of the North-Western countries, milk, butter and eggs could be obtained, dried fruits such as figs and raisins were possible, fresh meat was, it would seem, occasionally available, and fresh fish was easy to get.[171] It is true that these details are all taken from the 15th century when life may have been easier than in earlier times but in some degree this picture must apply also to the earlier centuries.

Fish – dried, salted, or fresh – was another staple of the medieval diet. Eels and herring were particularly common. In 11th-century England, at Wisbech in the Hundreds of Ely, William of Warenne had six fishermen who paid in three thousand five hundred eels. The Manor of Horningsea, which belonged to the Abbot of Ely, produced a thousand,[172] and eels were not only found in the Fens for quantities of them were also caught in Kent and Oxfordshire. Among the different ways of serving them in France towards the end of our period were salted eels, eels in galantine, and *Soringue d'Anguilles*, this last recipe including onions, parsley, ginger, cinnamon, cloves, pepper, saffron, vinegar, verjuice and wine.[173] It must have been good.

Herrings were extremely common. In the *Domesday Monachorum* the Manor of Sandwich paid 40,000 herring to the Archbishop of Canterbury who gave them to the monks.[174] The monks may or may not have been grateful for this benevolence. One view of the monastic diet is expressed with feeling in *Piers the Plowman*:

> 'Ich haue no lust, leyue me – to lenge a-mong monkes;
> For hij eteth more fisch than flesh – and feble ale drynken.'[175]

Guiot of Provins, in his own day, shared this emotion for he too had no desire 'believe you me' to linger among unsatisfied monks. But, although monks may have eaten 'more fisch than flesh' the fishy emphasis was by no means confined to the monasteries. It operated among the poorer classes of the populace and at Hawsted in Suffolk, for instance, the labourer during harvest time got 'two herrings per day, milk from the manor dairy to make cheese, and a loaf of bread'.[176] Fish was

[168] Wood-Legh, xxvi–xxviii; and see references in fn. 90.

[169] Salin, E., *La Civilisation Mérovingienne*, 440. For Roman recipes using honey with vegetables, see Apicius, III, xviii, 1b.

[170] See, for example: *Acc. Obed. Abingdon*, 53, 55; Neilson, N., *Economic Conditions on the Manors of Ramsey Abbey*, 71; Power, *Ménagier*, 295–6; Wood-Legh, passim.

[171] Wood-Legh, xxiv–xxvi.

[172] *VCH, Cambridge*, I, 381, 365; (*Domesday*).

[173] Power, *Ménagier*, 235, 267.

[174] *VCH, Kent*, III, 261.

[175] Langland, *Piers the Plowman*, C., Passus, VII, ll. 158–9.

[176] *Ibid*, Vol. II, 116, n. 304.

prominent too, though a little less markedly, on the tables of the wealthier merchants and the feudal nobility. Nor was it only in the Atlantic countries that herrings were usual for they were also eaten in Italy, as indeed were eels.[177]

There were, of course, all sorts of fish. Salmon was frequent, both in France and England, as were carp, tench, pike and roach. Crayfish were eaten in France and so were oysters. The latter in particular have a long history of popularity in England since they were eaten by the Early Iron Age citizens of Bagendon, near Cirencester, and in the middle of the 15th century they were favoured by the two old priests of Munden's Chantry at Bridport in Dorset.[178]

Meat was more prized than fish but it appeared less frequently on the tables of the poor. The 'tame-meat', with the possible exception of goats, pigs and pigeons, was not as good as it is now since inferior breeding and inadequate feeding produced smaller animals than those of modern times. Then again, most of the meat which was eaten during the winter had been salted, and not always efficiently salted, during the late autumn. Bacon, of course, was a stand-by and so, to some extent, were chickens.

The alternative to 'tame-meat' was game. This formed a considerable part of the upper-class diet but many a poor man, legally or illegally, was able to get 'something for the pot'. Among the illegal foragers was a hungry ancestor of the Sporting Parson, for on February 18th, 1292, we find an 'Order to Simon de Elleswrth, lieutenant of the justice of the forest on this side Trent, after taking a fine from Ranulf, parson of the church of Thornedon, to deliver him from the prison of Colecestre wherein he is detained for a trespass of venison in the forest of Essex....'[179] Lower down in the scale of hunting were rabbits, which were quite common, and in addition to these the dinner table was often graced by 'small birds', among which were partridges, quail, larks, pigeons, swifts and blackbirds.[180]

Finally, let us look at three different pictures of medieval English eating. The first is taken from the landowner class of the 7th century and shows the food-rent of a West Saxon property of ten hides, or about twelve hundred acres. The rent is: '10 vats of honey, 300 loaves, 12 "ambers" of Welsh ale, 30 of clear ale, 2 full-grown cows, or 10 wethers, 10 geese, 20 hens, 10 cheeses, an "amber" full of butter, 5 salmon, 20 pounds of fodder and 100 eels'.[181]

The second is Henry III's order for Christmas provisions at Westminster in 1240. Swans, cranes, herons or bitterns, peacocks, partridges, hares, roe-deer, and pickled boars' heads were some of the outstanding items of the royal feast, while in addition to these there were kids, lambs, pigs, hens, rabbits, lampreys, Yarmouth herrings, salmon, and salted shad.[182]

The third is a picture of life in a humble middle-class, or lower middle-class, household from 1453 to 1460. It is the household of William Savernak and John Trewen, the two priests of Munden's Chantry, in Dorset. Their most regular articles of food were bread, oatmeal, fish and peas. Eggs, milk, butter, and cheese were frequent purchases. Beef, mutton, and pork were not at all uncommon. Sometimes there was veal or lamb and 'as special treats, sucking pigs or chickens'. Almonds and raisins were bought and figs for Lent. A pottle of honey provided the sweetening for the year; salt was bought for preserving; and pepper, cloves, ginger and cinnamon gave some relish to the meals in this quiet and uneventful dwelling.

[177] Origo, *Datini*, 285 sq.

[178] France: Power, *Ménagier*, *passim*. England: *Roll*, *Swinfield*, II, xlvii; Clifford, E. M., 'Excavations at Bagendon, *ILN*, Feb. 1st, 1958; Wood-Legh, xxv.

[179] *Calendar of the Fine Rolls*, 20, Edward I, mem. 11.

[180] See, for example: Power, *Ménagier*, 234, 259, etc.; Origo, *Datini*, 98, 284, 285; *Roll*, *Swinfield*, II, xlvii; Chaucer, *Canterbury Tales*, Prologue, A, 349-52. For rabbits in Provençe, see *Cambridge Economic History of Europe* (Bibl. General), II, 326.

[181] *English Historical Documents*, I, Laws of Ine, cap. 70, I, p. 371.

[182] *Liberate Rolls*, Vol. II.

From their garden the two priests could get vegetables, from their orchard fruit, and they also had a vine which needed propping and which gave them grapes. They probably made some cider or perry, but ale was their usual drink and wine only appeared on very special occasions.[183]

Spiced Wine

Herbs and spices played an essential part in medieval cooking. Meat which was indifferent in summer and indifferently preserved in winter, fish which was dull when it was fresh and duller when it was salted, each needed seasoning to make it palatable. Ginger, cinnamon, and grains of Paradise – a sort of pepper – were widely used, as were saffron and nutmegs. The poor had to make do with garlic, mustard, parsley, clove carnations, paeony seeds, 'fynkelsede' or fennel seed, and any other herbs which they could find or grow.[184]

The Middle Ages spiced their drink for the same reasons that they spiced their food: to disguise its imperfections, to enliven its mediocrity, and to provide some variation in the monotonies of taste. Ale, or 'servicia', was the common drink of the English. Growtt, or groute, was a sort of ale, though whether it was a spiced ale is not at all clear. Ciromellum was the same as growtt; so was Idromellum, which looks like a variant writing of Hydromel but apparently is not. Among the ales which definitely were spiced were those called Bochet and Braket. Bochet, a French drink, was made of ale, honey, spices and water. Braket was English and was made with ale, honey and pepper although, with typical medieval confusion, it could be the same as Hippocras and Clarre which were made with wine and not with ale.[185]

Herbs or spices were sometimes put into those drinks which can more specifically be called honey-drinks. Mead, or methe, was basically made of honey and water; occasionally, however, spices were added. Metheglin was fundamentally the same as mead, though possibly it was stronger, and herbs were sometimes added to give it flavour. The history of both these drinks is largely rustic. Oxymel comes into the class of astringent drinks. It was made of honey and vinegar, sometimes with the addition of water, and was considered by the Anglo-Saxons to be a 'southern (or Italian) drink', this no doubt because of its association with Roman life. It seems unlikely that it was extensively drunk in the later Middle Ages. Hydromel, which also had Roman associations, was honey and water.

We do know, however, that spiced wines were very popular and there is no doubt that their manufacture was almost universal. In general they were classed as Piments, being thus named from the *pigmentarii* or dealers in drugs and spices. But when we find in the *Close Rolls* of Henry III '*ad pigmenta et alios potus preciosos conficiendos*'[186] we need not assume that the *pigmenta* were made by a royal apothecary since they were just as likely to have been made by one of the royal cellarers. Quite apart from the amount of aromatic wine that was made by merchants and taverners, a great deal of it must have been made 'at home' and very frequently it must have been made by the goodwoman of the house herself. Here, in the 'home Piments' of the Middle Ages we have the origin of the 'still-room' of later centuries.

Wine, honey, and spices – such was the generalized recipe for Piments. The

[183] K. L. Wood-Legh, *A Small Household of the XVth Century, passim.* This is indeed a valuable and enlightening work.

[184] Power, *Ménagier, passim*; Langland, *Piers the Plowman*, C. Passus, VII, 359–60; *Liberate Rolls*, 26, Henry III, mem. 3; 33, Henry III, mem. 1; Chaucer, *Romaunt of the Rose*, ll. 1359–72. For Tuscany, see Origo, *Datini*, 287 sq. For spices, etc., in 8th-century France, see Salin, E., *La Civilisation Mérovingienne*, I, 135–6.

[185] Growtt, groute (and growte): Stratmann, F. H., *A Middle-English Dictionary* (Bibl. Dictionaries). Ciromellum: Wright, *Vocabs.*, I, 772 (12). Idromellum: Wright, *Vocabs.*, I, 725 (26). Bochet: Power, *Ménagier*, 293. Braket: Arnold, 187, 188.

[186] *Close Rolls*, 32, Henry III, mem. 14 (A.D. 1247). Piment: *Close Rolls*, 28, Henry III, mem. 19; Ritson, III, 176, 177; *Nurture, Boke of*, l. 118; cf. the Roman *conditum* and the Cate pument of the 16th century A.D.

· hoe ·

ða ða heðranc ofðam piñe ðapcaið heðpuncen · ⁊læʒ
onhir ʒeælde unbeheled · Hiʃ ruñu ða cham ʒerſah hiʃ
ʒerceapu unbeheled · ⁊cyðde hic hir ꝧam ʒebroðrum ·
uc onſelda ·

ſem   hoe   cham   · iapıphapa ·

hap ða ſlode naʃ na ſcırʒeaıð

simplest, the most 'countrified', and probably the most common of the Piments was Gariofilatum. This was wine spiced with cloves – gillyflowers, or clove pinks – but it did not necessarily include honey. The *vina florata* recorded in the *Close Rolls* of 1236 may have been of the gariofilatum type although the suggestion has been made that they were sparkling wines; and indeed they may have been sparkling, *crémant* wines, *pétillant* with some remnant of their fermentation. It is more likely, however, that in this case 'floratus' bears its medieval meaning of 'scented', and thus the *vina florata* of 1236 and the 'tun of . . . (florati) wine' of the *Liberate Rolls* of 1242 were wines scented with flowers, and quite probably with clove pinks, so that each of them would in fact have been a gariofilatum.

But, as happens with some of the medieval wine-names, gariofilatum may have quite another meaning since it could have been Gillyflower Wine, made from honey (or sugar), water and the flowers of clove carnations. In all probability this latter was a drink only for the poor and I think we are justified in assuming that where gariofilatum occurs in the records it usually means an aromaticized grape-wine. Yet even here we must note that grape-wine gariofilatum was not always as innocent as it might seem. One of the medieval manuals remarks that some people put cloves into wine when they were doctoring it to prevent it turning and a certain amount of gariofilatum was thus made, not to satisfy the demand of the public, but to disguise the imperfections of the wine.[187]

The most esteemed of the Piments were Hippocras and Clarre. Hippocras was made from wine and sugar (or honey), cinnamon, ginger, and pepper, and was then strained. Clarre, or Clarry, was also made of wine, honey, and spices and, as the *Boke of Nurture* has it Clarey was sweet 'whañ it is newe'. But there could be variations in the recipes and while herbs might be added to Hippocras they could certainly be mixed with Clarre. Among those which went into this latter drink was, very possibly, the herb Clary. But a more basic meaning is that of a drink which is 'clear' and Clarre, *Claretum*, and Claret are names which all indicate that they were clear, or clarified, drinks.

Clearness of texture was the criterion of this type of naming and it was only natural that it should be applied also to 'clearness' of colour. Thus the medieval name Claret could also mean the same as the medieval name *Clairet, Clairet* being a pure wine which was light in colour. In the Chalonnais in the 14th and 15th centuries *Clairet* was used to mean a *vin rosé* and indeed the word is still used in the Gironde to describe wine which is run off the skins of red or black grapes after twenty-four hours. The medieval use of the words Claret and *Clairet* to mean the pale colour of a wine is underlined by the fact that as late as the 17th century the wine of Champagne could be described as 'claret and yellowish', 'claret' in this case meaning white or tawny.

The medieval meaning of the name Claret is thus quite different from its modern meaning but it seems that a devious thread can be glimpsed connecting the medieval to the modern significance. *Clairet* in the Middle Ages could mean a *vin rosé: vin rosé* can be a blend of red and white wines: and it seems most probable that *Clairet* bore just that meaning in the wine trade of medieval Bordeaux. And there may be yet another point of attachment between *Clairet* and Bordeaux since it is possible that *Clairet* was used to describe the medieval wines of Graves which are likely to

*Noah the Vintner:
from the Aelfric Pentateuch
mid 11th-century
English MS.
London, British Museum*

[187] *Close Rolls*, 20, Henry III, mem. 12; *Liberate Rolls*, 26, Henry III, mem. 12. Gariofilatum: *Pipe Roll*, 13, John, rot. 21d, mem. 1; *Liberate Rolls*, 17, Henry III, mem. 9; Petrus de Crescentiis, Bk IV, cap. xxxviii.

Tasting and Blending Wine from 'Livre des Prouffitz Champetres' Petrus de Crescentis, 1529 ed. London, British Museum

have had less colour than the wines of neighbouring vineyards. Be that as it may, it was a long time before the connection between the name *Clairet*, or Claret, and the place Bordeaux became intimate and it was not until long after the Middle Ages that Claret, always and unequivocally, came to mean to an Englishman what it means today – the blood-red wine of Bordeaux.[188]

'Yoxing and bolkynge'

On many occasions these aromatic wines, when mulled, would have soothed away the cold of a medieval winter. On other occasions they were used as stimulants and the old and scrawny husband in Chaucer's Merchant's Tale drank Clarre to increase desire. More generally, however, they were used at feasts and on special occasions as luxury-wines or 'liqueurs'. In the household of Humphrey, Duke of Gloucester, the dessert was comfits with caraway seeds, apples, wafers and Ypocras. The *Ménagier* of Paris notes in some detail 'the arrangements for the wedding feast that master Helye shall give on a Tuesday in May' and after enumerating the first part of the dinner goes on to say: 'Entremets: crayfish jelly, loach, young rabbits and pigs. Dessert: frument and venison. Issue: Hippocras and wafers. Sally-Forth: wine and spices.' Then, at the supper after this wedding feast, there shall be 'Dancing, singing, wine and spices, and torches for lighting'.[189]

Despite all these pleasantries we may still be inclined to consider that the manners of medieval eating were crude. It is true that the meals were eaten off trestle tables and the food out of bowls or from trenchers of bread. But, in the later Middle Ages, if not before, the tables of noble houses were carefully spread with cloths and the

[188] Hippocras: Ritson, III, 176; Chaucer, *The Canterbury Tales*, Merchant, E., l. 1807; *Nurture, Boke of*, ll. 121-76, 715; *Antiq. Cul.*, Forme of Cury, No. 191; Power, *Ménagier*, 226, 227, 299; Arnold, 187; cf. the Anomalin of Palestine in the 1st-6th centuries A.D. Clarre: Chaucer, *The Canterbury Tales*, Knight, A., l. 1471; Merchant, E., l. 1807; *Cal. Let. Bks. Lon.*, Vol. G, fo. clxvb, 1365; Arnold, 187, 188. Clarry: *Nurture, Boke of*, l. 120; Power, *Ménagier*, 327, recipes; *Antiq. Cul.*, 90. Clary Wine: I am much indebted to Mr F. Newman Turner of the Society of Herbalists for his advice on the uses of the herb Clary. See also *LWS*, II, 59, for 'slary' (*Salvia sclarea*) in a medicinal aspect; and see Appendix G, references for Renaissance to Modern Wines. Claret, claretum: Dioscorides, *Herbal*, Bk V, 8; *LWS*, II, X, 393; *Close Rolls*, 28, Henry III, mem. 19; Du Cange, *Glossarium* . . . (Bibl. Dictionaries); and for *Claret* see also Appendix G, references for Renaissance to Modern Wines. Clairet – in the Chalonnais: Gras, Pierre, MS. thesis, 'La vie rurale en Chalonnais aux XIVᵉ et XVᵉ siècles'. For this information I am much indebted to M. Jean Richard of Dijon. Champagne: *Maison Rustique*, 638, 640. At Bordeaux: Lafforgue, 49, 78.

[189] *Nurture, Boke of*, ll. 714-15; Power, *Ménagier*, 238-9.

*Noble Family at Dinner
from a 14th-century
manuscript*

construction of a trencher was no haphazard affair. Four-days-old bread was recommended for the best trencher, four slices being laid in the form of a square and one
slice on top of this absorbent platform. Furthermore the servants had to see that
everyone at dinner had their knife, spoon, and 'napkyn'.[190] Attention was paid to
the manners of servants as well as to those of noble children. Thus, while the
servants were commended not to be 'yoxing, ne bolkynge, ne gronynge',[191] neither
hiccuping nor belching, it was also found necessary to suggest to the noble young
that they did not wipe their noses on the towel which they used for drying their
hands.[192] They were warned in the *Boke of Curtasye* not to leave their spoon in the
dish, nor to lay it on the side of the dish, but to clean it. A reminder was issued not
to stroke cat or dog at table.[193] The most charming of these manuals is the *Babees
Book* whose task was to inculcate manners into the 'Bele Babees' or 'swete children',
all of them upper-class boys who waited or fed in the dining halls of the nobility.
Don't put your knife in your mouth, they were told, nor dip your meat in the salt-
cellar; when cheese is brought you must have a new trencher as well as a clean knife
to cut the cheese; when the meal is finished, you should clean your knife, put it in
its place and remain sitting until you have washed.[194] But one also comes across
recommendations which show that these Manuals were necessary to all classes and
which imply that the intricate ceremonial of a royal or ducal dinner could be
punctuated by unconventional behaviour. Guests were warned, when they were
sitting by a good man, not to put their knee under his thigh and they were exhorted
not to spit upon the table, that being regarded as the action of 'an uncurtayse mon'.
Servants, in their turn, were told not to grind or gnash their teeth and 'alle wey be

[190] *Nurture, Boke of,* ll. 56, 333–8;
l. 260.

[191] *Nurture, Boke of,* l. 298.

[192] *Urbanitas,* ll. 52–3, in Furnivall,
F. J., *Early English Meals and
Manners.*

[193] *Boke of Curtasye,* ll. 71–4, 107–8,
in Furnivall, F. J., *op. cit.*

[194] *Babees Book,* ll. 159–60, 162, 183–4,
190–3, in Furnivall, F. J., *op. cit.*

275

ware of thy hyndur part from gunnes blastynge' – a euphemism from the early age of gunpowder.[195]

Both the delight and the squalor of the Middle Ages have been subject to exaggeration. The Romantics are mesmerized by those unmechanical centuries and by the small brightness of the life which happened in them. They see the craftsman whose daily work was art as well as labour: the so-called Courts of Love in Provence: the community of guild life in the towns: peasants at a festival dancing by the edge of the forest which rings their little world: the soaring, intimate splendour of the Sainte Chapelle in Paris. The Antiseptics, on the other hand, see the dirt in the halls of the nobles, the sores of beggars, the horrible deformities, and the primitive detail of mediéval life. Unlike the Romantics, they smell the Middle Ages and are repelled by a thousand years of stale sweat.

Neither extreme is accurate: the craftsmen were by no means always artistic, and the intentions of Courtly love-singers were not always founded in purity. Filth in the streets did not mean that every housewife was a slut in her own home and the deformities of beggars were not much worse than they were in the Age of the Renaissance.

'thynges of complacence'

Towards the end of the Middle Ages a soft and sensuous current from the Mediterranean was beginning to make itself felt in North-Western Europe. One part of this current was a growing stream of commerce from South to North and one result of it was a gradual increase in luxury. The effects are visible in the domestic life of the time. Thus, for example, although the 'pese', which was made of wood or leather or sometimes of pottery, remained the common drinking cup, vessels of silver, pewter, and gilt were by no means unusual. In 1416–17 we find in the *Calendar of Letter Books of the City of London* '10 March, 4 Henry V . . . the guardianship of Robert and Elizabeth, children of Henry Wodewey, late skinner, together with divers goods and chattels, comprising (*inter alia*) a beaker of silver with the inscription *Benedictus deus in donis suis*, four plain pieces of silver, a dozen silver spoons weighing in all 64 oz., a basin and ewer, a dozen vessels of pewter (*stannei*), a bed of tapestry with three curtains and ceiler (*cellura*) of "carde" [an inferior kind of silk] . . . committed . . . to Nicholas Tunwell, grocer, who married the mother-in-law (*matrem in lege*) of the said orphans'. And in a long inventory of plate which comes from the Paston MSS. and which dates sometime after 1479 we read, among many others, the items: 'xij sylver spones, wereof my lady hath one . . . iij gilt spones . . . j gilte cup covered . . . a goblette of silver and gilt covered . . . j salte covered with a berall gairneshid. . . .'[196]

The general current of trade was fed in no small degree by the energy and enterprise of Genoese, Tuscans and Venetians and one representative of Italian commerce was Francesco di Marco Datini, a merchant of Prato in Tuscany. 'On the first page of Datini's great ledgers stood the words, "In the name of God and of profit",' and at the end of the 14th century he had branches or agents in Avignon, Pisa, Florence, Genoa, Barcelona, Valencia and Majorca. He even had an agent on the Balearic island of Iviza. Among the articles in which he dealt were Spanish wool,

[195] *Boke of Curtasye*, ll. 85–6, 117–20, and *Boke of Nurture*, ll. 301, 304, both in Furnivall, F. J., *op. cit.*; cf. Nineteenth Rule in Robert Grosseteste's *Rules*, in Walter of Henley's *Husbandry*.

[196] Wright, *Vocabs.*, I, 771/22; *Cal. Let. Bks. Lon.*, Vol. I, fo. clxxxiib; *Paston Letters, The*, III, 270 sqq.

Perugian veils, spices and sugar from the East, Tuscan wine, Spanish Malmsey, and slaves from the coasts of North Africa and the Black Sea.[197]

Yet Datini, though prosperous, was not one of the greater merchants of his time. The Rapondi of Lucca were bigger men than him. They had branches at Avignon, Paris and Bruges: they sold silks and spices, fruit from the Midi, and raisins from Corinth; they indulged in banking. Dino Rapondi bought fine and costly books for the library of Philip, Duke of Burgundy; and, when the Count of Nevers was taken prisoner by the Turks at Nicopolis in 1396 Dino was instructed to negotiate with the Sultan over payment of the spectacular ransom of 200,000 florins.[198] The Count was a valuable property: in modern terms his ransom is probably worth about £270,000 or $800,000.[199]

The expanding pattern of commerce is reflected in the traffic of wine up the Atlantic coasts of Europe. In 1237 'Ordiales', or wine from Castro Urdiales in the Spanish Province of Santander, was bought for King Henry III. In the next century wine of Portugal, shipped out of 'Lucebon', arrives at Sandwich on its way to Flanders. A few years later, in 1366, Algarbe – wine from the Algarve in the south of Portugal – is in England while in 1391 Riptage, which probably came from vineyards on the River Minho between northern Portugal and Spanish Galicia, was sold in London taverns. Osey, which was often, if not always, an Iberian wine, was becoming popular in England at this time and so was Ryvere, or Torrentyne, from the River Ebro in northern Spain. From south-western Spain came that wine of Lepe which Chaucer said was mixed and which certainly muddled the heads of the Londoners who bought it in Fish Street and Cheapside.[200]

Wines came into England too from Italy, the Adriatic, and the Aegean. From Italy came Vernage, Trubidiane and even 'Greek' wine from Tuscany, Apulia and Calabria. In 1365 Rybole appears in England and this may have been a wine from Istria. It was sold in the three sweet-wine taverns of London, as also was Romaney from the lands of Byzantium.[201]

The *Libel of English Policy* dwells graphically upon one aspect of the Mediterranean commerce:

> 'The grete galees of Venees and Fflorence
> Be wel ladene wyth thynges of complacence,
> Alle spicerye and of grocers ware,
> Wyth swete wynes, alle manere of chaffare,
> Apes, and japes. . . .'[202]

Such was the dominance of the Italians over these voyages from the Mediterranean to the Channel and the Low Countries, and such was the competition of the great galleys, that the English, to loosen the Italian grip, enacted one of the more picturesque of tariff regulations, ordering ten bowstaves to be imported with each butt of wine.[203] The reply of the Venetian Senate was, regrettably, of a duller nature and merely imposed an extra tax of four ducats a butt on wines loaded at Candia into foreign ships.[204]

The basis of the English cellar continued to be the Atlantic wines from Anjou, Gascony, and the Rhine. Nevertheless, and despite any commercial warfare, the

[197] Origo, *Datini*, 13, and Ch. 3.

[198] Roover, R. de, 'La communauté des marchands Lucquois à Bruges de 1377 à 1464', *Ann. de la Soc. d'Emulation de Bruges*, 86, 37–9, 1949.

[199] See Origo, *Datini*, 23.

[200] Ordiales: *Liberate Rolls*, 21, Henry III, mem. 13. Lucebon: *Close Rolls*, 23, Edward III, mem. 27. Algarbe: see fn. 159; also *Close Rolls*, 39, Edward III, mem. 4. Riptage: *Cal. Let. Bks. Lon.*, Vol. H, fo. cclx, 1391. Osey: Ritson, III, 177; *Cal. Let. Bks. Lon.*, Vol. H, fo. ccxivb, 1387; *Close Rolls*, 39, Edward III, mem. 4; 6, Richard II, mem. 10d; 19, Henry VI, mem. 36; 34, Henry VI, mem. 24; *Nurture, Boke of*, l. 119; *LEP*, 163. Ryvere, Torrentyne: see fn. 157. Lepe: see fn. 158.

[201] Vernage: see fn. 162. Trubidiane: see fn. 162. Greek: see fn. 167. Rybole: *Cal. Let. Bks. Lon.*, Vol. G, fo. clxvb, 1365; Simon, André L., *The History of the Wine Trade in England*, II, 205–6. Ribolla: Florio. On this question of the naming of Rybole, note that there is nowadays a Rebula wine in Yugoslavia; and see also V.V., *A.*, Dict. for the Rebolla *cépage*. Romaney: see fn. 161.

[202] *Libel of Eng. Policy*, 172; see also *Cal. State Papers Venetian*, I, No. 544.

[203] Cunningham, W., *The Growth of English Industry and Commerce* (Bibl. General), I, 433, fn. 4.

[204] *Cal. State Papers Venetian*, I, No. 544.

September: Treading Grapes from Queen Mary's Psalter 14th century London, British Museum

sweet wines of the South increased their popularity among the drinkers of England and this development was to influence the English palate for centuries to come. Indeed it marks the first great change in English drinking habits since the Romans left the island nearly a thousand years before. It is fitting that it should have happened at a time when the Renaissance was beginning to move beneath the medieval mind and when a new vision was beginning to attack the long triumph of the Gothic consciousness.

It is probable also that there was an increase of gaiety in these last centuries of the medieval era. But happiness is never absent from any civilization, however much that civilization may be haunted by a sense of guilt, and if many a man had tried in a monastery cell to atone for the fact that he was alive, many another had a hearty appetite for the joy and the pleasure which life could offer. Some found it in a cup of wine:

> '*Bevez bel a bevez bien,*
> *Vos le vostre e jo le mien,*
> Pari forma.'[205]

Others found it in the slow elaboration of beauty, as they did in the intricate, writhing world painted in the Book of Kells. There the long strands of decoration repeatedly end in narrow animals' heads until one feels that one is wandering through a dreaming Celtic forest designed by a master jeweller.

Elsewhere there was music and dancing: minstrels and acrobats at the wedding of Jehan du Chesne in Paris:[206] clerks at Liège forsaking their devotions at Easter to dance and sing before the crowned goddess-figure of one of their mistresses.[207] Flowers too: chaplets at weddings:[208] garlands in Chaucer's *Romaunt of the Rose*: Fortunatus dining in a room whose walls were decorated with festoons of ivy:[209] Roger de Walden, installed as Bishop of London, walking in procession with his canons, all of them garlanded with red roses.[210] And then we have this curious glimpse of frolics in London in the reign of Henry V: 'Proclamation at Christmas

[205] Jeanroy, A., et Langfors, A., *Chansons satiriques et bracchiques du XIII siècle*, Song xliii.

[206] Power, *Ménagier*, 246; and cf. 244.

[207] Helen Waddell, *The Wandering Scholars*, 149.

[208] Power, *Ménagier*, 247.

[209] Salin, E., *La Civilisation Mérovingienne*, I, 442.

[210] Amherst, 18.

forbidding night-walking, "mommyng" plays, and interludes, the wearing of false beards and masks, and ordering the hanging out of lanterns. . . .'[211]

Finally the contrasts, the hardship and happiness, of life in the medieval countryside. On the one hand are the 'peny-ale', the night-old worts, and the 'pece of bacun' which represented peasant hunger in *Piers the Plowman*[212] On the other are the mowing customs at Norwell in Nottinghamshire in the reign of Henry IV. These declare that a man

'. . . ought also, together with his companions, to mow the Lord's meadows in Northyng . . . for which he and the rest of the mowers . . . whose number is twenty-four, shall eat in the Prebendal-house as follows: first, they shall have bread and beer, potage, beef, pork, and lamb, for the first course; and for the second, broth, pigs, ducks, veal or lamb roasted; and, after dinner, they are to sit and drink and then go in and out of the hall three times, drinking each time they return, which being done, they shall have a bucket of beer, containing eight flagons and an half, which bucket ought to be carried on the shoulders of two men through the midst of the town, from the Prebendal-house unto the aforesaid meadow, where they are to divert themselves with plays the remainder of the day, at which plays the Lord shall give two pairs of white gloves.'[213]

It is not difficult to imagine the shouting and the laughter in that aforesaid medieval meadow.

[211] *Cal. Let. Bks. Lon.*, Vol. I, fo. ccxxiii.

[212] Langland, *Piers the Plowman*, A. Passus, VII, ll. 296–7.

[213] Rastall, W. D., *A History of the Antiquities of the Town and Church of Southwell* (edn of 1819), 150–1.

NOTE: References for wines listed in Appendix E, but not discussed in the text of this chapter: Antioche: Ritson, III, 176. Blanc: *Liberate Rolls*, 12, Henry III, mem. 6. Caprick: *Close Rolls*, 34, Henry VI, mem. 24; *Nurture, Boke of*, l. 120; cf. Caprick, in Appendix G, Wines, Renaissance to Modern. Carenum: see Wyne Cute. Carmignano: Origo, *Datini*, 17, 291. Chianti: Origo, *Datini*, 292. Corsica: Origo, *Datini*, 133; cf. Corsica, in Appendix G, Wines, Renaissance to Modern. Ew ardant: *Antiq. Cul.*, Forme of Cury, No. 189; cf. Origo, *Datini*, 289; and cf. Eau ardant, in Appendix G, Wines, Renaissance to Modern. Ferré: Godefroy; Rodier, XIV. Matringhale (a wine?): *Close Rolls*, 16, Henry VI, mem. 4. Melfi: Simon, André L., *The History of the Wine Trade in England* (Bibl. General), I, 282. Mondego: Edrisi, 222. Mountrosse: Ritson, III, 176. Cal. Let. *Bks. Lon.*, Vol. G, fo. cccxiib, 1373. Muscadelle: Ritson, III, 177; *Nurture, Boke of*, l. 118; cf. Turner, Cii, 25; and cf. Muscadine, in Appendix G, Wines, Renaissance to Modern. Muscat: V.V., *A.*, III, 374; and cf. Muscadine, in Appendix G, Wines, Renaissance to Modern. Potenza: as for Melfi in this footnote, above. Preignac: V.V., *A.*, I, 514. Rapolla: as for Melfi in this footnote, above. Rhodes: *Close Rolls*, 17, Henry VI, mem. 10. Rose, Coloure de: *Nurture, Boke of*, l. 114 and note. St Emilion: *Close Rolls*, 17, Edward I, mem. 3. Sancerre: *BdV*, 35. Sicera: see, for example *Pipe Roll*, 32, Henry II, rot. 6, mem. 2d; *Acc. obed. Abingdon*, 55; *VCH, Cambridge*, II, 70. Tente: *Close Rolls*, 3, Henry IV, mem. 7; and cf. Tent, in Appendix G, Wines, Renaissance to Modern. Verjuice: Petrus de Crescentiis, Bk IV, cap. xxiv; *Paston Letters*, Vol. III; for the Verjus vine see V.V., *A.*, II, 152. Vermaille: *Cal. Let. Bks. Lon.*, Vol. G, fo. ccxcvb, 1372; fo. cccvi, 1373; Vol. I, fo. cxxxiii, 1414. Vin fou: Rodier, 41.

CHAPTER SIX

The Renaissance and the Puritan Century

Primavera

In brilliant red doublets Italian horsemen cavort through a wood the colour of irradiated spinach. Beyond a violet pool pale greyhounds chase among the dark trunks of the trees. This is The Hunt, painted by Uccello in the 15th century. It was painted at a time when the movement of the Renaissance was gathering momentum, and it seems emblematic of the eager quest which animated so much of the Renaissance. But no longer was it, as it had been in the Middle Ages, the search for beatitude and the abstract Omnipotence. The hunt had changed in significance and become a quest for the curious and individual beauty of man.

Uccello manifested his delight in the patterns of the physical world. Botticelli demonstrated the beauties of the human body. But Botticelli saw the body as more than visual joy; he found it capable of expressing beauties which lay deep behind its physical appearance. Mantegna too saw it as a revealing creation and painted the unique, unrepeatable personality which was displayed through the medium of the flesh. And thus, when he painted the Marchese Lodovico Gonzaga and his family, he painted them not as religious puppets but as real people. It was not their piety so much as their humanity that was important.

But the movement of the Renaissance could not shake off the whole inheritance of the Middle Ages. Its mind, however humanist, however questioning, was still indelibly stamped by the tremendous impact of Christendom. Even among those Renaissance Italians who in their lifetime pretended to be pagan not a few received on their death-beds the last Sacraments of the Christian Church. And in the theology of Calvin – Calvin who started as a classical student and a humanist – there reappeared the insistence upon the guilty nature of man. There was here no rebirth of the classical spirit. The pagan culture was admired but the reality behind it was not appreciated.

Opposite:
Gozzoli, Benozzo
Detail from Vintage Scene
15th century

The Renaissance did not really understand Antiquity. Indeed, its task was otherwise: not understanding, but discovery, collection, and dissemination: Poggio discovering Latin authors 'lost' in the Abbeys of southern Germany; Federigo of Montefeltro collecting his library at Urbino, a library which, as well as Thomas Aquinas, Boccaccio, and the Church Fathers, included Sophocles, Pindar, and Menander; and, from north Italy, dissemination – Hesiod and Theocritus from Milan, Homer from Florence, and Aristophanes, Thucydides, Sophocles and Euripides from the Aldine Press at Venice.

But the Gothic vision prevailed and Antiquity became a distorted reflection in the backwash of the medieval mind. The result was a sort of romantic classicism. The educated classes of Europe (for the most part) accepted Antiquity as an embellishment or a decoration and not as a re-discovered dimension of experience. Ronsard produces the romantic bucolic, the shepherd with his flageolet in love with his Janette:

> 'Plus l'amoureux pasteur sur un troncq adossé,
> Enflant son flageolet à quatre trous persé,
> Son mastin à ses pieds, à son flanc la houlette,
> Ne dira plus l'ardeur de sa belle Janette.'[1]

The romantic note is sounded also, although in this case with a wistful optimism, by a commentator upon the English scene. Describing a harvest home in Berkshire, Hentzner says 'their last load of corn they crown with flowers, having besides an image richly dressed, by which, perhaps they would signify Ceres'.[2] An English 'Ceres' perhaps: but certainly not the great corn-goddess of the ancient Mediterranean.

[1] *Contre les Bucherons*', *Ronsard, Lyrics*, trs. Stirling, William, 114–15.

[2] Harrison, p. lxxxiv, quoting Hentzner.

The decorative aspects of this romantic classicism have appeared by the middle of the 15th century. At a banquet given by Philip, Duke of Burgundy, in 1453-4, the room was decorated with a tapestry which showed the life of Hercules. Jason, and monsters, were among the actors who entertained the Duke's guests. Other distractions were a fountain made of glass and lead, a group of twenty-eight musicians, and a high pillar which carried the statue of a naked woman. She was not, however, entirely naked. She wore a rich hat and – to some extent – a cloth covered with Greek writing. From her right breast flowed a continual stream of Hippocras.[3]

The old and the new were inextricably mixed at this banquet of the Duke of Burgundy. Outside the room the five doors were guarded by archers in grey and black. Inside the room were the mythological Heroes. The woman's nakedness was mitigated by Greek writing while her breast poured bountiful with Hippocras. The decoration may be Renaissance but the background is medieval. And again and again the rough background breaks through the new urbanity. The creatures of Rabelais, for all their mockery of an out-moded past, are still of the flesh and blood of the Middle Ages and the 'magic garment' of Shakespeare's Prospero is a fluttering relic of an earlier century. Even at the height of the Renaissance, and at a time when Leonardo da Vinci was a middle-aged man, Italy – the home of the Renaissance – could witness such a grotesque display of fanaticism as the '*auto da Fé*' inspired by Savonarola. A huge bonfire was made of (among other things) false beards, mirrors, lutes, chessboards, and the works of Boccaccio.

'When the pile was lighted, the Signoria appeared on the balcony, and the air echoed with song, the sound of trumpets, and the pealing of bells. The people then adjourned to the Piazza di San Marco, where they danced round in three concentric circles. The innermost was composed of monks of the monastery, alternating with boys, dressed as angels; then came young laymen and ecclesiastics; and on the outside old men, citizens, and priests, the latter crowned with wreaths of olive.'[4]

The old and the new were tangled also in the smaller incidents of life. Lucagnolo, a rival of Benvenuto Cellini, made 'a very large vase designed for the table of Pope Clement. . . . The vase was adorned with two fine handles, with masks both big and little, and clumps of beautiful foliage, and all worked with . . . perfect grace and art. . . .' Yet into this vase 'at dinner-time were thrown bones and the rinds of fruits'.[5] Then, at the Palace of Nonsuch in England – a Palace lavishly, even excessively, decorated – the presence-chamber was hung with fine tapestries but carpets were only put down where Queen Elizabeth herself would walk, the rest of the floor being strewn with straw or hay.[6]

A homelier picture, and one which comes from early Tudor England, is given us by some of the items of expenditure in the accounts of Katharine Countess of Devon: '. . . 1/4 mutton for the hawks . . . a gallon of honey against Christmas, 3s. 8d. . . . oats for fatting the swans against Christmas, 17d. . . . a doz. points for Dick the Fool . . . for mending Dick and Mug and Kit's clothes, 4d. . . . to buy two coats for Mug the fool when he went to London, 10s.'[7] The hawks and honey, and Dick and Mug, have still the savour of the Middle Ages.

[3]Marche, Olivier de la, *Mémoires*, Bk I, Ch. XXIX, 277-9.

[4]Burckhardt, J., *The Civilisation of the Renaissance*, 295-6.

[5]Cellini, 27-8.

[6]Platter, 191-2; for the decoration of Nonsuch, see Martin Biddle, '. . . Nonsuch, revealed in recent excavations' *ILN*, May 28th, 1960; and cf. Platter, 191.

[7]Brewer, *Henry VIII*, Vol. IV, Pt I, No. 771.

'... brown, beloved Bastard ...'

Herbs and spices continued to play an important part in everyday life. Sweet-smelling herbs such as rosemary and lavender were scattered among the rushes on the floors of houses, and herbs and spices, as well as other things, were put into beer and wine. Mum,* which was a speciality of Brunswick in Germany, was a beer which could include 'tops of *fir* and *birch*' and also herbs and ten unbroken eggs. The 'Bragget' of Tudor England must have been the same as the medieval Braket and thus either a Hippocras or else made with ale, honey, and pepper. Purl was compounded from ale or hot beer and wormwood or other herbs while Purl Royal, which was drunk in England in the 17th and 18th centuries, used the same herbs but was made with wine. In Lombardy in the first half of the 16th century rosemary was put into wine vessels and in the late 17th century in England it was said that lavender tops, or grains of Paradise, would preserve the wines of France.[8] *Vino mirrhato* – 'wine mixt with Mirrh' – occurs in Italy in the early 17th century but this seems to have been rather an exceptional mixture and the more commonplace meaning of *vino mirrhato* was 'wine mixt with wormewood'.

Other aromatic, or spiced and sweetened, wines were made in the Mediterranean and, most probably, in the Canaries as well. One of these was the Cate pument which Harrison records as being imported into Elizabethan England. Pument here is obviously Harrison's writing of piment so that the Cate pument would have been no more than a specially fine version of the piments (those mixtures of wine, honey, and spices) which had been drunk in earlier England.

We have already seen that the most famous and the most favoured of the medieval piments was Hippocras and, in England at any rate, Hippocras, both white and red, continued to be drunk until long after the end of the Renaissance. Some of it was what one might call 'involuntary' Hippocras since it is quite clear that the vintners of the 17th century used sugar and herbs or spices to amend a defective wine and the result, however inferior, would have been Hippocras.[9] But 'deliberate' Hippocras maintained a steady vogue. It was drunk in England under Elizabeth as it was under Charles I and Charles II. In 1662 Dr Christopher Merret gave to no less a body than the Royal Society an extensive recipe for making it, a recipe based on sherry and white wine and including Jamaica pepper, nutmegs, ginger, cloves, and sugar-candy.[10] From time to time Pepys drank Hippocras, on one occasion to soothe his stomach and on another to quieten his conscience:

> 'We went into the Buttery, and there stayed and talked, and then into the Hall again: and there wine was offered and they drunk, I only drinking some hypocras, which do not break my vowe, it being, to the best of my present judgement, only a mixed compound drink, and not any wine. If I am mistaken, God forgive me! but I hope and do think I am not.'[11]

But Hippocras was not only a reminder of the Middle Ages. It was also the fore-runner of the Negus of the 18th century. In 1576 George Gascoyne comments with

*References for the drinks and wines are listed in Appendix G, *Wines: Renaissance to Modern*. References for such drinks and wines will only be given in the footnotes to this, and succeeding chapters, when a particular incident is concerned.

[8] Boorde, *Introduction*, Ch. xxv (Lombardy); Houghton, *Collection*, Vol. II, 481, No. 392.

[9] *Vintners, The Art and Mystery of*; Houghton, *Collection*, Vol. II, 479, No. 391.

[10] Houghton, *Collection*, Vol. II, 486, No. 390 (395?) of Feb. 16th, 1699-1700. See also *Vintners, The Art and Mystery of*, 11.

[11] Pepys, Apr. 9th, 1664; Oct. 29th, 1663.

Anon.,
Triumph of Bacchus and
Ariadne
Florentine, late 15th century
London, British Museum

quite unnecessary disparagement: 'Yea wine of it selfe is not sufficient, but Suger, Limons, & sundry sortes of spices, must be drowned therein. To minister mater unto our vaine delights & to beguile our selves with the baite which dronkennesse doth therein lay for us.'[12] This, basically, is a description of the Georgian Negus and so far as the Georgians themselves were concerned they took the bait both merrily and often.

Osey, however, or at least under this name, does not seem to have outlasted its medieval career with anything like the same success as Hippocras. It was drunk to some extent by the Elizabethans and in the 17th century there is a recipe for making it from Bastard with, among other things, aniseeds, corianders, ginger, cloves, and lycoras. (This incidentally may, but only may, give us some clue to its medieval taste.) But by the latter half of the 17th century Osey is disappearing and the reason for this disappearance may well have been that its individual identity was merged into the general identity of Hippocras.

Bastard, too, was a medieval relic though one with a little more stamina than Osey. 'Brown and white bastard' says Elbow in *Measure for Measure*. 'Brown, beloved Bastard' writes Luke Hutton in 1638 in *The Blacke Dogg of New-gate*. 'Wines commonly compounded. Ipocris, Brown Bastard, White Bastard . . .' remarks *The Art and Mystery of Vintners* in 1682.[13] Whether always compounded or not, Bastard in the 17th century was usually a rich, sweet wine, the brown variety being the sweeter of the two, and most of it came, or was supposed to come, from the Iberian Peninsula.

I think *The Art and Mystery* was right in its sweeping statement that brown and white Bastards were two of the wines which were 'commonly compounded', and

[12]Gascoyne, George, *A Delicate Diet, for daintie mouthde Droonkardes*, 18. For the various kinds of Negus, see Ch. 8, p. 340.

[13]Shakespeare, *Measure for Measure*, Act III, Sc. ii; *Blacke Dogg*, A4; *Vintners, The Art and Mystery of*, 11. For medieval Osey and Hippocras, see Ch. 5, pp. 277, 285.

there can be little doubt that Bastard was often a *vin miellé*, a honied wine. This, in fact, is the meaning given in a French-English dictionary of 1611. There is certainly no question about the fact that Bastard was normally a sweet wine. But I am still inclined, as with the medieval Bastard, to doubt that it was invariably compounded and I think that the 'genuine' Iberian Bastard was a pure wine from the Bastardo grape.

In addition to the sweetened, there were also the bitter, wines. Of these Wormwood wine was the oldest, its history going back far beyond the Middle Ages although, as we shall see in the next chapter, distillation now gives it a new development. Here we need only note in passing that Pepys drank it on several occasions and once drank wormwood ale in 'a little house . . . which doubtless was a bawdy house'.[14]

Another of the bitter wines was the Italian Crespa of the early 17th century, a piquant, 'acid' wine with some suavity. It was usually made of 4/10ths old wine, 4/10ths sweet must which had only begun to ferment, 1/10th selected grapes, and 1/10th warm water. (The water was not essential.) The name Crespa comes from the fact that a draught of it made the eyebrows pucker but John Florio in *Queen Anna's New World of Words* (a delightful name for a dictionary) suggests a more vivid picture with the meaning which he gives to the related word *Crespatùra*: '. . . a frizling, a crisping, a wrinkling . . . as we say a crowes-foote in a womans face. . . .' The description is ungallant but it is graphic.

Then there was Rappis with its multiplicity of writings – Raspis, Respyse, Rapé, and Rap – and also with its confusing multiplicity of meaning. The least important meaning is that which Andrew Boorde attributes to Respyse. Respyse, he says in his *Dyetary of Helth*, is a wine made from berries and not from grapes, and this Respyse is therefore only a prolongation into the early 16th century of that medieval Raspice which was a raspberry, or a raspberry-flavoured, wine. It may have continued to find favour in country districts but it disappears from the more sophisticated circles and the other meanings are the ones which we meet most frequently. Then, by about the middle of the 17th century, they too disappear from the records and fall into disuse.

At first sight it seems possible to distinguish a basic difference between the wines which should be called Rappis and those which should be classed as Rapé. Rappis, it would seem, was basically an astringent drink whereas Rapé was basically a small wine made by the addition of ripe grapes to an existing wine. It is tempting to think that the confusion of meaning which existed with these names in medieval times is now being cleared up and that the different techniques are being given distinctive titles. But it is not so; and when we look at the various meanings which were attached to them we shall see that the confusion persisted.

Rappis, or Raspis, was a deliberately astringent drink. It was 'Raspish wyne, that is, whych biteth the tong'; or putting it another way, it was wine which 'dooth gette a certayn ponticite or taste like wormwood'. It was also 'greene or raspe wine'.[15] This is all quite clear, and, as we should expect, one method of making it was from sour and ripe grapes pressed together. But then there were other techniques which were to make it either from 'Raspishe wyne' and spices such as cinnamon and cloves or else from wine and sage leaves. And furthermore, far from

[14]Pepys, Mar. 21st, 1661-2.

[15]Morwyng, 390-1; *Maison Rustique*, 632.

being an astringent drink, in 1635 Raspis was classed by Thomas Heywood as a sweet wine.

Now let us look at Rapé. In the 17th century Rapé was usually made by filling a vessel with ripe grapes, pouring old wine over them and – sometimes – adding hot water. There is a certain analogy with Crespa which was both acid and suave but the purpose of the Rapé method was not to produce an acid or 'Raspish' wine but to make a small, economy wine which would tide a household over a year of sparse vintage. Thus the grapes were not put into the mixture to promote any deliberate astringency but to keep the small wine in heart for the whole of an insufficient year. The economy, as opposed to the astringent, aspect of Rapé is seen again in the variations of its technique, for a Rapé or Rappe wine could also be made from grapes, or grape husks, and water.

At this point we can re-state, and even extend, the apparently basic difference between Rappis and Rapé: Rappis was deliberately astringent, Rapé was deliberately economical; Rappis could include sour grapes, Rapé used only ripe grapes. But here enters confusion, for the use of ripe grapes in old wine was a technique not only for making Rapé but also for making Rappis. And then the preservation of grapes in must was an action related to the Rapé technique. But these grapes, which were considered great delicacies at table, were known as 'Rappez' and the miswriting of Rappez into Rappis was of course an easy one. Thus a delicacy made by a Rapé method passed easily under a Rappis title.

This is not the limit of confusion, for even Rapé by itself can have another meaning. In Champagne in the early 17th century 'rap wine' was made by putting wood chips into new wine, a type of concoction that was much the same as the *vin de coipeau* which appears in 1611 and which was 'new wine quickly made fit to be drunke, by Beechen chips first boyled then dryed, and afterwards put into the vessell'.

There we must leave the confusion and accept it as cheerfully as it seems to have been accepted by the drinkers of Tudor and Stuart times. Perhaps to them it was not confusion. Perhaps they knew precisely what they meant when they used one of the Rappis names. But if they did, we certainly do not.

Sack and Canary

Sack was one of the most popular of Elizabethan wines. It has also become one of the most famous since it was immortalized by the long, and oft-quoted, extravaganza put by Shakespeare into the mouth of Falstaff. 'A good sherris-sack hath a two-fold operation in it,' says Falstaff. 'It ascends me into the brain; dries me there all the foolish and dull and crudely vapours which environ it; makes it apprehensive, quick, forgetive, full of nimble, fiery and delectable shapes; which, delivered o'er to the voice, the tongue, which is the birth, becomes excellent wit. The second property of your excellent sherris is, the warming of the blood. . . .' And Sir John ends his paean of praise with the ringing declaration: 'If I had a thousand sons, the first humane principle I would teach them should be to forswear thin potations, and to addict themselves to sack.'[16] Another paean, although somewhat less robust, was pronounced by Robert Herrick in his *Welcome to Sack*:

[16] *Henry IV*, Pt II, Act IV, Sc. iii.

287

'But to forsake thee ever, co'd there be
A thought of such like possibilitie?
When thou thy selfe dar'st say, thy Iles shall lack
Grapes, before *Herrick* leaves Canarie Sack.'

and he continues:

'Thou mak'st me nimble, as the winged howers,
To dance and caper on the heads of flowers,
And ride the sun-beams. . . .'

The praised and famous name of Sack appears to have been a creation of the Renaissance, for Sack, at least as a wine-name, has no medieval history. It seems to have come into use about the beginning of the 16th century and it does not figure in the English records until the reigns of the earlier Tudors. Then Richard Layton, writing at the time of the Dissolution of the Monasteries, could remark that a certain Abbot, 'a very simple man' much favoured a concoction of 'white wine, sugar, burrage leaves, and seke, whereof he sips nightly in his chamber till midnight'.[17] A few years later Sack was used for the provisioning of garrisons and castles. In 1545 Malmseys – 'malvesyes' – and Sacks were among the victuals of Boulogne and in the same year there is a note of 'malmesey and sack for Garnesey castle'.[18] From about the same period, and certainly from the 1550's onwards Sack became popular among the civil drinkers of England[19] and its popularity increased until the poets bestowed upon it their loving and light-hearted gift of immortality.

Sack was thus an honoured word in England, honoured and frequent and much sung. It is all the more curious, therefore, that now we do not know exactly what the word meant.

We know, of course, the provenance of the wine for about that there is no doubt at all. The best Sack – 'Seres' or 'Sherris' or 'Sherris-sack' – came from Jerez de la Frontera. Other strong Sacks came from Malaga and the Canaries and the latter, as Canary Sack, achieved an especial popularity in late Tudor, and in Stuart, England. Indeed in 1634 James Howell, who was later appointed historiographer royal of England, called it the richest, best bodied, and most lasting wine.

Such were the principal Sacks but there were lesser ones which came from Galicia in north-western Spain and from Portugal. One of these was the 'kind of strong Spanish wine or sacke' which the Italians called *Vino Tibidrago*. This seems to have been the same as the wine which was variously known in the British Isles as Robdavie and Rubiedauy and we find in 1533 the record of a Portuguese ship which was laden with 'robdavies' and was one of four ships carrying wine to Waterford in Ireland. Robdavie may have been identical with the Ribadavia which came from the River Minho between Galicia and northern Portugal but from my reading of the evidence I think that it was not. It is more likely to have been the same as the wine called Roberdany which came from 'Robedillo' in 'hither Lusitania' and which was thus a wine either from Portugal or from Extremadura in western Spain. Alternatively the name may have been that of a style of Spanish or Portuguese wine and not the name of a wine from a particular vineyard area.

[17]Gairdner, *Henry VIII*, Vol. 13, Pt I, No. 1239.

[18]Gairdner, *Henry VIII*, Vol. 20, Pt II, Nos. 200 and 1010.

[19]TR, III, 514 sqq. (Bibl. General).

All these wines from all these different places were Sacks. But what does 'Sack' mean? Obviously it describes a general characteristic common to all the wines called Sacks. But what characteristic?

For many years there has been controversy over the meaning of the word and three different theories have been put forward to explain it. The most romantic, and the least tenable, suggests that the word Sack was derived from the Japanese Saké, the presumption being that there was some similarity in strength or taste between the European Sack and the Japanese rice-wine. There may very well have been a certain similiarity and it is true that some knowledge of rice wine was brought back to Europe by Marco Polo. 'Most of the people of Cathay drink wine of the kind that I shall now describe,' he says. 'It is a liquor which they brew of rice with a quantity of excellent spice in such fashion that it makes better drink than any other kind of wine; it is not only good, but clear and pleasing to the eye. And being very hot stuff, it makes one drunk sooner than any other wine.'[20] It is possible also that some knowledge of the Japanese Saké travelled back to Europe but I still see no reason to describe the European wine by the name of the Japanese drink. And furthermore we must remember that while Western explorers (in this case the Portuguese) did not reach Japan until 1542, 'seke' – which is a variant writing of Secke or Sack – appears in an English document of 1538.

The second theory, one widely accepted but now discarded, held that Sack was a corruption of 'seke' meaning 'dry' and that Sack was therefore a dry wine. 'Secke' does occur with a 'dry' meaning in Anglo-Norman but it does not have any specific relevance to wine.[21] Nor can it have any general relevance to Sack for Sack was often a sweet wine. In 1577, for example, *The Maire of Bristowe is Kalendar* stated that 'in this yeere came from Andoluzia suche sweete and pleasant secks in generall as by reporte the like was never knowen, as pleasant as bastards'. The point of the quotation is reinforced by the reference to Bastard since Bastard was commonly a rich, sweet wine. And then, in 1635, we get this from Thomas Heywood's *Philoco-thonista*: '. . . from the *Spaniard*, all kinds of Sacks, as *Malligo, Charnio, Sherry, Canary, Leatica, Palerno, Frontiniack, Peeter-see-mee, Vino deriba davia. . . .*'[22] Now, not all of these wines were rich but a number of them certainly were. Malligo often was; Charnio usually was; Leatica, or Leattica, was a rich Italian wine made from the *Aleatico nero* grape which may have been the same as the *Muscat noir*; Fronti-niack, from Frontignan, which was a favourite wine of James I of England, was a sweet and luscious muscat wine; and Peeter-see-mee was a rich, sweet wine from the Pedro Ximenez grape. It is quite clear that Sack was frequently a rich, sweet wine.

It is also clear that there was some strong connection between Sack and 'the Spaniard', for five of these Heywood wines came from the Iberian Peninsula and one – Canary – was made under Spanish influence. This brings us to the third theory of the meaning of the name Sack. It is a reasonable theory and, so far as I am aware, it is the one which currently holds the field.

It suggests that the name Sack is derived from the Spanish verb *sacar*, meaning 'to draw out' or 'to export', and that 'Sack' was therefore merely a name for ex-ported wine. The use of the verb, or a similar verb, is quite old enough and quite widespread enough to give the argument a respectable basis. An early 14th-century

October Vintage: from the Flemish Calendar early 16th-century MS. London, British Museum

[20] *Polo, The Book of Ser Marco*, trs., Ed., etc. Yule, Sir H., I, 441.

[21] *Munimenta Gildhallae Londoniensis* (Bibl. Ch. 5), Vol. III, Glossary, and *Liber Allus*, 724.

[22] Ricart, Robert, *The Maire of Bris-towe is Kalendar*, 60; Heywood, *Philocothonista*, 48.

[23] *The Black Book of the Admiralty*, Vol. II, 176-7 (Bibl. Ch. 5).

Changling

Simpleton

Fiends farewell M.

Sᵣ I Falstafe

Hostes

Clause

*Falstaff at the Boar's Head,
from Kirkmann's Drolls,
1672
London, British Museum*

French manuscript *Le Domesday de Gippewyz* (the *Ipswich Domesday*) uses the words '*saker hors*', and the translation, which was apparently made in the 15th century, renders them thus: 'And zif they fyndyn ony wyn that be corrupt and perlous to drynkyn for mannys body, or for to medelyn with newe wyn, a non with out havyng reward [regard?] to ony persone, the ballives of the toun shal doo shakyn out *saker hors* that wyn in the hie strete. . . .'[23] Furthermore, the word *saca* used in an export sense does occur in medieval customs documents and *sacar*, in the same sense, is used by Bartolomé Gutiérrez when writing about official negotiations concerned with the trade of Jerez in 1491: '. . . *todas las personas naturales y extranjeras, vecinos o no vecinos de Xerez, que quisieren sacar por el mar vinos de romania. . . .*'[24]

Sacar por el mar. So far, so good. The theory is attractive. We may well believe that Tudor merchants turned the Spanish *saca* or *sacar* into the English Sack in order to describe wines which were exported from Iberia and the Canaries, and that they later extended its usage to cover some of the wines which were exported from Italy and France.

But I do not believe that the theory is correct. I think that the answer lies in the simple face-value of the word sack. Sack wine is wine made with a sack. It is wine made from grape-juice strained through a bag or sack.

The technique is extremely ancient, and in fact it is one of the oldest recorded wine-making methods in the world. We find it in the 1st Dynasty of Egypt, when a sack-press, made of cloth or matting, was used to squeeze the juice out of the grapes.[25] It is true that this pressing technique seems to have been confined to Egypt and never to have spread to the rest of the ancient Mediterranean. But in wine-making history the sack has the double meaning of extraction and straining. When twisted, it acts as a press; when untwisted, it acts as a filter.

It is as a filter that the sack continues its progress through history. We see one – almost certainly a filter and not a mixing funnel – at the banquet of Rekhmara in Egypt in the 2nd millennium B.C. We meet it again in the Roman authors of the 1st century A.D. Columella, giving instructions on how to make vinegar from green figs, says that, after making the fluid, 'they let it percolate through small rush baskets or sacking made from butcher's broom' – '*postea in iunceis fiscellis vel sparteis saccis percolant . . .*' The poet Martial writes: 'and, that Alauda may drink his wine strained, anxiously . . . pass the turbid Caecuban through the bag . . .'

> '*et ut liquidum potet Alauda merum,*
> *turbida sollicito transmittere Caecuba sacco.*'[26]

I suggest, therefore, that the Tudor wine-name Sack was taken, in varying degrees of descent, from the Latin *saccus*, the Spanish *saco*, and the Italian *sacco*, each meaning a sack or a bag. The likelihood of my theory does not depend only upon the antiquity of the sack-technique, for there is contemporary evidence. An Italian wine-making manual of 1614 (and remember that, except in modern times, a wine-technique is always older than its first literary record) gives instructions for making '*vini . . . passati per il sacco*' and it comments upon the '*vino, che si fà con sachetti . . .*' The *sacco*, or *sachetti*, used in this method were pointed bags of coarse cloth hung over the vintaging tub and filled with grapes which had been partly crushed. The

[24] I am much indebted to Professor Peter Russell, of the University of Oxford, for his comments and advice on the early use of *saca*, etc. I should add that the opinions which I express on the origin of the wine-name Sack are my own opinions. The quotation from Gutiérrez is in González Gordon, 70-1. I am grateful indeed to Señor Manuel M. González Gordon for his help and hospitality in Jerez de la Frontera.

[25] See Ch. 2, p. 43.

[26] Rekhmara, see Ch. 2, p. 46. Columella: Colum., XII, 17, 2. Martial: Mart., XII, lx.

juice of the grapes dripped through the bags.[27] The result, when fermented, was Sack.

Interestingly enough, the three different theories – I am discounting the Saké theory – now run together and become included, one in the other: or rather, the theories of *sacar* 'to draw out' and 'secke' meaning 'dry' are both included in the *saccus* or *saco* explanation.

About the 11th or 12th century A.D. *sacar* was a legal word used in the transmission and acquisition of property. But it also came to bear a meaning, though still in the legal sense, of exempting oneself from fault, of purging oneself, of cleansing, purifying, or clarifying, and this, transposed into another sphere, is one effect of a sack-strainer upon a wine. Furthermore *sacar* took the meaning of 'to extract, to draw out' which, when again transposed into another sphere, could describe the action of a wine-making sack-strainer.[28] Thus although *saco* or *sacco* are the words from which, in my opinion, the English name Sack is derived, it is easy to see how, by resemblance in sound and similarity in meaning, the verb *sacar* is drawn into the orbit of any discussion about Sack.

It is even easier to see how 'secke' meaning *sec*, or 'dry', is drawn into the general discussion, for the sack-method need not necessarily make a sweet wine and some of the Sacks may well have been dry. But *sec* has no right to appear in the argument at all. Its appearance there is purely coincidental and is due only to the similarity of sound between *sec* and 'secke'.

As it happens we know that there were dry Sacks. In his *Dictionaire Anglois & François* of 1650 Robert Sherwood gives 'Sack (wine). *Vin d'Espagne, vin sec*'. Venner, writing in 1622, is more explicit: 'Canarice wine . . . is of some termed a Sacke, with this adjunct *sweete*, but yet very improperly, for it differeth not onely from Sacke in sweetnesse and pleasantnesse of taste, but also in colour and consistence, for it is not so white in colour as Sacke, nor so thin in substance.'[29]

The grounds for believing in the 'dry' theory of Sack were therefore apparently not unreasonable, and they were given further weight from the common English custom of mixing Sack with sugar, a custom which of course implied that the English Sacks were dry wines. The implication is unacceptable. The English had a remarkably sweet tooth and their sugaring of Sack need not necessarily have been done to turn a dry into a sweet wine but could equally well have been done to make a sweet wine even sweeter. The lust for sweetness was widespread. In England, says Fynes Moryson, 'Clownes and vulgar men onely use large drinking of Beere or Ale, how much soever it is esteemed excellent drinke even among strangers, but Gentlemen garrawse onely in Wine, with which many mixe sugar. . . . And because the taste of the English is thus delighted with sweetenesse, the Wines in Tavernes, (for I speake not of Merchants or Gentlemens Cellars) are commonly mixed at the filling thereof, to make them pleasant'. Then, writing about the Scots, Moryson says: 'They drinke pure Wines, not with sugar as the English . . .'; but, which shows that the English were not the only people with peculiar habits, he adds of the Scots: '. . . yet at Feasts they put Comfits in the Wine, after the French manner. . . .'[30]

The English put other things besides sugar into their wine. 'We have moreover Wine of the Vintners owne making conjured from the rest . . . Boxt *Alligant* with Sugar and Eggs,' says Thomas Heywood. 'Go brew me a pottle of sack finely,'

[27] Croce, Ch. x, 36–7; for an illustration of an '*ancien filtre dit manche pendante*' which is basically the same as the Rekhmara 'filter' and the Croce *sachetti*, see Nègre, E., et Françot, P., *Manuel Pratique de Vinification . . .*, etc. (Bibl. General), 267, 1941.

[28] See *Sacar* in Corominas, J., *Diccionario Critico Etimológico de la Lengua Castellana*; *saca* in the *Diccionario de la lengua española* of the Real Academia Española; also, in this latter, *pie* (7th meaning) for '*para exprimarla y sacar el mosto*'. Both these Dictionaries are in Bibl. Dictionaries.

[29] Sherwood's *Dictionaire* is in Bibl. Dictionaries; Venner, *Via recta*, 26–7.

[30] *An Itinerary*, IV, 176, 184; see also Platter, 170; and Venner, *Via recta*, 26.

commands Falstaff at the Garter Inn. 'With eggs, sir?' asks Bardolph and the fat Knight answers: 'Simple of itself. I'll no pullet-sperm in my brewage.' Then earlier in this same scene of *The Merry Wives of Windsor* Falstaff says to Bardolph: 'Go fetch me a quart of sack; put a toast in't.' The 'toast' custom seems to have been quite general for it existed also in Italy – 'in the shops where they sell Muskadines, there be continually boyes attending with little wigges of sweete bread and Junkets, which the Italians dip in the wine; and having thus broke their fasts in winter time, they commonly eate no more till supper'. These 'wigges' were small cakes and they appear again in England in 1661 when Pepys records: '. . . then home to the only Lenten supper I have had of wiggs and ale, and so to bed'.[31] It is a pity that, before he went to bed one night, Pepys did not tell us about Sack. He would have saved us much theorizing.

But at least we have a general idea. It was a Southern wine which could come from the Mediterranean but which more usually came from Iberia and the Canaries. It was wine made with a strainer. It was white or gold or tawny, and rarely, if ever, red. It was sometimes dry, more often sweet, and on occasions 'harsh and strong'. This latter was 'the Sherry sacke'.[32]

Sherry seal of 1468

Sherris and Sherry

'Sherry sacke', like 'Sherris-sack', came from Jerez de la Frontera in south-western Spain, and Jerez is the birthplace of modern Sherry. The obvious question, therefore, is this: was Sherry-sack like modern Sherry?

The answer is both yes and no. There must certainly have been some basic resemblance since the *terroir* of a wine-growing district determines the basic character of its wine. But then come the variations which can be played on the basic theme.

The first of these is the siting of the vineyards. In the Jerez area the vineyards differ according to their soil. There are the *albarizas* in which the soil is a white-ish chalk-lime. These produce the finest Sherry. In the second grade are the *barro* vineyards which contain less chalk but which give a greater amount of must. Thirdly there are the *arenas*, where the soil is sandy and which again produce more must than the *albarizas*. To say with any exactitude what an Elizabethan Sherris was like we have to know from which vineyard, or vineyards, that Sherris had been made. To know this is very difficult indeed.

The second variation can arise from the selection of the vines. What grapes grew in the ancient vineyards? How do they compare with the fruit of the modern vines?

In 1482, three of the varieties grown at Regla de Santa Maria (Chipiona), and perhaps at Jerez de la Frontera as well, were the *torrontes*, the *fergusano*, and the *verde agudillo*. *Torrontes* is a synonym of the *morrastel* which can give a good, rich red wine and these ancient *torrontes* vines may have been the same as the black-graped *morrastel*. The *fergusano* has some resemblance to the *mantuo de pilas* which is grown now at Jerez and whose green-gold grapes have a very sweet pulp. The *verde agudillo* may be the same as the *albillo peco* of Trebugena which, at any rate in modern times, is rare in the better vineyards of Jerez.[33]

It is true that these three vines – the *torrontes*, *fergusano*, and *verde agudillo* – were used for the making of *romania* wines but they may also have been used for the

[31]Heywood, P., 48; *The Merry Wives of Windsor*, Act III, Sc. v. Italy: Moryson, Fynes, *An Itinerary*, IV, 103. Pepys, Apr. 8th, 1664.

[32]Moryson, Fynes, *An Itinerary*, IV, 129; the dating of this comment is early 17th century.

[33]Varieties at Chipiona in 1432 (and *romania* wines): González Gordon, 71, 213. Ampelography - *Torrontes* and Morrastel: V.V., A., III, 384–7; see also VI, 248. Mantuo de Pilas: V.V., A., VI, 121–3. *Verde agudillo*, V.V., A., VI, 126.

making of Sherris, and the resemblance between the *fergusano* and the *mantuo de pilas* provides at least a slight link between the ancient and modern wines. There may be other resemblances, too, for some of the Sack may have been made from the *listán* of Andalusia, a white grape which is also called *palomino blanco* and which is widely grown in the modern vineyards. Another, and equally important resemblance must lie in the fact that the *Pedro Ximenez* grape went into the making of southern Spanish wines, and thus almost certainly into the making of Sack, and that the *Pedro Ximenez* grows now in the *albarizas* of Jerez.

The *Pedro Ximenez* is one of the better-known grapes of the Renaissance period. It is sometimes supposed to have been the Riesling, but wrongly so, since it is analagous to the Malvoisie and the Muscatel and it may have come to Spain from Greece.[34] It gives a rich, sweet wine, and wine made from it, or with its help, appears under various mis-writings of its name. We find it in Italy in the late 16th century as Perosimenez, and in England in the 17th century as Peter Seeme, Peter sa Meene, and the Sack called Peeter-see-mee. Some idea of what these wines were like, though only an approximate idea, can be gained from the modern PX. This, a contraction of *Pedro Ximenez*, is a very dark brown in colour and is very sweet indeed. It would certainly have appealed to the taste of the Renaissance English.

The third variation can arise in the treatment of the grapes and the making of the wine, and here it seems that the resemblances are more striking than the differences. Modern Finos are made from grapes which have been dried in the sun for about eight hours. Modern PX is made from *Pedro Ximenez* grapes which have been dried in the sun for fifteen days. It is extremely likely that these techniques were used in Tudor and Stuart times.

One of the reasons for asserting this is that a good deal of Sack was sweet. But Sherry, if left to itself, ferments into a dry wine. The sweetness in a sweet Sherry comes from blending and one of the liquors used in modern blending is PX from the heavily sun-dried grapes. Therefore a sweet Sherris-sack must either have been made from grapes which had been sun-dried for a long time or else from dry Sherris which had been blended with a sweetening liquor. I have no doubt that PX was used for this purpose.

Another liquor which is used in modern blending is *arrope*, or boiled-down must. It is very dark-brown in colour, has a smell of toffee, and is overwhelmingly powerful in the mouth. There is every reason to believe that *arrope* was used in Renaissance Jerez and there can be little doubt that it went into some of the wines which were drunk by Shakespeare in England.

It is possible also that Sherris had one of the particular characteristics of modern Sherry since it may have been worked upon by *flor*. *Flor*, the 'flower', is a *saccharomyces*, a minute organism which appears in wine. It is well known in the Jura district of France but its greater fame comes from Jerez de la Frontera. There it appears twice a year, in the Spring and Autumn, and it looks like flakes of chalk, or shreds of paper, floating on the surface of the wine. It lives in Fino sherries – in *Olorosos* it either does not, or is not allowed to, develop – and it gives to *Fino* the delicacy and the dry cleanliness which makes it a unique and exquisite wine.

It has sometimes been held that the beneficial aspect of *flor* was only realized about the middle of the 19th century. The assumption, therefore, is that there was no *flor*

[34] See V.V., *A.,*

294

sherry before about 1850. But the 'flowering' of wine was known, and clearly commonly known, in 1616 and although its meaning may not have been fully comprehended, its presence was not always regarded with aversion.[35] This does not mean that *flor* was actually encouraged at Jerez but I see no reason to assume that it was discouraged or that it was prevented from playing any part in the making of Jerez wine. And if it did play a part, then, of course, some of the Sherris-sack would have had some of the qualities of a modern Fino.

Yet another fact which we have to take into account when comparing ancient Sack and modern Sherry is the fact that modern Sherry is a fortified wine. It is given a dose of grape-brandy after fermentation and often another dose of brandy before it is exported, the amount of brandy varying according to the type of wine. The Sherry drunk in England, for example, ranges, speaking generally, from seventeen to twenty per cent of alcohol by volume. Now, we do not know that ancient Sack was fortified. It may have been, for brandy was known in Jerez by 1580 at the latest,[36] but although I think that export Sack quite probably was fortified, I would hesitate to express an opinion on how much, how often, and how well.

At this point we can say that there must have been a considerable degree of resemblance between the Sack which Falstaff drank and the Sherry which we drink today. But at this point also we must note the difference between them. It is an important difference and it is exemplified by the changing shape of Jerez itself.

Jerez is one of the prettiest of all the wine-making towns of Europe. Behind the white walls of the houses are patios tiled in black and white and in springtime there are both oranges and orange-blossom on the trees along the streets. Behind the white walls of the bodegas there are trees and gardens and an abundance of flowers – lilies, jasmine, and bougainvillaea. It seems almost that the fragrance of a fine Sherry comes in part from the flowers in the bodega gardens.

One of the curious, and I think unique, things about Jerez is the predilection which the Jerezanos have for keeping animals in their bodegas. The del Mérito bodega, for example, contains three alligators and a large aviary of budgerigars. In another part of the town there are the mice of González, Byass. These have been trained to climb a minuscule ladder and drink from the glass to which it gives access. When they are not engaged in having their *penultima* – as the 'last' drink of a series of rounds is optimistically called at Jerez – their faint squeaking is a constant and miniature music among the butts in the vast bodega. There is something reminiscently medieval about these private zoos for one cannot help being reminded of the strangely-assorted menageries which were kept by potentates of the Middle Ages.

In the middle of the 16th century Jerez was a walled city, dominated by heavy defensive walls and by the blunt, military towers which rose out of them.[37] Now it is a walled city but one of a different nature, for the striking emphasis of modern Jerez comes from the long, white walls of the bodegas where the wine is matured. These bodegas are huge and cool, with floors of beaten earth, and with long, high lines of oaken butts. The development of these bodegas reflects the development of sherry, not because their size is witness to increased production but because it is necessary to contain the Solera system.

Modern Sherry is a blended wine and modern Sherry is blended in a Solera. (There are *añadas* – unblended sherries – but they are seldom, if ever, sold and are

[35] *Maison Rustique*, 616.

[36] González Gordon, 472.

[37] See the interesting view of Jerez in González Gordon, 72.

kept for blending.) The simplest, and most generalized, way of envisaging a Solera is to think of it as a stack of butts three tiers high. The lowest tier holds the oldest wine. The next tier up holds the next-oldest wine. The highest tier holds the youngest wine. When the sherry is drawn off for drinking or for shipment it is drawn off from the butts of the lowest tier. These butts, none of which has been completely emptied, are then re-filled with wine from the second tier while the butts of the second tier are re-filled from the butts of the highest tier. The wine, therefore, moves down through the Solera, becoming aged, matured, and blended in its downward progress.

This description is accurate but it is over-simplified. To begin with, the wine in the highest tier need not be a very young, or a totally 'uneducated' wine and indeed everything in a good Solera must be over five years old. Then again a Solera may easily have more than three 'tiers'. And lastly, the 'tiers' of a Solera do not have to be ranged one above the other in a strictly geometrical pattern.

The system as a whole has yet a further complication, for the wine which is drawn from the 'lowest tier' of one Solera is not necessarily the wine in its final form. Sometimes it is. But on many occasions it is blended with wines from the 'lowest tiers' of other Soleras, this being done in order to produce a particular style of wine marketed by a particular shipper and demanded by his particular customers.

The purpose of the system is prediction, for, left to its own devices, Sherry is an unpredictable wine. The same grape-juice of the same vintage from the same vineyard will produce in one butt a delicate, dry wine and in another butt a wine which has more body and less dryness. It will take a year or more to develop these different characters and if the owner of a bodega left his wines to develop naturally he would never know how much of what sort of wine he would have in the years ahead of him. The Solera system enables him to control the wine and to predict his stock. It also enables him, year after year, and always with the same high quality, to produce the exact style of Sherry which his customer prefers. And, of course, the permutations which can arise from the blending of different Soleras means that the winemakers of Jerez can satisfy an enormously wide range of taste. Sherry remains always and distinctively Sherry as the features of a face remain always and distinctively the same; but within this sameness Sherry can be as varied as the expressions which come and go upon a human face. It is for this reason that, apart from being one of the best, it is also one of the most interesting, wines of the modern world.

The advantages of the Solera were not available to the men of the Renaissance, for the system did not develop until about the middle of the 18th century. No one seems to know when it actually did begin and it is quite possible that we might find its rudimentary form in the last half of the 17th century. Further back than that we cannot go and we can assume that the Sherris-sack of the Tudors was not matured and blended in the same way as modern Sherry. Their Sherris was not as uniformly good as ours; it was not as predictable; and it was not as varied. Their Sherris-Sacks would mostly have been harsh, strong wines, or rich, full-bodied wines and we might be tempted to translate this into terms of Finos and Olorosos. But the modern terms will not fit the ancient wines and all we can say is that Sherris-Sack was Sherry before Sherry became civilized.

The name Sack continued to be used in England throughout the 17th century

Weiditz, Hans
Measuring Wine Casks
Miniature, c 1530
Munich, Staatl. Graph.
Sammlung

and its use lasted until the beginning of the 18th century when Sack was drunk in London at the Lord Mayor's Show. But the name 'Sherry' appears as early as 1635 and from the Restoration onwards this title comes more and more into favour.[38] In 1693 a Londoner writes of the wine as 'a pert sort of wine which the Moderns call Sherry'[39] and in other quarters there are occasional touches of modernity. Bristol Milk is first recorded in 1634 and on June 13th, 1668, Pepys was much satisfied with a 'good entertainment of strawberries, a whole venison-pastry, cold, and plenty of brave wine, and above all Bristoll milk'.[40] It is clear that by this time the 'Milk' had achieved a considerable reputation. Then, in the Customs Records of 1697-8, we find that two and a quarter pipes of sherry are marked into London from the East Indies. This was a sea-voyage treatment which was believed by some connoisseurs to improve the wine,[41] and the belief persisted through the Georgian and Victorian Ages.

The Englishman's Cellar

In 1556 a complaint of the increase in the number of taverns at Oxford says plaintively that 'the poor scholars . . . will have wine whatever it cost' and it comments that the wines which the scholars preferred were Gascony, Sack, and Malmsey.[42] This was the basic pattern of English wine-drinking.

Gascon wines continued to be one of the mainstays of the English cellar. But Rhenish, too, played a part and though never as popular as Gascon, it not only maintained, but even increased, its popularity. Most of the Rhenish drunk in England was a white wine but there was some red as well. In 1542 a small amount

[38] Heywood, *P.*, 48; TR, VI, 413 sqq.; Fiennes, Celia, *The Journeys of Celia Fiennes*, 285.

[39] Ames, *Bacchanalian Sessions*, 5.

[40] Harrison, Godfrey, *Bristol Cream* (Bibl. General), 55. Pepys: as dated; and see fn. 1 to this entry of Pepys, the misleading comment of Byron.

[41] Public Records Office, Cust., 3, 1, Pt 1.

[42] *Cal. State Papers Dom.*, Addenda, Mary, Nov. 23rd, 1556.

of red Rhenish was made near Bonn and in 1663 Pepys, after eating 'very merrily' a dish of pease, went 'to the Rhenish wine-house, where we called for a red Rhenish wine called Bleahard, a pretty wine, and not mixed, as they say'. The latter part of Pepys' statement, which seems to imply that much red Rhenish was adulterated, is not, I think, as ominous as it sounds since it may not refer to adulteration at all but to a wine which became known in Germany as Schiller wine. This was an emergency wine, made after the long destruction of the Thirty Years War and when the German vineyards were being replanted. It was made from red and white grapes – that is to say, from any grapes which were available – and it could thus have been reddish, or pink, in colour as well as being described as 'mixed'.

Another German drink, or at any rate a drink which seems to have been of German origin, came into favour in England at about the same time. This was the 'Rhenish in the Must' which appealed to 'English *Ladies*' in the early 1660's. It was probably made out of Rhenish wine mixed with Rhenish must and its vogue appears to have been short-lived since its name is rare in the records. But one version of it was made out of white wine from La Rochelle, Nantes, or Cognac, together with clarified honey or sugar, and it was sometimes flavoured with 'a Decoction of *Clary* seeds, or *Gallitricum*''; thus it may have appeared in England under the more frequent names of Clary or Clary wine.

However much Gascon may have retained its place, and Rhenish increased in popularity, the emphasis of English drinking was strongly southern. The English palate loved the wines of Iberia and the wines that were shipped through 'the Streightes comonly called The Streightes of Marrock'. As it happens Straits Wine was often, perhaps even usually, wine from Malaga, but many other wines were shipped through those 'Streightes' which we now know as the Straits of Gibraltar: Cretan, Greek, Malmsey, Romania, Verde, and Vernage or Vernaccia: all of them Mediterranean, all of them welcomed in England.

A sidelight on the English attitude to Mediterranean wines is given to us by William Vaughan in his *Naturall and Artificial Directions for health* which was published in London in 1600:

'*What is the use of Muscadell, Malmesie, and browne Bastard?*
These kindes of wines are only for married folkes, because they strengthen the back.'[43]

Most 'folkes', however, liked Mediterranean wines whether they strengthened the back or not, and the wines which they liked most were Muscadel, Malmsey, and Romania. These were 'general' wines, that is to say they were not wines from any particular vineyard but were 'type' wines and the names were used to describe them in much the same way that (for other wines) we might now use the descriptions 'claret type', 'hock type' or 'burgundy type'.

Muscadel, the same as Muscadine, was wine made basically from muscat grapes and was usually a rich, sweet wine with an excellent bouquet. It is the 'Moscatello' which Florio records in 1611 and the 'Muscatello' which John Evelyn had in Italy in 1644. It was grown in many places in the Central and Eastern Mediterranean and it seems possible that it was even grown in some of the vineyards of Renaissance Germany.[44]

[43] Vaughan, W., *Naturall and Artificial Directions for health*, 11.

[44] 'Muscatella' in Germany: see Bacci, 338; but note that Bacci's information must often be treated with caution.

Malmsey had originally come from the Eastern Mediterranean especially from Crete, but the growing of it spread rapidly westwards. Some of the best Malmsey was made at Malaga. Other Malmsies were grown in the Azores, the Canaries, and Madeira, and as early as 1537 'Malvoisie of the Isle of Madeer in Portyngale' was received in London. Yet for a time the original eastern connection remained. Ammonius sent a skin of Cretan wine to Erasmus in 1515 while '*vini cretici*' were bought at Oxford throughout the 1530s and the 1540s. Rotimo, a Malmsey grown in the Rethymo vineyards of Crete, was shipped to England in the 6th century and at the same period the Eastern Mediterranean produced *Malvasia garba*, a special type of Malmsey which had been given a tang of astringency. This latter, however, was not common in England, and the usual Malmsey of the English was rich and sweet.

Strictly speaking, Romania was wine from the area of the medieval East Roman Empire and in 1596 Romania wine was specifically mentioned as being grown in Corfu and in north-western Greece. But we have already seen that a century earlier than this 'Romania' wines were being made at Chipiona in south-western Spain. There seems to have been no concealment about this act of copying and it is reasonable to say that the name 'Romania' – or Romnie or Rumrey, as it was variously written – was losing its strict territorial significance and was becoming the name of a type of wine. In general it seems to have been a white wine, for Tasso gives this colour to the Romanias; and it is interesting to note that not only does he give the same colour to the malmseys but that an early 17th-century meaning of Romania is 'a kind of Malmesie wine'.

It is difficult to say how much of the Romnie that was shipped into England had actually been grown in the Levant. A good deal of it, no doubt, for other wines were exported from the Aegean. Muscat was exported from Chios (or Smyrna), in 1607 and 'Cawos', which is presumably a mis-writing for Chios, turns up in England in 1637. Admittedly Chian was rare in English cellars but, as witness Rotimo and the *vini cretici*, it was not at all unusual for wines to be sent into England from the Greek east.

'Greek' wine also appears in the English records. Erasmus seems to have liked it for in 1511 from Queen's College he asks for Greek wine, but not too sweet. This, of course, as in the Middle Ages, would have come principally from southern Italy. It was not very common in Renaissance or Reformation England but we find it from time to time: as '*vino greco*' in 1576, and in 1664 as the two dozen bottles of white Greek wine from Syracuse which were bought for the cellar of the Earl of Bedford. In England its vogue was small but in Italy, on the other hand, it was much esteemed and widely drunk. There it had other uses, too, as we can see from the *Memoirs* of Benvenuto Cellini. During an attack on Rome Cellini was struck by a splintered piece of battlement. A friend of his heated a tile 'red-hot', sprinkled it with a handful of wormwood, poured 'excellent Greek wine' over it, and then 'when the wormwood was well soaked, he put it at once on my chest'. Cellini recovered his senses immediately.[45]

A wine which was rather more popular in Tudor England than Greek wine was the Vernaccia which mostly came from Tuscany, and which was made from the *vernaccia* grape. It appears under the verbal disguises of Vernage or Verunge, and

[45]Cellini, *Memoirs*, 56.

is described by one writer as 'a kind of wine like Malmesie'. Another Tuscan wine which achieved a certain, though rather later, reputation was Verde, or Verdera or Verdea, a delicate white Muscadine wine with a green tinge. Some of this was shipped to England in the 17th century but it was a difficult wine and had to be shipped in 'bottles' because the voyage tended to turn it into vinegar.

The southern emphasis in English drinking was an emphasis which had been carried over from the later Middle Ages. It continued into the Tudor and Stuart centuries but, as time went on, and as the Tudor period changed into that of the Stuarts, this emphasis lost its Mediterranean accent and became more markedly Iberian. Sacks and Canaries and the wines of Malaga, or 'Malligo', were mainly responsible for the change of accent but other wines from Iberian vineyards found their lesser place in the English favour: Tent, a rich red wine which came sometimes from Rota, near Jerez de la Frontera, sometimes from Alicant, and sometimes from other Spanish vineyards; Alicant itself, or 'Alligant', another rich red wine; and, of course, the 'Peeter-see-mee' of Andalusia.

Yet other names, though again in their lesser way, give witness to the Iberian interest. San Martyns was sent to King Henry VIII in 1513. This wine, which was much later known as Saint Martin, was a white wine and probably fairly rich, and it may have been grown between Madrid and Aranjuez. At all events it certainly came, as the documents put it, from the 'Kingdom of Toledo' or, more colloquially, from 'near the Court'. Ryvere, or Wyn ryvers, or wine from the River Ebro was imported into England and this name may have covered wine from Saragossa which was certainly known and appreciated. A telling comment upon it was written by Charles Longland to Vice-Admiral Badiley in 1656–7: 'Capt. Cox will deliver you a couple of chests of old Saragossa wine, a cup of which, in raw, cold weather, will not be amiss. . . .'[46]

From the River Minho, between Spanish Galicia and northern Portugal came Ribadavia, a light and delicate white wine whose name the dramatist Thomas Heywood contorted into the hiccuping jumble of '*Vino deriba davia*'. This sort of mis-writing, or mis-printing, was not, of course, at all uncommon and a Spanish red wine called Hollocke or Hollock also turns up in England as Hallacker. Portuguese wines suffered much the same fate in the eager web of the English language. Charneco, a wine which usually came from near Lisbon occasionally appears in England as 'Charnio' while Caprick, also from near Lisbon and also a rich wine, is recognizable among the Tudors as Capricke, Caprycke, and Caperikis.

Let us now look at some of the cellars of England and see how the pattern of drinking developed during the two centuries of poetry and puritanism. In 1524 Katharine Countess of Devon had Gascon, Claret, Malmsey, Ronnys (which must have been Rhenish) and a wine which was probably Muscadell in her cellar.[47]

Her choice is both medieval and renaissance but it is repeated in Stuart England, and it is repeated in the cellars of professional men as well as in those of peers. When William Whighte, a Midhurst doctor, died in 1631, his cellar contained three-quarters of a hogshead of claret, about a hogshead and a half of white wine, and a hogshead and a half of Sack. In 1665 Pepys finds that he has Claret, Canary, Sack, Tent, Malaga and an unnamed white wine, 'all in my wine cellar together; which' he adds proudly 'I believe, none of my friends of my name now alive ever had of

[46]*Cal. State Papers Dom.*, Vol. 1656–7, Jan. 1st, 227.

[47]Brewer, *Henry VIII*, Vol. IV, No. 771.

his owne at one time'. At about the same date the Earl of Bedford's cellar at Woburn displays the same preference for claret and for Spanish wines – Canary, Sherry Sack and Navarre – but he also has some Chablis and he buys a wine called Lybos. This latter, which is a very rare name in English wine-records, must have come from

Libos, near Fumel, in Gascony. A sign of modernity, or of approaching modernity, lies in the fact that in several years the Earl buys casks of Champagne. Then right at the end of our present period, and indeed reaching over into the early 18th century, the onset of modernity becomes even more noticeable, for as well as buying Navarre, Sack, 'Fayall', and Canary, the Earl of Bristol buys 'Obrian', 'Margoose Clarett' and 'Chateau Margou wine'.[48] These latter rank among the early instances of Château-named wines in English cellars.

The time which elapsed between the cellar of the Countess of Devon and that of the Earl of Bristol was the time which it took for England to transmute evolved medievalism into quasi-modernity and this was as true of wine as it was of many another side of English life. In so far as wine is concerned the use of Château names is one of the most important developments. Another, which is less important but still worth noting, is the gradual change in the meaning of the English word claret. During these two centuries it lost its medieval meaning of a spiced and sweetened drink, and it was less and less used to mean a wine that was pale or *rosé* in colour. The pale colour significance persisted in Europe, for in 1611 in France *Vin claret* meant *Vin clairet*, or wine that was made from red and white grapes, and in Italy at the same time Chiaretto or Chiarello meant a clear, light-coloured wine which had been quickly taken from the vat. In England, however, Claret came to mean a red wine, a blood-red wine, and one moreover which was often from Bordeaux. The modern English usage of the name began in Tudor times but even so it was not until the 18th century that Claret becomes the unequivocal English word for the dark-red wines of Bordeaux.

A slower development was the change of name from Rhenish into Hock. Rhenish continued as a name for German wine until the 18th century but from the Stuart period onwards it was gradually being ousted by the word Hock, or Hockamore, an English corruption of Hochheimer which meant wine from Hochheim on the Main.

The liking for Spanish wines was not merely an English idiosyncrasy. The Irish liked them too and although they drank French wines as well, yet those of Spain seem to have been more popular and when they could afford it the men of Ireland drank Spanish. They also drank, again when they could afford to, extreme quantities of Irish 'Usquebagh' which was mixed with raisins and fennel seed and was considered to be, of its kind, the best in the world. For the most part, however, they drank milk which they strained through an unclean handful of straw, and in other remarkable ways they seem to have preferred the simple life: '. . . I have seene,' writes a traveller, 'young maides starke naked grinding of Corne with certaine stones to make cakes thereof, and striking of into the tub of meale, such reliques thereof as stuck on their belly, thighes and more unseemely parts.'[49]

More sophisticated customs prevailed in Italy. Ingestars – a pleasant name for aperitifs – which were glasses of differently coloured wines, were set out on the inn tables, together with fruits, in order to tempt the appetite, while 'In Summer time, they set a broad earthen vessel full of water upon the Table, wherein little glasses filled with wine doe swimme for coolnesse'.[50] Some few years later at Padua, John Evelyn followed a local, but different, custom and drank his wine cooled with snow and ice. This, however, gave him a sore throat.[51]

[48] Whighte: for this information I am much indebted to Mr Francis Steer, who is editing Whighte's Inventory. Pepys: July 7th, 1665. Bedford: Bedford Cellar, 184 sqq. Bristol: Hervey Cellar, 168 sqq.

[49] Moryson, Fynes, *An Itinerary*, IV, 196–203. For drinking patterns, see Moryson, *loc. cit.*; and IV, 142; *Maison Rustique*, 642; Howell, Vol. II, Letter 55.

[50] Moryson, Fynes, *An Itinerary*, IV, 70.

[51] Evelyn, *Diary*, II, 472, 1645-6.

Oberon

The Renaissance may have liberated the mind but there still remained beliefs and emotions of a truly medieval barbarity. Witchcraft, with all that it involved, out-lasted the Renaissance by over a hundred years and the battle against it is a sordid story of exploited ignorance and willing sadism. The Bishop of Würzburg is stated to have put to death 9,000 witches and wizards within the years 1627-8 while nearly 1,000 were burnt in one single German principality during 1640-1.[52] This was during the Thirty Years War when whole tracts of Central Europe were ravaged and looted by mercenaries so that, perhaps, the proceedings of the authorities against reputed witches were a contemporary manifestation of the sort of mania that produces spy scares in times of war today.

The cruelty which human beings show to one another finds unhappy examples in the treatment meted out to these uncommendable women, for the stake was merely the final pain to which they could be subjected. Torture was a recommended technique. The *Malleus Maleficarum* thus counsels the would-be inquisitor as to his treatment of the presumed witch: '. . . after giving her holy water to drink, let him again begin to question her, all the time exhorting her as before. And while she is raised from the ground, if she is being tortured in this way, let the judge read or cause to be read to her the depositions of the witnesses with their names, saying: "See! You are convicted by the witnesses." '[53] Even the *Daemonologie* of James I of England includes the sentence '. . . further experience daylie proues how loath they are to confesse without torture . . .'[54]

Apart from chicanery, delusions of demonic possession, and sometimes indul-gence in the rites of a perverted paganism, the business of a witch was to meet the subterranean requirements of society: the achievement of revenge, the production of aphrodisiacs, and the procurement of abortions. In sophisticated circles in 17th-century Paris, where, in the classic phrase of Madame de Longueville, they 'did not care for innocent pleasures', sorcery and magic were among the most fashion-able diversions.

> 'Perdait-on un chiffon, avait-on un amant
> Un mari vivant trop au gré de son épouse,
> Une mère facheuse, une femme jalouse,
> Chez la devineuse on courait.'[55]

The 17th century seems to have been a flourishing time for women poisoners, often associated with black magic. The scandals associated with Frances Howard at the Court of James I – the substances which her apothecary confessed to providing her with included such things as 'powder of diamonds' (presumably glass) and 'great spiders' – the wholesale poisoning activities of Madame de Brinvilliers and the sensation caused by the association of the notorious Voisin with Madame de Monte-span are known to everyone; how many husbands or rivals of humbler rank were menaced by these activities will never be known. A number of the witch-women were no doubt evil or willing to implement, or pretend to implement the evil designs of others at a price; some were merely silly or insane; but for most of them their 'science' was not greatly removed from Oberon's command to Puck:

[52]*CMH*, Vol. 4, 423.

[53]*Malleus Maleficarum*, Pt II, question 16, 231.

[54]James I, *Daemonologie*, 30.

[55]La Fontaine, quoted in Jacques Boulenger, *The Seventeenth Century*.

'Fetch me that flower; the herb I shewed thee once.
The juice of it on sleeping eye-lids laid
Will make or man or woman madly dote. . . .'[56]

The fear of the supernatural world, the hope of profit from it, has lingered on. Except in our toleration of it, we are not so far from the 17th century.

The barbarity which human beings showed to each other was shown, also, although in lesser degree, to animals. Even the English do not seem to have developed that far-reaching fondness for animals which later became such a notable feature of their character. The Elizabethan Londoner, for example, took pleasure in 'whipping a blinded Bear, which is performed by five or six men, standing circularly with whips, which they exercise upon him without any mercy, as he cannot escape from them because of his chain: he defends himself with all his force and skill, throwing down all who come within his reach, and are not active enough to get out of it, and tearing the whips out of their hands, and breaking them'. The same Londoner also liked to watch a remarkably unimaginative form of bull-fighting. The bull was tethered in the middle of a sort of miniature bull-ring and dogs were sent singly against him. With his horns he speared and tossed them. An element of kindness broke in, however, for men held sticks beneath the dogs 'to break their fall, so that they could not be killed'.[57]

The Cult of Pleasure – and of Gloom

Although still disfigured by superstition and cruelty, life in the 16th and 17th centuries had a good deal of colour and gaiety, unless, of course, you happened to be in the path of one of the marauding armies, on the wrong side in religion, or poor or sick or out of your wits. In spite of continual wars, prosperity increased; the Renaissance extended not only the spiritual frontiers but the physical frontiers of the known world. From the 15th century onwards, the clothes of the fashionable young men around the Court, relieved of the former necessity of spending most of their active lives in suits of mail, had been growing more and more elaborate, in spite of Sumptuary Laws, though these, admittedly, were mostly aimed at the middle classes. Clothes were a cult at the Court of Queen Elizabeth, when favourite colours were 'pease porrige tawny' and 'goose-turd greene'.[58] Strange that the era of *Euphues* could find no romantic synonyms or needed to find none. Clothes grew ever more elaborate and resplendent; hair, or wigs, more luxuriant. The Puritans from the first signalled their distaste for the social order with cropped heads and sober broadcloth, with plain linen bands instead of elaborate lace collars.

Dancing was greatly enjoyed. Among the 'Revels' of Henry VIII we find one devised by Mr Harry Gyllforth 'that is to understand, a hill summit, thereon a golden stock branched with roses and pomegranates crowned, out of which hill issued a Morryke danced by the King's young gentlemen, as hynsmen, and thereto a lady'. The Revel Accounts supply some of the details of the festivity, for among the other items of expense we find '65 doz. bells for the dancers, the green, red, white and black knights, &c. . . . For the hire of 17 doz. bells while the gentlemen learned to dance, 5s. 3d. White and crimson sarcenet, for fools and minstrels. . . .'[59]

[56]*A Midsummer Night's Dream*, Act II, Sc. ii.

[57]Harrison, p. lxxix, quoting Hentzner; Platter, 168-9.

[58]Harrison, Bk II, Ch. VII, 172.

[59]Brewer, *Henry VIII*, II, Pt 2, 1494; Revel Accounts No. 2.

That was in 1511. In 1594 a *Madrigall to Foure Voyces* celebrated the morris thus:

'Ho! who comes here along with bagpiping and drumming?
O 'tis the morris dance I see, the morris dance a-coming.
Come ladies out, come quickly!
And see about how trim they dance and trickly.
Hey! there again! how the bells shake it!
Hey ho! now for our town! and take it!'[60]

A few years later William Kempe, who was one of the actors in the company which included William Shakespeare, danced the morris from London to Norwich, thereby winning, or maintaining, the reputation of being the 'greatest morris-dancer upon record'.[61] There was dancing after the play, too, and when Platter went to the theatre and saw 'the tragedy of the first Emperor Julius Caesar' he and the audience were entertained at the end of the tragedy by members of the cast dancing 'very marvellously and gracefully together as is their wont, two dressed as men and two as women'.[62]

The disapproval of the Puritan faction in England seems to have been directed more furiously against masques, dancing and play acting than against indulgence in drink, though as early as 1576 George Gascoyne produced his *Delicate Diet for daintie mouthde Droonkardes* 'wherein the fowle abuse of common carousing and quaffing with hartie draughtes is honestly admonished'. Gascoyne's tract, with its warning examples from classical and Biblical history, has served as a model for temperance advocates for some three hundred years though the classical allusions have tended to drop out. The Court of James I was notorious for drunkenness, among other unattractive characteristics; that of Charles I was more decorous and the pamphleteer William Prynne, before he had his ears cropped, dedicated to His Majesty a tract in which he besought him not to have 'his name profaned in every taphouse' by the drinking of continual 'Healthes'.[63] Pym introduced the Excise duty on strong drink in 1643; it may have been intended to discourage drunkenness but its more urgent object was to find money for Parliament in its struggle with the King, as is shown by the fact that in the following year the duty was extended to a variety of other commodities. That earnest Puritan, Colonel Hutchinson, fined his soldiers for drinking on the Sabbath; the fines were levied on the tavern keeper as well as the offender, but there is more than a suspicion that these penalties were as much directed to the promotion of military efficiency as to that of moral salvation. 'In our army we have the sins of men (drinking and wenching),' said a Royalist to his opponent, 'but in yours you have those of devils, spiritual pride and rebellion.'[64] Anyhow, the 'drinking side' lost the war, but although the playhouses were suppressed the taverns continued to flourish.

Smoking was one of the pleasures of the English and before the death of Queen Elizabeth, smoking was common in English ale-houses – 'the powder is lit in a small pipe, the smoke sucked into the mouth, and the saliva is allowed to run freely, after which a good draught of Spanish wine follows'. Captain Bobadill in Ben Jonson's *Every Man in his Humour*, acted in the year 1593, says to Matthew: 'We will have a bunch of radish, and salt, to taste our wine; and a pipe of tobacco, to close the

[60]Fellowes, E. H., *English Madrigal Verse 1588–1632*, 129, No. xviii.

[61]*Kempes Nine Daies Wonder*, Ed. Goldsmid, E., *passim*.

[62]Platter, 166; see also Harrison, p. lxxviii, quoting Hentzner.

[63]Prynne, *Healthes: Sicknesse*, 1628.

[64]*CMH*, Vol. IV, 335.

J. B. Vries after P. van der Brocht
Kitchen and Dining Room Scene
16th century

orifice of the stomach.'[65] The English addiction to the pipe represented perhaps an advance on the earlier Portuguese habit of stuffing the powdered leaf into the nose.[66]

Whether or not the free salivation increased the conviviality of the tavern – as it surely must have done after many a good draught of Spanish wine – the tavern was convivial enough without it and taverns proliferated, much, no doubt, to the satisfaction of Sir Walter Raleigh to whom the Queen had given licensing power.[67] The authority to give or refuse licences for taverns seems to have deteriorated very soon into a racket. In 1617 the notorious Mompesson, said to have been the original of Giles Overreach in Massinger's *New Way to Pay Old Debts*, and two others, were appointed Commissioners for licensing. But it was stated that 'most of the money went into the pockets of the Commissioners and the supervision was merely a means of extortion. Keepers of disorderly houses easily obtained licenses, while respectable people were kept out of the trade unless they would comply with the demands of the Commissioners'.[68]

The tavern was a multifold organism. Apart from occasional, and not so occasional, services rendered to the criminal profession, the taverns – or at least the bigger taverns – offered rooms that could be taken for private dinners. In some houses they could be taken for even more private amusements. Taverns could also be kept for the meetings of particular groups of friends and were thus, to a limited extent, the ancestors of the modern club. Of such was the 'Apollo' room kept at the *Devil* tavern for the use of Ben Jonson and his 'Clubbers'.[69] Spies – whom we should now call Intelligence Men – and emissaries of political factions used particular taverns for their contacts; the Puritans of London under Isaac Penington held their

[65] *Every Man in his Humour*, Act I, Sc. v, as printed in Waldron's *Miscellany*, 1792.

[66] Platter, 170–1. For an enthusiastic smoker in Elizabethan times, 1589, see Hall, Darrell, Appendix II. Portuguese use: Lewin, L., *Phantastica*, 287 sq.

[67] *Cal. State Papers Dom.*, Vol. 1598–1601, 341.

[68] Traill, *Social England*, Vol. IV.

[69] See, for example Simon, André L., *The History of the Wine Trade in England* (Bibl. General), III, 225–7.

meetings there.[70] The taverns did not close during the Commonwealth; on the contrary when Stage Coaches were introduced in 1658 the taverns came further into prominence. In 1647 George Foxe had petitioned Parliament not to allow more taverns than were necessary for travellers but he does not seem to have been very successful.

Then for mortals as well as for Immortals there was music in the taverns and if a traveller '. . . be solitary, the Musitians will give him the good day with musicke in the morning'. All classes went to the taverns, not only men but frequently women, while, at the very end of the 15th century and doubtless afterwards, those who did not keep a store of wine at home – and a considerable number, it seems, had no home cellar – bought their wine from the tavern. To the tavern also they resorted when they intended to have a party or, as it was phrased, 'when they mean to drink a great deal'.[71]

More than one traveller commented on the English love of music, '*Les Angloys, les uns avec les autres, sont joyeux, & ayment fort la musique*' says Perlin who, incidentally, had no great opinion of the English character.[72] How much they loved their music can be seen from the innumerable 'Madrigales', Canzonets, 'Ayres, Or, Fa las For Three Voyces', Songs, Sonnets, and Pastorals which fill the song books and a glance at these books of the Madrigalists and the Lutenists conjures up the happy noise of the Elizabethan and the Stuart English. One can imagine England echoing constantly with a warbling, twanging, fiddling and tinkling: 'Viols and Voyces', 'Little Short Aers to fiue and sixe Voices', Virginals, Lutes, Bass viols, the Orpharion, Theorbos, 'Irish Harpe', and – which must have been very popular – John Dowland's 'invention' in 1597 'for two to playe upon one Lute'.[73]

'. . . to goo to hys drynkeyng . . .'

The growth of comfort and order leads inevitably to thoughts of the simple life. This is one view of it in 1588.

> 'What pleasure have great princes
> More dainty to their choice,
> Than herdmen wild, who careless
> In quiet life rejoice,
> And Fortune's fate not fearing
> Sing sweet in Summer morning.
>
> · · ·
>
> O happy who thus liveth,
> Not caring much for gold,
> With clothing which sufficeth
> To keep him from the cold.
> Though poor and plain his diet,
> Yet merry it is and quiet.'[74]

This picture is another product of the romantic classicism of the Renaissance. The actuality is rather different. At the period when these verses were written 'a fully

[70] Pearl, Valerie, *London and the Puritan Revolution*, 1960.

[71] Moryson, Fynes, *An Itinerary*, IV, 175; Platter, 170; Sneyd, C. A., *A Relation . . . of the Island of England*, 21.

[72] Harrison, pp. lxxii, lxvi, quoting Perlin.

[73] Fellowes, E. H., *English Madrigal Verse 1588–1632, passim*.

[74] *Ibid*, 40–1.

*February: Torch Dance at
Feast
from* The Flemish Calendar
*early 16th century
London, British Museum*

employed labourer would only earn 10 pounds a year, while a carpenter's yearly
average, if he were lucky, would go up to 15 pounds'.[75] These figures may even err
slightly on the high side, and when one remembers that the cost of a peasant family
of four was £8 one can see that, while a labourer's life may have been merry and
quiet, he still had plenty of incentive for 'caring much for gold'. In fact it is more
than probable that the labourer was less well-off during the reign of Elizabeth than
his supposedly harassed counterpart was during the Wars of the Roses. Rough
estimates based on the figure of 100 for A.D. 1301 show that the cost of living had
risen to 210 in the reign of Henry VIII. Henry's debasement of the coinage and,
after 1550, the deluge of silver from Peru and Mexico, raised the figure by the end
of Elizabeth's reign to 700.[76] In the 17th century things were certainly no better for
the country people, if indeed they were no worse, since a family working on a
country estate would have earned on average just below £16 a year. There may of
course have been 'perks' and extra earnings of some sort, but it is doubtful how far
they would have gone to fill the gap between an income of £16 and an expenditure,
for a labourer and his wife with two children, of £21. 10. 0. A carpenter would

[75]TR, IV, 756–7; V, 672, 829–32.

[76]Clapham, Sir John, *A Concise
Economic History of Britain* (Bibl.
General), 186.

have been better off since his yearly wage would have been in the region of £25. 10. 0, but it seems clear that many an Englishman was hard put to it to make both ends meet.[77]

A comparison of wages and prices will show how expensive wine was – expensive, that is, to the labouring classes. In the period of the 1580s a fully employed labourer earned about 4/- a week, while a carpenter could average about 6/- a week. In 1589 the prices of wine were as follows, all by the gallon★: Claret and White wine 2/-, Sack 2/8d., Rhenish 2/9½d., and Muscadell 4/-.[78]

In the 17th century a labouring family in the country could have averaged about 6/- a week and a carpenter about 10/- a week. Wine prices in 1636 go thus, again all by the gallon: Claret and White wine 2/8d., Sack 4/-, Muscadine 4/8d. One might perhaps add a few other prices to fill in the background: 1602 – oysters 8d. the hundred, salmon (in February) 13/- each, lampreys 2/6d. each, butter (in November) 3½d. a lb., eggs 3/3d. the hundred; 1636 – cloves 10d. an oz., cinnamon and ginger 6d. an oz., sugar 1/4d. a lb.[79]

The workman's life was not particularly easy. According to the Municipal Regulation of Hours and Wages by the Common Council of London, the workman in winter in 1538 was supposed to work a twelve-hour day, beginning at six in the morning. At nine o'clock he had a quarter of an hour for breakfast, an hour at midday for his dinner, and at four o'clock in the afternoon, '... libertye to goo to hys drynkeyng by the space of one quarter of an houre onely ...'.[80] He must have needed that quarter of an hour's drinking.

Mainly he would have drunk beer and many of his betters would have done likewise: 'stale ale and strong beere ... beare the greatest brunt in drinking,' says Harrison. Later he comments: 'there is such headie ale & beere ... as for the mightinesse thereof among such as seeke it out, is commonlie called huffecap, the mad dog, father whoresonne, angels food, dragons milke, go by the wall, stride wide, and lift leg, &c. ... It is incredible to saie how our maltbugs lug at this liquor, euen as pigs should lie in a row, lugging at their dames teats, till they lie still againe, and be not able to wag'.[81]

There were, of course, other drinks: cider, mead, perry and 'wines' made with herbs and fruits, spiced and flavoured to make them more piquant.[82] But beer was the favourite, and the devotion to beer is roared out thus in the old song:

> 'Backe & syde goo bare, goo bare,
> Bothe hande & fote goo colde;
> But belly God sende thee good ale inowghe,
> Whether it be newe or olde.
>
> . . .
>
> Thowthe I goo bare,
> Take yow no care,
> I am nothynge colde;
> I stuffe my skynne
> So full within,
> Of joly goode ale & olde.'[83]

★For the size of Tudor, and later, measures, see Appendix H, below, *Measures, Medieval to Modern*.

[77]TR, v, 829-32.

[78]Prices: Hall, Darrell, 216, 223, 226; TR, v, 470; vi, 414.

[79]TR, v, 472; vi, 312, 395, 418, 442.

[80]Tawney, R. H., and Power, E., *Tudor Economic Documents*, I, 115.

[81]Harrison, 150, 295; see also Gascoyne, George, *A Delicate Diet for daintie mouthde Droonkardes*, 18.

[82]Hole, Christina, *The English Housewife in the 17th century*, 47-59.

[83]Percy Society, *Festive Songs*, Intro., Sandys, W., 22.

'Small Claret'

Mr Jorrocks, who was inclined to dismiss Victorian wines as less than a man's drink, would have been hard put to it in Renaissance times, when, even for those days, a good deal of the wine was small and unattractive. In the time of Henry VIII these small wines were so mediocre that their price was not even fixed by law. Buyer and seller were left to agree on a price as best they could and sometimes the wines could not be sold at all.[84] In the 17th century a number of the Charente wines which went by the name of 'Rochell' (so named after La Rochelle) were pale, hard, 'green' wines and rather acid, and an apt phrase used to describe them was 'hedge wines'.

Occasional mediocrity was noted also among some of the greater wines. In 1544 Vaughan said that he 'never drank . . . worse Renysshe wines' though it is doubtful if they could have been much worse than the Rhenish of 1529. This was so sour as to be almost undrinkable and was discourteously referred to as 'Anabaptist'.[85]

Among the small wines which were neither hedge wines nor mediocre great wines (great by the standards of those days) were the various economy wines such as the *acquarello* and the *vini schiappati* of Italy. *Acquarello*, which was the same as the modern *vinello*, was 'a kinde of small weake wine' and was made from grape-husks and water. The *vini schiappati*, or 'split' wines, were rather better. They were made of three parts grapes and one part water, the mixture being left for two or three days and then trodden. When they were finally ready they could be drunk by themselves or mixed with fatter wines, the purpose in each case being to 'stretch' the amount of wine available for household drinking.

Then, of course, there were wines which were natural but which were naturally small. Three of these came from Paris, from 'Argentoile', Montmartre, and Vanves. 'Argentoile', now the suburb Argenteuil, produced wines, some of them white, which were thin and not very strong but which, at the same time, were neither sour nor 'green'. Montmartre produced wine of much the same texture and so did Vanves. 'Sevre', or Sèvres, on the western outskirts of Paris, seems on the other hand to have grown rather bigger wines and one notes, in passing, that some of them were described as red or claret in colour.

We find the word 'claret' used also of the wines of Orleans. Some of these wines were red but others were 'yellowish, claret, and bright cleare' and in contradistinction to the wines of Paris the wines of Orleans were thought to be among the best of France. Whether they were appreciated for their strength or fineness we cannot be sure but some of them were certainly strong and they were recommended for those who were faint after 'too much use of women'.[86]

Small wines and bad wines continued to be made during these two centuries of the Renaissance and Reformation but we can assume that on the whole the quality of wine was better than it had been in the Middle Ages. We are entitled to make this assumption since it seems clear that there was an improvement in the methods of making the wine. The sack technique may not have been a Renaissance invention – or re-discovery – but its wide use must surely have been a Renaissance development. The same, perhaps, holds good of the *égrappoir*, and it is reasonable to believe that an increasing number of wines were made by some variant of the process which produced the *vini crivellati* of northern Italy. These were 'sieved' wines, the

[84] Gairdner, *Henry VIII*, Vol. 7, No. 1399; Vol. 17, No. 1206.

[85] Vaughan: Gairdner, *Henry VIII*, Vol. 19, Pt II, No. 757. 'Anabaptist': Deichmann u. Wolf, *Weinchronik* (Bibl. General).

[86] *Maison Rustique*, 641.

310

Mayer, Conrad
Family at Dinner
1645
Bad Berneck, Hist.
Bildarchiv

grapes being rubbed or squeezed on a sieve and thus separated from the stalks. A modern version of this laborious, but effective, *égrappoir* is that used at Château Mouton-Rothschild in the Médoc of France although at Mouton the grapes are shovelled by oak rakes across an oaken rack.

A technique which the Renaissance does seem to have invented, as opposed to having re-discovered or re-invented it, was that of sugaring the must before fermentation. This method was certainly known by the end of the 17th century, for specific mention is made of it in an English agricultural and commercial news-letter in 1700. The technique, however, was not only used to make wines which began sound but also to mend wines which had begun feeble. 'Our wine-coopers of later times,' says one of these same news-letters, 'use vast quantities of sugar or molossoes to all sorts of wines to make them drink brisk and sparkling, and to give them spirit; as also to mend their bad tastes: all of which raisins, cute and stum will perform.'[87] Cute, or Cutt, was the same as *vin cuit*, wine or must boiled down to a certain consistency. 'Soot', or 'Soet' as the 'Dutch' called it, was also used for fining and for improving the smell and taste of wine. It could be 'wine boyled to a consumption' or grape juice, or a mixture of honey, 'Liquorish', 'Long Almonds', and Sack or Gascony wine. Soot was also used as a sweetening syrup for wine and, among other purposes, for preserving Bastard and Malmsey.[88] Stum, which has been thought to be a contraction of the Latin *mustum*, and which also happens to be an anagram of 'must', was a little more complicated than Cute or Soot. It could be must which, by means of sulphur, had been prevented from fermenting or had been allowed only a partial fermentation. It could be a 'pure wine' which had been kept from fretting by racking and sulphuring. But the verb 'to stum' can also mean 'to fumigate a cask with sulphur ... to stop ... fermentation ... or to renew wine by mixing with stum'. Curiously enough, one authority states that 'Herring-rose preserves any *stum wine*' and the unpalatability of this thought is reinforced by a warning from the same authority: 'A little Stum put to Wine decayed, makes it ferment afresh and gives life and sweetness thereto, but offends the head and stomach, torments the guts, and is apt to cause looseness and some say barrenness in Women.'[89]

[87] Houghton, *Collection*, Vol. II, 479, No. 391; 484–5, No. 394 of Feb. 1699–1700.

[88] Merret, 215–16; *Art and Mystery of Vintners*, 2, 41; No. 39 on p. 41 repeats a Merret recipe of the 1660s but uses 'Soot' instead of Merret's 'Cute'.

[89] Merret, Dr C., *Some observations concerning the ordering of Wines*, 221–2.

This sounds rather worse than the late medieval recipe which counselled the cellar-man to suspend separately in the wine sugar and powdered seeds of rue and which added 'the rue has the quality of affecting the head'.[90]

A greater discovery during these two centuries was that of the power of sulphur. Unknown, or at least unused, during the Middle Ages, sulphuring had become a recognized practice by the end of the Puritan upheaval, when it was used to pre-serve wine or to put 'a little stop to fermentation'.[91] But it was also, and at last, used as a fumigant for the wine casks. 'Scent', as the *Art and Mystery of Vintners* calls it in 1682, may remind us of the '*encens*' recommended for that purpose by Petrus de Crescentiis at the end of the 15th and the beginning of the 16th century.[92] But the similarity is one of name rather than of composition. '*Encens*', as we have said in Chapter V, was probably the smoke of cedar wood while 'scent', although it embodies some herbal medievalism, is a more modern mixture. It was made thus: 'Take 4 ounces of Brimstone, a little Allom, a spoonful of Aqua-vitae, mix them together; when you have done, take a new piece of Canvas and dip therein, and have in readiness the powder of Antugus, 3 Cloves, 2 Races of Ginger, Orange-peel, and a little Coriander-seeds, well beaten together; then cast them upon the Canvas while it is warm, so keep it in a dry place.'[93]

With one important exception – the use of brandy, to which we shall come later – the other techniques show at the most only a gradual advance. For fining, white of egg seems to be more generally used and isinglass is also recommended.[94] On the other hand, the taste of resin is not absent from these centuries. At the height of the Renaissance, resin, together with herbs, was put into wine to cure its bad smell and some casks were still pitched inside and out up till the end of the 17th century.[95] A common method of curing indifferent Sack was the use of lime. Rightly or wrongly, Falstaff complained of it, but this form of 'plastering' was still advocated under the later Stuarts.[96]

The battle to keep wine drinkable, to prevent it going sour or turning into vinegar, was continual and although the importance of topping up a wine cask is recognized, it is only too clear that the battle was by no means won.[97] Cloudy, discoloured, and evil smelling wines were a common disappointment of life. In the English countryside 'vintners feed their fretting wines with raw beef' while their more sophisticated colleagues doctored unpleasant Rhenish with elder flowers, nut-megs and cloves.[98]

The Beginnings of Connoisseurship

After such a depressing recital of its frailties, it might appear surprising that wine was ever able, or even allowed, to age, but we find, for the first time since Imperial Rome, that the age of wine is becoming a subject for thought and discussion. Most wine, it is true, was still shipped in the few months after the vintage and was drunk in the year of its vintaging. But though it was considered that most of the wines of northern and western France reached their peak within half a year or at the most a full year after their making, it was recognized that the sweet wines of Anjou would keep well for two or three years. In the reign of Henry VIII, Rhenish would keep, and was kept, for six years and in Farquhar's play *The Twin-Rivals* a century and a

[90] Sigerist, Arnaldus, 31 (Bibl. Ch. 5).

[91] Houghton, *Collection*, Vol. I, 165, No. 61 of Sept. 1693; Vol. II, 479, No. 391.

[92] Petrus de Crescentiis, Bk IV, cap. xxxii.

[93] Art and Mystery of Vintners, 55; and see 59, 78; cf. *Maison Rustique*, 616; Morwyng, 87-8.

[94] *Maison Rustique*, 613; Houghton, *Collection*, Vol. II, 479, No. 391.

[95] Sigerist, Arnaldus, 29-30; *Maison Rustique*, 611; Houghton, *Collection*, Vol. II, 484-5, No. 394 of Feb. 1699-1700.

[96] Henry IV, Pt I, Act II, Sc. iv; *Art and Mystery of Vintners*, 74.

[97] *Maison Rustique*, 610; for unsound wines, see among others, *Art and Mystery of Vintners*, passim, and Houghton, *Collection*.

[98] Houghton, *Collection*, Vol. II, 479, 484-5, Nos. 391, 394.

half later, Balderdash says to Wouldbe: 'I have brought you a whetting-glass, the best old hock in Europe; I know 'tis your drink in a morning.'[99]

One would have expected the richer, stronger wines of the south to have kept more easily than their lean, northern cousins. To some extent this was so. The wine which the Squire of the Wood gave to Sancho Panza was wine from Ciudad Real and 'a good few years old too'. In less imaginative circles it was quite usual for the Spaniards to keep wine for two or three years and, though rarely, for very much longer. We have already seen that the longer Sherry Sack was allowed to lie, the better it was thought to be and that this was a matter of common knowledge, though not necessarily of common practice, is borne out by the early 17th-century advice that the wines of Spain would not be at their best before the fifth or sixth, or even the tenth, year. This rule, it is added, applies also to the wines of Italy, Provence and Gascony, but with regard to Gascony there appears to be some confusion since it is stated elsewhere in the same work that most of the Gascon wines, when grown in a hot, dry season, may be kept for three years.[100]

Here indeed are the beginnings of modern connoisseurship. They are the beginnings of an action that was to develop into quite unforeseeable splendour but they were still only the merest beginnings. A large part of civilized thirst continued to be quenched by wine that was either adolescent or adulterated. In some, in probably quite a number, of cases this adulteration was no more than the amount of *coupage* necessary to make an indifferent into a drinkable wine. Sometimes, however, it was open to a more equivocal interpretation as when, for instance, in London Malaga was 'added more or less to all Canaries'.[101] Frequently, the *coupage* amounted to fraud. Rhenish appears to have been the wine most commonly adulterated as well as most commonly counterfeited. French wines were sold as Rhenish in England – though of course not always; in the Netherlands it was forbidden to sell Rhenish and French white wine in the same tavern in case they should be mixed; while Rhenish, together with Hippocras, Alicant, Tent, and curiously enough, Frontignac, occurs in a list of wines that were 'commonly compounded'. Rhenish could be made from Rochelle wines and it could also be 'compounded' from dried lemon peel, white wine, damask-rose-water, and a branch of the herb Clary.[102] Muscadine was counterfeited with cute wine, coriander seeds and shavings of cypress wood.[103] For mending the colour of claret, sloes, damsons, black cherries or 'a strong decoction of beet roots' were unblushingly advocated.[104]

The purist may be shocked by some of these romantic concoctions. In a modern context his horror would be justified, but in that of the 17th century it would be misplaced. We must remember that there had been no real tradition of fine wine for twelve hundred years; men had to drink what they could get. Undoubtedly they tried to get the best, but unfortunately the best was not always, or not often, there to get. It was a rough world and we may, without undue exaggeration, compare its gastronomic roughness to a continual diet of curry and cowslip wine.

One view of adulteration is worth quoting, and for several reasons: it is quite alien to the attitude of the modern purist; it shows what must have been the attitude of many between the 5th and 17th centuries; and it was expressed as late as 1700:

'The things besides sugar and its compounds, now-a-days greatly used for mixture

[99]Markham, edn of 1616, 623-4, 631; Gairdner, *Henry VIII*, Vol. 21, Pt I, No. 768; George Farquhar, *The Twin-Rivals*, Act I, Sc. i.

[100]Don Quixote, Penguin edn, 549; Bacci, Bk VII, 363; Markham, edn of 1623, 143; edn of 1616, 623-4.

[101]Houghton, *Collection*, Vol. II, 484-5, No. 394 of Feb. 1699-1700.

[102]*Cal. State Papers Dom.*, Vol. 1611-18, 259; Moryson, Vol. IV, 62; *Art and Mystery of Vintners*, 11, 15, 27, 69.

[103]Houghton, *Collection*, Vol. II, 486, Nos. 390, 395 (?) of Feb. 16th, 1699-1700.

[104]Markham, edn of 1623, 152; *Art and Mystery of Vintners*, 4, 13, and *passim*; Houghton, *Collection*, Vol. II, 481, No. 392 of Jan. 1699-1700.

[with wine] are the juices of many fruits, as gooseberries, currants, and what not: but those which make the bulk are the juices of elder-berries and of the great grape, anglicè cyder, and if these be the worst, I do not see any great evil attends it.'[105]

For the first time since the Dark Ages the English lost their Crown of Inebriation. By almost universal consent it was awarded to the Flemings, the Dutch and the Germans. This is not to say that the English were remarkably temperate. They enjoyed their wine and they drank a lot of it, and they drank also considerable quantities of beer. The fleet drank wine and beer; there was little else for them to drink except brackish water.[106] A Fleming, however, in the vigorous phraseology of Andrew Boorde, gets as drunk as a rat, the Rhinelanders get drunk often, while the Dutch get very drunk, or 'cupshoten'.[107] Heavy drinking did not always bring out that sense of good will towards all men which some may consider natural to the German character, for on one occasion a party of Prussian farmers met together to carry out a bet that they would drink a certain quantity of wine. One of them, perhaps not feeling too well, tried to leave the party before the full sea of liquor was consumed. His companions caught him and roasted him upon a spit until he died.[108] Some desperate measures against intemperance or alcoholism were propounded in other countries. 'To drinke great store of Wine,' for example, 'and not to be drunke, you must eate of the rosted lungs of a goate.' The therapy for alcoholism is more laborious: 'To provoke hatred of Wine . . . mark diligently where the owle haunteth, that so you may get some of her egs, frie them, and give them to the drunken gallant to eate.'[109]

The Beginnings of Gastronomy

In spite of the 'maltbugs' of whom Harrison so much disapproved, the English were comparatively temperate, both in their eating and their drinking. Indeed, their moderate eating was contrasted favourably with the more enthusiastic intake of the Italians. For the most part the English had only two meals a day, dinner at eleven and supper at five, though the hours of eating were variable and tended to become later, mid-day and six o'clock in the evening. Their moderation at these meals, together with their decorous manners, were equally commended, and it was remarked that 'at the tables of the honourable and wiser sort' a great silence is observed. The lower classes of the country people were, however, convicted of 'verie much babbling' but it is also clear that loquacity, and for that matter satiation, were not unknown among their betters. An interesting, and I think a novel, factor is the interest in gastronomy. The majority of noblemen's cooks were 'musicall-headed Frenchmen and strangers' and the ladies of the court were able to provide 'delicat dishes of their owne deuising' in which, however, the most important ingredients were spices brought from Portugal.[110]

Sancho Panza confessed that the food to which he was accustomed was 'kid, beef, bacon, salt meat, turnips and onions'. He was also fond of mixed stews. He was, on the other hand, quite content with the 'two calves' feet stewed with chick-peas, onions and bacon', and he, and many Spaniards like him, must often have put up with shorter commons than those to which Sancho says he was accustomed.[111]

[105] Houghton, *Collection*, Vol. II, 487, Nos. 390, 395 (?) of Feb. 16th, 1699–1700.

[106] *Cal. State Papers Dom.*, Vols 1651-2, 1653-4, 1656-7, etc., *passim*.

[107] Boorde, *Dyetary*, Intro. Chs VIII, IX, XIII.

[108] Moryson, Vol. IV, 36-7.

[109] Markham, edn of 1616, 614.

[110] Harrison, Ch. VI, *passim*, and 272; Moryson, Vol. IV, 171-4; Warner, *Antiquitates Culinariae*, 133; for an adverse view of English manners see the biased account of Perlin.

[111] Don Quixote, 780, 849.

In England under Queen Elizabeth the poorer classes lived on brown bread and, whenever they could afford it, beef, mutton, veal, pork, chickens, eggs and fruit pies. Milk, butter and cheese were said to be consumed only by these poorer people, but the statement is not wholly accurate. The richer classes fed mainly on meat and game, geese and chickens and a certain amount of fish. At their smarter, or more formal, meals the prevalent delight in sweetness was met by an array of jellies, fruit conserves, 'marmalades', 'marchpaine' and sugarbreads. Two gastronomic specialities of England were brawn and venison pasty. Vegetables are remarkable for their almost total absence, but this unhealthy neglect was to some extent made up by the amount of fruit which they ate, apples, pears, quinces and strawberries, and some oranges and lemons.

Although this picture of Elizabethan eating is undoubtedly true, I think that it is not entirely so. Salads were quite common in the 17th century in England (as they were in some places on the Continent) and they were made of a wide variety of vegetables: chives, radishes, lettuce, bean-pods, asparagus and cucumbers. Another fresh salad called a 'compound Sallet' was made from red sage, mint, lettuce, violets, marigold and spinach. 'Preserved Sallets', some preserved with vinegar, included primroses, cowslips, gilly flowers and broom-flowers. We meet salads of much this type in Elizabethan times and, though not extensively used, they may not have been rare, particularly in the countryside.[112]

Nevertheless, when most Englishmen went to table they hoped or expected to eat meat. Fynes Moryson, commenting on his countrymen's passion for roasts, provides what is probably the first defence of the high protein diet. The Italians, he says, 'with a Charger full of hearbs for a sallet and with rootes and like meats of small price, would each of them eate two or three pennyworth of bread. And since all fulnesse is ill and that of bread worst, I thinke wee were more temperate in our dyet, though eating more flesh, than they eating so much more bread than wee did'.[113] In La Mancha the weekly diet of Don Quixote was 'stew, more beef than mutton, hash most nights, boiled bones on Saturdays, lentils on Fridays, and a young pigeon as a Sunday treat'.[114] In England the usual dinner of an Oxford student (who was poorer even than Don Quixote), was a ha'pennyworth of boiled beef with potage, bread and beer.[115] 'Wild' Darrell, in London from April to July 1589, lived almost entirely on meat: beef, mutton, chickens, bacon, pigeons, venison and buttered cold capon. A Friday meal was fish and cheese and among the fish which he ate were mackerel, conger, cockles and crayfish. He sometimes had radishes and a lettuce salad which he dressed with oil and sugar. Apart from these he ate practically no vegetables, though he made up for it with strawberries, and some oranges and lemons. With his meals he drank mainly claret, but occasionally Rhenish, Sack or Charneco.[116]

The desire, one might almost say the lust, of the English for meat was partly met by 'game'. Venison it seems was the most popular, but we must not think of it as meaning only deer, since boiled and roasted hares were also eaten as venison. Rabbits were, of course, the most usual form of game. Darrell ate a lot of them when he was in London and they must have been an important element in the country-man's diet: not only important but pleasant, for in this respect the English were lucky. Their conies were fat, tender and delicate, the best in Europe. In comparison

[112]Harrison, Ch. VI, *passim*; Moryson, Vol. IV, 171-3; Markham, edn of 1676, *The English House-Wife*, 51-4.

[113]Moryson, Vol. IV, 173.

[114]Don Quixote, 31.

[115]Warner, *Antiquitates Culinariae*, 133 (Bibl. Ch. 5).

[116]Hall, Darrell, Appendix II.

with the English rabbits German conies were 'more like rosted Cats'.[117] Venison, commonly baked in pasties, was eaten in England all the year round, a good deal of it preserved as best they could preserve it. John Husee, writing from London in 1538 to Lord Lisle, says 'I send by the bearer three does from the forest of Bere, part of them peppered and salted here'.[118]

In early Tudor England the 'wild meat' that was eaten was far more varied than we would now consider either desirable or palatable. Katharine Countess of Devon furnishes her table with woodcock, pigeon, teal, snipe, pheasant and partridge. But she also has swan, peacock and heron as well as, on occasion, gulls, cormorants and puffins.

Between the Wars of the Roses and the Restoration of the Stuarts one can observe little change in the dressings that were put to many of the dishes. The Green Sauce of the late Middle Ages was made of herbs, breadcrumbs, vinegar (or, of course, verjuice), pepper and ginger; yet in 1668 to 1669 the Duke of York was enthusiastic about 'the best universal sauce in the world' which had been taught to him by the Spanish Ambassador. This was made of pounded parsley and dry toast, with vinegar, salt and pepper, and scarcely differs from the medieval 'Grene Sawce'.[119] The most common sauce mixture in England, and probably also in France, during the 17th century was butter and vinegar (or verjuice), with the frequent addition of breadcrumbs and sugar. Saint-Simon mentions 'mutton dressed with gravy and garlic' as eaten by Louis XIV. Onions were often used in making sauces and so were cinnamon and mustard. One example of the lavish seasoning of food is in a 17th-century recipe for oyster pie which, apart from the 'greatest oysters drawn from the shells' contains currants, sugar, mace, cloves, cinnamon, nutmeg, dates, white wine and sweet butter. Some people added onions.[120]

One can argue that there is some development in taste, a developing sophistication, during these two hundred years. On the whole, the argument is justified, but it should not be taken too far. We find in 1675 the juice, the peel, or slices, of oranges and lemons being recommended with chickens, veal and pheasant. We find also in 1695 an 'omelet' made from eggs, cream and salt, fried in butter and served with sugar and the juice of oranges. On the other hand, in 1524, the Countess of Devon buys 100 sour and 50 sweet oranges and one may conjecture that at least some of these were used for dressings.[121] Darrell's oil and sugar dressing for his lettuce salad may be an indication of a growing simplicity, or refinement, of taste although Darrell was no gourmet and his diet would have been that of many another Elizabethan gentleman.[122]

Table Manners

Belching at table and rudeness to foreigners were among the accusations levelled against the English.[123] In at least one case, however, these criticisms were made by a prejudiced observer and the minor barbarism which they imply is not supported by other writers. On the contrary. With surprise and pleasure they record that the English were well mannered, generally sober and remarkably friendly. Erasmus writes in a letter of one of their more charming customs which was to kiss on meeting and parting and to kiss when they met again and parted once more: 'in short

[117] Hall, Darrell, Appendix II; Moryson, Vol. IV, 171.

[118] Gairdner, *Henry VIII*, Vol. 13, Pt I, No. 247.

[119] *Babees Book*, 172–5 (Bibl. Ch. 5); Pepys, *Diary*, Feb. 10th, 1668–9.

[120] Markham, edn of 1675–6, 75–8, 80.

[121] Markham, edn of 1675–6, 75–7; Houghton, *Collection*, Vol. I, 438, No. 67 of Oct. 1695; Brewer, *Henry VIII*, Vol. IV, Pt I, No. 771.

[122] Hall, Darrell, Appendix II; see also the salad dressings in Markham, edn of 1675–6, 52.

[123] Harrison, lxvii (Perlin).

Rembrandt van Rijn
Self-Portrait with Saskia
1635
Dresden, Gemälde Galerie

wherever you move all things are charged with kisses'.[124] The friendly urbanity of their manners did not of course touch all of them with its grace but it was clearly becoming widespread, as was the growing sophistication of their tables. In the houses of the nobility wine was served out to the company in silver jugs and goblets; and it was also drunk, not only in great houses, but also in those of the gentry, in fine glasses from Murano. Venice glass, outstanding in Europe, was much prized by the English, but it was comparatively expensive. Yet even those who could not afford these fragile delights decorated their pots and tankards of coloured pottery with silver or pewter. A curious refinement was their custom, in many cases, of not putting drinking vessels on the table. Each man called for the drink which he wanted at the moment when he wanted it. When he had drunk, the cup was returned to the cupboard.[125] This, it was noted, reduced the possibility of 'idle tippling'. Another reason may have been the lack of space on a well served table.

The amount of food, and the number of dishes, placed on the table at a banquet seems to us prodigious. Even what was described as 'an ordinary proportion which any good man may keep in his Family, for the entertainment of his true and worthy friends' numbered in the full service of its first course thirty-two dishes 'which is as much as can conveniently stand on one Table'. For this 'humble Feast' the dishes were: a shield of brawn with mustard, a boiled capon, boiled beef, a roast chine of beef, a roasted neat's tongue, a roast pig, baked chewets (a sort of spiced and sweetened pasty of shredded meat and mutton suet), a roast goose, a roast swan, a roast turkey, a roast haunch of venison, a venison pasty, a kid with a pudding in the

[124]*Cambridge Modern History*, Vol. I, 492.

[125]Harrison, 146-7. For glass in England, and elsewhere, see Ch. 8.

belly, an olive pie, two capons, and a sweet spiced custard. (Olive pie was not made with olives but of herbs, spices, veal and preserved fruit.) To make up the full service of this humble feast the housewife added salads, fricassees, sweetmeats and 'Quelquechoses', the latter being a fried dish made with eggs, cream, spices and chopped 'Pigs pettitoes' or, as its name implies, with anything that happened to be handy, such as small birds, oysters, mussels, cockles or fruit.[126]

The Lords of Language

It is strange to read of '. . . the great silence that is used at the tables of the honorable and wiser sort, generallie ouer all the realme'[127] of England, for the great discovery of the Renaissance was the use, not of silence, but of language and it was in England that language achieved a beauty which nowhere in the world has it achieved again. The Pentecost of the Apostles and the Pentecost of the Artists were both linguistic Magnificats. The first was the revelation of the one God: it was to bind man into a single attitude of thought and inspiration. The second was the revelation of multiplex man: by making language into a diversity, it enabled him to express himself in his diversity.

After the visitation of the cloven flames the Apostles spoke in different tongues and the mockers said of them that they were full of new wine. With some absence of wit (natural, perhaps, after the reception of a miracle) Peter pointed out that it was far too early in the day for them to be drunk. Metaphorically the mockers were, of course, right; the Apostles were filled with the unique vintage of Christianity. But their increased powers of communication did not alter the fact that they were communicating a single wine. With the Renaissance it was different. Italian (perhaps the earliest to mature), English, French, Spanish, Portuguese, German: six powers of expression, each grown in order to describe with a different beauty a different facet of western man: six wines to intoxicate the liberated individual.

The tongues of flame had been burning intermittently throughout the Middle Ages: in the *chansons de geste* of Provence, in the *cantigas de amigo* of Portugal: blazing up in The Canterbury Tales, and the Divine Comedy. But it was only at the Renaissance that they became a conflagration, leaping almost like a wildfire through Marlowe and Rabelais.

This spreading delight in language, this new eagerness to use words and to make poetry, runs fast, and sometimes wild, throughout emerging Europe. The people's songs, the *cossantes*, of medieval Portugal are lovely in their lyricism, but in their number they cannot compare with the multitude of Elizabethan madrigals, ballads, catches, and roundelays. From the pulpit outside St Paul's in London, sermons were given which had to last for three, or at a minimum for two, hours and to carry him through this marathon the preacher was supplied with bread and a bottle of wine.[128] This exhibition may have been a display of verbal acrobatics, but not necessarily more so than many a medieval exhortation. Now, however, the acrobatics could be more varied and complicated because the range of skill was greater: so great that it could achieve one of the most difficult acrobatics of language, the translation of a book so that a work of art in one tongue becomes a work of art in another. The alchemists of the Middle Ages attempted the transmutation of metals. The men of

[126]Markham, edn of 1675–6, 58, 75, 97–101.

[127]Harrison, Bk II, Ch. VI, 151.

[128]Platter, 177.

Distilling Scene
from The Art of Distilling
1692
Jasper Grinling Collection

the Renaissance and the Reformation transmuted minds: Chapman's Homer, Florio's Montaigne and Urquhart's Rabelais: these were works of the new art of discovering man by translating him in all the variations of his possibility. Even without interpreters Cellini translates himself for us in his autobiography as Montaigne does in his essays, and the way opens, though slowly, towards the distant humanism of the modern novel.

The Middle Ages were the passion of faith, the Renaissance the passion of art and the modern centuries are the passion of reason. At the turning point where medieval becomes modern, summing up the revolution of the Renaissance, stands a great declaration of faith. But it is of faith in man, not in God. Rembrandt translates himself for us in his series of self portraits: man the artist, growing through his strange power of imagination, intoxicated by the double splendour of the creation around him and the creation inside him, growing older into the terrible honesty of that face with the tired eyes, the worn skin, the red wine-flushed nose. The glory has been done, the power used, the purpose achieved. There is now the measurement of loss: of never the absolute, of nowhere the finality: of that which might have been done differently but can no longer be attempted: of moments that were wasted because they were not magnified. Sad, tired, wise, but with the courage to watch himself, even to the end. Man the measurer.

The 17th century, opening in a burst of vitality as warm as sunshine, was to darken with the clouds of war and rapine and to see, in the sack of Magdeburg and the reduction of Drogheda, two of the last and cruellest examples of massacre used as an instrument of policy, the last, that is, until our own day. The century had not heard the confident pronouncement of Jean-Jacques that man is born free, but it hastened to rivet chains upon itself. One repression succeeded another and no creed or faction which had the power refrained from tyranny, in lesser things as in great. The English Puritans closed the playhouses, forbade the Maypole and feasting at Christmas, and enjoined how every man over eighteen should spend the Sabbath. A little later the police of Louis XIV were searching houses, even those of foreign nationals, during Lent, for forbidden articles of diet. A party of monks, surprised at a feast with hams and pies and 'many bottles of wine' was sent to gaol. Small things, but indicative.[129]

The philosophy of the Renaissance had not marched with its astonishing artistic achievement. In many Universities Scholasticism still reigned and from the 15th century onwards the struggle between faith and reason had induced scepticism; it finds its most seductive expression in Montaigne. The discoveries of Copernicus and Galileo, the movements within both Catholic and Protestant Christianity for a simpler, more personal form of belief, all these currents of thought ran counter to each other until one man examined and correlated them and his work 'though severely methodical was at the same time the complete realization of the thought of his epoch and the starting point of future developments'.[130]

From the eyes of Rembrandt's self portraits, Man the Measurer looks out. In the first principle of René Descartes, the Man of Reason speaks: *Cogito ergo sum*. The order of priority will be challenged later but for nearly two centuries the conception of the Man of Reason, master of events, will determine the shape and colour of our civilization.

[129]Lewis, W. H., *The Splendid Century*.

[130]*Cambridge Modern History*, 778.

CHAPTER SEVEN

Damask Water

It is easy for us to conjure up the scene, for though it is archaic and comic, it is familiar to our imagination, from the pictures of Brueghel, Teniers and the Dutch and Flemish masters. By one window is a reading desk; three fat books sprawl on a wooden bench; at the far end of the room, among a litter of alembics, is a small furnace and behind the furnace is a leaded casement window looking out on to the countryside. In one corner of the room is the alchemist and somewhere, perhaps on the robe which he is wearing, are the astrological symbols of his art. It was a compound of magic and mysticism, of ignorance, and of ignorance disguised by the apparent meaning of sonorous names. The air of the room was supposed to be crowded with spirits and, if the alchemist were considered a great magician, to be crowded to overcrowding with these intangible instruments; his skill, so ran the belief, was to control them by the knowledge of their proper names, and by calling, rejecting or recalling them, to create from their controlled interaction a deliberate perfection. The rules of his craft were the studbook of superstition. In his various aspects the alchemist was the dedicated scholar, the suspect heretic, or the vagrant con man. Reputedly he could talk with the Invisible, and could stand unharmed between the four powers of Earth, Air, Fire and Water. His science was that of the compiler of horoscopes, the maker of almanacs and the mover of incantations. As late as 1800 Rowlandson could caricature him as Mr Hocus-Pocus, but he was none the less a scientist, for alchemy was the prelude to chemistry.[1]

People who believed, as most people did believe, that the earth was a thin and uncomfortable membrane between two supernatural worlds, one of demons and one of angels, found it natural to believe that the membrane was penetrated by supernatural spirits. They tended to assume that the heart of a thing was its spirit or essence. The idea is pagan and poetic and not particularly silly. The labour of the alchemists was to control these essences, and to make them breed. Their object

[1] Read, John, *Prelude to Chemistry: an outline of Alchemy, its Literature and Relationships*, London, 1936; and *The Alchemist in Art*, London, 1947.

321

Pieter Breughel the Elder, The Alchemist: London, British Museum

was to produce, each one according to his avarice or his dedication, the philosophers' stone which turned lead into gold or the philosophers' jewel whose radiance would open the shut doors of the universe. Inevitably, people believed that the alchemist held converse with spirits; and so beyond the casement window was the threat of torture and of the stake. The exercise of the art involved an element of risk, although the degree of that risk has probably been exaggerated; used adroitly, even with honesty, and above all with tact, the knowledge of spirits could bring a man power and amass him a moderate fortune. But for all their efforts to predict the choreography of the future as it would be danced out by the planets and by those under the power of the planets, the alchemists failed to see that they themselves had put a new step into the dance. Their preoccupation with medieval spirits was the discovery of modern spirits, for the alchemists were the first men who ever made brandy.

At a point between 16 and 17 per cent of alcohol, fermentation has to stop because that amount of alcohol kills the fermenting yeasts. Therefore, with or without the addition of sugar, wine cannot contain more than 17 per cent of alcohol. The normal range is between 7 per cent, which is very low, and 15 per cent, which is rather high. On average, good claret contains about 11 per cent of alcohol. In contrast, good brandy sold in Great Britain contains about 40 per cent of alcohol as do whisky and gin, these quantities being in some cases higher in the United States. (The strength of a distillation is, of course, a matter of taste or legality since the technique can produce absolute alcohol.) Thus, while neither Homer nor Horace drank anything stronger than 17 per cent, the men of the Renaissance could, and did, stupefy themselves with a potion three times as strong. The delights and the dangers were reflected in two of the many names which were given to the spirits: on the one hand, *aqua vitae*, the water of life: on the other, the *schnapsteufel*, the brandy devil as it was called in Germany in 1360.[2]

Distillation, in general terms and in so far as spirits are concerned, is the vaporizing of an alcoholic compound in order to separate the alcohol from the compound. The simplicity of the process resides in the fact that alcohol vaporizes at a lower temperature than water. Thus, in making brandy which in modern times is only properly made from grape wine, the wine is boiled to a temperature of between 75 and 100 degrees. The vapour is cooled and collected as a liquid which, to a greater or lesser degree, is concentrated, or pure, alcohol. This description is necessarily a rough one since the vapour boiled off the compound is not purely alcoholic although, of course, it can be redistilled – rectified – to obtain the pure alcohol.

The name brandy comes from the technique of distillation. 'Gebrannter' or 'geprannter Wein', 'brandwin', 'Brandewin' – burnt, distilled wine – were some of the names given to it in 13th- and 14th-century Germany. In other texts it is called 'aqua ardens' or 'ew ardant' – burning water – and this phraseology persists into the 17th century for in 1638-9 in England distillers are referred to as 'hot-water men'.[3] In some of these names we may detect a triple derivation: first, from the heat applied to the wine in order to distil it, second, from the fiery taste of the spirit and its heating effect on the throat or brain of the drinker, and third, from the fact that the distillate could be set alight and would burn. The flame to which we are accustomed on our Christmas pudding must have seemed to the alchemist to indicate the presence of an elusive and potent spirit. As of course it did.

This power to burn is to us only a matter of gastronomic fireworks but nineteen hundred years ago it had a curious moment of historical interest. Pliny says that Falernian was the only wine that took light when a flame was applied to it.[4] Now, ordinary wine of about 11 or 12 per cent alcohol will not burn, even when heated. Port wine, which contains about 22 per cent alcohol (since it is fortified with spirit), will burn under the same conditions though not with any vigour. The earliest historical distillates, which date from the 1st century A.D. in Alexandria, contained too much water to catch light, and it might thus seem that Pliny is recording the first proper distillation. If this were so, we should have to revise the historical perspective, but I think we must assume that it was not so. A boiled-down must was a popular drink among the Romans, who gave various names to the product according to the degree of reduction. Must boiled down to one-third was called *defrutum* and what Pliny is probably recording was an accidental ignition of the vapour noticed during the cooking of the must. His statement thus signifies only a moment of hesitation between the making of *defrutum* and the discovery of brandy. Over a thousand years were to pass before the hesitation became certainty.

Distillation was not used in the pre-Christian world, although the Babylonian

[2]Forbes, *SHD*, 96.

[3]Forbes, *SHD*, 91, 96; *Ménagier*, 8; *Cal. State Papers Dom.*, Vol. 1638-9, 244, 423.

[4]Pliny, Bk XIV, viii, 62.

drink *ulusin* has been translated as schnapps by one commentator, as we have noted in Chapter II. All the information which we have points to its discovery by Alexandrian experimenters in the 1st and 2nd centuries after Christ when Mary the Jewess, or her School of Alchemists, invented the still. Her labours are commemorated in the modern kitchen, perhaps inaccurately, by the *bainmarie*. Yet although the Alexandrians could distil they either could not, or did not, distil alcohol. It is generally supposed that the production of alcohol was an Arab technique whose secret they took with them into Arab Spain. It is, however, extremely doubtful that the Arabs knew alcohol and more than probable that it was discovered by 12th-century Christians at Salerno. By the middle of the next century the knowledge of distillation was common among the alchemist scholars and probably also among Italian apothecaries. A great step forward in the technique was made in the same century by Thaddeus Alderotti who invented, or improved, the method of cooling the vapour after it had been taken away from the cap of the still. It is possible that absolute alcohol was known in the time of Raymond Lull, though the alchemical writings once attributed to him are now considered apocryphal. Somewhere about 1400 it was known that spirit could be produced from corn.

By the early 15th century the drinking of brandy, whether distilled from wine, beer or corn, was becoming quite widespread, although its popularity was largely confined to Germany. Liqueurs – sweetened, aromaticized alcohol – spread in the 14th century from Italy to France but their popularity was never comparable with that of brandy, and the great day of liqueurs, as we understand them, was not to arrive for another four hundred years.

In the early Renaissance and, for that matter, until after the end of the 17th century, it is often difficult to know exactly what type of spirits were being drunk on any particular occasion. The tendency was to class all distillations under the heading of 'waters'. 'Hot waters', 'strong waters', or 'the water of life', and *ew ardant* or *aqua vitae*, were the most common designations and were used regardless of the compound from which the alcohol had been made. *Ew ardant*, for example, could mean in the 14th century alcohol distilled from wine and given one redistillation. At the same date, *aqua vitae* could mean a distillation of wine which had been four times rectified. But the various terms do not really follow any strict scale of quality or strength and it is obvious that both terms were also used, and very frequently, to mean simply a spirituous drink, whether crudely or competently distilled. The phrase 'hot water' may sometimes prove confusing, as in one 14th-century text where we find *ew ardant* served up with an elaborate pastry. Translated as hot water, which is accurate in medieval language, it could be taken to mean what we ourselves call hot water but from the context it is undoubtedly brandy and its appearance in a medieval cookery book is interesting, not so much because it was used as because it was so seldom used. Another confusion can arise from the fact that the word 'waters' was frequently applied to cosmetics and medical concoctions, as in Braunschweig's recipe for 'a good water for the palsy, not costly', which was to be made from herbs and distilled wine.[5]

The ethereal essence trapped by the alchemists quickly became the elixir of life lauded by the doctors, and the brandy devil which rendered so many of the Germans 'cupshoten'. Had the figure of Dionysios been invented at this time it would

[5]Forbes, *SHD*, 3–96; Sigerist, Arnaldus, *passim*; Braunschweig, *vertuose boke . . .*, cap. cc, xxxi.

Wenceslas Hollar, The Wine Market at Strasbourg; 17th century: André Simon Collection

have borne little resemblance to the Greek wine god. Instead, it would have been a blend of the Christian Romanesque and the German grotesque, angel winged and beaked like a demon with something as outlandish about it as the hydra-headed stills in the old illustrations. For climatic reasons it was only natural that the brandy habit should spread most rapidly in Germany and the Low Countries, and the men of these countries became the noted spirit drinkers of Europe. In the 16th century and after, the brandy which they drank was not distilled from wine but from corn and is more recognizable to us as aquavit, schnaps, or gin. By 1622 there appears in the *Constelyc Distilleerboec* the first published recipe in Dutch for Hollands Gin or Geneva. The latter name had nothing to do with the uninebriated Calvinist city but came from *aqua juniperi* or 'geneverbessenwater', made with juniper berries.[6] For a long time, until at least the 18th century, the confusion in names will persist and spirits will be known indiscriminately as brandy. One of the least objectionable habits of German drinking in the early 17th century was their custom, when going on a journey, of breakfasting on nothing but gingerbread and aquavit;[7] but the quality of the elixir must often have made it a demonic breakfast.

The English acquired an interest in spirits later than the Dutch and the Germans and their liking for 'strong waters' developed more slowly. It was not until the 18th century that their liking became an addiction and attained a degree of squalor unsurpassed by any other nation. Though spirits were imported into Elizabethan England – accompanied from the Low Countries by such miscellaneous objects as bottles, empty barrels, drinking glasses and chamber stools[8] – their consumption was not really widespread, the English rightly preferring to drink to their own greatness in wine and beer. The Scots also seem to have been tardy in the matter since, according to Moryson, they celebrated their national pride and national penury in unsugared wine and home-brewed ale. The latter may have been quite enough for them to cope with since, as Moryson remarks, it 'will distemper a strangers bodie'.[9] Some writers have claimed a very long pedigree for Scotch whisky and indeed,

[6]See Forbes, *SHD*, 160.

[7]Moryson, IV, 27.

[8]Hall, *History of Custom Revenue in England*, Vol. II, 236 sq.

[9]Moryson, IV, 184.

given the climate of Scotland, it would be surprising if some medieval farmer in his fastness had not discovered how to distil spirit from grain. The Exchequer Rolls record that a certain Friar John Cor was supplied with 'eight bools of malt for making aqua vitae' and it has been stated that whisky was a known and popular drink at the Court of James IV. Scottish usquebagh was imported into England during the 18th century and as late as the opening of Victoria's reign, but it was rectified and sold as gin. It was not until the discovery of the art of blending in the middle of the 19th century that Scotch whisky began to gain recognition as a drink; even then the tipple of the Victorian heavy 'swell' was brandy-and-soda, and remained so into Edwardian days.[10]

If Moryson did not encounter Scottish usquebagh, and he has left us no mention of it, he encountered, as we have noted in the previous chapter, a great deal of Irish usquebagh, which both sexes drank enthusiastically and which he considered the best in the world.

At the same time as the Irish were enjoying their usquebagh the English were distilling their own spirits from wine lees or from strong beer.[11] By 1639 the industry of the 'hot-water men' had reached a point where there was talk of the creation of a distillers' company in London.[12] A considerable part of English distillation would, however, have been done in home stills, and as early as 1565 the housewife was encouraged in this domestic necromancy by the publication of Peter Morwyng's *Treasure of Evonymus* whose recipes for distilled waters may have induced many a rustique hangover. But for the greater part the brandy drunk in Stuart England came from France, and some of it from Cognac, although in times of political difficulty with the French, and to some extent at other times, brandy came into England from Spain, Italy and Portugal.[13]

The greatest brandies in the world come from Cognac and it is curious to find that the origin of these remarkable liquors was due to economic distress and not to a stroke of genius. Around 1636 the growers in the Saintonge and Angoumois districts asked for a reduction of the tax on their wines, which had to be transported down the Charente, pointing out that the neighbouring provinces which were closer to the sea and not subject to these charges, were able to sell their wines abroad at a much better price. Nothing very much happened, however, until after the terrible winter of 1709 when nearly all the vines in the Saintonge country were destroyed by frost and had to be replanted.[14] Although the distilling industry had been active in Bordeaux in the 1550s, had a Gascon necromancer of those times prophesied that the once wild land of the Haut Médoc and the impoverished country of Saintonge would produce respectively the most subtle wine and the most subtle spirits in the world, he might have been accused of Gascon exaggeration. He would not indeed have been proved right for over two hundred years.

Neither the surroundings nor the spirits of Cognac were the same in 1630 as they are now. There would have been more trees on the low rolling hills, more corn in the fields, fewer vines. Between Rouillac, Jarnac, Segonzac and Jonzac, there would have been fewer of those huge walled farm-buildings which are now so typical of the Cognac country and whose ancestry is clearly Roman; their type occurred sometimes in Roman Britain.[15] Would there have been, then as now, in the spring-time, those thick masses of purple and of white lilac, which seem so appropriate in

[10]Read, John, *Alchemy at the Court of James IV of Scotland*, 60-7, quoted in Forbes, *SHD*, 101. Moryson, 197-8; Gilbey, *The Compleat Imbiber*, 28-9.

[11]Morwyng, 76; ALS, *HWE*, III, 367; Moryson, IV, 197.

[12]*Cal. State Papers Dom.*, Vol. 1638-9, 244, 423.

[13]See, for example, the import figures of 1697-8 in the Cust., 3, 1, Pt I, Public Records Office, London.

[14]Delamain, *Histoire du Cognac*, 18, 20.

[15]The Bignor villa, 4th century, is much larger and more complex than the Cognac farms but the same in principle. See *The Illustrated London News*, Dec. 29th, 1956.

Early Still
17th century
Messrs Hennessy and Co.

this country of -ac names? In all probability the grapes themselves were then different; they certainly were after the great frost of 1709 which made replanting necessary in the ruined vineyards. Much of the replanting was done with the Balzac grape (the Mourvèdre) which can give pleasant wine in Provence but which did not in the Charente. Modern cognac is largely made from the St-Emilion vine whose name in Italy is the Trebbiano.[16]

There is only one resemblance between the Charente brandy of the 17th century and the cognac of our own. The newly made wine would have been then, as it is now, distilled in the homes of the men who owned the vineyards. The technique would have been much the same, though less practised and less efficient. There the resemblance stops for modern cognacs are classified, aged and blended.

[16]Delamain, *op. cit.*, 15-20; Viala, Vermorel, Vol. II, 237, 255.

327

The classification of the modern vineyards of Cognac ranges from the Grande Champagne to the Bois Ordinaires: Grande Champagne, Petite Champagne, Borderies, Fins-Bois, Bons-Bois, and Bois Ordinaires: it is a scale of diminishing quality and the quality diminishes as does the amount of chalk in the soil. The raw brandy distilled by the wine growers of these districts is bought by the shippers and put into *barriques* in their cellars, warehouses or *chais*. In one of these, aptly named Le Paradis, and just across the slow, green river from Hennessy's main office, part of which was once a monastery, Hennessy keeps its hundreds and thousands of barrels of brandy. Each one of these is labelled in beautiful chalk copper-plate writing with the date and place of the vintaging. But in the strict sense of the term there is no vintage cognac, or very little, so far as the drinker is concerned. By far the greatest part of the cognac that is drunk is a blend of different ages.

Brandy ages in cask and it will continue to mature for anything up to half a century. Unlike wine, it will not mature in bottle. I have tasted an 1815 cognac which I can only describe as flat alcohol; an 1875, much smoother, was bitten into by its own bite; at the other end of this time scale a new cognac was raw and angry and choking, a violent highwayman of a drink. It is in its proper ageing that cognac becomes the perfection of brandy. But this ageing is expensive, for the alcohol evaporates year by year and the amount of maturing brandy which evaporates every day in the Cognac area is 25,000 bottles. Despite this welcome addition to the atmosphere I have never noticed any permanent feeling of inebriation in the town of Cognac.

Fine cognac is not only a mixture of brandy from different years but also of brandy from different districts, and far from this being a matter of counterfeiting or low cunning, it is a practice of high craft and considerable art. Desirable qualities of separate years are added together; so are those of separate vineyards; the result is a 'standard range' of cognacs to suit the inevitable variety of taste and income. In this respect, but in this respect only, cognac is like sherry. The blending process is, of course, a very different matter. In contrast to the slow solera system of Jerez, at Cognac brandy is run through pipes, at the junction of which they start their blending. Inside the blending vats the brandies are swirled round by huge oak propellers and if you put your nose to the open cover of the vat you will not be able to keep it there long. The smell is not the heady reek of fermentation, of must becoming alcohol, but the overwhelming anaesthesia of the alcohol itself.

These pipes and propellers might seem to obliterate any element of romance, to substitute mechanism for art. So, no doubt, to the starry-eyed wine lover, might the bottling plant: a huge web of red pipes with brilliantly polished stop-cocks, and a soulless array of arrow indicators and red lights. Nightmare is added to incongruity by the flat metal hands which come out of the bottling plant, curve suddenly round the bottle and disappear, leaving as a memento of their caress a clean label of title and maturity. The whole thing is unemotional, as efficient and unaffectionate as a power-house. But at the heart of the lights and stop-cocks and behind the grey, black-banded vats is the human artist. The taster is the arbiter of the blend and his work is vital. His art can be briefly, and incompletely, summed up in the phrase of a Cognac cellar-master: '*Il faut avoir du mémoire.*'

Apart from any question of the mechanical interventions in the modern Cognac process which in themselves are aids and not techniques, Charente brandy in the 17th century was quite different from what it is today. Except in very rare cases it would have been neither aged nor blended. Ageing would have been far too costly for the size of the industry and proper blending would have been beyond the powers of most distillers, as it would have been beyond their inclination. The cognac of that time was a raw young spirit. The palate of the time was not sophisticated enough to demand adult and educated brandy, but it had at least developed far enough to demand that its brandy should not taste bad. Since this often happened, the makers or the merchants were obliged to make their product more winsome by perfuming it with herbs or flowers,[17] as we have already noticed in the case of wine.

Not all brandy was really bad while very little brandy was really good. Attempts were made to improve it, but their success was not rapid. Nevertheless, the industry continued to grow in importance throughout the 16th and 17th centuries. As early as 1514, in Paris, appeared the corporation of '*sauciers-limonadiers-vinaigriers-distillateurs en eaux-de-vie*'. The distillers did not become a separate corporation until 1637 and the '*Statuts et Ordonnances pour La Communauté des Maîtres Limonadiers, Marchands d'Eau-de-Vie . . . de Paris*' registered in the Parlement in 1676 gave them some degree of monopoly in the buying, making, and selling of Eau-de-Vie either wholesale or retail.[18] That a large amount of the eau-de-vie made in France was still made from corn and not from wine is apparent from an '*Arrest du Conseil d'Etat du Roy*' issued in September 1693 which, with some exceptions, forbade the making of brandy from corn which should be better employed in making bread.[19] These ordinances had little long-term effect or at any rate did not seriously stop the production of brandy since in 1699 it was being sold '*porte-col*' at street corners, for which purpose the sellers had already been allowed by edict to have portable stalls or awnings of oilskin in order to protect their goods from the weather. These mobile hucksters, as they were condescendingly called, attracted mainly the poorer classes on their way to work; is it typically French that as well as brandy, their customers could also buy cherries in eau-de-vie?[20]

It is a far cry to the middle of the 19th century when Alfred de Vigny could pride himself on making the purest cognac – on his estate at Blanzac in the Fins-Bois.[21] Nevertheless brandy was achieving some aristocratic status in England for it begins to appear in 1680 in the cellar of the Earl of Bedford at Woburn. It continues to be stocked at Woburn during the last two decades of the century and it is interesting to see that its quality varies: 1686 – best brandy; 1693 – inferior brandy.[22] There is another side to the trade in England at this time for one of the many 'wives' of Farquhar's Sergeant Kite was the imagined, but representative, '. . . Peggy Guzzle, the brandy-woman, at the Horse-Guard in Whitehall'.[23]

The alchemists' discovery of 'burning water' was to have an important effect on the making and maturing of wine. The technique is known as 'fortification' and consists in adding spirit, in these days grape spirit, to the fermenting must in order to cut short the fermentation and thus retain some of the sweetness in the wine. It also, of course, increases the alcoholic content of the finished wine. Madeira, port and sherry are the best known fortified wines and their strength ranges from 16 to 23 per cent of alcohol by volume. (I should add here that fortification is not always used for the purpose of retaining sweetness and that a fortified wine can be a dry

[17]Delamain, *op. cit.*, 25-6; cf. in Ch. 6, p. 312, and Ch. 7, p. 331, the general use of herbs, flowers, and spices in the flavouring of drinks.

[18]Delamain, *op. cit.*, 16-17; Bibliothèque Nationale, Paris. MSS., F., Fr., 21668 (210); see also Bib., Nat., F., Fr., 21668 (216).

[19]Bib., Nat., Paris, F., Fr., 21668 (100); repeated in the Spring of 1694 for the same reason, Bib., Nat., 21668 (106).

[20]Delamain, *op. cit.*, 28-9.

[21]*Ibid*, 126-7.

[22]Bedford Cellar, 186 sq.

[23]Farquharson, *The Recruiting Officer*, Act 1, Sc. i.

329

wine.) Now, it has sometimes been stated that pagan man fortified some of his vintages. If this means fortification with spirits, the statement is almost certainly inaccurate. If it means fortification with *defrutum* or boiled-down must, then the statement is undoubtedly true. In order to avoid confusion we must differentiate the terms. To mean the strengthening of wine with *defrutum* I should like to use the word 'bodying' but I think it is too cumbersome. I shall therefore use 'thickening' and keep the word 'fortification' to mean the addition only of spirits.

So far as our knowledge goes at present, we can say that no wine was fortified before the 12th century A.D. And it is likely that the technique was not employed until the late 15th century. A suggestion has been made which would put the date back to the 14th century.[24] Chaucer described the intoxicating quality of the 'whyte wyn of Lepe'[25] and the idea has tentatively been put forward that its power must have been due to fortification. Mr Warner Allen, commenting on this suggestion, rightly remarks that if it is true this is the first recorded instance of a fortified wine.[26]

The suggestion is extremely interesting, but it is only a suggestion, and I think we would all agree that we must continue to eye it with affection, but some reserve. It is true that Chaucer knew a lot about the apparatus of distillation and he describes it for us in that splendid warning to greenhorns *The Canon's Yeoman's Tale*:

> '. . . sondry vessels maad of erthe and glas,
> Our urinales and our descensories,
> Violes, croslets, and sublymatories,
> Cucurbites, and alembykes eek,'[27]

and a good deal more of it. Chaucer was clearly familiar with the tricks, in all senses of the word, of the alchemist's art but the poet's emphasis is on alchemy and not distillation of alcohol. Brandy was well known in Europe in the 14th century and there is no reason why it should not have been used in Andalusia. But so far as I know there is no record of its use in fortification during this century. Furthermore, Bacci, giving towards the end of the 16th century a fairly detailed description of Spanish wines, says that Andalusia produced several sorts of wines, including natural wines, and he adds that it was a common practice to adjust them with a proportion of cooked wine so that they might withstand the rigours of exportation.[28] He may, of course, mean burnt wine, or brandy, but I think it more likely that he means cooked wine, *defrutum*. We cannot be certain since we do know that brandy was being made in or around Jerez at this date.[29]

We have to fall back upon the argument of silence. If 14th- or 15th-century vintners fortified their wines they may have decided to say nothing about it and to have hoped that the addition would have gone unnoticed. But if they had fortified them to any extent, the addition would have been noticed, commented upon, and somewhere recorded. By the 16th century, however, the silence is well and truly broken and although we still cannot say exactly where or how often wines were fortified, we do know that the practice was well known and widely encouraged.

The Treasure of Evonymus, which we have mentioned earlier, was translated into English by Peter Morwyng and published in England in 1565. Its subject is distilled

[24] See the comments of H. Warner Allen, *A Contemplation of Wine*, 74–5.

[25] *Canterbury Tales, Pardoner, C.*, 563, 570.

[26] Warner Allen, see fn. 24 above.

[27] *Canterbury Tales, Chanouns Yemannes Tale, G.*, 791–4.

[28] Bacci, 365.

[29] González Gordon, 472.

Patent for Wine, 1641
André Simon Collection

M.ͬ Alderman Abell and Richard Kilvert.

'waters' and it includes a recipe for 'domestic fortification' 'To preserve wyne that it be not troubled nor putrifyed, put to it the tenthe parte of *Aqua vitae*'. Morwyng adds, however, that for this purpose 'in dede sulphur is farre better'.[30] In the 1616 edition of the *Maison Rustique*, published in London, fortification is again described, but this time its purpose is to give a wine a good smell. The housewife or cellarman is recommended to 'infuse and steep in Aqua vitae the simples of such matter as you have your wine to smell of, and afterward straining the same Aqua vitae, to put it into the vessell amongst the wine'.[31] These tricks, which reflect to us the inferior quality of much of the wine, were, as we have already noticed, of common occurrence at the end of the 17th century.

From all these instructions one could argue that fortification was done by the distributor, the vintner or tavern-keeper, or by the ultimate customer in his own cellar. Little, it might seem, was done in the fermenting sheds of the wine farmers. This is a tenable theory and many a powerful wine, brisk and unbalanced, must have graced the tables, and turned the heads, of Puritan England.

Despite his mundane and increasing operations in the drink trade, the brandy devil retained, until the end of the 17th century, a quasi alchemical association. From the very start of European distillation both the art and its products were considered to be essentially a matter for apothecaries. Early distillers were doctors, not drinkers. Arnaldus de Villa Nova, the 13th-century Catalan, combined in himself the professions of writer, diplomat, alchemist, astrologer and physician. He predicted the advent of the anti-Christ and also thought it worth while recommending eye-bright wine, 'made from eyebright, or euphrasia in Latin' as a medicine for strengthening weak eyesight.[32] Very quickly, the distiller's art broadened out to include the making of cosmetics and perfumes. And in Dijon in the 14th century eleven stills were hard at work distilling the flowers of Burgundy, 'lavender, borage, salvia, violets, roses and lilies',[33] to make perfumed waters. If these fields of flowers were among the fields of vines, the meadows of Burgundy must have been truly fields

[30] Morwyng, 87–8.

[31] Markham, 612.

[32] Sigerist, Arnaldus, 36–7.

[33] Forbes, *SHD*, 91.

Wine Bottles
17th century
London, Victoria and Albert
Museum

of paradise. Those distillers who were professionals, as most of them were, moved in mixed company: 'in 1378 the Florentine painters were officially included in the same guild as the doctors and apothecaries, and in Bologna the *Arte degli Speziali* also included distillers, wax-makers and sellers of *acqua vitae*, rose-water, liquorice, honey and dried fruit, comfits, paints, rat-poison, and church wafers'.[34] By Elizabethan times at the latest, the art had become one for amateurs as well as professionals and the 'still room' became an important part of many a household. The alchemist's robe had been exchanged for the housewife's apron. We need not always think of her as potting venison with one hand and stirring the still-furnace with the other. She would often have used simpler methods of distillation, most if not all of which go far back into pagan times. She could have extracted her vegetable oils by pressing, by steeping or cooking, or by mixing with fats. Or she may have used a filtration technique, dripping the mixture through a cloth. Frequently, however, she would have used the alembic.

The number of things which she distilled were almost innumerable and often unnerving. Some of her decoctions were, of course, for 'painting colours' or, as we should say, cosmetics, waters for softening the skin, colouring the hair, and whitening the teeth.[35] These would have gone to fill the

> 'Cabinets with curious washes
> Bladders and perfumed plashes'

of which Richard Lovelace writes in his *Aramantha*, the nymph who 'banished Mercury from her sphere', together with 'all Iberian smells, amulets and pomander spells'. But Aramantha's simplicity was not the mode of the fine ladies of the period, whose cosmetic art long remained a semi-comic alchemy in which there still lurked a trace of danger, to the bedizened, perhaps, as well as to the beholder.

One of the favourite distillations used for making wafers, conserving quinces, perfuming gloves, or clearing the eyes, was rose-water.[36] Another favourite was

[34]Origo, *Datini*, 289 fn.

[35]Markham, edn of 1616, Ch. LXXI, 465.

[36]Markham, edn of 1675-6, 101, 102, 104, 108-9 (pagination of this edition is defective); cf. Sigerist, *Arnaldus*, 41.

that old friend of the centuries, wormwood wine, which, now that it was distilled into 'water of wormwood' was the absinthe of the High Renaissance.[37] *Eau clairette* was very popular in France and also as *Claret water* in 17th-century England. It was made from aquavite, cinnamon, sugar and old red Rosewater. The name appears to be a prolongation into the 17th century of part of the medieval meaning of the word Claret, which we have discussed earlier.

They seemed to have distilled nearly everything: black cherries and the stones of black cherries, bark of the elder tree, turnips, mints, marigolds, poppies and 'holi-hocke'. Not content with these creative labours they distilled honey, goat's blood, and swallows.[38] Is one to presume that this latter 'water' was any advance on the swallow nestlings sieved in wine which were recommended for energy in the *Leechdoms, Wort-cunning and Starcraft* of Anglo-Saxon England?

These 'waters' provided them with a wide range of medicines. Some of them were paradoxical – water of cloves, for instance.

'Take equal parts of cloves, ginger, and flowers of rosemary, infuse them in very good wine the space of eight days: distill the whole. This water comforteth the stomacke, assuageth the pains and wringings of the belly, killeth worms, and maketh fat folk to become leane, or maketh fat the leane, if they drink it mixt with sugar.'[39]

Others were unpalatable: remedies with more than a hint of sympathetic magic handed down from antiquity, given a new lease on life by the printing press and the home-still. Such was the distillation of bulls' dung (cows' dung for a woman sufferer) noted by Pliny as a remedy for dropsy.[40] Recipes of this kind appear in a book published in London in 1616, the year of Shakespeare's death, eight years after *Antony and Cleopatra*. Braunschweig, whose 'good water for the palsy' we have already noted, gives in his *vertuose boke of Distyllacyon*, instructions for making Water of Sorell and Mandrake water; these have a smockish air of country magic. But he continues with a recipe for 'Water of grounde wormes' and after saying '. . . than they shal be dystilled' adds firmly that 'the best be whiche be founde upõ the chyrch yarde or amonge graves . . .'[41] The housewife's still-room was indeed the borderland between witchcraft and marmalade.

Most of these recipes read like incantations and in this, as in their use and their compounding, they exemplify a world that was transmuting itself from the Middle Ages into the age of reason:

'Take two handfuls and a halfe of red Roses, Rosemarie flowers, Lauander and Spike flowers, of each a Pugill: of the sprigges of Thyme, flowers of Cammomile, flowers of small Sage, of Penyryall, and Marierome, of each a handfull: infuse them all in white wine the space of foure and twentie houres: then put them into the Stillitorie, sprinkling it with verie good white Wine, and scatter thereupon this powder following:
take an ounce and a halfe of well chosen Clouves, an ounce of Nutmegs, of Beniouin and Styrax calamita, of each two drammes, make them in powder: The water that shall be distilled, must be kept in a vessell verie well stopped.'[42]

It was called Damaske water.

[37] *Maison Rustique*, Ch. LXV, 452; see also Sigerist, Arnaldus, 41.

[38] *Maison Rustique*, Ch. LXV, 453 sq.; Ch. LXVI, 456-7; Ch. LXVII, 458; Braunschweig, *vertuose boke*, cap. xxxi.

[39] *Maison Rustique*, Ch. LXIX, 461.

[40] *Ibid*, 457; Plin., XXVIII, 68, quoted in Cockayne's *Leechdoms*, 1876.

[41] Braunschweig, *vertuose boke*, cap. cc, xxxi.

[42] *Maison Rustique*, 463.

CHAPTER EIGHT

The Age of Reason

Before, and behind, the Mirrors

Emblematic of this Age is the man whom James Boswell described in October 1763: 'He had on a blue garment, thick and long, a wig of amazing size, and a terrifying sword at right angles to his body. He was holding a book with both hands, raised almost to his eyes. . . . He held himself perpendicular, and he walked with measured steps, pursuing his studies.'[1] As an emblem this picture is less of a caricature than might at first be thought. The 18th century was a formal Age but the formality tended towards exaggeration and thus often became a caricature of itself. Dignity, delighted with itself, became pomposity and good manners became merely a technique of affectation. These are the natural exaggerations of any formalized society and they were not more frequent only because the Age was less formalized than it appeared to be. The silks and the swords were an attempt, on the whole, a successful attempt, to refine the ever present coarseness of life. 'Genteel' society was not insulated from the rough democracy of the streets. A robust callousness often amounting to cruelty disfigured the mind as much as smallpox disfigured the face and gin rotted the population. The humour of wit and intelligence was as prized as was the display of aesthetic sensitivity, yet the humour of caricature had a crude ferocity which mutilated what it mocked. One extreme of this civilization was the press gang, the cock fight, and the interested mob waiting for an execution at Tyburn Gallows. The other extreme is Voltaire's *Candide*, the music of Bach, and the urbane beauty of English architecture.

It was, though in a different way from the Renaissance, the Age of Individuality. The Renaissance saw the individual as a display of brilliance. It preferred the heroic gesture. The 18th century saw man primarily as a social animal made tolerable and tolerant by his reason. It was not interested in the artistic genius but in the average gentleman. The increasing use of mirrors, particularly in the salon, meant not only

Opposite:
Hogarth, William
Gin Lane, c 1751

[1]*Boswell in Holland*, 43.

335

Kneller, Sir Godfrey
1st Duke of Newcastle and
1st Earl of Lincoln (Kitkat
Club Series)
London, National Portrait
Gallery

that people could become accustomed to seeing their own faces, but were also able to see themselves moving in a social setting. The faces in the Rembrandt self portraits look out into the depths of space, into that '*silence éternal de ces espaces infinis*' by which Pascal was upset and haunted. The faces in the portraits of Hogarth and Romney are those of people who are conscious of being reflected in mirrors. As the Age progressed so also did the tendency for the gaze of the person to be reflected inside the personality. Rousseau, Chateaubriand, Goethe and Kant emphasized or dramatized this tendency. But it was in no sense confined to poets and philosophers. Gentlemen of wit and fashion were not immune from the pleasures of introspection. Boswell, the inimitable self-mirror, probed into his own hypochondria[2] and he was by no means the only sufferer from this disease of 'spleen', or melancholia. It is not unfair to say that, whereas the Renaissance had been the Age of Poetry, the Georgian era was the first great Age of Psychology and it is in this, as much as in its semi-scientific outlook and its invention (in France) of mathematical democracy, that it shows the true beginnings of the modern mind.

It was not mainly, or even generally, a time of preoccupied self-examiners. Far from it. It was a tough, virile, bustling, extrovert Age whose addiction to pleasure was tempered by curiosity and intelligence. The letter writers are a typical facet of the Age of Mirrors, reflecting with a brilliant and sometimes merciless clarity the world which amused or intrigued them. The urge to write, and the passion for print, was almost as strong in them, or perhaps on the whole even stronger, than the urge to get drunk. The contrast between extreme elegance and excessive intoxication is one of the contradictions of this time and although, until the French Revolution, the Age appears settled and self-confident, we can still call it the Age of Hesitation. Civilization had not completed the last stages of its climb out of the disaster of the Middle Ages, but by the end of this Georgian 'Century' Jane Austen's

[2] See Boswell's Column, *The Hypochondriak, passim.*

novels had been written, the railways were beginning, and the modern mind was about to triumph in the six competent decades of Victoria.

Some of the contradictions in the Georgian character are easily explicable, but others are less so. It was natural that there should have been a revolt against faith and a flowering of scepticism. With pride but, as it turned out, also with inaccuracy Voltaire could write of the Age of Louis XIV that during it *'la raison humaine en général s'est perfectionée'*.[3] It was equally natural that the scepticism of Gibbon and Hume and the utilitarian outlook of Jeremy Bentham should be balanced by the deeply religious charity of the Methodist Movement. It is a little less easy to understand the co-existence in time of Montesquieu's *Esprit des Lois* and the presence of State dwarfs at the Courts of Germany.[4] It is even more difficult to understand the contradiction between refinement and intoxication. For the first time in all its history Western Europe knew tea and coffee and though these non-alcoholic drinks became enormously popular, gross intoxication remained the curse of the Age. The history of wine in this period is of particular interest to the social historian since the contradiction in Georgian drinking habits illustrates with remarkable emphasis the contradictions in the Georgian character.

The Six-Bottle Men

The drinkers of this time were men of a hearty but not immoderate thirst. Goethe, even when taking a cure at Carlsbad, was ready to drink about two litres of wine a day.[5] Brillat-Savarin considered that a healthy man could live long if he drank two bottles of wine a day.[6] The peasants in Languedoc, however, needed three bottles of strong wine a day to keep them going.[7] But this was only commonplace drinking and examples of greater capacity are not rare. Doctor Johnson confessed that he drank three bottles of port at University College, Oxford, and was none the worse for it. Dr Alexander Webster, Boswell's uncle by marriage, was a five-bottle consumer of claret.[8] The poet James Thomson was obliged by his guests to agree that the allowance for one meal should be a bottle a head but, regarding this as a niggard amount, he placed a three-quart bottle before each man.[9] With apparent gravity Brillat-Savarin records that General Bisson drank eight bottles of wine for dinner every day without being thereby in any way incommoded.[10] Mytton, neither sane nor sober, used to drink four to six bottles of port wine every day: 'He shaved with a bottle of it on his toilet; he worked steadily at it throughout the day, by a glass or two at a time, and at least a bottle with his luncheon;' the remainder of his enormous ration was drunk after dinner and after supper.[11]

Mytton is a special case only for the magnitude of his intemperance, for the occurrence of drunkenness was only too common. *The Tatler* in 1709 commented that 'rural esquires . . . are drunk twice a day',[12] and they had not much improved at the beginning of the next century when a Dane travelling in Britain described a foxhunter and his friends. After dinner, when the foxhunter's wife had disappeared from the room, the men set about drinking in earnest; then 'about midnight the noisy crew reel into the drawing room . . . tea is then served to such of them as are capable of holding a cup; but the generality becomes speedily lost in a stupor. . . .' William Hickey was often, he tells us, 'as drunk as a beast', on one occasion he had

[3] *Siècle de Louis XIV*, Vol. I, 3.

[4] Lady Mary Wortley Montagu, *Letters*, Jan. 16th, 1717.

[5] Hallgarten, *Rhineland-Wineland*, 124.

[6] Brillat-Savarin, 125.

[7] Arthur Young, *Travels in France*, Vol. I, Ch. XVI, 457.

[8] Boswell, *Life of Johnson*, Vol. III, 245; for the possible dating of this deluge, see Vol. I, 104, fn.; *Boswell for the Defence*, 1769–74, fn. 3, 223.

[9] Aytoun Ellis, *Penny Universities*, 196.

[10] Brillat-Savarin, 74.

[11] Nimrod, *Life of Mytton*, 63–4.

[12] *The Tatler*, No. XIX of May 14th, 1709.

Hogarth, William
Midnight Modern
Conversation
Engraving
London, British Museum

his pocket picked, and on another he got into a hackney coach and 'vomited out of the coach window the whole way, to the great entertainment of the foot passengers'.[13] Such carousals led naturally to quarrels and although some of the outraged gentlemen were too drunk to get off the floor and reach their enemy, others were not quite so inebriated. They are described by young John Baber, who lived at Sunninghill in Berkshire between 1705 and 1707 and who wrote an amusing, interesting (and hitherto unpublished) diary called *The Annals of Staghunting*. Breaking into verse he describes the affray:

> 'Some two implacable Contenders rise
> From ye Symposiac Board, and kicking down
> Their Chairs, unsheath their Glitt'ring points, and stamp
> Directing at their Breasts deaddoing Stroaks.'[14]

Drunkenness was not only the ritual of the country squire – nor was it always his vice – but it was widespread in all classes. It is true that the poor might drink a lot of milk[15] and that in the middle of the century 'all classes in town and country were drinking tea in their own homes'.[16] This mitigated intemperance but it did not cure it. In June 1674 Narcissus Luttrell tells us that 'about this time Mrs Gwynn mother to Madam Ellen Gwynn being in drink was drowned in a Ditch near Westminster'.[17] In August 1764 Parson Woodforde records that '. . . poor Miss Milly Chiche . . . was dead; . . . I hope to God that she (poor dear creature) is happy. I believe verily that she was good to everyone, but herself, and I am afraid that drinking was her death. . . .'[18] Women were much less inclined to drink than men and of the inclination of the men there is no doubt at all. Swift complained of it among

[13]J. A. Andersen (A. A. Feldborg), *A Dane's Excursions in Britain*, Vol. I, 114–15; see also Turberville. *Johnson's England*, Vol. I, 339; William Hickey, *Memoirs*, Ed. Peter Quennell, 79–81.

[14]Baber, J., *Annals of Staghunting*, 26–7. For the opportunity of reading, and for permission to quote from, this interesting diary I am greatly indebted to Colonel John Baber.

[15]See J. A. Andersen, *op. cit.*, Vol. I, *passim*; and Vol. II, 13.

[16]Trevelyan, *Illustrated English Social History*, Vol. III, 91.

[17]Narcissus Luttrell, *Brief Historical Relation of State Affairs . . .*

[18]Woodforde, *Diary of a Country Parson*, Vol. I, 40.

the army and the youth of the nobility and gentry.[19] Doctor Johnson said he remembered the time 'when all the *decent* people in Litchfield got drunk every night, and were not the worse thought of'. The good Doctor's opinion on this point is perhaps open to some question since on another occasion he called the citizens of Litchfield the soberest in England and furthermore, when he remarked in the same context that 'our drinking less than our ancestors was owing to the change from ale to wine' he committed a manifest inaccuracy.[20] If there were inhibitions in the men of Litchfield there were certainly none in the 1780s in the men of the University of Cambridge where drunkenness was 'almost universal',[21] and Woodforde in the 1760s gives some graphic descriptions of drinking in the University of Oxford. On one occasion a gentleman called Mr Williams was bet half-a-crown 'that he drank 3 Pints of Wine in 3 Hours, and that he wrote 5 verses out of the Bible right, but he lost. He did it in the B.C.R., he drank all the Wine, but he could not write right for his life. He was immensely drunk about 5 Minutes afterwards'. At a later date when two companions of Woodforde's were drunk in the B.C.R. he himself had the strength to remain sober 'as I had made a resolution never to get drunk again, when at Geree's rooms in April last, when I fell down dead, and cut my Occiput very bad indeed'.[22] Such gaieties are of course not unknown in modern universities but taken as a whole Woodforde's *Diary* makes it clear that heavy drinking was a popular practice. He also comments, though not about Oxford, that '. . . I buried poor Thos Barnes this afternoon (who had been "a long time killing himself by Liquor") at Cary, aged 48'.[23]

England was not alone in this lust for comparative insensibility. Lord Chesterfield, writing to the Bishop of Waterford in 1747 remarks with disapproval that '. . . nine gentlemen in ten in Ireland are impoverished by the great quantity of claret, which, from mistaken notions of hospitality and dignity, they think it necessary should be drunk in their houses'.[24] Surprisingly enough, drunkenness was common in France, even among the upper classes, until about the middle of the 18th century.[25] It is hard to imagine a drunken satyr in lace ruffles and white wig, in the company of the exquisite and artificial shepherdesses painted by François Boucher.

On a November day in 1769 Parson Woodforde commented that his brother, who was an over enthusiastic drinker, 'spent the evening at the Angel at Cary and returned very much disguised in liquor. . . .'[26] The phrase is apt but the disguises of the 18th century in drink ranged from noise to nightmare. The wine-logged country squires merely turned themselves nightly into dull barbarians whereas the working classes, with the aid of rotgut gin, were able to divest themselves of any aspect of humanity.

Gin, Negus and Punch

It had taken a long time for the 'brandy devil' of late medieval Germany to become acclimatized in England but when it finally did so it achieved a success and a squalor which seemed to be truly diabolical. The fault was largely that of the men who governed England since in the reign of Queen Anne they allowed anyone who wished to distil what Doctor Johnson later called 'English malt brandy'.[27] In the

[19] Jonathan Swift, *A Project for the Advancement of Religion* . . .

[20] Boswell, *Johnson*, Vol. v, 59–60, and fn. 1, 60.

[21] Gunning, *Reminiscences . . . of Cambridge*, 24.

[22] Woodforde, *op. cit.*, Vol. I, 18, 31.

[23] *Ibid*, 99, dating Feb. 23rd, 1770.

[24] *Misc. Works of . . . Philip Dormer Stanhope, Earl of Chesterfield*, Vol. II, Bk III, Letter VIII.

[25] Franklin, A., *Vie privée d'autrefois*, Vol. 6, 127–32.

[26] Woodforde, *op. cit.*, Vol. I, 93.

[27] Boswell, *Johnson*, Vol. v, fn. 2, 346.

Boucher, François
Three cupids, 1754
National Trust, Waddeson
Manor

main, of course, the 'brandy' consumed by the populace was gin and despite the later efforts of legislators to cure the evil which they had encouraged they could not put a stop to the desire of a free people to poison themselves. The summary record of their ability to do so lives for us in the depraved figures of Hogarth's 'Gin Lane'.

The gin fury reached its peak half way through the reign of George II, and then began to decline, but spirits remained popular throughout the century. Woodforde drinks rum and water and gin and water, paying 3d. for a glass of the latter at Quantrells Gardens; he takes a bottle of gin on a fishing trip; when he entertains his friends at New College he gives them 'Arrac Punch' – Arrack being a spirit distilled from sugar cane and coming into England mainly from India and the East Indies. Rum came in from the West Indies and at Woodforde's ' . . . Frolic for my People to pay Tithe to me . . . They had to drink Wine, Punch, and Ale as much as they pleased; . . .' In addition to six bottles of wine and a quantity of ale they drank a gallon and a half of rum.[28] John Byng, later Lord Torrington, was accustomed to drink brandy and on one occasion in 1778 when he stayed at the Swan at Forest Row, Sussex, he had as much as half a pint of brandy with his dinner.[29]

When we think of 18th-century drinking we think of it mainly, and rightly, in terms of port, gin and punch but the latter was only a continuation of the spiced and sweetened drinks of ancient and medieval times. In January 1763, in a public house outside Whitechapel, Boswell drank 'some warm white wine with aromatic spices, pepper and cinnamon'.[30] This style of hippocras was a direct left-over from the Middle Ages and was less common in 18th-century England than negus and punch.

The negus which was invented by Colonel Francis Negus (d. 1732) was originally a mixture of wine, water, sugar, lemon and nutmeg.[31] More specifically, however, it came to mean a hot drink of this type made from port wine. Beaten eggs were sometimes added to it.[32] Variants of a negus, using toasted Seville oranges in the wine, were known as the Bishop when made with burgundy or claret, the

[28] Woodforde, *op. cit.*, July 27th, 1774; Dec. 3rd, 1776; June 5th, 1783; and *passim*; Aug. 18th, 1784.

[29] Torrington Diaries, 128, and *passim*.

[30] Boswell, *London Journal*, 154.

[31] Samuel Johnson, *Dictionary*.

[32] See Dennis Wheatley, *The Seven Ages of Justerini's*, 33-4.

Cardinal when made with old hock, and the Pope when made with Tokay.[33] Boswell, reminding himself to take care of his stomach, advised himself thus: 'Eat always some toast and drink a little negus at night, so as not to clog stomach at one meal.'[34] A form of cold negus, which could either be a beverage drink or a sweet dessert, was the syllabub. In 1741 in St James's Park in London it was a morning drink made of one-third Spanish wine and two-thirds milk fresh out of the cow which was milked on the spot.[35] More complicated recipes using wine, orange juice, lemon rind, sugar, cream and nutmeg, were published by Messrs Johnson and Justerini (now Justerini and Brooks of Bond Street, London) towards the end of the 18th century.[36]

The most popular of all these compounded drinks was punch and this was no doubt due to the predilection of the 18th century for spirits and the fact that punch, unlike negus, is a spiritous mixture. In its basic and original form it was made of rum, fruit – limes, lemons or oranges – sugar and water, but the recipes quickly multiplied until it could be made with brandy or arrack as well as rum, and with varying admixtures of tea, ale and milk. Shrub was a style of punch and a recipe in the reign of Queen Anne gives it as being made from brandy, lemons, white wine, water and sugar.[37]

A great deal of punch was drunk and the esteem in which the punch bowl was held can be seen from the number of times it occurs on the signs of public houses. At the beginning of its triumphant career a preference for punch carried with it a connotation of whiggery, claret being sometimes considered as a specifically Tory drink, but it speedily lost any party label which might have been applied to it and was eagerly drunk for its intoxicating and not for its political properties. It was served at most coffee houses as early as the reign of George II,[38] and in the 1780s it was one of the standard drinks at private college suppers in Cambridge, being put into a teapot to keep hot by the fire. Some of these teapots, it was remarked, were enormous.[39] The taste for punch moved, in a respectable way, into France somewhere about the end of the 18th or the beginning of the 19th century and it was served after dinner, accompanied, at least after a gourmet's dinner, by thin pieces of buttered and salted toast.[40] This, of course, is not to say that the Parisian 'one-for-the-road' was necessarily a hot drink for punch can be made either hot or cold. In various guises it was clearly much favoured in the Western Highlands of Scotland and four bowls of it (shared of course) once gave poor Boswell a severe hangover. He and his friends were, he says, '. . . merry to a high degree; but of what passed I have no recollection, with any accuracy'. He got to bed at five in the morning, woke at noon with a bad headache and a bad conscience. He discovered, however, a dram of brandy which he found an effective cure for his headache.[41]

To some extent, but only to some extent, the lust for heavy drinking declined towards the end of the 18th century, following the gradual diminution of the gin fever and helped by the growing taste for tea. By 1825[42] drunkenness had almost disappeared in France but even between 1774 and 1783 the 'ordinary drinking' of the French Court does not seem to have been immoderate. Mostly it drank wine (and probably most of this was *vin ordinaire*) and in addition some brandy, a small quantity of liqueurs and more beer than it drank cider and perry.[43]

The decline of drunkenness in England was less marked. 'I do fairly acknowledge,'

[33]Henderson, *History of Ancient and Modern Wines*, 285, and note t.

[34]*Boswell in Holland*, 113.

[35]Turberville, *op. cit.*, Vol. I, 183.

[36]Wheatley, *op. cit.*, 34-5.

[37]*The Pastry-Cook's Vade-Mecum*, 65-6.

[38]Aytoun Ellis, *op. cit.*, 203-4.

[39]Gunning, *op. cit.*, 45.

[40]Brillat-Savarin, 198, 202-3, 440.

[41]Boswell, *Johnson*, Vol. v, 258-9.

[42]Brillat-Savarin, 283.

[43]Archives Nationales, Paris, O1.793, Chambre aux deniers: dépenses, 1768, 1780-92.

wrote Boswell – 'The Hypochondriak' – in the *London Magazine*, 'that I love Drinking; that I have a constitutional inclination to indulge in fermented liquors. . . .'[44] In this he was no different from his English countrymen but, unlike many of them, he did at least confess that he continually feared this inclination. He took himself to task for being too merry with wine in society. He made resolutions to be sober but they were either not kept or they were not kept for long. He tried to limit his consumption and one of the disciplines which he imposed upon himself was four good glasses of wine at dinner and a pint after it.[45] Sam Johnson, who equally recognized the danger of the inclination, found himself better able to control it: 'I can't drink a *little*, child,' he said to Hannah More, 'therefore I never touch it.'[46] Indeed, for long periods of his life he was a total abstainer, unlike many of his compatriots who also found that they were unable to drink a *little*.

Elegance . . . and Champagne

These antics of intemperance must not obscure the fact that the Age was one of great elegance and considerable beauty. When we think of it we think of it first of all, perhaps, as the era of elegant building: the fine house, the lovely decoration, the landscape garden. The leaven of this development was already working strongly at the end of the 17th century. Celia Fiennes, during her journeys through England, notes a garden with '. . . fine flowers and greene dwarfe trees and oring and lemon trees in rows with fruite and flowers at once, and some ripe, they are the first oring trees I ever saw. . . .'[47] We may assume that the 'orings' and lemons were not used for making punch. Often she notes the bowling greens which belong to the big houses and she is vigilant to observe the fine and stylish gardens. With the breathlessness of inadequate punctuation she describes Patshull Park near Shrewsbury, a complex and formal pattern of clipped hedges, iron gates, statues and fountains, a grove of evergreens with avenues cut through it, gravel walks and grass plots, its Visto, its prospects, and its aviary of birds.[48] She is fascinated by the interiors of the houses which she visits but she is only at the beginning of that century that was to produce the splendours of the brothers Adam and the magnificence of Tiepolo.

Celia Fiennes chronicled the bad roads: Hogarth drew 'The Four Stages of Cruelty': Gibbon described the 'dull and deep potations' of the Fellows of Magdalen; yet despite all this it was a time, and the first time for many centuries, of a delicate and fragile beauty. The porcelain of Meissen and Chelsea, the pottery of Josiah Wedgwood, were part of the sophistication which delighted Boucher and Fragonard and which ended in the outrageous good taste of the Brighton Pavilion.

It is characteristic of this Age of Elegance that, during it, sparkling champagne should, for the first time in history, have been drunk and appreciated. This fresh, exhilarating northern wine, which has become almost synonymous with celebration was even then, at the outset of its career, the hallmark of smartness. The invention of sparkling champagne is one of the great drinking differences between modern times and all previous history. In order to put it into historical perspective, to see why it occurred towards the end of the 17th century, and to understand the uneven course of its development since that time, one must look backwards through the lens of the modern champagne vintage.

[44] Boswell's Column, 169, *On Drinking.*

[45] Boswell, *Johnson*, Vol. I, fn. 3, 13; Vol. II, fn. 1, 436.

[46] Boswell, *Johnson*, Vol. I, fn. 3, 103.

[47] *Journeys of Celia Fiennes*, 58.

[48] *Ibid*, 228–30.

*Goblet and Cover: glass
with cut and engraved
decoration
German, early 18th century
London, Victoria and Albert
Museum*

*Goblet, glass: stipple-
engraved
signed F. Greenwood fecit
English, engraved by Frans
Greenwood at Dordrecht,
c 1730
London, Victoria and Albert
Museum*

The champagne *vignoble*, east of Paris, lies around Epernay in the valley of the
Marne and stretches in a great eastward-facing sickle up towards Reims in the
northern plain. Between these two cities rises the Montagne de Reims which is not
of course a mountain but a huge rectangular lump, its flanks closed with vineyards,
its top crowned with a forest. South of Epernay, south of the Marne, is the *Côte-des-
Blancs* with the towns of Cramant and Avize. North of Epernay, and just north
across the river Marne, one climbs the southern flank of the mountain of Reims, up
towards Hautvillers which for wine lovers is perhaps the most famous place in the
champagne district. From Hautvillers, where a few of the vine leaves are red and
black, turning and dying, one looks down at the still, silver river and into the valley
pointed by clumps of poplars. The October sunlight has made the air a soft, gentle
gold, warm but with a hint of the distant winter. From Hautvillers one goes up on
to the top of the mountain, into the forest of Reims. Abruptly vineyards and wine
making have disappeared. Tangled underbrush, tall close trees, occasionally letting
through a patch of sun, the possibility of getting lost, and the possibility of meeting
a wild boar, take one back into the between-town landscape of the Middle Ages.
There are jays in the forest and magpies and on the north-east slope of the mountain
a windmill, a fox trotting along by a stream, and a quantity of cats hunting in the
grass verges of the road. Away to the north the grey bulk of the cathedral of Reims
crouches, watching the sun sink like a blood orange over the misty plain.

In the morning the air over the vineyards is like the wine of Champagne, clear, bright and brisk. In the village streets there are round, flat, dull purple cakes of pressed and dessicated grape skins. Out of a gate on a street corner spills an untidy tumble of skins and stalks. A stray runnel of must oozes out from under a village doorway. It is as though the actual villages had become vegetables and were suffering an irresistible organic change.

The grapes are gathered into deep, oval baskets and taken on carts and lorries to their local *pressoir*. The must runs from the press like the liquid out of a slow bath tap and at this stage of its life tastes – naturally – like sweet grape juice, not an enlivening drink. The must is run off into vats where it stays, or at least some of it stays, for about twelve hours when it is drawn off into barrels and sent straight to the buyers. Sometimes fermentation is quick to start and you see in the yard of the *pressoir* a barrel whose must is already fermenting and frothing out of the bung hole. Another is just beginning to 'move'. Most of it, however, does not start to ferment until it has arrived at the buyers, who are also the shippers and who give their names to the wines which they make from the raw must. Arrived at the shippers the barrels of must are put into huge sheds and assembled in lots which represent the various properties from which the must has been made and bought. As you walk among the barrels you can hear them 'talking'. One which is just beginning to 'move', crackles; one which is really 'moving', hisses; the carbonic acid gas coming out of the open bung hole of the fermenting barrel strikes one like a soundless blow in the face. But it also ferments in glass-lined tanks, which is more convenient though less romantic. From even a brief sniff at the bung hole of a fermenting cask one can understand why the sheds are locked during fermentation and why the workers are only allowed to go into them in pairs.

The fermentation of champagne must stops in the winter before all the grape sugar is fermented out of it. In the spring it will begin its secondary fermentation, the remaining sugar turning itself into alcohol and carbonic acid gas. If the wine is bottled before the secondary fermentation begins, then the resulting wine will be sparkling from the gas suspended in the wine. It is at this point, basically, that the wine of Champagne becomes sparkling champagne.

But this is by no means the whole story, for champagne is a blended wine, a product of the *cuvée*. This is not a dishonest practice. On the contrary, it is to the great benefit of the drinker for blending is necessary to produce consistently the finest result. Various growths are blended to make a harmony of their various qualities, each adding to the whole its own particular distinction of lightness, delicacy, fruitiness or body. Vintage champagne is almost entirely a blend of the fine wines of one year. Non-vintage champagne is a blend of the wines of two, or of several, years. Most champagne is a blend of wine made from the black Pinot noir, whose must is not allowed to remain on the grape skins lest it should take colour from them, and from the white Chardonnay, which has given its particular fame to the *Côtes-des-Blancs*. A champagne made only from white grapes is called *Blanc de Blancs*. It is a light delicate wine of which I myself am particularly fond but in general it lacks the body of a blended champagne.

When champagne is bottled in the spring, with a small amount of cane sugar added to it to help along the secondary fermentation, it begins its long education.

The bottles are taken down to cellars to age, and by law the wine has to age for at least a year. Fine wines are allowed to age for much longer. The ageing takes place in vast cellars dug out of the chalk and supposed to have been started by the Romans. In these cellars one's voice and one's footsteps accompany one like a detached presence alongside, a ghostly feeling intensified by the slimy smoothness of the chalk wall under one's hand and the thousand-fold silence of tilted bottles. They have been placed neck downwards in racks shaped like an inverted V. Daily each bottle is twisted, and slowly it is tilted, until finally it is vertical and upside down and the sediment in the wine has been twisted downwards into the neck of the bottle. There it stays until the *dégorgement*.

Dégorgement is using the gas in the wine to blow the sediment out of the bottle. Some shippers freeze the neck of the bottle so that the sediment comes out attached to the cork but the 'explosive' process is still common. When the cork and the sediment are out, a small but varying amount of liquor, made from old wine and cane sugar, can be added to the champagne to adjust its degree of dryness and sweetness to the tastes of different markets. Any extra space left in the bottle from the act of disgorging is made up with the same type of champagne as that already in the bottle. The bottle is then given its final cork and when that cork comes bang out of the bottle one should hold out one's glass.

It will thus be seen that three things are necessary in the making of good champagne: a good blender, a good bottle, and a good cork. It is for these three reasons that sparkling champagne began at the end of the 17th century.

The credit for beginning modern champagne goes to two monks, Dom Pérignon and Dom Oudart, both of whom worked in the Marne *Vignoble* in the last half of the 17th century, but the greater credit must go to Dom Pérignon. Neither of them, nor anyone else at the same time, 'invented' champagne for champagne had already invented itself. Throughout the Middle Ages, in the Renaissance, and during the 17th century, the wines of the Marne, if drunk young and during the spring, as was then customary, would have been in their secondary fermentation and would have been 'creaming' wines. The two monks imprisoned the fermentation inside a bottle and, instead of temporarily creaming, they made permanently sparkling, wine. Neither of them invented the bottle; and neither of them invented the cork, which was known long before their time. What they did do, and what Dom Pérignon did first, was to invent a more efficient cork and one that would keep the bubble in the bottle. He began to perfect the technique of producing clear white champagne wines and he began or he perfected (for those days) the technique of blending them. His love of good wine, his technical ingenuity, and his fine palate – (he was blind towards the end of his life which may have refined it still further) – have made him the monk on whom rests the modern fame of the Abbey of Hautvillers of which he was the cellarer.

Although the technique of sparkling champagne had been invented, it was to be over a century before it was fully mastered. One of the great difficulties was to keep the explosion in suspense. The fermentation inside a modern bottle builds up to a pressure of six atmospheres. After the experiments of François in the 1830s, the amount of carbonic acid gas produced from a given quantity of sugar in the wine became a matter of scientific calculation but before the 1830s the knowledge of fermentation pressure was inadequate. And where there was defective glass and excessive pressure the bottles went off like small bombs. They were bursting in the lifetime of Dom Pérignon[49] and they went on bursting until after the Napoleonic Wars. This was dangerous to the cellar workers and extremely expensive to the champagne producers but the situation was brought under control in early Victorian times and from a yearly breakage of anything from 15-40 per cent the figure has now been reduced to an average of only 1· per cent of all the bottles in the cellars. Another failure in the early history of champagne was due to the very success achieved by Dom Pérignon. Being himself a master-blender, he increased the popularity of champagne to such a point that his example was followed by eager imitators. But you cannot imitate a blend, for blending is a work of art and anyone who says that good champagne is 'just a mixture' is talking nonsense. Unfortunately, many of the champagnes of the late 17th and early 18th centuries were not made by artists and were in fact 'just mixtures', assuming of course that they were blended at all. A particular difficulty in the way of the sparkling champagne trade of England was that, from the reign of George II until the beginning of the 19th century there was a legal prohibition against the importation of wine in bottles.

In general we can say that from somewhere about 1670 to somewhere about 1770 sparkling champagne continued to be made and drunk and that for some years after 1770, in both France and England, still champagne was preferred.[50] In fact in 1775 the liking for 'sparkling, frothy *Champaigns*' was condemned as a 'depraved taste',[51] and an implicit example of champagne as a still wine is given by the same author when he advises that champagne should be put into iced water to cool its 'flask' for a quarter of an hour before drinking with the cork 'so loose . . . as . . . to give a free passage to the air'.[52]

Much of the champagne that was drunk during the 17th and 18th centuries was still wine, red or 'partridge eye' in colour. Still, red champagne, Bouzy *rouge* for example, is a mellow, fruity wine, reminiscent of burgundy but without the burgundy 'muscle'. Still, white champagne (which is pale gold), a refreshing, medium bodied, and very 'clean' wine, has a particular coolness in it, almost the taste of stone. Wines of these styles would have been drunk in England since the Restoration of Charles II, but seldom before.

The wines of the Marne had been known in England before King Charles returned from his travels, bringing with him a somewhat intimate knowledge of foreign customs and a liking for champagne. Its popularity as a smart drink was greatly increased by St. Evremond, a French gourmet who came to London in 1661 and who rated champagne as the finest of all wines. In a letter to the Count d'Olonne, also a gourmet and a member of the famous Ordre des Côteaux, who took their title from their knowledge of the best wine-producing Côteaux near Reims,[53] he mentions in particular the wines of Ay, Avenet, Auvilé (Ay, Avenay, Hautvillers), which were then known as 'river wines'. He also selects for mention the wines of Sillery and Versenai (Verzenay) – the 'mountain wines' grown in the sickle of vineyards facing east from the mountain of Reims. Highest of all he rated the wine of Ay, which he described as having 'the most exquisite agreeableness in regard of its Peach-taste which is peculiar to it'.[54] It is interesting to read a description of these river and mountain wines which was written almost exactly a hundred years after

[49]See for example, Houghton, *Collection*, Vol. I, 158, No. 56 of Sept. 1693.

[50]Barry, *Observations . . .*, etc., 425.

[51]*Ibid, loc. cit.*

[52]*Ibid,* 424.

[53]Boileau-Despreaux, *Satires*, Satire III, note.

[54]Des Maizeaux, *Works of M. de St. Evremond*, Vol. II, 97–8.

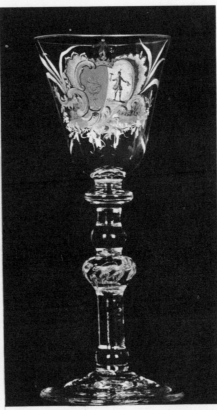

Wine-glass, painted in
enamel-colours
English, signed William
Beillby of Newcastle, c 1756
London, Victoria and Albert
Museum

St Evremond wrote to d'Olonne: '. . . *Champaign river* Wines are more delicate and
pale, than those which are distinguishable from them, by the name of *Mountain* grey
wines.' The best river wines at this date were considered to be 'Auvillers' and
'Epernay' while the best of the mountain wines were 'Selery' and 'St Thyery' (St-
Thierry).[55] Another writer, in the year in which Louis XVI was executed, describes
the river wine of Champagne as 'a clear white wine, pale as spring water, it is very
brisk and sparkling in the glass . . .' whereas the mountain wines, or at least some of
them, were known as '*Oeil de Perdrix*' or partridge-eye wines.'[56] This reddish colour
was given to the wine by an admixture of red grapes to the white at the time of the
pressing. The black grape skins must have been left in the juice for some hours after
the pressing since nowadays a good deal of champagne comes from black grapes
though the juice from them is perfectly clear since it is not allowed to remain on the
skins. It seems unlikely that the partridge-eye colouring was only due to careless
vinification since clear wine was both made and esteemed at that time and since
champagne, together with burgundy, was 'made with more care than any other
French wines'.[57] The colouring must, therefore, have been deliberately introduced
in order to satisfy the taste of the late 18th century.

In 1664 the Earl of Bedford bought for his cellar at Woburn three casks of Sillery
and he continued to buy it in subsequent years. This was wine not from Sillery itself,
at the northern end of the mountain sickle, but from Verzenay where the Marquis
de Sillery had his vineyards and made, so it was thought, the finest champagne.

[55] Barry, *Observations . . .*, 422.

[56] McBride, *Instructions . . .*, 15.

[57] Barry, *op. cit.*, 422.

347

It is probable that the Woburn champagne was intended to be drunk as a still wine but it is just possible that the Earl's cellarman bottled it up in the spring to try and make it sparkling. This possibility is indicated by a purchase in the same year of twelve gross of corks but it is no more than a possibility and I think we must generally assume that it was drunk at Woburn as a still wine.[58]

Whether still or sparkling, and whatever the vicissitudes of its making, it always remained the smart, and aristocratic, wine in England, and its consumption was of course limited. Sir Robert Walpole once smuggled some into the country and his cellar often contained champagne though in lesser quantities than fine claret for which he had a marked preference.[59] In France in 1782 the private cellar of Louis XVI contained in addition to the top-class burgundies, champagne from Pierry, Sillery, Ay, and Epernay.[60] It is more than likely that these were still champagnes since the sparkling wine was not then fashionable in France. It continued, however, in one style or another, to keep its aristocratic connotation and it had the mournful distinction of solacing the captivity of Louis XVI in the Temple. With his dinner this unfortunately unintelligent monarch had a bottle of champagne, a small carafe of Bordeaux, a small carafe of Malvoisie and a small carafe of Madeira.[61]

At the Restoration in England, champagne quickly acquired the reputation which it has never lost; that of being a party, a celebration, wine. Even in the middle of the 18th century it figures on the menu at Vauxhall Gardens where it is the most expensive wine, costing 8/- a bottle which was a large sum for those days. In comparison burgundy cost 6/- and claret 5/-, a bottle.[62] At this period also occurred what may have been the first instance of champagne being drunk from a woman's shoe, a habit which is supposed to have been so popular a hundred and fifty years later. *The Connoisseur* of June 6th, 1754, records the anecdote of the 'bloods' in company with a celebrated '*fille de joye*'. One of them pulled off her shoe, filled it with champagne and drank it off to her health. Carried away by the beauty of this compliment, and wishing to extend it further, he ordered the shoe to be dressed and served up for supper. The cook was equal to the occasion; he made a *ragoût* out of the upper part of the shoe, minced the sole, and, undefeated to the end, fried slices of the wooden heel in batter and put them as garnish round the dish. It must rank high as one of the most thoroughgoing and indigestible of all compliments.

The Glass of Fashion

Let us contemplate the man of fashion in another guise. It is James Boswell on the day of Count Nassau's dinner, October 14th, 1763: 'Dress in scarlet and gold, fine Swiss, white silk stockings, handsome pumps, and have silver-and-silk sword-knot, Barcelona handkerchief, and elegant toothpick-case which you had in a present from a lady.'[63] (In the same year Boswell also had a 'Leyden suit of green and silver'.) Let us imagine this fine figure at Count Nassau's reception, let us put a glass in his hand, and there we have a figure representing another aspect of the Age of Elegance. In this aspect it is the Age of Glass. And for the history of wine this is the most important aspect of the 18th century.

At the fall of the Roman Empire the art of glass making was not lost but for a thousand years it remained limited. There are some beautiful drinking horns of pale

[58] Bedford Cellar, 191-4.

[59] Walpole Cellar, 194, 201.

[60] Archives Nationales, Paris, MS., O1.793.

[61] Franklin, *Vie privée d'autrefois*, Vol. III, 213-14.

[62] Wroth, *London Pleasure Gardens*, 298-9.

[63] *Boswell in Holland*, 19, 45.

[64] British Museum.

[65] Dillon, *Glass*, 112.

blue glass from the Dark Ages of north-western Europe[64] while tumblers – literally tumblers since they were footless and had to be held in the palm of the hand – occur in their various styles in Anglo-Saxon and Merovingian graves.[65] In the 14th century a certain amount of glass was made in France and England though France was ahead of England both in quantity and style. For example, a French glass-maker in the Viennois made 'beakers with feet, known as hanaps'[66] whereas the 'cuppis to drinck and such lyke' made by the glass-makers at Chiddingfold in England from the 14th to the 16th century, along with a fairly sophisticated shape of bottle, were only rough tumblers.[67]

The domestic glassware of medieval north-western Europe was fern glass or forest glass. Modern glass, and in particular the transparent colourless crystal or *cristallo* glass does not begin until the Renaissance. Crystal glass was invented in 1463 and in the 16th century the Venetians, who had made the first completely transparent white glass since the Roman Empire, made *cristallo* famous, for the workmen of Murano could blow the glass to a bubble thinness and work it into a bewilderment of shapes.[68]

Venetian glass was much prized by the Elizabethans in England though the possession of Venice glasses was largely confined to the nobility and gentry who drank both wine and beer out of them. The rest of the English used pottery 'of sundry colours and moulds, whereof many are garnished with silver, or at the least-wise in pewter . . .'[69] and it is amusing to note that in October 1663, at the Lord Mayor's Banquet, Pepys had to drink and eat out of 'earthen pitchers and wooden dishes' which displeased him.[70] This, however, may have been an exceptional austerity as a result of the Civil War, since a considerable quantity of glass had been manufactured in England by the monopolist Sir Robert Mansell in the first half of the 17th century, and drinking glasses were not uncommon at this time.

We are so used to glass that it is difficult for us to imagine the exhilaration of the new brilliance of glass which spread over Europe in the 17th and 18th centuries. Venetian chandeliers like coruscating plants made of glass leaves and glass flowers; the simpler, but even more beautiful, chandeliers – the 'lustres' of 18th-century England and Germany which looked like falling but static fountains of cut crystal drops; the mirrors of the smart salon; and at the close of the 18th century, the glass pillars in the Café des Mille Colonnes in Paris;[71] for the first time in history this white elegance glittered throughout a civilization. To this display of grace the English made their own remarkable contribution for they not only invented fine lead glass but they made some of the most beautiful decanters and drinking glasses in Europe.

There had been lead in some early medieval glass but for all practical purposes fine lead glass was invented by Ravenscroft in 1675 in England and from that point begins the career of the famous 'Georgian' decanters and glasses.[72] The basic shapes of the English 18th-century wine glass can be seen in the patterns sent by Greene to Venice in about 1670. At that date, some years before Ravenscroft's invention, these fine glasses were to be made in Murano and they are for the most part English modifications of Venetian types.[73] They are glasses with pedestal stands and funnel-shaped bowls, the funnels ranging from the almost rectangular to the almost triangular, one of the latter being the long, thin 'flute'. There is a 'rounded funnel

21 Bottle Decanter
English, c 1740
André Simon Collection

[66]*Ibid*, 134.

[67]Thorpe, *History of English and Irish Glass*, 53-4, 56-7; and see also *loc. cit.*, 52.

[68]Thorpe, *op. cit.*, fn. 1, 52, 72; Dillon, *op. cit.*, 200, 214, 228.

[69]Harrison, W., *Elizabethan England*, Bks II and III, 89, 90.

[70]Pepys, Oct. 29th, 1663.

[71]Andrieu, P., *Fine Bouche*, 39.

[72]Dillon, *op. cit.*, 131; Thorpe, *op. cit.*, 124 sq.

[73]Thorpe, *op. cit.*, 111 sq., and fn. 1, 111.

bowl' which approximates in some degree to the modern tulip-shaped wine glass – the most satisfactory of all wine glasses. There is a brandy tumbler, almost square in section, and almost modern in look. There is also the Rhenish wine glass or rummer, a shape popular in 17th-century England and derived from the German *Roemer*. As early as 1600 the German *Roemer* had achieved the form which it retains today: a fairly squat, rounded bowl on a thick tubular stem which is covered with blobs of glass or 'prunts', the bowl and stem being mounted on a conical foot.[74] Some of these green glass rummers of the 17th century from Germany or the Netherlands are pale sea-green, remarkably lovely, and they are of course famous from their presence in Dutch still-life paintings.

The Abbé Manceaux suggested that Dom Pérignon invented the flute glass, presumably for the drinking of champagne.[75] This is clearly untrue since flute glasses were made in the first half of the 17th century.[76] The name itself has been the subject of some romancing but I think that it undoubtedly comes from a comparison between the long, thin drinking glass and the remarkably narrow ships called flutes which traded between London, Holland and the Baltic.[77] Thus, when the poet Richard Lovelace gives his thanks 'For elles of beere, flutes of canary',[78] he is not being hyperbolical. He means glassfuls and not shiploads of canary wine. There have also been several suggestions that the flute glass was either invented or particularly used for the drinking of champagne. I think we must regard the assumption as, at the very least, unproven. Flute glasses were used as ale glasses at the end of the 17th century as they undoubtedly were half way through the 18th century.[79] One of the curious things is that the modern champagne glass, with its shallow, saucerlike bowl, whose inefficient shape we are still at times forced to tolerate at weddings, appears as early as the first decade of the 18th century.[80] It was not necessarily used for champagne and it may be that its main use in Georgian times was to hold sweetmeats, which is just as well since it is about the least satisfactory design of glass for the drinking of wine.

For that matter the beautiful long stemmed, small bowled, trumpet glasses of Georgian England, for all their exquisite workmanship, were not best adapted for the drinking of fine wine. Nevertheless they had their effect, not only on the refinement of manners, but also on the refinement of wine, since the advent of clear glass meant that wine could at last be properly seen. The colour and the clarity of wine became important to the eye, an importance which was emphasised by the advent of the clear glass decanter.

Bottles, Corks and Corkscrews

But the outstanding act of this Age of Glass, insofar as wine is concerned, was its invention of the cylindrical bottle which at last made possible the proper maturing of wine. Earlier in this story we have seen that there were cylindrical 'bottles' in the Rhineland towards the end of the Roman Empire and that there was then a possibility of binning and maturing wine as we do it in the modern world. That possibility disappeared with the collapse of the Roman Empire and it was not until after the death of Dom Pérignon of Hautvillers, twelve hundred and fifty years later, that the possibility became the practice. It is sad to think that for a millennium and

[74] *Ibid*, 115. For the Roemer of 1600 see Dillon, *op. cit.*, Pl. xxxvii.

[75] Franklin, *op. cit.*, Vol. 6, 135.

[76] Thorpe, *op. cit.*, Vol. II, Pl. iv.

[77] *Cal. State Papers Dom.*, Vol. 1628–9, 33. See also Aytoun Ellis, *op. cit.*, 115.

[78] Lovelace, *Lucasta*, 'Being Treated'.

[79] Thorpe, *op. cit.*, Vol. II, Pl. xxi, and Vol. I, 183.

[80] *Ibid*, Vol. II, Pl. lxxii.

*Earliest illustration of a
Corkscrew, 1778
André Simon Collection*

a quarter of Western history the amount of matured wine in the Christian world
was so negligible that for the vast majority of Christians it was non-existent.

The cylindrical bottle is, however, of no use without a cork stopper. Each one
completes the other. A cork, properly driven into the neck of a bottle, will secure
the wine and allow it to mature in peace. But if the bottle is a standing bottle, if it
stands upon its base, and the bottom of the cork is not in contact with the surface
of the wine, the cork will dry up and shrink and will let enough air into the bottle
for the wine to begin changing into vinegar. The old 'globe and spike' bottle could
only stand on its base and the wine which it held could not mature. The cylindrical
bottle, lying on its side in the cellar, allowed the wine to come into contact with the
cork, kept the cork living and allowed the wine to mature without being destroyed.

In the Ancient World corks were sometimes used for sealing amphoras and sometimes, in a more modern sense, as jug stoppers. There is, for example, in the Stoa
of Attalos in Athens an early 5th-century jug which was found in the Agora together
with the cork which stopped it, neatly cut, with a small vertical hole in its middle.[81]
In this case the cork was used as what one might call a 'daily stopper' and the jug
was used as a 'daily decanter' and not as a long term storage vessel. This usage of
corks was perfectly familiar to Horace and had the Ancient World possessed the
cylindrical bottle (which towards the end of the Roman Empire did exist), and a
corkscrew to take the tightly fitting cork from the bottle neck, then they could
have matured wine as we do. But they seem to have lacked the experimental
curiosity. This type of curiosity was markedly lacking from the less competent
Middle Ages and it is not until the 16th century that we find the renaissance of the
cork. Dr Penzer has noticed the cork in England as early as 1530[82] and in *As You
Like It* Rosalind says to Celia 'I prithee, take the cork out of thy mouth, that I may
drink thy tidings'.[83] But they did not become common in England, nor apparently
in north-western Europe, until the end of the 17th century. Plugs of paper, wadding
or cloth, and wood served as stoppers and the vessels which they stopped were used

[81] *Hesperia*, XX, 50-1, Pl. 25. For
bringing this jug to my notice I
am much indebted to Miss Grace
and Miss Tallcott of the American
School of Classical Studies,
Athens. For cork-stopped amphoras, see Ch. 4, *Rome*, p. 210
and fn. 78.

[82] Penzer, N., *Book of the Wine
Label*, 23.

[83] Act III, Sc. ii.

as decanters.[84] By the middle of the Puritan century, however, the value – or should we say the expediency? – of the cork was becoming recognised. In July 1653 the Earl of Bedford buys twelve dozen stone bottles and a gross of corks, the latter costing him 4/-; in 1664 he orders twelve gross of corks; and in 1682 Sir Miles Stapleton bought a gross of corks at York for which he paid 2/3d.[85] By 1693 it was widely known that a corked bottle should be laid flat so that the wine should come into contact with the base of the cork in order to prevent it shrinking.[86]

The technique of the flush-fitting cork required the invention of the corkscrew. It was duly 'invented' about this time. The famous 'iron corkscrew' of Sedulius Scottus in the 9th century has been amply and wittily dealt with by Mr Warner Allen who suggests that it was a type of claw or pincer instrument to grip the projecting end of a cork or bung.[87] It is conceivable, however, that it may have been a version of the medieval *tarrer* and of the modern awl which is still used in some of finest cellars of the Médoc, where in order to draw wine for tasting from a two-year-old cask, an awl is drilled into the end of the *barrique*. To draw wine the end of the *barrique* is pressed, a jet of wine spurts out, and when the pressure of the hand is released the hole closes up. Whatever the shape of the early medieval corkscrew it was not that of the modern instrument, which under its 17th-century name and at the end of that century is incidentally described by Ned Ward: 'as regular as the worm of a *bottle-screw*'.[88] It assumes its modern name in the next century when, for example, Parson Woodforde quotes 'Gave Mrs Davie a very genteel steel Cork Screw this afternoon'.[89]

Though most of the so-called bottles of medieval England were of pottery or leather, glass bottles were made by the Chiddingfold glass-workers in the 15th and 16th centuries and were made in a comparatively sophisticated shape.[90] But until the end of the 17th century the bottle was used as a jug or decanter, to bring wine from the tavern or the cellar to the table where it was to be drunk. The usual shape of the 17th-century bottle was the 'globe and spike', like an onion with an upright tapering spout. This is also the general shape of the earthenware sack or wine bottles, the most delightful of which are the Lambeth jugs with blue lettering on a white ground. This globe-and-spike shape lasted into the 18th century and the common-ness of its use can be seen from its inclusion in two of the scenes from Hogarth's 'The Harlot's Progress'.[91] Most of these bottles are of green glass but there are squat, cylindrical, black glass bottles which date from the beginning of the Georgian era and are the ancestors of the later, long bottle. It was perhaps these globe-and-spike bottles of which Henri Misson de Valbourg was thinking when he describes a 'typical pub lunch' in London towards the end of the 17th century. It was remarkably like its modern equivalent except that you got it in a cook-shop and not in a tavern. You got meat (though then it was cooked on spits) and 'with this, a little Salt and Mustard upon the Side of a Plate, a Bottle of Beer, and a Roll; and there is your whole Feast'.[92] Gradually these squat bottles, particularly the globe-and-spike bottle, disappeared and the 18th century evolved, somewhere about 1760, the 'standard' cylindrical binning bottle which we can call, both in shape and in purpose, the modern bottle.

It is clear that both champagne and port must have contributed to the modern bottle, champagne because it had to have a flush-fitting cork, and port because it

[84] Dillon, *op. cit.*, 244, citing instances from the paintings of Teniers and Jan Steen.

[85] Bedford Cellar, 184, 191; *Household Books of Sir Miles Stapleton, Ancestor*, 39, July 1902.

[86] Houghton, *Collection*, Vol. 1, 158, No. 56 of Sept. 1963.

[87] Helen Waddell, *Medieval Latin Lyrics*, 325; H. Warner Allen, *A Contemplation of Wine*, 58 sq.

[88] Ned Ward, *The London Spy*, 341.

[89] Woodforde, *op. cit.*, Aug. 6th, 1781. There is an interesting collection of corkscrews at Château Mouton-Rothschild, in the Médoc.

[90] Thorpe, *op. cit.*, 56–7.

[91] Pls 3 and 6. It also occurs in a drunken scene by Hogarth called 'A Midnight Modern Conversation'. See dating of those in Appendix G.

[92] Misson, *Travels over England*, 146–7.

Seton, William
Will Fullerton and Captain
Lowis
Edinburgh, National
Gallery

had to be binned away and matured. But it is unlikely that either of these wines exercised a predominant influence since the taste for sparkling champagne died away and most of the port was drunk young. That the movement towards the cellar bottle was a general one can be seen by the growing use of bottles in Bordeaux in the 1720s and 1730s and by the growth of glass manufactories in that region which toward 1790 turned out nearly two million bottles a year.[93]

The clear glass decanter was specifically a development, and a beautiful development, of Georgian England. Among the wealthier and the upper classes it replaced the decanter jug and the decanter bottle,[94] the popularity of which can be imagined from Ravenscroft's price list of 1677 when he quotes wholesale prices for 'bottles' in sizes ranging from a quarter of a pint to a quart.[95] They were already becoming decorative as well as useful for some of these Ravenscroft bottles were '. . . all over nipt diamond waies'[96] but the great elegance of the decanter was to come in Georgian times when it replaced the serving bottle. The beauty and the transparency of the decanter made important the colour and the clarity of the wine which it was to hold. Another, if minor, elegance accompanied the evolution of the binning bottle and the smart decanter since the wine inside each of them had to be identified. The bottle in the cellar could be labelled by an attached piece of paper or wooden tag. Not so the decanter; and hence the invention of the 'bottle-ticket' or wine label, a removable hoop or plaque which carried the name of a wine and could be put on the decanter. Many of these bottle tickets achieved a distinction which later may have been equalled but has never been surpassed.[97] The cellar

[93] Lafforgue, *Vignoble Girondin*, 295.

[94] For a variant shape of these about 1690 and in the early 18th century, see Thorpe, *op. cit.*, Vol. II, Pl. lxxix.

[95] Thorpe, *op. cit.*, Vol. I, 127.

[96] *Ibid*, 133.

[97] See the full and expert treatment of this subject in Dr N. M. Penzer's *Book of the Wine Label*. The Victoria and Albert Museum, London, has published *Bottle Tickets*, H.M.S.O. 1958 – examples from the P. J. Cropper Collection.

bottle was not of course graced with these miniature beauties. Parchment labels were in use in the first half of the 18th century,[98] after which time the bottle began to adopt a distinctive, if less colourful modern guise with the advent of the printed label. One of the first of these, which has been published by Monsieur André Simon, appeared in 1756 on a port bottle[99] and even at this early date it is more complex and more 'modern' than the earliest burgundy labels which are merely slips of white paper overprinted in black with the simple name of the wine – Nuits, Vosne, Volnay, Montrachet.[100] In some respects, and despite the great improvements which were being made, the drinking of wine was still a simple business. The seals which are sometimes found on the shoulders of serving bottles have nothing to do with the nature of the contents. They were added by taverns, or by individuals, to identify their own property.[101]

The 18th-century bottle has mainly appealed to the mind of later generations not because of itself but because of its abuse. 'Three-bottle men' and 'Four-bottle men' are the fabulous figures of the Georgian era. I have often been asked whether we exaggerate the prowess of these mighty drinkers on the ground that the bottles which they used were smaller than those of today. It is difficult to decide this point but I do not think their consumption has been exaggerated; in fact I think we under-estimate their rollicking capacity. Gronow, writing of his youth in 1814 says: 'There were then four and even five bottle men' and he goes on to mention three peers who, 'wonderful to relate were six bottle men'. He thinks that 'the only thing which saved them was drinking very slowly and out of very small glasses' though from his own and similar accounts it does not seem to have saved them from very much.[102]

I have measured a number of bottles from the collection in the Ashmolean Museum at Oxford.* They show a wide variation of capacity but only two out of ten of them are smaller than the modern bottle. The standard British wine bottle of today holds $26\frac{2}{3}$ fluid oz.; all except two of the Ashmolean bottles which I have measured hold 28 to 34 fluid oz. and these larger size bottles date from about 1660 to 1817. Even the stubby cylindrical bottle of 1792, which looks quite small, holds 34 fluid oz. Bottles were of course made in many sizes and it is possible that the alcoholic giants of Georgian England drank from small bottles. I do not think so. Alternatively, if one is using 'bottle' in the sense of decanter and since, as we have seen, Ravenscroft made 'bottles' as small as a quarter of a pint, we cannot assume that these were the bottles used for the more saturated orgies. Ravenscroft also made a bottle that held a quart. The thirstier Georgians would regard the wine-accompanied dinner of today as nothing better than dwarf tantalization.

It is quite a different matter if we assess the drinking habits of our ancestors in the terms of their stated measures. In 1824 the English wine and beer gallons were standardized at 160 fluid oz. which is the modern British measure. Before that time the gallon measure, and therefore the quart and the pint, had varied very considerably, the wine gallon always holding less than that of today. In medieval and Elizabethan times it is probable that the wine gallon held about 104 fluid oz.; in the reign of Queen Anne a wine gallon would have held about 132 fluid oz.; while the Oxford wine gallon of 1737 held 140 fluid oz.* Thus, when Pepys gave his mother

*See Appendix H, *Medieval to Modern Measures.*

[98] Penzer, *op. cit.,* 32.

[99] *Bottlescrew Days,* 242 and 243-4.

[100] Musée du Vin, Beaune.

[101] Brise, Ruggles S., *Sealed Bottles,* 15-16.

[102] Gronow, *Reminiscences,* Vol. II, 34, 1892.

Canaletto, Rotunda, Ranelagh Pleasure Gardens, 1754: London, National Gallery

a pint of sack it would not have been more than three-quarters of a modern pint, or two reasonably filled modern tulip wine glasses.[103] On this showing the old lady was no soak. Similarly, the three-quart bottle produced by Thomson for each of his guests would only have held five modern pints. Even so it is more than enough. The Scotch pint, however, was about three Imperial pints so that when Boswell and his companions in Edinburgh consumed 'eleven pints of Scotch claret, two bottles of old hock and two of port' in addition to sundry drams of brandy and gin,[104] they were certainly consuming an intolerable deal of liquor.

Pleasure Gardens, Coffee Houses . . . and beyond

The contrasts in society, in the manners of the time, were extreme. An analogy might be taken perhaps from the differing shapes of the Georgian bottle. On the one hand there was the old globe and spike, rough, ready and coarse; on the other hand there was the refined decanter, elegant, sophisticated and frigid. Two scenes vividly illustrate the contrast.

Charles Moritz, a German travelling through England in 1782, describes the smart scene in the Rotunda at Ranelagh Pleasure Gardens. The Rotunda was 150 ft. in diameter and surrounded by a ring of sixty-two boxes in which you could get refreshments and above which was a gallery with other boxes. Apart from the light

[103]Pepys, Aug. 24th, 1660.

[104]*Boswell for the Defence*, 232, Edinburgh, July 9th, 1774.

355

given by its windows it was lit by chandeliers each one decorated with a gilt crown and one side of this enormous room was the orchestra.[105] Here, says Moritz, 'in a kind of magic rotundo, all the beau-monde of London move perpetually round and round . . . I now went up into the gallery, and seated myself in one of the boxes there . . . I looked down on the concourse of people, who were still moving round and round in the fairy circle; and then I could easily distinguish several stars, and other orders, of knighthood; French queues and bags contrasted with plain English heads of hair, or professional wigs; old age and youth, nobility and commonalty, all passing each other in the motley swarm'.[106]

The other scene also takes place in London but at the end of the 17th century. It is described by Ned Ward who kept a tavern next door to Gray's Inn and whose *London Spy* gives a pretty accurate reflection of the seamier side of London life. Into a tavern at Billingsgate where Ned 'happens to be', come a couple of seamen who

'. . . happened to espie a Hook drove into the Mantle-Tree, which they immediately converted to a very Comical use, laying violent Hands on my little Lord *Crowdero*, a "crooked Fiddler" who had come into the tavern and by the hind slit of his Breeches, hung upon him the Tenter, who being sorely affrighted at this unexpected Elevation, shot that into his Trousers which made the crooked Vermin out stink a *Pole-Cat*. In this condition, pendant like a *Play-House Machine*, or a *Brazen Cherub* over a Church Branch; he hung sprawling, begging with humble Submission to be set safe upon *Terra Firma*. All the time dripping his Guts upon the Hearth like a *Roasting Wood* cock; till at last, by rigling, he broke the string of his Breeches, and down came our Broil'd Scraper into his own Sauce. . . .'[107]

This vignette is coarse and vulgar; but it is less coarse than some of the customs of the time and to imagine this Age as a reality, to try and experience it as it really was, one must see the coarseness which lay beyond the glittering ambit of the chandeliers. The London mob at the Lord Mayor's Show indulged in antics which were better fitted for a pig-sty.[108] Beside the ferocity of the Georgian cartoonists our own satire has the pungent taste of skimmed milk. Rowlandson's grotesque caricatures seem part of a nightmare which is not always good-humoured. In commerce the slave trade was prosperous and in one year alone 50,000 slaves were shipped out of English ports.[109] Other nations of civilized Europe joined in this flourishing trade. In England the death penalty could be, but was not invariably, inflicted for trivial offences. Hanging was frequent and, to the spectators, popular. A noisy mob jostled round the triangular gallows at Tyburn while those who desired to watch the event in greater comfort could do so from convenient stands.[110] The most popular manifestations of the English sporting instinct were cock-fighting and bull-baiting. A lesser diversion was the sport of goose-riding. A goose 'with neck well greased was hung by the legs to a bar and the competitors, riding at speed beneath, tried to pull off the head'.[111] At the Marylebone Pleasure Gardens there was a garden orchestra, male and female singers, fireworks, and 'the rich seed and plum cakes, and the almond cheese-cakes made . . . by Miss Trusler'; footpads lurked outside the Gardens and guards had to be provided to escort the pleasure-seekers

[105] Wroth, *op. cit.*, 202.

[106] Moritz, *Travels . . .*, ed. Matheson, 46–50.

[107] Ward, *London Spy*, 43–4.

[108] *Ibid*, XII, 293–8.

[109] Trevelyan, *English Social History*, Vol. III, 92.

[110] Hogarth, *Industry and Idleness*, Pl. xi.

[111] Turberville, *op. cit.*, Vol. I, 374–5.

Rowlandson, Thomas
Vauxhall Gardens

from what is now Harley Street to what is now the West End of London.[112] Horace Walpole opens a chink in the Age of Grace when he writes to Sir Horace Mann in 1752: '. . . Seventeen were executed this morning, after having murdered the turnkey on Friday night, and almost forced open Newgate. One is forced to travel, even at noon, as if one was going to battle.'[113]

There was also of course, as we have already seen, plenty of 'bunging your eye'. To 'bung one's eye' is to drink a dram, or to drink heartily, and the less distinguished circles of Victorian England referred to beer and porter as 'bung-juice'. Students of the 18th century should note however that a 'bung-nipper' is not an alcoholic child but a common cut-purse.[114]

Over-bunging the eye took place even in fashionable society. Lord Granby, joining Lady Caroline Petersham's party on the way to Vauxhall Gardens 'arrived very drunk from Jenny's Whim'.[115] At a large party to which Sir Gilbert Elliot went after the Opera there were 'three young men so drunk as to puzzle the whole assembly'. Two of them were riotous and when Mrs Sheridan was trying to move away from their 'plain talk' she 'did not make her escape till her arms were black and blue and her apron torn off'.[116] Such boyish fun was not of course the rule and despite the complaint of Moritz at Vauxhall Gardens that 'women of the town . . . rushed in upon us by half dozens, and in the most shameless manner importuned us for wine'[117] the London Pleasure Gardens were on the whole remarkably decorous. They are a typical product of their Age and they illustrate the growing refinement of one side of Georgian life. The Jew's Harp House and Tea Gardens in Regent's Park was an inn which by 1772 boasted 'bowery tea gardens', skittle grounds and a tennis court; the Yorkshire Stingo, just south of the Marylebone Road, had large

[112] Wroth, *op. cit.*, 95–100.

[113] *Letters*, Mar. 23rd, 1752.

[114] *The Connoisseur*, No. 53 of Jan. 30th, 1755, 'On Dram-Drinking'; Partridge, *Dictionary of Slang*.

[115] Horace Walpole, *Letters*, to George Montague, June 23rd, 1750.

[116] Sir Gilbert Elliot, *Life and Letters*, Vol. I, 135–6, Mar. 8th, 1787.

[117] Mavor, *British Tourists*, Vol. IV, 18–20; Moritz, Charles P., *Travels . . . in 1782*.

tea gardens and a bowling green; Jenny's Whim, near Ebury Bridge in Pimlico, was a tavern (where Lord Granby got drunk) and also a pleasure garden in which there were 'flower-beds, a bowling green, a grotto, a cock-pit and a ducking pond' and when a customer trod upon an unsuspected spring a monster or a harlequin sprang up in the garden and '. . . huge fish and mermaids rose at intervals from the water on the pond'.[118]

Of all the London Pleasure Gardens Ranelagh was the smartest and Vauxhall the most continuously popular. Admission to Ranelagh cost half-a-crown in which were included tea and coffee, bread and butter. There were formal gardens with a circular temple of Pan, fireworks, and concerts – Mozart at the age of eight performed at Ranelagh, playing some of his own compositions on the harpsichord – but the great attraction of Ranelagh was the fashionable promenade in the Rotunda. Entrance to Vauxhall Gardens, on the south side of the Thames near Kennington Oval, was less expensive than Ranelagh, costing only a shilling. The Gardens, lit at night by over fifteen hundred lamps, were of a more rococo formality with 'pavilions, lodges, groves, grottoes, lawns, temples . . . cascades . . . porticoes, colonnades . . . rotundas . . . pillars, statues . . . paintings . . .' The alcoves of Vauxhall, much favoured for parties and less public assignations, were painted with scenes from contemporary life and the engravings made from them have left us a valuable and entrancing record. The paintings were often attributed to Hogarth, who did perhaps execute some of them, but the artist commissioned to do the work was Francis Hayman, a painter of great merit whose pictures are not unworthy of the better known master.

Vauxhall also gave musical concerts but it was famous rather for its suppers than its culture, and in particular for the 'wafer-like slices of beef and ham which were, on that account, considered expensive by the more economical or voracious

[118] Wroth, *op. cit.*, 113 sq.; and for the other Pleasure Gardens, below.

citizens'.[119] On the occasion of Lady Caroline Petersham's party at Vauxhall she herself took a hand in the cuisine: 'We minced seven chickens into a china dish, which Lady Caroline stewed over a lamp with three parts of butter and a flagon of water, stirring, and rattling, and laughing, and we every minute expecting to have the dish fly about our ears.' Rather naturally they 'had the whole concourse round our booth . . .'[120] Apart from chicken and meat the rest of the menu at Vauxhall was salad, bread, butter and cheese, tarts, custards and cakes, while the wine list ran from burgundy and champagne to 'old hock, with or without sugar', red port, sherry, beer and arrack.

The people of Restoration and Augustan England were extremely gregarious and although Society grew more and more conscious of itself as the 18th century progressed, and, to that extent, more and more snobbish, it never lost its strongly democratic instinct. At Vauxhall Gardens all classes mingled freely – at a shilling a head. The Pleasure Gardens were the most frivolous expression of the desire for company; the most important was the Coffee House. The first Coffee House in Christian Europe was set up at Oxford and by the end of the 17th century London alone had over two thousand of them.[121] They were disseminators of news, mouthpieces of criticism, commercial meeting places, and centres of political intrigue. They were cheap, warm, well-mannered, and open to all men. They were probably the most democratic institution which has ever existed. They were also, at the start of their career, non alcoholic, and by offering, for the first time in European history, a really palatable, and even exciting, alternative to liquor, they had a marked effect on the sobriety of the time. Their popularity declined in the 18th century but even so Coffee Houses were a part of University life at Oxford and Cambridge at the middle of the century and the Coffee House habit must have mitigated the worst rigours of University drinking. Coffee Houses continued to exist at the end of the 18th century when in them 'there generally prevails a very decorous stillness and silence . . . The greater part read the newspapers . . . the seats are divided by wooden wainscot partitions. . . .'[122] This is not greatly different from the description given by Ned Ward at the end of the 17th century: some scribbling, some talking, some drinking, the room smelling of tobacco, and the walls hung with gilt frames containing advertisements for 'Nectar and Ambrosia, May-Dew, Golden-Elixers, Popular Pills, Liquid-Snuff, Beautifying-Waters . . . Dentrifices, Drops, Lozenges, all . . . infallible as the Pope'.[123]

Early Clubs, of Several Kinds

One reason for the decline of the Coffee House is that it gradually changed its nature and turned into a club. White's, in St James's Street, grew out of White's Chocolate House, while Brooks's had its beginning in a house set up by Almack, these two being the first West End Clubs to have their own buildings. The St James's Club was founded in 1757 while Boodle's, first known as The Sçavoir Vivre, was 'a habitation and a name' in 1762. The Augustan Englishman was an extremely 'clubbable' person and clubs of every description, intelligent, eccentric, moral, and immoral appeared like an outbreak of strange fruit. Among the best of this new growth were the Dilettanti Society and the Sublime Society of Beefsteaks. Among the more

[119] *The Connoisseur*, No. 68 of May 16th, 1755. For Ranelagh, see also Horace Walpole, *Letters*, Apr. 22nd and May 26th, 1742, June 29th, 1744, and – a masquerade – May 3rd, 1749.

[120] See fn. 115.

[121] Aytoun Ellis, *The Penny Universities*, p. xiv, a most interesting work on the history of the coffee house.

[122] Mavor, *op. cit.*, Moritz, 50. See also Misson, *Travels*, 39.

[123] Ward, *op. cit.*, 11.

Medmenham Abbey, 1819
London, British Museum

eccentric – (although they are described by Ned Ward and may thus be creatures of his invention they can nevertheless be accepted as typical) – were The No-Nose Club, The Club of Ugly Faces, The Split-Farthing Club of Misers, and The Lying Club whose chairman was the member uttering the most 'stupendous Improbability'. Bob Weden's Cellar Club must have been one of the more depressing institutions. It was merely a drinking club whose members met in a small cellar at the Sign of the Still in the Strand. They drank bumpers of French brandy and 'sometimes they sat, without any adjournment, for half a Week together, scorning any other Refreshment than a Nod in a Chair. . . .' Even less salubrious associations were The Mollies Club, for homosexuals, and The Bawds Initiating Club, whose title is a masterpiece of short and accurate description.[124] Better known to us nowadays was The Hell-Fire Club whose amorous proceedings have been given notoriety by the rank of the participants and the suggestion of blasphemy. There were in fact many clubs which bore this name but the only one which has continued to tempt the imagination was The Hell-Fire Club of the 'monks' of Medmenham Abbey.[125] The fact that the male members of the club called themselves 'monks' or 'brothers' and that they entertained irregular 'nuns' in an atmosphere of seclusion and luxury does not necessarily mean that they were blasphemous. Some of the 'Knights of St Francis of Wycombe', as their founder, Sir Francis Dashwood, called them, had an antipathy to Roman Catholicism, but in the 18th-century idiom brothels were often referred to as 'nunneries' or 'abbeys' and brothel-keepers as 'abbesses'. William Hickey, who had much experience of these establishments, tells us that 'All the Lady Abbesses were dignified by the respectable title of Mother'.[126] The 'nuns' invited to Medmenham were all well-known courtesans and the 'orgies' enacted there can easily be given a name. They were probably much more commonplace than the Black Mass.

Whatever else the 'monks' did, they drank well. Their cellar included claret (which Wilkes seems to have preferred), port, Lisbon, calcavello, hock and Tenerif.*[127] They did not drink a great deal of spirits but they were no ascetics

*For the wines mentioned in this chapter, see Appendix G, *Wines, Medieval to Modern*.

[124]Ned Ward, *Compleat . . . Account . . . of Remarkable Clubs . . . in London*, 24-31, 51-5, 55-61, 203-27, 259-65, 265-9, 306-17.

[125]See in particular D. McCormick, *The Hell-Fire Club*.

[126]William Hickey, Alfred Spencer's edition, Vol. I, 71.

[127]McCormick, *op. cit.*, 75.

when it came to wine as one can see from the performance of 'Thomas de Greys and John of Henley' – (fictitious names which the monks assumed) – who managed at one sitting on September 29th, 1762, to work their way through two bottles of claret, four bottles of port and one of Lisbon.[128]

The Search for Claret

Claret was generally the wine preferred by the discriminating drinker in late 17th and in 18th-century England. It was also preferred by the Scots and the Irish. So marked was the English desire for fine claret that the best wines of Bordeaux were reserved for England. Despite all this, claret was not always easy to get in England since an almost continual state of political hostility existed between France and England throughout the 18th century. Nevertheless, by legal or illegal shipment, claret continued to find its way to England.

Its adversaries were not only the politicians. For the wine fakers were ready to make up the deficiency caused by political antagonism. Ames, hunting for claret through the London taverns in 1693, is bitterly disappointed, and exclaims:

> 'Claret was now grown so vicious,
> So counterfeit, poor, pall'd, dull, flat and insipid,
> That scarcely 'tis fitting for man to long lip at,'

and levels a general attack against counterfeiters for the '. . . *Damn'd stuff* which in their Vaults they brew'.[129] This depravity did not affect the men of taste who had enough money to buy what they liked and, when they could, ordered the best wines of Bordeaux. John Hervey, first Earl of Bristol, was fond of claret and although in 1691 he committed the misnomer of buying 'Hermitage Clarett', in the early 18th century he bought named wines from Graves and the Médoc: 'Obrian', 'Margoose Clarett', 'Pontack Clarett', 'La Tour' and 'Laffitte'.[130] Pontack usually means wine from a vineyard at Haut-Brion in Graves, and it took its name from the family who owned the vineyard from which, so Evelyn thought, came the best of the Bordeaux wines. One might observe here that in the early 18th century the territorial designation of Graves included also what we now call the Médoc, although by December 1800 when the third Viscount Gage bought three dozen Vin de Grave the designation may have become somewhat more precise.[131]

The taste of these eminent persons was followed by many others of varying degrees of nobility and wit. Sir Robert Walpole preferred Lafite, Latour, Margaux, and Haut-Brion,[132] while John Gay, author of *The Beggar's Opera*, described in a poem how he and his friends at the Devil Tavern, Temple Bar, unanimously chose 'Bourdeaux'.[133]

But for the majority of Englishmen in the 18th century the pattern of drinking was unmistakably Iberian. Some of the so-called Spanish or Portuguese wines may well have been claret shipped into England under a false *appellation*, and indeed smuggling introduced a considerable degree of flexibility into the wine trade of this century. Smuggling was widespread, savage, and countenanced by the respectable; its history is too well known to be repeated. Parson Woodforde's attitude is typical:

[128] *Ibid.*

[129] Ames, *Bacchanalian Sessions*, 8–9, 24.

[130] Hervey Cellar, *passim*.

[131] Account Book of the 3rd Viscount Gage, Sussex Archaeological Society.

[132] Walpole Cellar, 201.

[133] John Gay, *Poems*, 'Wine'.

361

in October 1781 he records in his Diary: 'Clerk Hewitt of Mattishall Burgh called on me this even' by desire of Mrs Davy to taste some smuggled gin which I liked and he is to bring me a Tub this week'; and, thirstily unrepentant, in May 1787 he writes: '. . . I bottled of this morning a Tub of Moonshine'.[134] The moonlight reception of gin could equally apply to the midnight traffic in claret.

The legal difficulties of importing claret into England, and, to a much lesser extent, the Francophobe prejudice against drinking French wines in England, were not the only reasons why the English drinker looked for consolation towards the Peninsula. There was behind him a long and strong tradition of drinking Iberian wines and the lack of claret would have been a real deprivation only to the better palates.

The Peninsular Wines

Quite apart from any question of port wine, the beverage wines of Portugal, particularly of Central Portugal, appeared frequently on English tables. 'Lisbon' was perhaps the most popular though some idea of its grading can be gathered from the example of Sir Robert Walpole. He kept the finest clarets for himself and his closer friends, while in his cellar, which also contained hock, old burgundy and champagne, he kept numerous hogsheads of white Lisbon (and of port) which were served at the great man's 'public' tables.[135] Sometimes, in the mid-18th century, it is known as 'old Lisbon',[136] but the adjective is more likely to have been a title of courtesy than an accurate description. 'Lisbon' was a general term covering the wines shipped out of the Tagus estuary. Sometimes they occur under the proper names of their vineyards such as Bucellas and Calcavella (Carcavellos) but the more usual classification was 'Lisbon' which covered the produce of all the vineyards around the city: Bucellas north-east of Lisbon, Charneco from the low, rolling country north and west of Lisbon (and a term which was on occasions extended to cover the vintages of Colares and Carcavellos), Carcavellos itself on the Lisbon estuary looking out towards the Atlantic, and Colares, on the north side of the Serra de Cintra where the land is spray-swept from the Atlantic and fields are screened and shielded by lines of cane fences. 'Lisbon' would also have included such wine as was grown on the southern side of the Tagus estuary, at Caparica (where there are still some vines) and such vineyards as may have existed on the north side of the Serra da Arrábida between Azeitão and Setúbal. For the most part the 'Lisbon' shipped to England in the late 17th and 18th centuries was white wine and from tasting the modern products of the vineyards we can, I think, obtain a very accurate idea of how they tasted to the Augustans.

Bucellas nowadays is a golden medium-bodied wine, Carcavellos (at least some of it) is a sweet wine, topaz brown, full bodied and strong; Colares, now usually a red wine, is dry and somewhat reminiscent of claret whereas the red wine from the Azeitão and Setúbal is purple dark, fairly heavily bodied, and more like a robust *vin ordinaire*. The red Colares takes its age well although in the 18th century it would seldom have been allowed to achieve that distinction. Colares also makes white wine and for that matter there are a number of light, pleasant white wines which come from the region north of Colares, between Torres Vedras and Caldas

[134] Woodforde, *op. cit.*

[135] Walpole Cellar, 201.

[136] TR, VII, 368 sq.

da Rainha. On the south side of the Tagus, Setúbal and Azeitão produce fine mos-
catel wines, sweet perfumed dessert wines which, in one version or another, have
been made from the 17th century and some of which may have come into Augustan
England either as Lisbon or as Caparica. It is of course impossible to say that today
we can drink Portuguese wines of exactly the same type and texture as those drunk
by the Georgians for we cannot be certain of the proportions of different grapes in
the vintages of 18th-century Portugal. Nor can we be certain of the degree to which
the gathered grapes were dried in the sun before pressing. But there is a remarkable
correspondence between a description of Carcavellos, written in 1793, and the
description of it which I have given today. It was then 'a white wine of an agreeable
sweetness, with a pungent taste'[137] and so it is in our own time. I do not think we
shall go far wrong if we assume a similar correspondence for the other Lisbon wines
of the two centuries.

The three most popular Spanish wines of the 18th century were Mountain,
Canary and Sherry, the word sack being progressively discarded and being replaced
by the more accurate, modern 'sherry'. Mountain is wine from Malaga and although
it was made in two styles, dry or sweet, the sweet was the most favoured. One of
the sweet styles, a luscious wine, was also called Malmsey, while another, rich and
sweet, was called Pedro Ximenes. To confuse the issue there was also a Mountain
wine which came from Corsica and as we have seen, there were Mountain wines
from the Champagne vignobles. But when 'Mountain' occurs in 18th-century
England as, for example, when John Byng refreshed himself on a journey with
'bread and cheese, and mountain wine',[138] we can be pretty certain that it meant
sweet wine from Malaga. Canary had been extremely popular in England during
the 17th century and the liking for it continued until about the middle of the 18th
century when it went out of fashion. It was known under a medley of names,
Canary, 'Palme', 'Palm sack', Vidonia, and Teneriffe. Most of these wines were
white and many of them were of a Malmsey style, rich and full bodied; but towards
the end of the 18th century Vidonia, whose name comes from the Vidogne grape –
the Chasselas de Ténériffe or Chasselas doré – which was considered the best brand
of Canary, was 'a dry white wine of a good body'.[139] It is likely that its dryness was
some reflection of the later taste for dry Spanish wines. It is thus likely that when
the dons of the senior Common Room at Christ Church, Oxford, bought 'white
Ténériffe' during the latter years of the Napoleonic Wars, they looked forward to
drinking a dry wine. It was quite expensive, costing 4/3d. a bottle – though cheaper
than sherry which cost 5/6d. It is clear that the dons liked Teneriffe since they went
on buying it until the mid 1820s when sherry becomes the dominant white wine
in the Common Room.[140]

Sherry was not then used as we use it now. It was not so much an apéritif as a
table wine. As an apéritif, hock, or Old Hock, seems to have been most usual.[141]
It is true that Boswell at the Shakespeare, when entertaining certain ladies by whom
he hoped to be entertained, ordered sherry but this can scarcely be called a whet in
the gastronomic sense. He drank quite a lot of it. He had a bottle of 'Choice Sherry'
with Miss Watts. The same evening having 'in a rich flow of animal spirits and
burning with fierce desire' picked up two pretty girls, he went back to the Shakespeare where the three of them had another bottle of sherry.[142] For more intellectual

[137] McBride, *Instructions* . . ., 23.

[138] Byng, *Torrington Diaries*, 103, dating 1785.

[139] McBride, *op. cit.*, 23.

[140] Christ Church Common Room Accounts, MS., C.R.2, dating 1806-24.

[141] Ned Ward, *London Spy*, 4; George Farquhar, *The Twin-Rivals*, Act I, Sc. i.

[142] Boswell, *London Journal*, 263-4.

recreation sherry was held in considerable esteem at the end of the century: so much so that from May 1796 until 1806 the Christ Church senior common-room bought nothing else except port and sherry.[143] At this date the English preferred it dry. 'Xerez, or Sherry, is a good dry white wine, in general use in Britain and much admired.'[144]

Among the other Spanish wines, one which was graded in England as of good quality, although it does not seem to have been drunk in any quantity, was 'Paca-retti' or, to give it its more usual name, Paxarete. This was made from the sweet Pedro Ximenez grape, the PX, but the wine was not always a heavy and luscious wine since it was described in 1775 as 'now much esteemed for its light, delicate taste, and fragrancy'.[145] A hogshead of Paxarete was shipped to England in 1818 for the Prince Regent by which time the 'light, delicate' tasting wine may have returned to its normal sweet richness.[146] A luscious wine would perhaps have gone better with the décor of the Brighton Pavilion, and the opulent tastes of the 'First Gentleman of Europe'.

Insofar as England is concerned, Madeira wine has a somewhat roundabout history. Shakespeare mentions it but it was known in London long before his time, for in 1537 there was imported some 'malvoisie of the Isle of Madeer in Portyn-gale'.[147] It continued to be bought, though in small quantities, throughout the 17th century, but its great period of triumph was the last half of the 18th century and the beginning of the 19th. And its sudden success was apparently due to the taste of English Colonists. Adam Smith in his *Wealth of Nations* shows how the greater commercial ease of its export into America and the West Indies spread a general liking for Madeira throughout the New World, a liking which was brought back after 1755 by English officers to England.[148] Twenty years later it was 'universally drank in England',[149] and in 1782 it figured in the private cellar of Louis XVI of France.[150] By that time it was well known that a long sea voyage helped the final quality of the wine though in these days opinions differ as to the real value of its sea travel.

The main reason for its sudden rise to fame in the middle of the 18th century must have been that it then first began to be a fortified wine, a technique which, as we shall see with port, was not properly applied to certain Portuguese wines until this date. Undoubtedly before, though much more so after, the advent of fortifi-cation, Madeira was a rich or sweet wine. The three main modern classifications of Madeira can give us some idea of its permutations in the 18th century: Sercial is the driest, dry but rich; Bual (and Verdelho) is a rich, smooth wine that needs age, a great age if possible, and an 1840 Bual which I drank in 1950 was a very remark-able wine, fine and full and with what one can only call a 'tremendous smoothness'; then finally, and again needing great age, is the sweetest of the Madeiras, the Malmsey. A peculiarity in the making of Madeira, and one not employed in any other great vineyard, is the technique of keeping the young wine for a time in heated vessels. This technique was well known in ancient Rome though whether it reached the island of Madeira from a knowledge of classical authors, or was 're-invented' there by local genius, is a matter for conjecture. The increasing refusal of the modern world to leave fine wines to age makes it probable, and sad, that our grandchildren will never drink superb Madeira.

[143] Christ Church C.R. Accounts.

[144] McBride, *op. cit.*, 29.

[145] Barry, *op. cit.*, 443.

[146] Croft-Cooke, R., *Sherry*, 155. For the possibility of its return to sweetness, see McBride, *op. cit.*, 29, dating 1793.

[147] *Henry IV*, Pt I, Act I, Sc. ii; Gaird-ner, *Henry VIII*, 12, Pt II, No. 751.

[148] Bk IV, Ch. IV, 4–5 of Vol. II.

[149] Barry, *op. cit.*, 443.

[150] Archives Nationales, Paris, MS., O1.793.

Heda, William Claes
Breakfast Table, 1600
Dresden, Gemeente Galerie

Old Hock, Sweet Muscat and Wine from the Cape

Although Hock continued to be drunk in England throughout the Augustan Age, and although it had its occasional devotees such as Sir Robert Walpole, it is clear that it was not drunk to any great extent and that when it was it was drunk either as an apéritif or as a bewildered beverage. In 1763 Boswell supped at The Queen's Head in Holborn with his printer and his bookseller – a lesson to aspiring authors – and at this supper 'every man drank his bottle of Rhenish with sugar'[151] – no lesson for an aspiring gourmet. At about the same date the menu at Vauxhall Gardens included Old Hock, with or without sugar, which cost 5/- or, and rather ominously less expensive, Rhenish and sugar.[152] The reason for the bewilderment of a potentially fine wine is two-fold: a great increase in planting in the Rhineland had led to the production of quantity as opposed to quality wine, a common and self-destructive act which abased the reputation of the wine and led, towards the end of the 18th century, to a crisis of over-production; the second reason is, I think, that Rhenish wines always tended to be harsh since the *Spaetlese* technique was only discovered (at Johannisberg) at this particular time.[153] This does not merely mean a late picking of the grapes since the need for full ripening, for leaving the berries on the vine as long as possible, was known in the early history of mankind. It means what we now call the *Beerenauslese*, the picking of grapes only when they are over-ripe, 'sleepy' and suffering from the 'noble rot' which comes from an ill-sounding fungus named *Botrytis cinerea*. In fact the fungus is the drinker's friend since it disposes of some of the water in the grape berry. It leaves the grapes shrivelled into apparently hopeless senility but it makes the splendour of the great Sauternes and the magnificence of the finest Hocks. When one walks through the vineyards and sees this 'noble rot' which has nothing noble in its appearance, one can understand why it took so long for wine makers to discover that it was a friend and not an enemy.

[151] Boswell, *London Journal*, 297. For Walpole's hock, see Walpole Cellar, 201.

[152] Wroth, *op. cit.*, 298-9.

[153] Langenbach, *Wines of Germany*, 37.

Italian wines, both red and white, continued to be imported into England, mostly Tuscan wines passing under the general title of 'Florence'. One of these, in the 17th century, was a red 'muscadine' wine called Leattica and made from the *aleatico nero* grape which may in fact have been the same grape as the Muscat noir. The white and red Florence wines, when genuine and well made, probably had a certain degree of delicacy but carelessness or mal-culture diminished their fineness as they did at the same time with Chianti, and a once delightful wine, which still however kept 'freshness and beautiful deep colour', now had a 'disagreeable roughness' and found no favour with the English.[154] Among the lesser French wines shipped into England were the sweet Muscat wines of Lunel and Frontignan in Languedoc where sweet and liqueur wines are still made today from Muscat grapes[155] and wine from Jurançon near Pau in the western Pyrenees. This was in all probability the 'Navarre' wine of which a certain amount was drunk in England at the end of the 17th century, and although Pepys did not think a great deal of it it was still exported from France in the 18th century and then appreciated for its vigour. Today Jurançon is made from small vineyards curiously tucked away among the woods of the Pau foothills, an attractive, but to the casual traveller an elusive, *vignoble*. The best Jurançon wine is white and it is particularly prized for its outstanding sweetness which to some extent recalls a Sauternes. For my own taste I prefer the dry white Jurançon (also called *blanc de blanc*), a wine that is soft and smooth as silk but still has a slight hardness of stone to give it bite. It has also a delicate bouquet which I find I have variously described as of flowers, or nectarines, or of the vine itself, as if the wine had been made with the leaves and the flowers as well as with the grapes of the vine.

For the first time in history wine was shipped into Europe from vineyards beyond the homeland of Western civilization. Counting Madeira and the Canary Islands as 'European', then the distinction of creating the first trans-oceanic vineyards belongs to the New World of America where the Spaniards fostered wine-growing in Mexico and California. But the first trans-oceanic shipments came from South Africa. There, in the last decades of the 17th century, vineyards spread rapidly over the country outside Cape Town, at Stellenbosch, Wynberg and Somerset West. The arrival of the Huguenots at the Cape in 1688 brought extra skill and vitality to South African viticulture and although the production of wine went on increasing, particularly in Drakenstein and Stellenbosch, there was no corresponding increase in quality. The exception was the wine of Constantia which was rated by European gourmets as a wine of some distinction. Constantia, or 'Cape wine' as it was also called, was red or white, the red being considered the best wine, while the white was of a syrup-like body and 'full in the mouth'. Boswell drank Constantia in 1772 at a dinner with Mr Foote.[156] The *Vin du Cap* which occurred in the cellar of Louis XVI at Versailles would not have been the wine of Cap-Breton, which at that period was favoured for its delicacy, but the wine of Constantia as was also the *Vin du Cap* nominated by Brillat-Savarin as the contribution of Africa to a gourmet's dinner.[157]

It might seem that English taste coarsened during this Age, drowning itself in gin, punch, and bad port. But this is only one side of the picture. The other side manifests an increasing range of choice and discernment. And the English palate takes a new interest in the wines of Burgundy and the Rhône Valley.

[154]Barry, *op. cit.*, 442.

[155]Gage Cellar, 1301, 'Lunelle', de Secondat, *Mémoire . . .*, 65.

[156]McBride, *op. cit.*, 21; *Boswell for the Defence*, 93.

[157]Archives Nationales, Paris, MS., O1.793, de Secondat, *op. cit.*, 65; Brillat-Savarin, 330.

The vineyards of the Côtes du Rhône run sporadically from Lyon down through Vienne (whose Pyramide is among the finest restaurants in Europe), the Côte Rôtie, Hermitage, Tain, to Tavel, Châteauneuf-du-Pape, and Avignon. It is fitting that the Rhône vineyards should make great wines since the valley is one of the routes by which the vine travelled up out of Greek and Roman Provence into Burgundy and the Rhineland. Even today this valley gives one the impression that it is still a feeler of the Roman south pushing its way northwards towards the countries of mist and Celts and Germans. The valley makes splendid wines which for some reason, and with the possible exception of Tavel *rosé*, have tended to lose popularity in 20th-century England. It is hard to see why this is so. The red wines are rich and strong and vigorous but to be at their best they must age and they will age for many years. Hermitage, for example, which is rough when young, with age becomes regal. The dry, white Hermitage also needs age to soften its initial roughness and then becomes a fine wine, although in my view the finest white wine of the Rhône valley is that which comes from a small and picturesque vineyard, Château Grillet, a few kilometres south of Vienne. It is a pale, white wine, dry, clean, scented, skilled and excellent, a vintage to which one can accurately apply the phrase 'a wine of beauty'. It is, alas, difficult to get (almost impossible in England), since its production is naturally very limited and one can only find it in a few of the best restaurants. If I were offered any vineyard in the world I would hesitate long before refusing Château Grillet. It may be nowadays that the fine and the rich wines from the terraced hillside vineyards of the Côte Rôtie and Hermitage as well as the big red wines from the rough, stony vineyards of Châteauneuf-du-Pape where the vines are unwired bushes, mostly unstaked, and where the yellow brown earth sticks to the fingers, are not allowed to age and thus achieve their proper distinction. If so, it is a pity for we are missing an experience.

We cannot be sure how long these wines were allowed to age in the 17th and 18th centuries though it would have been more at the end of the 18th than at the end of the 17th century. From 1690 onwards the first Earl of Bristol, who showed excellent taste in his choice of the greatest clarets, bought Hermitage and he continued buying Rhône wines until 1737. They must, therefore, have had some distinction. 'Hermitage Clarrett' must be a red or *rosé* wine: so perhaps was the 'Côte Rôty': and he had the good sense to buy eighteen gallons of 'white Coindrieux' from vineyards at Château Grillet. He may also have bought white as well as red Hermitage for, towards the end of the century, the white was more sought after than the red.

A gradual improvement in road communications and a growing use of the glass bottle enabled the English to extend their connoisseurship to the Burgundian wines of the Côte d'Or. But Upper Burgundy still remained the most landlocked of the great European vineyards. Its wines had to travel by road and the roads of the 18th century, though they were rapidly being salvaged from a state of incompetent medievalism, were variously quite good and quite impossible.[158] The amount of travel, and the urge to travel, were both increasing fast but the majority of country people before the Industrial Revolution were as localized as the East Anglian villagers who, in Celia Fiennes' irritated phrase, knew 'scarce 3 mile from their

[158] For English roads, see Celia Fiennes, *Journeys, passim*; and cf. *The Torrington Diaries*, eighty to a hundred years later, p. 91, etc. For France, cf. Brillat-Savarin, 323.

home'.[159] The localization of Burgundy wine had never of course been as complete as that of the East Anglian villager; it had travelled to Paris in the Middle Ages and to England in the Renaissance; but the difficulties of its transport can be seen from the fact that, apart from Paris, its greatest market was Belgium. The wines were taken northwards from Dijon on massive carts, some of which would carry fifteen barrels. Often they went in convoy, the first cart being decorated with a gigantic bouquet.[160] Apart from the natural hazards of the roads there were also the unnatural hazards of man, for a cask of burgundy in transit was often tapped, enjoyed, and topped up with water.[161] Nevertheless, in spite of all the difficulties, burgundy (and henceforward when I use the simple word burgundy I shall mean the wine of the Côte d'Or) continued to expand its foreign markets and to overcome both ignorance and caution.

There were times when the caution was justified. In the early 17th century the wines of Burgundy (and in this case the phrase probably meant both upper and lower Burgundy) were harsh, rough and sour, and St Evremond, writing towards the end of the same century, states that they have lost almost all 'their old Reputation with the Citizens'.[162] This lamentable result had probably been brought about by indifferent viniculture, partly no doubt to an over-planting of the Gamay grape, the 'disloyal Gamay', which may have satisfied the greed of the producer but not the taste of the client.

The great wines of the Côte de Nuits and the Côte de Beaune are now made principally from the Pinot noirien which is the same as the Pinot noir of Champagne. The great white wines, Meursault, Montrachet, and Corton-Charlemagne, are made principally from the Chardonnay. The Gamay does not give great wines. But there is another factor which one must take into account in all the later history of Burgundy, and it is characteristic of the viticulture of the Côte d'Or. This is the extreme division of the ownership of the vineyards. There are few singly owned 'Château' properties in the Côtes, Romanée-Conti and La Tâche being two of them. Mostly they are parcelled out between many owners: Clos Vougeot, for example, has thirty principal owners: Charmes, at Meursault, has thirty-two: Montrachet has eleven. To put this piecemeal ownership into more general terms one can go to the statistics of 1950: there were then 9,219 hectares of *appellation* and non-*appellation* vineyards in the Côte d'Or and they were divided between 19,079 *viticulteurs*.[163] It is not uncommon for the bigger proprietors to have a dozen or more parcels of vines in different vineyards of the Côte. Clearly this system tends to create differences, however slight, between the wine-making of one *vigneron* and that of another. This perhaps accounts for the apparent secrecy of the Burgundy vintage.

The Golden Slope in September is truly golden and the lovely fawn-coloured villages among the vines are drenched with sunshine. In the village streets, contemptuously resistant to the motor car, sleep the 'dust dogs' of the Côte d'Or. These animals are unique in my vineyard experience: they are hot and happy and, covered in dust from the vintaging lorries, are almost indistinguishable from the street on which they sleep. Their contented somnolence is typical of the lazy look of the Slope for, apart from the pickers in the vineyards, nothing appears to be happening. The fermentation in the Côte d'Or is for the most part tucked away in small barns

16th-century Goblets, Glasses and Ewers London, Victoria and Albert Museum

[159]Fiennes, *op. cit.*, 145.

[160]Rodier, 57-8.

[161]Arnoux, 47.

[162]Des Maizeaux, *Works of St. Evremond*, Vol. II, 97-8.

[163]Poupon et Forgeot, *Les Vins de Bourgogne*, 130, quoting the *Journal Officiel*.

and out-houses, some of them so small that there is scarcely room to climb into the vat between the top of the vat and the ceiling of the shed. It is a private, personal and family business, this making of wine on the Golden Slope and, although perhaps I am prejudiced, I think that they can make the finest red wine in the world. The great burgundies do not have the subtlety, nor the variety, of the fine clarets but to drink the generous, mellow strength of a great red burgundy is to experience the soul of wine. If a man who has never drunk wine wants to understand what all the fuss is about, give him a glass of great burgundy; unless he is a barbarian he will understand. If he wants to feel in his blood the history of wine, give him claret; it will take him time but he will grow into the history.

This multiple ownership of the Burgundy vineyards existed to some extent in the early 18th century and, when each small proprietor made his own wine, the sins of the maker were visited upon the client. But the conditions of wine-making then did not basically differ from those which are observed today and the skilled proprietor could have made a welcome wine. There is no doubt that he did so. St Evremond's view was not long maintained and even in the early 18th century burgundy was not only bought by connoisseurs but was beginning to be classified. By the last quarter of the century it was considered, as was champagne, to be 'made with more care than any other French *Wines*' and it was then 'generally imported pure'.[164]

In England it was a wine for men of taste and fashion. They not only stocked it in their cellars but expected to find it when they went out on a frolic. At the Rose in 1691, 'Where the Beau's and the Sparks with their Mistresses Feast',[165] there was Burgundy wine and seventy years later it was the second most expensive wine on the menu at the Vauxhall Pleasure Gardens.[166] In the early 18th century the Earl of Bristol buys Burgundy, though not a great deal, and in this case it seems to have been chiefly to satisfy a woman of taste and fashion since one entry in the cellar account records '12 flasks of Burgundy wine "for dear wife"'. It was expensive for it cost 6/- a bottle, as dear as the burgundy sold retail at Vauxhall. The prices which the Earl paid were usually higher than those which he paid for the finest clarets though white burgundy was much cheaper. The interesting thing about the cellar accounts is that they show the beginnings in England of a classification of the growths of the Côte d'Or. Among the entries which merely name it 'Burgundy' are others which name it by its vineyard: 'St George-wine' (Nuits-St Georges) or 'White Muljo Burgundy' (Meursault).[167] This classification was, not unnaturally, more precise at Versailles in 1782 where Louis XVI had 'Chambertin, Romanée S. Vincent' (Romanée Saint-Vivant?) 'Tache' (La Tâche), 'Richebourg' and 'Vougeot', all of them from the Côte de Nuits, and 'Beaune' from the Côte de Beaune.[168]

We can see the differences, and the likenesses, between the 18th century and modern Burgundy wines in the picture which is given to us by Sir Edward Barry, writing in 1775, and Arthur Young, writing in 1792. The classification is becoming more precise and more or less modern in pattern but we may be surprised at the ageing frailty of some of the wines. Sir Edward Barry divides them up into 'Wines de Garde' and 'primeurs'. As the Wines de Garde, those which should be allowed to age, he names Nuits and Chambertin, of which Chambertin was generally

The Wedding of Sir Henry Unton, 1597
Anonymous
London, National Portrait Gallery

[164] Barry, *op. cit.*, 422.

[165] Ames, *A Farther Search after Claret*, 16.

[166] Wroth, *op. cit.*, 298–9.

[167] Hervey Cellar, *passim*. See Walpole Cellar, 201, for Sir Robert Walpole's stocks of Burgundy.

[168] Archives Nationales, Paris, MS., O1.793.

Rowlandson, Thomas
from the 'Comforts of
Bath', 1798
London, British Museum

thought, he says, to be the best wine of Burgundy. The wines of Nuits were of deep velvet colour and should be kept until their second, third, fourth or fifth year. This is not really long enough for a great red burgundy. Of the 'primeurs' he names 'Volnet', 'Pomard' and 'Chassagne'. None of the 'primeurs', he says, would last more than two years except Chassagne which would live for three or four. Volnay would only last for one year. And though they are still lightish wines which mature quickly, some of them will nowadays age for much longer than a year. They were then 'in colour a little deeper than the *eye of a partridge*'. Pommard, on the other hand, was then 'of the colour of fire' and although Volnay wines are still lighter coloured than those of Pommard, both of them are darker than they were in the 18th century.[169] Arthur Young expounds his classification with an almost medieval richness of orthography. 'Clos de Veaujeau', he says, was the most famous vineyard of Burgundy whose wine sold at the highest price, both its red and its white wine being equal in quality and cost. (It still makes a small amount of white wine at Clos Blanc de Vougeot.) Of the other growths of 'Nuys', whose productivity was never great, he lists 'St George, Romané, La Tashe, de Vaume' (Vosne) 'Richebourg, Chambertin, and Côte roté'. The last name may be a mistaken inclusion of the wines of the Côte Rôtie among the wines of the Côte d'Or, or it may have been a local name for one of the vineyards in, perhaps, Vosne. At 'Beaume' (the Côte de Beaune) he lists as the finest wines 'after the *Clos de Veaujeau* . . . Volny, Pomar, Aloes' (Aloxe), 'Beaume, Savigné' (Savigny-les-Beaune), 'Mulso' (Meursault – this is the Earl of Bristol's 'Muljo') 'and Maureauché . . .' (Montrachet). By the time of the French Revolution the classification of the Côte d'Or was becoming modern.[170]

Clos de Vougeot, like the other clerical vineyards, was confiscated by the revolutionaries and the last cellarer of the Abbey, which had owned the Clos since the

[169] Barry, *op. cit.*, 430, 432–3.

[170] Arthur Young, *Travels in France*, Vol. II, Ch. x, 16, 17. For Modern Burgundy, see Rodier; Poupon et Forgeot, Lichine, *Wines of France*, etc.

Middle Ages, had a name which seems to ring out from the disappearing past. He was called Dom Goblet. His departure symbolically marks the end of medievalism in wine-making, but long before he departed the scene was being shifted towards modernity by the efforts of a new type of wine merchant. It is in this century that the wine-shipper begins to assume his modern form and it is to these men that we must give much of the credit for the classification of growths and the maturing of vintages. In the Côte d'Or whose export trade in wine had for a time been largely in the hands of Belgians, commercial houses were being founded in the middle of the 18th century and the Burgundians themselves started to take over the marketing of their own wines. In Bordeaux the Château wines had asserted their individuality and the trade in Bordeaux wines had expanded greatly as a result of its exports to America and the French Colonies. An inevitable consequence was a growing commercial organization. In Cognac the great shipping houses were being founded: Martell in 1705, Ranson and Delamain in 1725, and Hennessy in 1765. In Jerez and Cadiz, shipping businesses were being founded by both the Spaniards and the British: Harvey by 1780, de la Riva at the middle of the century, and Duff Gordon in 1772, while in 1792 an energetic young man called George Sandeman, who had interests in Oporto as well as in Jerez, was selling Sherry in the British Isles. In Oporto, Crofts, then Phayre and Bradleys, Taylor, Fladgate, and Yeatman (then Bearsley), Koepke (established as general merchants as early as the middle of the 17th century), Warre's (then Clark) in 1718 and, towards the end of the century in 1790, George Sandeman. In north-western Europe the same double commercial process of discrimination and expansion was at work. In the Rhineland, brokers began to travel through the wine-growing areas picking out the most likely wines which would fetch the best prices. In Champagne, many of the world famous shippers set up their houses in the 18th century: Ruinart in 1729, Moët et Chandon in 1743, Lanson in 1750, Veuve Cliquot in 1783 and Heidsieck in 1785. The thirst of the world was being organized.

Augustan Eating

So, also, was the gastronomy of Europe. In the 1760s the restaurant was invented in Paris, some suppose by a man called Boulanger in the rue des Poulies, while others give the honour to Roze and Pontaillé who began in the rue des Poulies but moved to the rue Saint-Honoré.[171] There had, of course, been eating houses before this date. In all the larger towns of France, at the turn of the 17th and 18th centuries, there were *auberges* where one could eat at a fixed hour and at a fixed price. These, however, were really in the class of the 'ordinarys' which in general had neither the range of dishes nor the fixed price per dish that were characteristic of the later restaurant. England had at least two famous ordinarys, Pontack's, run by a Frenchman, and Locket's, both in London and both famous for their luxurious cuisine. Ames, in the middle of his diatribe against quack vintners, praises Locket for his 'Ortland' (? ortolan) 'Dainties' and 'rich Champaign', an almost Edwardian menu. Defoe describes Pontack's as 'a constant ordinary for all comers at very reasonable prices' but a meal at Pontack's could cost as much as two guineas a head, a sum whose equivalent few of us could imagine paying in these days. It would

[171] Andrieu, *Fine Bouche*, 20 sq.

Engraved Dickenson, after
H. Bunbury
A Chop House
mid 18th century

appear to have become more fashionable and more expensive until it was pulled down in 1780.[172] For the most part an Englishman who went out to eat went into a Cook Shop where he chose the meat he wanted while it was still upon the spit and ate it upon the premises. All classes who could afford it went to these Cook Shops when they felt so inclined and there, for a shilling, could eat themselves full. The fare which they provided was usually only meat, of which there was a choice, bread and beer.[173] They were the origin of the 18th-century chop-houses such as Betty's and Dolly's, or Dolly's Steak-house in Paternoster Row which was patronized by Boswell who was not averse to what, on another occasion, he called 'a jolly profusion of smoking, juicy beef-steaks'.[174] The ordinarys and the beef-steak-houses may have lacked the refinements of French cooking but they suited the English taste and they were not all as depressing as some travellers considered them. Woodforde, when he dined at the Ordinary at the King's Head, Norwich, on June 1st, 1787, had 'fryed soals', boiled beef, a Pudding, and a fore-quarter of lamb with cucumber and lettuce. For this snack he paid a shilling. Torrington, in 1785, did in fact complain of the 'same dull round of "mutton and beef for steaks . . . fowls and ducks . . . veal for cutlets . . ." ', adding that French inns did not suffer from this lack of imagination. On the other hand, in 1789, he and his friends had a 'fowl . . . with a large quantity of thick beef steaks, flank'd by a stack of asparagus, each one foot in height', which, he remarked, 'satisfied me: (who had not eaten for two hours)'.[175] In his travels Torrington found a number of good English inns but his good fortune, or his cleverness, was not always shared by other voyagers.

As we might expect, the standard of English cooking varied a great deal. Moritz, who probably lacked both good fortune and cleverness, at least in the matter of gastronomy, laments in 1782: 'An English dinner, to persons in my situation, generally consists of a piece of half boiled, or half roasted, meat and a few cabbage

[172] Ames, *A Farther Search after Claret*, 9; Misson, *op. cit.*, 147; Ned Ward, *The Quack-Vintners*, 21.

[173] Misson, *op. cit.*, 146–7; cf. Boswell, *London Journal*, 86 (he liked it).

[174] Boswell, *London Journal*, 86, 154, etc.; *The Connoisseur*, No. 19 of June 6th, 1754.

[175] *Torrington Diaries*, 98, 202.

leaves, boiled in plain water; on which they pour a sauce made of flour and butter, the usual method of dressing vegetables in England'; the coffee which he found in England was also a dismal thing, most frequently brown water. Neither of these complaints is totally inapplicable today. But he found compensations: excellent wheat bread, good butter and Cheshire cheese and, above all, the 'incomparably good' buttered toast.[176] Another Gothic traveller did confess that, at Kelso, he 'suffered considerably from the vast columns of smoke and fumes of whiskey' at the local inn, but he cheerfully adds that he and his friend were given 'a very decent apartment, and supped on excellent steaks of ribs of beef, and pickled cabbage'.[177] James Woodforde (whose enchanting *Diary* is, for the gastronome, a combined bedside book and nightmare) once dined 'at the Chaplains table . . . upon a roasted Tongue and Udder' and wrote down the sage memorandum, 'N.B. I shall not dine on a roasted Tongue and Udder again very soon'.[178] For most of his life, however, the good parson ate well and I cannot resist quoting the dinner which he ordered for Christmas Day at New College, Oxford: they had

'two fine Codds boiled with fryed Souls (sic) round them and oyster sauce, a fine sirloin of Beef roasted, some peas soup and an orange Pudding for the first course, for the second, we had a lease of Wild Ducks rosted, a fore Qu: of Lamb and Sallad and mince Pies. . . .'[179]

The diet of all but the poorest of English was bread, meat and puddings. Of these three, bread was the least, and meat the most, important. The favourite was beef, followed by mutton, while rabbits filled in many a hungry corner. A certain quantity of vegetables accompanied the meat, though not always and not to a very much greater extent than in Elizabethan times. A certain amount of fruit was also eaten, much more in fact than has often been supposed: and here one might remark that the idea of the Englishman being, throughout his history, an exclusive carnivore has a great deal of truth but also some exaggeration. Fish was not at all uncommon on the English menu though, after meat, the most popular dish was the pudding. Basically it was either what we would call a plum-duff or a suet pudding, but there were innumerable variants of this twin theme. Sometimes it was boiled with meat, sometimes put into the belly of a roasted pike, and sometimes it was '. . . a baked plumb Pudding of the Custard Kind. . . .'[180]

The English were massive, but not gigantic, eaters. At their dinner, in the middle of the day, they ate largely but their supper was usually moderate and their breakfast frugal. The 'English breakfast' of bacon and eggs was not an invention of the Georgians; instead they had tea, and sometimes cocoa or chocolate, toast, bread and butter, and honey.[181] The poorest, of course, had none of these refinements and they had to subsist on much the same diet as the medieval poor. In the Lake District, they ate clap bread, butter, cheese and beer.[182] As a drink, milk was not an uncommon alternative in the northern parts of the kingdom, while in the West Country the countryman's can was filled with cider. For those of even moderate means there were many delicacies. There was potted venison, potted char from Windermere (sometimes with sweet spices), cured woodcocks, lampreys, pickled mushrooms, and pickled oysters. There were also, for the more affluent palates,

[176] Mavor, *op. cit.*, Vol. IV. Moritz, 14.

[177] J. A. Andersen (Feldborg), *A Dane's Excursions*, Vol. II, 6–7, dating early 19th century.

[178] Feb. 17th, 1763.

[179] Dec. 25th, 1773.

[180] See for example, Misson, *op. cit.*, 313–16; Woodforde, *Diary, passim*; but in particular July 24th, 1767, Nov. 13th, 1769, June 4th, 1777, Oct. 21st, 1779, Nov. 25th, 1784, June 12th, 1787, and Oct. 31st, 1787; also Torrington, *passim*.

[181] Andersen (Feldborg), *op. cit.*, Vol. I, 199; Woodforde, *op. cit.*, Jan. 2nd, 1775, Apr. 10th, 1775; Turberville, *op. cit.*, 342–3.

[182] Fiennes, *op. cit.*, 196.

The 'Table d'Hôte'
early 19th century
André Simon Collection

'ruffs and rees' which came from the Fen country of East Anglia and were fattened up and sold at a high price to the London market.[183]

Both in England and in France the 'genteel' time for dinner was between two and three o'clock in the afternoon while supper was a late meal, sometimes at nine but more usually at ten or eleven at night. Country people, who were not of the gentry, tended to keep earlier hours. William Hickey, in a rather condescending account of a visit to a middle-class household at Chelsea, says 'we dined at one, drank tea at five, and supped at half-past eight, retiring to our respective bed-chambers rather before ten'. 'Provincials' in France had their dinner at midday. As the century went on, the times of dining and supping came later in both countries, the most fashionable time for dinner in England being towards five and in Paris towards six o'clock. Supper was very late indeed in fashionable England, and in Paris it finally disappeared and was replaced by a midday *déjeuner* as the other meal of the day. Thus the hours of fashion in Paris at the beginning of the 19th century reverted to what they had been for the nobility under Louis XIV.[184]

The system of serving up a meal remained much the same in England as it had been at the Renaissance. Each of the two or more courses of a dinner was composed of a number of assorted dishes of different foods and, generally speaking, instead of progression there was replacement. To use a somewhat involved simile, the Georgian dinner was like the rounds of a boxing match whereas the modern dinner is like the acts of a play. This is generally, but only generally true, for, particularly

[183]Fiennes, *op. cit.*, fn. 1, 74, fn. 13, 148, 191; Houghton, *Collection*, Vol. IV, 112-13, 265-71, *et passim*; *The Pastry-Cook's Vade Mecum*, 46; Torrington, *op. cit.*, 352-3.

[184]Hickey, Quennell's edn, 174; Woodforde, *op. cit.*, Aug. 21st, 1768; Brillat Savarin, *op. cit.*, 70, 357; Turberville, *op. cit.*, 343-6; Franklin, *Vie privée d'autrefois*, Vol. 8, 109-20.

374

in France, some idea of development was being introduced into the meal. Another custom which had lasted over from the Renaissance was that of leaving the wine and the glasses on a serving-table or sideboard from which a guest could call for a drink when he wanted it. Once again there were exceptions to this custom but it persisted in France until the middle of the 18th century and the modern habit of putting glasses and bottles, or decanters, on the table during a meal was not common until just before the French Revolution. There were exceptions in England too but any serious drinking was done after a meal when the women left the dining-room and resigned themselves to a later meeting with their unsteady consorts.

On the whole the manners of the French were in advance of those of the English but the influence of France on the English table, and further afield, extended only to fashionable circles. Some aristocrats employed a French chef and a few went so far as to seek out the finest, or the most famous, chef and to import special delicacies, such as Périgord pie from France which Lady Anne Millar recognized at a Court Ball at Caserta in 1771 where also 'the Coffee room was furnished like the Coffee Houses of Paris precisely'. But the robust, insular and commonsensical stomachs of the majority of Englishmen regarded French cooking with a mixture of pity and terror. It is amusing to see that, even then, at the beginning of the 18th century the English had already assumed some of their traditional attitudes towards the French. With great pleasure and equal inaccuracy they imagined that the French lived miserably with starvation at their elbow and that when they did eat they ate nothing but herbs and roots. In fact the French ate plentifully and used less 'Herbs, Pulse, and Roots' than the English. But the English liked their prejudice and they cherished it; it persisted as a stock theme with the cartoonists; and insofar as the poorest classes of each country were concerned the English may well have been right.[185]

They may also have confused the issue by confusing herbs and spices. English taste had become much plainer since the days of Queen Elizabeth and though they did not ignore spices they used them with less overwhelming enthusiasm. During the reign of Louis XIV the French, on the other hand, were much addicted to the use of both perfumes and spices in their cooking, a preference which lasted until towards the end of the 17th century and which may have continued a legendary existence in the determined imagination of the Island Race. Rose water, musk, and ambergris were commonly used in the fashionable cuisine of France.[186]

Louis XIV was a great eater and his august example was not ignored by his subjects. The food of the Grand Siècle consisted very largely of *ragoûts*, or varieties of stew. Soups were very popular, far more so than in England. Lavarenne in his *Cuisinier François*, which was published in 1651 and republished in 1653, mentions 120 soups, one of which was made of eggs, raspberries and milk. Asparagus, artichokes, mushrooms and truffles were also popular as were *Nulles* which were sweet and scented custards, and sometimes garnished with flowers. One of Lavarenne's sauces, the *Sauce poivrade*, gives some indication of the taste of the time: it was made of vinegar, salt, onion or spring onion, lemon rind and pepper.[187]

One small but important difference in the *cuisines* of the two countries – the use of wine in cooking – can be noticed in this general period and it has persisted ever since. For one example, among the accounts of the Office of the Ordinary of the King in March 1768, we find a purchase from the royal wine merchants of '*vin de*

[185] Franklin, *op. cit.*, Vol. 6, 106, 110; Turberville, *op. cit.*, 345; Misson, *op. cit.*, 125, 313-16; Woodforde, *op. cit.*, Aug. 28th, 1783; Acton, *The Bourbons of Naples*, 154.

[186] Franklin, *op. cit.*, Vol. III, 128-30; cf. Brillat-Savarin, 373 sq.

[187] François-Pierre de la Varenne, *Le Cuisinier François*, 2nd edn, 1652, 91, 99, 117-18, 179, 265, 270-1.

'The National Contrast',
c 1780
André Simon Collection

poisson'. It would have made less onerous than they already were the theoretical austerities of fish days and days of fasting.[188]

The outstanding pre-eminence of France as a nation of gourmets began towards the end of the 17th century and triumphed in the early decades of the 18th century. One of the signs of its beginning was the creation, as early as the middle of the 17th century, of one of the first 'Wine and Food Societies' of Western Europe. This was the Ordre des Côteaux, among whose members were (apparently) St Evremond and (certainly) his correspondent the Count d'Olonne, and all of whom prided themselves on their niceness of taste. St Evremond reacts strongly against the popularity of the *ragoûts* and admonishes d'Olonne: 'Look upon all . . . kitchen compositions, call'd Ragous, or Kick-shaws, to be little better than Poison. . . .' They will, he says, ruin the taste by their inclusion of pepper, vinegar, and onions. He prefers the simplest sauces and for seasoning recommends salt and orange as the most general, but 'Fine Herbs' as being more wholesome and 'more exquisite than Spices'.[189]

By the reign of Louis XV the gourmet view of eating had definitely established itself. In 1739 when François Marin produced his *Dons de Comus, ou les Délices de la Table* we already have an anticipation of the 'scientific gastronomy' of Brillat-Savarin. The approach is almost entirely modern as are some of the menus in 1740 collected by Brillat-Savarin himself.[190] One menu is particularly interesting since it shows that the *service russe*, that is to say the modern progression of a meal's courses which is commonly supposed to have been introduced into England about 1860, already existed in France a hundred years earlier.

[188] Archives Nationales, Paris, O1.793 (104).

[189] Boileau-Despreaux, *Satires*, Satire III; Des Maizeaux, *Works of St. Evremond*, Vol. I, 19; Vol. II, 98 sq.

[190] Franklin, *op. cit.*, 205–6, see especially the preface to the *Dons de Comus*, written by two Jesuits; Brillat-Savarin, fn. I, 315.

Gronow, whose reminiscences reflect the manners and tastes of a generation earlier than his own, mentions the restaurant Brinvilliers in the rue de Richelieu, which was 'far superior to any restaurant of our day and the wines were first-rate'. Brinvilliers was celebrated for his *suprême de volaille* and his *côtelette à la Soubise*. That this sophistication was little emulated in England is evident from his gloomy account of 'a grand dinner' at which 'the universally adored and ever popular boiled potato was eaten with everything'. Gronow is insular enough to consider our vegetables 'the best in the world' though 'they were never honoured by an accompanying sauce and generally came to the table cold'. The Clarendon Hotel, he says, was 'the only public hotel at which you get a genuine French dinner and for which you seldom paid less than three or four pounds, your bottle of Champagne or Claret costing you a guinea'. One wonders what happened to that 'miserable-looking' public house at Eastbourne where Hickey had 'as fine a dish of fish as ever was seen at Billingsgate, with excellent lobster and oyster sauces . . . followed by a pair of tender well-dressed chickens . . . and good old Cheshire cheese'. This, with two bottles of claret, cost eighteen pence a piece, including the wine. Unless there was something wrong with Hickey's arithmetic by the end of that dinner, the miserable-looking public house could not have been making much profit. On another occasion, however, 'at the Royal Hotel in Pall Mall', a dinner for fifteen people cost him 'rather more than forty pounds' which is much nearer to the Clarendon's prices in 1814.[191]

However much the delicacy of the French taste may have increased, the vigour of the French appetite was unimpaired. Oysters were much eaten in both France and England (Woodforde records a payment of 1/6d. - about 15/- modern - for eighty oysters), and they were sometimes eaten in quantities which make the normal modern performance look merely effeminate. At Versailles in 1798 Brillat-Savarin resolved to do justice to an acquaintance of his, Laperte, who was a profound admirer of the shell-fish. Brillat-Savarin managed to eat three dozen but Laperte was stopped at his thirty-second dozen and then only because his host wanted to get on with the dinner.[192] At the other extreme of this type of gastronomy were the Viennese in 1717 who were so fond of oysters that they had them sent from Venice and ate them 'very greedily, stink or not stink'.[193] The double jewel in the crown of French gastronomy was considered by Brillat-Savarin to be the truffled turkey and to ennoble those who shared his view he coined the titles *Dindoniphiles* and *Truffivores*.[194] We may agree with both of his titles though not with both sides of his choice.

The increasing attention paid to the quality of the food and the service of the meals is important, not only because it shows the taste of the time but because it is paralleled, as one would expect, by an increasing attention paid to the quality and the service of the wines. When Lady Mary Wortley Montagu was in Vienna in 1716 she noted that the dinners of the 'first people of quality' were served on dishes of silver or of the finest china. But the thing which surprised her was the great variety of wines served at these dinners - often as many as eighteen different wines - and that a list giving the names of the wines was laid, together with the napkins, upon the plates of the guests.[195] A little over a hundred years later one of the modern rules for the serving of wines was formulated, or at least published, by

[191] Gronow, *op. cit.*, Vol. I, 51–74; Hickey, *op. cit.*, Ed. Quennell, 207-8.

[192] Brillat-Savarin, 104; Woodforde, *op. cit.*, Oct. 20th, 1785.

[193] Lady Mary Wortley Montagu, *Letters*, Jan. 1st, OS., 1717, from Vienna.

[194] Brillat-Savarin, 91–3, 108-13.

[195] Lady Mary Wortley Montagu, *op. cit.*, Sept. 8th, OS., 1716.

Oporto
engraving from C. Seller,
'Oporto old and new'
London, 1899

Brillat-Savarin who pronounced that the progression of the wines at a meal '*soit des plus lampants au plus parfumés*'.[196] Eccentricities did, however, occur, since at Hamburg in the 1770s where it was the custom for the rich, even at ordinary meals, to have a particular wine for each course, the wines selected were 'Malaga for fresh beans and fresh herrings, Burgundy with fresh peas, Champagne with oysters, Port or Madeira with costly salted fish'.[197] These permutations must often have produced dreams of a truly Gothic magnitude.

Georgian Port: the Legend and the Facts

The correspondence between the food which a country eats and the wine which it prefers to drink is seen at its most striking in 18th-century England. The amount of port drunk by the Georgian English has become legendary and when one remembers that most of it was a coarse, rough, heavy wine one may wonder how it became the English national drink. The reason for their drinking it in quantity is of course partly political since the customs duties were loaded in its favour; but the reason for their drinking it with liking, and even with fervour, is due to the fact that their diet was highly carnivorous. The heavy groundwork of meat called out for a deluge of strong wine and the call was abundantly answered. Add to this a loyalty to intoxication and the reasoning is completed. There is no doubt at all that they drank for effect and not for taste. Dr Johnson himself admitted that it was not the flavour but the effect which he desired, although at one time in his life he did try to amend the taste of his port wine by pouring into it a syrup called capillaire.[198] Such was the story and it may well be true for the good Doctor was no gourmet although in this instance he may have been showing sound common sense since the quality of 18th-century port was frequently lamentable.

Port is now, and for a century and a half has been, one of the great wines, and it fully deserves its title. To see how it became what it is, and why its early career was so troubled, we have to look backwards from its modern definition. Modern port

[196] Brillat-Savarin, 198.

[197] Friedlaender, *Darstellungen aus der Sittengeschichte Roms*, trs. Freese, and Magnus, 7th edn, *Roman Life and Manners*, Vol. II, 162.

[198] Boswell, *Life of Johnson*, edn of 1831, Vol. I, 481–2.

is grown in a legally limited area of the Douro, some forty to eighty miles up the Douro river from Oporto. It can be a red or a white wine, although most port is red. It is fortified with grape brandy. It is blended at Vila Nova de Gaia, on the other side of the Douro from the city of Oporto. It is matured in cask or in bottle. It is a product of care, skill, and art. In its earliest history it was none of these things and much early 18th-century port was not even grown along the Douro.

The wine trade between England and Portugal goes back into medieval times but the wines that were shipped out of Portugal were seldom, if ever, wines of the Douro. They were mostly from the Minho in the north or from Lisbon. Towards the end of the 17th century the trade between England and Portugal was 'triangular': ships sailed from England to Newfoundland where they caught fish: from Newfoundland they sailed to Portugal (and Spain) where they sold their fish, bought wine, and sailed back to England. The English traders who were resident in Portugal were general merchants, wine being only one of the commodities which they handled. At this period there were indeed vineyards of the Douro but they were not big and they were not many and when we come across 'Port' in England at this time it is more likely to mean Portuguese wine than port wine.[199]

The movement towards port wine began in the last decades of the 17th century. The 'triangular' trade was sometimes, so it would appear, direct, as it had been in the Middle Ages. English factors were resident in the north of Portugal at Monção, at the port of Viana do Castelo, and in a lesser degree at Oporto itself. It is at this time that 'Port' occurs with a sudden and increasing frequency in English records and it seems to me quite clear that the word covers Portuguese wine in general as well as wine shipped out of Oporto. In the Customs Accounts of 1697-8, for example, there are entries for 'Portugall wine' and for 'Port' whereas four years earlier an English writer specifically refers to 'Portoport' which he describes as 'a very strong Bodied Wine . . . but not very Palatable, and therefore not so much drunk as other wines'.[200] This latter is clearly ordinary wine from the Douro, that is to say, Douro port wine before it became modern. The other imports of both red and white port which occur at this time may be wines from anywhere in Portugal and they will not necessarily have been shipped out of North Portuguese ports.[201]

The position then at the end of the 17th and the beginning of the 18th century was this: a prohibition on the import of French wines into England meant that a good deal of claret was shipped from Bordeaux to Oporto whence it was shipped to England as Wine of Portugal or Oporto Wine, or 'Port'. The prohibition also favoured the legitimate trade in Portuguese wines but none of these, with the possible exception of Colares, was really full-bodied. While they were acceptable to the English market few of them were strong enough to satisfy the robust inclinations of the country squire. The strongest natural (unfortified) wine in Portugal is natural Douro wine which is now, of course, never drunk outside Portugal. It is still drunk domestically on the Douro and very good it is. But it is not a great wine and it is not port. It is a first class *vin ordinaire*, strong, full bodied, vigorous with a trace in it of 'Douro burn', dry, full of alcohol, and almost black in colour. This is what port would be if port were not fortified, blended or matured. I have a particular liking for it and I should like to be able to drink it in England. I have been

[199]Gairdner, *Henry VIII*, Add., Vol. I, Pt I, No. 526; *Cal. State Papers Dom*, Vol. 1595-7, 172; Vol. 1653-4, 81; Ralph Davis, 'Merchant Shipping in the Economy of the Late Seventeenth Century', *Economic History Review*, 2nd Series, Vol. IX, No. 1, Aug. 1956, 59 sq.; Sellers, *Oporto, Old and New*, passim, but in particular 113-14.

[200]Public Records Office, London, Cust., 3, 1, Pt I; Salmon, *English Physician*, 926.

[201]For red and white port, see Bedford Cellar, passim; Ames, *Search after Claret, Farther Search after Claret*, passim; TR, VI, 413 sq. See also Cockburn, *Port Wine and Oporto*, 97.

lucky enough to have had sent to me from the Douro some bottles of this natural red wine from one of the finest *quintas*; for six months it kept all its vigour and flavour; then it began to lose its distinction and was either unwilling to begin ageing or was entering upon a troublesome adolescence. I have cited this personal experience because the 'port' that was drunk by the early Georgians, when it did come from the Douro and not from somewhere else in Portugal, was this natural, unfortified, heavy *vin ordinaire*.

Basically it was a wine that would satisfy the cold and carnivorous English squire. But only basically for in its early days it was badly made and was a coarse drink whose only merit lay in its power to produce stupefaction. A coincidence of English taste and English politics gave it the necessary impetus towards a great future.

As early as 1654 British merchants had been allowed an especially favoured position inside Portugal. The Treaty of Commerce made by John Methuen in 1703 merely extended the existing dominance of British traders. It provided that English cloth should be allowed into Portugal and that Portuguese wines should be allowed into Great Britain on the payment of a customs duty a third less than that paid on wines from France. Encouraged by the British shippers, who were steadily moving down from Viana and the north and basing themselves on Oporto, the Douro vineyards began to expand to meet what the shippers hoped would be a vast increase in trade.

They were not immediately right. The import of Portuguese wine into England increased, but not dramatically; then six years after the Treaty it fell, and it fell drastically. The reason was undoubtedly the bad quality of the natural Douro wines, made with speed and carelessness for a market that was ready to welcome them and forced to reject them. It was at this point that the invention of modern port became essential to the energetic merchants of Oporto.

Modern port wine is made by the addition of grape brandy to the fermenting must. This dose of brandy stops the fermentation and prevents all the sugar in the must from fermenting out into alcohol. The wine is then in a condition to be blended, to become mellow, and to mature. This technique was invented in the 18th, though it was not perfected until the 19th, century. We cannot be certain who did invent it but we can, I think, be certain that he invented it for the wrong reason. It was not fortified to retain some of its sugar but to enable it to maintain even a vestige of life after the rigours of the voyage to England. The brandy, a very small dose, was not added during but after fermentation, and it was hoped that it would both preserve and disguise the wine.

This is a somewhat contentious view and there are many who hold that port was first invented for the right reason and that brandy was put in to stop the ferment. I do not think this is so. When one has read the wine-making manuals of earlier centuries, going back from the 17th century to the Renaissance, it is made clear that the fortification technique was certainly widely known and almost certainly widely used. Its use was merely to keep the wine in condition and to prevent it from turning sour. The spirits were put into the wine after fermentation, and very often after shipment, and they literally fulfilled their name of *eaux de vie* since they were the strong waters that kept the wine alive. The practice, and the reason for the practice, continue throughout the 18th and into the beginning of the 19th century.

In 1785 de Secondat tells us that some of the wines of Guienne were fortified with brandy which, he adds, foreign customers were supposed to prefer to the natural wine. John Wright in 1795 records that 'It hath been, and is still the practice in Porto, to complete the batching or mixtures of all their red wine with Portuguese Brandy'. His additional comment is that 'Brandy . . . is . . . absolutely necessary to make small or bad wines keep'. A printed cellar book among the papers of the third Viscount Gage at the turn of the 18th century instructs the 'Butler's Assistant' that poor red port should be improved with the addition of brandy and that the best method of 'managing' claret 'is to feed it every two or three weeks with a pint or two of French brandy'. This manual, which throws a rather startling light on the drinking habits of the time, adds among its other instructions that 'Bucella' wine, a 'tender wine', 'should be fed with a little brandy, for, if kept in a place that is either too hot or too cold, it will be in danger of turning foul'.[202]

Towards the end of the century Douro wine was fulfilling two of the conditions of modern port. It was being blended or, to use John Wright's words, batched and mixed, and it was being matured. That these practices, which have been normal in Vila Nova de Gaia since Victorian times, were in use in the late 18th century does not mean that they were universal. Indeed it is clear that they were not. A great deal of the port that was drunk in Britain in the 1790s was only a year old.[203] On the other hand, the advantage of maturity was widely recognized; Wright himself, neither an original nor an imaginative writer, lays down the law about it and concludes that good, well-kept port tends towards perfection when it has been three to five years in wood and one to three years in bottle; Torrington, a plain and pungent commentator who drank port habitually, remarks that pleasure is much destroyed by drinking port when only a year in bottle and because of his travels through England he spoke from experience; from the 1740s onwards the designation 'Old Red Port' is not exceptional and the fact that both shippers and customers recognized the value of maturity makes it certain that the better shippers, of whom there were many, endeavoured honestly to please their customers in this respect.[204]

Their efforts to uphold and to increase the good name of port were only too often vitiated by the avarice of their less reputable colleagues in Portugal and the dishonesty of their competitors in England. The adulteration and counterfeiting of port wine became a minor industry of considerable scope. It was resented by the discriminating, tolerated by the masses, and it continued to prosper. In his *Farewell to Wine* (1693) Ames speaks of being offered a 'Red Port' 'so spiritless and flat' with

> '. . . as many different tastes
> As can be found in Compound pastes
> In Lumber pye or soporifrous Methridate.'[205]

Obviously this 'Wine from Portugal' never saw the Douro. In 1775 Sir Edward Barry notes that '. . . large quantities of *nominal Port* Wines are made' in England 'without any *Port* Wine in them'.[206] As late as 1844 Baron Forrester, that doughty defender of pure wine, fulminated against the faking and adulteration of port in Portugal itself.[207] One of the commonest adulterations during this century and a half was the use of elderberries to colour the wine; another and not uncommon

[202] de Secondat, *op. cit.*, 89; John Wright, *Essay on Wines*, 20–1; see also *Ibid*, 14, 21; Account Book, etc., of the 3rd Viscount Gage; Cellar Book, 'A New and Complete Cellar Book of The Butler's Assistant, by James Farley', 2nd edn, 1846, 3.

[203] John Wright, *op. cit.*, 14, 43; TR, VII, 353.

[204] John Wright, *Ibid*, 30; Torrington, *op. cit.*, 211; TR, VII, 358 sq.

[205] Ames, *Bacchanalian Sessions*, 21–2.

[206] Barry, *op. cit.*, 440.

[207] Forrester, J. J., *Wine Trade of Portugal*, 3 sq.

form of artistry was to blend Benecarlo, now Benicarlos, a thick, strong, red wine from the Province of Valencia in eastern Spain into 'thin, pale Port', a trick that was also performed in the 18th century with claret.[208]

The fight against adulteration was a hundred years' war fought out inside Portugal. The first great battle was the formation in 1756 of the Companhia Geral, or the General Company of Agriculture of the Wines of the Alto Douro, a monopoly company set up by the Portuguese ostensibly to improve the quality of port wine and the conditions of the port wine growers, but deeply motivated all the same by jealousy of English dominance in the port wine trade. Being a monopoly, with power to accept or reject the wines grown in the Douro vineyards, it was only natural that its workings should have been lubricated with bribery. The British merchants hated it but their self-righteous condemnation of its aims and activities was sometimes open to the charge of intellectual dishonesty. However misconceived the Company may have been in its creation and however corrupt in its dealings, some of the British merchants were themselves no candidates for sainthood and in fact the Company did help forward the proper development of port wine. One of its better acts was officially to define the limits of the Douro *vignoble* in which, and only in which, port wine could be made. On the whole, however, it was a restrictive nuisance rather than a wise discipline and the great magnificence of port wine was brought about by the skill of English shippers and at a time when the Company had disappeared.

The second great battle against adulteration and malpractice was fought as a sort of Robin Hood action by one English shipper against the rest of the trade. Baron Forrester, a much beloved and extremely sincere member of an Oporto shipping firm, grew enamoured of the idea that port wine was falling into disrepute because it was counterfeited or adulterated with Bairrada wines, while the port actually made in the Douro vineyards was coloured with elderberry, loaded with brandy and sweetened with *jeropiga*. (*Jeropiga*, which can be either white or red, is nowadays merely a Douro wine which is deliberately made sweet; it is used, according to need, in the blending of port wine and its use is both legitimate and beneficial.) There was without doubt some truth in Forrester's accusations, but his gloomy picture was exaggerated and when he urged that Douro wine should be fully fermented, that its fermentation should not be stopped by brandy and that the sugar should be allowed to ferment right out into alcohol, he was not advocating the purity but the destruction of port. It is the brandy check to the fermentation that makes port capable of becoming a great and mellow wine. Without the check it would become a full-bodied wine of less distinction than claret. Bravely Forrester fought a battle which he was bound to lose but his passionate campaign, by re-emphasizing the need for honest well-made port, benefited the wine trade he loved in a way which he had not intended.[209]

It is scarcely necessary to add here that the proper blending of port wines with each other is a skilled practice which at its highest becomes art. As with champagne and sherry it is designed to bring the best out of the wine and to give the customer the style of port which he prefers. Even vintage port wine is a blend, or almost always a blend, but in this case only of the finest wines of the one particular vintage year. There are few greater wines than a superb vintage port but it would not be so

[208] Houghton, *Collection*, Vol. II, 487, No. 390-5 (?) of Feb. 16th, 1699-1700; *Art and Mystery of Vintners*, 68; Forrester, *op. cit.*, 13; John Wright, *op. cit.*, 17, 53; de Secondat, *op. cit.*, 89.

[209] Forrester, J. J., *op. cit.*, *passim*; Forrester, J. J., *Observations on . . . Attempts . . . to reform the abuses . . . in the making of Port Wine*; and cf. Letter of Offley, Webber and Forrester of Nov. 28th, 1845, to their correspondents.

wonderful if it were not blended. For example, I have drunk in the Douro a vintage port made on a first class *quinta* in an outstanding year; it had been neither blended nor refreshed; it had aged much quicker than its blended companions and although it was beautiful it was not as great as the port of that vintage which had been through the 'school' at Vila Nova de Gaia. I should like to think, in all humility, that Baron Forrester would have agreed.

I feel quite sure that James Boswell would have approved of modern port, particularly after some of the stuff which he induced himself to drink. In July 1763 he gives a description of the wine which can stand as the general epitaph on 18th-century port. 'A bottle of thick English port is a very heavy and a very inflammatory dose. I felt it last time that I drank it for several days, and this morning it was boiling in my veins.'[210] Blackstrap, others called it, horrible bad port, or 'bad, thick port' and 'puckering port'.[211] 'O *vinho abafado*' – a smothered wine – was Baron Forrester's dismissal of its quality.[212] But, however it was made and however it was described, it was part of the Englishman's heritage and nothing could stop him drinking it. A pint of port was a normal dinner ration for Torrington; a citizen's family at Vauxhall's Pleasure Gardens ordered a bottle of port after their supper; while the Olympian fastness of the Christ Church Senior Common-room at Oxford solaced itself between 1796 and 1806 on nothing else but port and sherry. The most favoured nectar was port.[213]

Baron Forrester

Growth of Scientific Viticulture

With a fanfare of trumpets the 17th century proclaimed the beginnings of the Age of Science. Newton, Boyle and Harvey put reason in the place of necromancy and demonstrated that the invisible world was indifferent to man and unaffected by supplication. They showed, however, that it could be known by thought and to some extent controlled by human beings and thus they emancipated the mind a hundred and fifty years before their countrymen emancipated the slaves. The application of science, the technical use of the mind, was a growing factor throughout the 18th century. The drainage of the Fens done in the 17th century by the Bedfords with the advice of Dutch engineers was carried on throughout the 18th century and completed at the beginning of the 19th. Bridgewater and Brindley cut their canals into the surface of England while 'Turnip' Townshend and Coke, of Norfolk, showed how the surface of the land could be improved by rational agriculture.

This technical movement was slower on the Continent than in England but it begins nevertheless to affect the vineyards of Europe. Methods of planting are noted, varieties of grape are listed, and methods of making are criticized. This century and a half sees the beginning of the first scientific viticulture since the fall of the Roman Empire. But the progress was slow and sporadic and whereas on the one hand you have a classification of vines, on the other you have pruning by the moon. (The course of the moon is still watched today by some Ligurian wine-makers though perhaps for calendar rather than for superstitious motives.)[214]

In northern Italy, vines continued to be grown high, trained up trees and festooned from one tree to another: or, as John Gay puts it,

[210] Boswell, *London Journal*, 303.

[211] John Wright, *op. cit.*, 26; Torrington, *op. cit.*, 326, 391.

[212] *Wine Trade of Portugal*, 6-10 (English), 6 (Portuguese).

[213] Torrington, *op. cit.*, *passim*, *The Connoisseur*, No. 68 of May 15th, 1755; Christ Church Common Room Accounts, MS., C.R.2.

[214] Locke, Vol. x, *Observations . . .*, 330-1.

'. . . in fields grotesque and wild
   They with implicit curls the oak entwine,
   And load with fruit divine his spreading boughs;
   Sight most delicious!'[215]

Gay's description was felicitous though not particularly accurate since the fields were neither grotesque nor wild and the trees used to support the vines were not oaks but, among others, willows or fruit trees.[216]

In French vineyards vines were grown low. The height varied of course with the vineyard. At 'Mr Pontac's vineyard near Bourdeaux' (Haut-Brion) some of the vines were allowed to grow to a height of four or five feet while others were trained about a foot from the ground 'between little low stakes or laths'. At Clos de Vougeot in Burgundy the vines were kept to a height of two or three feet.[217] Stakes or props were usual in Burgundy and Bordeaux, but they were not universal in France since in Languedoc they were not employed and the vines had to support themselves. But the greatest difference which we should notice between a modern French vineyard and that of the 18th century would be the way in which the vines were planted. Nowadays, for the most part, they are planted in long, regular rows although there are some vineyards where this practice is not followed. In the 18th century, however, the reverse was the case: vines planted in rows were the exception – at Cahors for example – the general method, if it can be called a method, was that of promiscuous planting. The vines were not arranged in rows but planted apparently at random and this was the method adopted in Champagne and in Burgundy. It disappeared from the vineyards of Bordeaux long before it was discarded in those of the Côte d'Or and the Marne Valley. Another great difference, which would not have been so noticeable to us, was that many of the vines were anything from 80 to 200 years old, the plants being the old European stocks which can live to a great age. In nearly all modern vineyards in Europe these European stocks are now grafted on to American roots to protect them from phylloxera and although this grafting does not impair the quality of the wine it does diminish the age of the vine plant. Modern grafted vines, as we shall see later, have only at most half the life of the old ungrafted European stocks.[218] It may well be that this comparative shortness of life does in some small degree affect the quality of the finest wines, although the mere fact of grafting does not. Pre-phylloxera wines could have been made from much older plants and may have had a richness and staying power which would be exceptional in modern vintages. The astonishing age of some of the pre-phylloxera clarets may seem to support this argument, but it is impossible to decide one way or the other and in any case it is now irrelevant since there are practically no vines on their own European roots and the vintages made from grafted vines are brought as near to perfection as anyone could desire.

In the making of the wine there was a similar variation in technique and a similar gradual but sporadic improvement. At one end of the scale is the comment of John Locke towards the end of the 17th century: 'In the kuve . . . as well as all other parts of their making wine, they are, according to their manner, sufficiently nasty: the grapes often are also very rotten, and always full of spiders.' Locke's philosophical outlook was also unable to view with equanimity the sight of their treading

[215]John Gay, *Poems*, 'Wine'.

[216]Lady Mary Wortley Montagu, *Letters*, Letter of July 10th, 1748; Arthur Young, *Travels in France*, etc., Vol. II, Ch. III, 238 sq.

[217]Locke, *op. cit.*, 331; Arthur Young, *op. cit.*, Vol. II, Ch. X, 16.

[218]Locke, *op. cit.*, 330; Arthur Young, *op. cit.*, Vol. II, Ch. X, 7, 16. For some of the vines grown in French vineyards, see de Secondat, *Mémoires . . .*, *passim*.

the wine with their naked feet since the dirt carried into the wine by the feet 'were enough to set one's stomach ever after against this sort of liquor'.[219] At the other end of the scale, and a century later, Arthur Young notes with approval the great care exercised in the Champagne vineyards where the pickers examine the bunches and take out every unsound grape.[220]

More notable, however, than the gradual improvement in the growing of wine was the sudden development in the technique of making the wine. The *Spaetlese* or late gathering and the *Beerenauslese*, or the late and selective gathering of over-ripe, 'sleepy' grapes were discovered in Germany, and from their sugary and wrinkled sleep was made some of the finest wine of Europe. We have already mentioned this accidental discovery at Johannisberg, but in 1783 which made a '*Jahrhundertwein*' there is an explicit record of *Edelfaeule*, the 'noble rot'.[221] The shippers of the Douro put brandy into fermenting grape juice and invented port. It was during this century, or at the latest in the first part of the 19th century, that the solera technique began to be commonly used in Jerez de la Frontera. It is indicative of the technical attitude of the Age that a writer should even suggest the freezing technique for 'Hock-makers'. When it is used nowadays, which is not often, the wine is artificially refrigerated but the method devised in 1793, and of course the only possible method, was to leave the wine out on a frosty night and take the ice off the next morning, thereby decreasing the water content of the wine.[222] This technique was not an 18th-century invention since, literally, bitter experience would have taught it to Rhineland wine-makers from very early times. This bitter experience need only have been a combination of rain, frost and ripe grapes. If these three happened together the berries become frozen, and by the freezing of the water in the berries the richness of the grape juice is thereby increased. *Eiswein* sometimes happens in our own time but only infrequently and in small quantities. There was some, for example, in 1949.

The outstanding technical development we have already discussed: it was the invention of the cylindrical bottle which enabled wine to be easily and properly matured. From the vineyard to the dinner table the conception of wine was radically altered. An incentive was given to classify 'growths' to produce fine wine, to watch it and manage it in the grower's or the shipper's cellar, and finally to drink it in conditions of connoisseurship. The full development of this process was not achieved until Victorian times but the development was steadily growing throughout the later 18th century. Yet in the emerging modernity of this period there are reminders of the long, undiscarded, past: oxen working in the vineyards of the Médoc; the fining of wine by whisking white of egg into it with a 'fouet' made of the bristles of a wild boar bound with a ring to an iron rod.[223]

The Quack Vintners

The inventiveness of every century has always been misapplied by greedy, stupid or dishonest people. The 18th century was no exception, and possibly more wine was faked or adulterated than at any other time in history. So much was this the case that in 1775 there was said to be practically no genuine claret in Britain. The same writer observes that genuine sherry can be procured 'by a proper application'

[219] Locke, *op. cit.*, 336.

[220] Young, *op. cit.*, Vol. I, Ch. x, 383.

[221] Deichmann u. Wolf, *Wein-chronik.*

[222] McBride, *Instructions . . .*, 19.

[223] de Secondat, *op. cit.*, 81, 84.

and that Rhenish wines 'can be got genuine'.[224] The adulteration, or to call it by a kinder word, the *coupage*, was practised at both ends of the wine trade, by the growers or shippers on the Continent and by the merchants in England. Bordeaux wine was blended with wine from Cahors, or with heavy Spanish wine from Benecarlo and Alicante. Italian wines, chiefly Tuscan, were darkly reputed to be used in lightening heavy port or making artificial claret and burgundy.[225]

Alum and litarge were among the substances put in the wine by the growers and although various forms of adulteration were prohibited by the French at the end of the 17th century, it is not likely that the prohibition had much effect. Inquisitive citizens, or angry drinkers, were sometimes a nuisance to the cheerfully adulterating peasant; such a citizen was 'le sieurr Benoist Gersant de la Benardiere' who pounced on a peasant of Aumont, found that in a sack on his shoulder he was carrying alum and litarge, and had him arrested and flung into gaol.[226]

The ingenuity of the English found expression in actual counterfeiting of wine and in this fraudulent art they excelled, both by their energy and their shamelessness. We have mentioned Ames's complaints of manufactured port and adulterated claret. They made a great deal of port, a considerable quantity of Madeira and more Mountain wine than Spain itself could produce. The basis for this latter brew was mead, or cider and honey. They condescended also to work the lesser magic of adulteration – 'improving' was one of the euphemisms – and they improved sherry with mellow Lisbon wine and a quantity of honey.[227] These distortions of drinking, the 'mending' or the 'making' of wine, may seem to us improper but when we look back and see the things that had been mixed with wine throughout the Middle Ages, the Renaissance and in the Puritan century we cannot be surprised that the mixtures were both committed and consumed.

From Damaske Water towards Chartreuse

A more reputable activity of science was the development of liqueurs. Distillation had made them possible and had changed the spiced and sweetened medieval drinks into the flavoured and sweetened spirits which are modern liqueurs. On the one side they trace their descent from Hippocras and on the other from the alchemists, and their immediate ancestry lies in the various 'Waters' of the Renaissance and Reformation, which we have considered in Chapter VII. Their refinement into a modern form is mainly the achievement of the 18th century and the honour in which they were held by Brillat-Savarin is proof of the excellence which they had then attained.

At the start of their modern career, however, they were still regarded as medicinal. The most famous of them was the *rossolis* or *rossoly* which Fagon made for Louis XIV when his immense appetite began to impair his stomach, and which was generally drunk at dessert. This was made from the seeds of *anise*, and from fennel, dill, coriander and caraway, all of which were crushed and macerated for three weeks in a stoppered glass vessel. Spirits were then added together with water of camomile and sugar and the mixture, once it had been filtered, was ready for the royal patient.[228] The liqueur was also held in esteem, though perhaps not for the same reason, by the King's subjects and in 1676 it was officially allowed to be sold

[224] Barry, *op. cit.*, 438, 443, 447.

[225] Arthur Young, *op. cit.*, Vol. II, Ch. X, 3; Barry, *op. cit.*, 436, 442; de Secondat, *op. cit.*, 89.

[226] Bibliothèque Nationale, Paris, *Fonds Français*, 21, 664 (125); see also *Fonds Français*, 21, 664 (142).

[227] Barry, *op. cit.*, 440, 443; John Wright, *op. cit.*, 20; McBride, *op. cit.*, 29; Gage Accounts, James Farley . . ., Cellar Book (see fn. 202 above).

[228] Vallot, D'Aquin et Fagon, *Journal de la Santé du Roi Louis XIV*, 435.

Wine-glass with wheel decoration
English, c 1750
London, Victoria and Albert Museum

Wine-glass, cut on the wheel
English, c 1750
London, Victoria and Albert Museum

on the streets of Paris.[229] At the same time the street vendors were allowed to sell *populo* brandy and other liqueurs and essences. *Populo* was only a light, delicate *rossolis* and *rossolis* itself was for a time little more than a generic name for one class of liqueur based on brandy and sugar. The number of herbs in it could vary, spices such as cinnamon were sometimes added, and it could be scented with musk or ambergris.[230]

As the 18th century went on, liqueurs began to individualize themselves and to define their own individuality. But the process took time and even at the middle of the century there was still a welter of 'Strong Waters' whose names and recipes varied with the inventiveness of their makers. There were: *frangipane*, angelica water, juniper water, and *eau de mille fleurs*. There were: *eau nuptiale*, *Belle de Nuit*, *Huile de Cythère* '*qui est merveilleux pour accélérer les accouchements*' and *Huile de Vénus*, though the authentic recipe for this was said to have died with its inventor, a certain Monsieur Cigogne.[231] Perhaps the last survivor of this amorous sounding group is that *Parfait Amour* which Edwardian dandies were thought to have offered to nubile young ladies and which is still in the distillers' repertoire.

In 1749 a young Italian from Bologna called Justerini arrived in London and set up in business with an Englishman named Johnson, thus founding the firm of Johnson and Justerini, now Justerini and Brooks of Bond Street. Among the recipes which he brought with him from Bologna were those for making ratafia, orange

[229] Bibliothèque Nationale, Paris, 'Statuts et Ordonnances pour la Communauté des Maîtres Limonadiers . . .', F., Fr., 21668 (201).

[230] Franklin, *Vie privée d'autrefois*, Vol. 23, 167-9.

[231] *Ibid*, Vol. 6, 143; Poncelet, *La Chymie du Goût et de l'Odorat*, Articles VI and XIX, 1756.

brandy, and Aqua Mirabilis.[232] Justerini's activity gives a good picture of the transitional stage between Renaissance 'Water' and the modern liqueur.

If we ever regard some of these old recipes as being ludicrous in their complexity, as being romanticized alchemy or mere herbal enthusiasm, we have only to remember that modern Benedictine is said to include 30 different herbs and modern Chartreuse 130. Both of these, as well as many other modern liqueurs, are made from old recipes and they are one of the very few ways in which we can sensually experience the world of the French Revolution and the Prince Regent, for they are the same to us as they were to Talleyrand.

The 'home still-room' is now for most of us an impossible experience and even though 'country wines' continue to be made in the recesses of England they have no period charm and very often they have no charm at all. The old still-room passes slowly perhaps and a fragrant, muslin whiff of its passing is preserved for us in the letters of Jane Austen. 'We must buy currants for our Wine,' she writes, and on another occasion says in a postscript, to Miss Alethea Bigg:

'The real object of this letter is to ask you for a receipt, but I thought it genteel not to let it appear early. We remember some excellent orange wine at Manydown, made from Seville oranges, entirely or chiefly & should be very much obliged to you for the receipt, if you can command it within a few weeks.'[233]

The refinement of liqueurs is typical of the growing sophistication of the Age. Good taste asserted a widespread, and for the most part genuine, ascendancy. Beautiful glass, silver and china: the finest furniture ever made in Europe: interior decoration that has been incessantly copied but seldom surpassed: an exterior architecture that still holds the imagination: all these things are part of a quickening move towards the civilization of ordinary life.

A growing emphasis on the quality of things, on the quality of the texture in which one lived, could not fail to have an effect on wine and although the effect was slow it was nevertheless marked. It is illustrated with particular clarity in the case of Bordeaux. There had been a rough classification of these wines made at Bordeaux itself in 1647. It was made in terms of selling prices and it shows that of the red wines those of the Palus were the most popular, followed by the red wines of Barsac and Sauternes. The red wines of Graves and the Médoc come third. For white wines these districts rank almost equal in the scale of prices.[234] It seems surprising that wines from the Palus, low-lying vineyards which produced thick wines, should have been so popular but that was due to commercial buying from Holland. Their comparative price had fallen by the first half of the 18th century by which time although they still went to Holland they had found a market in the West Indies and in America.

General though it is, and apart from the Palus wines, this classification of 1647 is not in its upper levels greatly at variance with any classification that has since been made. Furthermore, its generalization was soon to be broken down by a connoisseur who wanted a particular wine from a particular area. 'Aubryan' appears in Restoration England and under its other name of 'Puntack' it is sought and desired towards the end of the century. In the first two decades of the next century the first Earl of

[232] Wheatley, *Seven Ages of Justerini's*, 12 sq.

[233] *Jane Austen's Letters*, 290, 477.

[234] Lafforgue, *Vignoble Girondin*, 293.

Bristol not only buys 'Obrian' and 'Pontac' but also 'Chateau Margou', 'La Tour', and 'Laffitte'. The Earl of Bristol's taste was shared by Sir Robert Walpole and by the end of the 18th century the phrase 'first growth clarets' is becoming a not unusual designation.[235] As individual taste became more refined and more insistent the individuality of the better vineyards became more important and more pronounced. Gradually wine became a thing that could not only be enjoyed but could also be perfected.

Great tracts of rough and careless taste were left unaffected by the activity of the gourmets and one can only contemplate with alarm the mishandled and manufactured wines which lurked in the more barbaric areas of thirst. There were gaps also in the splendid apparatus of domestic comfort. Lady Mary Wortley Montagu writes from Blankenburg – admittedly it was December – and comments upon 'our (English) obstinacy in shaking with cold six months in the year, rather than make use of stoves. . . '[236] A generation before this cri de coeur Celia Fiennes takes time out to remark upon 'a Water house' at Norwich which was to supply piped water into some of the households in the town. The fact that she mentions it also at Derby shows that at length cleanliness was becoming easier than Godliness.[237] Even so, while it was becoming easier, it was still less common. Sanitation remained largely and dangerously medieval. There were, it is true, a few water closets in Georgian houses but they were more helpful in producing disease than in promoting comfort. The commode, of course, was there for the sick or the sophisticated, but for the most part men and women toiled out into the backyard or garden to the unwholesome inconvenience of the privy and the cesspit. It is incomprehensible that human beings, with all their inventive genius, should for so long have tolerated this state of affairs but, after all, they had been used to it for thirteen hundred years. Only an ingrained indifference can explain the unseemliness of the French nobility who in the middle of the 17th century relieved themselves against tapestries and in fireplaces. The power of elegance, however, was clearly irresistible and we may note with pride that under Louis XVI there was each morning a special and general clearing of excretus in the palace which the King was then honouring with his presence.[238]

The same applied to England. 'I wish you could see the villas and seats here!' writes Horace Walpole. 'The country wears a new face; everybody is improving their places. . . . The dispersed buildings, I mean, temples, bridges, &c, are generally Gothic or Chinese, and give a whimsical air of novelty that is very pleasing.'[239] The idea of the villa worked like a fever in the blood of the English. Prosperous London merchants insisted on having villas in the countryside surrounding their city. Thus began, and it began at this time, the long honeymoon of the Englishman with the 'weekend in the country'. Many of these villas were whimsical but they would not always have pleased the fastidious taste of Horace Walpole. A writer in The Connoisseur of September 1754, fascinated by the novelty of this weekly London trek, describes how he visited the proud possessor of one of these villas or 'Boxes'. He went, of course, on Sunday and found the 'Seat' without difficulty. It was built on the side of a public road. On the other side of the road a hedge cut off all the view 'except from the garrets, from whence indeed you have a beautiful vista of two men hanging in chains on *Kennington* Common, with a distant view

[235]TR, VI, 413 sq. (entry of 1669); Hervey Cellar, *passim*; Walpole Cellar, 201; McBride, *Instructions . . .*, 13.

[236]*Letters*, Dec. 17th, O.S., 1716.

[237]Fiennes, *Journeys*, 147, 169-70.

[238]Franklin, *Vie privée d'autrefois*, Vol. 7, 18, 171, and Vol. 7, Appendix, 31-4.

[239]*Letters*, Aug. 2nd, 1750.

of St *Paul's* Cupola enveloped in a cloud of smoke'. The hall of the villa had been decorated with care; on one wall hung a map of London and on the other 'the Death of the Stag, by the happy pencil of Mr Henry Overton, finely coloured'; 'close by the parlour door, there hung a pair of stag's horns, over which there was laid across a red roccelo and an amber-headed cane'. A roccelo was a knee-length cloak, fashionable at the time. In the parlour itself there was a picture of the owner's wife 'in the habit of a shepherdess, smelling to a nosegay, and stroaking a ram with gilt horns'. The villa garden was 'a yard about thirty feet in length, and contained about a dozen little pots ranged on each side with lillies and coxcombs supported by some old lamps painted green with bowls of tobacco-pipes on their tops. At the end of this garden he made me take notice of a little square building . . . which he told me an Alderman of great taste had turned into a Temple, by erecting some battlements and spires of painted wood on the front of it; but concluded with an hint, that I might retire to it upon occasion'.[240]

The 'follies' of the Age, the artificial ruins, the impractical shepherdesses, the mis-applied Gothic and the 'Chinese taste', were exaggerations and for that reason they gained an exaggerated importance in the mind of later generations. In retrospect it is easy to overlook the normal and to see only the outrageous. Most outrageous of all the follies of the 18th century was the insensate gambling of a small fraction of the English upper classes. The enormity of the sums that were won or lost makes them appear grotesque; even more grotesque, even more the final exaggeration, was the appearance of the men who won and lost them. Among the young men of quality who gambled at Almack's were those who '. . . turned their coats inside outwards for luck . . . they put on pieces of leather . . . to save their lace ruffles; and to guard their eyes from the light, and to prevent tumbling their hair, wore high-crowned straw hats with broad brims, and adorned with flowers and ribbons; masks to conceal their emotions when they played at Quinze'. Misson writes disparagingly of the 18th-century Beaux as 'creatures compounded of a Periwig and a Coat laden with powder' but adds that the generality of Englishmen dressed 'in a plain uniform Manner'.[241]

The Georgian Beaux, like the Shepherdesses of Boucher and Fragonard, seem remote and indeed beyond reality, as though they moved in a bright and pointless masquerade. . . . Remote also from Augustan reality seem to be the men who four years later and three thousand miles away put their signatures to a Declaration of Independence. They were remote because even in 1776 they were ahead of their Age and were moving into the 19th century. There was nothing new about the ideals of the American rebels; they had been said before, in different ways and at different times, in Europe. What was new was that, in the words of one of their later poets, the leaders of the American rebels could say:

> 'Come my tan-faced children,
> Follow well in order, get your weapons ready,
> Have you your pistols? have you your sharp-edged axes?'[242]

and to show that this was no peasant rising but the beginning of a nation they could add: 'Pioneers! O pioneers!'

[240]No. 33 of Sept. 17th, 1754.

[241]Horace Walpole, *Last Journals*, Feb. 1772; Misson, *op. cit.*, 16.

[242]Walt Whitman, *Leaves of Grass*, 'Pioneers! O Pioneers!'

CHAPTER NINE

Victorian Triumph

In Europe since the Renaissance it has been normal for one Age to react against the Age which has gone before. A young generation rebels against the behaviour pattern of its parents. It breaks out of the cage and constructs another pattern for itself which, of course, becomes another cage. This happens in civilizations as well as in families and it accounts for the intensity of our reaction to the Age of Victoria.

The Victorians are not as distant from us as we sometimes imagine. Their modes of thought dominated us until 1939 and to a considerable extent they dominate us still. Hence the violence of our reaction, and also the misunderstanding with which we view it since it is difficult not to be prejudiced against the parental cage. We regard the Victorians as self-righteous, self-deluded, self-satisfied, priggish and pompous and – the final condemnation – of a surpassing prurience.

The accusation is not true. There were of course canting, hypocritical Victorians as well as those whose dull minds were made even more tedious by profound conceit. Such men were not peculiar to Victorianism. On the contrary, it is the continual movement of intellect which gives a distinctive flavour to the Victorian Age. The men, and the women, of that time were unsparing critics; they criticized themselves and they criticized society; they challenged faith and destroyed tradition; at whatever cost to their own peace of mind they insisted upon knowledge and the integrity with which they sought, and used it, put a profound tension into their emotional life. It was from beginning to end an Age of mental revolution and, so far as the intellect is concerned, it was one of the greatest Ages in history. Nor was it a quiet, chilly revolution, conducted in science laboratories and university lecture rooms. Controversy was public and vociferous; convictions passionately held were attacked with equal passion; the air vibrated to a continuous thunder, as the giants of the Age hurled at each other massive rocks of argument and eloquence. The Victorians were a passionate people.

Georgian Survivals

Georgian England reached over into the early years of Queen Victoria's reign. Duelling continued until 1843. In 1840 Thackeray went to see François Benjamin Courvoisier hanged and though the huge crowd was decorous he found the spectacle degrading.[1] Nevertheless it remained a popular attraction for sightseers until it was abolished in 1868.

For a few years only the street life of London maintained an old-fashioned atmosphere. In 1837 there were performing dogs on the street, acrobats and a butcher who 'serenades his young mistress with the cleaver and the bones; the Italian boy delights all the ears of those who hear with his hurdy-gurdy . . . the streets are horribly noisy . . . the road is not macadamized, or asphalted, or paved with wood . . . men are perpetually jostling, quarrelling, and fighting; the coaches, those of the short stages with two horses, and for long stages with four, are always blowing their horns and cracking their whips . . . it is not in silence either that the women who carry baskets full of fish on their heads go along the street, nor is the man silent who goes with the pack donkey loaded on either side with small coal; and the wooden sledge on which is the cask of beer, dragged along by a single horse, makes by itself as much noise' as all the carriages in 1888.[2] The change was well begun in the early 40s by which time there were something like 700 omnibuses carrying a daily load of 60,000 passengers. Nor was London any longer a dark city. Pall Mall it is true had been lit by gas as early as 1807 but in the early 40s '. . . the metropolis now burns gas in every square, street, alley, lane, passage, and court'.[3] Sunday seems still to have been a day of pleasure for some of the population, at least for the lower classes of London who went up the Thames to Richmond on a 'Steam Packet' and diverted themselves by smoking, swearing and drinking.[4]

In the middle 30s the English countryside remained much the same as it had been in Georgian times. Augustus Hare, looking back on his childhood in Sussex at this period, remembers the silence and seclusion of the countryside and remembers also that 'the flail, as well as the sickle and scythe, were then in constant use at Hurstmonceaux, where oxen – for all agricultural purposes – occupied the position which horses held now'.[5] By 'now' he means 1896. Howitt in his *Boy's Country Cook* shows us two sides of rural life: for a boy 'it was just as good fun to go with old Samuel Davis with this cargo of crabs in a cart to Kidsley Park to press them in the ancient crab press, which stood in the orchard, into verjuice': and on the other hand not so much fun for the poor lad of about seven who had been sent out to work on a 'cold, raw, foggy day in February'. He was dressed in a blue carterfrock and carried a wooden clapper with which to scare the birds. For seven hours he patrolled this wet ploughed field 'singing his song with a melancholy voice and sounding his clapper'. In the end he cried because the silence frightened him.[6]

The seclusion and the loneliness did not last for many years. By 1848 the old coaching days were disappearing and railways were spreading over the countryside. Moreover the 'tourist' – a specifically modern phenomenon – had already appeared and by 1838 a number of these intrepid English tourists were each year visiting the Scottish Highlands, Derbyshire, Wales and Ireland.[7]

For the poor, malnutrition was a constant threat and a frequent actuality. Poverty

[1] Thackeray, W. M., *Works*, 13 vols, 1898; Vol. III 'Going to see a man hanged'.

[2] Besant, *Fifty Years Ago*, 54, 58-9.

[3] Knight, *London*, Vol. I, 32, III.

[4] Howitt, *Rural Life of England*, Vol. II, 312 sq.

[5] *The Years with Mother*, 15.

[6] pp. 76, 114.

[7] Howitt, *Rural Life of England*, Vol. II, 384.

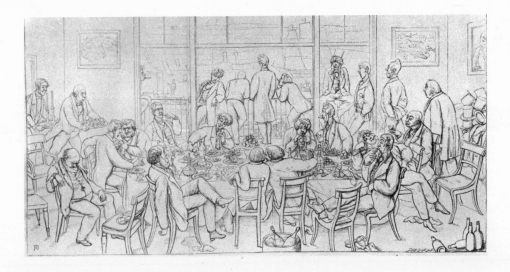

R. Dalziel
Dinner down the River,
c 1850
from 'The Bird's Eye View
of Society'
André Simon Collection

was a little less harsh to the countryman and the townsman who had small gardens in which they could grow a few vegetables, keep a few chickens and a pig. Basically however, the diet of the poor depended upon bread and potatoes, flour for puddings, rice, oatmeal, barley and vegetables with a little meat or fish.[8] In the countryside the rent night supper, given twice a year by the landlord to his tenants was somewhat more cheerful being '. . . a regular old English one, of roast beef, plumpudding, pigeon-pies, roast fowls, fruit-tarts, when the season permitted, and plenty of ale and pipes'.[9] Among the more prosperous farmers the eating was sometimes gargantuan. Howitt describes one such entertainment – obviously not an everyday occurrence – given by one such farmer to his friends and neighbours. The guests, having had breakfast at home, arrived between 10 and 11 o'clock in the morning and immediately sat down to lunch which consisted of 'a boiled ham, a neat's tongue; a piece of cold beef; fowls and beef-steak-pie; tarts, and bread, cheese and butter; coffee for the ladies, and fine old ale for the gentlemen. . . .' At 1 o'clock they had dinner. This was a two-course affair but the number of the courses has no relevance to the quantity of the victuals. The first course was of roast beef, veal, lamb, hams, turkeys, geese, game, pigeon-pies, peas, potatoes, cauliflowers, kidney beans, lettuces, washed down by ale and porter and 'wine for those that will'. For the second course they had plum puddings, fruit tarts, cheese-cakes, syllabubs, whipped creams and jellies. For the dessert there were walnuts, almonds, raisins, fruits and confections and '. . . the wine circulates – foreign and English – port and sherry – gooseberry and damson – malt and birch – elderflower and cowslip. . . .' Later on in the day there was tea and later still a supper of hot game, fowls and fresh pastry.[10] Some element of rhapsody may have crept into this description but one cannot dismiss it as wholly exaggerated. Equally rhapsodic, though clearly quite unexaggerated is the description of a visit paid by Mr Willis, an American, to the Duke of Gordon at Gordon Castle in Scotland. There were seldom less than thirty for dinner at the castle though on the night Willis arrived there were over ninety. They dined shortly after seven and a 'band of music' played during dinner, only ceasing its labours when the ladies left the table. Even though the men did not

[8] *Early Victorian England*, Young, Peel, I, 126 sq., chapter on 'Homes and Habits'.

[9] Howitt, *Boy's Country Book*, 289.

[10] *Rural Life of England*, Vol. I, 128 sq.

appear to drink a great deal they sat on until 11 o'clock when they adjourned to the drawing-room. 'Cards, tea, music, filled up the time till 12, and then the ladies took their departure, and the gentlemen sat down to supper. I got to bed somewhere about 2 o'clock. . . .' At breakfast, attended by at least some of the women, the men read their letters or the newspapers. For the rest of the morning 'the ladies were generally invisible and the gentlemen rode or shot, or played billiards, or kept in their rooms'. There was a light lunch at two and the afternoon was passed in riding or driving in carriages. The scenery had all the enchantment of a genuine aristocratic idyll: 'velvet sward', shrubs in clumps, deer in a park graced by ornamental gates and 'in the hollows of the woods' gamekeepers lifting their hats to the Duke's guests as they rode or drove by in their afternoon's pleasure.[11]

Prince Pückler-Muskau, a Prussian who travelled through England in 1828 and 1829, remarked that the English had admirable taste in spending their vast wealth,[12] and Willis's September experience at Gordon Castle would have confirmed the Prince in his view. Pückler-Muskau's observations on English life are often vivid and although many of them refer to customs which changed under Victoria some of the scenes he describes are typical of English upper class life until late Victorian times. On taking leave of his hostess 'in her own room' he found 'a floor covered with splendid camellias, in baskets, looking as if they grew there'. Their effect was heightened because it was in February.[13] On another occasion, this time in June, he went to 'an interesting breakfast' given by the Kitchen Club which was a club for shooting at pigeons. 'On one side,' he says, 'was a row of tents; in the largest of which a table was spread with viands, from one o'clock to six and furnished with a constant supply of iced Moselle and Champagne.'[14] If for pigeon shooting we substitute archery, at which the young women could display their clothes and their figures, and later on croquet, at which they could display their tempers, this type of open-air party became one of the hallmarks of Victorian country house life. One thing which is not Victorian is the meaning which he gives to the word 'breakfast'; his meaning is nearer to that exemplified by Gronow who wrote, of the fashionable Café Tortoni in Paris, 'in the early parts of the day, Tortoni's became the rendezvous of duellists and retired officers, who congregated in great numbers for breakfast; which consisted of cold pâtés, game, fowl, fish, eggs, broiled kidneys, iced champagne, and liqueurs from every part of the globe'.[15] This, as we shall see, was by no means the normal Victorian breakfast.

Until the late 20s there were still characters who exhibited a Georgian eccentricity. The Marquis of Hastings shortly before his death 'ordered that his right hand should be cut off immediately after his death, and sent to his wife. A gentleman . . . out of real tenderness, and with her previously obtained permission, cut off his mother's head, that he might keep the skull as long as he lived. . . .'[16] Admittedly these incidents occurred some ten years before Queen Victoria came to the throne and in Victorian times necrolatry took on forms which may have been just as morbid but were certainly less personal. A later, and gayer, note is struck by Augustus Hare. He dined at Bath with Walter Savage Landor whose rooms 'were entirely covered with pictures, the frames fitting close to one another, leaving not the smallest space of wall visible. . . . Mr Landor lived alone with his beautiful white Spitz dog Pomero, which he allowed to do whatever it liked, and frequently to sit

[11] *Ibid*, Vol. I, 30 sq. For the 'vie de château' see also Pückler-Muskau, III, 311–15.

[12] Pückler-Muskau, *Tour in England* . . ., Vol. III, 179.

[13] *Ibid*, III, 317.

[14] *Ibid*, IV, 351 sq.

[15] *Reminiscences and Recollections*, Vol. II, 283–4.

[16] Pückler-Muskau, *op. cit.*, Vol. III, 180.

in the oddest way on the bald top of his head. He would talk to Pomero by the hour together, poetry, philosophy, whatever he was thinking of, all of it imbued with his own powerful personality, and would often roar with laughter until the whole house seemed to shake'.[17] He also records that in 1857 Mrs Grote, wife of George Grote the historian of Greece, lunched with him in his Oxford rooms. He was, he records, 'enchanted with Mrs Grote . . . though her exterior – with a short waist, brown mantle of stamped velvet, and huge bonnet, full of full-blown red roses – was certainly not captivating. . . . She had a passion for discordant colours, and had her petticoats always arranged to display her feet and ankles, of which she was excessively proud. . . . Mrs Grote sat with one leg over the other, both high in the air, and talked for two hours, turning with facility to Saffi on Italian Literature, Max Müller on Epic Poetry, and Arthur on Ecclesiastical History, and then plunged into a discourse of the best manure for turnips and the best way of forcing Cotswold mutton, with an interlude first upon the "harmony of shadow" in water colour drawing, and then upon rat hunts at Jemmy Shawe's – a low public house in Westminster'.[18]

One distinctive continuation of Georgian manners was the method of serving dinner. The system which we generally follow nowadays is based on the *service russe*, the courses of a meal following each other in a definite and deliberate procession and each course being of a particular type of food. Another distinctive feature of the *service russe*, and at the time when it was properly introduced into England this was perhaps its most distinctive feature, was that the food was carved or cut up away from the table and only then handed round by the servants. The *service russe* began to be introduced into England in the 50s but it was not until the 70s that it was generally triumphant over its rival the *service français*.[19]

The *service français* was the older method of dining and it was the system followed by the Georgians. In general it consisted of two courses, all the many dishes of each course being placed on the table at the same time and being carved at, and served from, the table itself. Thus for the first course of a dinner to sixteen or eighteen people in 1855 there would be on the table at the same time soup, fish, boiled turkey, Ragout of Palates, Croquets of Poultry, Galantine of Veal, Fillets of Rabbits, sweetbreads, mushroom sauce, Venison or Haunch of Mutton, Mutton Cutlets and Sorrel Sauce, Tendons de Veau ä la Poulette, Tongue, Vol au Vent of Oysters, Curry of Chicken, a sauce, and gravy or currant jelly. There was, however, a vestige of progression in this meal which was accompanied by the system of 'removes'. Thus the soups, of which there were two, one at the top and one at the bottom of the table, were, as one writer cryptically says, 'removed by four fishes' and these in their turn were removed by the meats and poultry. For the rest it was a shambles since 'every man helps the dish before him . . . if he wishes for anything else, he must ask across the table or send a servant for it'. On the table for the second course of this dinner there were: Poulard Larded, Soufflé, Jelly, Aspic of Chicken, Artichokes, Tourte, Cream, Fondeau, Wild Ducks, Salad of Fillets of Soles, Seakale, fancy pastry, cream, a sauce and a gravy. The second course was sometimes followed by a sort of savoury dessert consisting of cheese and celery, radishes or cucumbers. Wine it seems was seldom drunk with this course although it was not infrequently accompanied by ale – sometimes thirty years old; beer or toast and

[17] *The Years with Mother*, 57–8.

[18] *Ibid*, 107–8.

[19] See for example, Beeton's *Complete Etiquette for Gentlemen* (edn of 1876), 27 sq.

R. Dalziel
A State Party, 1861
from 'The Bird's Eye View
of Society'
André Simon Collection

water were also served. Finally came the dessert proper: fruit, olives, preserved and crystallized fruits, biscuits, cakes, filberts, ices and preserved ginger. 'Occasionally zests are served at the close of the dessert: these consist of anchovy or biscuits, devilled game or poultry, grills, and such like.' With awe one learns that 'soon after the ladies retire to the drawing-room, coffee and tea are handed round to them, with fancy biscuits and cakes. . . .'[20]

For inconvenience, delay and confusion the *service français* is hard to beat and it is incredible that it lasted so long. It is often thought that it disappeared in the 70s but in fact it lingered on for dinner until the end of the century and for lunch until Edwardian times.[21] It was among the upper classes that the *service russe* spread first and most rapidly and here again, although it is often assumed that it was an innovation of the 50s, and not really accepted until the 60s, we can trace its introduction into England to an earlier date. We have already seen, in Chapter VIII, that it existed in France before the Revolution,[22] and one can see the tentative beginnings of it in England in 1829. All the dishes of each course were still placed upon the table and the only variant was to send the servants round with the dishes. Pückler-Muskau, himself a German, calls this 'the more convenient German fashion' and it is clearly one step towards the *service russe*. The 'German' compromise was still being observed in England in 1855.[23] It was, however, only a compromise and although we may say that the *service russe* exercised some influence, this influence was not decisive until the middle of Queen Victoria's reign.

At the same time as the service of dinner was developing into its modern form, so also was the timing of the day's meals. The modern 'foursome' – breakfast, lunch, tea and dinner – replaces the 'Georgian threesome' – breakfast, dinner, supper. At the beginning of the period, for example, Oxford and Cambridge dined at 4 o'clock and the general middle class custom was to dine in the middle of the day.[24] Much the same system was observed in Germany, at any rate among the middle classes, who dined at twelve or one and had supper at 7 o'clock in the evening.[25] The

[20] *The Butler*, by an experienced servant, 91 sq., 1855; Pückler-Muskau, *op. cit.*, Vol. III, 83-7; Besant, *op. cit.*, 121.

[21] Beeton, *Book of Household Management* (edn of 1893), 12; (edn of 1906), 1681.

[22] Ch. 8, p. 376.

[23] Pückler-Muskau, *op. cit.*, Vol. III, 83 sq.; *The Butler* . . ., 95.

[24] Besant, *op. cit.*, 87, 157.

[25] Howitt, *Rural and Domestic Life of Germany*, 231.

English upper classes, however, dined between seven and eight. In general we can say that, at any rate in England, the lower classes maintained, and have still maintained, the Georgian pattern whereas the middle and upper classes adopted the modern system. But during the time of transition the same names were used for different meals. To clear away any ambiguous meanings it is easier to consider each meal separately.

Chocolate with a piece of bread or biscuit had by the 40s become 'the universal breakfast of Spain'.[26] A summer breakfast in middle class Germany was coffee and bread, the latter being 'mostly without butter'.[27] In upper and upper middle class England breakfast assumed more heroic proportions. It was usually served about 9 o'clock though at house parties it could be at 10 o'clock or even as late as eleven. There was tea or tea and coffee and 'besides the colder dishes on the sideboard there is frequently served . . . boiled eggs, fried eggs and bacon, mutton kidneys, devilled fowl, broiled cutlets, broiled fish, potted fish, and meats . . . besides bread of various kind and shapes, and butter in the butter coolers'. The butter coolers were perhaps not universal.[28] In the United States the attitude to breakfast was quite as robust. There were coffee, tea or cocoa – (and the writer comments favourably on American as against English coffee, a criticism that is still justified) – together with hot rolls baked that morning, steak, or chops, or ham and eggs, liver or fried tripe. Melons, eaten at the beginning of breakfast, were quite common as were roasted tomatoes and fried potatoes. Radishes were sometimes eaten as a relish for breakfast and in winter 'it is hard for the American ro rise from his . . . breakfast without his buckwheat cakes' which 'are eaten with butter and treacle or sugar cane molasses'. In New England a favourite Sunday breakfast was baked pork and beans and brown bread.[29]

All this seems straightforward in meaning although excessive in quantity. There was, however, another type of 'breakfast', a luxurious example of which was that described by Gronow at the Café Tortoni in Paris. This in fact meant lunch or *dejeuner à la fourchette* but the ambiguous phraseology lasted, as far as Paris is concerned, until as late as 1882.[30] It is curious to note that even today in some of the British West Indian islands the word 'breakfast' is used to mean an early lunch.

In the upper strata of English society at the end of the Georgian period, lunch was sometimes nothing but a glass of wine and bread or biscuits; at the same time 'luncheon' which was then also called the second breakfast, was coming into vogue though it was generally only eaten by women. A generation later, and then called either a *dejeuner à la fourchette* or luncheon, it was becoming an accepted part of the day's eating. It was an informal meal mainly consisting of cold meats though there were sometimes puddings when the children took their 'dinner' at their parents' 'luncheon'. The old-fashioned breakfast was thus splitting up into the modern breakfast and the modern lunch, the modern note being emphasized by the development of lunch from the earlier cold to the later hot meal.[31]

Tea was drunk by the lower classes when they could afford it and by the upper classes after dinner. Afternoon tea was not yet a British institution and at the beginning of our period was only the fad of a few fashionable women. A charming custom which is now, though alas only too seldom, known as the 'wine merchant's tea' and which consists of a glass of wine and a dry biscuit, prevailed in the country

[26] Ford, *Gatherings from Spain*, 143.

[27] Howitt, *Rural and Domestic Life of Germany*, 231.

[28] *The Butler . . .*, 65; see also Pückler-Muskau, *op. cit.*, Vol. III, 193-4, 311 sq.; Howitt, *Rural Life of England*, Vol. I, 30 sq.; Peel, Mrs C. S., *A Hundred Wonderful Years*, 115-16.

[29] Towle, *American Society*, Vol. I, 266-70.

[30] Gronow, *Reminiscences and Recollections*, Vol. II, 283-4; Dickens, *Dictionary of Paris* – 'Restaurants at fixed prices', 215 *et seq*.

[31] Cosnett, *Footman's Directory*, 78; Pückler-Muskau, *op. cit.*, Vol. III, 311 sq.; *The Butler . . .*, 66-8; Peel, Mrs C. S., *op. cit.*, 115-16.

towns of England in the 30s and doubtless lingered on through the 40s. When a visitor came to call, and in particular when one woman called upon another, out came the biscuits and the decanters and the visitor was offered port or sherry. 'In some houses it was not port and sherry that were placed upon the table but "red" and "white". I do not know,' says Besant, 'whether the red was currant or raspberry, but I think that the white was generally cowslip.'[32] It was not long, however, before the teapot replaced the decanter and afternoon tea became a settled feature of Victorian England. Two separate influences helped to establish it as a regular meal: the growing lateness of the dinner hour which made it necessary and the growing temperance of the Victorians which made it non alcoholic.

It was only gradually that the hour of dinner became later, shifting backwards from half past six to half past seven, though even at the beginning of the period the aristocracy was tending to adopt the later time. This led, though again only gradually, to the disappearance of the late supper, but the disappearance was not as complete as some had supposed for even in Edwardian times there were often sandwiches between 10 and 11 o'clock in the evening for any guest who, already having had four meals in the day, might still feel himself in danger of starvation.

By the middle of Queen Victoria's reign the English system of eating had assumed its modern form. They ate far more than we do and their cooking was not altogether the same as ours, but in its essentials our modern practice was established before the death of Dickens. We cannot say this about the drinking habits of the Victorians. They evolved throughout the period, in some cases, radically, but they did not attain the modern pattern until after the First World War. In the same way that, at the beginning of the era, most of the countryside was still 'the old England' so also was much of the drinking. Some of it indeed was medieval. As late as 1858, beer was drunk for breakfast by farmers and labourers, as it was by a number of undergraduates. At Cambridge breakfast parties 'the tankard was passed round as the finish'. The home brewing of beer was widespread, particularly in the country, and as late as the middle 50s it was the responsibility of the butler to superintend the brewing. Even at upper class dinner parties it was quite usual for strong ale or porter to be served with the cheese-dessert.[33]

Another relic of English history, Medieval, Renaissance and Georgian, was the 'still-room'. This was a vital part of every English country home, the precinct (as was the cheese room) of the farmer's wife and her daughters or a tributary state in the empire watched over by the housekeeper in a great mansion. Here were made the tea and coffee, the jams, lavender water, medicines, cordials and 'country wines'.[34] Not only did the manufacture of country wines – though in ever-decreasing quantities – last throughout the Victorian period but it has continued until today, and in fact there seems recently to be some revival of interest in their manufacture. I remember them being made on a country estate in the 1930s and remarkably potent they were. When Victoria came to the throne 'wine' in a middle class household usually meant either port or sherry but it could mean cowslip, ginger, or gooseberry.[35] Donovan in his *Domestic Economy* of 1830 gives recipes for making wine from ripe or unripe gooseberries, currants, strawberries, raspberries, elderberries, and damsons. Of the wine made from unripe gooseberries he says 'the wine thus produced will generally be brisk and similar in all its qualities (flavour excepted)

[32] Besant, *op. cit.*, 92. For 'afternoon tea' see *Early Victorian England*, Young, Peel, I, 97, 99, 126 sq., chapter on 'Homes and Habits'. For 'after-dinner tea', see also Pückler-Muskau, *op. cit.*, Vol. III, 83-7, 311-15.

[33] Besant, *op. cit.*, 165; *The Butler...*, 10; Cosnett, *op. cit.*, 111; Pückler-Muskau, *op. cit.*, Vol. III, 83 sq.

[34] Besant, *op. cit.*, 165-6; Howitt, *Rural Life of England*, Vol. I, 128 sq.; *Early Victorian England*, Young, Peel, Vol. I, 83, chapter on 'Homes and Habits'.

[35] Besant, *op. cit.*, 165-6, and see 92.

to the wines of Champagne, with the strength of the best Sillery'.[36] Besant, writing of the years between 1837 and 1887, and saying that by the latter date these British wines were almost extinct, describes them in terms of apparent admiration: '. . . The cowslip, delicate and silky to the palate; the ginger, full of flavour and of body; the redcurrant, rich and sweet – a lady's wine; the gooseberry, possessing all the finer qualities of the grape of Epernay; the raisin with fine Tokay flavour: or the raspberry, full of bouquet and of beeswing.'[37] Saintsbury, whose remarks cover the end of the Victorian and the whole of the Edwardian epochs, comments that according to a friend of his, rhubarb wine could be 'really worth drinking'. 'Raisin wine,' he himself adds, 'can be doctored into something not unlike a coarse Tent; and "orange" into something by no means distantly suggestive of sherry and bitters. But all these are amiable "fakings", brandy being the chief accessory to the fact.'[38] Does Saintsbury's description, I wonder, give us a clue to the orange wine which Jane Austen desired to make?[39]

Other concoctions which were being made at the end of the Georgian period, and which would also have been made for a time in the still-rooms of early Victorian England, were ginger beer, which included powdered ginger, and spruce beer which was compounded with the help of 'essence of spruce'.[40] One of the odder beverages was toast and water which was drunk by all classes until the 60s. The recipe is perfectly simple and remarkably unexciting; you toast a slice of stale bread until it is brown but not black, put it into a jug, pour over it clean, boiling water, cover the jug, and let the mixture stand until it is quite cold. The more refined practitioners strained the resulting mixture before they put it on the dining-room sideboard. Among the upper classes it was drunk at lunch and at dinner with the cheese-dessert. It died out of English life towards the end of the century and it is not likely that many wept at its passing.[41]

Victorian Drinking Patterns

The Georgians drank memorable quantities of Punch and negus. The Victorians, in their more temperate way, carried on this tradition. Negus, 'made of port or sherry and hot water, sweetened and spiced' accompanied the dancing and card games of lower middle class parties.[43] In the 50s Punch, as well as grog and beer, 'were the most common drinks at Evans's Supper Rooms in London',[44] and in the 40s one may notice a variant of Punch which, in the slang of the semi-criminal lower classes, was called 'hot flannel' and was made from beer and gin, with eggs, sugar and nutmeg.[45] Punch, not in the form of 'hot flannel' but in the guise of *Punch à la Romaine*, or 'Roman punch', was popular among the upper classes throughout the whole of the period. It was a vigorous drink as we can see from a recipe of 1869 which recommends that it should be 'made of "chablis" syrup, lemon juice; freeze it, add two whites of egg of Italian meringue, and when about to serve add rum and champagne'.[46] In early Victorian times it appeared, together with other drinks, at ball suppers. This is reasonable; but one notes with surprise that in the 60s and even as late as Edwardian times, this Punch had become part of the formal dinner.[47] With an alternative or accompanying *sorbet*, for example, a *sorbet au rhum* (much the same as 'Roman punch' though without the champagne and the whites of egg)

[36]Vol. I, 287–98.

[37]*Fifty Years Ago*, 171–2.

[38]*Notes on a Cellar Book*, 95. For Tent see Appendix H, *Wines, Renaissance to Modern*.

[39]*Jane Austen's Letters*, see fn. 233, Ch. 8, and Ch. 8, p. 388. For recipes in 1893 see Mrs Beeton, *Book of Household Management* (edn of 1893), 1197 sq.

[40]Cosnett, *op. cit.*, 290.

[41]Recipes, *Apicius Redivivus . . .*, No. 463 (Bibl. Ch. 8); Cosnett, *op. cit.*, 290. Use of, *The Butler . . .*, 69, 97; *Early Victorian England*, Young, Peel, Vol. I, Ch. II, 138, 'Homes and Habits'.

[42]Footnote deleted.

[43]*Early Victorian England*, Young, Peel, Vol. I, Ch. II, 121, 'Homes and Habits'.

[44]Sala, *Twice Round the Clock*, 340–2.

[45]*Sinks of London Laid Open . . .*, Modern Flash Fictionary (Anon).

[46]Gouffé, *Royal Cookery Book*, 564–5.

[47]*Early Victorian England*, Young, Peel, Vol. I, Ch. II, 120, 'Homes and Habits'; Gouffé, *op. cit.*, *loc. cit.*; Rey, *Whole Art of Dining*, 43.

or a *Kirschenwasser sorbet* (made of chablis and syrup frozen, and 'Kirschenwasser' added instead of rum before serving) it was in the 60s served together with the roasts; in Edwardian times, however, 'Roman punch' was served between the joint and the roast game. This apparent, but slight, difference in service may be purely verbal and it is quite likely that whenever it was served at a Victorian dinner, it came between two courses, or at least it was intended to be drunk between the courses.

Hot wine, either in the form of Punch or of mulled wine, was drunk on fitting occasions but its popularity declined throughout the century and has continued to decline until today. Nevertheless it had its devotees. At the *Ange Gabriel* young prostitutes and their ponces used to refresh themselves with snails and 'great bowls of hot wine'.[48] At what may well have been the same wine shop, since it also was in the rue Pirouette in Paris, Zola describes the counter at the end of which 'bowls of Punch and warm wine circled with brass were bubbling, over the brief blue and pink flames of a gas burner'.[49] Colette has a charming story of herself and her father electioneering in the 80s in a cold Burgundian autumn when, after the election meeting was over, 'at the nearest tavern the hot wine would be steaming on the embers, with the flotsam and jetsam of lemon peel and cinnamon bubbling on its purple swell'.[50] Colette's appreciation of hot burgundy was shared by Americans who compounded for themselves in the 90s a drink called a 'Locomotive', deriving its name no doubt from its power to haul the drinker firmly and safely to bed on a cold night. It was made from two yolks of eggs, one ounce of honey, one liqueur

[48] Andrieu, *Fine Bouche*, 106.

[49] *Savage Paris*, trs. D. Hughes and M-J. Mason, London, 1955, 26.

[50] *My Mother's House*, trs. Troubridge, U. V., and McLeod, E., London, 1953, 40–3.

glassful of curaçoa, a few drops of essence of cloves, and a pint of good, hot burgundy.[51] The 'Locomotive' is thus only a modern extension of the technique which made the medieval piment and the *calida* of Ancient Rome.

It 1825 occurs the delightful phrase 'wine-connors'.[30] It was used to designate those who were wine-knowers or wine-tasters: those in fact who were connoisseurs.[52] Using it in its widest sense we may ask: what of the wine-connors of early Victorian times? What wines did they drink with their meals, and in what sequence did they drink them?

We find a continuing difference between the French and the English habits of drinking. The first difference lies in the taking, or the non-taking, of the *apéritif*. In France one took an *apéritif* before meals: in England one did not. This generalization can be argued but the argument will deal only with exceptions which do not affect its general truth. That such a difference between the drinking habits of the two countries should have existed at all may seem to us surprising: to explain it as being due to a difference in climate is not convicing: a possible, and certainly a more likely, reason is that it stems from the different emphasis which the peoples of the 'Mediterranean' and the 'Gothic' areas attach to the drinking of wine. Basically Mediterranean Man considers wine as an integral part of his meal and a pleasant, but minor, adjunct to his conversation. Basically again, Gothic Man when he thinks of wine, considers a carouse. This too is a generalization to which there are exceptions: the Ancient Greeks inclined on occasion towards the carouse: at festival time in modern Spain or Portugal it is not unknown for the reveller to become his own wine skin. In Gothic countries, on the other hand, the drinking bout is by no means the inevitable conclusion to a friendly evening: among the eagerly intemperate Georgians it was, for example, not at all rare to find men who took their wine with dignity and discretion. Nevertheless, and although they are only basic, almost always subconscious, and often modified by individual sophistication, these differences in outlook do exist and they do influence the social habits of the southern and the northern peoples.

Throughout the 19th century in France the '*coup d'avant de wermuth*' was the most usual *apéritif*. Later in the century, and as alternatives to *wermuth* (which still remained the most popular) one took an absinthe or 'A Bitter', both of them being mixed with water although the 'Bitter' was often mixed with curaçoa or with cassis; at evening in the cafés Madeira was quite a popular *apéritif*.[53]

The Victorians and Edwardians in England displayed an almost total lack of interest in the purpose or pleasure of the *apéritif*. Around the middle of the century sherry-and-bitters was occasionally taken but for the most part the time before dinner was enlivened only by hunger or impatience.[54]

Early in the 19th century it was the custom of the French, at their finer or more elaborate dinners, to drink their ordinary wine neat, immediately after, and only after, the soup. This was called the '*coup d'après*'. For the rest of the meal the ordinary wine – if it continued to be drunk – was always mixed with water unless, as Grimod de la Reynière says, one is a provincial, or no fine wines are being served. The fine wines were served between courses or in the latter part of the meal. Sillery (champagne) was served after the roast meat and if Punch was given it was drunk, usually iced but sometimes hot, towards the end of dessert.[55] A curious feature of these

[51] Beeton, *Book of Household Management* (edn of 1893), 1223 sq. But see Besant, *op. cit.*, 170, for cold versus hot grog in 1888.

[52] Jullien, *Wine Merchant's Companion and Butler's Manual*, trs. Hilton, 1.

[53] Henderson, *History of Ancient and Modern Wines*, 127-9, and see 112, fn. a; Dickens, *Dickens's Dictionary of Paris* (1882), 47 sq., 82.

[54] Footnote deleted.

[55] Grimod de la Reynière, *Manuel des Amphitryons*, 274, 299; Henderson, *op. cit.*, 127 (but he is doubtless using, in part or in whole, Grimrod de la Reynière; see Henderson, *op. cit.*, 112, fn. a).

Ball Supper at the Galerie de Diane
Tuileries; 1869
ILN, February 27th, 1869

smart dinners was the *coup du milieu*. This appears to have been an alternative to the Sillery which consisted of a small glass of bitter liquor, or of spirits, usually Swiss 'extract of absinthe' or Jamaica rum or very old Cognac brandy. The purpose of the *coup du milieu* was to give a tonic 'to the fibres of the stomach and to accelerate the peristaltic movement which produces digestion'; and, carried away by the beauty of health, or comfort, Grimod adds passionately '. . . *sous aucun prétexte on ne peut se dispenser de le boire*'.[56]

This system was never adopted in England. There was never, or almost never, a *coup d'avant*. Wine was, of course, drunk during meals – by the upper classes – but it was not, in the strict sense of the term, *vin ordinaire*: nor was there such a thing as the *coup d'après*. So far as one can tell the English did not mix water with their wines: not at any rate with the wines which they drank at dinner. Professor Saintsbury remarks that 'Our ancestors, I regret to say, had rather a habit of putting water into wine'.[57] He does not give the source of his information nor does he define the period to which he refers but from the context of his remark it seems that he refers to the Georgians, and perhaps also to the early Victorians and that the watered wine, as he himself suggests, was merely grog.

The English never made a point of serving their finer wines between the courses of a meal and although they did serve them towards the end of dinner, the range of wines was limited and their gastronomic quality under-emphasized. As we have already seen,[58] strong ale appeared with the cheese-dessert while with the succeeding dessert of fruit and preserves sweet wines were sometimes served and decanters were put on the table. These decanters usually contained claret, port, and sherry, or less frequently, Madeira. I have nothing against drinking claret right at the end of dinner (though not with the dessert), and I think it a pity that we ourselves do

[56]Grimod de la Reynière, *op. cit.*, 296–7.

[57]*Notes on a Cellar Book*, 164.

[58]p. 398.

not observe such a custom. It is clear, however, that the early Victorians did not regard their late-dinner claret as a dominant wine. They preferred port or sherry. Indeed, at the beginning of Victoria's reign, claret, together with burgundy, Rhône, and Sauternes was only drunk in England by the upper classes. For their after-dinner drinking, middle class people confined themselves to port and sherry, varied sometimes with Madeira or occasionally with Lisbon. For practical purposes 'wine', to the majority of the English, meant port or sherry.[59]

Here we see made plain the second great difference between the French and English drinking in the 19th century. France, rather naturally, drank its own wines and George Augustus Sala, after describing a typical dinner in a reasonably well-off French bourgeois household in 1839, states that 'Sound bordeaux or burgundy' accompanied the meal. One may note his additional comment that '. . . not the faintest whisper of champagne' was heard at these middle class dinners.[60] At the beginning of the century in Paris the white wine served at the 'ordinary' – or *table d'hôte*[61] – was Chablis and although at the less expensive *tables d'hôte* one could get beer it was customary to include a carafe of wine in the dinner.[62] It was, of course, French wine.

Nineteenth-Century Cellar Books

English drinking, as we have seen, was still dominated by that Iberian influence which had been powerful under the Tudors and the Stuarts and almost overwhelming in the Georgian century. Sack, Charneco, Canary, Tent, Madeira, Malaga, Lisbon, Port and Sherry continued to be sought in the English market,★ and it was not until the middle of the century that the Iberian influence began to lose its vigour. This is not to say that there were no French wines in England. Claret, Sauternes, Champagne, some Burgundy, Rhône, and Chablis were drunk in early Victorian times, but only at the tables of the upper class. It would be equally untrue to say that Iberian wines did not appear in France where, at the beginning of the century, Madeira was well known, the dry 'Packarets' (Paxarete) were considered pleasant, and where Malaga and the 'Wine of Xeres', the latter being dry and slightly bitter, were both drunk at dessert.[63] But however much they were appreciated in France, they merely added a detail of elegance to the general, and indeed inevitable, preference of the French for the wines of their own country.

Various cellar books of the 19th century exemplify the English taste for Iberian wines. From the 20s until the 50s in the Senior Common Room of Christ Church, Oxford, the favourite, and overwhelmingly the favourite, wines were of course port and sherry; but when a don wished to vary his choice beyond these two he bought brandy or Madeira, a regular, but limited, amount of claret, a small amount of hock, and towards the end of the period a little Sauternes and Chablis and a certain amount of Moselle. But one also finds in these S.C.R. Accounts that from 1806 until 1824 Teneriffe (certainly on some and probably on all, occasions a white Teneriffe) was bought, while a small quantity of 'Spanish wine' was purchased in 1840 and of 'Bucellas' in 1854.[64]

These Accounts from Oxford give us only a partial reflection of the taste of the

★For these wines (and many others mentioned in this chapter) see Appendix H, *Wines, Renaissance to Modern.*

[59]Pückler-Muskau, *op. cit.*, III, 83 sq.; Besant, *op. cit.*, 165-6; Cosnett, *op. cit.*, III, 113.

[60]*Living London . . .*, 480.

[61]Grimod de la Reynière, *op. cit.*, 294.

[62]See for example, 'Chez Flicoteaux', Pl. Sorbonne, Paris – a students' *table d'hôte*, 1810-48; Andrieu, *op. cit.*, 96.

[63]Beauvilliers, *L'Art du Cuisinier*, II, 349-51.

[64]*Christ Church Common Room Accounts*, MS., C.R.2, *passim.*

G. du Maurier
'A Sleepy Hollow in the
Old Country'

time. Another mirror is the memory of Sir Walter Besant which, looking back at Cambridge in the 30s, recorded that 'there was a great deal of solid drinking among the men, both Fellows and undergraduates. The former . . . drank the good old college port; the latter sat in each other's rooms and drank the fiery port which they bought in the town'.[65] Other mirrors exist for us in the cellar books of the big houses of England. Two of these, the Ashburnham MS. and the Goodwood cellar books, give us a detailed and interesting picture.

In 1845 the Ashburnham cellar held a considerable quantity of port, a large, though not so large, quantity of Madeira, and a much smaller quantity of sherry. The only other Iberian wine which figures in this year is a small lot of 'Calcavello'. Of the French wines, claret is the most prominent but there is not a great deal of it. Most of the claret was designated merely 'St Estephe', the rest of it being 'Bell Raimi 1825', though there were also in the same bin eight bottles of claret which are darkly described as being 'not good'. There is a moderate amount of burgundy, some Chablis, and small amounts of champagne and 'Masdew', the latter being a wine grown between Perpignan and Collioure at the eastern end of the Pyrenees. Of the other wines worth mentioning in the present context there was a little Tokay, both dry and sweet, some Sicilian wine, quite an amount of Smyrna, red and white, a little of it sweet, and a considerable quantity of 'Hock'.[66]

The Goodwood cellar of the Duke of Richmond and Gordon shows much the same general pattern. Of all the bottles of wine in the cellar in May 1845, 2,077 were Iberian and 1,091 were French. For the rest there were 23 bottles of German, and 137 of Cape wine from South Africa. In detail, however, this cellar differs from Ashburnham for it contains more sherry than port, and only a small quantity of Madeira. Assuming that the very small amount of Malmsey in Ashburnham was Malmsey from Teneriffe, or at least from the Canary Islands, then in addition to port, sherry and Madeira, the only other Iberian wines in Ashburnham are Malmsey

[65] Besant, *op. cit.*, 157.

[66] Ashburnham MS., 2734, Sept. 1845.

and 'Calcavello'. Goodwood, on the other hand – again in addition to its port, sherry and Madeira – has Calcavella, Bucellas, Malaga, Vidonia (a dry wine from the Canaries, which was often called Teneriffe), 'Paxaretta' and Lisbon. There is much more claret in proportion to port, sherry and Madeira in Goodwood than there is in Ashburnham. Goodwood has far more champagne and far less hock. Another notable feature is the large quantity of Cape wine.[67]

Some idea of the actual consumption of these wines can be gained from the amounts drunk from the Goodwood cellar during the five days of Race Week in July 1845: Best Claret – 64 bottles, Light Claret – 57, Port – 100, Sherry – 176, Madeira – 14, Champagne – 162, Bucellas – 2, and Hock – 12.[68] (One might mention that out of these totals the kitchen took 10 bottles of Port, 10 of Sherry, 7 of Madeira and 4 of Brandy.) Admittedly Race Week is a special occasion and to some extent created special conditions, but even so these figures cannot help reflecting the general preferences of the English upper class.

Looking at the Ashburnham Records for 1836 and 1840 one can see that its contents varied, though not, I think, to the extent of upsetting the general pattern. Champagne occurs, as do 'Johanisberg', Moselle, and 'Sauterne'. There is some white burgundy and Hermitage. Cape wine is listed but it disappears after 1840 as does Marsala though this may be the wine which later appears as Sicilian. Cyprus, and a wine vaguely called Muscat, are stocked. Among the Iberian wines we find Tent, Mountain (presumably from Malaga and some of it dated 1769), Seges (from Sitges near Barcelona), Malaga and Lisbon. It is curious to find that, in these years, Sack and Pontac continue to be used as names, thus endowing the cellar book with a faint redolence of late Stuart England.

The popularity of sherry in England is confirmed by scattered incidents. Frith, the painter of 'Derby Day', relates in his memoirs that when he was bringing his mother from Harrogate to London in 1837 or 1838, they stopped at a tavern along the road and his mother, giving him a bottle, told him to go in and get it filled with the best sherry which they had.[69] Frith later tells us that his fellow artist Turner was in the habit of offering him brown sherry and that Turner, on his death bed, had the courtesy to offer 'fine brown sherry' to the doctor who was attending him.[70] When the friends who were going to take Thackeray to see Courvoisier hanged in public called at his house at 4 o'clock on the morning of the execution, after a breakfast of tough fowl, 'the wing even as hard as a board' Thackeray suggested some sherry and soda-water as 'it clears the brains famously'.[71] It is somewhat paradoxical that at Granada in Spain in the 1840s sherry was only sold as a liqueur while at the best houses in Seville one glass only was drunk and this as a '*chasse*'. On account of its aid to the digestion it was called the '*golpe medico*'.[72] It was thus a Spanish version of the French *coup du milieu*.

The wines of Burgundy and the Rhône play only a minor part in these English cellar accounts from which I have quoted. During this period, that is to say during the first half of the 19th century, some burgundy, and on occasion white burgundy, was drunk in England. Chablis makes a small appearance as do the Rhône wines of Hermitage and St-Péray. Beauvilliers, in 1814, extols the red wines of Hermitage but points out that, to be really good, they must be allowed to mature.[73] It seems that they usually got this allowance for they continued to maintain a high reputa-

[67]Goodwood Cellar Books, May 6th, 1845.

[68]*Ibid, loc. cit.*

[69]Frith, *Victorian Canvas*, Ed. N. Wallis, 52–3.

[70]*Ibid*, 71, 76.

[71]See fn. 1. For Saintsbury's view of 'sherry and seltzer' as 'a mistake' see *Notes on a Cellar Book*, 27.

[72]Ford, *Gatherings from Spain*, 162.

[73]*Op. cit.*, 345.

Frith, William Powell, Derby Day, 1858: London, Tate Gallery

tion. At the same date Beauvilliers comments favourably on the wines of Auxerre and Tonnerre and adds that, in a good year, the wine of Beaune, which had a beautiful red colour, could match up to the First Growths. The wines of Burgundy, he says, were ranked by gourmets above all other French wines.[74] Even discounting his slight prejudice in their favour it is clear that Burgundy produced some excellent wines and although they became more important in English drinking in the last half of the century, they never, and they never have, obtained in England the general estimation which should have been their due.

Thackeray – (by chance Thackeray again!) – drank burgundy with *bouillabaisse*. The details of this error are that it was Chambertin and in Paris. In his younger days, at the same inn, he accompanied his *bouillabaisse* with claret. Youth is its own excuse; but, in years of maturity, to deface Chambertin – no.[75] The Ballad in which these *mésalliances* are preserved for posterity is both jocular and sentimental and may therefore be excused as a poetic escapade, rather than the recollection of an actual gastronomic delight. But the smacking of poetic lips over the recipe, the pungency recollected in tranquillity! He may not have remembered much about the wine but he remembered the dish:

> Green herbs, red peppers, mussels, saffron,
> Soles, onions, garlic, roach, and dace:
> All these you eat at Terré's tavern
> In that one dish of Bouillabaisse.

[74] *Ibid,* 342.

[75] *The Ballad of Bouillabaisse.*

406

Revolution, not Rebellion

The Georgian framework was too small to contain the growing population and, in particular, to cope with the rapidly growing urban and industrial population. Harsh conditions in the factories bred either apathy or bitterness; Chartism seemed to be an explosive attack upon society; the 'Hungry Forties' broadened the scope of misery. To the men of that time it must often have seemed that England was on the verge of revolution.

Feelings of insecurity could only have been sharpened by the knowledge that there was no organization capable of maintaining regular and continuous civil order. The answer to a rioting mob was the military. It is true that there were special police who could be called upon in an emergency and that the military was used as seldom as possible, but the fact remained that the police system of the country was fragmentary and inefficient. Individual violence was easy and fear of its happening was no mere vapourish timidity. It was not until the 40s and 50s that the system of County Constabularies was organised and became widespread.

Life faced other insecurities. In 1831 in England, out of the children under five years of age one in three died.[76] In 1836 the expectation of life was 55 years for 'Gentlefolk' at Bath and 25 years for labourers in the same city; in Manchester it was 38 for 'Gentlefolk' and 17 for labourers.[77] Inadequate medicine, sporadic hygiene, and archaic sanitation all helped to produce these depressing figures. In upper class houses fresh air was not considered a necessity and in lower class houses it was often an impossibility. In medicine the anaesthetic and antiseptic revolution was beginning: chloroform in 1847 and antiseptic surgery in 1865: yet although the medical press had begun to exert its influence as early as the 1820s, the revolution took time to gather momentum and to replace ignorance by knowledge.

The need for knowledge was stressed by the outbreaks of cholera in 1831-2 and 1848-9; in 1832 it caused rioting at Exeter and in London in September 1849 it killed 300 people a day.[78] The closets which were in use in upper class houses at this time were inefficient and unventilated. They combined a degree of convenience with the probability of illness. For the poorer people in both town and country the closet was rudimentary while the cesspit system was, to say the least of it, unsophisticated. A *Footman's Directory* of 1825 recommends the weekly cleaning out of the water-closet,[79] and it is hard to believe that even this reluctant treatment was meted out to the backyard privy – known in the lower class slang of the 1840s as 'Mrs Jones's Counting-house'.[80] Old cesspits, being replaced at need by new ones, were often left to infect the ground. The earth of London was impregnated with filth. Polluted water was pumped by the Lambeth and the Southwark Water Companies to their unhappy clients and in South London in 'miles upon miles of open sewer ditches' the drainage 'was left to rot and putrefy in close propinquity to the houses and to poison the air. . . .'[81] In Leeds in the 30s 'whole streets were floating with sewage'.[82]

Cholera again in London in 1853 and 1854 added its weight to the vehement humanitarian protest of Shaftesbury and Dickens against the enforced squalor of the poor. It is almost impossible to believe that human beings could exist in such conditions of horror. Perhaps 'existence' is too dignified a word for the domestic

[76] *Early Victorian England*, Young, Peel, Vol. I, Ch. II, 141, 'Homes and Habits'.

[77] Young, G. M., *Victorian England*, fn. 1, 24.

[78] Peter Cunningham, *Handbook of London, Past and Present*, liv; Skinner, *Journal of a Somerset Rector*, 298 sq.; *Early Victorian England*, Young, Mottram, Vol. I, Ch. III, 157 sq., 'Town Life'.

[79] Cosnett, *op. cit.*, 229.

[80] *Sinks of London Laid Open . . .*, Modern Flash Dictionary.

[81] Jephson, *Sanitary Evolution of London*, 72-3.

[82] *Early Victorian England*, Young, Mottram, Vol. I, Ch. III, 167, 'Town Life'.

scene described in evidence given to the Metropolitan Sewers Commission in 1847 – 'I have also seen in such places human beings living and sleeping in sunk rooms with filth from overflowing cesspools exuding through and running down the walls and over the floors. . . .'[83] Just off New Oxford Street in London, 2,850 people lived in 95 'wretched houses'.[84] There are only too many examples of similar abominations.

In 1848 Europe was alive with revolution. England, becoming more and more critical of the misery in which many of her people lived, growing more and more impatient at the incompetence of the old Order to deal with that misery, might also have seemed ready for upheaval. But, in that same year, and instead of revolution, she got her first Public Health Act.

This is a typical instance of the English Victorian attitude. England was in fact undergoing a profound revolution for she was creating the basis of the modern, democratic, Welfare State. It was an administrative revolution, gradual, determined, and pervading. Its distinctive feature was not so much that it valued efficiency as that it was guided by knowledge. At last we have the methodical collection of figures which, together with the census returns (the census was begun in 1801) made possible some scientific analysis of the ills and the needs of society. It was the beginning of the age of statistics. But, however much this revolution was devoted to the creation of an efficient (and enlightened) bureaucracy, however much it attempted to put dispassionate knowledge into the work of administration, it was also motivated by a religious impulse.

Evangelical religion was a powerful force in the early part of this century. Its moral vigour and its earnestness of purpose turned strongly towards humanitarian action. It was behind the anti-slave movement and it fought against the appalling conditions in the factories. It is again typical of early Victorian England that the impetus of a social reform should have been religion on the one hand and rationalism on the other. Where Evangelical religion stirred the conscience, Utilitarian Philosophy activated the mind. The views of Jeremy Bentham coincided with the statistical temper of the time. Nonconformist Utilitarian thinking, with 'Radical realism', produced a hard, devoted efficiency that made the revolution unanswerable.

England in the 30s and the 40s may seem to us to have been riper for armed, or at least violent, revolt than in fact she was. Despite the incidence of squalor, injustice, and hunger, the purchasing power of wages in general was rising,[85] and even in the 'Hungry Forties' there were areas of prosperity. Trade unions had already been made legal and thus working class agitation, however opposed or obstructed, was not the conspiracy of outlaws. Furthermore, the growing use of machinery demanded a growing application of skill and the master-mechanic was making his way in the hierarchy of industrial labour. The major influences of the time, religious, economic, and intellectual, were in England antipathetic to rebellion; what they wanted, and what they got, was a peaceable, painstaking and intelligent revolution. They had not got all of it by 1860 but by then the work of the pioneers had brought modern England safely out of the troubled break up of the old Order. The magnitude of the achievement gives an heroic stature to the men who created it.

[83]Jephson, *op. cit.*, 18–19.

[84]Peter Cunningham, *op. cit.*, 369; *Sinks of London Laid Open*, 19. For examples in the 60s and early 70s see Taine, *Notes on England*, 29-31.

[85]Sir John Clapham, *Economic History of Modern Britain*, Preface, vii.

Gestures of Retreat

It is only natural that a society exposed to the pressure of continual reform and increasing complexity should from time to time react against the pressure and momentarily attempt some form of retreat. This happened in England through most of the Victorian Age, manifesting itself in various forms of romanticism, all of which turned back to admire an idealised conception of the Middle Ages. In each case the conception which they admired was a misinterpretation of reality. The Pre-Raphaelites – the 'Brotherhood' which began in 1848 with Millais, Holman Hunt and Dante Gabriel Rossetti – generally misinterpreted the practice of early Italian art. Pugin believed that the excellence of architecture depended upon the religious and moral purpose of the architect; to him its most perfect expression was 14th-century English Gothic. Ruskin, in his turn, trumpeted the exclusive virtues of earlier Gothic and Romanesque. William Morris, convinced (rightly) that the craftsman ought to find artistic joy in his work, believed (wrongly) that the Middle Ages were the golden period of this joyous self-expression. Rousseau and Châteaubriand, Wordsworth and Shelley, had done their work of extending the range of the imagination, encouraging introspection, extolling solitude and the beauties of untamed nature. Victorian poetry continued to follow this line and another strong influence was the fusion of the Gothic and Romantic elements, stimulated by the publication of the old English and Scottish ballads by Thomas Percy and Sir Walter Scott and by the folk tales collected by the brothers Grimm. This influence indeed spread widely across northern Europe, producing Scottish tartans in the most unlikely places. The 'Gothic' interest in the horrific and mysterious attained perhaps its highest expression in Poe's *Tales of the Grotesque and Arabesque*. In the hands of lesser men these trends produced a crop of pseudo-historical romancing and fantasies of excited morbidity.

The Challenge to Orthodoxy

The two forces of reorganization and mechanization might drive the Victorian into a gesture of retreat. But there was yet a third pressure which he was compelled to meet: the challenge to his religious faith. There had, of course, been previous attacks upon Christianity: Hume and Voltaire, for example, on the intellectual level, and Tom Paine on that of political agitation. But, however much religion may have been weakened in France, in England it maintained, and even increased, its strength. The Puritan impulsion, still deeply dependent upon the Bible, though gentler now than it had been in the days of Cromwell, continued to be a social dynamic. It was a potent influence on the Evangelicals; its moral earnestness spread from the middle into the upper classes; its humanitarian emphasis speeded the work of early Victorian reform.

We have seen the Puritans in the 17th century pouring out their wrath upon masques and dancing; some 19th-century Evangelicals also frowned on mixed dancing and even Byron, no Puritan, had in 1813 launched an anonymous attack upon the impropriety of the Waltz.[86] But what to us is perhaps most repugnant in the Victorian religious attitude is illustrated in a book called *The Successful Merchant* which was published in London in 1852. It was a tribute to the commercial success

[86]Wesley, *Works*, Vol. VII, 34; Byron, *The Waltz*, published anonymously in 1813 but included in the 1824 edn of the poet's work.

J. J. Chalon, 'Le Restaurant', 1820

of Samuel Budgett, an aptly named merchant of Bristol who died in 1851. In the 'great warehouse in Nelson Street, Bristol' he allowed, indeed he encouraged, the use of one room as a chapel where the men who breakfasted on the premises could worship for half an hour before their breakfast. The worship consisted of scripture reading, prayer, and a hymn, and it is worth noting that on the chapel table lay *Fletcher's Family Devotion* and *Wesley's Hymns*. Comment upon the character and the achievement of Mr Samuel Budgett is given in this book by a 'Minister of Religion'. He quotes one of the Budgett workmen (who had been helped by S. Budgett), as saying that 'the secret of Mr Budgett's success in business lies in his true religion'. And, remarks the Minister of Religion, the workman 'was right. Never have I witnessed such a remarkable instance of a firm of mercantile men being guided by the Saviour's injunction "Seek ye first the kingdom of God and His righteousness, and all these things shall be added unto you"'. The book was dedicated to 'The Young Men of Commerce'.[87]

The unctuous smugness and the intellectual dishonesty – or perhaps it is kinder to say the intellectual frailty – of this 'Minister's' comment were not typical of Victorian religion which, on the contrary, was being tested by criticism and scoured by self-examination.

Hippolyte Taine observed that Scottish Protestantism was 'a religion whose practice and dogma resemble a hedge of thorns'[88] and his description might well be applied, though in a different sense, to the Anglican Christianity of mid-Victorian England. The thorns of doubt afflicted both those who felt that denial was impossible and those who felt that belief was dishonest. The fervour of the

[87] Arthur, W., *The Successful Merchant*, 14-15, 256.

[88] *Op. cit.*, 283.

410

Methodists and the Evangelicals may have slowed, but it could not stop, the movement of rejection. The loss of faith had begun before Victoria came to the throne.[89] It was due to many causes, to apathy, to rationalism, to discontent at the uninspired voice which sounded from what the polite called the pulpit and the irreverent the 'autem cackle tub'.[90] The Tractarian movement of the 30s was a defence and not a counter-attack. The attack came from rationalism which spread among the educated classes of England as it did among the same classes in Germany, and the crucial point of attack was the literal truth of the Bible. Geology had become popular in the 30s with the publication of Lyell's *Principles of Geology* and geology was to cast doubt upon the biblical age of the world. In 1857 Neanderthal man appeared and the embarrassing questions raised by this discovery became inescapable with the publication two years later of Darwin's *Origin of Species*. The battle between science and the Book of Genesis was fully engaged and the logic of this disbelief could not fail to make honest men question at least some of the tenets of their religion. This mental revolution, whose turning point had occurred in 1859, was, like the administrative revolution, intelligent and earnest, and – this is typically Victorian – the men who lost their faith in religion kept their faith in morality. They believed in 'right-doing' just as fervently as any Evangelical with the same integrity of conscience and of purpose.

Victorian Tastes: in wine and other things

A streak of incurable earnestness ran through the whole period and thus, while the Victorians were usually ready to criticize, they were generally reluctant to laugh. Their sense of humour was not sophisticated; at its weakest it could produce the joker who, at suppers in the 30s, poured melted butter into coat pockets;[91] at its most acceptable the later, and heavy-handed humour of *Punch*. The Victorian sense of the comic was refreshed, and even uplifted, by the spectacles of a Distinguished Person sliding desperately upon banana peel. And if the majority of them were deaf to laughter, they were also blind to beauty. Seldom can a high civilization have been cursed by such lamentable taste. Their furniture was pompous, their paintings sentimental, their ornaments innumerable, and their buildings hideous. The same exaggeration and lack of taste characterized their decoration and their clothes. Fringed and tasselled pelmets, trellised wallpaper, striped and flowered fabrics of green, maroon, and tan diminished any feeling of space which might have been left in the already overcrowded rooms. The crinoline only served to emphasize the lack of space for in 1860 'a fashionable woman needed an area of 20 to 25 square feet in which to stand comfortably without compression'.[92] Colours were heavier than in the 40s and were used in sharp contrast – purple, lilac, black, royal blue, claret, magenta and dark green. But beauty, at any rate so far as sex is concerned, is in the eye of the beholder and the girls of the 50s and 60s doubtless looked charming, embellished, when they went to balls, with prim, round, paper-frilled bouquets and otherwise decorated with pseudo Gothic or copied Renaissance jewellery.[93]

Still, if aesthetics wilted, knowledge flowered and in the growth of detail and of classification we can see another movement of the statistical mind. The growing

[89] For some instances of irreligion see Taylor, G. R., *The Angel-Makers*, 48; Skinner, *op. cit., passim.*

[90] *Sinks of London Laid Open . . .*, Modern Flash Dictionary.

[91] Besant, *op. cit.,* 100.

[92] *Connoisseur Period Guides, Early Victorian Period,* 131 (chapter on 'Costume' by Anne M. Buck); see also Yarwood, Doreen, *English Costume*; Truman, Nevil, *Historic Costuming*; Laver, James, *Victorian Vista*, Pl., p. 148.

[93] *Early Victorian England*, Young, Peel, Vol. I, Ch. II, 102, 'Homes and Habits'; Connoisseur Period Guides, *Early Victorian Period,* 146-7, chapter on 'Jewellery' by J. F. Hayward.

attention to detail, and to accuracy of detail, had a marked effect on the attitude to wine. Vintage dates and style-descriptions occur more frequently in cellar books and wine lists. This type of classification was not entirely new; one finds it for example in the magnificent wine list of Astor House, New York, in 1839;[94] but its regular application is the work of the later Victorians. In 1836, for example, the Ashburnham cellar book has Claret, Light Claret, and Pontac.[95] In 1845 the Goodwood cellar book lists Best claret (Vintage 1834) and Light claret (La Rose), but from 1845 until 1859 it mentions only Best claret and Light claret, the latter being sometimes additionally described as La Rose.[96] In 1862, however, there are six clarets, five of them named and two of them dated. The same general process is particularly noticeable with sherry. In 1836 Ashburnham just has 'Sherry' as does Goodwood in 1845 and 1855. But in the late 60s and early 70s the Goodwood classification is far more detailed and includes Manzanilla and Amontillado. The Christ Church Accounts follow much the same pattern though 'Amontillada' makes its appearance in 1846.[97] A Wine List of Harvey's of Bristol in 1867 has sixteen sherries – and, curiously enough, puts Rota Tent under the heading of Sherry.[98] This growing emphasis on discrimination affected, and was affected by, a parallel development in the vineyards for in 1855 came the great classification of the wines of the Gironde and a few years later the classification of the Cognac vineyards into areas of differing quality.[99]

The role of sherry in Victorian drinking was quite different from what it is in our own days. The Victorians took over the Georgian habit of mind and considered sherry, not as an *apéritif*, but as a wine. Indeed, Mrs Beeton states in her *Complete Etiquette for Gentlemen* of 1876 that 'sherry is the dinner wine'.[100] This was clearly not true of all dinners of all classes at this time and since some of the other wine-lore in the early editions of the same work is inaccurate, one accepts this particular statement with reservation. It cannot, however, be rejected entirely. Other instances display the older attitude: on Christmas Eve, 1847, at Goodwood there were seventeen to dine and there was a dance and the wines brought up from the cellar were two bottles of port, one bottle of Best claret and ten bottles of sherry; in the 80s and 90s that eager gourmet, Professor Saintsbury, was accustomed to give his guests sherry towards the end of dinner.[101] As a matter of fact, Saintsbury gives indirect support to Mrs Beeton's dictum since he writes that the lightest sherries, and in particular Manzanilla, can be drunk as a beverage with almost any food and adds that the 'medium sherries . . . are, perhaps, more the wine of all occasions than anything else . . . with food or without it'.[102]

The sherry of which Mrs Beeton speaks would not have been the dry sherry which appeals to our modern taste. The vogue for dry sherries – the finos which have been worked on by the *flor* – began in England in the 70s but even then the wine was not, in our sense of the words, really dry. It is tempting to put the change of taste, or rather the beginning of the change, further back than the 70s; in 1845 we find the listing of a Pale Dry Sherry and the same description occurs in another cellar book in 1862.[103] Remembering that a dry and slightly bitter wine of 'Xeres' was drunk in 1814,[104] one might assume that the taste had spread to the more cosmopolitan of the English aristocracy. There is, however, no proof of this assumption and even though Harvey's in 1867 were shipping a Vino de Pasto –

[94] Published by André L. Simon in *The Gourmet's Week-End Book*, 253-7; cf. the interesting wine lists of 1803 and 1847, *Ibid*, 244 sq.

[95] Ashburnham MS., 2732.

[96] Goodwood Cellar Books.

[97] *Common Room Accounts*, MS., C.R.2.

[98] Published by Godfrey Harrison, *Bristol Cream*, 114.

[99] Delamain, *Histoire du Cognac*, 70.

[100] p. 44.

[101] Goodwood Cellar Books, Saintsbury, *Notes on a Cellar Book*, 218, 223, etc.

[102] *Loc. cit.*, 17–18, 22.

[103] Ashburnham MS., 2734, Goodwood Cellar Books.

[104] Beauvilliers, *op. cit.*, 351.

Doré, Gustave
The Derby: Lunch
from 'London'
London, British Museum

(a dinner sherry which, at least a few years later, was sometimes dry) – and also a Manzanilla,[105] we must continue to believe that the Victorians until the 70s, and many of them for much longer, drank what we would call medium and rich sherries.

The same change of taste, from sweet to dry, happened also with champagne, beginning in the 60s and becoming general in the 70s. Until the middle of the century it had been a 'difficult' wine, young and unstable, sometimes 'sparkling' as we know it, sometimes merely 'creaming' or 'foaming'. Scientific research and improved technique enabled it to become a stable, dependable wine, more consistent in quality and much lower in price and as a result its popularity increased so enormously in England that champagne becomes a feature of later Victorian drinking. One set of figures alone dramatically illustrates this development in the champagne trade: in 1844–5, so states the Chambre de Commerce de Reims, 4,380,214 bottles of champagne were exported from France, while from 1869–70 France exported 13,858,839 bottles, all of them being sparkling wines.[106] Another and more colourful illustration of its popularity is given by Taine at the Derby. In a

[105]Godfrey Harrison, op. cit., 114.

[106]Archives Nationales, Paris, F12, 2525.

413

W. Dickes
Champagne Bottling: 'The
Production Line'
early 19th century

description as vivid and detailed as Frith's 'Derby Day' he enumerates the tents and booths, gipsies, dancers, and musicians, carts, cabs, private omnibuses and 'four-in-hands, each with its basket of pies and pastries, cold meats, melons, fruit and wine, especially champagne'. Yet the old Iberian pattern persisted for when one of Taine's party was invited to drink with some new acquaintances, he was offered 'a glass of port, sherry, stout or ale'. Taine himself appears to have been no horse-player and remarks of the whole race meeting: 'No doubt I am lacking in enthusiasm, but I find it like watching a game played by insects.' The insects, however, enjoyed themselves, especially after the big race, and the consequent eating and drinking, were over: 'Twenty-four gentlemen triumphantly set up seventy-five bottles on their omnibus – they had drunk them all. Parties bombarded each other with chicken-bones, lobster shells and divots of turf. Two parties of gentlemen had got down from their omnibus and were boxing ten against ten; one had two teeth broken.'[107]

In 1837 champagne had been rare and regarded either as an extravagance or as a wine to be drunk only at special celebrations.[108] In 1855 it was beginning to be drunk with meals, thus starting a habit which became dominant in late Victorian times. A not uncommon sequence of wines at a dinner in the 50s was sherry or Marsala after the soup and with the fish, and with the 'entrees' (or third course) champagne or sparkling Moselle.[109] Another mid-century menu illustrates the continued emphasis on sherry, the delight in sparkling wines, and the habit of drinking good table wine at the end of the meal. The occasion was a dinner given by Sir

[107]Taine, *Notes on England*, 32–6.

[108]Besant, *op. cit.*, 165–6.

[109]*The Butler . . .*, 95 sq.

William Hardman at his club, his guests being George Meredith, Dante Gabriel Rossetti and a certain Dr Liveing. Hardman's comment was: 'I flatter myself they never sat down to a better selected meal in their lives.' For your judgment also here it is:

'Oysters, bearded, brown bread and butter Côtelettes de Saumon à l'Indienne	Chablis
Filets de Boeuf grillés au beurre d'Anchois Epinards au jus Côtelettes d'Agneau à l'Italienne	Amontillado
Fricassée de Poulet à la Marengo Choux-fleurs au gratin Omelette aux Fraises Maccaroni au gratin	Sparkling Hock

Wine after dinner: Chambertin
Coffee: Dry Curaçao
Cigars: ad libitum.'[110]

Meredith, after this dinner, was in excellent shape.

We have already seen that in Paris at the beginning of the century a *coup du milieu* was drunk immediately after the roast.

The shock treatment of the *coup du milieu* imported into Victorian dinner parties in the 60s may well have been necessary since the Victorians possessed heroic appetites, and it was not only at dinner that they indulged them. They prepared themselves for the day by a breakfast which could include eggs, kidneys, cutlets, fish and cold dishes. In the middle of the day they had a lunch which, both for business men and country families, was not radically different from what it is today, and usually, though not invariably, they were temperate in their lunch-time drinking. Sir William Hardman tells the story of a friend of his who went to dinner with a public-house keeper in Hackney. They dined at three on a Titanic meal accompanied by 'Cooper' – a half and half mixture of stout and porter. This was followed by hot spirits and water, 'well sweetened'. Tea, at 7 o'clock, merely consisted of cress, shrimps, and an enormous pile of muffins. Tea was followed by still more 'Cooper'. This may seem, in every sense, an outstanding occasion but a fondness for muffins after a large meal was an eccentricity shared by quite a number of the mid-Victorians. Toast, bread and butter, and muffins, together with tea and coffee, were handed round in the drawing-room after a dinner party by which time, one might have thought, they would have been superfluous.[111]

For the hungrier, and less affluent, London gourmet of the 40s there was the baked-potato man who patrolled the streets with his 'locomotive cookshop' and for a half-penny retailed a hot potato seasoned with butter, pepper and salt. For a penny the late theatregoer could buy a sandwich from the ham sandwich man.[112] Another vanished feature of the Victorian scene was the marrow bone. At small parties these were served with the cheese-dessert, after the second course. They were popular in the 50s and also in the 60s, as can be seen from the menu of the Saturday

[110]Hardman, *op. cit.*, 114.

[111]Hardman, *op. cit.*, 106-10, including the comments of his editor; *The Butler* . . ., 100-1.

[112]Knight, *London*, Vol. IV, 317-19; ed. Smith, A. R., *Gavarni in London*, 101-6.

evening dinners of 'Our Club' founded by Douglas Jerrold and attended mainly by writers, publishers and artists. They dined at Clunn's in Covent Garden on fish, boiled beef, pigeon pie, rump steak and marrow bones, finishing off the evening with punch.[113] In 1899 you could still get marrow bones at the Blue Posts in Cork Street, London, but they were then considered to be old-fashioned British food.[114]

Another, and excellent, form of British food – the oyster and woodcock lunch – may perhaps have been considered somewhat old-fashioned, or provincial, at the end of the century,[115] but the oyster at least could look back upon a career of almost universal popularity. The Victorians ate far more oysters than we do now. In the 40s in London they ate them at Oyster Rooms, to which they went for supper rather than for dinner, and in the 80s they could get them, as the Londoner can get them now, at Rule's, Wilton's and Scott's.[116] In Paris they were, of course, also very popular and, according to Gérard de Nerval, one method of eating them (at the Restaurant Baratte) was sprinkled with shallots which had been chopped, peppered, and soaked in vinegar.[117] They were a favourite food in the eastern part of the United States. Pickled oysters were eaten in considerable quantities in Cincinnati in the early 30s. Sala comments on the underground oyster cellars 'on Broadway Pavement' in the 50s and an American writer of the 60s calls them the national dish. 'There is,' he says, 'scarcely a Square without several oyster saloons; they are above ground and under ground, in shanties and palaces. They are served in every imaginable style – escalloped, steamed, stewed, roasted 'on the half shell', eaten raw with pepper and salt, devilled, baked in crumbs, cooked in pâtés, put in delicious sauces on fish and boiled mutton'. With some pride he continues 'the English oyster is but a poor shrivelled pigmy of a dish in comparison. . . .'[118] They were the first course at what a New York newspaper in 1822 described as 'a Good Sunday Dinner'. The entire menu was thus:

Oysters
Potage Printanier Royal
Broiled Salmon Ravigote
Saddle of Lamb
Succotash
Roast Woodcock
Tomato Salad
Macédoine of Fruits
Dessert, Cheese, and Coffee

Sala comments on this menu 'Tomato Salad is just beginning to be appreciated in civilized English houses' and points to one of the differences between American and English eating.[119]

Other differences existed then and have continued to exist. Even in 1852 an American farmer visiting England could observe of the young men of Chester that, on Sunday night, they each drank their glass or two of beer 'as in an American town they would take ice cream'.[120] With prejudiced astonishment (and she was prejudiced), Frances Trollope remarks at the beginning of the 30s that the Americans

[112] Knight, London, Vol. IV, 317–19; Ed. Smith, A. R., Gavarni in London, 101–6.

[113] The Butler . . ., 95; Hardman, op. cit., 200.

[114] Newnham-Davis, Dinners and Diners, 47.

[115] Ibid, 46.

[116] Knight, London, Vol. IV, 316; Dickens, Dickens's Dictionary of London, 205.

[117] Andrieu, op. cit., 105.

[118] Frances Trollope, Domestic Manners of the Americans, 254–6; Sala, Twice Round the Clock, 326; Towle, American Society, Vol. I, 272.

[119] Sala, Living London, 407; cf. Towle, op. cit., 270, etc.

[120] Olmsted, Walk and Talks of an American Farmer in England, 149.

*Vintage in the Médoc
from 'Château Loudenne',
1889
Messrs W. & A. Gilbey,
Ltd*

'mix things together with the strangest incongruity imaginable. I have seen eggs and oysters eaten together; the sempiternal ham with apple sauce; beefsteak with stewed peaches. . . .'[121] Both at this time and in the 60s it was rare for the Americans to drink anything but water with their meals.[122] Towle, an American, writing in 1869 tells us that good wine was rare in American hotels and that even poor wine was expensive in comparison with European prices. As the cheapest and the best he recommends 'the native Catawba and wild grape wine' and also mentions California Hock and Sparkling Catawba.[123] Anthony Trollope, writing in 1862, records that, in his experience, wine in American hotels was costly and bad. It was indeed costlier for the usual price was $2 (or 8/-) a bottle whereas St Julien Claret was only three shillings a bottle (retail) in London. When they did drink wine with their dinner in hotels they drank champagne but in the normal course of events they drank before dinner and at the bar, a drink, whatever it was, invariably costing a dime (or fivepence).[124]

While these observations are, of course, accurate, they still do not give us the whole of the picture. We have already noticed the remarkable wine list of Astor House, New York, which offered to its clients in 1839, fourteen Hocks and fifteen clarets and thirty-nine Madeiras, among which were 'Wedding Wine' at eight dollars a bottle and 'Caroline, an old Family Wine' at five dollars a bottle. There were also champagne, sherry, burgundy, port, Sauterne, and one Moselle.[125] Other evidence from this period shows that Americans were not only buying, but were increasingly buying, European wines. In 1830 the United States imported 1,854,839 gallons of French wines and this figure, still for French wines, rose to 3,184,873 gallons in 1839. In 1830 the United States took from France 440,910 gallons of wine brandy and in 1839 they took 1,902,376 gallons.[126] It is unlikely that all of this wine was used for distillation in the States, or blending, and in fact Americans of the 60s, or at least some Americans, continued to drink European wines.

They also drank 'country wines'. In idyllic terms Towle describes life in August

[121]*Op. cit.*, 254-6.

[122]Frances Trollope, *op. cit.*, 254-6; Towle, *op. cit.*, 270.

[123]Towle, *op. cit.*, Vol. I, 327.

[124]Anthony Trollope, *North America*, Vol. II, 403.

[125]See fn. 94.

[126]*Archives Nationales*, Paris, F12, 2525.

and September on a Connecticut farm twelve miles from Hartford and the picnics which the young people had there in the woods at which they drank 'bottles of gooseberry and currant wine, of cider and lemonade. . . .'[127] Among the drinks which were served in New York bars at this time were Claret Punch, Brandy Cocktail, Mint Julep, Gin Sling, and Sherry Cobblers. The latter, made of sugar, sliced oranges, crushed ice and sherry, and sometimes with the addition of pineapple or other fruit, was very popular as indeed it was in the late 40s in London where it was much favoured by the customers – after a polka for example – at the 'Casino', which had originally been the Adelaide Gallery. The Sherry Cobbler was not of course a cocktail and it was drunk through a straw or, by the young couples at the Casino, through two straws, but from the technique used by New York barmen who mixed these various drinks, it is plain that we are at the beginning of the cocktail era.[128]

The Classic Age of Claret

At the accession of Queen Victoria in 1837, claret appeared in England only at the tables of the upper classes. At the death of Queen Victoria in 1901 it was beginning to disappear from those same tables. And yet one can say that the reign of Victoria was the classic Age of Claret. This was due to many factors, to increase of wealth and of population, and, not least, to the 19th-century passion for classification and to Mr Gladstone's views of Free Trade.

The quality-listing made at Bordeaux in 1855 for the *Exposition Universelle* is the most famous wine classification in the world. It has been accepted for over a hundred years and it is, with certain reservations, acceptable today. Classification by quality was not a new thing in Bordeaux; there had been a rough one in 1647, another in 1767; and it was thus a long tendency which culminated in the great classification of 1855. This covered the fine wines of the Médoc, and of Sauternes and Barsac and it crowned the five Royalties of Bordeaux: Château Lafite (Château Lafite-Rothschild) and Château Latour, both of Pauillac, Château Margaux of Margaux, Château Haut-Brion of Graves, and Château d'Yquem of Sauternes: to which, by universal acclamation, must now be added Château Mouton-Rothschild of Pauillac. Haut-Brion won its place in this classification as a First Growth of the Médoc even though it is in fact a Graves and indeed there was no official classification of the Graves vineyards until 1953; nor was there, for that matter, such a classification for the wines of Saint-Emilion until 1955. Apart from assuring the quality of its wines – insofar as such a thing is possible in viticulture – the Bordeaux classification gave a much-needed index to the multiplicity of Château names, whose number had increased to the point where it could only bewilder the ordinary wine lover. The index-value may well have been the most important value of the classification in world markets. The ordinary man who likes his wine likes also to have a simple method of grading its quality relative to other wines; very reasonably he wants some simple landmarks in a complicated wine list. And since, perforce, he cannot have the experience of growers or shippers or gourmets he must rely on others to provide his own landmarks. The Bordeaux Classification is experience expressed with simplicity. I believe myself that, if there had been a similar classification of the

[127] *Op. cit.*, Vol. II, 133-40.

[128] Towle, *op. cit.*, Vol. I, 268, 285; Smith, *Gavarni in London*, 14-15.

fine wines of Burgundy (assuming this to have been feasible), it would have had a marked effect on the sale abroad of the wines of the Côte d'Or.[129]

The men of Bordeaux and the drinkers of England found somewhat unexpected aid in the massive intellect of Mr Gladstone. The Cobden-Gladstone Treaty of 1860 lowered the British duties on French wines. St Julien claret had been three shillings a bottle in England in 1839; in September 1860 it was two shillings a bottle. In 1867, 'Médoc' was 1/6d. a bottle as it was in 1893.[130] These were the lower prices for what one must call 'ordinary Médoc claret' but they did their job and after Gladstone had permitted grocers to have an off-licence there appeared the derisory appellation of 'grocer's claret' as well as 'grocer's port'. Though the derision may sometimes have been merited, French wine became a popular beverage. Dr Robert Druitt, a London physician, whose 'Report on the Cheap Wines' was dedicated to Mr Gladstone, considered that 'at and above eighteenpence a bottle Bordeaux wine can be had, retail . . . fit for the table of any gentleman' . . . 'Below eighteenpence good Bordeaux wine may be got retail if the consumer take some pains to choose it and keep it a little'.[131] We cannot vouch for the good doctor's palate but he reads impressively. Exports from Bordeaux to England doubled between 1859 and 1863.[132] The United States, it may be noted, at this time imported as much claret as Great Britain.

The reputation of the wines of Bordeaux, already high, was raised still higher by the outstanding vintage record of the 70s. In the ten years from 1870 to 1879 only two (1873 and 1876) produced indifferent wines; another two years (1872 and 1879) produced medium wines; while of the remaining years four produced fine wines and two (1874 and 1875) produced great and famous vintages. The last vintage of this decade, that of 1879, although it did produce some good wine, was ominous for the future since in that year the vineyards were scarred by the spreading ravages of the phylloxera.

It has always seemed to me that the Médoc *vignoble* is a typical creation of the Victorian era. Historically this is not true, or only partly true; aesthetically it is tenable. But it is tenable only of the Médoc, for the other vineyards of the Gironde have different, and for the most part, older atmospheres. The Côtes de Blaye and the Côtes de Bourg, on the north side of the Gironde, have a Latin look. The grey, or fawn, farmhouses among the pine woods look as ancient as the yellow earth of the vineyards and the old, fawn-coloured churches. In the early spring among the black, stubby vine-stocks there are strips of vivid mustard yellow of willow withes used to tie up the bundles of vine prunings. In the early autumn the gardens are full of morning glory, yellow and purple dahlias, and pink geraniums. It is a curious out of the way part of the *vignoble*, seemingly remote from visitors and imbued with a memory of Imperial Rome. Some of this Latin flavour, though with a strong dash of medieval, clings to the old town of St-Emilion. It sits on and against a cliff in which have been hollowed out 'catacombs' and an old church. Vines sweep up the cliff to the edge of the plateau on which stand Château Ausone and Château Canon. North-west of Canon, and on the edge of Pomerol, is Château Cheval-Blanc, perhaps the most famous of the First Great Growths of St-Emilion. A short distance north again, and in Pomerol, is Château Pétrus, the pre-eminent Great Growth of the Pomerol vineyards. At Libourne, the river port for these two

[129] Lafforgue, *Vignoble Girondin*, 292 sqq. A number of books give the Bordeaux Classification: see Lafforgue, *op. cit.*, 296–8; Alexis Lichine, *Wines of France*, 259 sqq., who also gives the other Gironde classifications. Mr Alexis Lichine, *op. cit.*, 92 sqq., gives a suggested and most interesting Côte d'Or classification. Cf. that suggested in 1855 by Lavalle, Rodier, *Vin de Bourgogne*, 268 sqq.

[130] Harrison, *Bristol Cream*, 114; Beeton, *Book of Household Management* (edn of 1893), 33–4.

[131] Druitt, Robert, *Report on Cheap Wines*, 57.

[132] Lafforgue, *op. cit.*, 265.

*Cuvier: Press House
Grapes coming in from
Vineyard
from 'Château Loudenne',
1889
Messrs W. & A. Gilbey
Ltd*

districts, and at St-Emilion itself one can get magnificent lampreys *à la Bordelaise* and larks wrapped in goose's liver. There is nothing half-hearted about the gastronomy of the Gironde.

St-Emilion looks southwards across the Dordogne and over the valley lands of Entre-deux-Mers which, with four other wine districts, lies between the Dordogne and the Garonne. It produces ordinary wines, both red and white, and some of the white wines at least, soft and agreeable, are 'better than ordinary'. Entre-deux-Mers has some historic importance but it has no historic appearance: it just looks fertile.

South, over the Garonne, is Sauternes, which includes Barsac and which has an atmosphere as distinctive as the splendour of its wines. It is rich, contented, luxurious country. The villages seem to be dispersed, and sunk, among the vines. There are slow streams and peaceful woods shadowed in jade and black. In September the air is lazily golden, sweet and golden like the wines, until the district – the loveliest in the Gironde *vignoble* – takes on the atmosphere of an 18th-century idyll. Even Château d'Yquem, despite its battlements and pointed towers, is perfectly at home in this gentle and sophisticated dream.

It is a strange contrast to walk down the neat rows of vines and see the grapes from which these wonderful wines are made. By the time they are ready for picking they are brown, shrivelled, and dusted with the grey of the *pourriture noble*. This 'noble rot' is caused by the fungus *Botrytis cinerea* which, under the right climatic conditions of heat and humidity, feeds on the sugar and the organic acids of the grape, but more on the acids than the sugar, and produces the sweet pulp from which the great Sauternes are made. The rotted grapes are picked singly, one by one, and the harvest, which can if necessary be stopped for some days and then restarted, may take up to six weeks – sometimes even longer. There is the story of the picker who did a row of vines and, at the end of it proudly presented four rotted grapes. If you take a grape which has suffered this transformation, and you squeeze it, the result may seem disappointing for out of the wrinkled skin comes a morsel

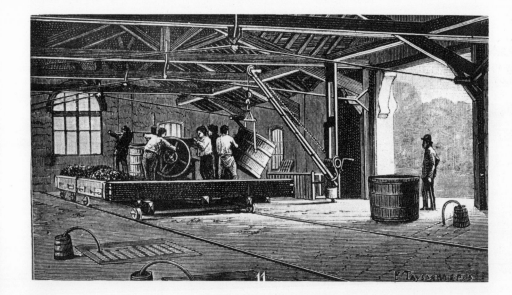

*Égrappoir in Médoc
from 'Château Loudenne',
1889
Messrs W. & A. Gilbey
Ltd*

of pulp, small, yellow and sticky. But out of such grapes are made some of the finest wines of the Gironde. We have already noticed a record of the 'noble rot' at Johannisberg in the 18th century and there may, indeed must, have been occasions when it accidentally influenced the making of Sauternes, but it did not become either general or deliberate until the 19th century and we can class the development of the technique as a Victorian success.

At Yquem the *chais* are behind the Château itself, long, low buildings which are cool and efficient and so clean that they seem to have been polished. Yquem is the star show-piece of Sauternes, but at Château Coutet, down the hill and hidden behind its trees, you find the same spick and span atmosphere in the *chais* and this rigorous cleanness persists through the district. When the grapes are harvested they come into the *chais* and go through an *égrappoir*, a horizontal, revolving drum whose general function is to separate the grapes from their stalks. The grapes are then pressed and the juice, without the skins, is left to ferment in *barriques*. Sulphur is necessary to control the fermentation of these sweet wines but great care is taken by the majority of growers, and certainly by the growers of the fine wines, to see that it is used in such small quantities as will achieve control without affecting the taste. Fine Sauternes spends three years in wood and then goes into the bottle in which it will pass the remainder of its long life. Sometimes this life will be as long as sixty years but more often it will reach its maturity at somewhere between twenty and forty. But, as in everything else, the modern world is in a hurry; great wines are being drunk younger and younger and it may be that many of the Sauternes also will meet their end before they are ready.

At first sight the Médoc is disappointing. The countryside is basically flat, with gentle slopes and with hollows which one can scarcely call valleys. The villages have a prosaic charm but they do not enchant. The woods are not dramatic. The vineyards look out over the estuary of the Gironde which is wide, dull, and often muddy brown. And yet the Médoc is fascinating.

*The Vintage Cart
Built at Pino Terinese
early 19th century
Pessione, Turin, Wine
Museum*

It is an Alice-through-the-Looking-Glass creation. The vines, in their neat, green rows, are the squares on a gigantic chessboard. The pieces on this board are a curious mixture of the functional, the fantastic, and the elegant. Tall, grey and white water towers, bluntly modern; the pointed turrets of Château Pichon-Longueville, and the semi-Palladian front of Château Margaux. Château Cos d'Estournel displays its Chinese pagoda towers while Château Langoa Barton sits with a graceful 18th-century serenity behind its round lawn, its double flight of steps, and its terrace with orange trees in square, white tubs. This *mélange* of style is truly Victorian. Church spires are also pieces on this chess-board and signposts bearing the great names of the Châteaux direct you from one set of squares to another. At the inter-section of vineyard roads there is often a crucifix and in the villages a sort of basset-dog which seems peculiar to the Médoc. There is the occasional, tattered palm tree and in the grass at vintage time there are small mauve cyclamen. At Pauillac, down by the waterfront and the dusty roadside under the trees where the men play *boule*, you may find an itinerant circus, with a clown in baggy, brown check trousers and a woman trapeze artiste in black tights. The third member of the troupe, a young girl still in the puppy-fat stage, tries to do hand-stands with only moderate success. 'Surprise presents' (at fifty francs a time) are handed out to the *aimable société*, consisting mainly of mothers and their children, who much to their surprise receive useful objects such as cigarette holders.

There is an earnestness about the Médoc vintage which also seems to me Victorian. No blatant gaiety disturbs the serious work of making wine. The drums of the Douro, the open and urgent bustle of Champagne, have no place in the harvesting of the Médoc. It is true that at the end of the vintage there may be dancing, the presentation of a bunch of grapes and flowers, and the election of 'Mr and Miss Vintage'; but these somewhat artificial reflections of pagan antiquity are a mere frolic. There is nothing Dionysiac about the Médoc vintage. It is, on the contrary, undemonstrative almost to the point of public disappearance and when the visitor is shown into a *chai* he may well feel that he is being privileged to visit for a moment the *atelier* of a busy and preoccupied artist, the private workshop of a Michelangelo of alcohol.

There is nothing diffident about the men who do the work. They are quiet and expert and they are fully aware that they are co-operating in a great work of art. They are, and they *know* (often rightly), that they are producing one of the unique excellences of civilization. Their attitude to the wine they make tends to become one of reverence before a great beauty. This attitude is so infectious that I once found myself, on the terrace at Lafite, walking softly so as not to awaken the sleeping wine.

There is nothing romantic about the making of Médoc wine except the fact that great wine is being made. The act looks like an orderly and repeated transition from farmyard to laboratory. A cart, drawn by two horses, rumbles into the yard of the *chais*. On the cart are two large wooden tubs full of black grapes. The tubs are lifted off the cart by a winch and tackle, swung through an opening in the wall of the *chai* and tipped into a broad, shallow receiving tray. From the tray the grapes are shovelled into a mechanical *égrappoir* (but not at Latour where the grapes are rubbed on a table) which churns out the stalks at one end and sends the grapes, partly mashed, up a pipe to the fermenting vats. These vats, the *cuves*, are huge and cavernous and the grapes, spat into them from the pipe, fall and splash far down in the darkness. If, while the *cuve* is being filled, you peer down into this darkness through the trap door in the lid of the *cuve*, you see a vast fruit salad of grapes rising slowly up into sight. When the *cuve* is filled to about a metre from the top, the trap door is shut down, the top of the *cuve* is plastered over (when this is necessary to help fermentation) and a tube let into the lid of the *cuve* to allow the explosive part of the fermentation to escape. If it is a cold vintage and the fermentation is slow to start, then a small quantity of the must has to be heated. It comes to the *chai* in a conical bucket, which has a long horzontal handle projecting on either side so that it can be carried by two men, and it looks like the sticky, slightly frothy, dark pink beginning of jam. But it is not jam for this 'starter must' may not be allowed to boil, and indeed may not be heated above 70° centigrade (160 Fahrenheit); it is thus not the same as the ancient Roman *defrutum* or *siraeum* which were both must reduced in quantity by boiling. In a bad year, when the sugar content of the grapes is too low, *sucrage* is a permissible technique, but only after it has been sanctioned by law.

When the *cuve* is filled and plastered over it looks like a cottage in a scientist's fairy tale for the huge wooden vat is covered with a thin roof of what might be icing sugar from which the grey vent-tube sticks up like a small chimney. The resemblance to a laboratory, albeit an unusual one, is increased by the scene which takes place at a table set against a wall of the *chai*. There the proprietor, Ronald Barton (for this is Château Langoa Barton), his nephew Anthony, and the *maître de chai*, are discussing the acid and sugar tests taken from the grape juice in the receiving tray.

The laboratory atmosphere is not, of course, special to Bordeaux. In these days of scientific viniculture you find it throughout the wine trade. At one end of Europe are the hydraulic presses in the surgically clean pressing rooms of German vineyards, where the heavy top-plate assembly swings gently and quietly sideways to drop into the stave-circled pressing bed. At the other are the spotless tasting rooms of the port wine shippers at Vila Nova de Gaia. The poetic traveller may deplore the lack of drama, the absence of apparently romantic treaders, the preoccupation with sugar-content rather than with unlimited singing. He may feel that the beauty is going out of the vintage. And this may be so, but it does not matter because it is going into the wine.

If you made this statement to a man of Bordeaux he would regard it as so trite that it could only have been made by a man who was not of Bordeaux. The wine growers of the Gironde accept the truth of the statement as a matter of fact and not of faith. The expression of this fact varies according to personality: the admiring enthusiasm of the proprietress at Château Canon in St-Emilion: the commanding confidence of the cellar-master at Yquem in Sauternes: the quiet dedication of Monsieur Portet, the director at Lafite and the irrepressible delight of M. Marjary, director at Mouton, in the Médoc.

The absorption in excellence does not vary from one fine château to another but the details of its production do. At Château Latour they bring in the grapes on the same type of horse cart as that used at Langoa Barton, but at Latour the grapes are then put on to a wooden, slatted table where they are rubbed by hand through the slats and thus unstalked. They are shovelled from the receiving tray beneath the table into the usual, double-handled, conical buckets. These are carried, with military precision, by two men, one at either side, up a double ladder to the *cuve* into which the grapes are tipped. At Château Mouton-Rothschild the grapes are dealt with on the first floor. Once again the grapes arrive in their tubs on horse carts. They are hoisted up by crane, tipped on to a receiving platform, and shovelled down a chute on to the *égrappoir* table. They are rubbed through this table, and un-stalked, by blunt-ended wooden rakes. The stalks are put on to another *égrappoir* table where men in black rubber gloves pick up the bunches of stalks and fling them hard on to the slats, thus shaking through any remaining grapes and a portion of the stalks. From the mobile *égrappoir* platform, which runs on rails along the shed, the must is shovelled into one of the waiting *cuves*. Here, as at Latour, is the combination which seems to exemplify the modernizing of viniculture: wooden shovels, rubber boots, and electric presses.

The wine of the Médoc ferments in the *cuves* for anything from four or five days to three weeks. Roughly speaking, the shorter the fermentation the sooner the wine will be drinkable; the longer it ferments the more tannin it will contain, the longer it will live and the more time it will take to be drinkable. Tannin comes from the pips, stalks, and the grape skins themselves, and also, so it is said, from the new oak barrels in which the wine is matured. It gives a bitter taste to young wine but this disappears with maturity and, although the longevity of fine wine is due chiefly to the proper balance of the constituents of the grape, tannin does help to maintain it in good health. A corollary of this is that the wine needs less time to mature in barrel. Good Médoc wine should stay in *barriques* for two and a half years before being bottled, but nowadays the tendency is to bottle before the third year. It is difficult to know which is the cause, and which the effect, of this unhappy develop-ment. In the Médoc it is sometimes said that the consumer demands wine which can be drunk younger; others say that it is due to the merchants and shippers who desire to sell a vintage sooner than it used to be sold and also to lessen the cost of the wine by shortening the time in which it must lie unsold in cask. The first of these theories is certainly true, and when one thinks of the amount of money locked up in the maturing *barriques* it is reasonable to assume that there is at least some truth in the second. One may excuse the development by pleading the impatience of the customer or the necessities of commerce, but one cannot regard it without dismay. It would be foolish to suggest that fine and fully matured wine will become a thing of the past: but it may well become a thing that is only for the very few.

It is an impressive sight to see in the cellars of the Médoc the long lines of *barriques*, each holding 225 litres of maturing wine, and each plugged loosely in its bunghole with a small, solid glass tumbler which is easily removed so that the cask can be topped up with wine every few days. It is also an impressive delight to be the guest of one of the hospitable men who make these wines and to wander in taste across the wide range of clarets. This range is, I think, one of the reasons for the abiding popularity of claret for there is a Médoc wine to suit almost every palate. One *cru* will be firm but graceful: another 'feminine' and delicate: yet another big in body and magnificent in poise. All of them, however, and this is another reason for their popularity, have an innate elegance, that quality of unhesitant fineness which is the essence of civilization.

Phylloxera, the 'Devastator'

If the Victorian Age was one of prosperity for European vineyards, it was also one of danger. In the 50s, Oidium, a powdery mildew, did considerable damage in the vineyards and was only defeated in the end by spraying the vines with sulphur dust. But, before it was controlled, this fungus spread over Europe. In 1853 it was on the Moselle and it went south-west also to the Douro, Jerez, and even to Madeira whose vineyards it almost completely destroyed. Some thirty years later, in the 1880s, another fungus, the Peronospera, attacked some of the vineyards and did its quota of damage. A chemical method of control using copper was instituted, but Peronospera has not been abolished and it has appeared again in the last decade. These fungus attacks were bad enough; but in the 60s there appeared in Europe a pest so lethal that it threatened the entire destruction of the European vineyards.

The pest is a vine-louse, *Phylloxera vastatrix*, the 'devastator'. On American wild vines, which are its natural home, the Phylloxera performs a somewhat complicated life-cycle. It begins with one species which lives on the vine leaves. In the summer, and after the course of two or three generations of these insects, some move down the vine to its roots. They breed the root species, or *radicolae*, which look like tiny, nightmare ant-eaters fitted with beaks. In the autumn these *radicolae* produced winged phylloxeras which fly to other vines. These winged phylloxeras lay eggs which produce wingless male and female insects, of which the females, having been fertilized, lay an egg. From this egg, in the Spring, comes a female which moves from the bark of the vine to the young leaves where, without herself having been fertilized by a male, she lays several hundred eggs from which come the leaf-feeding phylloxeras, from which, in their generation, come the root-

425

feeding phylloxeras: and so on, and so on, as the cycle repeats its protean ingenuity.

On a European vine the life-cycle is simpler, being devoted almost entirely to producing the root-feeders. This fact is of no consolation to the *vigneron* since European vines are highly susceptible to the phylloxera and are destroyed by its attack upon the roots. Phylloxera was brought to Europe from the United States and was first discovered in England in 1863. In 1864 it was identified in the Midi of France and in 1869 it appeared in the Gironde. At the end of the 60s it was in the Douro. It was not, however, until the last quarter of the century that it developed to the full its powers of destruction. In France, at its worst, it is said to have devastated two and a half million acres of vineyards. It ravaged the vineyards of Madeira, destroyed whole plantations of vines in the Douro, destroyed almost completely the vineyard of the Grande Champagne in Cognac, and partly destroyed the other vineyards of this area, ate its way in the 80s through the vineyards of Bordeaux and of Jugoslavia, appeared in Champagne in 1892 and in Jerez in 1894. Ironically enough, it also turned to attack vineyards in the United States. It did not harm the vines of the Eastern States, to which it was native, but in California, where European vines had been planted in the 50s and 60s, it was able to destroy as it destroyed in Europe.

There appeared to be no cure. Chemical controls were expensive and inefficient. Slowly and relentlessly the vineyards of Europe were being exterminated. It seemed likely that less and less fine wine would be made in the world, and the crisis makes this moment of wine history the most dramatic since the vine went to Greece. When the remedy was discovered it was found to be as American as the pest itself for the only method of saving European vines was to graft them on American roots.

American native vines are used for this purpose – such as *Vitis riparia* and *Vitis rupestris* – which are immune to phylloxera and are used as roots to carry the European grafts, so that now by far the greater part of good European wine is grown on American roots. In this way the vines are safe while the wine made from them retains its old, European qualities. There has from time to time been some argument as to whether modern wines differ in quality from those grown on European roots. With one reservation it would seem that they do not. The reservation is this: American rooted vines live for about a quarter of a century whereas ungrafted European vines live for half a century, and often much longer: it is thus possible that wine made from the longer lived, ungrafted European vines would have the greater 'guts' and longevity. For example, I drank in 1958 a bottle of Château Lafite 1875 and this pre-phylloxera claret, then eighty-three years old, was a big, healthy, robust wine. Admittedly it was the finest claret of the 70s, and perhaps one of the finest ever vintaged; admitted also that we cannot now set against it in comparison a post-phylloxera claret of equal age; yet nevertheless one is inclined to wonder. On the other hand the great consensus of expert opinion is that the fine wines we drink now are equivalent to those drunk by the 'pre-phylloxera Victorians' and indeed it is difficult to imagine finer wines than those which the Great Growths now offer to us.

Despite the phylloxera, there are still pure European vines in Europe and wine is still made from them. There are some at Quinta do Noval in the Douro; until immediately after the Second World War the Romanée-Conti in the Côte d'Or was still planted with European roots though now it has been replanted with grafted vines; but the most important exception to the rule of the grafted vine is West Germany. About half of the German vineyards make their wine from grapes grown on non-American roots. The Palatinate is one of the least affected of the German wine districts though perhaps the best known vineyards which are still on European roots are those on the Moselle at Bernkastel and Graach. Not all of these latter, and lovely, vineyards are pure European and when replanting becomes necessary they are planted with American roots. These vineyards on the Middle Moselle are still comparatively free of the Phylloxera, the *Reblaus*, but recently it appeared round Niederemmel which is also on the Middle Moselle. There is of course no doubt that, as things are at present, the number of German vineyards planted with non-American roots will constantly diminish since the *Reblaus* is constantly spreading its attack and forcing the wine growers to think of replanting on the resistant American roots.

In Burgundy the war against the Phylloxera had a secondary, but important, effect. When the growers of the Côte d'Or replanted their vineyards with American roots they changed the old method of promiscuous planting for the modern system of arranging the vines in regular rows. The ancient method existed also in some parts of the Marne Valley before the advent of the Phylloxera as it did too in some of the vineyards of Chablis. By the time these great vineyards had been replanted and re-ordered, the shape of medieval viticulture retreated still further into the past. It is not that the old method was in all cases wrong but that it was in most cases impractical, since the modern use of chemicals, and later of machines, demands a regular spacing between the rows of vines.

In general, the Victorian Age was a time of prosperity for wine growers and shippers. Nevertheless a *vigneron* born in 1820 and, as an old man, looking backwards from the end of the century would have seen the sixty years of his adult working life as years of difficulty and despair relieved only at intervals by a blessed prosperity. He would remember the triple attack of Oidium, Peronospera and Phylloxera. If he had been a man of the Midi or the Gironde he would have remembered the abundant vintages of 1840 and 1841 and the disastrous drop in prices which followed as a result. He might have remembered it being said in 1842 that more than half the properties of the Médoc were up for sale.[133] He might equally remember that one of the causes of this crisis had been the desire of many growers to produce quantity and disregard quality.[134] If he had been an Alsatian he would have remembered the annexation by Germany in 1871 and, because of the German connection, an emphasis in the Alsace vineyards on quantity rather than quality. (He would not, of course, have been able to see the return of Alsace to quality production after 1919.) If he had been a Californian he would have seen in his own country the pattern of over-production, slump, and phylloxera.

In a century of rising demand, and increasing transport, it was inevitable that there should be sporadic over-production and this, paradoxically enough, was made worse by the phylloxera. Spreading devastation, and the consequent drop in harvests, gave to the unaffected vineyards an opportunity to fill the gap. Naturally, and eagerly, they filled it; in the first place from Italy and the Adriatic and from

[133] *Ibid*, 262.

[134] *Ibid*, 262–3.

427

Spain and Portugal, and in this latter connection it is interesting to note that in 1898 Lisbon had the highest production figure of any wine district in Portugal.[135] In the second place the scarcity gave impetus to the production of wine in Tunisia and Algeria, and in Algeria the impetus continued to such an extent that in 1907 the Midi of France was faced with a serious crisis due to the competition from Algerian wines. And in the third place the newer wine-producing territories such as California and South-eastern Australia used this opportunity with varying success, to fill their own markets with their own produce.[136] The oldest of the overseas commercial *vignobles*, the Cape Province of South Africa, was of course still making wine; Canada, at this time one of the youngest entrants into the business, began to plant its wine-vineyards in 1857.

Once the phylloxera was over, French wines had no great difficulty in reasserting their place in the world market. One might have expected that French vineyards would have regained and even increased their pre-phylloxera size. During the end of the 18th and the first half of the 19th centuries there had been a continuous increase in the vineyard area of France: in 1788 there were 1,567,700 hectares: by 1860 this had risen to 2,205,409 hectares.[137] In the face of continually rising demand after 1860 one might have assumed a continual (though interrupted) rise in the area of plantation. This was not always so. Phylloxera had taught the expensive lesson of replanting and in the process the less economic vineyards were allowed to disappear. In 1877, before the phylloxera, there were 282,000 hectares of vines in the two Charentes; nowadays there are 70,000.[138] In the Department of the Gironde in 1875, before the phylloxera, there were 188,000 hectares of vines; in 1939 there were 131,500 hectares.[139] In Burgundy in 1875 there were over 30,000 hectares of vines; at the end of the Second World War there were only about 10,000 hectares, since many of the lesser vineyards had never been replanted.[140] In Portugal, also, the same thing happened and one can still see, in parts of the Douro valley and the valleys running off it, abandoned terraces which are slowly disappearing into a wineless hillside.

Old Customs and New Science

Old-fashioned customs lingered on into this Age of developing science. At the beginning of the 19th century the wines of Pommard and Volnay in the Côte d'Or were pale, slightly pink wines – the colour known as *oeil de perdrix* – and were made from a mixture of white and black grapes.[141] At Valdepeñas in La Mancha the wine was carelessly made and was kept in the cellars in big pottery jars.[142] (Huge jars are still used today in the wine-making of Valdepeñas and one can see them also in the vineyard country near Tarancón outside Madrid.) The brimstone matches used for fumigating wine barrels have a definitely medieval ring since the brimstone was often mixed with aromatics 'such as powdered ginger, cloves, cinnamon, the iris of Provence, thyme blossoms, lavender, marjoram, etc.'; the 'Strasbourg matches', which in 1825 were considered by some to be the best obtainable, were 'covered with the leaves of violets'.[143] A curious custom (perhaps not archaic) in some parts of Germany was the use of wooden mallets to crush the grapes in the tubs, although at the same time, in 1841, they were also mashed in a sort of *égrappoir*

[135]Cincinnato da Costa, *O Portugal Vinicola*, xxvi.

[136]For discussion of this subject, see Lafforgue, *op. cit.*, 257 sqq.; Carosso, *California Wine Industry*, 99 sqq., *et al.*

[137]*Archives Nationales*, Paris, F12, 2525.

[138]Delamain, *op. cit.*, 93.

[139]Lafforgue, *op. cit.*, 272.

[140]Rodier, *op. cit.*, 68-9.

[141]*Ibid*, 40.

[142]Ford, *Gatherings from Spain*, 148.

[143]Jullien, *Wine Merchant's Companion*, 27.

placed over the vat.[144] In Cyprus, in 1851, the grapes were 'raised with shovels and carried into rooms paved with marble, a little sloping on one side. They are there bruised with a flat mallet and squeezed three or four times under small presses'.[145] Even today, in the Loire Valley, the grapes are partly squashed by hand with a wooden pestle – a *fouloir à main*.[146] But these were only stray chords in the score of a developing symphony whose four movements dwelt on the themes of sulphur, copper, sugar, and air. The new symphony of wine making was being written by chemists. Sulphur was coming into general use to defeat Oidium, to sterilize casks, and to control fermentation. Copper was coming into use against mildew. Sugar was at last scientifically employed to aid fermentation of wine and the making of champagne. Before 1832 Chaptal – hence *chaptalization* – discovered or rationalized, the technique of sugaring wines: that is to say, adding sugar to the must to increase the alcoholic content of the wine: and in many of the north-westerly European vineyards this practice is legally permitted in a bad year. Gall distributed this technique in Germany, with particular benefit to the wine growers of the Moselle. Without sugaring, they might have given up their attempt to grow Moselle wine from Riesling grapes, and had they abandoned the Riesling, Moselle would not be the fine wine which we know today. Champagne had improved at the beginning of the century, due to the adoption by some, not all, of the makers of what was basically the modern technique of *dégorgement*.[147] This method of freeing the wine from its sediment helped the quality of champagne but to produce it in quantity was still an expensive business since until the discoveries of François in 1836 (see Chapter VIII) the makers had only an imperfect control of the secondary fermentation inside the bottle. The capacity to estimate the amount of unfermented sugar enabled the makers to reduce the number of burst bottles in their cellars, as

[144]Howitt, *Rural and Domestic Life of Germany*, 55.

[145]Redding, Cyrus, *A History and Description of Modern Wines*, 293, 1851.

[146]*House and Gardens Wine Book*, 1959, 60.

[147]Simon, André L., *Champagne*, 40–1.

we have seen, and also to reduce the cost of champagne to the eager consumer. Thus, by a natural sequence, were made possible those vast accumulations of bottles which the shippers have to build up to meet the world demand for champagne.

The *leitmotiv* of the new symphony was bio-chemical and it was written into the score by Louis Pasteur. His contribution, which came, appropriately enough, at the middle of the century was the study of wine as a living thing. There had been before his time attempts to study fermentation. In 1785 the Academy of Florence had offered a prize, won by the Italian Fabroni, for a theory of fermentation which could be applied to making wine live longer and also to live better during transport. The fact that a prize was offered for this purpose throws an interesting light on the quality of Italian wine at this period. But it was not until Pasteur began his study of yeasts as living organisms, that the great advance was made. Interested by the condition called '*l'amer*' which every year deteriorated large quantities of the best wines of Burgundy (which throws a significant light on the quality of burgundy), he studied the life of wine in sickness. He investigated the action of air upon wine and, showing how this action varied according to the amount of air in the container with the wine, he showed its importance as an element in the proper, and to some extent controlled, maturing of good and healthy wine. The combination of oxygen and wine was, he thought, the essence of maturation.[148] Many vignerons in the many centuries before Pasteur must have thought of wine as a living thing, as a strange and temperamental semi-animal, but their attitude would have been made out of intuition and experience. After Pasteur it was made out of knowledge.

The mixture of old and new is seen most clearly in the German wine trade. We are accustomed nowadays to the lengthy and accurate titling of German wines: for example, *Rüedesheimer Berg Burgweg, Riesling, Spätlese, Kabinett*. First of all comes the name of the vineyard: Rüedesheimer Berg Burgweg; then Riesling, the name of the grape from which the wine is made, though this does not always occur; next the type of harvesting, in this case Spätlese, or a late gathering of grapes which have been allowed to ripen long upon the vines; finally the description *Kabinett* to show that it is one of the finest wines of that particular vineyard. Sometimes a cask number is added after the title, the reason for this being that in Germany each single pressing matures in its own cask, unlike the Médoc where all the pressings of the quality grapes of one vineyard are mixed together to make a single Château wine. This process is called 'equalizing'. And in fact it is beginning to be adopted in some of the German vineyards. It is not at all improbable that the practice will spread.

There are, of course, shorter German wine-titles: *Schloss Vollrads Kabinett*, for example. Here, Schloss Vollrads is the name of the Estate – one of the finest in the Rheingau – but the description *Kabinett* is itself qualified by the colour of the capsule on the bottle, as happens with some of the other fine Rheingau wines, different ones being used by some Estates to indicate the lateness of the harvesting, or the condition – 'ripe' or 'sleepy ripe'. There are of course simpler titles which are merely geographical; Bernkastel, for instance, means wine from the Bernkastel area. Liebfraumilch only means wine which is grown in one, but not necessarily any specific one, of the Rhine vineyard districts. It may be added that in most cases the date of the vintage precedes the title of the wine.

At the beginning of the 19th century it was rare to find German wines carrying

[148]Pasteur, *Études sur le vin, passim.*

Diners, 1899
Bad Berneck, Hist.
Bildarchiv

anything but a general district title. More detailed designations became commoner in the 1820s and the 1830s but, even so, they were not of widespread application. As late as 1837, for example, Deinhard & Co. (then Deinhard and Jordan) were offering Hocks and Moselles under general district titles: *Rudesheim, Hochheim, Geisenheim: Zeltingen, Winningen, Wehlen.* Their wines were, however, given vintage dates and one or two of them, such as '*Johannesberg, Castle*', had a more detailed designation.[149] A German wine bought in 1838 at Christ Church, Oxford, was just called 'Markobrunner' though this is some advance on a district name since Markobrunn is a particular vineyard in Erbach.[150] In the 30s the Ashburnham cellar book does distinguish 'Johanisberg' but goes little further than this, while from 1845 until 1895 the entries in the Goodwood cellar books are 'Hock' and 'Moselle', being only infrequently given a vintage date.[151] Remembering the Old Hock which was on the menu at Vauxhall Gardens in the middle of the 18th century, it is like welcoming an old Georgian character to find that in 1851 Deinhard's were offering to their customers 'Best Brown Old Hocks of 1822 and 1811, etc., etc.'. The favour in which Brown Old Hock was held, at least in England, may account for the considerable age of some of the Hocks which Deinhard's were offering in their price list of 1837. They then quoted a 'Johannesberg, Castle' of 1783, a Rudesheim of 1794 and a 'Markobrunn' of 1806. Some Rhine wines will live for a long time so that the cask of 'Johannesberg, Castle', almost certainly 'filled up' from time to time, could have been replenished with 1783 wine from another vessel, and not necessarily 'refreshed' with a younger wine. In any case, that particular 'Johannesberg, Castle' would basically have been of the 1783 vintage

[149] *The House of Deinhard & Co.* (booklet), 10.

[150] *Christ Church Common Room Accounts*, MS., C.R.2.

[151] Ashburnham MS., 2732, Goodwood Cellar Books, *passim.*

431

*The First Course
from a print by Genzmer
Bad Berneck, Hist.
Bildarchiv*

and it would have become dark in colour and, probably, *madérisé*.[152] The Old Hock
of Georgian England (when it was genuine and when it was good), may have been
a wine of this type although one may doubt that it was usually as old as those offered
by Deinhard to the mid-Victorians.

It is therefore reasonable to assume that a 'solera' system was to some extent in
use in German vineyards in the last half of the 18th century (if not before) and in
the first half of the 19th century. Changing taste and greater classification of vintages led to the disappearance of this system in the marketing of the finer German
wines. In 1846, however, it was in general use in the making of sherry at Jerez de la
Frontera where it has, of course, remained in use ever since. Richard Ford describes
Jerez at this time as a 'rich and popular town, when seen from afar, rising in its vine-
clad knoll . . . characterized by these huge erections' – the bodegas, of which more
than a thousand were registered at the Custom House for the Jerez district. In commenting on the wine made by the Jerezanos, Ford says that 'fine pure sherry is of a
rich brown colour, but in order to flatter the conventional tastes of some English,
"pale old sherry" must be had, and colour is chemically discharged at the expense
of delicate aroma' and he adds that few of the really fine sherries were allowed out

[152] *The House of Deinhard*, fn. 149
above, 16. For comments on these
Deinhard wines I am much indebted to Messrs Deinhard and
Co., London. See also Ch. 8,
p. 365.

of the bodegas until they were ten or twelve years old.[153] Ford is clearly accurate when he describes the life of Spain, but when he is describing Jerez wine making his accuracy is sometimes open to question; nevertheless we can accept most of his statements even if, out of due caution, we have to tone them down.

For the greater part of the 19th century the views taken of the ageing of wine were somewhat different from those which we take today. The tendency in Germany was to keep wine in the cask longer than we should keep it. Eight or ten years was a general time suggested in 1825 for 'Rhenish'. The same time was also suggested for the keeping of Bordeaux in wood whereas now the fine wines of the Médoc are bottled in the second or third year after the vintage.[154] A somewhat curious set of figures for the maturing and longevity of the wines of the Gironde was given by Petit-Lafitte in 1868. The wines of the Palus, wines grown in the low, river vineyards of the Dordogne and Garonne, and the Gironde itself would, he says, reach maturity – that is to say, the full development of their quality – in fifteen to twenty years and would live indefinitely; the *Vins de Côtes* (and all these figures seem to relate only to red wines), would mature in ten to fifteen years and live for twenty-five to thirty; the *Vins de Graves* would mature in six to eight years and live for ten to fifteen.[155] White Hermitage, says Redding in 1876, 'is the finest white wine France produces' and he adds that 'real white Hermitage' will keep for a hundred years 'without the least deterioration'.[156] The fine wines of the Côte d'Or of Burgundy are nowadays bottled in about the third year after the vintage. In 1825, however, 'Light and fine wines, those of Volnay ... and other delicate wines should commonly be bottled a year after harvest. The wines of Pomard, Vosne, Chambertin, Corton, Alox, etc. ... should remain in the cask during three, four, and five years'.[157] Pasteur, in 1866, remarks that Clos Vougeot averaged six years in wood before it was bottled whereas 'Pomard', Volnay, Chambertin, and Romanée were bottled at the end of three or four years.[158]

Adulteration in Victorian Times

It is difficult to decide whether the 18th or the 19th century wins the title of the Golden Age of Adulteration. Judged by volume, the 19th century ought to be awarded the Crooked Crown. The Victorians complained as much as the Georgians had done and although some of the Victorian complaints are suspect in the accuracy of their detail there is no doubt that they were based upon a general and depressing truth. Misunderstanding or exaggeration made them credit this Victorian malpractice with a meaning and a scope which it did not have. Still, it was bad enough.

Prince Pückler-Muskau, surveying England in the late 1820s, took a decidedly poor view of the London wine merchant. 'Gourmands,' he remarked, 'must ever miss the finest wines, even at the best tables in London,' since they insisted on buying their wine from the London wine merchants who insisted on adulterating the wines which they sold. As a sad morsel of evidence he adds 'these wine merchants ... adulterate the wine to such a degree, that one who was lately prosecuted for having some thousand bottles of port and claret in his cellars which had not paid duty, proved that all this wine was manufactured by himself in London. ...'[159] The single incident may be true, but the general imputation is false. It is false for two quite

[153] *Gatherings from Spain*, 155–8.

[154] Jullien, *op. cit.*, 48–9.

[155] Quoted in Lafforgue, *Le Vignoble Girondin*, 51.

[156] Cyrus Redding, *History of Modern Wines*, 135.

[157] Jullien, *op. cit.*, 48–9.

[158] Pasteur, *op. cit.*, 111–12.

[159] Pückler-Muskau, *op. cit.*, Vol. III, 104–5.

opposite reasons: in the first place, sound wine was drunk in England: and in the second place, the wine was often adulterated before it reached England. (I am here using the word adulteration in the widest sense, to include improper blending, unnecessary fortification, and the use of extraneous materials.) In the time of the Prince Regent a claret sold on the London market, and made specifically for that market, was blended with Hermitage, this being 'infinitely more to the taste of an Englishman than . . . delicately-flavoured wine'.[160] *The Wine Merchant's Companion* of 1825 tells us that Bordeaux wines sent to London (but not to Paris) were blended with wines from the South of France and that this was done to satisfy the English taste.[161]

The English also, it would seem, preferred their wines to be fortified. In the 1820s many wines grown in the South of France and used to strengthen 'weak, good, pure wines' were fortified with brandy – apparently to satisfy the English market.[162] Foreign visitors to England remarked upon the peculiar taste of the English. At dinner, writes Pückler-Muskau, 'glass jugs filled with water happily enable foreigners to temper the brandy which forms so large a component part of English wines'.[163] Hippolyte Taine remarks that the English palate of the 1860s needed 'to be scratched or scraped' and in this connection points out that the wines which they drank, the port and sherry, were 'very full and strong and, furthermore, blended with brandy – a practice which ruins their subtler qualities. But if they were pure the English would find them insipid: our wines of Bordeaux, and even of Burgundy, are too light for them'.[164] Whatever the truth of his statement, he, like Pückler-Muskau before him, missed the point. Both sherry and port, which were the wines so widely consumed in England, are quite properly blended with brandy and to say that the Victorian English liked these wines is not necessarily to say that they liked their wines to be over fortified. Indeed in 1860 an English wine merchant offered to the public a port that was 'free from Cognac' (a curious idea),[165] and the Master of the Queen's Household writes from Windsor Castle in 1845 that 'We are partial here to Sherry without the Brandy but with a good body'.[166] Another point which may have eluded the Prussian Prince and the French historian was that some wines, quite apart from port or sherry, had to be fortified to stand the sea voyage while others were dosed with brandy to keep them alive in English cellars. Cape wines, for example, were reputed in 1855 to be fortified so that they should travel safely to England, where they arrived with a 'hot, fiery taste'.[167] One may wonder whether Pückler-Muskau's statement about tempering wine with water explains Professor Saintsbury's cryptic reference to the habit of 'Our ancestors' mixing wine with water; and whether these two together explain the startling Edwardian instruction that glasses for water should not be put on the table 'unless asked for during the meal for mixing Bordeaux or spirits with mineral water'.[168]

A worse practice, and one that was strictly dishonest, was the use of extraneous substances to disguise a wine. We have already come across the Battle of the Elderberries in the port wine trade.[169] Other substances used, at least in the 1820s, were iris, violet, raspberries or 'syrups perfumed by these plants' by which 'common wines . . . imbibe a bouquet, by which they are taken for good wines by bad judges'.[170] But one must not assume that such 'cosmeticizing' of wine was commonplace in Victorian times. On the contrary, there were many growers, shippers, and

[160] Gronow, *Reminiscences and Recollections . . .*, Vol. I, 141–2.

[161] Jullien, *op. cit.*, 75–6; and see *op. cit*, 72–5.

[162] *Ibid*, 75–6.

[163] *Op. cit.*, Vol. III, 83–7.

[164] *Op. cit.*, 47–8.

[165] Quoted by André L. Simon in *The Gourmet's Week-End Book*, 195.

[166] Quoted by R. Croft-Cooke, *Sherry*, 165.

[167] *The Butler . . .*, 26.

[168] Pückler-Muskau, *op. cit.*, Vol. III, 83–7; Saintsbury, *op. cit.*, 164; Rey, *The Whole Art of Dining*, 8.

[169] Ch. 8, pp. 381–2.

[170] Jullien, *op. cit.*, 70–1.

merchants – more than ever before – of great skill and the highest integrity who produced more fine wine than the world had ever known.

Their great enemy was the faker. By manufacturing counterfeit wine and then labelling it as the real article, he could ruin the reputation of an entire *vignoble*. Among connoisseurs bad wine does not drive out good; but among the mass of ordinary drinkers, who are not interested in becoming connoisseurs and who are interested only in getting sound wine, the experience of, let us say, a counterfeit port may induce a long-lived suspicion of all port. The view is unfair but very understandable. How far, in fact, the suspicion of counterfeiting altered the drinking habits of the Victorians is not easy to assess. In 1876, for example, Mrs Beeton in her *Complete Etiquette for Gentlemen* warns the aspiring, or the would be, gentleman that 'such a thing as pure port is seldom, if any, found in this country. A great deal of cheap French wine is sold here for port'. She adds, moreover, that 'immense quantities' of champagne were manufactured in England.[171] Whatever the truth in the statement and however much the hopeful gentleman thought it socially prudent to avoid champagne, the Victorians as a whole disregarded the awful warning and drank more and more champagne. As for Mrs Beeton's crisp utterance about port, good port wine continued to be drunk in England, but the cheaper styles of port wine may well have become suspect as they must certainly have done a few years later in the early 1880s when the cheapest 'port wines' were fortified with Hamburg Spirit, and when manufactured port was shipped from Hamburg to England.[172] Yet, despite these and other malpractices of the least reputable merchants, good port and fine port were widely popular in England at the end of the century. Sherry, however, suffered a lamentable fate, due also it might seem to the manufacturing enthusiasm of Hamburg and in early Edwardian times it had lost most of its pride and much of its place in upper class English homes.[173] It was still drunk in England by those who knew, and liked, genuine sherry and the genuine wine was offered, in many styles, by the best wine merchants. But one can see it diminishing in importance in some of the cellar books of the period and although its decline may have been due in part to competition from the cocktail there seems no doubt that this was one case of bad wine driving out good. The slump in sherry in England lasted until the 1920s and the rise of the sherry party, the first of these – so far as I am aware – having been given by Mr Charles Williams, of Messrs Williams and Humbert in London in 1924 or 1925. Since those days it has regained much of the esteem in which the mid-Victorians held the wine of Jerez but it is still not as important a word in the drinker's vocabulary as it rightly should be. Fine sherry is a great wine.

Inns, Coffee Houses and Restaurants

In the 1820s the upper class Englishman began to drink less. Harder drinking was becoming 'unfashionable',[174] but among other classes and at universities it lasted on until the 1840s.[175] Various incidents from the first half of the Victorian Age are worthy of a place among the chronicles of intemperance. Skinner records at Camerton in 1830 that 'White told me afterwards that the reason he had not rung' (the church bells) 'for the last two Sundays was because he had gotten drunk

[171] p. 43.

[172] Cockburn, *Port Wine and Oporto*, 35; see also 31 (1868, a) and 36 (1887, a).

[173] Allen, Warner H., *No. 3 St. James's Street*, 203 sqq.; and *A Contemplation of Wine*, 151.

[174] Pückler-Muskau, *op. cit.*, III, 83–7.

[175] Besant, *op. cit.*, 157; *Early Victorian England*, Young, Peel, Vol. I, Ch. II, 117, 'Homes and Habits'.

Saturday night, and had too bad a headache in the morning to bear the sound of bells'.[176] At a later date Frith tells the story of a friend of Mark Lemon, editor of *Punch*. This friend often used to get rather drunk and on one occasion Lemon observed 'Look at B— he is trying to peel an apple with the nut-crackers. . . .'[177] Taine, describing England between 1859 and 1871, confirms that drunkenness was rare in the upper classes, but he is not so consoling about other strata of the populace. I am not quite sure that the figures which he was given (doubtless in good faith) were always accurate but his own observations are beyond question. 'During the last few days,' he wrote, 'I have twice been down to Chelsea and both times came across men lying dead drunk on the pavement.' Nor do we have any reason for rejecting his next sentence: 'My friend who lives in that district often finds working girls and women in the same condition.'[178] Spirits were the curse – or if you consider their poverty, the consolation – of the lowest classes. In the 1840s rum had a certain vogue and 'The twopenny dram of pure Jamaica is preferred' by the begging vagrants.[179] Brandy was also drunk but the mainstay of urban intemperance was gin, some of which was no doubt 'jigger-stuff' or illicitly distilled spirit.[180] Gin was the most cherished companion of the 'Bingo boys', or male dram drinkers, and of the 'Bingo mots', or female dram drinkers who referred, possibly with reason, to the landlord of a gin shop as a 'Diddle cove'.[181]

Auguste Barbier took an elevated but accurate view of the matter, in a poem called *Le Gin*:

> '*Du gin, du gin! – à plein verre, garçon!*
> *Dans ses flots d'or, cette rude boisson*
> *Roule le ciel et l'oubli de soi-même;*'

Other writers were interested less in the colour of the substance than in the colour of its results. Taine describes what he calls the 'common people' when rotted by bad gin: 'They can be seen in, among other places, the low streets down by the Thames: the faces are apoplectic and swollen, the scarlet colour so dense that it is almost black; eyes dead, bloodshot, like those of a raw lobster.' He merely adds: 'The primal brute – brutalized.'[182] Besant relates that he once saw in a public house near the West India Docks in London a man 'in rags; his knees bent as he walked, his hands trembled, his eyes were eager. And, wonderful to relate, the face was perfectly blue – not indigo blue, or azure blue, but of a ghostly, ghastly corpse-like kind of blue, which made one shudder. Said my companion to me, "That is gin." '[183] To this blue result may have been due some of the many slang names for gin such as 'blue ruin' and 'blue tape'. But blue was not a monopoly colour for we also find it called 'white tape', 'white face' (Australian), or even 'white port' or 'white wine'. 'Jackey' was another name for it as was the ominous expression 'stark naked' while a glass of gin could be graphically described either as a 'flash of lightning' or a 'shove in the mouth'.[184] Still, however much it may have debased the drunkard, the favourite morning drink of the fishmongers in Billingsgate Market was gin and milk and it probably did no harm at all to these worthy handlers of unlimited herrings.[185]

[176]Rev. John Skinner, *Journal of a Somerset Rector*, 236.

[177]*Victorian Canvas*, ed. Nevile Wallis, 77.

[178]*Op. cit.*, 116, 216–17.

[179]*Sinks of London Laid Open*, 36.

[180]Barrère and Leland, *Dictionary of Slang . . .*; and Partridge, *Dictionary of Slang*.

[181]*Sinks of London Laid Open . . .*, Modern Flash Dictionary.

[182]*Op. cit.*, 42–3.

[183]*Op. cit.*, 167–8.

[184]*Sinks of London Laid Open . . .*, Modern Flash Dictionary; Barrère and Leland, *op. cit.*; Partridge, *op. cit.*; for a 'blue-ruin' shop' in 1821–2, see Amateur, *Real Life in London*, II, 204.

[185]Sala, *Twice Round the Clock*, 12.

Cruickshank, George
Tavern Scene, c 1840

On the whole, however, people were becoming more temperate and although some of this happy result was due to a continuing Puritan impulse and to the work of the Temperance Movement, most of it was due to the nature of the time, to the increasing emphasis on, and opportunity for, respectability, and the growth of a bourgeois civilization. Nevertheless, the influence of the Temperance Movement was considerable and though its ultimate triumph was Prohibition in the United States it had some Victorian influence on English life. The immortal William McGonagall of Dundee celebrated the Movement in 'A Tribute to Mr Murphy and the Blue Ribbon Army':

> 'All hail to Mr Murphy, he is a hero brave,
> That has crossed the mighty Atlantic wave,
> For what purpose let me pause and think –
> I answer, to warn the people not to taste strong drink.
>
> . . . . .
>
> The more's the pity, I must say,
> That so many men and women are by it led astray,
> And decoyed from the paths of virtue and led on to vice
> By drinking too much alcohol and acting unwise.'

An even more curious, but perhaps equally praiseworthy, effect of the Blue Ribbon feeling appeared in 1906 when 'At the first meeting of the Parliamentary Labour Party, Keir Hardie was elected chairman and at his desire every Labour M.P. pledged his honour that he would abstain from alcoholic drinks throughout the parliamentary session'.[186] Whatever one may think about the quality of the Victorian achievement one can at least be grateful for the enormous increase in convenient civilization. It developed the restaurant and created the modern hotel. But as early

[186]Rattray, R. F., 'The Decline and Fall of the Labour Party', *Quarterly Review*, London, July 1957.

as the 1820s the English inns were described as excellent. A foreign traveller describes a breakfast which he had at Woburn: 'In the middle of the table smoked a large tea-urn, prettily surrounded by silver tea-canisters, a slop-basin and a milk-jug. There were three small Wedgwood plates, with as many knives and forks, and two large cups of beautiful porcelain: by them stood an inviting plate of boiled eggs, another "ditto" of broiled "*oreilles de cochon . . .*"; a plate of muffins, kept warm by a hot-water plate; another with cold ham; flaky white bread, "dry and buttered toast", the best fresh butter in an elegant glass vessel; convenient receptacles for salt and pepper, English mustard and "*moutarde de maille*"; lastly a silver tea-caddy, with very good green and black tea. This most luxurious meal . . . was, moreover, very cheap; for it was charged in the bill only two shillings. . . .'[187] At the middle of the century the inns seem to have been just as good for an American farmer describes The Red Lion in a village near Liverpool. Of the kitchen he remarks: '. . . You would think the fireplace a show-model, for the very bars of the grate were glistening. It is all glowing with red-hot coals; a bright brass tea kettle swings and sings from a polished steel crane-hook, jack and all like silver; the brass coalscuttle, tongs, shovel, and warming pan are in a blazing glow, and the walls and mantelpiece are covered with bright plate covers, and I know not what other metallic furniture, all burnished to the highest degree. . . . We hesitated to cross the clean scoured, buff, tiled floor with our muddy shoes. . . .'[188] In London in 1869 the public house, that is to say the public house designed for the middle classes, and not the gin palace or the beer house, was splendid with Victorian luxury. 'The

[187]Pückler-Muskau, *op. cit.*, Vol. III, 193-4.

[188]Olmsted, *Walks and Talks of an American Farmer in England*, 90-4.

furniture is all new and beautifully polished, the seats are generally exquisitely soft and covered with crimson velvet, the walls are ornamented with pictures and pier-glasses, and the ceiling is adorned in a manner costly and rare. . . . Let us suppose it is about nine or ten in the evening. . . . In this box are two or three old friends discussing a bottle of claret . . . pass on; here are some bagmen, red with port and redolent of slang. In the next box are three or four young fellows drinking whisky and smoking cigars. . . .'[189]

In the 1840s there were many forms of eating house in London. There were 'dining-rooms' or cook-shops at which the menu was usually meat and vegetables, pastry, or cheese and bread. At the better dining-rooms a plate of roast beef cost sixpence to eightpence. There were many houses which kept a 'table-d'hote' or 'ordinary', 'that is, a dinner ready for all comers at a fixed hour in the day, and at a fixed charge. . . .' Reasonably enough, these houses tended to attract the same clientele day after day. Somewhat lower down the scale there were 'alamode-beefhouses' which served soup and bread at fourpence or sixpence a plate. A lower class of soup house sold 'a basin of prime soup, potatoes, and a slice of bread' for twopence or threepence. There were oyster rooms which were popular for suppers and in the City of London there was a custom both pleasant and sensible. This was what one might call the public-house-with-grid-iron. The customer went to a butcher shop a few doors away from a public house of his choice. He chose and bought a steak or a chop and took it to the public house where it was taken from him by a waiter and cooked 'on an enormous grid-iron, the bars of which are so constructed as to save a great portion of the fat from the meat. For this service the small sum of one penny only is charged, in addition to an equally moderate charge for bread, potatoes, and whatever drink may be called for'.[190]

In the London coffee shop, at the beginning of the 20th century, you could get, as well as tea, coffee or cocoa, a cooked meal and 'a selection of the daily papers was provided for reading while eating'.[191] This type of coffee house was almost entirely a development of the Victorian Age. In 1815 there had not been more than about twelve of them in London but in 1840 they numbered about 1,800. And it is interesting to note that a coffee house keeper, giving evidence to a committee set up by the House of Commons in 1840, stated that 'At the present moment besides a great number of newspapers every day, I am compelled to take in the highest class of periodicals. For instance, we have eight or nine quarterly publications, averaging from four shillings to six shillings each; and we are constantly asked for every new work that has come out'. This particular house was frequented mainly by solicitors, lawyers' clerks, and commercial men. There were coffee houses also for the humbler section of the populace and in one of them nine newspapers were provided. It was also about this time that the coffee house keepers were obliged by the demands of their customers to sell cooked food, and thus became the type of coffee shop which was later met with in Edwardian London.[192] But the coffee shops were for men only and the increasing employment of young women in offices and shops in Edwardian times brought about the development of the tea-shop which many of us now accept as a convenient, if not exciting, part of our daily life.[193]

The system in Paris in the 1880s was in general similar to that in London. In Paris there were three types of restaurant, the restaurant à la carte, the restaurant at fixed

[189]Ritchie, Ewing J., *The Night Side of London*, 253.

[190]Knight, *London*, Vol. IV, 314–16.

[191]Willis, *op. cit.*, 136–8.

[192]Knight, *op. cit.*, Vol. IV, 317 sqq.

[193]Willis, *op. cit.*, 137–8.

price, and the *établissement de bouillon*. The first of these, the restaurant à la carte, corresponded to what the English simply called a restaurant. The most famous of these were the Café Anglais (which had '*cabinets particuliers*' on the *entresol*) at the corner of the Boulevard des Italiens and the Rue de Marivaux, the Maison Dorée at the corner of the Boulevard des Italiens and the Rue Laffitte, Bignon in the Avenue de l'Opéra, the Café de la Paix in the Place de l'Opéra, the Café Riche at the corner of the Boulevard des Italiens and the Rue Lepeletier, and Lapérouse on the Quai des Grands Augustins.[194] Maxim's, which began as 'Maxime et Georges' in the early 1890s, had become world famous by 1900.[195] At some of these restaurants (in 1882) a bottle of Volnay or of Nuits would cost four or five francs which was equivalent then to 3/4d. or 4/2d. a bottle, or – at the exchange then ruling – 80 cents to a dollar in U.S. money.[196]

The restaurants at fixed prices corresponded to the English 'ordinary' and, as in England, each one tended to become the rendezvous of a particular clientele. They served both breakfast and dinner and one may note here that the word 'breakfast' still means the '*déjeuner à la fourchette*'. Their prices, which usually included wine, ranged from 1/3d. to 2/6d., or 30 to 60 cents U.S., for breakfast and 1/8d. to 4/2d. – or 40 cents to a dollar U.S. – for dinner.

The third type of eating place was an *établissement de bouillon* which was usually just called '*un bouillon*'. These *bouillons*, whose menus were à la carte, and whose prices were moderate, filled the place which in England was filled by the 'dining-rooms' and 'alamode-beefhouses'. They served soup, or fish, or roast meat, and in them *vin ordinaire* usually cost a franc a bottle – 10d. English or 20 cents U.S. – whereas a bottle of Mâcon or Bordeaux cost Fr. 1.20 the bottle – 1/- British or 24 cents U.S. As some standard of comparison to these Parisian prices one may remember that the retail price of ordinary claret in England at this time was about 1/8d. a bottle.[197]

By 1899 in London, dining in a restaurant was becoming an accepted custom and in some hotels, such as for instance the Berkeley, Piccadilly, it was even possible for women to lunch or dine without a male escort. Hotels were becoming smart and social: among them were the Hotel Cecil in the Strand, the Savoy, the Hotel Continental in Regent Street, the Hotel Victoria in Northumberland Avenue and, of course, Claridges, as splendid then as it is now. 'It takes a great number of men,' wrote one commentator, '– six, I think – to open the doors of Claridges and to show the visitor into the hall. . . .' Among the restaurants were the Holborn Restaurant, the Trocadero, the Avondale in Piccadilly which had many American clients, and Dieudonné's in Ryder Street. Dieudonné was another 'of the places where ladies can dine by themselves, without fear of any inconvenience . . .' and the decor no doubt compensated for the absence of an escort. The first floor room of Dieudonné's was 'all in white . . . the two pillars in the centre of the room are white, the great dumb-waiter is white, the walls are white. There are delicately-painted panels, with gentlemen and ladies in powder and silk and brocade limned upon them; the ceiling is the work of an artist, and there is here and there a touch of gold in the framing of a screen or the capital of a pillar'. The wall brackets were graced by white, and pink, shades and 'on the tables there were flowers in vases of silver'.[198]

[194]Dickens, *Dickens's Dictionary of Paris (1882)*, 215 sq.

[195]Andrieu, *Fine Bouche*, 189 sqq.

[196]Dickens, *op. cit.*, fn. 194 above, 215 sq., 157.

[197]*Ibid*, 215 sq., 87 sq., 157.

[198]Newnham-Davis, *Dinners and Diners, passim*.

The big London hotels of the late Victorian Age introduced to England a new idea of luxury but, however luxurious they may have been, it would seem that in comfort and modernity the American hotels were ahead of them. The Americans had begun long before the British and although Anthony Trollope did not like American hotels, his comments in the 60s make it clear that they were more comfortable and more modern than any in Europe except possibly in Switzerland. One of the particular differences between the American and the English hotel (apart from the fact that in America sanitation was generally much better), was the fact that, as well as there being many small tables in the hotel restaurants, there were also '. . . long tables extending in parallel rows completely across the spacious hall. Each will accommodate one hundred guests or more; and the people all sit demo-

Luncheon Table, laid for eight
Mrs Beeton, Household Management
London, 1891 edition

cratically at table together'. In the early 60s the cost of a room and 'as many meals as the guest can contrive to eat' was almost always 2½ dollars – or 10/- British – a day. Wine, however, usually cost 2 dollars – or 8/- – a bottle.[199]

Edwardian Eating – and Drinking

By the time of the Edwardians the system of eating had become modern though the amount that they ate has, to the moderns, become fabulous. A suggested dinner in 1906 in England is one which most of us now would consider a banquet. If we had the money to afford it we would not have the time to cook it, and if we had the time to cook it we would not have the appetite to eat it. The first course – the meal comes to us by courtesy of 'Mrs Beeton' – was usually soup, but that was often preceded by an *Hors d'oeuvre* '. . . such as caviare, croûtons, sardines, oysters, or other little *appétisants*. . . .' These, and the soup, having been disposed of, the second course was fish. Then came the '*entrées*' or 'made dishes', followed by joints, and then by the poultry and game. After these, and in case anyone was still hungry, came savoury dishes, then sweets, then cheese and celery, finalized, as we might now say, by a dessert of fruit.[200] To upset still further the modern digestion I quote another writer of the time: 'The menu of the "*Déjeuner à la Fourchette*"' – (still the old name for lunch) – 'is generally composed of "Hors d'oeuvre variés" or soup, followed by either fish or eggs, a lightly prepared meat dish such as "Navarin aux Primeurs", Goulash, calf's head, tongue and spinach, etc.; grilled meat such as "*Entre-côte*", mutton chops, etc., and salad, sweets, cheese, fruit, etc.'.[201] This was a menu for lunch in European hotels or restaurants and we do not have to believe that each course was necessarily eaten by each customer. Nor do we have to believe that the

[199]Trollope, *North America*, Vol. II, 395, 403; Towle, *American Society*, Vol. I, 315 sqq.

[200]Beeton, *Household Management* (edn of 1906), 1689.

[201]Rey, *The Whole Art of Dining*, 51.

Edwardian English ate heavily of each course at their dinner parties. Compared with the modern English, however, they ate heavily.

Having had four meals a day, breakfast, luncheon, 'Afternoon Tea', and dinner, the Edwardian was usually disinclined to add supper to the rhythm of refreshment. Supper, as a standard meal, had almost entirely disappeared in later Victorian times. Charles Dickens (the son), had remarked in 1882 that 'In Paris as in London suppers are almost a relic of the past. . . . We live too fast nowadays to eat suppers'.[202] His comment is all the more delightful in that it was made before the invention of the motor car and the aeroplane. It has often been said that the real reason for the decline of supper in Victorian times was the growing lateness of the Victorian dinner which had settled down to a time between seven and eight in the evening. This cannot, however, be the sole reason since in the late 1820s dinner in the big country houses of England was at seven or eight in the evening and there was 'a light supper of cold meats and fruits' just before midnight.[203] Suppers remained in vogue, of course, at balls in private houses and in Edwardian times at restaurants after the theatre. On the Continent at the end of the Edwardian era suppers could be very much later than in England and could last nearly all night, thus continuing a pleasant custom of the Parisian supper which, in 1903, began about two o'clock in the morning and was aptly named the *collation en ambigu*.[204]

The Edwardian English clearly considered that asceticism was not a vital part of sport. A sample menu for an open air lunch at a race meeting or picnic shows that the 'Luncheon table hampers' could contain the following assortment of food:

Hors-d'Oeuvre Variés
Mayonnaise de Saumon
Médaillons de Homard à la Russe
Boeuf braisé à la Gelée
Jambon d'York
Poulet Rôti. Langue à l'Ecarlate
Galantine de Volaille
Pâte de Foie Gras Truffé
Suprêmes de Volaille St-James
Salade Coeurs de Laitues
Gelée Macédoine
Crème Parisienne
Gateau Princesse
Blancmange aux Amandes
Patisserie assortie

Dessert

Café

The usual drink at such nourishing frolics was champagne.[205]

For those who think that this simple meal was merely an occasional extravagance, a special picnic for a large house party or a smart luncheon at the Races, let me add a Shooting Lunch from the unexcited pages of Mrs Beeton.

[202] *Dickens's Dictionary of Paris*, 247.

[203] Pückler-Muskau, *op. cit.*, Vol. III, 159, 311–15.

[204] Grimod de la Reynière, *Almanach des Gourmands*, 162; Rey, *op. cit.*, 86.

[205] Rey, *op. cit.*, 112–15.

'Menu for Luncheon for a Shooting Party.

Fillets of Sole in Mayonnaise. Iced Lobster Soufflé. Braised Beef with Savoury Jelly. Dressed Ox-Tongue. Fillets of Duckling with Goose Liver Farce. Braised Stuffed Quails. Roast Pheasant in Crust. Japanese Salad. Border of Rice with stewed Prunes. African Cakes. Savoury Cheese Fingers. Cheese. Dessert.'[206]

It is an heroic feast to fill the interval between the morning and the afternoon slaughter.

A more formal occasion in England was the 'At-Home Tea' which was a reception attended by anything up to a hundred people. So far as eating went it was a comparatively modest entertainment, offering only sandwiches, cakes, pastries, biscuits, bread and butter, fresh fruit, ices, jellies and blancmange. As alternatives to tea or coffee there was claret cup and the inevitable champagne.[207]

Extravagance made its appearance, not only in the food on the dining table but in the decoration of the table itself. Ever since the early 19th century, flowers, fresh or artificial, had been used to bring an extra beauty to the dining-room.[208] But a simple beauty was not always enough for the Edwardians and simplicity gave place to the sophistication, and sometimes the exaggeration, of a minor art. Smilax, said one author, was very popular for table decoration since 'it so easily lends itself to any kind of pretty effect on the cloth'. Maidenhair fern and wild asparagus fern were often used and it was suggested that 'Small silver or bronze ornaments or *statuettes* representing rustic figures or Cupids placed here and there among the flowers, add greatly to the beauty of the decoration and form a pleasing contrast'. For the more enterprising, or for the more agile, it was suggested that 'If there is a lamp hanging from the ceiling over the centre of the table, this may be made use of to suspend from it four trails of Smilax with china roses or primroses interlaced. The ends of the trails may be fastened either to the corners of the table with drawing pins or secured with the candlesticks or any other ornament'.[209]

The basic formula for the Edwardian at dinner is summarized in Professor Saintsbury's quotation: 'a bottle of sherry, a bottle of sham, a bottle of port, and a shasscaffy'.[210] But this is only the basic formula and it has many variations, some of which we may find unusual and even unacceptable. In general, we may note two things: the dominance of champagne and the decline of claret.

Although the cocktail had been invented by Edwardian times, the cocktails of that era were generally sweeter than they are now and it was not until after the First World War that they became drier and more widely drunk. Cocktails were drunk before an Edwardian dinner, but not frequently, and in fact it was quite usual for there to be no apéritif at all. When apéritifs were drunk in England they were 'French or Italian Vermouth, Sherry and Angostura, Gin and Orange Bitters, Quinine Dubonett, Byrrh, or an American cocktail'.[211] Then came the Hors-d'oeuvre. The first surprise comes with the oysters for it was recommended that they should be accompanied by either Chablis or Montrachet, which is reasonable, or by 'Sauterne or Haut Barsac' which is unreasonable. Despite the fact that sherry was losing its popularity, it was still customary to drink sherry with the soup. Here Mrs Beeton provides the second surprise with the observation that 'Sometimes a glass of . . . mineral waters with whisky is served with the soup . . .' but from other

[206] Beeton, *Household Management* (edn of 1906), 1729.

[207] Rey, *op. cit.*, 59–61.

[208] *Early Victorian England*, Young, Peel, Vol. I, Ch. II, 120, 'Homes and Habits'.

[209] Rey, *op. cit.*, 11 sqq.

[210] (Quoting Foker), *Notes on a Cellar Book*, 213.

[211] Rey, *op. cit.*, 152.

evidence it seems clear that the word 'sometimes' should carry the meaning of 'only occasionally'.

From this point in the dinner the progression of wines varied according to the size of the party and the taste or conventionality of the host. The standard routine was to serve champagne and claret but it was not rare to find that only champagne was served from the fish until the dessert. 'In Paris,' wrote Newnham-Davis in 1899, 'no man dreams of drinking champagne, and nothing but champagne, for dinner; but in London . . . ninety-nine out of a hundred Englishmen, in ordering a little dinner for two, turn instinctively to the champagne page of the wine-card.' One reason for the popularity of champagne, thinks Newnham-Davis, is the heavy English atmosphere: if he means the climate, he is wrong but if he means the atmosphere inside a restaurant then he was probably right. His other reason is that of '. . . women thinking no dinner complete without champagne'. Of this singular and unimaginative practice he adds: 'It is wrong. . . .'[212]

Those with a more varied taste gave hock – still hock, be it noted – with the fish or else the white wines that were recommended to go with oysters (Saintsbury once gave a dinner at which he served 'Ch. Yquem, 1870', with grilled red mullet). With the Entrées one was allowed to serve a good red burgundy and with the joint a good red claret.

Then came the roast and some more surprises. At the bigger dinners, and particularly at those where the guests were mainly or mostly men, an interval occurred between the joint and the roast. Considering the number of courses, this seems eminently sensible. But the interval was one for reinvigoration as well as for rest, and a sorbet or Punch à la Romaine was applied to the jaded palate. Here we go back to the 'Roman Punch' and the sorbets which in the 1860s were served with the roasts, and, in a sense, still further back to the Paris of Napoleon when the '*Coup du milieu*' was drunk immediately after the roast.[213] During this interval Edwardian 'gentlemen generally smoke a Russian cigarette', again a sensible practice in order to clear the palate. Frith, the painter, says that he had heard of smoking during dinner as being a fashion in foreign countries and he was surprised, and pleased, at 'the introduction of cigarettes . . . beginning, I think, after the fish . . .' at a dinner party given by Ouida at the Langham Hotel in London.[214]

After the interval, the roast, which was usually 'tame or wild birds'. And with the roast, iced champagne. This was indeed an eccentricity since champagne does not go best with game although it is tolerable with capons or ortolans. The Edwardians, however, liked it that way.[215] After this phantasy, yet one more, for in 1891 claret was considered to be the only wine which could *follow* champagne. Claret was drunk with the sweet and with the dessert and, for example, 'dessert claret' was among the wines at the Trocadero in Shaftesbury Avenue in 1899. By Edwardian times, however, claret was beginning to lose this unenviable position. It had other uses and it is pleasant to find that, in the terms of employment of a governess in a household of the Duchess of Richmond and Gordon in the 90s was the stipulation that she should receive 'a glass of cold claret at eleven o'clock in the morning'. A civilized custom.[216] But so far as dinner was concerned, port replaced claret as the wine for dessert.[217]

The popularity of champagne, or of what Tennyson rather loosely called 'the

[212]Rey, *op. cit.*, 152 sqq.; Beeton, *Household Management* (edn of 1906), 1471 sqq.; Newnham-Davis, *op. cit.*, xx; Saintsbury, *op. cit.*, 211 sqq.

[213]Gouffé, *Royal Cookery Book*, 564-5; Grimod de la Reynière, *op. cit.*, 296; Rey, *op. cit.*, 43.

[214]Rey, *op. cit.*, 43; Frith, *Victorian Canvas*, Ed. N. Wallis, 220-1.

[215]Rey, *op. cit.*, 43, 153.

[216]Rey, *op. cit.*, 9; Warner Allen, *No. 3 St. James's Street*, 205-6; Newnham-Davis, *op. cit.*, 108; cf. menus in Saintsbury, *op. cit.*, 211 sqq. For the information on the governess's claret I am indebted to Hilda, Duchess of Richmond and Gordon.

[217]Warner Allen, *No. 3 St. James's Street*, 205-6; Rey, *op. cit.*, 153.

foaming grape of eastern France' and the success of the champagne technique, were responsible for the appearance of other sparkling wines on the London market. In 1906 you could get Sparkling Burgundy, Sparkling Chablis, and Sparkling Saumur.[218] Port also was subject to the flattery of imitation and in the same year, in London 'California Port' was offered, retail, at 2/7d. a bottle.[219] At an even earlier date, in 1876, another port-style American wine, the 'Mustang . . . of Texas . . .' was known in London and, says Mrs Beeton happily, 'The Mustang grape yields a wine hardly distinguishable from the best port.'[220] The name seems oddly chosen.

In the last quarter of the 19th century and in the Edwardian decade, trans-ocean wines became more and more known to the island British. As well as Mustang in 1876, there was another wine 'of Texas' called El lasco, while in 1893 Londoners could buy Australian red wines - 'Carbinet Grape', 'Hermitage' and 'Burgundy'. In 1906 they could buy Californian wines called Claret, Burgundy, Chablis, Hock, Moselle, and Sauterne. They could also buy Californian Sherry and had a choice of Blackberry Brandy or California Grape Brandy.[221]

In general, though with a few startling variations, the Victorians and the Edwardians drank their wines at much the same temperature as we do ourselves today. Champagne was drunk iced and for this, as for other cooling purposes, an ice pit was kept near the (country) house. Another method of cooling wines, in the middle of the century at least, was to use glass coolers for the wine glasses. The coolers were filled half full of spring water and the wine glasses were turned down in them. Wine coolers were also in use and it is interesting to find that in 1855, sherry was sometimes cooled by being put into ice and water. The cooling of sherry (which is a civilized practice) lasted into Edwardian times when it was drunk slightly warmer than champagne and at the same temperature as sparkling hock and moselle. After the Edwardians the custom lapsed and reappeared only - and only too slowly - in our own day. One variation from modern usage can be found a hundred years ago when 'Burgundy is considered best at the temperature in which it is taken from the cellar'. The wisdom of this is debatable; but even odder things happened to claret. Saintsbury, who was born in 1845, speaks of three successive attitudes towards claret. First of all it was iced and there were even ' "marsupial" claret jugs with a pouch for ice'. Then came the time when it was warmed or, perhaps as often, heated. Last, and more recently, it was allowed to come up to room temperature.[222] I do not hold with icing, or chilling, a good claret but, in the summer, 'ordinary' claret can be pleasant when slightly chilled and it is only fair to observe that some experts in the Haut Médoc drink their fine clarets at a temperature which in England would be considered too cold.

The End of a Chapter

In 1900 The Annual Register could write that '. . . the outlook at the end of the year which closed the 19th century could hardly fail to arouse misgivings as to the future in all but the imperviously self-satisfied'.[223] The Boer War did not prove to be a satisfying experience. Some, in varying degrees of emotion or inaccuracy, were inclined to cast doubt about the ethical content of the White Man's Burden, though it was a 20th-century wit who described it as 'usually a bag of the Black Man's

[218] Tennyson, In Memoriam, finale, v. 20; Beeton, Household Management (edn of 1906), 1471.

[219] Simon, André L., History of the Wine Trade in England, Vol. I, p. x (advertisement).

[220] Complete Etiquette for Gentlemen (edn of 1876), 44-5.

[221] Ibid, loc. cit., Beeton, Household Management (edn of 1893), 33-4; Simon, André L., History of the Wine Trade in England, Vol. I, p. x (advertisement).

[222] Early Victorian England, Young, Peel, Vol. I, Ch. II, 81, 'Homes and Habits'; The Butler . . ., 72, 85-6; Rey, op. cit., 153-4; Saintsbury, op. cit., 67-8.

[223] Annual Register, 1900, Vol. I, 246.

Hopkins, Arthur
The Dinner Party, 'My
first Season', 1890

gold'.[224] Some, like Jack London, were appalled by the slow murder (or if you prefer it, the slow suicide) of the very poor. These boding voices might 'mar the merriment' but, whatever the iniquity which they denounced, for many people in north-western Europe, in England, in the United States of America, the Edwardian years were golden beyond compare. More people lived in comfort than had ever been comfortable before. Prosperity multiplied the rich and produced a glossy, opulent world whose extravagance was usually redeemed by sophistication and good manners. Frederick Willis, who worked in the silk hat trade in London at that time, has remarked upon the efficiency of the rich. They 'knew what was first class in service and goods and respected the tradesman who could supply it'.[225] Whatever the morals of the rich, they at least took care – or they at least attempted – to observe the rules of disguise and although we may consider them dishonest they would probably have regarded the publicity of modern sinning as being either dull or barbarous. Those women who did attract publicity were fabulous and beautiful creatures: Cléo de Mérode and Irma de Montigny – and so many others who demonstrated that beauty is its own reward.

To some, as to the unfortunate girl in the immortal lyric, life may have seemed a gilded cage. Society moved according to the 'Seasons': winter at Monte Carlo or in Cairo: London in the early summer: later, for the English the German Spas such as Marienbad or Homburg: and for the smart French, Dieppe: during the autumn the English relaxed by entertaining each other in their country houses. Monte Carlo was not of course the only fashionable place on the Riviera and on the other coast of France Biarritz achieved a spectacular vogue.

In all these places, luxury flourished under the flood of money, and if one had to

[224]The late Hugh Kingsmill.

[225]Willis, *101 Jubilee Road*, 22.

447

pick out three symbols of opulence one would select the Casino at Monte Carlo, Maxim's in Paris, and the Waldorf-Astoria in New York. Some of the manifestations of wealth seem to us a little comic – for example, at the Holborn Restaurant in London, '. . . a howling swell with tuber roses in the buttonhole of his frockcoat and a lordly moustache'.[226] Others, a little eccentric: 'A very wealthy lady of Chicago, noted for her daring feats as an expert climber in Switzerland, once gave a dinner on the roof of her house. The guests, being all amateur climbers, were previously invited to attend the dinner in mountaineer garb. The house was transformed into a miniature copy of Mont Blanc; the lady herself received the guests at the entrance, and after being fastened with ropes in the usual manner, they climbed to the summit guided by the hostess, where a sumptuous dinner was waiting for the merry mountaineers.'[227] Others were delightfully extravagant: when New York was suddenly gripped by a craze for bicycling, Lilian Russell '. . . became the talk of the town. In a white serge cycling costume with stylish leg-of-mutton sleeves, you saw her pedalling up through the Park. . . . Her bicycle was a national sensation, entirely gold plated, its mother-of-pearl handle-bars with her monogram in diamonds and emeralds; the hubs and spokes of its wheels were set with many jewels that sparkled in the sun. . . . "Diamond Jim" Brady . . . always rode a gold-plated bicycle with silvered spokes . . . sometimes, however, he rode a triple bicycle, with a beautiful girl perched behind him and his factotum, Dick Barton, on the third saddle'.[228]

The full development of Edwardianism, of Edwardian Society and Edwardian manners, could best be seen in London. At five o'clock in the afternoon, the Park was a glitter of carriages as Society showed itself to itself, the gleam on the coats of the horses, on the polish of the carriages, on the cockaded top hats of the coachmen and footmen, was the gleam of a polished world, an assured and still a small world, that would move on its golden way through Ascot and Goodwood and Cowes. The value which it set upon good manners was not one peculiar to itself. Other classes in London observed their own courtesies. 'To remain seated in bus, train, or tram while a woman was standing was unthinkable'; and, less practical but more romantic, 'no young man worthy of his salt ever went to meet a young woman without offering her flowers, which he bought ready made up. Tiny roses with a maidenhair fern background were the most popular. On Saturday night all the young women with male escorts at the theatres and music halls would be wearing the nosegays. The flower girls of London regarded this custom as their chief staff of life'.[229]

In 1900, Freud published his *Traumdeutung* which was to show man the darkness inside himself.[230] The Viennese professor was the herald of the 20th century. Earlier ages had thought (in their optimistic moments) that if you opened up man you would disclose an angel. Freud opened him and showed an untamed child crying in the darkness. Psychology, perhaps, might cure his unhappiness but he could be tamed only by the conventions of society. It may be that, compared to us, the Edwardians were wiser in their generation.

[226] Newnham-Davis, *op. cit.*, 20.

[227] Rey, *op. cit.*, 127.

[228] Lloyd Morris, *op. cit.*, 212.

[229] Willis, *op. cit.*, 121-2.

[230] *Die Traumdeutung*, Leipzig and Vienna, 1900.

CHAPTER TEN

Drinking in America

BY JOHN N. HUTCHISON

When one considers the fairly barbaric drinking habits of its early colonizers, and the inhospitality of the land to the first viticultural attempts, it is a marvel that the United States today has any degree whatever of civilization in matters of alcoholic beverage.

Add to these gloomy facts the basic Puritanism which still shadows the American spirit, then recall that this undercurrent came to the surface in the 20th century in the infamous Prohibition, beginning in 1923, and ending in 1933-4, and the expectations are dreary, indeed.

But the United States is a flexible, adaptable, changing nation, and what one President, in 1928, called a 'noble experiment', was by the next President cheerfully discarded, and probably forever. It is likely that Franklin D. Roosevelt, on the crest of a new tide of confidence and modernity, killed forever the long-lingering attitude that drink, however moderate, is outright sinful.

To the adventurous few who first saw the New World, the grape was one of its impressive characteristics. The Vikings, now credited with landing on the North American mainland long before Columbus had even reached islands in the Caribbean, referred to the country as Vineland. And hundreds of years later, two men who saw the Carolina coast in 1584 reported a land 'full of grapes', as did also Captain John Smith in 1606, who reported, 'we made neere twentie gallons of wine'. The London Company sent French experts to Virginia in the early 17th century to try to grow grapes: Charles II encouraged American viticulture; the Huguenots, Swedes and Dutch, according to Philip Wagner, an American oenologist, also tried. And all failed, he thinks, because the native American phylloxera and severe climate promptly killed the European varieties which the colonists hoped to establish.

But with the development of a certain elegance in 18th-century America, when merchant and planter classes had the means and appetites to imitate European manners, wine became fashionable in the seaboard colonies. Madeira became a status drink, even while rum was a staple of New England. And on the tables in the mansions of the Tidewater country from Georgia to Delaware, rich cotton and tobacco planters served the best European vintages they could order from abroad. Among those who could afford it, wine was a popular colonial beverage.

Randy and convivial Benjamin Franklin founded a small club early in the 18th century, and records that he often drank wine in the company of its members. It was Franklin who said 'Wine is a constant proof that God loves us and loves to see us happy'. As a colonial lobbyist in England, and as an American diplomat in France, Franklin was a noted host. As an American scientist, he, too, attempted to introduce European vines into American husbandry. Franklin wrote some bouncy tavern songs, and he devised a comical rationale for the providential proportions of the human arm. He wrote to a French friend:

'. . . If the elbow had been placed closer to the hand, the forearm would have been too short to bring the glass to the mouth; and if it had been closer to the shoulder . . . the forearm would have been so long that it would have carried the glass beyond the mouth.' Franklin surmised that an ingenious Creator had seen to it that neither of these faulty designs had produced a limb unsuited to a most important function. Some two hundred years later, the Broadway musical comedy, *Ben Franklin in Paris*, introduced a song, 'God Bless the Human Elbow'.

George Washington, the farmer-soldier who was first President of the United States, stocked his Virginia house with wine. He described his own tastes as plain: 'A glass of wine and a bit of mutton are always ready,' but the recipes written down by his wife, Martha, indicate that food at Mount Vernon was often as elaborate as it was hearty. Wine was frequently used in her cooking, and was regularly served. Port and sherry, as well as dry reds and whites, are often mentioned in accounts of the Washingtons' hospitality.

Washington's contemporary, Thomas Jefferson, was a wine enthusiast, both before and after his Presidency. He opposed high taxes on wine: 'No nation is drunken where wine is cheap.' Jefferson, probably the most remarkable American intellect of his day, had a fine cellar at Monticello, the classic home he built on a Virginia hilltop. This literate, liberal, inventive, successful man, was also a gourmet. He often did his own marketing. He maintained a tiny pond for keeping live trout ready for the kitchen. Among the ingenious details of his house is a dumb waiter built to carry wine bottles from the cellar to the dining-room.

Jefferson kept careful cellar accounts. They show an early taste for dessert wines, including sherry and 'Pedro Ximenes' and he advised a successor President to bring in 'vin blanc liquoreaux de M. Fourdan', 'vin de Ledarion, something of a port character but higher flavored', and 'the wine of Florence called Montepulciano'. But in later years, Jefferson acquired a taste for drier wines.

Wines, being imports, were too expensive for the common man. The early Americans were a robust people of robust appetite, and from the earliest days they made and drank great quantities of beer, rum and whiskey. Beer was brewed as early as 1637 by the Massachusetts Bay Colony, and the Pilgrims reported that they would have sailed far beyond Plymouth Rock to Virginia had their ship's supply of beer not run out. Americans are great beer drinkers, but for something like a century their taste has been for brews of the German Bohemian types, highly carbonated, low in alcohol, and chilled. From 1880 until Prohibition parched the land, beer was the great light beverage of the ordinary man. 'Rushing the growler', which meant going to the corner saloon with a pitcher or pail for draft beer to take home, was a working family custom. The pitcher or bucket was neatly wiped around the rim with a bit of butter. The butter somehow inhibited the formation of the deep collar of foam with which the saloon keeper could make the container look deceptively full. The film of butter kept him honest.

A Dutchman opened a brewery in America in 1637; William Penn was an important commercial brewer; most colonial households brewed their own. Straight on until the enactment of the hated Volstead Act, America was dotted with breweries, large and small. Throughout Prohibition, some breweries, with the aid of corrupt local authorities, continued to produce beer, many householders risked severe penalties to make their own 'home brew', and a few large, reputable companies turned out 'near beer', a beer from which the alcohol was extracted. Occasionally, a discreet notice in a country café might be read by the customer: 'Near Beer Here. Real Beer Near Here.'

Americans very early on were big consumers of rum. Rums of wide variety were brought by American ships from the West, and strong, dark rum much like today's issue rum in the Royal Navy was distilled in New England from West Indies molasses. Rum is still a very popular drink in the United States because it mixes so well in tall drinks and punches, and because good American rums, reasonable in price, are made in the Virgin Islands and Puerto Rico.

But the great hard drink of the United States is whiskey. It became, in the 18th century, an important item of commerce. Small distilleries by the score, up and down the seaboard, turned out rye and barley whiskeys without let or hindrance until 1791. Then the hard-pressed new government, seeking funds, slapped on an excise tax. The indignation was so great that tax collectors were tarred and feathered, militia were called out to put down rioting, and the violence entered the history books as 'The Whiskey Rebellion'. Many resentful distillers moved West to Indiana and Kentucky and began to use maize in their product. An early distillery in Bourbon County, Kentucky, gave the name to America's best known type of whiskey. 'Bourbon', by law, must be made from a mash which is at least 51 per cent maize, always called 'corn' in America. But 'corn' whiskey, still made to some extent, is entirely made from corn.

In contrast to Europe, the American colonies, and the States which they became, were a land of relative plenty and little class distinction. If the ordinary man was a rude and rustic fellow, he was generally a well-fed one. Food and drink formed the principal bounty in a life where rich land and game and fish and fruit were there for any man rugged and willing enough to make them his own. Life was elegant only for the wealthy, but life was satisfying, in creature terms, for any who pursued it with spirit. Meals were plain but hearty. Drink was copious. The population of such a raw and mainly agricultural economy was predominantly engaged in hard outdoor labour, producing big appetites and vigorous recreation. Despite the inhibiting Puritan heritage, social life was often boisterous, and characterized by

451

neighbourhood parties, dances, husking bees, barn-raisings and other vigorous community exercises at which heaps of 'vittles' were washed down with beer, home-made fruit wines, punches, cider and milk. The tradition of the head of the family as a 'good provider' has persisted in the face of the swift revolution which, in the 20th century, has changed a rural nation into an urban one.

The idea of plenty for everyone was a commonplace as soon as the earliest colonists survived their first few years of crisis. A Frenchman travelling in Virginia with a party of twenty persons in 1686 wrote of the ease with which a country gentleman lodged and entertained the whole group: 'He had great Store of Good Wine and other Things to drink, and a Frolic ensued.' The London magazine for July 1746 has a fascinating report from America:

'All over the Colony, an universal Hospitality reigns; full Tables and open Doors, the kind Salute, the generous Detention, speak somewhat like the old Roast-beef Ages of our Fore-fathers, and would almost persuade one to think their Shades were wafted into the Regions, to enjoy, with greater extent, the Reward of their Virtues. (What is said here is most strictly true, for their Manner of Living is quite generous and open: Strangers are fought after with Greediness, as they pass the Country, to be invited. Their Breakfast Tables have generally the cold Remains of the former Day, hash'd or fricasséed; Coffee, Tea, Chocolate, Venison-Pasty, Punch and Beer, or Cyder, upon one Board; their Dinner, Good Beef, Veal, Mutton, Venison, Turkies and Geese, wild and tame, Fowls, boil'd and roasted; and perhaps somewhat more, as Pies, Puddings, etc., for Dessert: Suppers the same, with some small Addition, and a good hearty Cup to precede a Bed of Down. And this is the constant Life they lead and to this Fare every Comer is welcome.)'

But always, as Americans prospered, there were aspirations to elegance on the part of many, and fine cooking and fine wines were the commonest expressions of affluence. By the middle of the 19th century, great hotels and elaborate Continental menus and impressive wine lists were major attractions in large cities. With the growing interest in dining out came the first successful efforts to produce domestic wines. In 1830 the first vineyards had been planted in the harsh climate of Northern New York State. The bitter winters of this area are too severe for most varieties of *vitis vinifera*, the European grape, but the stony soil, bordering the Finger Lakes, is hospitable to native America grapes descended from those Leif Ericson and Captain Smith found entangled in the trees so long before. By 1840, an Ohio millionaire named Nicholas Longworth was producing similar wines from steep slopes above the Ohio River that are now in the heart of the city of Cincinnati.

At about the same time, the Mexican general governing Alta (northern) California, was planting a vineyard he named Lachryma Montis, north of San Francisco, and two men, Benjamin Wilson (the grandfather of the World War II General George S. Patton) and a Frenchman named, quite appropriately, Jean Louis Vignes, began producing wines commercially in the neighbourhood of Los Angeles. The modern wine industry of the United States was under way.

In New York and Ohio, winter temperatures can drop to fifty degrees of frost, but the growing season is long, and *vitis labrusca* grapes, some European rieslings, and some new European hybrids, thrive. Native American grapes with names like Catawba, Niagara, Delaware, Elvira and Dutchess produce wide ranges of wines.

The New York industry, although very small compared with that of California, turns out a range from sherry on through red and white table wines and including champagne. The Taylor Wine Company is the largest producer of 'champagne' in the United States and one of the largest in the world. The sparkling wines of the Finger Lakes area are excellent, as are the dry white still wines. This is not to say that the other New York wines fall short in quality, but to wine drinkers accustomed to wines made from the vinifera, the completely different taste of the native wines takes some getting used to.

There are 7,000 acres in wine grapes in New York, and 450 growers; but one company, Taylor, is responsible for about half the total output.

New York law permits the addition of non-grape sugar to the wines, a practice sternly forbidden in California.

Ohio's wine industry, too, is based upon native American grapes. But the unique aspect of Ohio wines is that most of them come from one firm, and their grapes come mostly from a tiny island, roughly the size of the City of London's square mile. The island is in Lake Erie, its highest point is fourteen feet above lake level, and the entire grape acreage – 570 – belongs to Meier's Wine Cellars, which brings the grapes to the mainland for pressing.

New York's 7,000 acres of wine grapes, plus the few hundred in Ohio, and bits and pieces of wine land in Maryland, Virgina, Missouri, Michigan, Washington, Arkansas and other scattered states still only turn out 15 per cent of the American production. All the rest come from California.

California has been growing grapes for nearly two hundred years. The growers receive some £55,000,000 a year for their table grapes, their raisins and their wine. Of the latter, they turn out more than 130,000,000 imperial gallons a year.

It all started with Father Serra. Junipero Serra was probably the most important man in the history of California. He was a Franciscan friar of enormous drive and vision. The Spaniards had known about California since the early 1500s; Juan Cabrillo and others had sailed north along the American coast all the way to what is now British Columbia. And yet the Spanish exploiters of Mexico, little interested in anything but the 'conversion' of the Indians and the seizure of valuables they could ship to Spain, ignored the real riches of California for more than two hundred years. Father Serra knew better.

In 1769 he took a party of daredevils across the blistering wastelands north-west of Mexico City to the uninhabited harbour of San Diego, now in southern California. And there, in the names of God and the King of Spain he built the first of a chain of twenty-one 'missions'. Into the soil by that mission, as at the rest of them later, he put some vines from a Spanish grape, still today called the Mission grape, and still grown by the thousands of tons in California.

Vitis vinifera had been introduced to California. The Mission grape produced the sacramental wines for the big stone and adobe churches, and table wines for the friars and the travellers who moved north along the 'Mission Trail', El Camino Real – the King's Highway which is still the main route north. The last of the twenty-one missions – at Sonoma, north of San Francisco, was built in 1823. Most of the missions still stand.

In the same year that the mission in Sonoma was dedicated, nearly 500 miles to the north, a Missourian settler in Los Angeles planted 4,000 vines. He was the first man to make California wine to sell. But the Missourian, Joseph Chapman, was no expert. Soon on his heels came Vignes, a Bordeaux cooper, who brought over French vintners. He spurned the local leather flasks and clay bottles; he introduced good French cuttings. And he developed El Aliso – a great *hacienda* of legendary hospitality on the land where the Los Angeles railway station now stands. In 1840 Vignes shipped El Aliso wines as far as San Francisco, to the immense *ranchos* and *presidios* of Mexican grandees living in a style seldom known before or since anywhere on earth.

The Spaniards had had California within their reach for more than two centuries before they realized what it really could mean to them. By the time the penny dropped, their hold was slipping; the great free-wheeling, high-living, swashbuckling days of California's history were in the short period of Mexican rule before the American takeover.

Spanish royal grants had shared California out among the missions and a few favoured families. The result was vast domains; some of them ranches of hundreds of thousands of acres, with great herds of cattle supporting rancher nobility in a rude luxury with no counterpart in North America. In these great sprawling houses hospitality exceeded anything a rich Virginia planter could have imagined. There was constant 'open house', with banquets, and riding contests, and bullfighting and bearbaiting. Great entourages set out from one *rancho* by coach and in the saddle, to visit friends at other *ranchos*, where they might be guests for weeks at a time, before going on to a second, or yet another welcoming host. Whole steers were barbecued at great feasts, barrels of wine and brandy were drunk. One of the best known of such treks survives today in shrivelled fashion – 'Los Rancheros Visitaderos'.

This silver-saddled, hidalgo elegance was reaching its peak when the California Gold Rush swept Northern California into a period of still greater opulence.

San Francisco was founded in 1776 as a tiny military outpost subordinate to the *Presidio* of Monterey, seat of the Governor of Alta California. The huge and wonderful bay – 450 square miles of salt water – had still only a scattering of people on its shores when the discovery of gold brought it to life with a rush in 1849. It became a city of tents and flimsy wooden shanties, looking on a harbour jammed with ships abandoned by gold-hungry crews. Within a few years it was a city of the careless rich, eager to spend. Promoters brought an opera company from Peru, and knocked out the wall between two adjoining saloons to make room for its performance. Pianos were imported from France. A shipowner made a fortune taking laundry to be done in Hawaii, 1,100 sea miles away, because nobody wanted to bother with the laundry business in San Francisco. Champagne from Europe was chilled with ice shipped down from Alaska. This rumbustious, swirling life, deep in gold dust and merchants' profits, called for drink.

Whiskey poured across the bars, but there was a great demand for the best, and damn the expense. This not only brought in some good French and German vintages, and gave rise to some hotels of surprisingly high quality. It also encouraged some enterprising arrivals to try wine-making in Northern California.

One of them was Agoston Haraszthy.

This restless, adventurous Hungarian was a man Father Serra would have understood. Haraszthy, from a noble Hungarian family in what is now part of Jugoslavia, arrived in the United States in 1840, having left his productive home estate for reasons never made quite clear. He settled in Wisconsin, a North Central state where, as a dashing, active man, he founded a town, established a number of business firms, wrote a travel book, and finally went back to Hungary, to bring back his parents, his wife, and his three sons. In 1848, the whole family set out by ox team for San Diego, in Southern California. The Count, as Agoston Haraszthy was known, was involved in a bewildering succession of promotions – planting vineyards, building a town, contracting to put up buildings, holding various public offices. Then, in 1852, he moved near to San Francisco, where he planted the grape which was to become the mainstay of red table wine production there – the Zinfandel, possibly imported from Hungary, but whose origin is uncertain.

It is difficult to write briefly about the erratic, hustling Haraszthy. In San Francisco he grew wines, operated a gold refinery, and minted coins. Then he founded a new winery in a county to the north, Sonoma. He is deservedly called the father of modern commercial wine-making in America, but he was finally a personal failure in the process. By 1868, after two dozen promising careers, he was in Nicaragua, distilling rum, operating a sawmill, and struggling against yellow fever which killed his wife. This astonishing man is thought to have been eaten by an alligator when he fell into a Nicaraguan stream in 1869!

But despite the problem of what to leave out of an account of Haraszthy's life, he was the outstanding influence in the establishment of American wines. He returned to Europe to select and import tens of thousands of European cuttings. In twenty years of spirited agitation, he helped increase California wine production by fiftyfold, and the winery he built in Sonoma County is today one of the best in the nation.

Wine began to take on new importance in the United States during the years in which Haraszthy lived there. In 1842, Nicholas Longworth pulled the cork from a bottle of Catawba he had grown in Cincinnati. Like the wine Dom Perignon had made by accident in the 17th century, it was sparkling. Longworth promptly went into production, and by 1850, producers in his state were turning out in a year 135,000 bottles of champagne. Out in California, Benjamin Wilson produced sparkling California wines in 1855, and large quantities of such wines are made today. Several brands, like Korbel, Beaulieu, Almaden and Masson, are truly fine.

In the 1870s, eating and drinking in America began to achieve, in a few hotels and restaurants, a standard seldom before approached outside private homes. By the 1880s there were many restaurants in New York, Boston, Baltimore, Chicago, New Orleans and San Francisco which were well worth a gourmet's attention. And twenty years later – in the Gay Nineties – sophisticated American tastes were reflected in the cooking and the wine lists of George Rector's, and Delmonico's, and the old Astor in New York; the Palace Hotel and the Clipper in San Francisco; the Palmer House in Chicago, and several restaurants in the French Quarter of New Orleans. The plains in between may have been filled with potroast and potatoes in the heavy, Teutonic cooking which typified most of America, but there were chefs and sommeliers who were as knowing as anyone, in the few cities where appetites were educated and income was adequate. In the 1880s two pages of fine print carried the menu of the old Palace, in San Francisco. There were nine soups, six entrées and ten joints. There were forty-one wines on its list, including an 1874 Château Léoville and twelve California wines. There were also Guinness and Bass, at two shillings a bottle. When the great Hotel Del Monte opened in 1888 in Monterey, California, it had an elaborate menu in impeccable French, a good list of French and German vintages, and twenty California wines, including five from Arpad Haraszthy and Company. Arpad was a son of Agoston.

It was a period of good living, and it continued to develop in spite of the provincialism and isolationism of the United States. The mass of Americans, familiar with beer and whiskey, was ignorant of wine, but New York and San Francisco diners continued to develop their interest. It is interesting, in parenthesis, to note that the per capita consumption of wine in the United States today is said to be twice that of the United Kingdom. California wines began to make some reputation in England in the 19th century; in 1894, Charles Oldham of the London firm now known as Grierson, Oldham and Adams, delivered a paper on California wines, for which he predicted 'a high place in public estimation'. His firm shipped 'Big Tree' wines and brandy from California, and listed a 'very fine old claret' at twenty-five shillings a dozen. A 'splendid' folle blanche brandy was listed at sixty-one shillings per dozen.

American wines were being shipped in the early 1900s to many parts of the world, although never in large quantities, and they were making an admirable mark for themselves in their own country. All was going well until Prohibition. With that backward act, the United States underwent a peculiar and unhealthy change. A nation with extraordinary respect for law shocked itself with its disobedience. Large segments of the population which would not have condoned other violations felt a moral obligation to flaunt Prohibition. People who would not have defied reasonable regulation, and who had relatively little interest in drinking, began to make at home such beverages as dandelion and elderberry wine, or to send away for 'wine bricks' – solid cakes of raisins, mailed with yeast and instructions. Home brew was made by householders whose appetites were more appeased by defiance than by the beer. A contest for a new word describing resistance to Prohibition put a new noun into the language: 'scofflaw'.

A great deal of whiskey and rum was smuggled in by sea or across the borders. Every small town and country crossroads had its bootlegger or 'moonshine' distiller; every city had speakeasies. Although illegal beer and contraband wine could be bought, whiskey, being more concentrated, was popular because of its superior portability. A quart of whiskey was easier to hide than two gallons of beer, and it kept without spoiling.

The worst consequence was the corruption of American taste. People were encouraged by necessity to drink bad things furtively. Drunkenness was the least of the result; men were crippled, blinded or killed by 'Jamaica ginger', wood alcohol, canned heat and other substitutes for potable drink.

By 1934, when Prohibition was removed from its place in the national Constitution, there were few wineries or wine-makers available. Vineyards which had developed good varietal grapes had either disappeared, or had been put into rather common grapes. It was nearly ten years before a new wine industry found its footing again. The nation had been through a sad, silly period, imposed on it by an aggressive minority while a timid majority failed to speak up. The temperance movement and the bootleggers thought it a triumph.

The United States still has many county or municipal 'local option' areas which are either bone dry or permit only weak beer. There are numerous states which allow, or operate bottle shops, but where liquor cannot be bought by the drink. The range of official attitudes toward liquor is very wide. In the national capital, Washington, the customer may *sit* at a bar and drink beer. (He may not stand.) He may only drink hard liquor while *sitting* at a *table*. If he should want to join friends at another table, he must ask the waiter to carry his drink there; he may not be on his feet with a drink in his hand.

There are places in the United States where drink may only be served where food is served. There are places where drink may not be served where food is served. There are states where diners bring their own bottles and pay the waiter to bring them glasses and minerals. In some states (Virginia, bordering on Washington, D.C., is one) beer and light wines may be drunk in public, but anything stronger, including sherry, may not. In fact, almost anything you may say about liquor regulation in the United States is true, somewhere, because the country is a huge confederation of fifty half-independent nations.

California is noted for having voluminous laws about everything. Its liquor controls are detailed, closely enforced, but generous. Bars are open from 10 a.m. to 2 a.m., and beer, wine and hard liquor in great variety both American and imported, are sold in liquor stores, drug stores, tobacco shops, supermarkets and other outlets.

Californians, by now greatly diluted by immigrants from other American states (it now has more than seventeen million population) still exhibit some of the generous, expansive traits of the Mexican Dons and rowdy Fortyniners. They are hospitable, healthy, extroverted; they eat, drink and play heartily. In a nation which does not consume much wine, Californians are knowledgeable winelovers. Of the forty-nine Wine and Food Society chapters in the United States, twenty-two are in California.

Most California wineries offer tastings and tours to the passing public. Some of the best wineries are beautiful, park-like estates with vine-covered stone *chais*, cool stone caves, oak-shaded lawns. Wine-growing is not merely respectable in California; it is a status occupation, as it is in Bordeaux. Some of the finest contributions to American wine-growing have been made, as they were by Longworth in Ohio, by gentleman vintners in California. The late Ambassador and industrialist, J. D. Zellerbach set up Hanzell Vineyards with the intention of sparing no expertise or expense to make the best possible wine. Fred McCrea, San Francisco advertising executive, owns the small but great Stony Hill Winery; Frank Bartholomew, chairman of United Press International owns and operates Haraszthy's old winery in Sonoma County. Ignace Paderewski, the Polish pianist and statesman, bought a California vineyard in the 1920s.

There are high-quality big vineyards, too. The Paul Masson complex in Santa Clara County, south of San Francisco, is one. It ships its wines to London, as do the fine Beaulieu Vineyards in Napa County. Other notable wines come from Martini, Heitz, Beringen, Inglenook and Krug.

San Francisco is in the centre of a wine area now producing some of the best wines on earth - clean, full and pure. Soil, climate, technique, enthusiasm, and a University of almost limitless resources have combined to raise winemaking to formidable levels of skill and quality. The future of California competition with the wines of the world is suggested in the enterprise shown by Almaden Vineyards. This winery, founded in 1852, was forced by the rising value of its own land to move most of its operation from Santa Clara County to a new area in San Benito County, farther south of San Francisco. Employing the best consultants on soil, climate, and varietal grapes, Almaden planted 3,500 acres. The grapes are *vitis vinifera* varieties on *vitis vinifera* root stocks, in a vast educated gamble based on assurance from viticultural scientists that phylloxera will not attack them. Phylloxera, say the California savants, has never attacked vineyards grown at the altitude of the vast Almaden vineyards at Paicines, on mountain land. The vines are now delivering excellent vintage table wines, and a Blanc de blancs champagne.

The state of California undertook in 1880 to make grape growing and wine making scientific. It established then, at an agricultural branch of its great University, a department of viticulture and oenology. Later another such department was set up at a State College. In each of these, degrees are awarded to an increasing number of highly trained graduates who enter the growing wine industry. Intensive research in experimental vineyards is unceasing. New hybrids are developed, new cultivating and harvesting methods are devised, new ageing processes, pest controls and sanitation methods are discovered and, always and forever, new students are taught to recognize a good wine. Quality is the goal they seek.

The growers, who draw heavily on these massive State resources, are well organized. They support a State Wine Advisory Board, to which they pay assessments on their gallonage. Some of these funds go to the Wine Institute, established in 1934 to promote high quality and develop the wine trade.

The Institute has fifty full-time employees with headquarters in San Francisco. It works ceaselessly to persuade more Americans to appreciate wine; and it conducts and supports research. It has a fine wine library, and a dedicated staff. It is probably then the largest single influence improving American wine habits – still undeniably primitive in many large areas.

The long history of American wine, with its trouble and its triumphs, may be at a threshold devoutly hoped for by Agoston Haraszthy, but about which his son, Arpad, was somewhat pessimistic. Said the son, 'The great obstacle to our success . . . is, that the average American is a whisky-drinking, water-drinking, coffee-drinking and consequently dyspepsia-inviting subject, who does not know the use or value of pure light wines taken at the proper time and in moderate quantities. The task before us lies in teaching our people how to drink wine, when to drink it, and how much of it to drink.'

Well put. And in the hundred years since he said it, long steps have been taken in the task he set. Spared another aberration like Prohibition, the Californians, the New Yorkers, and the Ohioans may soon awaken the rest of America to the greatness of their own vintages. The world will follow on.

APPENDIX A: WINES OF EGYPT AND THE ANCIENT MIDDLE EAST

ABYDOS – North-west of Thebes, Nile Valley.

ALALAḤ – Ancient: Alalaḥ, modern: Tell 'Atshānah, Plain of Antioch, Syria.

ALEXANDREOTIC – The same as Mareotic.

ALONTITH – Palestine. Old wine, clear water, and balsam.

AMABANU – Northern Mesopotamia (?).

AMMONITE – Presumably from Ammon, north-east of the Dead Sea; modern Jordan.

AMOR – A district probably between modern Latakia, Tripolis and Homs; modern Northern Lebanon and Western Syria.

'ANDJET – Busiris, Nile Delta.

ANOMALIN – Palestine. Wine, honey, and pepper.

ANTYLLAN – Ancient Antylla, Nile Delta.

ARANABANIM – Northern Mesopotamia (?).

ARIAN – Ancient: Aria, modern: Herat, Afghanistan.

ARSINOITIC – Ancient: Arsinoë and Crocodilopolis, modern: Faiyûm, Egypt.

ARVAD – Arvad, on the coast between Tripolis and Laodiceia – modern Latakia – Syria.

ASALLU – Presumably the same as Izallan.

ÁŠ-AN – Sumeria. Probably palm-wine.

BABYLONIAN – Babylonia.

BACTRIAN – Ancient: Bactria, modern: Northern Afghanistan, and part of Turkmenistan.

BAHRIYEH – 'Northern' oasis; modern: El Baharia Oasis, south-west of the Faiyûm, Egypt.

BERYTIAN – Ancient: Berytus, modern: Beirut, Lebanon.

BETH LUBAN – Possibly from modern Lubban, north-west of Jerusalem, Palestine.

BETH RIMMAH – Possibly from modern Beit Rima, north-west of Jerusalem, Palestine.

BILAK – Probably the Harran area, North-west Mesopotamia.

BITÂTIM – Northern Mesopotamia (?).

BIT-KUBATI – Ancient Elam; South-west Persia.

BITTER WINE – Palestine.

BŠ – Egypt. Is this 'irp bš – white wine?

BUTO – Buto, North-west Nile Delta.

BYBLINE – Ancient: Byblus, modern: Gebal, Lebanon.

CARMANIAN – Southern Persia.

CARMEL – Palestine.

CHALYBONIAN – Originally from ancient Beroea, or Chalybon; modern Aleppo; Syria. Later at Chalybon; north of Damascus, Syria.

CHALYMONIAN – The same wine as Chalybonian.

CHARU – An ancient Egyptian name for Palestine and Syria.

COPTIC – Ancient Coptos, Thebaïd, Egypt.

DAKHEL – Oasis of Dakhel; modern Dakhla Oasis, Upper Egypt.

DIDA – Babylonia. Possibly a herbal drink.

DIOSPOLAN – Ancient Diospolis parva; Thebaïd, Upper Egypt.

DSDS – Oasis of Dakhel, Upper Egypt.

EASTERN SIDE, WINE OF – Probably the Eastern Nile Delta.

'EBIR NARI – Harran area, North-west Mesopotamia.

ELEPHANTINE – District of Elephantine, near modern Aswân, Upper Egypt.

EN-GEDI – Jordan Valley, Palestine.

ESNEH – Egypt.

FERGANIAN – Iranian region.

GEŠTIN DÙG-GA – Assyria. 'Sweet wine.'

GEŠTIN-KALAG-GA – Assyria. 'Strong wine.'

GIBEON – Gibeon, modern el-Jib, Palestine.

GURDELI – Palestine. White wine; also a nickname for an inferior white wine.

ḤABUR – North-west Mesopotamia. Another name for wine from the Ḥarran area.

HARDAI – Cynopolis, Nile Delta.

ḤARRAN – The Harran area of North-west Mesopotamia.

HATTULIM – Possibly from Kefr Hatla, north of Gilgal, Palestine.

HEBRON – South of Jerusalem, Palestine.

HELBONIAN – The same wine as Chalybonian.

HELIOPOLIS – Presumably near Heliopolis, Nile Delta.

HEMY – Hemy (Hmy), near Lake Mareotis, Nile Delta.

ḤILBUNIM – Apparently the same wine as Helbonian.

ḤĪLĪṢṬON – Palestine. A *vin de paille*.

ḤM – Possibly in the Nile Delta, near Lake Mareotis.

HONIED WINE – Palestine.

HULBUNU – Probably ancient Elam, South-west Persia. A wine known in Sumeria.

HYRCANIAN – Ancient: Hyrcania, southern shore of the Caspian, modern: Northern Iran and Southern Turkmenistan.

ḤZMW – Egypt.

'IMET – Ancient: 'Imet, modern: Nebesheh, south-east of Tanis, Nile Delta.

'IRP – The ancient Egyptian word for wine.

IZALLAN – 'Izallu', or Izallam; probably ancient Elam, South-west Persia.

KALḪU – Ancient: Kalḫu or Calah, modern: Nimrud, Tigris.

KANEKEME – Nile Delta.

ḲARINA – 'From Assia'; either from Asia Minor or from Essa, a town east of the Lake of Tiberias, Sea of Galilee. A sweet wine. Can it be *Karynon*? – see Greek List.

KARUHIM – Palestine. The same as Keruthin.

KAS-GEŠTIN – Sumeria. A name for grape-wine.

KAS-GIG – Sumeria. A drink made from approximately equal parts of date-wine, of paste, and of old liquor.

KAS-KAL – Sumeria. A drink made from $\frac{1}{3}$ date-wine and $\frac{2}{3}$ fermented grain.

KEFAR SIGNAH – Possibly Sukneh, near Jaffa, Palestine.

KERUTHIN – Possibly from Coreae (Korea), Jordan Valley, Palestine.

KHÂRGEH – Modern: Oasis of El-Khârga, Upper Egypt.

KHOR – Palestine, and Syria.

KURUNNU – Assyria and Babylonia. 'Strong drink'; date-wine, or possibly a kind of beer.

LAODICEIAN – Ancient: Laodiceia, modern: Latakia, Syria.

LOWER EGYPT, WINE OF – Nile Delta.

MAREOTIC – Lake Mareotis, near Alexandria, Nile Delta.

MARGIANAN – Ancient: Margiana, modern: Southern Turkmenistan.

MAZUG – Palestine. Wine mixed with water; diluted wine.

MEGIDDO – Ancient Megiddo, Plain of Esdraelon, south-west of Sea of Galilee, Palestine.

MEMPHIS – Presumably near Memphis, Egypt.

METHEN – (belonging to Methen); perhaps in the Faiyûm, or in the Nile Delta.

MRS – Egypt. Must (?).

MSK – Ancient: Ugarit, modern: Ras Shamra, coast of Syria.

MYRRH WINE – Palestine.

NHAM. T – A city of ancient Egypt.

OMPHACIUM – Egypt (but also made in the Aegean).

PELUGTO – Near Tiberias, Galilee, Palestine. Possibly the same wine as that of Perugitha.

PELUSIAN – Ancient Pelusium, district of modern Port Said, Nile Delta.

PERUGITHA – Northern Israel. Possibly near Tiberias in Palestine.

PESINTIṬON – Palestine. '*Absinthiatum*', a bitter wine.

PETRITAN – Most probably from Petra in ancient Nabataea (modern Jordan).

PRAISED BE HORUS WHO IS IN THE FRONT OF HEAVEN – Possibly at Memphis, Egypt.

RETENU – The ancient Egyptian term for Palestine. Upper Retenu is Palestine and sometimes includes the Lebanon. Lower Retenu is the plain of Syria.

SAND-DWELLERS, WINE OF THE – The 'Sand-dwellers' were the inhabitants of Northern Sinai.

SEBENNYTIC – Ancient: Sebennytus, Nile Delta.

SEMADAR – Palestine.

SEN(?)PU – Egypt. (Perhaps in the Western Nile Delta.)

SHARON – Plain of Sharon, Palestine.

SHEDEH – Egypt. Must (?).

SHÎLOAN – Shiloh, near Mt Ephraim, Central Palestine.

SHUSHU – Northern Mesopotamia (?).

ŠIKARU – Assyria and Babylonia. 'Strong drink', often translated as 'date-wine'.

SIMMINI – Possibly the same as Zimzini.

SIMMŪQĪM – Palestine. Raisin wine.

SMOKED WINE – Palestine.

SOGDIAN – Ancient: Sogdiana, modern: Uzbekistan.

SOUR WINE – Egypt; Palestine; (and Island of Cos, Aegean).

SOUTHERN POOL, WINE OF THE – Presumably Egypt; exact location uncertain.

SPICED WINE – Palestine.

STRIP-WINE – The same as Taeniotic.

SÛḤAM – Northern Mesopotamia (?).

SYENE – Syene (Swny), probably quite near Lake Mareotis, Nile Delta.

TAENIOTIC – Nile Delta.

TAMAD – Palestine. Wine made from grape-husks steeped in water.

TANIS – Ancient: Tanis, Eastern Nile Delta.

TBUI – A district of ancient Egypt.

THARU – Nile Delta.

THEBAN – Ancient: district of Thebes, modern: Luxor, Nile Valley.

THEL – Probably at Tell Abu Sêfeh, $1\frac{1}{2}$ miles east of El-Ḳanṭareh, Nile Delta.

'THREE-LEAF' WINE – Palestine. Wine from a three-year-old vine.

TILA – Palestine. A strong, acrid wine, or wine mixed with pepper.

ṬILIA – Palestine. 'An inferior kind of wine.'

TIROSH – Palestine. New wine, perhaps more usually must.

TRIPOLITICAN – Tripolis; Phoenicia.

TUHIMMU – Northern Mesopotamia (?).

TYLOS – Ancient: 'island of Tylos', modern: Bahrein, Persian Gulf. Vines grew here – 4th century B.C.

TYRIAN – Ancient: Tyrus, Phoenicia, modern: Tyre, Lebanon.

UA-WINE – Egypt. This name occurs on a Stele of the 3rd Dynasty.

VAN – District of Lake Van in ancient Armenia (modern Turkey).

WAZYT – Nile Delta; perhaps from vineyards at Buto.

WESTERN RIVER, WINE OF – Western Nile Delta; most probably meaning the Canopic arm of the Nile.

WESTERN SIDE, WINE OF – Probably the Western Nile Delta.

WORMWOOD WINE – Palestine.

YAYIN – Palestine. A term for fermented wine.

YAYIN HA-ṚEKAḤ – Palestine. A term for spiced or aromatic wine.

YAYIN MEBUSHAL – Palestine. Boiled wine.

YAYIN MEYUSHSHAN – Palestine. A term for three-year-old wine.

YAYIN TAPUḤIM – Palestine. Cider.

YAYIN YASHAN – Palestine. A term for one-year-old wine.

YEN NESEK – Palestine. Wine which, to Jews, had been defiled because the 'heathen' may have dedicated it as libation wine for a 'heathen' idol or god.

YEN TEMARIM – Palestine. A term for date-wine.

YEN ẒIMMUḲIN – Palestine. Raisin-wine.

ZAHI – Western Syria, and in particular Phoenicia.

ZIMZINI – Northern Mesopotamia (?).

References for wines listed in Appendix but not discussed in the text of Chapter 2 will be found in note 207 of that chapter.

APPENDIX B: ANCIENT GREEK WINES

ABATES – Cilicia, Asia Minor. A laxative wine.

ACANTHIAN – Ancient: Acanthus, Chalcidice, Macedonia.

ACRAGAN – Ancient: Acragas, modern: Agrigento, Sicily.

AMBLADIAN – Amblada, Pisidia, Asia Minor.

AMBRACIOTAN – Ambracia, north-west coast of Greece.

AMPHIAS – The Greek name of a bad wine.

APAMEIAN – Apameia, Phrygia, Asia Minor.

ARIUSIAN – Ariusia, a district of the Island of Chios, Aegean.

ARNE – Boeotia, Central Greece. Homeric dating.

AROMIAN – Aroma, near Nysa, Mt Mesogis, Asia Minor. The best kind of Mesogitan wine.

ATTIC – Attica, Greece.

BIBLINE – Probably Thrace. It may also have been the name of a vine. Hesiodic dating; and later.

BOSPORAN – Ancient: Cimmerian Bosporus, modern: Straits of Kerch, Southern Russia.

CALPIAN – Ancient: Calpe, Bithynia, modern: Turkey.

CARYSTIAN – Arcadia, Central Peloponnese, Greece.

CATACECAUMENITAN – Lydia, North-west Asia Minor.

CHERSONESIAN – Ancient: Chersonesus Taurica, modern: Kerch, Crimea, Southern Russia.

CHIAN – Island of Chios, Aegean.

CILICIAN – Cilicia, southern coast of Asia Minor.

CLAZOMENIAN – Clazomenae, Ionia. Coast of Asia Minor, near Smyrna.

CNIDIAN – Cnidos, Caria, Asia Minor.

COAN – Island of Cos, Aegean.

COLOPHONIAN – Colophon, Ionia, Asia Minor.

CORCYRAEAN – Ancient: Corcyra, modern: Corfu.

CORINTHIAN – Corinth, Peloponnese, Greece.

CRETAN – Island of Crete. Minoan and Mycenaean dating.

CYPRIAN – Island of Cyprus.

CYZICAN – Cyzicus, Propontis, Asia Minor.

DECELEAN – Decelea, north of Athens, Attica.

DELIAN – Island of Delos, Cyclades, Aegean.

DEUTERIAS – Greek. 'Wine' made from grape-skins soaked in water.

EPHESIAN – Ephesus, Asia Minor.

EPIDAUROS – Epidauros, Acte (Argolis), Peloponnese. Homeric dating.

ERYTHRAEAN – Erythrae, Ionia, Asia Minor.

EUBOEAN – Euboea, Aegean.

EUREAN – Thessaly, Greece. Coin information.

EUROMIAN – Euromus, Caria, Asia Minor.

'FIVE HILLS' – Sparta, Peloponnese, Greece.

GLEUCOS – γλτύκος : Greek for sweet new wine, but more usually 'must' – unfermented grape juice.

HALICARNASSIAN – Halicarnassus, Caria, Asia Minor.

HEPSEMA – 'Wine' boiled till it is sweet.

HERACLEOTAN – Probably Heracleia Pontica, Bithynia, Asia Minor.

HIPPODAMANTIAN – Asia Minor?

HISTIAIA – North-west Euboea, Aegean. Homeric dating.

ICARIAN – Island of Icaria, Sporades, Aegean.

ISMARAN – Ismarus, Maronea, Thrace. Possibly Homeric dating. Probably the same as Maronean.

ISSAN – Ancient: Island of Issa, modern: Vis, Jugoslavia, Adriatic.

ITHACAN – Homeric 'Ithaca', Adriatic. Possibly the same as Leucadian, assuming that Homeric 'Ithaca' is identified as Leucas.

KAPNEOS – καπνίας : Greek for the 'smoky' vine, describing the colour of its grapes. It may later have been used for 'smoked wine'.

KARYNON – Greek. κάροινον : sweet wine boiled down.

KNOSSOS – Knossos, Crete. Mycenaean dating.

LAMPSACAN – Lampsacus, Hellespontine, Phrygia, Asia Minor.

LEMNIAN – Island of Lemnos, Northern Aegean. Homeric dating. Re-export from Maronea or Thasos (?).

LESBIAN – Island of Lesbos, Aegean.

LEUCADIAN – Leucas, Adriatic.

MAEONIAN – Maeonia, Lydia, Western Asia Minor.

MAGNESIAN – Probably Magnesia, Ionia, Asia Minor.

MARONEAN – Maronea, Thrace.

MEILISSIAN – Epidauros, Peloponnese.

MELIAN – Island of Melos, Sporades, Aegean.

MELITENE – Melitene, Cappadocia, Asia Minor.

MELITION (?) – Pylos, Western Messinia, Peloponnese. Mycenaean dating.

MELITITES – Probably made all over the Greek and Roman worlds. 'Honey-wine', made of must or wine, honey, and salt, 'brought just to the boil'.

MENDAEAN – Mende, Pallene, Chalcidice, Macedonia.

MESOGITAN – Mt Mesogis, Ephesus, Asia Minor.

METHYMNIAN – Methymna, Island of Lesbos, Aegean.

METROPOLITAN – Metropolis, north of Colophon, Ionia, Asia Minor.

MILETAN – Miletus, Ionia, Asia Minor.

MONARITE – Melitene, Cappadocia, Asia Minor.

MYCENAE – Mycenae, Argolis, Peloponnese, Greece. Mycenaean dating.

MYCONIAN – Island of Myconos, Cyclades, Aegean.

MYNDIAN – Myndus, Caria, Asia Minor.

MYSIAN – Mysia, North-west Asia Minor.

MYSTIAN – Mystus, Asia Minor (?).

NASPERCENIAN – From Pontus, Northern Asia Minor.

NAXIAN – Ancient: Naxus, modern: Capo Schiso, Eastern Sicily. Coin information.

NAXIAN – Island of Naxos, Cyclades, Aegean.

OENEATIC – Probably from Oenoe, Island of Icaros (Icaria), Sporades, Aegean.

OMPHACITES – The same as *Omphacium*.

OMPHACIUM – Aegean. The juice, or the dried pulp, of unripe or only partly ripe grapes.

ORCHOMENOS – Orchomenos, Boeotia, Greece. Middle Helladic dating.

ORETIC – Probably from Histiata Orĕus, North-west Euboea, Aegean.

OXYMEL – Possibly made all over the Greek and Roman worlds. Honey, vinegar, salt, and rain-water, heated ten times to boiling point, then kept till cold.

PALAIKASTRO – Palaikastro, Eastern Crete. Mycenaen dating.

PEDASOS – Peloponnese, probably on the Gulf of Messinia, Greece. Homeric dating.

PEPARETHIAN – Island of Peparethus, off Northern Euboea, Aegean.

PHAISTOS – Southern Crete. Minoan dating.

PHLIAN – Phlius, south-west of Corinth, Peloponnese, Greece.

PHORINEAN – From Phoron in Attica (?).

PHRYGIAN – Phrygia, Asia Minor. Homeric dating.

PHYGELITES – A name used by Dioscorides for a wine which grew near Ephesus, in Asia Minor.

POLLIAN – Syracuse, Sicily.

PRAMNIAN – Near Ephesus, Island of Icaros, Island of Lesbos, near Smyrna, and most probably elsewhere. Homeric dating.

PRODROMON – The same as *protropon*.

PROTAGION – Greek. Probably the same as *protropon*.

PROTROPON – Greek; in particular from Cnidos and Lesbos. 'Must' which bleeds from grapes before pressing and wine made from it.

PROTROPUM – The same as *protropon*.

PSITHIAN – The Greek name for a vine and for the raisin-wine made from its grapes.

PTELEAN – Possibly from Pteleum, in modern Othris, East-central Greece.

PYLOS – Pylos (modern Epano Englianos), Western Messenia, Peloponnese, Greece. Mycenaean dating.

RHODIAN – Island of Rhodes, Aegean.

SAMIAN – Island of Samos, Aegean.

SAPRIAS – 'Saprias oinos' – old, mellow wine.

SCIATHIAN – Island of Sciathos, Northern Sporades, Aegean.

SCYBELITES – Galatia, or Pamphylia, Asia Minor.

SELGEAN – Pamphylia, Southern Asia Minor.

SICYONIAN – Presumably from Sicyon, north-west of Corinth, Peloponnese, Greece.

SINOPIAN – Sinope, Paphlagonia, Asia Minor.

SMYRNAN – Smyrna, Ionia, Asia Minor.

SPARTA – Sparta, Peloponnese, Greece. Mycenaean dating.

SYBARITAN – Gulf of Tarentum, Southern Italy; from ancient Sybaris.

TELMESICAN – Telmesus, Lycia, Asia Minor.

TENEDIAN – Island of Tenedos, North-east Aegean. Coin information.

TENIAN – Island of Tenos, Northern Cyclades, Aegean. Coin information.

THASIAN – Island of Thasos, Northern Aegean.

THERAN – Island of Thera, Southern Aegean.

TIRYNS – Tiryns, Argolis, Peloponnese, Greece. Mycenaean dating.

TMOLITAN – Mt Tmolus, Lydia, Asia Minor.

TRAPEZIAN – Trapezus, south-east coast of the Euxine (Black Sea), Asia Minor.

ὑπόχυτος– 'doctored wine'.

ZACYNTHIAN – Ancient: Zacynthus, modern: Zante, Adriatic.

References for wines listed in Appendix but not discussed in the text of Chapter 3 are in note 170 of that chapter.

APPENDIX C: ANCIENT ROMAN WINES

ABSINTHITES – Wine with wormwood.

ADRANUMENITAN – Ancient Adranum, Mt Etna, Sicily.

ADRIAN – Po Estuary and Venezia, North-east Italy.

AEQUAN – Territory of the Aequi, east of Rome and north of the Fucine Lake, Central Italy.

AIGLEUCOS – Pliny's writing of *Gleucos*. *See:* Greek List. The same as *semper mustum*.

ALBAN – Latium, Italy.

ALLOBROGIAN – The name of a pitch-flavoured grape which grew, in particular, in the Rhône Valley, France. Viennan wine was made from it.

ALUNTIUM – Ancient: Aluntium, modern: Southern Filadelpho, North-east Sicily. A kind of must was produced at Aluntium.

AMINEAN – The name of the top-ranking vine of the Romans, probably the same as the later *Greco bianco*.

ANADENDRITES – Wine from an *anadendras* vine, which grew up trees.

ANCONITAN – Ancona, east coast of Italy.

APIAN – The apiana, or 'bee-vine', or Muscat. Possibly the same as the Greek psithian and the medieval Muscatel.

ARDEATAN – Neighbourhood of Ardea, Latium, Italy.

ARICIAN – Ancient: Aricia, modern: Ariccia, south of the Alban Lake, Latium, Italy.

BAETERRENSAN – Ancient: Beterrae, modern: Béziers, near Narbonne, France.

BAETICAN – Ancient: Baetica, modern: Andalusia, Southern Spain.

BALIARICAN – Ancient: Baliarides or Baleares, modern: Balearic Islands, Spain.

BALISCAN – From the Balisca vine, which grew in Dyrrachium (modern: Durazzo, Adriatic) and in Spain. *See: Coccolobis.*

BARINE – Probably ancient: Barium, modern: Bari, Apulia, Italy.

BASILIC – Presumably the same as the Balisca vine. See: *Baliscan.*

BENEVENTINE – Ancient: Beneventum, modern: Benevento, Samnium, Southern Italy.

BÉZIERS – France. See: *Baeterrensan.*

BITURICA – The name of a vine. Possibly the same as the *Biturigiaca*.

BITURIGIACA – The name of a vine which grew, probably, at Bordeaux. Possibly the same as the *Biturica*.

BORDEAUX – See: *Biturigiaca.*

BURDIGALA – Modern: Bordeaux, France. See: *Biturigiaca.*

BURGUNDIAN – Ancient: Pagus Arebrignus, probably the modern Côte de Beaune and Côte de Nuits, Burgundy.

BUXENTINE – Ancient: Buxentum (Pyxus), modern: Policastro, Lucania, Italy.

CAECUBAN – Bay of Amyclae, Latium, Italy.

CAERETAN – Ancient: Caere, modern: Cervetri, Etruria, Italy.

CAESENIAN – Ancient: Caesena, modern: Cesena, Romagna, Adriatic coast, Italy.

CALDUM – A hot drink; wine and hot water.

CALENIAN – Ancient: Cales, modern: Calvi, Latium, Campania, Italy.

CAPUAN – Capua, Campania, Italy.

CARPETAN – Modern: Valdepeñas, La Mancha, Spain.

CARSEOLAN – Carseoli, in the territory of the Aequi, east of Rome.

CATANAEAN – Ancient: Catana, modern: Catania, Eastern Sicily.

CAUCINIAN – Latium, Campania, Italy. A growth of Falernian from the highest *climat* of the Falernian *vignoble.*

CAULINE – Near Capua, Campania, Italy.

CIRCUMCIDANEUM – The same as *Circumsicium.*

CIRCUMSICIUM – Wine from grapes cut from the 'cake' of the first pressing, and then pressed again; or from the chopped 'cake', which is then pressed again.

COCCOLOBIS – The Spanish name of the Balisca vine. See: *Baliscan.*

CONDITUM – Aromatic, spiced wine.

CONFUSUM – Mixed, or blended, wine.

CONSENTIAN – Ancient: Consentia, modern: Cosenza, Calabria, Italy.

CORSICAN – Island of Corsica.

COUM – Coan wine, see Greek List.

CRETICUM – *Vinum Creticum*, Cretan wine.

CRHYSATTICON – A syrup, or an artificial wine.

CUMANUM – Possibly a wine from Cumae, near Naples, Campania.

DECOCTUM – Must, boiled down.

DEFRUTUM – Must reduced by boiling.

DEUTERIAS – See: Greek List. The same as *Lora*.

ERBULAN – Location unidentified. A very light and delicate wine. (Ath-E, i. 27c.)

EUGENIA – The name of a vine imported into Italy from Taormina, Sicily, and grown in Alban territory. See: *Alban*.

FAECATUM – Lees-wine. Pressed, or made, from the dregs or lees of wine.

FALERNIAN (1) – Latium, Campania, Italy.

FALERNIAN (2) – Latium, Campania, Italy. A growth of Falernian from the lowest *climat* of the Falernian *vignoble*.

FAUSTIAN – Near Sinuessa, Latium, Campania, Italy. A growth of Falernian from the middle *climat* of the Falernian *vignoble*. In Pliny's day Faustian was the best Falernian.

FAVENTINE – Ancient: Faventia, modern: Faenza, Romagna, Italy.

FORMIAN – Ancient: Formiae, modern: Formia, Latium, Italy.

FUNDANIAN – Ancient: Fundi, modern: Fondi, Latium, Italy.

GAURAN – Ancient: Mt Gaurus, between Cumae and Naples, modern: Monte Barbaro, Campania, Italy.

GEMINIANUM – Wine from a particular property near Pompeii, Campania, Italy.

GENUAN – Ancient: Genua, modern: Genoa, Liguria, Italy.

GRAVISCAN – Ancient: Graviscae, just north of modern Civita Vecchia, Tuscany, Italy.

HELVIOLAN(?) – Territory of the Helvii (?), Southern Rhône Valley, France. *Helvola* was also the name of a vine – *q.v.*

HELVOLA – Columella has this as a vine. Pliny gives *helvola* but also 'the small helvia', or *helvium*. See: Helviolan.

HEPSEMA – The same as *Sapa*, and *Siraeum*.

HYDROMEL – Water and honey.

IOTALINE(?) – Corrupt text. It might be Italiot. It was the Sicilian name for a copy style of Mamertine. Some grew near Syracuse.

ITALIOT(?) – See: Iotaline.

LABICAN – Ancient: Labicum, south-east of Rome, near modern Frascati, Latium, Italy.

LAEETANIAN – Territory of the Laeetani, north-east coast of Spain, between modern Barcelona and Gerona.

LAGARITAN – Ancient: Lagaria, near Thurii, Gulf of Taranto, Southern Italy.

LALETANIAN – Probably the same as Laeetanian.

LATINIENSIAN – West coast of Italy, probably the coast of Latium.

LAURONENSIAN – Probably the district of ancient Lauro in modern province of Valencia, Spain.

LEUCOGAEAN(?) – Perhaps from the Leucogaean hills, Campania, Italy.

LITERNINE – Ancient: Liternum, modern: Torredi Patria, coast of Campania, Italy.

LORA – 'After-wine', made from grape-skins soaked in water. The same as *deuterias*.

LUNENSAN – Ancient: Luna, near modern La Spezia and Carrara, Italy.

MAECENATIAN – Possibly from the Rimini-Ravenna-Bologna area; Romagna, Adriatic coast. Less possibly from Etruria, Italy.

MAMERTINE – Ancient: Messana, modern: Messina, Sicily.

MARIANUM – Wine from a particular property near Pompeii, Campania, Italy.

MARSIC – Territory of the Marsi, east of Rome and south of the Fucine Lake, Central Italy.

MASSIC – Ancient: Mons Massicus, modern: Monte Massico, Latium, Italy.

MASSILIAN – Ancient: Massilia, modern: Marseilles, France.

MESOPOTAMIAN – From near Gela, Southern Sicily.

MORONIAN – Ancient: Moron, modern: Almerim, north-east of Lisbon, Portugal.

MOSELLE – Ancient: Mosella, modern: Moselle Valley, Germany.

MULSUM – Wine and honey, or must and honey, mixed. See: *Melitites* – Greek List.

MURGENTINA – A vine imported into Italy from Sicily. Also called the *Pompeiana*.

MUSTUM TORTIVUM – The same as *Circumsicium*.

MUTINE – Ancient: Mutina, modern: Modena, Emilia, Italy.

NARBONENSIAN – Ancient: Gallia Narbonensis, modern: Provençe, France.

NOMENTAN – Ancient: Nomentum, modern: Mentana, north-east of Rome in Sabine territory, Central Italy.

NOMENTANA – The name of a vine, likely to have been the ancestor of the *teinturier mâle*. It probably made the Nomentan wine – *q.v.*

OINOMELI – The same as *mulsum*.

OPIMIAN – The outstanding recorded vintage-year of ancient Rome, 121 B.C.

OXYMEL – Honey, vinegar, salt, and rainwater, heated to boiling point ten times, cooled, and kept till old.

PAELIGNIAN – Abruzzi, Italy.

PASSUM – *Vinum passum*, raisin wine.

PATAVIAN – Ancient: Patavium, modern: Padua, Italy.

PETRINENSIAN – Ancient: Petrinum, near Sinuessa, Campania, Italy.

PICENIAN – Ancient: Picenum, Adriatic coast between Ancona and the R. Sangro, Italy.

PIPERATUM – Peppered wine.

POMPEIAN – Pompeii, Campania, Italy.

POMPEIANA – Another name for the *Murgentina* vine.

POTITIAN – A particular growth – the best – of *Mamertine*, and so called from its original grower.

PRAENESTINE – Ancient: Praeneste, modern: Palestrina, south-east of Rome, Latium, Italy.

PRAETUTIAN – Northern Adriatic coast of Italy.

PRECIAN – From the name of a vine, which produced quite a good quality of wine.

PRIVERNATIAN – Ancient: Privernum, modern: Priverno, Latium, Italy.

PROTAGION – See: *Protagion* – Greek List.

PROTROPUM – See: *Protropum* – Greek List.

PSITHIAN – See: *Psithian* – Greek List.

PUCINE – Near the R. Timavus, Gulf of Trieste, Adriatic.

RHAETIC – The name of a vine and of a Roman Alpine province. Rhaetic wines came from the Northern Po Valley, including the district of Verona, and probably that of Aquileia.

RHEGINE – Ancient: Rhegium, modern: Reggio, Calabria, Italy.

ROSATUM – Rose wine. It can also be a rose conserve.

SABINE – District of ancient Reate and Amiternum, north-east of Rome.

SAPA – The same as *Hepsema* and *Siraeum*. Must boiled down to one-third. See: *Defrutum*.

SEMPER MUSTUM – The same as *aigleucos*.

SERVITIAN – Probably from Apulia or Lucania, Southern Italy.

SETINE – Setia, Latium, Italy.

SIGNINE – Ancient: Signia, modern: Segni, Latium, Italy.

SIRAEUM – Must boiled down to a third. The same as *Hepsema* and *Sapa*.

SPIONIAN – *Spionia* was the name of a vine, particularly suited to the district of Ravenna, Italy.

SPOLETINE – Ancient: Spoletium, modern: Spoleto, Umbria, Italy.

STATANIAN – The Statanian vineyards were in Latium, next to the Falernian *vignoble*.

STATONIENSIAN – Ancient: Statonia, between modern Orvieto and modern Orbetello, Tuscany, Italy.

SULMONIAN – Sulmo, Abruzzi, Italy.

SURRENTINE – Sorrento, Campania, Italy.

TARENTINE – Ancient: Tarentum, modern: Taranto, Apulia, Italy.

TARRACONENSIAN – Ancient: Tarraco, modern: Tarragona, North-east Spanish coast.

TAUROMENITAN – Taormina, Sicily.

TEMPSAN – Tempsa; near modern Nicastro, Calabria, Italy.

THURINE – Ancient: Thurii, near the site of ancient Sybaris, Calabria, Italy.

TIBURTINE – Ancient: Tibur, modern: Tivoli, east of Rome, Latium, Italy.

TIRONIANUM – Wine from a particular property near Pompeii, Campania, Italy.

TREBELLICAN – Four miles from Naples, Campania, Italy.

TREBULAN – Modern: Maddaloni, south of Caserta, Campania, Italy. Probably also the name of a vine.

TRIFOLINE – Campania, Italy. So called because it matured in three years.

TURDETANIAN – South-west Andalusia, Spain.

ULBAN – Near ancient Cumae, Campania, Italy.

VATICAN – Ancient: district of Mons Vaticanus, modern: Vatican and neighbourhood, Rome.

VEIENTAN – Veii, north of Rome.

VELITERNAN – Ancient: Velitrae, modern: Velletri, Latium, Italy.

VENAFRAN – Ancient: Venafrum, modern: Venafro, Samnium, Southern Italy.

VERONIENSAN – Verona, Northern Italy. See: *Rhaetic.*

VESUVIAN(?) – Mt Vesuvius, Campania, Italy.

VIENNAN – Ancient: Vienna, modern: Vienne, Rhône Valley, France.

VINUM PICATUM – Pitched wine, or wine with a natural taste of pitch.

VIOLATIUM – Violet wine.

APPENDIX D: MEASURES AND MONEY OF THE ANCIENT GREEK WORLD

THE AMPHORA

The question of the capacities of Greek amphoras is intricate and difficult and it is one which I am certainly not competent to discuss. This Appendix is designed, however, to give only a general view of ancient measures and hence I have taken the liberty of offering a few general indications. It is for this reason also that I have not given measures in decimal figures but have confined myself to giving them in approximate litres and gallons and in approximate fractions of litres and gallons. (Gallon figures are in both British and United States equivalents.) For those who wish to go further into the matter I give select bibliographies for the amphora and the pithos, as well as for some measures of the Middle East and Egypt which are not listed in this Appendix.

AMPHORAS OF THE GREEK WORLD

It is doubtful if there was any 'standard' amphora for the ancient Greek world as a whole. There do appear to have been attempts to standardise the capacities of certain amphoras but these attempts seem to have been made on a city basis. Thus, in any discussion of measurement, the word amphora by itself is more or less meaningless and it has to be qualified by a territorial designation, such as Chian, Rhodian, Thasian, etc.

On the other hand, the various jar 'standards' – if they were standards – may have obtained some inter-city recognition so that, for example, the Athenian buyer could have known how much Chian wine he was buying, and need not (or should not) have feared that he was buying a short measure. In this case the necessary standard would have been one of minimum capacity, and it is quite likely that some such standards existed. There seems also to have been some tolerance upwards and over the minimum; but here again it must have been limited by the merchant's natural desire not to sell, let us say, 25 litres of wine for the price of 22. And furthermore, when taxes or rents were paid in kind, it would have been important to have jars whose capacities were more or less known.

Here are some of the capacities about which we have some knowledge:

Panathenaic amphoras of the early 5th century B.C. held, or could hold, 12 *choes* and were thus equal to a *metretes*. If we give this *chous* the value of c $3\frac{1}{4}$ litres, then these amphoras would have held c 39 litres or c $8\frac{1}{2}$ gallons British and c $10\frac{1}{4}$ gallons U.S.

Chian amphoras of the 5th-4th centuries B.C. often held c 22 litres or a little under 5 gallons British and c $5\frac{3}{4}$ gallons U.S.

Mendean amphoras at certain times seem to have varied between c 26 and c $32\frac{1}{2}$ litres, or c $5\frac{3}{4}$ and $7\frac{1}{2}$ gallons British and c $6\frac{7}{8}$ and $8\frac{1}{2}$ gallons U.S.

Cnidian amphoras of the 2nd-1st centuries B.C. vary in capacity from 27 to 34 litres, or c 6 to c $7\frac{1}{2}$ gallons British, and c $7\frac{1}{8}$ and 9 gallons U.S.

It is possible that in the Roman period the 'Greek' amphora commonly, or perhaps one should say frequently, held c 26 litres, or c $5\frac{3}{4}$ gallons British and c $6\frac{7}{8}$ gallons U.S. But one must remember that 'amphoras' could be small as well as large and that fractional sizes could exist at the same time as the larger containers. It may not be without interest to note that, of the Mycenaean stirrup-jars which have been excavated, the most usual size is c 12-14 litres, or c $2\frac{1}{2}$-3 gallons British, and c $3\frac{1}{8}$-$3\frac{3}{4}$ gallons U.S., although this, it seems, might rise to c 18 litres, or c 4 gallons British and c $4\frac{1}{2}$ gallons U.S.

AMPHORAS OF THE ROMAN WORLD

In Roman times standardisation seems to have become more pronounced. The *amphora Capitolina*, or 'standard' amphora, of Rome held 26 litres, or c $5\frac{3}{4}$ gallons British and c $6\frac{7}{8}$ gallons U.S. In Roman terms it was equal to one *quadrantal* – 2 *urnae* – 8 *congii*.

But there were other capacities. Some amphoras of the 1st century B.C., which were possibly intended to contain oil, held from 22-40 litres, c 5-9 gallons

British and *c* $5\frac{3}{4}$–$10\frac{1}{2}$ gallons U.S., while some of the Monte Testaccio amphoras, which carried wine and oil from Spain to Rome in the 2nd century A.D., held about 50 litres or 11 gallons British, and about $13\frac{1}{4}$ gallons U.S. And there could have been, of course, smaller as well as larger sizes.

AS (ROMAN) – A weight or a coin. In the period 150–90 B.C., there were 16 *asses* to the *denarius*. Under the Empire the *as*, a copper coin, remained at 16 to the *denarius*.

CHOUS (GREEK) – A liquid measure sometimes equal to *c* $3\frac{1}{4}$ litres or *c* $5\frac{1}{2}$ pints British and *c* $6\frac{7}{8}$ pints U.S. There were 12 *cotylai* to a *chous* and 12 *choes* to a *metretes*. The 'Greek' *chous* was roughly equivalent to the Roman *congius*. But note that the 'Greek' *chous* could vary; for example there were eight Chian *choes* to seven Athenian *choes*.

CONGIUS (ROMAN) – A liquid measure, holding *c* $3\frac{1}{4}$ litres or *c* $5\frac{1}{2}$ pints British and *c* $6\frac{7}{8}$ pints U.S. The *congius* was roughly equivalent to one value of the 'Greek' *chous* and there were 8 *congii* to the Roman 'standard' *amphora*. There were 12 *heminae* to a *congius*. (See: *Chous*.)

COTYLE (GREEK) – A small measure of liquid (and dry) capacity, equal to *c* $\frac{1}{4}$ litre or *c* $\frac{1}{2}$ pint British and *c* $\frac{1}{2}$ pint U.S. There were 12 *cotylai* (liquid) to the *chous*. (But note the varying capacity of the *chous*.)

CULLEUS (ROMAN) – A large liquid measure, equal to 20 Roman 'standard' amphoras, and holding 524 litres or *c* 116 gallons British and *c* $138\frac{3}{8}$ gallons U.S. It is thus almost equivalent to the modern Pipe of Port wine.

CYATHOS (GREEK) – A gourd or ladle. The smallest unit of Greek liquid (and dry) measurement. The *cyathos* – *c* 1/25th of a litre or *c* 1/14th of a pint British and *c* 1/12th pint U.S. There were 6 *cyathoi* to a *cotyle*. The Roman *cyathus* was about equal to the Greek *cyathos*. (But see: *Cotyle* and *Chous*.)

CYATHUS (ROMAN) – A small, liquid (and dry) measure roughly equal to the Greek *cyathos*: i.e. *c* 1/25th of a litre or *c* 1/14th of a pint British and *c* 1/12th pint U.S. (See: *Cyathos*.)

DENARIUS (ROMAN) – About 170 B.C. the *denarius* became the standard silver Roman coin. It was equal to 4 *sesterces* and 16 *asses*. The silver *denarius* was equivalent to the Attic *drachma*.

DOLIUM – The *dolium* was a large jar used for fermenting or storing wine. Its capacity varied between 20 and 70 amphoras. (See: *Amphora*; cf. *Pithos*.)

DRACHMA (GREEK) – This small coin was equal to 6 *obols*. The Attic *drachma* was equivalent to the Roman silver *denarius*. (But some *drachmas*, i.e. the Aeginetan and Phoenician, varied in value from the Attic *drachma*.)

HEMINA (ROMAN) – A liquid (and dry) measurement, equal to *c* $\frac{1}{4}$ litre or *c* $\frac{1}{2}$ pint British and *c* $\frac{1}{2}$ pint U.S. The Roman *hemina*, of which there were two to the Roman *sextarius*, was equivalent to the Greek *cotyle*.

JUGERUM (ROMAN) – A land measurement which equalled 28,800 sq. Roman feet. The *jugerum* is $\frac{5}{8}$ of an acre or $\frac{1}{4}$ of a *hectare*.

METRETES (GREEK) – A large, liquid measure, holding 12 *choes* and equal to *c* 39 litres or *c* $8\frac{1}{2}$ gallons British and *c* $10\frac{1}{4}$ gallons U.S. (But see: *Chous*.)

MINA (GREEK) – The silver *mina* was equivalent to 100 Attic *drachmae* or to 100 Roman *denarii*. (The *mina* of gold was worth five times the silver *mina*.)

OBOL (GREEK) – The *obol* was a small coin, of which there were 6 to a *drachma*. The *obol* was, therefore, equivalent to 1/6th of the Roman silver *denarius*. (But note that there were approximately three Aeginetan to four Attic *obols*.)

ORCA – A large vessel sometimes (as in Spain – Varro, I, xiii, 6) used for fermenting must. (See *Colum*. 12, 15, 2 – storage of figs in *orchae*.)

PITHOS – A storage container, static or semi-static, for wine, oil, grain, etc. A common Mediterranean vessel, the *pithos* had a long history and varied greatly in capacity.

Mesopotamia. At Nimrud (ancient Calah) the capacity of some storage jars was over 2 *homers*, the *homer* being *c* 187 litres or *c* 41 gallons British and *c* $49\frac{3}{8}$ gallons U.S.

Anatolia. Pithoi in the shrine of Beycesultan, *c* 2400 B.C. held $45\frac{1}{2}$–68 litres, or *c* 10–15 gallons British and *c* 12–18 gallons U.S. Those in the Burnt Palace, of *c* 1900 B.C., held $4\frac{1}{2}$–$13\frac{1}{2}$ litres, about 1 to 3 gallons British and *c* $1\frac{1}{4}$–$3\frac{1}{2}$ gallons U.S.

Crete. Pithoi in the Later Minoan cellars of Knossos have been estimated to hold between 185 and 277 litres, *c* 40–61 gallons British and *c* $48\frac{7}{8}$–$73\frac{1}{8}$ gallons U.S.

Mycenaean. The jars in the wine magazine of the Palace of Nestor in the South-west Peloponnese are estimated to have held somewhere about 200 litres, *c* 44 gallons British or *c* 52¾ gallons U.S., whereas the jars in the 'oil' magazine of the Palace were only about one-third of this capacity.

(Compare the Roman *Dolium*.)

QUADRANTAL (ROMAN) – The same volume as the 'standard' Roman *amphora*, i.e. 26 litres, or *c* 5¾ gallons British and *c* 6⅞ gallons U.S.

SCRIPULUM (ROMAN) – A weight, equal to 1/24th of an oz. (Also a measure of area.)

SESTERCE (ROMAN) – See: *Sestertius*.

SESTERTIUM (ROMAN) – 1,000 *sestertii*.

SESTERTIUS (ROMAN) – A *sesterce*, a small coin, of which there were four to the *denarius*.

SEXTARIUS (ROMAN) – A liquid (and dry) measure of *c* ½ litre or *c* 1 pint British and *c* 1 pint U.S. There were two *heminae* to the *sextarius*.

TALENT – A weight, equivalent to 60 *minae*.

URNA (ROMAN) – A liquid measure holding *c* 13½ litres, *c* 3 gallons British or *c* 3½ gallons U.S., and thus about half the capacity of the 'standard' Roman amphora.

APPENDIX E: MEDIEVAL WINES

For the confused medieval meaning of some of the following *appellations*, see discussion in the text of Chapter 5.

ALGARBE – Algarve, Southern Province of Portugal. Possibly also wine shipped down the River Guadiana.

ALGRADE – Same as *Algarbe*.

ALICANTE – Alicante, South-east Spain.

ANDEGAVIA – A name for Anjou, France.

ANJOU – Area of Angers and Saumur, Loire, France.

ANTIOCHE – Presumably Antioch, in ancient Syria.

ARGENTUEIL – Argenteuil. North-west Paris.

AUÇUERRE – The same as *Auxerre*.

AUSSAI – Alsace (?); or modern Auxey-Duresses, Côte d'Or, Burgundy (?). Its identification with *Osey* – q.v. – has been suggested, but the identification is questionable.

AUVILER – Hautvillers, Epernay, Champagne.

AUXERRE – Auxerre, Yonne (near Chablis), Lower Burgundy, France.

BASTARD – Spain, Portugal.

BIAUNE – Beaune, Côte d'Or, Burgundy.

BLANC – England, 13th century. A general term for white wine.

BOCHET – Paris, 14th century. A drink compounded of ale, honey, spices and water. See: *Braket*, below.

BRAKET – England, 15th century. The same as *Hippocras* and *Clarre* – q.v. But it could also be made with ale, honey, and pepper, when it was much the same as *Bochet* – q.v.

CAEREN – Anglo-Saxon England. Same as *Wyne Cute* – q.v.

CAMPELYTE – England, 15th century. Tuscany (?), Italy. But, in 1650, Campole was the name of a white grape and *Campelyte* may thus have been a wine named from a grape and not from any specific vineyard area.

CAMPLETES – A variant spelling of *Campelyte* – q.v.

CAMPOLET – A variant spelling of *Campelyte* – q.v.

CANDY – Candia – Island of Crete. A sweet wine. Also known as *Candia Malmsey*. See: *Cret, Malmsey*.

CAPRICK – Of uncertain provenance. Its most likely origins are Portugal and Spain; slightly less probable are mainland Italy and Capri; least probable is Cyprus.

CARENUM – See: *Wyne Cute*, below.

CARMIGNANO – Carmignano, west of Florence, Tuscany, Northern Italy.

CHABLIES – Wine, generally speaking, from the modern Chablis country, Lower Burgundy, France.

CHALON – France, 6th century. Chalon-sur-Saône (ancient Cabillonum), Burgundy, France.

CHIANTI – Tuscany, Northern Italy, 14th century.

CIROMELLUM – England, 15th century. This was *Growtt* – q.v. – a type of ale. See: *Idromellum*.

CLAIRET – France. Generally used in the 14th and 15th centuries in France to describe wine by its colour, the colour being between blood-red and white. In the Chalonnais it meant vin rosé. In the Gironde it probably meant a blend of red and white wine, and it may also have meant wine from Graves. Contrast *clairet* with *claret* – q.v.

CLARET – Drunk in England in Anglo-Saxon times and throughout the Middle Ages. *Claret* could mean the same as *clairet*, i.e. a wine which in colour was between dark-red and white; but the usual medieval meaning is that of a drink made of wine, honey, herbs, and spices. It was also called *claretum*. It could thus be the same as *Clarre*, *Clarry*, and *Hippocras*, all of which were styles of *Piment* – q.v. It is possible that a variety of the herb Clary was used in the making of *claret*. Cf. *Clairet*.

CLARRE – The same as *Claret* and *Hippocras*, q.v., wine, honey, and spices, although it could be made with ale, when it was the same as one style of *Braket* – q.v.

CLARRY – The same as *Claret* and *Hippocras* – q.v.

CORSICA – Island of Corsica.

CRET – Candia – Island of Crete. *Cret*, though much or most of it was grown in Crete, was also *Cret*, i.e.

Cretan style wine grown elsewhere. For Crete, see also: *Candy, Grenache, Malmsey.*

CRETICUM – The same as Cret – *q.v.*

CYPRUS – Island of Cyprus. Some was sold as *Malmsey* – *q.v.* – though not as good as Candian Malmsey. See also: *Caprick*, above; *Greek*, below.

ESPAIGNE – Spain. Some of this was white wine.

ESPERNAI LE BACHELER – France, 13th century. Epernay, Champagne.

EW ARDANT – England, late 14th century. In the *Forme of Cury* this is translated as hot water. Possibly, however, it means *aquavite*. See: Renaissance to Modern List. See: *Eau ardant* – Renaissance to Modern List.

FERRÉ – France. A kind of wine. It may have been a wine into which a hot iron had been plunged. On the other hand *vin de fer* has been in modern usage a term for a *vin vert*, or a young, astringent wine.

FRANEBOYSE – 13th century. Probably a raspberry, or raspberry-flavoured, wine.

FRONTIGNAN – Frontignan, Hérault, France, 8th century, etc.

GALANT – Burgundy. Called '*galantwyn*' in medieval London. Same as *Wyne Cute* – *q.v.*

GARIOFILATUM – 12th, 13th centuries. Wine, spiced with cloves or gillyflower. It may also have been Gillyflower Wine, made from sugar, water, and clove carnations.

GARNARDE – 14th century. Probably Granada, Spain.

GAZETIC – Gaza, Philistia, Palestine. Known of in, and possibly imported into, France in the 5th and 6th centuries.

GAZITINE – Same as *Gazetic* – *q.v.*

GERNARDE – A Chaucerian name for, probably, *Garnarde* – *q.v.*

GRECO – Same as *Greek* – *q.v.*

GREEK – Tuscany, Northern Italy; but mainly Apulia and Calabria, Southern Italy. A sweet, white wine, sometimes in the style of *Cyprus* – *q.v.* – wine. It was probably named from the greco vine. It was on occasion called *Latin* – *q.v.* – wine.

GRENACHE – Candia – Island of Crete; possibly also Italy. So named from the Grenache vine. See: *Cret*.

GROWTT – 12th–15th centuries. A sort of ale. Variant spellings are *groute, growte*, etc. See: *Ciromellum*, above; *Idromellum*, below.

HIPPOCRAS – England, 14th, 15th centuries; Paris, 14th century. *Hippocras* was made from wine, cinnamon, ginger, pepper, etc., and sugar, then strained. It was the same as *Claret, Clarre*, and *Clarry* – *q.v.* – and was a style of *Piment* – *q.v.* In 14th-century Paris it was used as a 'liqueur', as it was in 15th-century England. See also: *Braket*.

HYDROMEL – See: *Muret*, below.

IDROMELLUM – England, 15th century. This, apparently, was *Growtt* – *q.v.* – a type of ale, and not a variant writing of *Hydromel* – *q.v.* See: *Ciromellum*, above.

LATIN – Apulia and Calabria, Southern Italy. See: *Greek*, above.

LEPE – Most probably ancient Illipula, modern Niebla, between Seville and Huelva, South-west Spain. (But there is a modern village of Lepe between Huelva and Ayamonte.) Chaucer has 'whyte wyn of Lepe'. *Lepe* may also have been a general term for wine coming from, or through, Seville.

MALAGA – Malaga, Southern Spain.

MALEVESYN – A variant of *Malmsey* – *q.v.*

MALMSEY – Candia – Island of Crete; Cyprus; Southern European vineyards; (later from the Canaries and Madeira). The name was used for a style of wine, the best quality of which grew in Crete. It was also called Cret – *q.v.* See: *Candy, Cyprus, Rotimo*.

MALVASIA – A variant writing of *Malmsey* – *q.v.*

MALVOISIE – A variant writing of *Malmsey* – *q.v.*

MATRINGHALE – Unidentified. This wine (?) appears in England in 1438.

MEAD – Basically made of honey and water. Spices were sometimes added. Also called *methe*. See: *metheglin*, below.

MELFI – Melfi, Central Italy.

METHE – Same as *mead* – *q.v.*

METHEGLIN – Basically made of honey and water. Herbs were sometimes added. See: *mead*, above.

MEURON – France. This may have been a name for mulberry or blackberry wine, or wine flavoured with these berries. Variant spellings, *mouron, mûron*. See: *Moretum* and *Muret*, below.

MONDEGO – River Mondego, Beira Litoral, Central Portugal. *c* 1154. At this date there were a number of vineyards along the course of the Mondego river.

MORÉ – See: *Muret*, below.

MORETUM – This may have been mulberry or black-berry wine, or wine flavoured with these berries. Cf. *meuron* and *muret* – *q.v.*

MOSSAC – Probably a variant writing of *Muissac'* – *q.v.*

MOUNTROSSE – Possibly from Monterosi, north of Rome, or, more likely, from Monterosso al Mare, La Spezia, North-west Italy. A sweet wine.

MOUSSELE – Probably the Moselle. See: *Oblinquo, de* – below.

MUISSAC' – Moissac, Tarn et Garonne, South-west France.

MURET – France. A sort of wine, sometimes *hydromel* – i.e. honey and water. '*Muret*', or '*more*' could also be used to mean 'dark red' or 'black' as a wine colour; hence possibly a drink coloured by the addition of mulberries or blackberries. See: *Meuron* and *Moretum*, above.

MUSCADELLE – Candia – Island of Crete, etc. A sweet wine made from Muscat grapes.

MUSCAT – Southern France; and probably elsewhere round the Mediterranean. Wine made from the Muscat grape.

OBBLENC – Same as *Oblinquo, de* – *q.v.*

OBLINQUO, DE – Possibly the Moselle. The identification of this wine as Moselle is uncertain.

ORDIALES – Castro Urdiales, Province of Santander, Northern Spain.

OSEY – Spain and Portugal.

OXYMEL – Drunk in Anglo-Saxon England. Made of vinegar and honey, sometimes with the addition of water.

PALME – Probably from Palermo, Sicily; an alternative is the Island of Marjorca, Balearics.

PICTAVIA – A name for Poitou, Western France.

PIMENT – Wine mixed with honey and spices. *Claret*, *Clarre*, *Clarry*, and *Hippocras* were all styles of *Piment*.

POITIERS – Poitiers, Poitou, France.

POTENZA – Potenza, Central Italy.

PREIGNAC – Preignac, Sauternes, Bordeaux, 6th century.

PROVENCE – Provençe, France.

RAPÉ – The same as *Raspice* – *q.v.*

RAPOLLA – Rapolla, near Melfi, Central Italy.

RAPPIS – The same as *Raspice* – *q.v.*

RASPETUM – The same as *Raspice* – *q.v.*

RASPICE – England, 13th, 15th centuries. A 'wine' made of must fermented with grape clusters and other wine; or wine so made as to have some astringency; or such astringent wine with herbs or spices added to it. But 'raspice' may occasionally have meant raspberry, or raspberry flavoured, wine.

REC – Wine shipped, or drunk, after its racking. Many variant spellings, *Rek'*, etc.

REK' – Variant spelling of *Rec* – *q.v.*

RETHYMO – See: *Rotimo*.

RHENISH – Western Germany. Usually this meant wines grown on, or shipped down, the Rhine, but it could also mean Alsatian wines and German wines in general. Much Rhenish was white.

RHODES – Island of Rhodes, Aegean.

RIPTAGE – Almost certainly from Iberia or the Mediterranean and probably from the River Minho, Northern Portugal. Most probably a sweet, or at least a heavy, wine.

ROCHELLE – La Rochelle, Charente-Maritime, France. Much wine was shipped through La Rochelle to England. See: *Vermaille*, below.

ROMANEY – Yugoslavia; Adriatic islands; Greece; Bulgaria; Asia Minor. The derivation of the name is almost certainly from Rūm (Rumania) the medieval East Roman Empire.

ROMPNEY – Probably the same as *Romaney* – *q.v.*

ROSE, COLOURE DE – This name appears in 15th-century England. It has been suggested as meaning lees of red wine. It is more likely to have meant vin rosé. It may have been *Vin de Rosette*, or *Vin Rosetique*, for both of which see Renaissance to Modern List.

ROTIMO – Island of Crete. A type of *Malmsey* – *q.v.* – from the Rotimo (Rethymo) vineyards of Crete.

RUMNEY – A variant writing of *Romaney* – *q.v.*

RYBOLE – Probably from Istria, Italy, and Jugoslavia. Note that there is now a Rebula wine of Jugoslavia. It is possible, however, that the medieval *Rybole* was another name for *Vin cuit*, or grape juice boiled down, as was *Ribolla* – *q.v.* Renaissance to Modern List.

RYVERE – River Ebro; possibly modern Rioja, Logroño, etc.; but more probably Saragossa and Tarragona. It was also called 'of the river'. An early 16th-century variant is 'Wyn ryvers'.

ST EMILION – England, 1289. Modern: St Emilion, Bordeaux.

ST JOHN – At or near St Jean d'Angely: Charente, France.

SANCERRE – Sancerre, Berry, France.

SAREPTAN – Sarepta, Phoenicia, 5th century.

SICERA – Cider.

TENTE – Spain.

TIRE – This wine may have been named from the tirio grape (the same grape perhaps as the tiro), and may have come from Calabria, Southern Italy, and from Sicily. But some Tire wine almost certainly came from Tyre, in the Lebanon.

TORRENTYNE – River Ebro, Northern Spain. See: *Ryvere*, above.

TREBBIANO – Tuscany and the Marches, Northern Italy. So named from the medieval trebbiano vine of Tuscany.

TRUBIDIANE – Possibly the same as *Trebbiano* – q.v. Was *Diana* – see Renaissance to Modern List – a name corrupted from *Trubidiane?*

TYRE – The same as *Tire* – q.v.

UBLINQUO – The same as *Oblinquo, de* – q.v.

VERJUICE – Juice of unripe fruit, and grape juice from unripe grapes, used in cooking and sometimes for making mustard. The Verjus grape was once common in North-west Europe but verjuice could be made from any grape.

VERMAILLE – Red wine. Sometimes refers to wine from Gascony or La Rochelle. See: *Rochelle*, above; *Wasconia*, below.

VERNACCIA – See: *Vernage*, below.

VERNAGE – Italy; probably mainly from Northern Italy. It was wine made from the vernaccia grape.

VINEQUYT – The same as *Wyne Cute* – q.v.

VIN FOU – Burgundy. Fermented must of unpressed grapes.

VIN SANTO – Tuscany, Northern Italy. In modern Tuscany it is made from partly dried grapes, fermented slowly and for a long time. If fully fermented it can be dry; if partly fermented, sweet. Some modern *vin santo* is made from malvasia or trebbiano grapes.

WASCONIA – A name for Gascony: when applied to wine, it included Bordeaux, Guyenne, Périgord, etc. See: *Vermaille*, above.

WYNE CUTE – *Vin cuit*, cooked must, grape juice boiled down. It is the same as the Anglo-Saxon *Caeren*, from Latin *carenum*. In medieval times it was also called *Vinequyt* and, in Burgundy, *Galant*.

XERÈS – Jerez de la Frontera, South-west Spain, *c* 1154.

YPOCRAS – The same as *Hippocras* – q.v.

References for wines listed in Appendix but not discussed in the text of Chapter 5 are in note 228 to Chapter 5.

APPENDIX F: MEDIEVAL ENGLISH VINEYARDS

EXPLANATORY NOTES

1. Brackets indicate a vineyard which is, or may be, listed under another name: i.e. [Stoke] is the same as Severn Stoke.
2. A question mark indicates that the evidence on which the entry is based is either inconclusive in itself, as in Cholsey, Berks, where the word 'Vineyard' may have another meaning, or inconclusive as to whether a plantation of vines, or only a few vines, is meant. Cambridge, Peterhouse, is an example of this latter class. For a discussion of evidence, see Chapter 5, pages 237–43.
3. An asterisk indicates that the location of a vineyard is particularly uncertain, as in Eseham, Yorks, and Colton, Kent.
4. The sign ✠ indicates an ecclesiastical vineyard: the letter **R** a royal vineyard. Wherever possible these signs have been applied to designate the first status of a vineyard; see, for example, Belvoir, Lincs, and Lincoln, Lincs. Where neither of these two signs occurs the vineyard is assumed to have been established by, or have belonged to, a lay owner. In seven cases, however, the original ownership is very doubtful. These cases are: Barking, Cambridge, Peterhouse, Cambridge, Trinity Hall, Chart Sutton, Leeds, Santlac, and Winchester (2).
5. References to the vineyards are in Chapter 5, notes 46–63. VCH references are given as well as those of *Domesday* folios, since VCH volumes usually contain their county section of Domesday. In addition, VCH, Somerset, 1, has the 'Exon Domesday' and the 'Geld Inquest': VCH, Kent, III, the 'Domesday Monachorum': and VCH, Cambridge, 1, the 'Inquisitio Comitatus Cantabrigiensis'.

STATISTICAL SURVEY

1. *Period*. The centuries covered are the 10th to the 16th. The end date – with one exception, Abberton, Worcs – is the Dissolution of the Monasteries. Abberton is included because its date is near enough to the Dissolution to make most probable the existence there of a pre-Dissolution vineyard; it is not, hover, counted in any statistic except that of the total number of definite and possible vineyards listed.
2. *Probabilities*. For a discussion of the terms used in Latin texts, such as *vinea*, *vinarium*, etc., and their use as evidence for the existence of vineyards, see Chapter 5, page 240. For a discussion of the possible meanings of 'Wynyard' and 'Wynyates', see Chapter 5, page 240.
3. *Measurements*. The Domesday measure of the *arpent* is given by Sir Henry Ellis, *A General Introduction to Domesday Book*, 1, 117, as being *c* 1 acre. I have used this equation in listing the size of Domesday vineyards.
4. *Counties*. Twenty-four English counties seem to have had vineyards, ranging from Worcestershire with 17 – (excluding Abberton and Alvecherche) – and Essex with 16 – (excluding Barking and Thurrock, West) – to Bucks and probably Devon, each of which had one, Hants which almost certainly had at least one, and Norfolk which probably had one. For complete listing see, in this Appendix, Medieval English Vineyards by Counties.
5. *Figures*. Total number of definite and possible vineyards listed (excluding duplicates and counting 'all', as in Belvoir, Lincs, as being no more than 2) 139
Total of definite pre-Conquest vineyards listed   2
Total of *Domesday* vineyards listed   39
Total of listed vineyards occurring between the Conquest and 1100 and not recorded in *Domesday*   5
Total number of listed vineyards apparently established in the 12th century   33
Over the whole period:
Total of definite and possible royal vineyards . .   11
Total of definite and possible church vineyards   52

Total of definite and possible lay vineyards... 67
Total of vineyards whose original ownership
is very doubtful........................ 8

6. *Extent. Domesday* records *c* 123 acres of vineyard in thirty-five vineyards. The average extent of the *Domesday* vineyard was thus *c* 3½ acres. Of the thirty-five *Domesday* vineyards whose size is re-corded, eight were of *c* 5 acres or over, two were of *c* 4 acres, seven of *c* 3 acres, eleven of *c* 2 acres, six of *c* 1 acre, and one of *c* ½ acre. The largest size recorded in *Domesday* is *c* 12 acres at Bisham, Berks. The next two in size are Belchamp Walter, Essex, with *c* 11 acres and Waltham, Great, Essex, which had *c* 10 acres.

MEDIEVAL ENGLISH VINEYARDS BY COUNTIES

BEDFORDSHIRE
Eaton Socon
Kemeston
Warden ? ✠ 2

BERKSHIRE
Abingdon ✠
Bisham
Burghfield
Cholsey ? ✠
Tidmarsh
Wallingford
Watchfield **R** ★ (probably Berks)
Windsor **R**

BUCKINGHAMSHIRE
Iver

CAMBRIDGESHIRE
Cambridge: Peterhouse ?
Cambridge: Trinity Hall ?
Ely ✠
Kennet
Thorney ✠

DEVON
Teinton: Bishopsteignton ✠ ★

ESSEX
Ashdon
Barking ? ★
Belchamp Walter
Castle Hedingham
Colchester
Debden
Hadleigh

Maldon 2
Maplestead, Great
Maplestead, Little
Mundon
Rayleigh
Stambourne [or Toppesfield]
Stebbing
Thurrock, West ?
[Toppesfield] See: Stambourne
Walden
Waltham, Great

GLOUCESTERSHIRE
Bisley
[Gloucester, Vale of]
Prestbury ✠
Prinknash
Stonehouse
Tewkesbury
Westbury

HAMPSHIRE
Beaulieu ✠
Winchester ? 2
(two or more)

HEREFORDSHIRE
Hereford **R**
Ledbury ✠
Litley ✠
Mavordine ★

HERTFORDSHIRE
St Albans ✠
Standon
Ware

HUNTINGDONSHIRE
Buggenden ✠ ★
Huntingdon **R**
Ramsey ✠
Somersham Manor ✠

KENT
Berton ✠
Brook ✠
Canterbury, St Martins ✠
Chart Sutton
Chertham ✠
Chislet ✠
Colton ✠ ★ ★
Erith ?
Halling ✠
Hollingbourne ✠
Kennington **R** ★
Leeds
Norflet ✠
Rainham
Rochester ✠
Tenham ✠

LINCOLNSHIRE
Belvoir 2
(two or more)
Lincoln 2 **R** ✠ ★ (2)
(one might be Buggenden)
Spalding ✠

LONDON
Holborn ✠
Holborn
Smithfield, East
Westminster **R**

479

MIDDLESEX
Coleham
Kempton
Kensington
Staines ✠

NORFOLK
Eresham ★

NORTHAMPTONSHIRE
Ashby
Peterborough ✠
Rockingham **R**

SHROPSHIRE
Purlai ★
Shrewsbury ✠

SOMERSET
Bath ✠ ★
Curry, North **R**
Dumster
Glastonbury ✠
Lyncombe
Meare ✠

Minehead
Muchelney ✠
Pamborough in Wedmore ✠
Portbury ? 2
Timberscombe

SUFFOLK
Barking ✠
Bury St Edmunds ✠
Clare
Ixworth
Lavenham

SURREY
Chertsey ✠
Croydon

SUSSEX
Beeding
Santlac ★

WILTSHIRE
Bradford on Avon ✠
Lacock
Malmesbury ✠

Tollard Royal
Wilcot

WORCESTERSHIRE
Abberton
Alvecherche ✠
Broadwas ✠
Bushley
Chaddesley 4
Cotheridge 2
Fladbury
Grimley ✠
Hallow ✠
Hampton, Great and
    Little ✠ 2
Leigh ✠
Pershore ✠
Ripple
Severn Stoke. Possibly **R**
[Stoke]

YORKSHIRE
Eseham ✠ ★
Kyrketon ✠ ★
[York]

APPENDIX G: WINES: RENAISSANCE TO MODERN

ABANELLO – Italy.

ABSINTHII AQUA – A type of *Wormwood Wine*.

ACQUARELLO – Italy.

AETNA – Mt Etna, Sicily.

ALBA FLORA – Majorca, Balearic Islands.

ALBANA – Italy.

ALBANELLO – Italy.

ALBANO – Albania.

ALEATICO – A name taken from the Aleatico grape. A variant wine-name is *Leattica*.

ALICANT – Alicante, South-east Spain.

ALLIGANT – A variant spelling of *Alicant*.

ANNADEA – Anadia, north of Coimbra, Central Portugal.

ARGENTOILE – Argenteuil, a north-western suburb of Paris: (not the Argenteuil, south-east of Tonerre, in the Dépt of the Yonne).

ARGOSTOLA – Argostólion, Island of Cephalonia, west coast of Greece.

ARINTO – Portugal.

ARRACK – Mainly East Indies.

AUBRYAN – A variant spelling of Haut-Brion. Pessac, Graves, Bordeaux.

AUXERRE – Auxerre, Yonne, near Chablis, Lower Burgundy.

AY – Near Epernay, Marne. Champagne.

BACKRAG – Bacharach, Rhine, Germany.

BAIRRADA – Central Portugal.

BASTARD – Spain; Portugal; some from Corsica.

BEAUNE – Beaune, Côte d'Or, Burgundy. Sometimes included wine of Dijon.

BENECARLO – Province of Valencia, East Spain.

BLANQUET – Département de l'Aude, Midi, France.

BLANQUETTE DE LIMOUX – Département de l'Aude, Midi, France.

BLEAHARD – Probably from the Rhineland.

BONECARLOS – A variant spelling of *Benecarlo*.

BRAGGET – Presumably the same as *Braket* – q.v. Medieval List.

BRONTE – Bronte, Mt Etna, Sicily.

BUCELLAS – Bucelas, north-east of Lisbon.

BUDA – Budapest, Hungary.

CALCAVELLA – Carcavelos, on the Tagus, west of Lisbon.

CAMARATE – Olivais, on the Tagus, north-east of Lisbon near Charneca and Sacavém.

CANARY – Canary Islands.

CAPARICA – Most probably from or near, Caparica, southern coast of the Tagus Estuary, Portugal. (Bacci has 'In *Lusitania Caparica* . . .')

CAP BRETON – Capbreton, Bayonne, Landes. Gascony.

CAPE – Cape Province, South Africa.

CAPRICK – Of uncertain provenance. Its most likely origins are Portugal, and Spain; slightly less probable are Mainland Italy and Capri; least probable is Cyprus, as suggested by Henderson.

CARCAVELOS – Carcavelos, on the Tagus, west of Lisbon. The same as *Calcavella*.

CARIÑENA – Cariñena, between Calatayud and Saragossa, Aragon, Spain.

CARRASPADA – Spain.

CASTELLI ROMANI – Alban Hills, Rome.

CATE PUMENT – Sometimes either from the Canaries, Iberia, or the Mediterranean area, or from all three.

CAWOS – Presumably Island of Chios, Aegean.

CEPHALONIA – Island of Cephalonia, west coast of Greece.

CERAGUZA – Probably from Saragossa, Spain.

CHAOS – Presumably Island of Chios, Aegean.

CHARNECO – Portugal; and perhaps also from Spain.

CHIANTI – Tuscany, Northern Italy.

CHIARETTO – Northern Italy.

CHIOS – Island of Chios, Aegean.

CLARET WATER – The same as *Eau clairette*.

CLARY WINE – England; probably also Italy and the Mediterranean.

COLARES – Colares, near Sintra, north-west of Lisbon.

COMMANDERIA – Island of Cyprus.

CONSTANTIA – Vineyards of Great and Little Constantia, near Cape Town, South Africa.

CORSICA – Island of Corsica.

COUSSYE – Presumably from the area of Coucy-le-Château, east of Laon and north of Soissons, France.

CRESPA – Northern Italy.

CRETAN – Island of Crete.

CUTE – *Vin cuit* – grape juice boiled down to a desired consistency.

CUTT – The same as *Cute*.

CYPRUS – Island of Cyprus.

DIANA – (?). It may have been wine grown near, or shipped down, the River Guardiana, and thus wine either from Spain or Portugal, possibly the same as the medieval *Algarbe*. On the other hand, the name could be a corruption of *Trubidiane*.

EAU ARDANT – France. *Aquavite*.

EAU CLAIRETTE – France; (also England?).

EAU DE BOUCHET – France.

FLORENCE – Florence, Tuscany, Italy.

FRONTIGNAN – Frontignan, Hérault, Languedoc, France.

GALLICIA – Galicia, North-west Spain.

GASCONY – Gascony, South-west France.

GREEK – Central and Eastern Mediterranean; but principally Southern Italy; some from Tuscany.

GRILLET, CH. – Near Condrieu, Rhône Valley, France.

GRISO – Northern Italy.

HERMITAGE – Tain, Drôme (Rhône Valley), France.

HOCKAMORE – An English corruption of 'Hockheimer', meaning *Hock*.

HOUBRION – A variant spelling of Haut-Brion. Pessac, Graves, Bordeaux.

JURANÇON – Near Pau, in the Basses Pyrénées, France.

KIAN – This may mean Chian wine but it can mean a Cayenne sauce.

KOLLOSERWEIN – Haloze, Slovenia, Jugoslavia.

LEATTICA – Italy, particularly Tuscany. See: *Aleatico*.

LISBON – Lisbon, and surrounding districts.

LUCINA – Most probably from Lucena, south of Cordoba, Spain.

LUNELLE – Lunel, Hérault, Languedoc, Southern France.

LUSENNA – A variant writing of *Lucina*.

LUTTENBERGER – Ljutomer, Slovenia (Southern Styria), Jugoslavia.

LYBOS – Libos, near Fumel, Lot-et-Garonne, Gascony, France.

MADEIRA – Island of Madeira.

MALAGA – Malaga, Southern Spain.

MALLIGO – A variant spelling of *Malaga*.

MALMSEY – Originally Eastern Mediterranean, especially Crete; later the Mediterranean generally; Southern Spain, the Canary Islands, Madeira, the Azores.

MALVASIA DI BOSA – Island of Sardinia.

MALVASIA GARBA – Mediterranean; probably in particular from Crete.

MARCEILLES – (?). This is most probably a variant spelling of *Marcella*.

MARCELLA – This may be a variant spelling of *Marsala*. Or it could mean wine from Marseilles, or from Marseillan near Beziers, Hérault, France.

MARGOOSE – A variant writing for Château Margaux, Médoc, Bordeaux.

MARSALA – Western Sicily.

MASDIEU – Between Perpignan and Collioure, Roussillon, Pyrénées Orientales, France.

METHUEN WINE – Probably Portugal.

MONTILLA – Montilla, south of Cordoba, Spain.

MONTMATRE – Montmartre, Paris.

MOUNTAIN – Mostly from Malaga, Southern Spain.

MULJO – Most probably from Mersault, Côte d'Or, Burgundy.

MULSO – Mersault, Côte d'Or, Burgundy.

MUM – Brunswick, Germany. A type of beer.

MUSCADEL – Mainly the Mediterranean; but also South-west France, Portugal, etc.

MUSCADINE – Mainly the Mediterranean; but also from other vineyards.

MUSCADINE WINES – Muscadine, or Muscatel wines (i.e. wines made from muscat grapes) named in this List are: *Caparica* (?), *Cephalonia*, *Charneco* (?), *Chios* (?), *Cyprus*, *Florence*, *Frontignan*, *Leattica*, *Lunelle*, *Malaga*, *Marcella* (?), *Muscadel*, *Rivesaltes*, *Rota*, *Seges*, *Setubal*, *Smyrna*, *Syracuse*, *Tintilla de Rota*, *Verde*, and *Vino Santo*.

NAVARRE – Western Pyrénées.

NERAC – Nérac, Lot-et-Garonne, France. See: *Vin Rosetique*.

NIKARINE – River Neckar, South-west Germany.

NOUSSA – Probably from Thessaly, Northern Greece.

OBRIAN – A variant spelling for Haut-Brion. Pessac, Graves, Bordeaux.

OSEY – Spain and Portugal.

PACARETTI – Southern Spain. A variant spelling of *Paxarete*.

PACKARET – Southern Spain. A variant spelling of *Paxarete*.

PALM – Although this can mean wine from Majorca, in early 18th-century England it usually meant wine from the Canary Islands.

PAXARETE – East of Jerez de la Frontera, South-west Spain; and other districts of Southern Spain.

PEDRO XIMENES – Southern Spain.

PEROSIMENEZ – Southern Spain. A variant writing for Pedro Ximenes.

PETER SA MEENE – Southern Spain. An English corruption, as was also 'Peter Seeme', of *Pedro Ximenes*.

PICKERWEIN – Pekre, Slovenia (Southern Styria), Jugoslavia.

PIQUETTE – France.

PONTAC – Bordeaux.

PRINAC – Preignac, Sauternes, Bordeaux.

PROSECHO – Istria, Italy.

PURL ROYAL – England. A mixture of wormwood, or other herbs, with wine.

PX – Southern Spain. PX is a contraction of *Pedro Ximenes*.

RAPÉ – France; and perhaps elsewhere under other names.

RAPPIS – France; and the Mediterranean area.

RHENISH – Western Germany, particularly the Rhineland; probably at times including Alsace.

RHENISH IN THE MUST – Germany or the Low Countries; also 'manufactured' elsewhere.

RIBADAVIA – Ribadavia, River Minho, Galicia, North-west Spain.

RIBOLLA – Apparently another name for *Vin cuit*.

RITTERSBERGER – Ritoznoj, Slovenska Bistrica, Slovenia, Jugoslavia.

RIVESALTES – Riversaltes, north of Perpignan, Roussillon, Pyrénées-Orientales, France.

ROBDAVIE – Portugal and Spain. Perhaps the same as *Rubiedauy*.

ROBERDANY – Robedillo, in 'hither Lusitania'; possibly in Estremadura, Western Spain; or Portugal? Possibly the same as *Rubiedauy*.

ROCHELL – La Rochelle, Charente-Maritime, France.

ROMANIA – Area of the medieval East Roman Empire; probably in particular from Corfu and North-west Greece; also South-west Spain; possibly also the Canary Islands.

ROMNIE – A variant spelling of *Romania*.

ROTA – Rota, near Jerez de la Frontera, Province of Cádiz, South-west Spain.

ROTIMO – Island of Crete.

RUBIEDAUY – Spain; perhaps also Portugal.

RYVERE – River Ebro, North-east Spain.

SACAVEEM – On the Tagus, north of Lisbon.

SACK – Mainly from Andalucia and particularly from Jerez de la Frontera; also from the Canary Islands; and some from Galicia and Portugal. Some possibly made in Italy (?).

ST GEORGE AUSBRUCH – St George, near Pressburg (modern: Bratislava), Czechoslovakia.

SAN MARTYNS – From the 'Kingdom of Toledo'; it may possibly have come from Pinto, between Madrid and Aranjuez.

SANTORINI – Island of Santorini (modern: Thera), Cyclades, Southern Aegean.

SARAGOSSA – Sarragossa, River Ebro, North-east Spain.

SARDINIAN – Island of Sardinia.

SECKE – A variant spelling of *Sack*.

SEGES – Sitges, south-west of Barcelona, Spain.

SERES – Jerez de la Frontera, south-west Spain. A variant spelling for Jerez.

SETÚBAL – Area of Setubal and Palmela, southern side of the Tagus Estuary, Portugal.

SEVRE – Sèvres, western outskirts of Paris.

SEXARD – On the Danube, between Buda and Esset.

SHERRIS – Jerez de la Frontera, South-west Spain. Shakespeare's 'sherris' or 'sherris-sack'.

SHIRAZ – Shiraz, South-west Persia.

SHRUB – England. A cordial – and to some extent a variant form of *Punch*.

SICILIAN – Island of Sicily.

SILLERY – Principally from Verzenay, Champagne; from the vineyards of the Marquis de Sillery; also from Sillery itself, on the northern side of the Montagne de Reims.

SMYRNA – Smyrna (modern: Izmir), Turkey.

SOSTRATTA – Northern Italy.

STRAIS WINE – Mediterranean.

SYRACUSE – Syracuse, Sicily.

TENERIFFE – Canary Islands.

TENT – Rota, near Jerez de la Frontera, Province of Cádiz, South-west Spain; but probably also from Alicante and Malaga, Southern Spain.

TERMO – Lisbon, Portugal.

THERA – Island of Santorini (Thera), Cyclades, Southern Aegean.

TINTILLA DE ROTA – A wine from *Rota*.

TOKAY – Tokaj, North-east Hungary.

VANVES – South Paris.

VERDE – Tuscany, Northern Italy.

VERDEA – The same as *Verde*.

VERDERA – The same as *Verde*.

VERDONA – Canary Islands.

VERJUS MIELLÉ – A form of Verjuice.

VERNACCIA – Italy; including Sardinia.

VERNAGE – Italy; including Sardinia. An occasional English name for *Vernaccia*.

VIDONIA – Canary Islands.

VILACHO – A variant writing for *Vipao*.

VIN CUIT – Grape-juice boiled down.

VIN DE COIPEAU – Apparently France.

VIN DE ROSETTE – Another name for *Alicant*.

VINELLO – Italy. A 'wine' made from grape-husks and water.

VINI CRIVELLATI – Turin district; but perhaps elsewhere in Italy.

VINI SCHIAPPATI – Turin district; but perhaps elsewhere in Italy.

VIN MIELLÉ – French version of honied wine.

VINO COTTO – The same as *vin cuit*.

VINO DE PASTO – Jerez de la Frontera, South-west Spain.

VINO MIRRHATO – Italy; and perhaps other countries as well.

VINO SANTO – Island of Santorini (modern: Thera), Cyclades, Southern Aegean.

VINO TIBIDRAGO – An Italian name for a kind of Spanish Sack.

VIN ROSETIQUE – Nérac, Lot-et-Garonne, France.

VIN SANTO – Tuscany, Northern Italy.

VIPAO – Either from Villach, Carinthia, Southern Austria; or from the Vipacco area, near Gorizia, north of Trieste, the latter being the more likely.

WORMWOOD WINE – Europe.

WYNE COURSE – Island of Corsica.

APPENDIX H: MEASURES, MEDIEVAL TO MODERN

Medieval, and later, measures of capacity varied from country to country and also from district to district. To take three examples: in the late 15th century, according to Arnold's *Chronicle*, the *aum*, or 'awme', was 50 gallons at 'Dordreight' and 35 gallons at 'Andwarp'; the *butt*, or *botte* (Edler), held differing amounts in Sicily, Cyprus, and Bruges; and John Houghton, in his *Collection*, gives a curious table of varied weights and measures in England at the end of the 17th century (Houghton, *Collection*, Vol. I, No. 46 of June 1693). Efforts at standardisation were made but achieved only limited success and in Great Britain, for instance, uniformity was not reached until the early 19th century.

Unless specifically labelled as modern, all measures in this Appendix are presumed to be those of the period from which they have been cited. Fluid ounces are reckoned in modern British terms. Modern equivalent measures are given to the nearest quarter fraction.

A Select Bibliography, together with the abbreviations of Authorities used in this text, is given at the end of this Appendix.

AMBER – Generally 4 bushels or 32 gallons (Prior, Offprint, 36, 45).

ANFORA – (Amphora) In medieval Venice this held 518½ litres, or 114 modern British gallons and 136¾ modern American gallons (Edler, 29, 319).

AUM – (*Awm, ohm*) The *aum* may have held 36 gallons. Arnold, however, has the 'awme' as 50 gallons at 'Dordreight' and 35 gallons at 'Andwarp', dating late 15th century. The modern *aum* holds 30 gallons. (Gairdner, Henry VIII, 18, Pt II, No. 449, 22; TR, IV, 640; Arnold, 189-90.)

BARILE. BARILE CORNUTO – See: *Barrel.*

BARREL – The medieval *barile* of Florence held about 45½ litres, or *c* 10 modern British gallons and *c* 12 modern American gallons. The medieval *barile cornuto* of Pisa held about 68 litres, or *c* 15 modern British gallons and *c* 18 modern American gallons. Towards the end of the 15th century the English

barrel of wine held 31½ gallons. The 16th-century English barrels of wine and ale were of different sizes. (Edler, 43-4, 319; TR, IV, 205; Hall and Nicholas, 29; Prior, Offprint, 19, 45.)

BLACKJACK – See: *Bombard.*

BOMBARD – Dr Johnson's *Dictionary* has 'A barrel, or large vessel for holding liquour'. In medieval, or late medieval, times it may usually have been a leather jug or bottle, often large. It was also called a *Blackjack*. Falstaff was called 'that huge bombard of sack' (Henry IV, Pt I, Act II, Sc. 4). In *c* 1634 these vessels were described as 'Leather Jackes which are tipped with siluer' (Hall and Nicholas, 52; Heywood, *Philocothonista*).

BOTTE – See: *Butt.*

BOTTLE – Medieval bottles were made of leather or pottery, glass bottles being rare. They were used as jugs and 'decanters', and not as storage vessels. Glass bottles became common in the 17th century but they were not used for maturing wine until the 18th century.

The size of the bottle varied. 'Memorandum – To send hom wyn and ij quart botelys' wrote Thomas Howes in October or November 1454 (*Paston Letters*, I, 307). These 'botelys' may have held 26 fluid ounces. 'Item, a bottell for wine of a potell . . .' (*Paston Letters*, III, 407, Inventory). This 'bottell' may have held 52 fluid ounces, and it can probably be dated about 1474.

(See also: Thorpe, W. A., *A History of English and Irish Glass*, Bibl. Ch. VIII, I, 56-7, 127, 133, for the early Chiddingfold bottles.)

The following are measurements of bottles in the Ashmolean Museum, Oxford (Ashmolean):

1. Globe and spike bottle, green glass. No. 1896-1908. M.68.
   Dating: 1647-63.   31 fluid ounces
2. Globe and spike bottle, green glass. No. 1924-512.
   Dating: 1682.   33 fluid ounces

3. Globe and spike bottle, green glass. No. 1916–19.
   Dating: 1685. $33\frac{1}{2}$ fluid ounces
4. Small globe and spike bottle, green glass. No. 1915. 6.
   Dating: 1695–1712.   16 fluid ounces
5. Globular. No. 1913. 928.
   Dating: 1709.   33 fluid ounces
6. Globular. No. 1896–1908. M.64.
   Dating: 1715. $27\frac{1}{2}$ fluid ounces
7. Stubby cylindrical bottle, black glass. No. 1909. 953.
   Dating: 1792.   35 fluid ounces
8. Long cylindrical bottle, black glass. No. 1919. 17.
   Dating: 1817.   28 fluid ounces
   The modern British standard bottle. $26\frac{2}{3}$ fluid ounces
   There are 6 modern British bottles to the modern British gallon.

BUSHEL – In medieval England the bushel could mean 8 gallons, but it varied. It may sometimes have been equivalent to the *modius* – q.v. (Prior, Offprint, 45).

BUTT – In 1488 there was a butt of 48 Venetian gallons used for the shipment of Candy wines. In Naples, or in Sicily, the butt (*botte*) held about $454\frac{1}{2}$ litres, or *c* 100 modern British gallons and *c* 120 modern American gallons. In Cyprus it held about 491 litres, or *c* 108 modern British gallons and *c* $129\frac{1}{2}$ modern American gallons. In Bruges it held about $909\frac{1}{4}$ litres, or *c* 200 modern British gallons and 240 modern American gallons.

In 1443 a butt of Rhenish in England held 36 gallons – cf. the *aum*. In 1510 in England the butt of Malmsey wine held 100–105 gallons whereas towards the end of the 15th century it held 126 gallons by Statute.

The modern butt of sherry holds about 491 litres, or 108 modern British gallons and $129\frac{1}{2}$ modern American gallons.

(*Cal. State Papers Venetian*, I, No. 544; Edler, 319; TR, IV, 205, 640, 648.)

CESTRE – See: *Sestre*.

DOLEUM – (*Dolium*) As a general rule this meant a tun, or cask. In 15th-century England the *doleum* equalled the *tun* and held 252 gallons but before this time the capacity of the *doleum* varied considerably. See: *Tun*. (*MLWL*, TR, III, 509, 511, and *passim*; IV, 639; Prior, Offprint, 19, 46.)

FAT – In England in 1443 the *fat* may have held 36 gallons. Cf. the *aum*. The *fat* may, however, also have held more (TR, IV, 640).

GALLON – Until 1824 there were two gallon measures in England, one for wine and one for ale, that for ale being the larger.

It is likely that the medieval and Elizabethan wine gallon held 104 fluid ounces, or *c* 3 litres and *c* $\frac{3}{4}$ of a modern American gallon. (See: Prior, Offprint, 17, for the light London gallon.) The Queen Anne wine gallon, containing 231 cubic inches, would have held about $132\frac{1}{2}$ fluid ounces, or *c* $3\frac{3}{4}$ litres, and *c* 1 modern American gallon. The Oxford wine gallon of 1737 held 140 fluid ounces. The English wine, and beer, gallons were standardised in 1824 at 160 fluid ounces, which is the modern British standard measure. This modern British gallon is equal to *c* $4\frac{1}{2}$ litres and *c* $1\frac{1}{4}$ modern American gallons.

In comparison, the Oxford ale gallon of 1670 held 168 fluid ounces, or *c* $4\frac{3}{4}$ litres and *c* $1\frac{1}{4}$ (1·26) modern American gallons. But the Oxford ale gallon of 1778 held 160 fluid ounces, the present British standard measure. See: *Quart, Pint*. (*Munimenta Gildhallae Londoniensis*, Vol. II, Pt I, 383 – Liber Custumarum; *Cal. State Papers*, 1581–90, 110; Prior, Offprint, 9. For variant weights and measures, see: Hall and Nicholas, 52; Houghton, *Collection*, Vol. I, 132 sq. Oxford measures are in Ashmolean.)

HOGSHEAD – In England towards the end of the 15th century, and also later, it held 63 gallons. Modern hogsheads vary from 46 to 72 modern British gallons, or *c* 209–*c* $327\frac{1}{4}$ litres and *c* $55\frac{1}{4}$–*c* $86\frac{1}{2}$ modern American gallons. The modern hogshead of Burgundy and Claret holds 46–48 modern British gallons, or *c* 209–*c* $218\frac{1}{4}$ litres and *c* $55\frac{1}{4}$–*c* $57\frac{1}{2}$ modern American gallons (TR, IV, 205; V, 448; cf. Edler, 320 – *Pippa*; and see also: Hall and Nicholas, 21).

LAGENA – A gallon (Prior, Offprint, 47).

LITRE – There are 4·54 litres to the modern British gallon.

MODIUS – (*Mui, muid*, etc.) In 9th-century France this may have equalled a hogshead which might have held 63 gallons (see: Power, Eileen. *Medieval People*, 171–2). Later, in France and England, the *modius* may have held 16 gallons (Sheppard, p. xxvii). But Prior, Offprint, 47, has the *modius* or *muid* as being a measure of 16 small *sextarii* or 8 gallons – cf. *Bushel*.

The 'old French' *muid* was at one time 72½ gallons (Henderson, 386).

See: *Sestre*.

MUI, MUID, MUYS – See: *Modius*.

OHM – See: *Aum*.

PECE – See: *Pese*.

'PES' – 'I sen my lady a lytyll pes of Renysch wyne of the best, of x. gallons . . .' (*Paston Letters*, Lumen Haryson to Sir John Paston, *c* 1490?). But for *Pes* as a measure of length or weight, see: Prior, Offprint, 48, and *passim*.

See: *Pese*.

PESE – A common name for a drinking cup. Many variant spellings (Wright, *Vocabs*, I, 771, 22). See: *Pece*, etc., in *Paston Letters*, Inventory of Sir John Fastolf's Goods, A.D. 1459, and *passim*. Cf. '*Pes*'.

PINT – It is likely that the medieval and Elizabethan wine pint would have held 13 fluid ounces, or *c* $\frac{1}{3}$ litre. The Queen Anne wine pint would have held about 16½ fluid ounces, or *c* $\frac{1}{2}$ litre. In 1737 the Oxford wine pint held 17½ fluid ounces. The modern British pint holds 20 fluid ounces, or just over half a litre (·568 litre).

Thus the Elizabethan wine gallon would have held about 5 modern standard British pints. The Queen Anne wine gallon would have held about 6½ modern British standard pints.

In comparison, the Oxford ale pint of 1670 held 21 fluid ounces, whereas the Oxford ale pint of 1778 held 20 fluid ounces which is the modern standard British pint measure. See: *Gallon*, and cf. *Pinta*. (*Cal. State Papers*, 1581–90, 110; Hall and Nicholas, 22; Prior, Offprint, 17).

The modern American pint contains 16 fluid ounces as against 20 fluid ounces to the modern British pint.

PINTA – In Paris this measure held just over 1½ modern British pints, which is just under a litre and about $\frac{1}{4}$ modern American gallon. The old *pinte* of Paris held a little less than a litre (Edler, 319; *Dict. Acad. Française*; cf. Henderson, 386).

PIPE – In 15th-century England the pipe held 126 gallons. In the same century, however, the pipe of Spanish white wine held 100–105 gallons. The modern pipe of port holds 115 modern British gallons, or 522¾ litres and 138 modern American gallons. (TR, I, 172; IV, 205, 640; cf. Edler, 320 – *Pippa*.)

PIPPA – See: *Pipe*.

PRICHPOTTUS – 15th century. A vessel holding 4 gallons. (*MLWL*.)

POTTLE – This was a measure of ½ gallon, or a pot holding about this quantity; but the measure may sometimes have varied (*Oxford English Dictionary*; Prior, Offprint, 20, 48). Dr Johnson's *Dictionary* has: 'It is sometimes used licentiously for a tankard, or pot out of which glasses are filled.' In medieval England glasses would, of course, have been comparatively rare.

PUNCHEON – In the 15th and 16th centuries in England this held 84 gallons, the same quantity as the *tercian* (TR, IV, 205; Prior, Offprint, 49).

QUART – TR apparently has the English quart of the 13th and 14th centuries as being equal to the quart of 1866 and thus holding 40 fluid ounces. He also has its alternative measure as being probably 9 gallons. Prior gives it, in 1395, as being 8 gallons.

Considered, however, as a sub-division of the gallon, it is likely that the Elizabethan wine quart would have held 26 fluid ounces, or *c* $\frac{3}{4}$ litre. The Queen Anne wine quart would have held about 33 fluid ounces, or nearly 1 litre and $\frac{1}{4}$ of the modern American gallon. The Oxford wine quart of 1737 held 35 fluid ounces. The modern British standard quart holds 40 fluid ounces, or just over 1 litre and about $\frac{1}{3}$ of a modern American gallon.

In comparison the Oxford ale quart of 1670 held 42 fluid ounces, whereas the Oxford ale quart of 1778 held 40 fluid ounces which is the modern British standard measure. (TR, I, 172; Prior, Offprint, 19–20; Ashmolean.)

RUNDLET – (*Runlet*) A small cask of varying measure. On occasions during the last half of the 15th century the rundlet held 15 gallons, 16 gallons, and 18½ gallons, the latter by Statute. Prior gives it as 18½ gallons. In 1665, however (at Eton), it held 8 gallons and 12½ gallons. In the earlier 17th century there was a rundlet of between 6 and 7 gallons and a runlet of 11 gallons. (TR, IV, 205, 648; VI, 413, 416, 417, 419; Prior, Offprint, 49; *Paston Letters*, A.D. 1466, John Paston's Funeral. See also: TR, V, 447; Gairdner, Henry VIII, 19, Pt I, No. 67.)

See: *Runlet*.

RUNLET – See: *Rundlet*. But see also definition in the *Oxford English Dictionary* of smaller runlets varying from a pint to 4 gallons. (And see: Gairdner, Henry VIII, 19, Pt I, No. 67.)

SESTERCIUM – See: *Sestre*.

SESTRE – The *sestre* may have measured 1 gallon and there may have been 16 *sestres* to the *modius* – *q.v.* (Sheppard, p. xxvii). In 1241 in English the *Sestercium* of wine held a gallon (*Cal. Pat. Rolls*, 25, Henry III, mem. 8). But for smaller *sextarii*, see: Prior, Offprint, 47; also: *Setier* and *Sextary*, below.

Cestre may have meant 4 gallons (Prior, Offprint, 34).

SETIER – (*Sestre* – Godefroy) A measure holding 8 *pintes* in France: probably about 12 modern British pints or just over 6¾ litres and just over 1¾ modern American gallons (*Dict. Acad. Française*). Cf. *Pinta*.

SEXTARY – In England the sextary varied from 2 to 6 gallons. On average it probably meant about 5 gallons, though the sextary of sweet wine meant, at least on occasion, 2 gallons. But the sextary could mean an allowance served to a mess at a meal when it signified about 5 gallons. The ale sextary often measured a larger quantity. (TR, I, 172, 619; IV, 639,

650; Simon, André L., *The History of the Wine Trade in England*, I, 352; Hall and Nicholas, 15; Prior, Offprint, 31 sq.)

STOUP – When used in the 13th century for honey it measured 3½–5 gallons (Prior, Offprint, 35, 49).

TERCIAN – See: *Puncheon*.

TIERCE – In England in the 15th century the tierce, by Statute, held 41 gallons, a measure which continued into Tudor times (TR, IV, 205; Prior, Offprint, 49). But it could also be, and later was, 42 gallons (TR, V, 449; *Oxford English Dictionary*).

In France the *tiercel* and the *tierçuel* were measures of wine (Godefroy).

TONEGALLA, TON MASCULL, TONNEL, ETC. – See: *Tun*.

TONNEAU – See: *Tun*.

TUN – In 15th-century England the tun held 252 gallons, and it would seem that the *ton mascull* held the same amount. The *tun*, or *tonegalla*, or *tonnel* – many variant spellings – could also mean just a large cask. (TR, I, 172; IV, 205; *Oxford English Dictionary*; *MLWL*; Prior, Offprint, 50.)

See: the Parisian tun, etc., under *tonello* in Edler, 301, 320; and see: *Doleum*, above.

The modern tun holds 252 gallons, or *c* 1145½ litres and *c* 302½ modern American gallons. The modern French *tonneau* holds 190 gallons or 863¼ litres and 228 modern American gallons. In modern Portugal *tonel* is often used to mean a storage cask, the capacity of which can be very large indeed.

BIBLIOGRAPHICAL ABBREVIATIONS

(Key to the Abbreviations used in Footnotes, Lists, etc.)

Acc. Obed. Abingdon – *Accounts of the Obedientiars of Abingdon Abbey*, ed. Kirk, R. E. G., Camden Society, 1892.

Adamič – Adamič, France, Ministry of Agriculture, Ljubljana, and Ljubljana University. Lecture on Yugoslav wines arranged by Messrs Richard and William Teltscher Ltd, London, Feb. 1959.

AJA – *American Journal of Archaeology*.

ALS, *HWE* – Simon, André L., *History of the Wine Trade in England*, 3 vols, London, 1906–9.

Ames, *Bacchanalian Sessions* – Ames, Richard, *The Bacchanalian Sessions . . . with A Farewell to Wine*, London, 1693.

Ames, *FSC* – Ames, Richard, *A Farther Search after Claret . . .*, etc., London, 1691.

Ames, *SAC* – Ames, Richard, *The Search after Claret . . .*, etc., London, 1691.

Amherst – Amherst, Hon. Alicia, *A History of Gardening in England*, 3rd edn, London, 1910.

Amherst Tablets – Pinches, T. G., *The Amherst Tablets*, Pt I, London, 1908.

Amphitryons – Reynière, Grimod de la, *Manuel des Amphitryons*, Paris, 1808.

Anat. Studs. – *Anatolian Studies*, Journal of the British Institute of Archaeology at Ankara.

Ancient Charters – *Ancient Charters, Royal and Private, prior to A.D. 1200*, Pt I, ed. Round, J. H., Rolls Series, London, 1888.

Andrieu – Andrieu, P., *Fine Bouche*, London, 1956.

Antiq. Cul. – Warner, Richard, *Antiquitates Culinariae* (containing The Forme of Cury), London, 1791.

Apicius – Flower, Barbara, and Rosenbaum, Elizabeth, *The Roman Cookery Book*, London, 1958.

Apicius Redivivus – Anon., *Apicius Redivivus; or The Cook's Oracle*, London, 1817.

Arnold – *Arnold's Chronicle or The Customs of London*, London, 1811.

Arnoux – Arnoux, *Dissertation sur la Situation de Bourgogne, sur les vins quelle produit . . .*, London, 1728.

Ashburnham MSS. – Ashburnham MSS. (Cellar Books, etc.), East Sussex Record Office, Lewes.

Assyrian Domesday – Johns, C. H. W., *An Assyrian Domesday Book*, Assyriologische Bibliothek, Leipzig, 1901.

Ath-E – Athenaeus, *Deipnosophists*, trs. Gulick, Prof. C. B., Loeb Classical Library, 7 vols.

Ath, F. – Athénée de Naucratis, *Les Deipnosophistes*, Vol. I, Bks I and II, ed. and trs. Desrousseaux, A. M., and Astruc, C., Soc. d'Édition, 'Les Belles Lettres', Paris, 1956.

Auson. – Ausonius, *Mosella: Epigrams: Epist.*, trs. White, H. G. Evelyn, Loeb Classical Library, 2 vols, 1919, 1949.

Bacci – Bacci, Andrea, *De naturali vinorum historia . . .*, etc., Rome, 1596.

Barbazan et Méon – Barbazan et Méon, *Fabliaux et Contes des Poètes François des XI, XII, XIII, XIV et XVᵉ Siècles*, 4 vols, Paris, 1808.

Barry, *Observations* – Barry, Sir Edward, *Observations . . . on the Wines of the Ancients . . .*, etc., London, 1775.

BCH – *Bulletin de Correspondance Hellénique*, Athens, Paris. (Name of contributors given thus: BCH,   .)

BdV – *La Bataille des Vins*, d'Andeli, Henri, *Fabliaux et Contes des Poètes François des XI, XII, XIII, XIV et XVᵉ Siècles*, Barbazan et Méon, Vol. I, Paris, 1808.

Beauvilliers – Beauvilliers, A., *L'Art du Cuisinier*, 2 vols, Paris, 1814.

Bedford Cellar – Cellar of the Earl of Bedford, *Life in a Noble Household, 1641–1700*, Gladys Scott Thomson, London, 1937.

Bêt Khallâf – Garstang, J. (and Sethe, K., on the inscriptions), *Mahâsna and Bêt Khallâf*, Egyptian Research Account, London, 1903.

Blacke Dogg – Hutton, Luke ('L. H.'), *The Discovery of a London Monster, called, The Blacke Dogg of New-gate*, London, 1638.

Blowbol. – *Colyn Blowbols Testament*, printed in Vol. I of *Remains of the Early Popular Poetry of England*, ed., etc. Hazlitt, W. Carew, 4 vols, London, 1864–6.

Boorde, *Introduction* – Boorde, Andrew, *Introduction of Knowledge*.

Boorde, *Dyetary* – *Dyetary of Helth*, ed. Furnivall, F. J., Early English Text Society, London, 1870.

Boswell – Boswell, James, see Bibliography to Ch. 8.

Breasted, *ARE* – Breasted, J. H., *Ancient Records of Egypt*, 5 vols, Chicago, 1906–7.

Brewer, *Henry VIII* – Brewer, J. S., *Letters and Papers, Foreign and Domestic of the Reign of Henry VIII*, Rolls

Series, London. Vol. I, 2nd edn revised, Brodie, R. H., 1920, etc.; Vol. II, etc., 1st edn, 1864, etc.

Brillat-Savarin – Brillat-Savarin, A., *Physiologie du Goût*, Belley, 1948.

BSA – Annual of the British School at Athens, London.

CAH – Cambridge Ancient History, 2nd edn, Cambridge, 1924, etc.

Cal. Docs. Fr. – Calendar of Documents preserved in France, Vol. I, A.D. 918–1206, H.M.S.O., London, 1899.

Cal. Inquisitions – Calendar of Inquisitions Post Mortem, etc., P.R.O., London.

Cal. Let. Bks Lon. – Calendar of Letter-Books preserved among the Archives of the Corporation of the City of London, Letter-Books A-K, 1275–1422, ed. Sharpe, R. R., London, 1899, etc.

Cal. Pat. Rolls – Calendar of the Patent Rolls, H.M.S.O., London, 1901, etc.

Cal. Select Pleas Lon. – Calendar of Select Pleas and Memoranda of the City of London, ed. Thomas, A. H., 1932.

Cal. State Papers Dom. – Calendar of State Papers, Domestic Series, Rolls Series, London.

Cal. State Papers Venetian – Calendar of State Papers, Venetian, etc., Rolls Series, London, 1864, etc.

Camden Misc. XV – Camden Miscellany, Select Tracts and Table Books relating to English weights and measures . . ., Hall and Nicholas.

Cart. Mon. Ram. – Cartularium Monasterii de Rameseia, 3 vols, Rolls Series, London.

Cart. Sax. – Cartularium Saxonicum, Walter Birch, London, 1885, etc.

Cato – Cato, *De Agri Cultura* in Cato and Varro, trs. Hooper, W. D., and Ash, H. B., Loeb Classical Library, 1934.

Cellini – Cellini, Benvenuto, *Memoirs*, Everyman edn, London.

Charleton, *Mysterie* – Charleton, W., *The Mysterie of Vintners* (published London, 1669).

Christ Church Acs. – Christ Church Common Room Accounts, MS. C.R.2, Christ Church, Oxford.

Chron. Abb. Ram. – Chronicon Abbatiae Rameseiensis, Rolls Series.

Chron. Mon. Abingdon – Chronicon Monasterii de Abingdon, ed. Stevenson, J., 2 vols, Rolls Series, London, 1858.

CIL – Corpus Inscriptionum Latinarum.

Close Rolls – Close Rolls preserved in the Public Record Office, H.M.S.O., London, 1902, etc.

CMH – Cambridge Medieval History.

Coins, Brit. Mus. – Coins, British Museum, *A Guide to the Principal Coins of the Greeks from circ. 700 B.C. to A.D. 270*, London, 1932.

Coleman-Norton – Coleman-Norton, P. R. (ed.), *Studies in Roman Economic and Social History in honor of Allan Chester Johnson*, Princeton, 1951. The authorship of individual chapters is indicated thus: Coleman-Norton, West, etc.

Colum. – Columella, *De Re Rustica*, trs. Ash, H. B., 3 vols, Loeb Classical Library, 1948.

Connoisseur – The Connoisseur, National Magazine Co., London.

Contenau – Contenau, G., *Everyday Life in Babylon and Assyria*, trs. Maxwell-Hyslop, K. R., and A. R., London, 1954.

Corominas – Corominas, J., *Diccionario Critico Etimológico de la Lengua Castellana*, 4 vols, Madrid, 1954.

Cotgrave – Cotgrave, Randle, *A French-English Dictionary*, London, 1650 (and 1611).

Croce – Croce, G. B., *Della eccellenza e diversità de i vini, che nella Montagna di Torino si fanno . . .*, etc., Turin, 1614.

Cunn., *GEI* – Cunningham, W., *Growth of English Industry and Commerce . . .*, etc., Cambridge, 1882.

Curia Regis Rolls – Curia Regis Rolls, Public Record Office, H.M.S.O., London, 1922, etc.

Davies, *Butler – The Butler*, by an Experienced Servant. (*The Wine Department*, by J. B. Davies), London, 1855.

Deinhard – Messrs Deinhard and Co. (Coblenz and London), *Yesterday and Today*, London, 1958–9.

Dekker – Dekker, Thomas, *Dramatic Works*, ed. Shepherd, R. H., 4 vols, London, 1873.

de Secondat – de Secondat, *Mémoires sur l'histoire naturelle . . .*, including his *Mémoire sur la culture des vignes de la Guienne et sur les vins de cette Province*, Paris, 1785.

Dill, *RSG – Roman Society in Gaul in the Merovingian Age*, London, 1926.

Dion, *Rev. Hist.* – Dion, Prof. R., 'Le Commerce des Vins de Beaune au Moyen Age', *Revue Historique*, Vol. CCXIV, Oct.-Dec. 1955.

Dioscorides, *Herbal – The Greek Herbal of Dioscorides*, ed. Gunther, R. T., Oxford, 1934.

DS – Daremberg-Saglio, *Dictionnaire des Antiquités Grècques et Romaines*, Paris, 1877.

Dubberstein – Dubberstein, Waldo H., 'Comparative Prices in Later Babylonia (625–400 B.C.)', *The American Journal of Semitic Languages and Literatures*, LVI, 1939.

Dunbabin – Dunbabin, T. J., *The Western Greeks*, Oxford, 1948.

DWM – Loeschcke, Dr S., *Denkmaeler v. Weinbau a.d. Zeit d. Roemerherrschaft an Mosel, Saar u. Ruwer*, Weinmuseum, Trier, 1933.

Edict. Dioc. – Frank, Tenney (ed.), *An Economic Survey of Ancient Rome*, Vol. v, Appendix, *The Edict of Diocletian on Maximum Prices* by Elsa Rose Graser, John Hopkins Press, Baltimore, 1940.

Edrîsî – Edrîsî, *Description de l'Afrique et de l'Espagne par Edrîsî*, ed. and trs. Dozy, R., and de Goeje, M. J., Leyden, 1866.

Erman – Erman, A., *Life in Ancient Egypt*, trs. Tirard, H. M., London, 1894.

Evelyn, *Diary* – Evelyn, John, *Diary*, ed. Beer, E. S. de, 6 vols, Oxford, 1955.

FAC – *Attic Comedy, The Fragments of*, ed., trs., etc. Edmonds, J. M., 2 vols, Leiden, 1957, 1959.

Florio – Florio, John, *Queen Anna's New World of Words, or Dictionarie of the Italian and English tongues . . .*, London, 1611.

Forbes, *SHD* – Forbes, R. J., *Short History of the Art of Distillation*, Leiden, 1948.

Ford, *GS* – Ford, Richard, *Gatherings from Spain*, London, 1846.

Forme of Cury – Warner, Richard, *Antiquitates Culinariae* (containing *The Forme of Cury*), London, 1791.

Forrester, *Observations on . . . Attempts . . . to reform . . . abuses* – Forrester, J. J., *Observations on the Attempts lately made to reform the abuses practised in Portugal, in the making and treatment of Port Wine*, 1st Part, Edinburgh, 1845.

Frank – Frank, Tenney, and others, *An Economic Survey of Ancient Rome*, 5 vols, Baltimore, 1933–40. The authorship of individual chapters is indicated thus: Frank, Collingwood, etc.

Franklin, *Vie privée* – Franklin, Alfred, *La vie privée d'autrefois*, 27 vols, Paris, 1887–1902.

Frith – Frith, W. P., *Memoirs*, edited by Nevile Wallis as *A Victorian Canvas*, London, 1957.

Froissart – Froissart, Messire Jehan, *Histoire et Chronique de*, 4 vols, 1574.

Fussell – Fussell, G. E., *The English Rural Labourer . . . Tudor to Victorian times*, London, 1949.

Gage Cellar – *Account Book of the 3rd Viscount Gage*, Sussex Archaeological Society, Lewes (Accession No. 741).

Gairdner, *Henry VIII* – Gairdner, James, *Letters and Papers, Foreign and Domestic of the reign of Henry VIII*, Rolls Series, London.

Galen – *Oeuvres Anatomiques, Physiologiques et Médicales de Galien*, trs. Daremberg, C., 2 vols, Paris, 1854, 1856.

Genouillac, *TSA* – Genouillac, H. de, *Tablettes Sumériennes Archaiques*, Paris, 1909.

Ges. Abb. Mon. S. Alb. – *Gesta Abbatum Monasterii Sancti Albani Walsingham*, ed. Riley, 3 vols, Rolls Series, London.

Gest. Pont. Ang. – William of Malmesbury, *De Gestis Pontificum Anglorum*, ed. Hamilton, N. E. S. A., Rolls Series, London, 1870.

Giraldi Cambrensis Op. – *Giraldi Cambrensis Opera*, ed. Brewer, J. S., Dimock, J. F., and Warner, G. F., 8 vols, Rolls Series, London, 1861–91.

Glossographia – Blount, T. B., *Glossographia: or a Dictionary . . .*, etc., 3rd edn, London, 1670.

Glotz, *AGW* – Glotz, G., *Ancient Greece at Work*, London, 1926.

Godefroy – Godefroy, F., *Dictionnaire de l'ancienne langue française et de tous ses di'ctes du IXe au XVe siècle*, Paris, 1881–1902.

González Gordon – Manuel Ma. González Gordon, *Jerez-Xeres-Scheris: Noticias sobre el Origen de esta ciudad, su historia y su vino*, Jerez de la Frontera, 1948.

Goodwood Cellar – *Goodwood Cellar Books* (*Duke of Richmond and Gordon*), West Sussex County Archives, Chichester, Sussex.

Gras, MS. – Gras, Pierre, *La vie rurale en Chalonnais aux XIVe et XVe siècles*, MS. thesis of the École des Chartes.

Gronow – Gronow, R. H., *Reminiscences and Recollections*, 2 vols, London, 1892.

Gunton, *Peterburgh* – Gunton, Symon, *History of the Church of Peterburgh*, London, 1686.

Hall, Darrell – Hall, H., *Society in the Elizabethan Age* (Appendix II – The Darrell Papers), London, 1887.

Harrison – Harrison, W., *Harrison's Description of England in Shakspere's Youth*, ed. Furnivall, F. J., 2 vols, New Shakspere Society, London, 1877–8. (Unless otherwise specified, the volume referred to is Part I.)

Harrison, *Prolegomena* – Harrison, Jane, *Prolegomena to the study of Greek Religion*, New York, 1957.

Hazor Exhib. – *Hazor in Galilee*, An Archaeological Exhibition arranged by the Anglo-Israel Exploration Society at the British Museum, 1958 (Catalogue).

Hebrew Deeds – *Hebrew Deeds of English Jews before 1290*, ed. Davis, M. D., London, 1888.

Henderson – Henderson, A., *The History of Ancient and Modern Wines*, London, 1824.

Herodotus – Herodotus, *The Histories*, trs. Selincourt, A. de, Penguin Books, London, 1954.

Hervey Cellar – Hervey, John, 1st Earl of Bristol, *The Diary of, 1688–1742*, Ernest Jackson at Wells, 1894.

Hesp. – *Hesperia*, Journal of the American School of Classical Studies at Athens.

Heywood, P. – *Philocothonista*, etc., London, 1635.

Hist. Tech. - A History of Technology, Singer, C., Holmyard, E. J., Hall, A. R., Williams, 2 vols, Oxford, 1954, 1956.

Hor., *Carm.* - Horace, *Odes*, trs. Bennett, Loeb Classical Library, 1924.

Hor., *Epist.* - Horace, *Epistles*, trs. Fairclough, Loeb Classical Library, 1926.

Hor., *Sat.* - Horace, *Satires*, trs. Fairclough, Loeb Classical Library, 1926.

Houghton, *Collection* - Houghton, John, *A Collection for the Improvement of Husbandry and Trade . . .*, etc., revised Richard Bradley, 4 vols, London, 1727-8.

Howell - Howell, James, *Familiar Letters (Epistolae Ho-Elianae)*, 8th edn, London, 1713.

Howitt, *Rural England* - Howitt, W., *The Rural Life of England*, 2 vols, London, 1838.

Huguet - Huguet, E., *Dictionnaire de la Langue Française du Seizième Siècle*, Paris, 1925, etc.

Iliad - Homer, *The Iliad*, trs. Lang, A., Leaf, W., and Myers, E., London, 1949.

ILN - Illustrated London News, London.

Iraq - Iraq, Journal of the British School of Archaeology in Iraq.

Jackson, *Bury - Jackson's Guide to Bury*, new edn, 1867.

JEA - Journal of Egyptian Archaeology, Egypt Exploration Fund, London, 1914, etc. Names of contributors are given thus: Gardiner, *JEA*.

Jeanmaire - Jeanmaire, H., *Dionysos, Histoire du Culte de Bacchus*, Paris, 1951.

Jewish Enc. - The Jewish Encyclopedia, 1906.

JNES - Journal of Near Eastern Studies, University of Chicago Press.

John of Salisbury - *The Letters of John of Salisbury*, Vol. I, 1153-61, ed. Millor, W. J., and Butler, H. E., revised, Brooke, C. N. L., London, 1955.

Juvenal - Juvenal, *Satires*, trs. Ramsay, G. G., Loeb Classical Library, 1918.

Keruynge - The Boke of Keruynge, printed in *Early English Meals and Manners*, ed. Furnivall, F. J., London, 1931.

Kleberg - Kleberg, J. V. B., *Hôtels, Restaurants et Cabarets dans l'Antiquité Romaine*, Uppsala, 1957.

Lafforgue - Lafforgue, G., *Le Vignoble Girondin*, Paris, 1947.

Lambard, *Kent* - Lambard, William, *Perambulation of Kent*, London, 1656.

Lambarde, *Dict. Ang. Top.* - Lambarde, William, *Diction-*

arium Angliae Topographicum et Historicum, London, 1730.

La Rosa, *VR* - Quinta de la Rosa, Douro, Portugal, *Vintage Records*.

LEP - Libel of English Policy, printed in Vol. II of *Political Poems and Songs*, ed. Wright, T., Rolls Series, London, 1861.

Letters . . . Henry VIII - Letters and Papers . . . of the Reign of Henry VIII . . ., Addenda, 1 vol., H.M.S.O., London.

Leyel, *HD* - Leyel, Mrs C. F., *Herbal Delights*, revised edn, London, 1947.

Liberate Rolls - Calendar of Liberate Rolls, Public Record Office, H.M.S.O., London, 1916, etc.

Locke, *Obs.* - Locke, John, *Observations upon the Growth and Culture of Vines and Olives*, Vol. x of Locke's Works, 11th edn, 10 vols, London, 1812.

Lucas - Lucas, A., *Ancient Egyptian Materials and Industries*, 3rd edn, revised, London, 1948.

Lutz, *VB* - Lutz, H. F., *Viticulture and Brewing in the Ancient Orient*, Leipzig, 1922.

LWS - Leechdoms, Wortcunning, and Starcraft of Early England, ed. Cockayne, O., 3 vols, Rolls Series, London, 1864-6.

Madox - Madox, T., *The History and Antiquities of the Exchequer of the Kings of England*, 2 vols, London, 1769.

Maison Rustique - Maison Rustique: or The Countrey Farme (revised by Gervase Markham), Stevens and Liebault, trs. Surflet, R., London, 1616. This is the edition used for the Medieval, and Renaissance to Modern, Wine Lists.

Markham - Markham, G., *The English House-Wife*, London, 1683. In the edition of 1695 entitled *A Way to get Wealth*, Markham, G., London.

Mart. - Martial, *Epigrams*, trs. Ker, W. C. A., 2 vols, Loeb Classical Library, 1947, 1950.

Mart. - *Martial's Epigrams*, trs. Francis, A. L., and Tatum, H. F., Cambridge, 1924.

Maxwell Lyte - Maxwell Lyte, Sir Henry, *A History of Dunster, and of the families of Mohun & Luttrell*, London, 1909.

McBride, *Instructions* - McBride, Duncan, *General Instructions for the Choice of Wines and Spirituous Liquors*, London, 1793.

Meir - Blackman, A. M., *Rock Tombs of Meir*, Archaeological Survey of Egypt, 6 vols, Vol. III (Memoir 24); Vol. v (Memoir 28), London, 1914-53.

Ménagier - Ménagier de Paris, Le, trs. Eileen Power, London, 1928.

Merret - Merret, Dr Christopher, *Some Observations con-*

cerning the ordering of Wines (published in London, 1669, with W. Charleton's *Mysterie of Vintners*).

Milner – Milner, John, *History and Survey of the Antiquities of Winchester*, 2nd edn, 2 vols, 1809.

Mirmeki – Michalowski, K., and others, *Mirmeki*, Wykopaliska Odcinka Polskiego, WR, 1956 (with resumé in French), Warsaw, 1958.

Mishnah – *The Mishnah*, trs. etc. Danby, H., Oxford, 1933.

MLWL – *Medieval Latin Word List*, Baxter, J. H., Johnson, C., and Abrahams, P., Oxford, 1934.

Monasticon – *Monasticon Anglicanum*, Sir William Dugdale, ed. Caley, Ellis, and Bandinel, 6 vols, London, 1817-30.

Morwyng – Morwyng, Peter, *Treasure of Evonymus . . . A new booke of destillatyon of waters . . .*, London, 1565.

Moryson, *Itinerary* – Moryson, Fynes, *An Itinerary*, 4 vols, Glasgow, 1907-8.

Mun. Gild. Lon. – *Munimenta Gildhallae Londoniensis*, Liber Albus, etc., Rolls Series, London, 1859, etc.

Murashû – *Murashû Sons of Nippur, Business Documents of*, Babylonian Expedition of the University of Pennsylvania, Series A, Cuneiform Texts, Hilprecht, H. V., and Clay, A. T., Vols IX, X, Philadelphia, 1898, 1904.

Mycen. Docs. – Ventris, M., and Chadwick, J., *Documents in Mycenaean Greek*, Cambridge, 1956.

Nares, *Glossary* – Nares, Robert, *A Glossary; or Collection of Words . . . etc. . . . in the Works of English Authors, particularly Shakespeare and his Contemporaries* (first pub. 1822), New Edn, ed., etc. Halliwell, J. O., and Wright, Thomas, London, 1888.

Neilson – Neilson, N., *Economic Conditions on the Manors of Ramsey Abbey*, Philadelphia, 1899.

Newman Turner, *Corresp.* – Correspondence with Mr F. Newman Turner of the Society of Herbalists, London.

Nurture, Boke of – John Russell's *Boke of Nurture*, printed in *Early English Meals and Manners*, ed. Furnivall, F. J., Early English Text Society, London, 1931.

OCD – *Oxford Classical Dictionary*, 1949.

Odyssey – Homer, *The Odyssey*, trs. Butcher, S. H., and Lang, A., London, 1935.

OED – *Oxford English Dictionary*, Oxford, 1933.

Olivier – Olivier, G. A., *Voyage dans l'Empire Othoman, l'Egypte et la Perse*, 3 vols, Paris, 1801-7.

OPV – *O Portugal Vinicola*, Cincinnato da Costa, B. C., Lisbon, 1900.

Origo, *Corresp.* – Correspondence of the author with the Marchesa Iris Origo.

Origo, *Datini* – Origo, Iris, *The Merchant of Prato* (Francesco di Marco Datini), London, 1957.

Ovid, *Met.* – Ovid, *Metamorphoses*, trs. Miller, F. J., 2 vols, Loeb Classical Library, London, 1956, 1958.

Panégyr. Lat. – *Panégyriques Latins*, ed., trs. Edouard Galletier, Vol. II, 1952, 3 vols, Paris.

Pasteur – Pasteur, L., *Études sur le vin*, Paris, 1866.

Paston Letters – *The Paston Letters*, ed. James Gairdner, 3 vols, London, 1895.

Pastry-Cook's Vade-Mecum – *The Pastry-Cook's Vade-Mecum*, London, 1705.

Pell Records – *Issues of the Exchequer: Henry III-Henry VI*, ed. Devon, F., London, 1837.

Penzer, *BWL* – Penzer, N. M., *The Book of the Wine-Label*, London, 1947.

Periplus – *The Periplus of the Erythraean Sea*, trs. Schoff, W. H., New York, London, 1912.

Petrus de Crescentiis – *Le Liure des Prouffitz champestres et ruraulx* (Liber ruralium commodorum), Paris, 1529.

Pinchbeck Register – *The Pinchbeck Register relating to the Abbey of Bury St Edmunds*, etc., ed. Lord Francis Hervey, 2 vols, Brighton, 1925.

Pipe Roll – *Pipe Roll*, 31, Henry I, *Magnum Rotulum Scaccarii vel Magnum Rotulum Pipae*, ed. Hunter, J., Commissioners of the Public Records, London, 1833.

Pipe Roll – *Pipe Roll, Great Roll of the Pipe, et sqq.*

Platter – Platter, Thomas, *Travels in England: 1599*, trs. and ed. Clare Williams, London, 1937.

Plin. – Pliny (the Elder), *Natural History*, trs. Rackham, H., 10 vols, Loeb Classical Library, 1938.

Polyb. – Polybius, *Histories*, trs. Paton, W. R., 6 vols, Loeb Classical Library, 1927.

PWK – Pauly-Wissowa-Kroll, *Real-Encyclopaedie d. klassischen Altertumswissenschaft*, 1893, etc.

Pyramid Texts – Mercer, S. A. B., *The Pyramid Texts*, 4 vols, London, 1952.

Quibell, *Ramesseum* – Quibell, J. E., *The Ramesseum*, Egyptian Research Account, 1896, London, 1898.

Ras Shamra – *Ras Shamra, Mission de*, directed by C. F-A. Schaeffer, Haut-Commissariat de la République Française en Syrie et au Liban, Service des Antiquités, Bibl. Archéologique et Historique, Paris (various vols and authors).

Redding – Redding, Cyrus, *A History and Description of Modern Wines*, London, 1876.

Reg. Prior. Wigorn. – *Registrum . . . Prioratus Beatae Mariae Wigorniensis*, ed. Hale, W. H., Camden Society, London, 1865.

Ricart, *Kal.* – Ricart, Robert, *The Maire of Bristowe is*

Kalendar (*Ricart's Kalendar*), ed. Lucy Toulmin Smith, Camden Society, London, 1872.

Ritson – Ritson, J. (ed.), *Ancient Engleish Metrical Romancees*, 3 vols, London, 1802.

Rodier – Rodier, C., *Le Vin de Bourgogne*, 3rd edn, Louis Damidot, Dijon, 1943.

Roll . . . Swinfield – *Roll of the Household Expenses of Richard de Swinfield, Bishop of Hereford: 1289 and 1290*, ed. Webb, J., 2 vols, Camden Society, London, 1854.

Ros., *SEHH* – Rostovtzeff, M., *The Social and Economic History of the Hellenistic World*, 3 vols, Oxford, 1941.

Ros., *SEHR* – Rostovtzeff, M., *The Social and Economic History of the Roman Empire*, Oxford, 1926.

Rot. Sel. Angl. (*Placita*) – *Rotuli Selecti ad Res Anglicas et Hibernicas . . .*, etc., Public Records, London, 1834.

Saintsbury, *Cellar Book* – Saintsbury, George, *Notes on a Cellar-Book*, London, 1953.

Salin – Salin, E., *La Civilisation Mérovingienne*, Paris, 1949.

Salmon, *EP* – Salmon, William, *The Compleat English Physician: or, The Druggist's Shop Opened*, London, 1963.

Sigerist, *Arnaldus* – Sigerist, H. E., trs. and ed. *The Earliest Printed Book on Wine* (Arnaldus de Villa Nova), New York, 1943.

Sidonius – Sidonius, Gaius Sollius Apollinaris, *Poems and Letters*, trs. Anderson, W. B., 2 vols, Loeb Classical Library, 1936.

Sino-Iranica – Laufer, B., 'The Grape Vine', *Sino-Iranica*, Vol. xv, No. 3, 220 *et sqq.* (Publication 201; Anthropological Series), Field Museum of Natural History, Chicago, 1919.

Somner – Somner, W., *The Antiquities of Canterbury*, London, 1640.

Speechly – Speechly, William, *A Treatise on the Culture of the Vine*, 2nd edn, London, 1805.

Stow, *Annales* – Stow, John, *Annales, or a Generall Chronicle of England*, London, 1631.

Strab. – Strabo, *Geography*, trs. Jones, H. L., 8 vols, Loeb Classical Library, 1917.

Stratmann – Stratmann, F. H., *A Middle-English Dictionary*, Oxford, 1891.

Suet. – Suetonius, *The Twelve Caesars*, trs. Graves, Robert, Penguin Classics, London, 1957.

Syll. Foed. – *Syllabus of Rhymer's Foedera*, Rolls Series, London, 1869.

Talmud-B. – *The Babylonian Talmud*, ed. Epstein, I., 35 vols, London, 1935-52 (references are page references).

Talmud-J. – *Le Talmud de Jérusalem*, trs. Schwab, M., 11 vols, Paris, 1871-89 (references are page references).

Tanzer – Tanzer, Helen H., *The Common People of Pompeii*, The Johns Hopkins University Studies in Archaeology, No. 29, Baltimore, 1939.

Tell El-Amarna – *Tell El-Amarna, The City of Akhenaten*, Pts I-III, Frankfort, Peet, Pendlebury, Woolley, and others, Egypt Exploration Society, London, 1923, etc.

Theophr., O. – Theophrastus, *Concerning Odours*, in Enquiry into Plants, trs. Hort, Sir A. F., 2 vols. Loeb Classical Library, 1916.

Theophr., P. – Theophrastus, *Enquiry into Plants*, trs. Hort, Sir A. H., 2 vols, Loeb Classical Library, 1916.

Thompson, *Botany* – Thompson, R. C., *A Dictionary of Assyrian Botany*, London, 1949.

Tommaseo, Bellini – Tommaseo, N., and Bellini, B., *Dizionario della Lingua Italiana*, Turin, 1929.

TR – Thorold Rogers, J. E., *A History of Agriculture and Prices in England*, 7 vols, Oxford, 1866-1902.

TR, *SC* – Rogers, J. E. Thorold, *Six Centuries of Work and Wages*, London, 1903.

Turner – Turner, W., *A new Boke of the natures and properties of all wines that are commonly used here in England*, London, 1568.

Varenne – Varenne, François-Pierre de la, *Le Cuisinier François*, 2nd edn, Paris, 1652.

Varro – Varro, *Rerum Rusticarum* in Cato and Varro, trs. Hooper, W. D., and Ash, H. B., Loeb Classical Library, 1934.

VCH – The Victoria History of the Counties of England, ed. Doubleday, H. A., Page, W., Salzman, L. F., etc., London, 1900-35; Oxford, 1935.

Venner, *Via recta* – Venner, T., *Via recta ad Vitam Longam . . .*, 2nd edn, London, 1622.

Vickery – Vickery, K. F., 'Food in Early Greece', *Illinois Studies in the Social Sciences*, xx, No. 3, University of Illinois, 1936.

Virey, *Rekhmara* – Virey, P., *Le Tombeau de Rekhmara, Mémoires . . . de la Mission Archéologique Française au Caire*, Vol. 5, Pt 1, Paris, 1889.

Virgil – Virgil, *Georgics*, trs. Lewis, C. Day, London, 1940.

Vispré – Vispré, F. X., *A Dissertation on the Growth of Wine in England . . .*, Bath, 1786.

Vizetelly, *FAP* – Vizetelly, H., *Facts about Port and Madeira . . .*, etc., London, 1880.

V.V., *A.* – Viala, P., and Vermorel, V., *Ampélographie*, 7 vols, Paris, 1901-10.

Waddell, *WS* – Helen Waddell, *The Wandering Scholars*, Penguin Books, London, 1954.

Walpole Cellar – Ch. vi, by J. H. Plumb, of *Studies in Social*

History: A Tribute to G. M. Trevelyan, ed. Plumb, J. H., London, 1955.

Ward, *London-Spy* – Ward, Ned, *The London-Spy*, introduction Ralph Straus, London, 1924.

Warner Allen, *GWP* – Allen, H. Warner, *Good Wine from Portugal*, London, 1957.

Woodforde – Woodforde, Rev. James, *The Diary of a Country Parson, 1758-1803*, ed. Beresford, J., 5 vols, Oxford, 1924, etc.

Wood-Legh – Wood-Legh, K. L., *A Small Household of the XVth Century* (The Account Book of Munden's Chantry, Bridport), Manchester University Press, 1956.

Wright, *Vocabs.* – Wright, Thomas, *Anglo-Saxon and Old English Vocabularies*, ed. Wuelcker, R. P., 2nd edn, 2 vols, London, 1884.

Xen., *An.* – Xenophon, *Anabasis*, trs. Loeb Classical Library.

Xen., *Oec.* – Xenophon, *Oeconomicus*.

Xen., *Symp.* – Xenophon, *Symposium*, trs. Loeb Classical Library.

Young, *Travels in France* – Young, Arthur, *Travels during The Years 1787, 1788, and 1789 . . . in France*, 2 vols, Bury St Edmunds and London, 1792, 1794; Vol. II is the second edition of 1794.

INDEX

añadas, 295-6
anadendras, 155
anadendrites, 155, 467
Anatolia, 68, 81, 102, 121, 267
Anau, 29
Anaxandrides, 98
Ancona, 158-9n., 169, 467
Andalusia, 154, 164, 218, 234, 267, 289, 294, 300, 330 (see also Baetica)
Andegavie, 267, 474
'Andjet, 78n., 461
angelica water, 387
Angostura, 444
Angoulême, 265
Angoumois, 326
Anjou, 250, 263, 267, 277, 312, 474
Annadea, 481
Anna Perenna, 215-16
anomalin, 78, 274n., 461
Anthesteria, 31, 108, 124-6
Antinous, 95
Antioche, 279n., 474
Antiphanes, 146
Antyllan, 78n., 201-2n., 461
Apameian, 150n., 452
apéritif, 98, 204, 401, 444
Aphrodite, 76-7
Apian vine, 158, 174-5n., 467
Apicius, 193-7
Apollo, 105, 123, 143
Apollodorus, 148
Appii Forum, 167
Apulia, 157, 166, 277
Apy, Tomb of, 51
aqua ardens, 323
aqua juniperi, 325
Aqua Mirabilis, 388
aqua vitae, 323, 324, 326, 331, 332
aquavit, 325
Aquileia, 158-9
Arabs, 324
Aragon, 265-6
Arammu, 68
Aranabanim, 78n., 461
Aranjuez, 300
arbustum vineyard, 176-8
Arcadia, 88, 104
Archestratus, 135, 149
Archilochus, 107, 121, 126

Archpoet, 261
Ardea, 156n., 173, 467
arenas, 293
Arganil, 234
Argentueil (Paris), 265, 310, 462, 481
Argolis, 98
Argostola, 481
Aria, 65, 461
Ariadne, 87, 121, 125, 126
Arician, 155-6n., 467
Arinto, 481
Aristophanes, 97, 99, 104, 106, 107-8, 112, 125, 127
Aristotle, 127
Ariusian, 137-8n., 467
Arkansas, 453
Armagnac, 264
Armenia, 32, 65
Arnaldus de Villa Nova, 331
Arne, 98, 464
Aroma, 147-8n., 464
aromatic wine, see under wine
Arpad, 456
Arrack, 341, 342, 481
Arras, 252-3
arrope, 294
Arsinoitic, 78n., 461
Artenis, 88, 119
Artemis Brauronia, 116
Arvad, 47, 461
áš-an, 59, 461
Asallu, see Izallu
Ascra, 104
Ashburnham Cellar Book, 404-5, 412, 431
Ashmolean Museum, 355
Asia Minor, 79-80, 104, 151, 202
    vineyards, 162, 175-6
    viticulture, 32
    wines, 76, 98, 130, 137, 146-8, 202
Assyria, 55, 58, 61
Astor House, Wine List of, 412, 417
Atalanta, 77
Aten, Wine of the House of, 45, 46, 50, 51
Athenaeus, 108, 113, 130, 149
Athene, 100, 119
Athens, 88, 104, 106, 107, 114-15, 116, 137-8, 146

Attica, 92, 94, 104, 106, 113
    festivals, 124-6
    vineyards, 104, 128
    viticulture, 104
    wines, 92, 115, 125, 130
auberges, 371
Aubryan, see Haut-Brion
Auçuerre, 265, 474 (see also Auxerre)
Augustan England, 359-78 (see also under Georgian)
Augustus, 154, 158, 200 216
Aunis, 265
Ausonius of Bordeaux, 162-3, 195-6, 227-30, 231
Aussai, 474
Austen, Jane, 336-7, 388, 399
Australia, 428, 446
Auvergne, 231
Auvilé, see Hautvillers
Auvillers, 347 (see also Hautvillers)
Auxerre, 265, 406, 474
Auxey, 233
Avenay, 346
Avenet, see Avenay
Avignon, 367
Avize, 343
Ay, King, 36
Ay, wine of, 346, 348
Azag-Ban, 55
Azeitão, 362-3
Azores, 299

Baber, John, 338
Babylon, 66
Babylonia, see Mesopotamia
Bacchanalia, 216
Bacchus, 118, 121, 216 (see also Diony-sos)
Bacchylides, 143, 144
Bacci, Andrea, 330
Backrag, 481
Bacon, Roger, 244
Bactria, 65, 461
Baeterrensan, 162, 208, 455
Baetica, 159-60n., 202, 455
Bagendon, 271
Bahriyeh, 46, 461
Baiae, 181, 195, 215
Bairrada wines, 382, 469
Balearic Islands, 160, 202, 455

Baliarican, *see* Balearic Islands

Balisca vine, 160n., 455
  wine, 467

Baltimore, 456

Balzac vine, 327

Baragnon, Bernard, 253

barbarians, 229-32, 244

Barbier, Auguste, 436

Bari, 157, 467

barrel, *see* cask

barro vineyards, 293

Barry, Sir Edward, 369-70, 381

Barsac, 388, 418, 420

Bartholomew, Frank, 458

Basilic vine, *see* Balisca

Bastard, 285-6, 289, 298, 311, 462, 481

Bastardo grape, 286

Bataille des Vins, 263, 264-5

Bath, 394, 407

Bazas, 227

Bearsley shipping house, *see* Yeatman

Beaulieu, 456, 458

Beaujolais, 259

Beane, 231, 233, 259, 265, 369, 406, 481
  Côte de, 251, 368, 369, 370
  Musée du Vin, 186, 211

Beauvilliers, A., 405-6

Bede, 238

Bedford, Earl of, 299, 301-2, 329, 347-8, 352

Bedfordshire, 240

'bee-vine', *see* Apian

beefsteak-houses, 372

beer, 29-30, 33, 51, 55-6, 59, 163, 236, 263, 284, 309, 341, 395, 398, 399, 416, 450-1, 457-8
  barley, 33, 55-6, 84
  ginger, 399
  spruce, 399

Beerenauslese technique, 365, 385

Beeton, Mrs, 412, 435, 442, 443-4, 446

Beirut, 67, 75, 461

Bêl, 120

Belchamp Walter, 239

Belgium, 210, 242, 368, 371

Bell Raini claret, 404

Belle de Nuit, 387

Belvoir, Priory of, 233

Benecarlo, 382, 386, 481

Benedictine, 388

Beneventine, 157, 212, 467

Benicarlos, *see* Benecarlo

Bentham, Jeremy, 337, 408

Berkshire, 239, 282

Beringer, 458

Bernkastel, 427, 430

Berytian, *see* Beirut

Besant, Sir Walter, 398, 399, 404, 436

Beth Luban, 75, 461

Beth-Pelet, 181

Beth Rimmah, 75, 461

Beycesultan, 80, 81

Bèze, 233
  Clos de, 264

Béziers, 161, 162

Biaune, *see* Beaune

Bibline, 99-100, 134-5, 147, 464

'Big Tree' wines, 457

Bilak, 61, 461

Bilbilis, 160

binning, 212, 350-2

Bischholz, 264

Bisham, 239

Bisson, General, 337

Bit-Kubati, 65, 461

Bitâtim, 78n., 461

Bithynia, 146, 147

bitters, 401, 444

Biturica vine, 162n., 208, 467

'Bituricus' vine, *see* Biturica

Biturigiaca vine, 162n., 467

Blanc, 279n., 474

blanc de blanc, *see* Jurançon

Blanc de Blancs (champagne), 344

Blanquet, 481

Blanquette de Limoux, 481

Blanzac, 329

Bleahard, 298, 481

blending, 146, 192, 258, 294, 295-6, 328-9, 344-6, 382-3, 434-5

Boccaccio, 282, 283

Bochet, 272, 462

Boeotia, 98, 102, 104, 109n., 112, 113, 121, 128

Bois Ordinaires, 328

Bologna, 332, 387

Bonecarlos, *see* Benecarlo

Bonn, 298

Bons-Bois, 328

Boorde, Andrew, 286, 314

Bourbon, 451

Bordeaux, 168, 227-8, 263, 326, 353
  classification, 388-9, 418-19
  Côtes de, 263
  merchants, 258
  trade, 263-4, 273, 371
  vineyards, 162, 232, 384, 419-25, 426
  wines, 164, 208, 209, 214, 263-4, 273-4, 302, 361-2, 386, 388-9, 418-25, 433, 434, 440 (*see also* claret)

Bordeaux, Archbishop of, 235

Borderies, 328

Bosporus, 129-30, 136, 464

Boston, 456

Boswell, James, 335, 336, 340, 341-2, 348, 355, 363, 365, 366, 372, 383

Botrytis cinerea, 365, 420

bottles, 209-10, 212, 350-5

Boulogne, 288

Bouzy, 346

Brabant, 242

'Braggett', 284, 481

Braket, 272, 284, 462 (*see also* Hippocras *and* Clarre)

brandy, 322-31, 339-40, 341, 399, 403, 405, 434, 436

brandy, California, 457

Blackberry, 446
  California Grape, 446
  Cocktail, 418
  corn, 324, 325, 329
  grape, 25, 295, 380-1
  malt, 339
  orange, 387-8
  populo, 387

Braunschweig, 324, 333

Brillat-Savarin, A., 337, 366, 376, 377-8, 386

Brinvilliers, Madame de, 303

Brioni Grande, 225

Bristol, Earl of, 302, 361, 367, 369, 389

Bristol Milk, 297

Britain, Roman, 163-5, 210, 227, 267, 326